In Conflict and Order

Understanding Society

Eleventh Edition

D. Stanley Eitzen

Emeritus, Colorado State University

Maxine Baca Zinn

Michigan State University

PEARSON

Boston   New York   San Francisco
Mexico City   Montreal   Toronto   London   Madrid   Munich   Paris
Hong Kong   Singapore   Tokyo   Cape Town   Sydney

Senior Series Editor: Jeff Lasser
Series Editorial Assistant: Erikka Adams
Senior Development Editor: Jane Buchbinder
Senior Marketing Manager: Kelly May
Production Editor: Won McIntosh
Editorial Production Service: Nesbitt Graphics, Inc.
Composition Buyer: Linda Cox
Manufacturing Buyer: JoAnne Sweeney
Electronic Composition: Nesbitt Graphics, Inc.
Interior Design: Glenna Collett
Photo Researcher: Sarah Evertson
Cover Administrator: Joel Gendron

For related titles and support materials, visit our online catalog at www.ablongman.com

Between the time website information is gathered and then published, it is not unusual for some sites to have closed. Also, the transcription of URLs can result in typographical errors. The publisher would appreciate notification where these errors occur so that they may be corrected in subsequent editions.

ISBN: 0-205-48494-8

Printed in the United States of America
10 9 8 7 6 5 4 3 2   RRD-VA 10 09 08 07

Contents

6 Social Control 133

7 Deviance 161

PART THREE The Study of Society 191

8 Structural Sources of Societal Change: Economic and Demographic 191

PART FIVE   Human Agency   521

18 Human Agency: Individuals and Groups in Society Changing Social Structures   521

Preface

Many introductory students will be exposed to sociology in only one course. They should leave that course with a new and meaningful way of understanding themselves, other people, their society, and other societies. The most fundamental goal of this book, then, is to help the student develop a sociological perspective.

This goal is emphasized explicitly in the first chapter and implicitly throughout *In Conflict and Order: Understanding Society*, Eleventh Edition. The sociological perspective focuses on the social sources of behavior. It requires shedding existing myths and ideologies by questioning all social arrangements. One of the most persistent questions of the sociologist is, Who benefits from the existing customs and social order and who does not? Because social groups are created by people, they are not sacred. Is there a better way?

Although there will be disagreement on the answers to these questions, the answers are less important, sociologically, than is the willingness to call into question existing social arrangements that many people consider sacred. This is the beginning of the sociological perspective. But being critical is not enough. The sociologist must have a coherent way to make sense of the social world, and this leads us to the second goal of *In Conflict and Order*: the elaboration of a consistent framework from which to understand and interpret social life. *In Conflict and Order*, Eleventh Edition, is guided by the assumption that there is an inherent duality in all societies. The realistic analysis of any one society must include both the integrating and stabilizing forces, on one hand, and the forces that are conducive to malintegration and change, on the other. Society in the United States is characterized by harmony and conflict, integration and division, stability and change. This synthesis is crucial if the intricacies of social structure, the mechanisms of social change, and the sources of social problems are to be understood fully.

This objective of achieving balance between the order and the conflict perspectives is not fully realized in this book, however. Although both perspectives are incorporated into each chapter, the scales are tipped toward the conflict perspective. This imbalance is the conscious product of how the authors, as sociologists and teachers, view the structure and mechanisms of society. In addition to presenting what we believe is a realistic analysis of society, this imbalance counters the prevailing view of the order perspective, with its implicit sanctification of the status quo. Such a stance is untenable to us, given the spate of social problems that persist in U.S. society. The emphasis on the conflict approach, on the other hand, questions existing social arrangements, viewing them as sources of social problems, a position with which we agree. Implicit in such a position is the goal of restructuring society along more humane lines.

That we stress the conflict approach over the order model does not suggest that *In Conflict and Order* is a polemic. On the contrary, the social structure is also examined from a sympathetic view. The existing arrangements do provide for the stability and maintenance of the system. But the point is that, by including a relatively large dose of the conflict perspective, the discussion is a realistic appraisal of the system rather than a look through rose-colored glasses.

This duality theme is evident primarily at the societal level in this book. But even though the societal level is the focus of our inquiry, the small-group and individual levels are not ignored. The principles that apply to societies are also appropriate for the small social organizations to which we belong, such as families, work groups, athletic teams, religious organizations, and clubs. Just as important, the sociological perspective shows how the individual is affected by groups of all sizes. Moreover, it shows how the individual's identity is shaped by social forces and how in many important ways the individual's thoughts and actions are determined by group memberships. The linkage of the individual to social groups is shown throughout *In Conflict and Order*. The relationship of the individual to the larger society is illustrated in special panels that examine societal changes and forces impinging on individuals and the choices available to us as we attempt to cope with these societal trends.

Organization of the Book

The book is divided into five parts. Part One (Chapters 1 through 3) introduces the reader to the sociological perspective, the fundamental concepts of the discipline, and the duality of social life. These chapters set the stage for an analysis of the structure (organization) and process (change) of U.S. society. The emphasis is on the characteristics of societies in general and of the United States in particular.

Part Two (Chapters 4 through 7) describes the way in which human beings are shaped by society. The topics include the values that direct our choices, the social bases of social identity and personality, the mechanisms that control individual and group behavior, and the violation of social expectations—deviance. Throughout these chapters we examine both the forces that work to make all of us living in the United States similar, and those that make us different.

Part Three (Chapters 8 through 12) focuses on social change and social inequality. This section begins with a chapter showing how three major social forces (globalization, the new immigration, and the aging of the population) affect human behavior and social life. Among other things, these structural changes affect social stratification by class and race. These are the topics of the remaining chapters in this section. We examine how societies rank people in hierarchies. We also examine the mechanisms that ensure that some people have a greater share of wealth, power, and prestige than do others, and the positive and negative consequences of such an arrangement. Other chapters focus on the specific hierarchies of stratification: class, race, and gender.

Part Four (Chapters 13 to 17) discusses another characteristic of all societies: the presence of social institutions. Every society historically has developed a fairly consistent way of meeting its survival needs and the needs of its members. The organization of society into families, for example, ensures the regular input of new members, provides for the stable care and protection of the young, and regulates sexual activity. In addition to discussions of the family, chapters in Part Four are devoted to education, the economy, the polity, and religion. The understanding of institutions is vital to the understanding of society because these social arrangements are part of its structure, resist change, and have a profound impact on the public and private lives of people.

Part Five (Chapter 18) examines social changes that occur from the bottom up. The goal of this chapter is to combat the strong structural determinism bias of the earlier chapters by focusing on how human beings, individually and collectively, change social structures.

Themes of the Book

As in previous editions, *In Conflict and Order* incorporates four themes: diversity, the struggle by the powerless to achieve social justice, the changing economy, and globalization. First, although there are separate chapters on race, class, and gender, these fundamental sources of differences are infused throughout the book and in the photographs. This emphasis is important to an understanding of the diversity in society as well as the structural sources of inequality and injustice. Second, the tendency toward structural determinism is countered by Chapter 18 and various examples of human agency throughout the book: the powerless organizing to achieve power and positive social changes (for example, civil rights, gay rights, rights for people with disabilities, and gender equity in sports). Third, the sources and consequences of the structural transformation of the economy are examined. This is a pivotal shift in the U.S. economy with significant implications for individuals, communities, the society, and the global economy. And, fourth, the focus is often shifted away from the United States to other societies through descriptions, panels, and tables. This global perspective is important for at least two reasons: to illustrate the universality of sociological concepts and to help us understand how the world is becoming ever more interdependent.

These four themes—diversity, the struggle by the powerless to achieve social justice, the changing economy, and globalization—are important concepts to consider sociologically. We see that social problems are structural in origin and that the pace of social change is accelerating, yet society's institutions are slow to change and meet the challenges. The problems of U.S. society are of great magnitude, and solutions must be found. But understanding must precede action, and that is one goal of *In Conflict and Order*.

The analysis of U.S. society is a challenging task. It is frustrating because of the heterogeneity of the population and the complexity of the forces impinging on U.S. social life. It is also frustrating because the diversity within the United States leads to many inconsistencies and paradoxes. Furthermore, it is difficult, if not impossible, for people in the United States to be objective and consistently rational about their society. Nevertheless, the sociological study of U.S. society is fascinating and rewarding. It becomes absorbing as people gain insights into their own actions and into the behavior of other people. Understanding the intricate complex of forces leading to a particular type of social structure or social problem can be liberating and can lead to collective efforts to bring about social change. This book attempts to give the reader just such a sociological perspective.

Finally, we are unabashedly proud of being sociologists. Our hope is that you will capture our enthusiasm for exploring and understanding the intricacies and mysteries of social life.

Features

To help students develop and foster their sociological perspective, we integrate the following features throughout the book.

- Human Agency boxes show how individuals and groups can become empowered to achieve positive social change.
- Globalization boxes present examples of the interconnections among the world's peoples.
- Diversity boxes address tolerance and understanding of a wide range of groups, institutions, choices, and behaviors.
- A Closer Look boxes elaborate on specific topics in detail, including "Learning to Hate"; "The Internet's Private Eye"; and "The New Welfare Policy: A Critique."
- Research Methods boxes explore different stages and facets of the research process in the social sciences.
- End-of-chapter-pedagogy includes Chapter Reviews, Key Terms, Study Questions, and suggestions for Further Reading and Using the Web.

New to This Edition

This eleventh edition of *In Conflict and Order,* while retaining the structure of the earlier editions, is different and improved in the following ways:

- **New Globalization boxes** include an international view on gay marriage, a look inside the mind of a suicide bomber, globalization's affect on disease, the stock market, pollution, and job insecurity, and more.
- **More information about the changing economy,** including extensive coverage of the rise of multinational corporations, outsourcing and off loading jobs, the decrease in work benefits, the increasing gap between the wealthy and everyone else, the hidden welfare system that supports big business, and "the best democracy money can buy."
- **New coverage of popular contemporary topics,** including the Internet as a surveillance tool, the widening inequality gap, the rise in cosmetic surgery, social cognitive theory of socialization, body image, the implications of the Patriot Act, terrorism, downward pressure on wages, "benefits insecurity," poverty level employment, work-related injuries by race, the decline of unions, campaign finance reform, a critique of the "No Child Left Behind" legislation, and religion in public schools, and the rise of professional sports leagues for women.
- **Updated statistics** reflect rapid changes in society and the intransigence of many social problems.
- **More incisive cartoons.**

A Note on Language Use

In writing this eleventh edition of *In Conflict and Order*, we have been especially sensitive to our use of language. Language is used to reflect and maintain the secondary status of social groups by defining them, diminishing them, trivializing them, or excluding them. For example, traditional English uses masculine words (man, mankind, he) to refer to people in general. Even the ordering of masculine and feminine, or of Whites and Blacks, with the discussion or reference to one category consistently preceding its counterpart, subtly conveys the message that the one listed first is superior to the other. In short, our goal is to use language so that it does not create the impression that one social class, race, or gender is superior to any other. The terms of reference for racial and ethnic categories are changing. Blacks increasingly use the term African American, and Hispanics often refer to themselves as Latinos or Latinas. In this book, we use each of these terms for each social category because they often are used interchangeably in popular and scholarly discourse.

Also, we do not use the terms America or American society when referring to the United States. America should be used only in reference to the entire Western hemisphere—North, Central, and South America. The use of America as a reference to only the United States implies that the other nations of the Western hemisphere have no place in our frame of reference.

On Supplements

Instructor's Supplements

Instructor's Manual and Test Bank

Chalane E. Lechuga of the University of New Mexico and Ray O'Connor of Holyoke Community College.

For each chapter in the text, the Instructor's Manual provides At-a-Glance grids that link main concepts to key terms and theorists as well as to other supplements. Each chapter includes a chapter overview, learning objectives, chapter outline, suggested activities, suggested films and readings. The Test Bank contains a multitude of questions in Multiple Choice, True False, and Short Answer and Essay question formats. Available in print, and electronically through the Allyn & Bacon/Longman Instructor's Resource Center.

Computerized Test Bank. The printed Test Bank is also available through Allyn and Bacon's computerized testing system, TestGen EQ. This fully networkable test generating software is available on a multiplatform CD-ROM for Windows and Macintosh. The user-friendly interface allows you to view, edit, and add questions, transfer questions to tests, and print tests in a variety of fonts. Search and sort features allow you to locate questions quickly and to arrange them in whatever order you prefer. Available on request to adopters. Also available electronically through the Allyn & Bacon/ Longman Instructor's Resource Center.

PowerPoint Presentation

Beth H. Tracton-Bishop: College of Saint Elizabeth

These PowerPoint slides, created especially for the eleventh edition, feature lecture outlines for every chapter. Each PowerPoint chapter includes figures and tables that are represented in the text. PowerPoint software is not required, as a PowerPoint viewer is included. Available on request to adopters. Available on a CD-ROM for Mac or Windows, and electronically through the Allyn & Bacon/Longman Instructor's Resource Center.

The Sociology Digital Media Archive IV. Updated for 2006. Want more electronic presentations in your classroom? This CD-ROM contains hundreds of graphs, charts, and maps that you can use to build PowerPoint slides to supplement your lectures and illustrate key sociological concepts. If you have full multimedia capability, you can use the DMA's video segments and links to sociology Web sites. Available on request to adopters.

Allyn & Bacon Transparencies for Introductory Sociology. Updated for 2006, this package includes 125 color acetates featuring illustrations from this text and other current Allyn and Bacon sociology titles. Available on request to adopters.

Allyn and Bacon/ABC News Sociology Videos. This series of videos contain programs from *Nightline, World News Tonight,* and *20/20.* These videos are perfect if you like to use news footage and documentary-style programs to illustrate sociological themes. Each video has an accompanying User's Guide (available electronically through Allyn and Bacon's Supplements Central Web site). Available titles are *Poverty and Stratification, Race and Ethnicity, Gender, Deviance,* and *Aging.* Available on request to adopters. Contact your Allyn and Bacon/Longman representative for details.

Sociology Video Library. Third-party videos are available on every major topic in sociology. Some of the videos are from Films for the Humanities and Sciences and Annenberg/CPB. Some restrictions apply. Contact your Allyn and Bacon/Longman representative for details.

The Video Professor: Applying Lessons in Sociology to Classic and Modern Films
Anthony W. Zumpetta, West Chester University

This manual describes hundreds of commercially available videos that represent nineteen of the most important topics in Introductory Sociology textbooks. Each topic lists a number of movies, along with specific assignments and suggestions for class use. Available in print, and electronically through the Allyn & Bacon/Longman Instructor's Resource Center.

Student Supplements

Addison-Wesley Higher Education Tutor Center (Access Code Required). Tutoring from qualified sociology instructors by phone, e-mail, or fax is available for your students during evening hours on all material covered in the text. Access to the Tutor Center is available on request when a Tutor Center Access Card is packaged with a new copy of this text.

Study Guide with PowerPoint Lecture Outlines
Payton Andrews, Cape Fear Community College

This student workbook is designed to help students prepare for quizzes and exams. Every chapter in the text contains Chapter Overviews, Learning Objectives, Key Terms, supplemental reading material, and fill-in-the-blank questions with a corresponding word bank to encourage students to practice their skills. There is an additional practice exam section that contains questions in multiple choice, true false, and short essay formats with a corresponding answer key. PowerPoint lecture outlines are provided as study and note-taking aids.

Introduction to Sociology Website. This Web site features practice texts including multiple-choice, true/false, and essay questions; Learning objectives, flashcards, annotated Web resources and student activities. There is also a link to the research database Research Navigator™ (access code required). Additionally, the website includes the *eThemes of the Times for Introductory Sociology*, the full text of thirty articles from the *New York Times* chosen to complement the various topics in this course.

New! VideoWorkshop for Introductory Sociology. VideoWorkshop is a supplement that brings sociological concepts to life with high quality video footage, on an easy-to-use CD-ROM. The VideoWorkshop CD-ROM contains two kinds of video-television news stories, and interviews with prominent sociologists, who discuss some of the important research studies and debates within their fields. Each video segment is paired with a set of observation questions and activities in the accompanying *Student Guide*. The *Student Guide* also includes assignments based on viewing popular films that illustrate sociological themes. The VideoWorkshop *Student Guide With CD-ROM* is packaged on request with this text. The *Instructor Guide With CD-ROM* includes the complete contents of the *Student Guide*, plus an overview of each video segment, and teaching suggestions.

Online Course Management

Introduction to Sociology WebCT and Blackboard Courses. For colleges and universities with **WebCT™** and **Blackboard™** licenses, our *Introduction to Sociology* online course cartridges for these formats feature preloaded content—some specifically for this book and some generic content that is organized topically. (Contact your sales representative for additional information.) In addition, we also convert all test items in our Test Bank for WebCT™ and Blackboard™ (on a CD-ROM or electronically through our Instructor's Resource Center), for uploading to your course.

Additional Supplements

Research Navigator™ (Access Code Required). Students receive a six-month subscription to this valuable research database when the text is packaged with the *Research Navigator Guide* for Sociology (see below). ResearchNavigator's powerful search engines provide access to thousands of full-text articles from scholarly social science journals and popular magazines and newspapers, including a one-year archive of the complete *New York Times*.

Research Navigator Guide: Sociology. This reference guide includes tips, resources, activities, and URLs to help students learn the basics of Sociology. The first part introduces students to the basics of the Internet and the World Wide Web. Part two includes over thirty Net activities that tie into the content of the text. Part three lists hundreds of World Wide Web resources for sociologists. The guide also includes information on how to correctly cite research, a guide to building an online glossary, and an access code for the ResearchNavigator site. Packaged on request with the text.

Building Bridges: The Allyn and Bacon Guide to Service Learning
Doris Hamner

This manual offers practical advice for students who must complete a service-learning project as part of their required course work. Packaged on request with this text.

Careers in Sociology, Third Edition
W. Richard Stephens, Eastern Nazarene College

This supplement explains how sociology can help students prepare for careers in such fields as law, gerontology, social work, business, and computers. It also examines how sociologists entered the field. Packaged on request with this text.

Breaking the Ice: A Guide to Understanding People From Other Cultures, Third Edition

Akiiki Daisy Kabagarama, Montgomery College

Breaking the Ice helps students better understand and interact with people from other cultures, encouraging them to react and draw on their experiences. The concept of culture is discussed fully, and both its unifying and divisive elements are examined. Exercises found both throughout the text and at the end of each chapter are aimed at helping readers discover their own biases. Packaged on request with this text.

College and Society: An Introduction to the Sociological Imagination

Stephen Sweet, Ithaca College

This supplemental text uses examples from familiar surroundings—the patterns of interaction, social structures, and expectations of conduct on a typical college campus—to help students see the ways in which large society also operates. Available for purchase separately or packaged with this text at a special discount.

Themes of the Times for Introductory Sociology. This collection of recent articles from the New York Times, all related to the study of sociology, can be packaged upon request with this text.

Acknowledgments

We want to thank the following reviewers for their critiques of the eleventh edition: Denise Bullock, Indiana University East; Kate Hovey, Albuquerque Technical Vocational Institute; Joyce M. Johnson, Santa Rosa Junior College; Chalane Lechuga, University of New Mexico; Nathan Pino, Georgia Southern University; Dean Purdy, Bowling Green State University; and Andrea Stepnick, Belmont University.

We especially thank Amy Fitzgerald and Jessica Mills of Michigan State University and Janis Johnston from Colorado State University for their research assistance on this edition.

D. Stanley Eitzen

Maxine Baca Zinn

About the Authors

D. Stanley Eitzen
Colorado State University

Maxine Baca Zinn
Michigan State University

D. STANLEY EITZEN is professor emeritus in sociology from Colorado State University, where previously he was the John N. Stern Distinguished Professor. He received his Ph.D. from the University of Kansas. Among his books are: *Social Problems*, which was awarded the McGuffey Longevity Award for excellence over multiple editions in 2000 by the Text and Academic Authors Association and *Diversity in Families* (both coauthored with Maxine Baca Zinn); *Experiencing Poverty: Voices from the Bottom* (with Kelly Eitzen Smith); *Solutions to Social Problems: Lessons from Other Societies; Solutions to Social Problems from the Top Down: The Role of Government* (with George H. Sage); *Solutions to Social Problems From the Bottom up: Social Movements* (with Kenneth L. Stewart); *Paths to Homelessness: Extreme Poverty and the Urban Housing Crisis* (with Doug A. Timmer and Kathyrn Talley); *Sociology of North American Sport* (with George H. Sage); and *Fair and Foul: Rethinking the Myths and Paradoxes of Sport*. He has served as the president of the North American Society for the Sociology of Sport and as editor of *The Social Science Journal*.

MAXINE BACA ZINN is professor of sociology at Michigan State University, where she is also senior researcher in the Julian Samora Research Institute. She received her Ph.D. from the University of Oregon. Her books include: *Women of Color in U.S. Society* (with Bonnie Thornton Dill) and *Gender through the Prism of Difference* (with Pierrette Hondagneu-Sotelo and Michael Messner). She is the coauthor (with D. Stanley Eitzen) of *Social Problems* and of *Diversity in Families*, both of which won McGuffey Awards for longevity from the Text and Academic Authors Association. She has served as president of the Western Social Science Association. In 2000, she received the American Sociological Association's Jessie Bernard Award in recognition of her career achievements in the study of women and gender.

The Sociological Perspective

Life appears to be a series of choices for each of us. We decide how much schooling is important and what field to major in. We choose a job, a mate, and a lifestyle. But how free are we? Have you ever felt trapped by events and conditions beyond your control? Your religious beliefs may make you feel guilty for some behaviors. Your patriotism may cost you your life—even willingly. These ideological traps are powerful, so powerful that we usually do not even see them as traps. Have you ever felt trapped in a social relationship? Have you ever continued a relationship with a friend, a group of friends, a lover, or a spouse when you were convinced that this relationship was wrong for you? Have you ever participated in an act, which later seemed absolutely ridiculous, even immoral, because other people wanted you to? Most likely your answers to these questions are in the affirmative, because the people closest to us effectively command our conformity.

At another level, have you ever felt that because of your race, gender, age, ethnicity, or social class certain opportunities were closed to you? For example, if you are an African American football player, your chances to play certain positions on the team (usually quarterback, center, offensive guard, and kicker) will probably be limited regardless of your abilities. If you are a woman, you may want to try certain sports or jobs, but to do so would be to call your femininity into question.

Even more remotely, each of us is controlled by decisions made in corporate boardrooms, in government bureaus, and in foreign capitals. Whether we retain employment may not be the consequence of our work behavior but rather the result of corporate decisions to move a plant overseas or to outsource the work offshore. Our tastes in style are decided on and manipulated by corporate giants through the media. Rising or declining interest rates can encourage corporate decisions to expand or contract their businesses, thus affecting employment.

Those same interest rates can stimulate or deter individuals and families who seek to purchase housing and automobiles. A war in the Middle East reduces the supply of oil, raises the price dramatically, and thus restricts personal use in the United States. The weather in China and Russia affects grain prices in the United States, meaning bankruptcy or prosperity for individual farmers and high or low prices for individual consumers. So, too, with soaring inflation rates in a country, as occurred in 1999 when Brazil, which grows 10 percent of the world's soybean crop, devalued its currency, causing a rapid decline in the world price of soybeans and a decline of 10 percent or more in the price for U.S. farmers.

Finally, we are also trapped by our culture. We do not decide what is right or wrong, moral or immoral. These are decided for us and incorporated inside us. We do not decide what is beautiful and what is not. Even the decision on what is important and what is not is a cultural bias embedded deep inside each of us.

Sociology

Sociology is the discipline that attempts to understand these social forces—the forces outside us that shape our lives, interests, and personalities. In John Walton's words, "Sociology explores the determinants of individual and collective behavior that are not given in our psychic or biological makeup, but fashioned in the broader arena of social interaction" (Walton, 1990:5). As the science of society and social behavior, sociology is interesting, insightful, and important. This is true because sociology explores and analyzes the ultimate issues of our personal lives, of society, and of the world. At the personal level, sociology investigates the causes and consequences of such phenomena as romantic love, violence, identity, conformity, deviance, personality, and interpersonal power. At the societal level, sociology examines

"I'm a social scientist, Michael. That means I can't explain electricity or anything like that, but if you ever want to know about people I'm your man."

and explains poverty, crime rates, racism, sexism, pollution, and political power. At the global level, sociology researches such phenomena as societal inequality, war, conflict resolution, immigration patterns, and population growth. Other disciplines arc also helpful in understanding these social phenomena, but sociology makes a unique contribution.

The insights of sociology are important for individuals because they help us understand why we behave as we do. This understanding is not only liberating but a necessary precondition for meaningful social action to bring social change. As a scholarly discipline, sociology is important because it complements and in some cases supersedes other disciplines concerned with understanding and explaining social behavior.

Assumptions of the Sociological Perspective

To discover the underlying order of social life and the principles that explain human behavior, scientists have focused on different levels of phenomena. The result of this division of labor has been the creation of scholarly disciplines, each concentrating on a relatively narrow sphere of phenomena. Biologists interested in social phenomena have focused on organic bases for behavior. Psychological explanations assume that the source of human behavior lies in the psyches of individuals.

The understanding of human behavior benefits from the emphases of the various disciplines. Each discipline makes important contributions to knowledge. Of the three major disciplines focusing on human behavior, sociology is commonly the least understood. The explicit goal of this book is to remedy this fault by introducing the reader to the sociological ways of perceiving and interpreting the social world. Let us begin by considering the assumptions of the sociological approach that provide the foundation for this unique, exciting, and insightful way of viewing the world.

Individuals Are, by Their Nature, Social Beings. There are two fundamental reasons for this assumption. First, human babies enter the world totally dependent on other people for their survival. This initial period of dependence means, in effect, that each of us has been immersed in social groups from birth. A second basis for the social nature of human beings is that throughout history people have found it to their advantage to cooperate with other people (for defense, for material comforts, to overcome the perils of nature, and to improve technology).

Individuals Are, for the Most Part, Socially Determined. This essential assumption stems from the first assumption, that people are social beings. Individuals are products of their social environments for several reasons. During infancy, the child is at the mercy of adults, especially parents. These people shape the infant in an infinite variety of ways, depending on their proclivities and those of their society. The parents have a profound impact on the child's ways of thinking about himself or herself and about other people. The parents transmit religious views, political attitudes, and attitudes toward how other groups are to be rated. The child is punished for certain behaviors and rewarded for others. Whether that child becomes a bigot or integrationist, traditionalist or innovator, saint or sinner depends in large measure on the parents, peers, and other people who interact with her or him.

The parents may transmit to their offspring some idiosyncratic beliefs and behaviors, but most significantly they act as cultural agents, transferring the ways of the society to their children. Thus, the child is born into a family and also into a society. This society into which individuals are born shapes their personalities and perceptions. Peter Berger has summarized the impact of society:

> Society not only controls our movements, but shapes our identity, our thoughts and our emotions. The structures of society become the structures of our own consciousness. Society does not stop at the surface of our skins. Society penetrates us as much as it envelops us. (Berger, 1963:121)

The individual's identity is socially bestowed. Who we are, how we feel about ourselves, and how other people treat us are usually consequences of our social location (which is determined by our social class, race/ethnicity, gender, and sexuality) in society. Individuals' personalities are also shaped by the way we are accepted, rejected, and defined by other people. Whether an individual is attractive or plain, witty or dull, worthy or unworthy depends on the values of society and the groups in which the individual is immersed. Although genes determine one's physiology and potential, the social environment determines how those characteristics will be evaluated. Suggesting that human beings are socially determined is another way of saying that they are similar to puppets. They are dependent on and manipulated by social forces. A major function of sociology is to identify the social forces that affect us so greatly. Freedom, as Reece McGee has pointed out, can come only from a recognition of these unseen forces:

> Freedom consists in knowing what these forces are and how they work so that we have the option of saying no to the impact of their operation. For example, if we grow up in a racist society, we will be racists unless we learn what racism is and how it works and then choose to refuse its impact. In order to do so, however, we must recognize that it is there in the first place. People often are puppets, blindly danced by strings of which they are unaware and over which they are not free to exercise control. A major function of sociology is that it permits us to recognize the forces operative on us and to untie the puppet strings which bind us, thereby giving us the option to be free. (McGee, 1975:3)

Thus, one task of sociology is to learn, among other things, what racism is and to determine how it works. This is often difficult because we typically do not recognize its existence—because we have been puppets, socialized to believe and behave in particular ways. To say that we are puppets is too strong, however. This assumption is not meant to imply a total **social determinism** (the assumption that human behavior is explained exclusively by social factors).* The puppet metaphor is used to convey the idea that much of who we are and what we do is a product of our social environment. But there are nonconformists, deviants, and innovators. Society is not a rigid, static entity composed of robots. While the members of society are shaped by their social environment, they also change that environment. Human beings are the shapers of society as well as the shapees. This is the third assumption of the sociological approach.

---

*Advocates of social determinism are guilty of oversimplifying complex phenomena, just as are genetic determinists, psychological determinists, geographical determinists, and economic determinists.

Individuals Create, Sustain, and Change the Social Forms within Which They Conduct Their Lives. Even though individuals are largely puppets of society, they are also puppeteers. Chapter 2 describes this process of how people in interaction are the architects of society. In brief, the argument is that social groups of all sizes and types (families, peer groups, work groups, corporations, communities, and societies) are made by people. Interacting people create a social structure that becomes a source of control over those individuals (that is, they become puppets of their own creation). But the continuous interaction of the group's members also changes the group.

There are four important implications of this assumption that groups are human-made. First, these social forms that are created have a certain momentum of their own that defies change. The ways of doing and thinking common to the group are viewed as natural and right. Although human-made, the group's expectations and structures take on a sacred quality—the sanctity of tradition—that constrains behavior in the socially prescribed ways.

A second implication is that social organizations, because they are created and sustained by people, are imperfect. Slavery benefited some segments of society by taking advantage of other segments. A free enterprise system creates winners and losers. The wonders of technology make worldwide transportation and communication easy and relatively inexpensive but create pollution and waste natural resources. These examples show that there are positive and negative consequences of the way people have organized themselves.

The third implication is that through collective action, individuals are capable of changing the structure of society and even the course of history. Consider, for example, the social movement in India led by Mahatma Gandhi that ended colonial rule

Successful social movements usually require a leader with extraordinary personal attributes (charisma) to challenge and inspire followers to join in a common quest to change society.

by Great Britain, or the civil rights movement in the South led by Martin Luther King, Jr., that ended segregationist laws, or the failure of the attempted coup by Communist hardliners in the summer of 1991 because of the refusal of Soviet citizens and soldiers to accept it.

The final significance of this assumption is that individuals are not passive. Rather, they actively shape social life by adapting to, negotiating with, and changing social structures. This process is called **human agency**. A discussion devoted to this meaningful interaction between social actors and their social environment, bringing about social change, is reserved for the final chapter. Human agency provides the crucial vantage point and insights from the bottom up, and whereas most of this book examines social life from the top down, occasional panels will highlight human agency throughout the text.

The Sociological Imagination

C. Wright Mills (1916–1962) in his classic *The Sociological Imagination* (1959) wrote that the task of sociology was to realize that individual circumstances are inextricably linked to the structure of society. The **sociological imagination** involves several related components (Eitzen and Smith, 2003):

- The sociological imagination is stimulated by a willingness to view the social world from the perspective of others.
- It involves moving away from thinking in terms of the individual and her or his problem, focusing rather on the social, economic, and historical circumstances that produce the problem. Put another way, the sociological imagination is the ability to see the societal patterns that influence individuals, families, groups, and organizations.
- Possessing a sociological imagination, one can shift from the examination of a single family to national budgets, from a poor person to national welfare policies, from an unemployed person to the societal shift from manufacturing to a service/knowledge economy, from a single mother with a sick child to the high cost of health care for the uninsured, and from a homeless family to the lack of affordable housing.
- To develop a sociological imagination requires a detachment from the taken-for-granted assumptions about social life and establishing a critical distance (Andersen and Taylor, 2000:10–11). In other words, one must be willing to question the structural arrangements that shape social behavior.
- When we have this imagination, we begin to see the solutions to social problems not in terms of changing problem people but in changing the structure of society.

Problems with the Sociological Perspective

Sociology is not a comfortable discipline and therefore will not appeal to everyone. To look behind the closed doors of social life is fraught with danger. Sociology frightens some people because it questions what they normally take for granted. Sociologists ask such questions as: How does society really work? Who really has power? Who benefits under the existing social arrangements and who does not? To ask such questions means that the inquirer is interested in looking beyond the commonly accepted official definitions. As Berger has put it, the "sociological perspective involves a process of 'seeing through' the facades of social structures" (Berger, 1963:31). The underlying assumption of the sociologist is that things are not as they seem. Is the mayor of your town the most powerful person in the community? Is the system of justice truly just? Are professional sports free of racism? Is the United States a meritocratic society in which talent and effort combine to stratify the people fairly? To make such queries calls into question existing myths, stereotypes, and official dogma. The critical examination of society will demystify and demythologize. It sensitizes the individual to the inconsistencies present in society. Clearly, that will result if you ask: Why does the United States, in the name of freedom, protect dictatorships around the world? Why do we encourage subsidies to the affluent, but resent those directed to the poor? How high would George W. Bush have risen politically if his surname was Hernandez and his parents had been migrant workers? Why are people who have killed Whites more likely to be sentenced to death than people who have killed African Americans? Why are many women opposed to the Equal Rights Amendment? Why, in a democracy such as the United States, are there so few truly democratic organizations?

The sociological assumption that provides the basis for this critical stance is that the social world is human-made—and therefore not sacred. Belief systems, the economic system, the law, the way power is distributed—all are created and sustained by people. They can, as a result, be changed by people. But if the change is to correct imperfections, then we must understand how social phenomena work. The central task of this book is to aid in such an understanding of U.S. society.

The sociological perspective is also discomforting to many people because an understanding of society's constraints is liberating. Traditional sex roles, for example, are no longer sacred for many people. But while this understanding is liberating from the constraints of tradition, it is also freedom from the protection that custom provides. The acceptance of tradition is comfortable because it frees us from choice (and therefore blame) and from ambiguity. Thus, the understanding of society is a two-edged sword—freeing us, but also increasing the probability of frustration, anger, and alienation.

Sociology is also uncomfortable because the behavior of the subjects is not always certain. Prediction is not always accurate, because people can choose among options or be persuaded by irrational factors. The result is that if sociologists know the social conditions, they can predict, but in terms of probabilities. In chemistry, on the other hand, scientists know exactly what will occur if a certain measure of sodium is mixed with a precise amount of chlorine in a test tube. Civil engineers armed with the knowledge of rock formations, rainfall patterns, type of soils, wind currents, and temperature extremes know exactly what specifications are needed when building a dam in a certain place. They could not know these, however, if the foundation and building materials kept shifting. That is the problem—and the source of excitement—for the sociologist.

The political proclivities of people in the United States during the past few decades offer a good example of shifting attitudes. In 1964, the Republican candidate for president, Barry Goldwater, was soundly defeated, and many observers predicted the demise of the Republican Party. But in 1968, Richard Nixon, the Republican, won. He won again in 1972 by a record-setting margin, leading to the prognostication that the Democratic Party would no longer be viable. Two years later, however, Nixon resigned in disgrace, and in 1976 the Democratic candidate, Jimmy Carter, was the victor. In 1980, President Carter was defeated by Ronald Reagan, and a number of liberal senators were defeated by conservatives. These wide swings seemed to stop as Reagan was reelected in 1984, and he was succeeded four years later by his loyal vice president, George H. W. Bush. But Bush was defeated by Democrat Bill Clinton in 1992, leading some observers to predict the end of the Republican era. Then Clinton's first two years in office, and the timidity of the Democratic majorities in the House and Senate, led to the Republicans winning majorities in the House and Senate in 1994 and ushered in what appeared to be a new era of conservatism. By 1996, however, the Republican blueprint (the "Contract with America") was no longer viable. President Clinton was reelected, although the Republicans held majorities in the House and Senate. In 1998, when Clinton was a lame duck president and involved in a serious scandal, it seemed obvious that Republicans would increase their majorities in the House and Senate. Actually, they lost seats in the House and stayed even in the Senate. Later, Clinton was impeached by the House but acquitted by the Senate, and President Clinton's approval ratings by the public stood at 70 percent. Then, in the election of 2000, Al Gore, Clinton's vice president, won the popular vote but was narrowly defeated in the electoral college (and, dare we say it, in the Supreme Court). George W. Bush began his presidency without a popular mandate, but given the events of September 11, 2001, and the military actions afterward, Bush's approval rating soared to over 80 percent. In Bush's second term, however, his approval ratings plummeted below 40 percent. He and the Republican majorities in the House and Senate overreached on several issues leading to the possibility of Democratic gains in 2006 and 2008.

What does the future hold? History reveals that as long as human beings are not robots, their behaviors will be somewhat unpredictable. International events, economic cycles, scandals, and other occurrences will lead to shifts in political opinions and shifts in the prevailing political ideology.

In sum, "sociology excites a unique set of reactions—it bores some and frightens others. . . . Sociology is extraordinary because it can be regarded as both trivial and threatening" (Walton, 1990:4). Students tend to react to sociology in either of these ways. One reaction is that sociology is the trivial and tedious examination of the obvious. Sociology for them is boring. After all, they have lived in families, communities, and society. They know social life. To them, we argue, immersion in social life does not equate with understanding social life. As Zygmunt Bauman has written: "Deeply immersed in our daily routines, though, we hardly ever pause to think about the meaning of what we have gone through; even less often have we the opportunity to compare our private experience with the fate of others, to see the social in the individual, the general in the particular; this is precisely what sociologists can do for us" (Bauman, 1990:10).

To be sure, we are all sociologists of sorts because we know how to behave socially, we intuitively understand social distance, and we have "street smarts." Many go through life knowing how to behave socially, but they do so unconsciously, without being analytical about things social. Most go through life accepting social boundaries of class, race, gender, and sexuality without understanding that they are social constructions. And many are manipulated by advertising, the media, preachers, and politicians.

To understand social life requires more than social experiences. It requires a perspective—the sociological perspective—that leads to sociological questions and analysis. With this perspective, students will find excitement and engagement in looking behind the facades of social life and finding patterns in human behaviors (seeing the general in the particular).

A second common reaction by students to sociology is that they find this inquiry threatening. Sociology is subversive—that is, sociology undermines our foundations because it questions all social arrangements, whether religious, political, economic, or familial. Even though this critical approach may be uncomfortable for some people, it is necessary for understanding human social arrangements and for finding solutions to social problems. Thus, we ask that you think sociologically. The process may be scary at first, but the results will be enlightenment, interest, and excitement in all things social.

The Historical Development of Sociology

Sociology emerged in Western Europe in the late eighteenth century during the Enlightenment (also known as the Age of Reason). Spurred by dramatic social changes such as the Industrial Revolution, the French Revolution, urbanization, and capitalism, intellectuals during this period promoted the ideals of progress, democracy, freedom, individualism, and the scientific method. These ideas replaced those of the old medieval order, in which religious dogma and unquestioned obedience to royal authorities dominated. The new intellectuals believed that human beings could solve their social problems. They also believed that society itself could be analyzed rationally. Out of this intellectual mix, several key theorists laid the foundation for contemporary sociological thought. We focus briefly on the contributions of four: Auguste Comte, Karl Marx, Emile Durkheim, and Max Weber. We further elaborate on the sociological explanations of Marx, Durkheim, and Weber throughout this book.

Auguste Comte (1798–1857): The Science of Society

The founder of sociology was a Frenchman, Auguste Comte, who coined the word *sociology*—from the Latin *socius* ("companion," "with others") and the Greek *logos* ("study of")—for the science of society and group life. Comte sought to establish sociology as a science free of religious arguments about society and human nature (his initial name for the discipline was social physics) using the Enlightenment's emphasis on **positivism** (knowledge based on systematic observation, experiment, and comparison). Comte was convinced that, using scientific principles, sociologists could solve social problems such as poverty, crime, and war.

Emile Durkheim (1858–1917): Social Facts and the Social Bond

Durkheim provided the rationale for sociology by emphasizing social facts. His classic work *Suicide* (Durkheim, 1951, first published in 1897) demonstrates how social factors explain individual behavior (see Chapter 2). Durkheim focused on **social facts**—social factors that exist external to individuals such as tradition, values, laws, religious ideology, and population density. The key for Durkheim was that these factors affect the behaviors of people, thus allowing for sociological explanations rather than biological and psychological reasoning.

Durkheim was also interested in what holds society together. His works show how belief systems bind people together; how public ceremonies and rituals promote solidarity; how labeling some people as deviant reaffirms what society deems to be right; and how similarities (shared traditions, values, ideology) provide the societal glue in traditional societies, while differences (division of labor) provide the social bond in complex societies.

Durkheim made invaluable contributions to such core sociological concepts as social roles, socialization, anomie, deviant behavior, social control, and the social bond. In particular, Durkheim's works provide the foundation for the order model that is found throughout this book (see Chapter 3).

Karl Marx (1818–1883): Economic Determinism

Karl Marx devoted his life to analyzing and criticizing the society he observed. He was especially concerned with the gap between the people at the bottom of society and the elite, between the powerless and the powerful, the dominated and the dominant. Marx reasoned that the type of economy found in a society provides its basic structure (system of stratification, unequal distribution of resources, the bias of the law, and ideology). Thus, he was vitally interested in how the economic system of his day—capitalism—shaped society. The owners of capital exploited their workers to extract maximum profits. They used their economic power to keep the less powerful in their place and to benefit unequally from the educational system, the law, and other institutional arrangements in society. These owners of capital (the ruling class) also determined the prevailing ideas in society because they controlled the political system, religion, and media outlets. In this way, members of the working class accept the prevailing ideology. Marx called this **false consciousness** (believing in ideas that are not in a group's objective interests but rather in the best interests of the capitalist class). Social change occurs when the contradictions inherent in capitalism (see Chapter 13) cause the working class to recognize their oppression and develop **class consciousness** (recognizing their class interests, common oppression, and an understanding of who the oppressors are), resulting in a revolt against the system.

Marx made extraordinary contributions to such core sociological concepts as systems of inequality, social class, power, alienation, and social movements. Marx's view of the world is the foundation of the conflict perspective, which is infused throughout this book.

Max Weber (1864–1920): A Response to Marx

Although it is an oversimplification, it helps to think of Weber's thought as a reaction to the writings of Marx. In Weber's view, Marx was too narrowly deterministic. In response, Weber showed that the basic structure of society comes from three sources: the political, economic, and cultural spheres, not just the economic, as Marx argued. Similarly, social class is not determined just by economic resources, but also includes status (prestige) and power dimensions. Political power does not stem just from economic resources, as Marx argued, but also from the expressive qualities of individual leaders (**charisma**). But power can also reside in organizations (not individuals), as Weber showed in his extensive analysis of bureaucracy (see Chapter 2). Weber countered Marx's emphasis on material economic concerns by showing how ideology shapes the economy. Arguably his most important work, *The Protestant Ethic and the Spirit of Capitalism* (Weber, 1958, first published in 1904) demonstrates how a particular type of religious thought (the protestant belief system) made capitalism possible. In sum, Weber's importance to sociology is seen in his mighty contributions to such core concepts as power, ideology, charisma, bureaucracy, and social change.

Sociological Methods: The Craft of Sociology

Sociology is dependent on reliable data and logical reasoning. These necessities are possible, but there are problems that must be acknowledged. Before we describe how sociologists gather reliable data and make valid conclusions, let us examine the kinds of questions sociologists ask and the two major obstacles sociologists face in obtaining answers to these questions.

Sociological Questions

To begin, sociologists try to ascertain the facts. For example, let's assume that we want to assess the degree to which the public education system provides equal educational opportunities for all youngsters. To determine this, we need to do an empirical investigation to find the facts concerning such items as the amount spent per pupil by school districts within each state and by each state. Within school districts we need to know the facts concerning the distribution of monies by neighborhood schools. Are these monies appropriated equally, regardless of the social class or

racial composition of the school? Are curriculum offerings the same for girls and boys within a school? Are extra fees charged for participation in extracurricular activities, and does this affect the participation of children by social class?

Sociologists also may ask comparative questions—that is, how does the situation in one social context compare with that in another? Most commonly, these questions involve the comparison of one society with another. Examples here might be the comparisons among industrialized nations on infant mortality, murder, leisure time, or the mathematics scores of sixteen-year-olds.

A third type of question that a sociologist may ask is historical. Sociologists are interested in trends. What are the facts now concerning divorce, crime, and political participation, for example, and how have these patterns changed over time? Table 1.1 provides an example of trends over time by examining the living arrangements of children by race and ethnicity.

TABLE 1.1

Percentage Distribution of Living Arrangements of Children by Race and Hispanic Origin.[a]
Selected Years, 1970–2000

	1970	*1980*	*1990*	*2000*[b]
All children				
Two parents[c]	85	77	73	69
Mother only[d]	11	18	22	22
Father only[d]	1	2	3	4
No parent	3	4	3	4
White, non-Hispanic				
Two parents[c]	90	83	81	77
Mother only[d]	8	14	15	16
Father only[d]	1	2	3	4
No parent	2	2	2	3
African American				
Two parents[c]	58	42	38	38
Mother only[d]	30	44	51	49
Father only[d]	2	2	4	4
No parent	10	12	8	9
Latino(a)				
Two parents[c]	78	75	67	65
Mother only[d]	—	20	27	25
Father only[d]	—	2	3	4
No parent	—	3	3	5

[a]Persons of Hispanic origin may be of any race. Estimates for Blacks include Hispanics of that race.

[b]Numbers in these years may reflect changes in the Current Population Survey because of newly instituted computer-assisted interviewing techniques and/or because of the change in the population controls to the 1990 Census-based estimates, with adjustments.

[c]Excludes families where parents are not living as a married couple.

[d]Because of data limitations, includes some families where both parents are present in the household, but living as unmarried partners.

—Data not available.

Source: Adapted from U.S. Department of Health and Human Services, *Trends in the Well-Being of America's Children and Youth: 2002.* Washington, DC: U.S. Government Printing Office, p. 41.

The three types of sociologist questions considered so far determine the way things are. But these types of questions are not enough. Sociologists go beyond the factual to ask why. Why have real wages (controlling for inflation) declined since 1973 in the United States? Why are the poor, poor? Why do birth rates decline with industrialization? Why is the United States the most violent (as measured by murder, rape, and assault rates) industrialized society? (See the panel titled "A Closer Look: Thinking Like a Sociologist" for an example of sociological questions applied to a particular social occurrence.)

a Closer Look

Thinking Like a Sociologist

An article in the *New York Times* (Henneberger and Marriott, 1993) reported a disturbing social trend— male teenagers, apparently to demonstrate their manhood, were abusing or showing disrespect to girls in ever greater numbers. These incidents included verbal abuse, such as yelling explicit propositions, and physical abuse, such as fondling girls and other sexual assaults. This story also reported a nationwide survey of junior high and high school students, which found that more than two-thirds of the girls and 42 percent of the boys reported being touched, grabbed, or pinched on school grounds.

A sociologist interested in adolescence, courtship patterns, or gender might wish to research this apparent trend. The particular research questions of the sociologist depend on his or her interests and theoretical orientation. For our purposes, though, some likely questions might be the following.

Factual Questions
Is sexually oriented abuse aimed at females by adolescent males common today? The authors of the *New York Times* article interviewed only fifty adolescents. If it is common, is it more an urban phenomenon or is it found in the suburbs and rural areas as well? Is it more concentrated in the Northeast or is it found throughout the United States? Is this behavior pattern more prevalent among the youth in some racial and ethnic groups than others? Is it related to social class? And, if the reported incidents occur most often among the disadvantaged in society, is this an accurate measure or the result of the bias of the criminal justice system?

Comparative Questions
Is this trend limited to the United States or is it found in other societies as well? If so, are these societies similar to the United States in affluence, religious heritage, and economic activities?

Historical Questions
How do the current adolescent behaviors compare with those behaviors at other times in the United States? Have there been times in U.S. history when adolescent gendered behavior was less abusive and more courtly? If so, have the changes become gradually more abusive or has sexual abuse among teenagers varied according to some social condition such as the level of economic affluence or gender inequality?

Theoretical Questions
Assuming that the facts indicate that male teenagers are especially abusive to females now, the important question is, Why? Sociologists persuaded by the theoretical perspective of the order model (which is discussed in Chapter 3) might ask questions such as: How have the socialization patterns of youth changed from an earlier, more genteel time? Is the loosening of family ties (higher rates of separation/divorce/remarriage) the reason? Are these behavioral changes congruent with the changes in values? Are changing gender roles invoking this hostile response by males? Is this type of violence the result of a culture of poverty that idealizes a tough "macho" image? Conflict theorists, on the other hand, would ask quite different questions: Are patterns of male aggression toward females correlated with poverty rates, unemployment rates, and low wage rates? Is this form of violence related to a changing economy in which opportunities are becoming more limited because of technology and global competition? Does male abuse of females increase as the degree of inequality in a society increases?

A **sociological theory** is a set of ideas that explains a range of human behavior and a variety of social and societal events. "A sociological theory designates those parts of the social world that are especially important, and offers ideas about how the social world works" (Kammeyer, Ritzer, and Yetman, 1997:21).

Chapter 3 provides two competing theories that guide many sociologists. In that chapter there is a quote from Michael Harrington: "The data of society are, for all practical purposes, infinite. You need criteria that will provisionally permit you to bring some order into that chaos of data and to distinguish between relevant and irrelevant factors" (Harrington, 1985:1). Thus, theory not only helps us to explain social phenomena, it also guides research.

Problems in Collecting Data

A fundamental problem with the sociological perspective is that bane of the social sciences—objectivity. We are all guilty of harboring stereotyped conceptions of such social categories as African Americans, hard hats, professors, gays and lesbians, fundamentalists, business tycoons, communists, the rich, the poor, and jocks. Moreover, we interpret events, material objects, and people's behavior through the perceptual filter of our religious and political beliefs. When fundamentalists oppose the use of certain books in school, when abortion is approved by a legislature, when the president advocates cutting billions from the federal budget by eliminating social services, or when the Supreme Court denies private schools the right to exclude certain racial groups, most of us rather easily take a position in the ensuing debate.

Sociologists are caught in a dilemma. On the one hand, they are members of society with beliefs, feelings, and biases. On the other hand, though, their professional task is to study society in a disciplined (scientific) way. This latter requirement is that scientist-scholars be dispassionate, objective observers. In short, if they take sides, they lose their status as scientists.

This ideal of value neutrality (to be absolutely free of bias in research) can be attacked from three positions. The first is that scientists should not be morally indifferent to the implications of their research. Alvin Gouldner has argued this in the following statement:

> It would seem that social science's affinity for modeling itself after physical science might lead to instruction in matters other than research alone. Before Hiroshima, physicists also talked of a value-free science; they, too, vowed to make no value judgments. Today many of them are not so sure. If we today concern ourselves exclusively with the technical proficiency of our students and reject all responsibility for their moral sense, or lack of it, then we may someday be compelled to accept responsibility for having trained a generation willing to serve in a future Auschwitz. Granted that science always has inherent in it both constructive and destructive potentialities. It does not follow from this that we should encourage our students to be oblivious to the difference. (Gouldner, 1962:212)

Or, put another way, this time by historian Howard Zinn, explaining his style of classroom teaching:

> I would start off my classes explaining to my students—because I didn't want to deceive them—that I would be taking stands on everything. They would hear my point of view in this course, that this would not be a neutral course. My point to them

was that in fact it was impossible to be neutral. *You Can't Be Neutral on a Moving Train* [the title of Zinn's memoir] means that the world is already moving in certain directions. Things are already happening. Wars are taking place. Children are going hungry. In a world like this—already moving in certain, often terrible directions—to be neutral or to stand by is to collaborate with what is happening. (Quoted in Barsamian, 1997:37–38)

The second argument against the purely neutral position is that such a stance is impossible. Howard Becker, among others, has argued that there is no dilemma—because it is impossible to do research that is uncontaminated by personal and political sympathies (Becker, 1967; see also Gould, 1998:19). This argument is based on several related assumptions. One is that the values of the scholar-researcher enter into the choices of what questions will be asked and how they will be answered. For example, in the study of poverty, a critical decision involves the object of the study—the poor or the system that tends to perpetuate poverty among a certain segment of society. Or, in the study of the problems of youth, we can ask either of these questions: Why are some youths troublesome for adults? Or, Why do adults make so much trouble for youths? In both illustrations, quite different questions will yield very different results.

Similarly, our values lead us to decide from which vantage point we will gain access to information about a particular social organization. If researchers want to understand how a prison operates, they must determine whether they want a description from the inmates, from the guards, from the prison administrators, or from the state board of corrections. Each view provides useful insights about a prison, but obviously a biased one. If they obtain data from more than one of these levels, researchers are faced with making assessments as to which is the more accurate view, clearly another place in the research process where the values of the observers have an impact.

Perhaps the most important reason why the study of social phenomena cannot be value-free is that the type of problems researched and the strategies used tend either to support the existing societal arrangements or to undermine them. Seen in this way, social research of both types is political. Ironically, however, there is a strong tendency to label only the research aimed at changing the system as political. By the same token, whenever the research sides with the powerless, the implication is that the hierarchical system is being questioned—thus, the charge that this type of research is biased. Becker has provided us with the logic of this viewpoint:

> When do we accuse ourselves and our fellow sociologists of bias? I think an inspection of representative instances would show that the accusation arises, in one important class of cases, when the research gives credence, in any serious way, to the perspective of the subordinate group in some hierarchical relationship. In the case of deviance, the hierarchical relationship is a moral one. The superordinate parties in the relationships are those who represent the forces of approved and official morality; the subordinate parties are those who, it is alleged, have violated that morality. . . . It is odd that, when we perceive bias, we usually see it in these circumstances. It is odd because it is easily ascertained that a great many more studies are biased in the direction of the interests of responsible officials than the other way around. (Becker, 1967:240, 242)

In summary, bias is inevitable in the study and analysis of social problems. The choice of a research problem, the perspective from which one analyzes the problems, and the solutions proposed all reflect a bias that either supports the existing social arrangements or does not. Moreover, unlike biologists, who can dispassionately observe the behavior of sperm and the egg at conception,* sociologists are participants in the social life they seek to study and understand. As they study race riots in cities, children living in poverty, or urban blight, sociologists cannot escape from their own feelings and values. They must, however, not let their feelings and values render their analysis invalid. In other words, research and reports of research must reflect reality, not as the researcher might want it to be. Sociologists must display scientific integrity, which requires recognizing biases in such a way that these biases do not invalidate the findings (Berger, 1963:5). When research is properly done in this spirit, an atheist can study a religious sect, a pacifist can study the military-industrial complex, a divorcée can study marriage, and a person who abhors the beliefs of the Ku Klux Klan can study that organization and its members.

In addition to bias, people gather data and make generalizations about social phenomena in a number of faulty ways. In a sense, everyone is a scientist seeking to find valid generalizations to guide behavior and make sense of the world. But most people are, in fact, very unscientific about the social world. The first problem, as we have noted, is the problem of bias. The second is that people tend to generalize from their experience. Not only is one's interpretation of things that happen to him or her subjective, but there also is a basic problem of sampling. The chances are that one's experience will be too idiosyncratic to allow for an accurate generalization. For example, if you and your friends agree that abortion is appropriate, that does not mean that other people in the society, even those of your age, will agree with you. Very likely, your friends are quite similar to you on such dimensions as socioeconomic status, race, religion, and geographic location.

Another instance of faulty sampling leading to faulty generalizations is when we make assumptions from a single case. An individual may argue that African Americans can succeed economically in this country as easily as Whites because he or she knows a wealthy African American. Similarly, you might argue that all Latinos are dumb because the one you know is in the slowest track in high school. This type of reasoning is especially fallacious because it blames the victim (Ryan, 1976). The cause of poverty or crime or dropping out of school or scoring low on an IQ test is seen as a result of the flaw in the individual, ignoring the substantial impact of the economy or school.

Another typical way that we explain social behavior is to use some authority other than our senses. The Bible, for example, has been used by many people to support or condemn activities such as slavery, capital punishment, war, homosexuality, or monogamy. The media provide other sources of authority for individuals. The media, however, are not always reliable sources of facts. Stories are often selected

---

*Scientists are subject to the political, cultural, and social influences of the times and places in which they live. Thus, even the seeming objectivity of biologists watching and interpreting the behavior of sperm and egg at conception is questionable. Biologists have long assumed that sperm are the more active participants in conception while the egg is passive (which fits, of course, with the patriarchal model). But new research shows that rather than being forceful swimmers, sperm flounder around, meandering sideways and even moving away from the egg. The egg, on the other hand, has now been found to actively grab the sperm. Also, we now know that rather than the genes in the sperm activating the development program in the passive egg, the genetic material in the egg alone guides development in the first few hours after fertilization. These new findings have been known since 1964 "but research indicating an active role for the egg 'just sat there,' says anthropologist Emily Martin of Princeton University. 'No one knew what to do with it'" (Begley, 1997:56).

Research Methods

Standards for Objectivity and Integrity in Social Research

Social scientists must contend with the essential problem of credibility of their research. How is objectivity possible, though, when they cannot escape their personal values, biases, and opinions? The answer lies in the norms of science.

Sociologists share with other scientists norms for conducting research that minimize personal bias. Their research must reflect the standards of science before it is accepted in scholarly journals. These journals function as gatekeepers for a discipline. What they accept for publication is assumed by their readers to be scientific. The editors of scholarly journals send manuscripts to referees who are unaware of the identity of the authors. This system of anonymity allows the referees to make objective judgments about the credibility of the studies. They review, among other things, the methods used to assess validity and reliability. Validity is the degree to which a study actually measures what it purports to measure. Reliability is the degree to which another study repeating the same methods would yield the same results.

To guide sociologists, their professional association, the American Sociological Association, has a code of ethics, which includes a number of standards for objectivity and integrity in sociological research.

1. "Sociologists adhere to the highest possible technical standards that are reasonable and responsible in their research, teaching, practice, and service activities. They rely on scientifically and professionally derived knowledge; act with honesty and integrity; and avoid untrue, deceptive, or undocumented statements in undertaking work-related functions or activities."

2. "Sociologists conduct research, teach, practice, and provide service only within the boundaries of their competence, based on their education, training, supervised experience, or appropriate professional experience."

3. "In research, teaching, practice, service, or other situations where sociologists render professional judgments or present their expertise, they accurately and fairly represent their areas and degrees of expertise."

4. "Sociologists maintain the highest degree of integrity in their professional work and avoid conflicts of interest and the appearance of conflict."

5. "Irrespective of their personal or financial interests or those of their employers or clients, sociologists adhere to professional and scientific standards in (1) the collection, analysis, or interpretation of data; (2) the reporting of research; (3) the teaching, professional presentation, or public dissemination of sociological knowledge; and (4) the identification of Implementation of appropriate contractual, consulting, or service activities."

Source: American Sociological Association, 1997. "Code of Ethics." Washington, DC: American Sociological Association, pp. 4–7.

---

because they are unusually dramatic, giving the faulty impression of, for example, a crime wave or questionable air safety (see the panel titled "Research Methods: Standards for Objectivity and Integrity in Social Research").

Our judgments and interpretations are also affected by prevailing myths and stereotypes. We just "know" certain things to be true, when, actually, they may be contradicted by scientific evidence. As examples, six common beliefs about the poor and racial minorities are presented and discussed.

1. *Most homeless people are disabled by drugs, mental disease, or physical afflictions.* The facts show, however, that the homeless, for the most part, are not "deficient and defective" but rather not much different than the non-homeless. People are not homeless because of their individual flaws but because of structural arrangements and trends that result in extreme impoverishment and a shortage of affordable housing (Timmer, Eitzen, and Talley, 1994).

2. *African American and Latino youth are more likely than White youth to smoke tobacco and be heavy binge drinkers of alcohol.* The facts belie this myth (Centers for Disease Control study, report in McClam, 2000; *Chronicle of Higher Education*, 1998; *U.S. News & World Report*, 1999).

3. *Welfare makes people dependent, lazy, and unmotivated.* Contrary to this image, however, the evidence is that most daughters of welfare recipients do not become welfare recipients as adults (Sklar, 1993). Put another way, most women on welfare did not receive welfare as children (Center on Social Welfare and Law, 1996).

4. *Welfare is given more generously to the poor than to the nonpoor.* Farm subsidies, tax deductibility for taxes and interest on homes, low-interest loans to students and victims of disasters, and pork-barrel projects are examples of government welfare and even the dependency of nonpoor people on government largesse. Most important, these government handouts to the nonpoor are significantly greater than the amounts given to the poor (see Chapters 10 and 14).

5. *African Americans are similar in their behaviors.* Blacks are not a monolithic group, with members acting more or less alike. A study by the Rand Corporation, for example, found that about 1 in 100 young, high-ability, affluent Black women from homes with two parents become single, teenage mothers (for White women in this category, the chances were 1 in 1,000, explained, in part, by the much greater willingness to use abortion). In contrast, a poor Black teenager from a female-headed household who scores low on standardized tests has a 1 in 4 probability of becoming an unwed teenage mother (for White women in this category, the odds were 1 in 12) (cited in Luker, 1991:76–77). In the words of Kristin Luker, "Unwed motherhood thus reflects the intersecting influences of race, class, and gender; race and class each has a distinct impact on the life histories of young women" (Luker, 1991:77).

6. *Unmarried women have babies to increase their welfare payments.* Three facts show that this belief of political conservatives is a myth (Carville, 1996:23–24; Males, 1996): (a) From 1972 to 1996, the value of the average Aid to Families with Dependent Children (AFDC) check declined by 40 percent, yet the ratio of out-of-wedlock births rose in the same period by 140 percent; (b) states that have lower welfare benefits usually have more out-of-wedlock births than states with higher benefits; and (c) the teen out-of-wedlock birth rate in the United States is much higher than the rate in countries where welfare benefits are much more generous.

Conventional wisdom is not always wrong, but when it is it can lead to faulty generalizations and bad public policy. Therefore, it is imperative to know the facts, rather than accept myths as real.

A similar problem occurs when we use aphorisms to explain social occurrences. The problem with this common tactic is that society supplies us with ready explanations that fit contradictory situations and are therefore useless. For instance, if we know a couple who are alike in religion, race, socioeconomic status, and political attitudes, that makes sense to us because "birds of a feather flock together." But the opposite situation also makes sense. If partners in a relationship are very different on a number of dimensions, we can explain this by the obvious explanation: "opposites attract." We use a number of other proverbs to explain behavior. The problem is that there is often a proverb or aphorism to explain the other extreme:

- Absence makes the heart grow fonder.
  Out of sight, out of mind.

- Look before you leap.
  He who hesitates is lost.
- Familiarity breeds contempt.
  To know her is to love her.
- Women are unpredictable.
  Isn't that just like a woman.
- You can't teach an old dog new tricks.
  It's never too late to learn.
- Above all, to thine own self be true.
  When in Rome, do as the Romans do.
- Variety is the spice of life.
  Never change horses in the middle of the stream.
- Two heads are better than one.
  If you want something done right, do it yourself.
- You can't tell a book by its cover.
  Clothes make the man.
- Many hands make light work.
  Too many cooks spoil the broth.
- Better safe than sorry.
  Nothing ventured, nothing gained.
- Haste makes waste.
  Strike while the iron is hot.
- Work, for the night is coming.
  Eat, drink, and be merry for tomorrow you may die.
- There's no place like home.
  The grass is always greener on the other side of the fence.

These contradictory explanations are commonly used and, of course, explain nothing. The job of the sociologist is to specify under what conditions certain rates of social behaviors occur.

Sources of Data

Sociologists do not use aphorisms to explain behavior, nor do they speculate based on faulty samples or authorities. Because we are part of the world that is to be explained, sociologists must obtain evidence that is beyond reproach. In addition to observing scrupulously the canons of science, there are four basic sources of data that yield valid results for sociologists: survey research, experiments, observation, and existing data. We describe these techniques only briefly here.*

Survey Research. Sociologists are interested in obtaining information about people with certain social attributes. They may want to know how political beliefs and behaviors are influenced by differences in sex, race, ethnicity, religion, and social class. Or sociologists may wish to know whether religious attitudes are related to racial antipathy. They may want to determine whether poor people have different

---

*See the section titled "For Further Reading" at the end of this chapter for references on the methods of sociology. Methodological footnotes and "Research Methods" panels focusing on methodological issues and procedures appear occasionally throughout this book to give insight into how sociologists obtain, analyze, and interpret data.

values from other people in society, the answer to which will have a tremendous impact on the ultimate solution to poverty. Or they may want to know whether voting patterns, work behaviors, or marital relationships vary by income level, educational attainment, or religious affiliation.

To answer these and similar questions, the sociologist may use personal interviews or written questionnaires to gather the data. The researcher may obtain information from all possible subjects or from a selected **sample** (a representative part of a population). Because the former method is often impractical, a random sample of subjects is selected from the larger population. If the sample is selected scientifically, a relatively small proportion can yield satisfactory results—that is, the inferences made from the sample will be reliable about the entire population. For example, a probability sample of only 2,000 from a total population of 1 million can provide data very close to what would be discovered if a survey were taken of the entire 1 million.

Typically with survey research, sociologists use sophisticated statistical techniques to control the contaminating effects of confounding **variables** to determine whether the findings could have occurred by chance, to determine whether variables are related, and to see whether such a relationship is a causal one. A variable is an attitude, behavior, or condition that can vary in magnitude and significance from case to case.

Sociologists may use personal interviews to gather data on the beliefs and behaviors of people to determine if they vary by age, sex, race, ethnicity, religion, social class, or region.

Experiments. To understand the cause-and-effect relationship among a few variables, sociologists use controlled experiments. Let us assume, for example, that we want to test whether White students in interracial classrooms have more positive attitudes toward African Americans than Whites in segregated classrooms have toward them. Using the experimental method, the researcher would take a number of White students previously unexposed to Blacks in school and randomly assign a subset to an integrated classroom situation. Before actual contact with the Blacks, however, all the White students would be given a test of their racial attitudes. This pretest establishes a benchmark from which to measure any changes in attitudes. One group, the control group, continues school in segregated classrooms. (The **control group** is a group of subjects not exposed to the independent variable.) The other group, the experimental group, now has Blacks as classmates. (The **experimental group** is a group of subjects who are exposed to the independent variable.) Otherwise, the two groups are the same. Following a suitable period of time, the Whites in both groups are tested again for their racial attitudes. If this posttest reveals that the experimental group differs from the control group in racial attitudes (the **dependent variable**), then it is assumed that interracial contact (the **independent variable**) is the source of the change. (The dependent variable is a variable that is influenced by the effect of another variable. The independent variable is a variable that affects another variable.) As an example of a less contrived experiment, a researcher can test the results of two different treatments on the subsequent behavior of juvenile delinquents. Delinquent boys who had been adjudicated by the courts can be randomly assigned to a boys' industrial school or a group home facility in the community. After release from incarceration, records are kept on the boys' subsequent behavior in school (grades, truancy, formal reprimands) and in the community (police contacts, work behavior). If the boys from the two groups differ appreciably, then we can say with assurance, because the boys were randomly assigned to each group, that the difference in treatment (the independent variable) was the source of the difference in behavior (the dependent variable).

Observation. The researcher, without intervention, can observe as accurately as possible what occurs in a community, group, or social event. This type of procedure is especially helpful in understanding such social phenomena as the decision-making process, the stages of a riot, the attraction of cults for their members, or the depersonalization of patients in a mental hospital. Case studies of entire communities have been very instrumental in the understanding of power structures (Dahl, 1961; Hunter, 1953) and the complex interaction patterns in cities (Whyte, 1988). Long-time participant observation studies of slum neighborhoods and gangs have been insightful in showing the social organization present in what the casual observer might think of as disorganized activity (Gans, 1962; Liebow, 1967; Whyte, 1956).

Existing Data. The sociologist can also use existing data to test theories. The most common sources of information are the various agencies of the government. Data are provided for the nation, regions, states, communities, and census tracts on births, deaths, income, education, unemployment, business activity, health delivery systems, prison populations, military spending, poverty, migration, and the like. Important information can also be obtained from such sources as business firms, athletic teams and leagues, unions, and professional associations. Statistical techniques can be used with these data to describe populations and the effects of social variables on various dependent variables.

Chapter Review

1. Sociology is the science dealing with social forces—the forces outside us that shape our lives, interests, and personalities. Sociologists, then, work to discover the underlying order of social life and the principles regarding it that explain human behavior.

2. The assumptions of the sociological perspective are that (a) individuals are, by their nature, social beings; (b) individuals are socially determined; and (c) individuals create, sustain, and change the social forms within which they conduct their lives.

3. The sociological imagination involves (a) a willingness to view the social world from the perspective of others; (b) focusing on the social, economic, and historical circumstances that influence families, groups, and organizations; (c) questioning the structural arrangements that shape social behavior; and (d) seeing the solutions to social problems not in terms of changing problem people but in changing the structure of society.

4. Sociology is uncomfortable for many people because it looks behind the facades of social life. This requires a critical examination of society that questions the existing myths, stereotypes, and official dogma.

5. The basis for the critical stance of sociologists is that the social world is not sacred because it is made by human beings.

6. Sociological research involves four types of questions: factual, comparative, historical, and theoretical.

7. The development of sociology was dependent on four European intellectuals: (a) Auguste Comte was the founder of sociology. His emphasis was on a rigorous use of the scientific method. (b) Emile Durkheim emphasized social facts (sociological explanation for human behavior) and the social bond. (c) Karl Marx wrote about the importance of economics in understanding social stratification, power, and ideology. (d) Max Weber, in reaction to Marx, demonstrated that social life is multidimensional and that ideology shapes the economy.

8. Sociology depends on reliable data and logical reasoning. Although value neutrality is impossible in the social sciences, bias is minimized by the norms of science.

9. Survey research is a systematic means of gathering data to obtain information about people's behaviors, attitudes, and opinions.

10. Sociologists may use experiments to assess the effects of social factors on human behavior. One of two similar groups—the experimental group—is exposed to an independent variable. If this group later differs from the control group, then the independent variable is known to have produced the effect.

11. Observation is another technique for obtaining reliable information. Various social organizations such as prisons, hospitals, schools, churches, cults, families, communities, and corporations can be studied and understood through systematic observation.

12. Sociologists also use existing sources of data to test their theories.

13. Sociology is a science, and the rules of scientific research guide the efforts of sociologists to discover the principles of social organization and the sources of social constraints on human behavior.

Key Terms

Sociology
Social determinism
Human agency
Sociological imagination
Positivism
Social facts

False consciousness
Class consciousness
Charisma
Sociological theory
Value neutrality
Sample

Variable
Control group
Experimental group
Dependent variable
Independent variable

Study Questions

1. How would sociologists differ from psychologists in studying such phenomena as divorce and racism?
2. Peter Berger has said that "the sociological perspective involves a process of 'seeing through' the facades of social structure." What does this mean? Give examples.
3. To what extent are you shaped by your social environment? Provide examples of the social facts (Durkheim) that affect you.
4. Speculate (sociologically) on why sociology developed where and when it did.
5. Apply the sociological imagination to the social problem of poverty.
6. Are you comfortable or uncomfortable with the sociological perspective? Elaborate.
7. How do sociologists minimize bias in their research activities?

For Further Reading

The Sociological Perspective

Zygmunt Bauman, *Thinking Sociologically* (Cambridge, MA: Basil Blackwell, 1990).

Bennett M. Berger (ed.), *Authors of Their Own Lives: Intellectual Autobiographies by Twenty American Sociologists* (Berkeley: University of California Press, 1990).

Peter L. Berger, *Invitation to Sociology: A Humanistic Perspective* (Garden City, NY: Doubleday Anchor Books, 1963).

Peter Berger and Hansfried Kellner, *Sociology Reinterpreted* (Garden City, NY: Doubleday Anchor Books, 1981).

Randall Collins, *Sociological Insight: An Introduction to Non-Obvious Sociology*, 2nd ed. (New York: Oxford University Press, 1992).

Kai Erikson (ed.), *Sociological Visions* (Lanham, MD: Rowman & Littlefield, 1997).

Ann Game and Andrew Metcalfe, *Passionate Sociology* (Thousand Oaks, CA: Sage, 1996).

Ann Goetting and Sarah Fenstermaker (eds.), *Individual Voices, Collective Visions: Fifty Years of Women in Sociology* (Philadelphia: Temple University Press, 1995).

Charles Lemert, *Social Things: An Introduction to the Sociological Life* (Lanham, MD: Rowman & Littlefield, 1997).

C. Wright Mills, *The Sociological Imagination* (New York: Oxford University Press, 1959).

John Walton, *Sociology and Critical Inquiry: The Work, Tradition, and Purpose*, 2nd ed. (Belmont, CA: Wadsworth, 1990).

The Historical Development of Sociology

Tom Campbell, *Seven Theories of Human Society* (New York: Oxford University Press, 1981).

Randall Collins and Michael Makowsky, *The Discovery of Society*, 3rd ed. (New York: Random House, 1984).

R. P. Cuzzort and Edith W. King, *Social Thought into the Twenty-First Century*, 6th ed. (Fort Worth, TX: Harcourt, Brace, 2002).

Charles Lemert (ed.), *Social Theory: The Multicultural and Classic Readings* (Boulder, CO: Westview, 1993).

Ken Morrison, *Marx, Durkheim, Weber: Formations of Modern Social Thought* (Thousand Oaks, CA: Sage, 1995).

George Ritzer, *Sociological Theory*, 3rd ed. (New York: McGraw-Hill, 1992).

Alan Sica, *Social Thought: From the Enlightenment to the Present* (Boston: Allyn and Bacon, 2005).

The Craft of Sociology

Robert R. Alford, *The Craft of Inquiry: Theories, Methods, Evidence* (New York: Oxford University Press, 1998).

Earl R. Babbie, *The Practice of Social Research*, 10th ed. (Belmont, CA: Wadsworth, 2004).

Howard S. Becker, *Tricks of the Trade: How to Think about Your Research While You're Doing It* (Chicago: University of Chicago Press, 1998).

W. Lawrence Neuman, *Social Research Methods: Qualitative and Quantitative Approaches*, 5th ed. (Boston: Allyn and Bacon).

Web Resources

http://www.asanet.org/

The American Sociological Association is a non-profit association "dedicated to advancing sociology as a scientific discipline and profession serving the public good."

http://socserv2.mcmaster.ca/w3virtsoclib/

WWW Virtual Library: Sociology contains links to many websites related to sociology. The links include information about online sociological journals, related fields, and work done by contributors to the emergence of sociology (Marx, Durkheim, and Weber).

http://www.sociologyonline.co.uk/

An interactive website that includes polls and quizzes on different topics, such as race, class, and gender. It also has a library with links to different sites on theory.

http://www.pscw.uva.nl/sociosite/

SocioSite has an extensive list of influential sociologists, with links to each, which contain information about their work and other pertinent information. The site also has other options, such as searching journals related to sociology.

http://ryoung001.homestead.com/index.html

Sociologist At Large "has been introducing students and non-students to the Sociological Perspective since 1999." It contains information in terms that are very accessible for those new to sociology.

http://trochim.human.cornell.edu/kb/qual.htm

This site offers information on the various types of qualitative methods of research that are used in sociology, such as participant observation and in-depth interviewing.

http://odwin.ucsd.edu/glossary/

This is a glossary of social science computing and data terms, which can be searched for definitions relevant to research.

http://www.latrobe.edu.au/aqr/

The Association for Qualitative Research is an international organization for those with an interest in qualitative research. The site has a journal that can be downloaded.

http://ericae.net/ft/tamu/vpiques3.htm

This site offers a guide to developing questionnaires. It includes descriptions of problems that may arise and how to avoid them.

The Structure of Social Groups

An experiment was conducted some years ago when twenty-four previously unacquainted boys, age twelve, were brought together at a summer camp (Sherif and Sherif, 1966). For three days the boys, who were unaware that they were part of an experiment, participated in campwide activities. During this period, the camp counselors (actually, they were research assistants) observed the friendship patterns that emerged naturally. The boys were then divided into two groups of twelve. The boys were deliberately separated in order to break up the previous friendship patterns. The groups were then isolated from each other for five days. During this period the boys were left alone by the counselors so that what occurred was the spontaneous result of the boys' behavior. The experimenters found that in both groups there developed (1) a division of labor; (2) a hierarchical structure of ranks—that is, differences among the boys in power, prestige, and rewards; (3) the creation of rules; (4) punishments for violations of the rules; (5) argot—that is, specialized language such as nicknames and group symbols that served as positive ingroup identifications; and (6) member cooperation to achieve group goals.

This experiment illustrates the process of social organization. The counselors did not insist that these phenomena occur in each group. They seemed to occur naturally. In fact, they happen universally (Liebow, 1967; Whyte, 1956). The goals of this chapter are to understand the components of social structure that emerge and how these components operate to constrain behavior. Although the process is generally the same regardless of group size, we examine it at two levels—the micro level and the societal level, also known as the macro level.

The Micro Level

Social Organization

Social organization refers to the ways in which human conduct becomes socially organized—that is, the observed regularities in the behavior of people that are due to the social conditions in which they find themselves rather than to their physiological or psychological characteristics as individuals (Blau and Scott, 1962:2). The social conditions that constrain behavior can be divided into two types: (1) **social structure**—the structure of behavior in groups and society; and (2) culture—the shared beliefs of group members that unite them and guide their behavior.

Social Structure. Sociology is the study of the patterns that emerge when people interact over time. The emphasis is on the linkages and networks that emerge and that transform an aggregate of individuals into a group. (An **aggregate** is a collection of individuals who happen to be at the same place at the same time. A **group** is a collection of people who, because of sustained interaction, have evolved a common structure and culture.) We begin, then, with social interaction, the basic building block of groups. When the actions of one person affect another person, **social interaction** occurs. The most common method is communication through speech; the

a Closer Look

The Isolating Effects of E-Mail

Americans send more than ten times more e-mail messages a day than pieces of first-class mail.

"As more and more of us go online, we become accustomed to e-mail's mix of intimacy and anonymity. . . . Gone are intonation, affect, facial expression; e-mail offers only bare words, without even the nuances of handwriting" (Sklaroff, 1999:55). Chatrooms on the Internet are something like coffeehouses where like-minded people share their interests. This allows scholars, for example, from around the world to regularly interact. This is good but it is quite different from the bonds that emerge from regular face-to-face interaction. As sociologist Philip Slater says, "A community life exists when one can go daily to a given location and see many of the people he knows" (quoted in Oldenburg, 1997:32).

John L. Locke, a professor of communications, argues in *The De-Voicing of Society* (1998) that e-mail, voice mail, fax machines, beepers, and Internet chatrooms are robbing us of ordinary face-to-face talking. Talking, he says, like the grooming of apes and monkeys, is the way we build and maintain social relationships. Ironically, these incredible communication devices that combine to connect us in so many dazzling ways also separate us from intimate relationships. Our connections are now superficial—even devoid, often, of human contact:

Our great-grandparents lived very differently. They could see and hear their communicants. Messages were wrapped in blankets of feeling. Voices moved, faces flashed. From an averted gaze, a grin, or a catch in the voice, our great-grandparents knew when other people were ill at ease or saying something not quite true. They knew from the tone of the voice, set of jaw, and focus of the eyes when their associates "meant business."

How times have changed. We great-grand-children trade thoughts on a daily basis with people we do not know and will never meet. The social feedback mechanisms that were handed down by our evolutionary ancestors—systems that were designed and carefully tuned by hundreds of millennia of face-to-face-interaction—are rarely used nowadays, and there is a potential for miscommunication and mistrust as never before in human history. (Locke, 1998:18–19)

The new forms of communication reduce face-to-face interaction in other ways. Some people now work out of their homes, communicating with colleagues and clients through faxes and e-mails rather than standing around the water cooler at work. Even when physically with other employees at work, more and more communication is done over the Internet. Virtual conferences now often take the place of meetings with business associates. Human contact is also reduced when we shop, invest, bank, pay bills, play games, and do research over the Internet.

written word; or a symbolic act such as a wink, a facial expression, or gestures such as a wave of the hand or the raising of a finger (which finger is often crucial). (See the panel titled "A Closer Look: The Isolating Effects of E-Mail.")

Behavior can also be altered by the mere presence of other people. The way we behave (from the way we eat to what we think) is affected by whether we are alone or with other people. Even physical reactions such as crying, laughing, or passing gas are controlled by the individual because of the fear of embarrassment. It could even be argued that, except in the most extreme cases, people's actions are always oriented toward other human beings whether other people are physically present or not. We, as individuals, are constantly concerned about the expected or actual reactions of other people. Even when alone, an individual may not act in certain ways because of having been taught that such actions are wrong.

Social interaction may be either transitory or enduring. Sociologists are interested in the latter type because only then does patterned behavior occur. A case of enduring social interaction is a **social relationship**. Relationships occur for a number of reasons: sexual attraction, familial ties, a common interest (for example, collecting coins or growing African violets), a common political or religious ideology, cooperation to produce or distribute a product, or propinquity (being neighbors). Regardless of the specific reasons, the members of a social relationship are united at least in some minimal way with the other members. Most important, the members of a social relationship behave quite differently than they would as participants in a fleeting interaction.

Once the interaction is perpetuated, the behavior of the participants is profoundly altered. An autonomous individual is similar to an element in chemistry. As soon as there is a chemical reaction between them, however, the two elements become parts of a new entity, as Olsen (1976) notes:

> The concepts of "elements" and "parts" are analogous to terms in chemistry. By themselves, chemical elements— sodium and chlorine, for instance—exhibit characteristics peculiarly their own, by which each can be separately identified. This condition holds true even if elements are mixed together, as long as there is no chemical reaction between them. Through a process of chemical interaction, however, the elements can join to form an entirely new substance—in this case, salt. The elements of sodium and chlorine have now both lost their individual identities and characteristics, and have instead become parts of a more inclusive chemical compound, which has properties not belonging to either of its component parts by themselves. In an emergent process such as this, the original elements are transformed into parts of a new entity. (37)

Olsen's description of a chemical reaction is also appropriate for what arises in a social relationship. Most sociologists assume that the whole is not identical to the sum of its parts—that is, through the process of enduring interaction, something is created with properties different from the component parts.* The two groups of boys

---

*This assumption—the realist position—is one side of a fundamental philosophical debate. The nominalist position, on the other hand, argues that to know the parts is to know the whole. In sociology the realist position is dominant and is found in the words of Emile Durkheim (1958) and in the classic work by Charles Warriner (1956). The minority nominalist position in sociology is represented most prominently by George Homans (1964).

artificially formed at the summer camp, for example, developed similar structural properties regardless of the unique personalities of the boys in each group. Although groups may differ in size or purpose, they are similar in structure and in the processes that create the structure. In other words, one group may exist to knit quilts for charity while another may exist to commit terrorist bombings, but they will be alike in many important ways. Their social structure involves the patterns of interaction that emerge, the division of labor, and the linking and hierarchy of positions. The social structure is an emergent phenomenon bringing order and predictability to social life within the group.

Culture. The other component of social organization is culture—the shared beliefs of a group's members that serve to guide conduct. Through enduring social interaction, common expectations emerge about how people should act. These expectations are called **norms**. Criteria for judging what is appropriate, correct, moral, and important also emerge. These criteria are the **values** of the group. Also part of the shared beliefs are the expectations that group members have of individuals occupying the various positions within the group. These are **social roles**. The elements of culture are described briefly here for the micro and macro levels and in detail in Chapter 4. To summarize, social organization refers to both culture and social structure. Blau and Scott describe how these operate to constrain human behavior:

> The prevailing cultural standards and the structure of social relations serve to
> organize human conduct in the collectivity. As people conform more or less closely
> to the expectations of their fellows, and as the degree of their conformity in turn
> influences their relations with others and their social status, and as their status in
> turn further affects the inclinations to adhere to social norms and their chances to
> achieve valued objectives, their patterns of behavior become socially organized.
> (Blau and Scott, 1962:4–5)

Norms

All social organizations have rules (norms) that specify appropriate and inappropriate behaviors. In essence, norms are the behavioral expectations that members of a particular group collectively share. They ensure that action within social organizations is generally predictable. Some norms are not considered as important as others, and consequently are not severely punished if violated. These minor rules are called **folkways**. Folkways vary, of course, from group to group. A particular fraternity may expect its members to wear formal dress on certain occasions. In a church, wine may be consumed by the parishioners at the appropriate time—Communion. To bring one's own bottle of wine to Communion, however, would be a violation of the folkways of that church. (Could you imagine an announcement in your church bulletin that Communion will be next Sunday—B.Y.O.B.?) These examples show that folkways involve etiquette, customs, and regulations that, if violated, do not threaten the fabric of the social organization.

Violation of the group's mores, on the other hand, is considered important enough that it must be punished severely. (**Mores** are important norms, the violation of which results in severe punishment.) This type of norm involves morality—

in fact, mores can be thought of as moral imperatives. In a sorority, for instance, examples of the violations of mores might be disloyalty, stealing from a sister, and conduct that brings shame to the organization, such as dealing drugs.

Status and Role

One important aspect of social structure is composed of the positions of a social organization. If one determines which positions are present in an organization and how they are interrelated, then the analyst has a structural map of that social group. The existence of positions in organizations has an important consequence for individuals—the bestowing of a social identity. Each of us belongs to a number of organizations, and in each we occupy a position, or **status**. If you were asked, "Who are you?" chances are you would respond by listing your various statuses. An individual may at the same time be a student, sophomore, daughter, sister, friend, female, Baptist, Sunday school teacher, Democrat, sales clerk, U.S. citizen, and secretary-treasurer of the local chapter of Weight Watchers.

The individual's social identity, then, is a product of the particular matrix of statuses that she or he occupies. Another characteristic of statuses that has an important influence on social identity is that these positions in organizations tend to be differentially rewarded and esteemed. This element of **hierarchy** (the arrangement of people in order of importance) of status reinforces the positive or negative image individuals have of themselves depending on placement in various organizations. Some individuals consistently hold prestigious positions (bank president, deacon, Caucasian, male, chairman of United Fund), while others may hold only statuses that are negatively esteemed (welfare recipient, aged, Latino, janitor), and some people occupy mixed statuses (bus driver, thirty-second-degree Mason, union member, church trustee).

Group memberships are vital sources of our notion of our own identity. Similarly, when they know of our status in various organizations, other people assign a social identity to us. When we determine a person's age, race, religion, and occupation, we tend to stereotype that person—that is, we assume that the individual is a certain type. Stereotyping has the effect of conferring a social identity on that person, raising expectations for certain behaviors that, very often, result in a self-fulfilling prophecy. This phenomenon is heightened when considering an individual's **master status**, which is a status that has exceptional significance for social identity. The master status trumps all other statuses when a situation or an individual is evaluated by others. For most of us, our occupation is a master status because it informs others of our educational attainment, skills, and income. But it may also be the status of African American, or athlete, or ex-convict, or having acquired immune deficiency syndrome (AIDS).

The mapping of statuses provides important clues about the social structure of an organization, but the most important aspect of status is the behavior expected of the occupant of a status. To determine that an individual occupies the status of father does not tell us much about what the group expects of a father. In some societies, for example, the biological father has no legal, monetary, or social responsibility for his children, who are cared for by the mother and her brother. In U.S. society, there are norms (legal and informal) that demand that the father be responsible for his children. Not only must he provide for them, but he must also, depending on the customs of the family, be a disciplinarian, buddy, teacher, Santa Claus, and tooth fairy.

The behavior expected of a person occupying a status in a group is that person's **role*** (the behavioral expectations and requirements attached to a position in a social organization). The norms of the social organization constrain the incumbents in a status to behave in prescribed and therefore predictable ways, regardless of their particular personalities. Society insists that we play our roles correctly. To do otherwise is to risk being judged by other people as abnormal, crazy, incompetent, and/or immature. These pressures to conform to role demands ensure that there is stability in social groups even though member turnover occurs. For example, ministers to a particular congregation come and go, but certain actions are predictable in particular incumbents because of the demands on their behavior. These demands come from the hierarchy of the denomination, from other ministers, and most assuredly from the members of the parish. The stability imposed by role is also seen with other statuses, such as professor, janitor, police officer, student, and even president of the United States.

The expectations of behavior of members in the various statuses are not to make behavior totally predictable, however. Occupants of the statuses can vary their behavior within limits. There are at least three reasons for this.

- First, personality variables can account for variations in the behavior of people holding identical statuses. People can be conformist or unconventional, manipulated or manipulators, passive or aggressive, followers or inspirational leaders, cautious or impetuous, ambitious or lackadaisical. Personality traits can make obvious differences in the behavior of individuals, even though individuals may face identical group pressures.

- A second reason role does not make social actors robots is that the occupants of a status may not receive a clear, consistent message as to which behavior is expected. A minister, for example, may find within his or her congregation individuals and cliques that make conflicting demands. One group may insist that the minister be a social activist. Another may demand that the pastor be apolitical and spend time exclusively meeting the spiritual needs of the members.

- Another circumstance leading to conflicting expectations—and unpredictability of action—results from multiple group memberships. The statuses we occupy may have conflicting demands on our behavior. When an African American politician, for example, is elected as mayor of a large city, as has been the case in Los Angeles, Chicago, Detroit, Philadelphia, Baltimore, and Atlanta, he or she is faced with the constraints of the office on one hand, and the demands of the African American constituency on the other. Other illustrations of conflicting demands because of occupying two quite different statuses are daughter and lover, son and peer-group member, and businessperson and church deacon. Being the recipient of incompatible demands results in hypocrisy, secrecy, guilt, and, most important for our consideration, unpredictable behavior.

---

*This section introduces the concept of role as it is appropriate to the context of social organization. We elaborate on it in Chapter 4.

Although role performance may vary, stability within organizations remains. The stability is a consequence of the strong tendency of people in a social organization to conform. Let us look briefly at just how powerfully roles shape behavior. First, the power of role over personal behavior is seen dramatically as one moves from one status to another. Think about your own behavior at home, at church, at school, in the dorm, at a party, or in a parked car. In each of these instances you occupy multiple statuses and face conflicting role expectations, resulting in overall inconsistent behavior but likely behavior that is expected for each separate role.

The power of role to shape behavior is also demonstrated as one changes status within an organization. The Amish, for instance, select their minister by lot from among the male adults of the group. The eligible members each select a Bible. The one choosing the Bible with the special mark in it is the new pastor. His selection is assumed to be ordained by God. This individual now has a new status in the group—the leader with God's approval. Such an elevation in status will doubtless have a dramatic effect on that person's behavior. Without special training (the Amish rarely attend school beyond the eighth grade), the new minister will in all likelihood exhibit leadership, self-confidence, and wisdom. Less dramatically, but with similar results nonetheless, each of us undergoes shifts in status within the organizations to which we belong—from first-year student to senior, bench warmer to first team, assembly-line worker to supervisor, and from adolescent to adult. These changes in status mean, of course, a concomitant shift in the expectations for behavior (role). Not only does our behavior change but so too do our attitudes, perceptions, and perhaps even our personalities.

A dramatic example of the power of role over behavior is provided by an experiment conducted by Philip Zimbardo, who wanted to study the impact of prison life on guards and prisoners. Using student volunteers, Zimbardo (1972) randomly assigned some to be guards and others to be inmates. By using subjects who were not associated with a prison, the researcher could actually study the effects of social roles on behavior without the confounding variables of personality traits, character disorders, and the like.

Zimbardo constructed a mock prison in the basement of the psychology building at Stanford University. The students chosen as prisoners were arrested one night without warning, dressed in prison uniforms, and locked in the cells. The guards were instructed to maintain order. Zimbardo found that the college students assigned the roles of guard or inmate actually became guards and inmates in just a few days. The guards showed brutality and the prisoners became submissive, demonstrating that roles effectively shape behavior because they have the power to shape consciousness (thinking, feeling, and perceiving). Interestingly, Zimbardo, who is a psychologist, concluded that social factors superseded individual ones: "Individual behavior is largely under the control of social forces and environmental contingencies rather than personality traits, character, will power or other empirically unvalidated constructs" (Zimbardo, 1972:6).

Finally, roles protect individuals. The constraints on behavior implied in the role provide a blueprint that relieves the individual from the responsibility for action. Thus, the certainty provided by role makes us comfortable. Gay rights, to name one contemporary movement, is aimed at liberation from the constraints of narrowly prescribed sex and gender roles. But to be free of these constraints brings not only freedom but also problems. So, too, when one is freed from the constraints of a particular community, job, or marriage, the newfound liberty, independence, and excitement are countered by the frustrations involving ambiguity, choice, loneliness, and responsibility.

Social Control

Although they vary in the degree of tolerance for alternative behaviors, social groups universally demand conformity to some norms. In the absence of such demands, groups would not exist because of the resulting anarchy. The mechanisms of social control are varied. They can occur subtly in the socialization process (see Chapter 5) so that people feel guilty or proud, depending on their actions. They can occur in the form of rewards (medals, prizes, merit badges, gold stars, trophies, praise) by family members, peers, neighbors, fellow workers, employers, and the community to reinforce certain behaviors. Also common are negative sanctions such as fines, demerits, imprisonment, and excommunication, which are used to ensure conformity. More subtle techniques, such as gossip or ridicule, are also successful in securing conformity because of the common fear of humiliation before one's friends, classmates, co-workers, or neighbors.

An example of a particularly devastating and effective technique is the practice of shunning the sinner used by some of the Amish and Mennonite religious sects. No one in the religious community, not even the guilty party's spouse and children, is to recognize his or her existence. In one celebrated case, Robert Bear was the victim of shunning. He took the case to court on the grounds that this practice was unconstitutional because it was too severe. Since the shun had been invoked, Bear's wife had not slept with him, his six children were alienated from him, and his farm operation was in ruin because no one would work for him or buy his produce. The courts ruled, however, that it was within the province of the church to punish its members for transgressions. The severity of the shun is an extremely effective social control device for the Amish community, guaranteeing, except in rare cases, conformity to the dictates of the group.

Whatever the mechanism used, social control efforts tend to be very effective, whether within a family, peer group, organization, community, or a society. Most of the people, most of the time, conform to the norms of their groups and society. Otherwise, the majority of the poor would riot, most of the starving would steal, and more young men would refuse to fight in wars. The pressure to conform comes from within us (internalization of the group's norms and values from the socialization process) and from outside us (**sanctions** [or the threat of sanctions], social rewards or punishments for approved or disapproved behavior), and we obey. In fact, what we consider self-control is really the consequence of social control. These constraints are usually not oppressive to the individual. Indeed, we want to obey the rules.

Primary and Secondary Groups

A **social group** is an organization created through enduring and patterned interaction. It consists of people who have a common identity, share a common culture, and define themselves as a distinct social unit. Groups may be classified in a number of ways, the most significant of which involves the kind and quality of relationships that members have with each other. Sociologists have delineated two types of groups

A primary group is composed of members intimately involved with each other. The members have a strong identification, loyalty, and emotional attachment to the group and its members.

according to the degrees of intimacy and involvement among the members — primary and secondary.

Primary groups are groups whose members are the most intimately involved with each other. These groups are small and display face-to-face interaction. They are informal in organization and long-lasting. The members have a strong identification, loyalty, and emotional attachment to the group and its members. Examples are the nuclear family, a child's play group, a teenage gang, and close friends. Primary groups are crucial to the individual because they provide members with a sense of belonging, identity, purpose, and security. Thus, they have the strongest influence on the attitudes and values of members.

Secondary groups, in contrast to primary groups, are much larger and more impersonal. They are formally organized, task oriented, and relatively nonpermanent. The individual member is relatively unimportant. The members may vary considerably in beliefs, attitudes, and values. Americans are greatly affected by this type of group. The government at all levels deals with us impersonally. So, too, do our schools, where we are a number in a computer. We live in large dormitories or in neighborhoods where we are barely acquainted with people near us. We work in large organizations and belong to large religious organizations.

Secondary groups spawn the formation of primary groups. Primary groups emerge at school, at work, in an apartment complex, in a neighborhood, in a church, or in an army. In other words, intensely personal groups develop and are sustained by their members in largely impersonal settings.

The existence of primary groups within secondary groups is an important phenomenon that has ramifications for the goals of the secondary group. Two examples from military experience make this point. In World War II the German army was organized to promote the formation of primary groups. The men were assigned to a unit for the duration of the war. They trained together, fought together, went on furloughs together, and were praised or punished as a group. This was a calculated organizational ploy to increase social solidarity in the small fighting units. This worked to increase morale, loyalty, and a willingness to die for the group. In fact, individuals often became more loyal to their fighting unit than to the nation (Shils and Janowitz, 1948).

In contrast, the U.S. army in Vietnam was organized in such a way as to minimize the possibility of forming primary groups. Instead of being assigned to a single combat unit until the war was over, soldiers were given a twelve-month tour of duty in Vietnam. This rotation system meant that in any fighting unit, soldiers were continually entering and leaving. This constant rotation prevented the development of close relationships and a feeling of all for one and one for all. Because each soldier had his own departure date, his goal was not to win the war but to survive until he was eligible to go home. This individualism made morale difficult to maintain and loyalty to one's unit difficult if not impossible to achieve. It also made the goal of winning the war less attainable than would a system that fostered primary groups (Moskos, 1975).

Bureaucracy: The Ultimate Secondary Group

A **bureaucracy** is a hierarchical formal organization characterized by rationality and efficiency—that is, improved operating efficiency and more effective attainment of common goals. As an organization grows in size and complexity, there is a greater need for coordination if efficiency is to be maintained or improved. Organizational efficiency is maximized (ideally) under the following conditions (Weber, 1947:329–341):

- When the work is divided into small tasks performed by specialists.
- When there is a hierarchy of authority (chain of command), with each position in the chain having clearly defined duties and responsibilities.
- When behaviors are governed by standardized, written, and explicit rules.
- When all decisions are made on the basis of technical knowledge, not personal considerations.
- When the members are judged solely on the basis of proficiency, and discipline is impartially enforced.

In short, a bureaucracy is an organization designed to perform like a machine. The push toward increased bureaucratization pervades nearly all aspects of U.S. life, including government (at all levels), the church (for example, the Catholic Church and the Methodist Church), education (all school systems), sports (the National Collegiate Athletic Association [NCAA], athletic departments at big-time schools, professional teams), health care (hospitals, health maintenance organizations, Blue Cross/Blue Shield), corporations (General Motors, IBM), and even crime (the Mafia) and fast-food chains. The increasing bureaucratization in social life is called **McDonaldization**, coined by George Ritzer. By this he means "the process by which the principles of the fast-food restaurant are coming to dominate more and more sectors of American society as well as the rest of the world" (Ritzer, 1996:1).

The benefits of bureaucracy include a division of labor that promotes efficiency, specific expectations of members, rewards based on achievement rather than favoritism, and expertise for specific tasks coordinated to accomplish complex goals.

There is also a significant downside to bureaucracy. Ironically, while created for efficiency, bureaucracies often foster the opposite result by having too many regulations—individuals evade responsibility by passing the buck, and creativity is stifled by rules. Blind obedience to rules and the unquestioned following of orders mean that new and unusual situations cannot be handled efficiently because the rules do not apply. Rigid adherence to the rules creates automatons. Robert Merton (1957) observes that "adherence to the rules, originally conceived as a means, becomes transformed into an end-in-itself" (199). Most significant, there is the danger that Max Weber feared from the **"iron cage" of rationality**; that is, bureaucracies can be dehumanizing. As summarized by Ritzer (1996):

> In Weber's view, bureaucracies are cages in the sense that people are trapped in them, their basic humanity denied. Weber feared most that these systems would grow more and more rational and that rational principles would come to dominate an accelerating number of sectors of society. Weber anticipated a society of people locked into a series of rational structures, who could move only from one rational system to another. Thus, people would move from rationalized educational institutions to rationalized work places, from rationalized recreational settings to rationalized homes. Society would become nothing more than a seamless web of rationalized structures; there would be no escape. (21)

Power of the Social Group

We have seen that primary and secondary groups structure the behavior of their members by providing rules, roles, and mechanisms of social control. The result is that most of us, most of the time, conform to the expectations of social groups.

© G. Oliver Reprinted by permission.

Let us examine some illustrations of the profound influence of social groups on individuals, beginning with Emile Durkheim's classic study of suicide.

The Group Affects the Probability of Suicide. One's attachment to social groups affects the probability of suicide. Suicide would appear on the surface to be one area that could strictly be left to psychological explanations. An individual is committing the ultimate individual act—ending one's own life—presumably because of excessive guilt, anxiety, and/or stress. Sociologists, however, are interested in this seemingly individual phenomenon because of the social factors that may produce the feelings of guilt or the undue psychological stress. Sociologists are not interested, however, in the individual suicide case, as psychologists are, but in a number of people in the same social situation. Let us look at how sociologists would study suicide by examining in some detail the classic study by the nineteenth-century French sociologist Emile Durkheim (1951). Durkheim was the consummate sociologist. He reacted to what he considered the excessive psychologism of his day by examining suicide rates (the number of suicides per 100,000 people in a particular category) sociologically. Some of the interesting results of his study were that single people had higher rates than married people, childless married people had a higher rate than those with children, the rate of city dwellers exceeded that of rural people, and Protestants were more likely to be self-destructive than Catholics or Jews. Societal conditions were also correlated with suicide rates. As expected, rates were higher during economic depressions than in periods of economic stability, although surprisingly high rates were found during economic booms.

Durkheim went an important step beyond just noting that social factors were related to suicide rates. He developed a theory to explain these facts—a theory based on the individual's relationship to a social organization. Durkheim posited three types of suicide—the egoistic, altruistic, and anomic—to illustrate the effect of one's attachment to a group (society, religion, family) on self-preservation. **Egoistic suicide** occurs when an individual has minimal ties to a social group. The person is alone, lacking group goals and group supports. This explains why married people are less likely to commit suicide than are single people, and why married people with children are not as likely to kill themselves as are married people who are childless. Being an important part of a group gives meaning and purpose to life. This lack of group supports also explains why Protestants during Durkheim's day had a higher suicide rate than did Catholics. The Catholic religion provided believers with many group supports, including the belief in the authority of religious leaders to interpret the scriptures. Catholics also believed that through the confessional, sinners could be redeemed. Protestants, on the other hand, were expected to be their own priests, reading and interpreting God's word. When guilty of sin, Protestants again were alone. There was no confessional where a priest would assure one of forgiveness. The differences in theology left individual Protestants without religious authority and with a greater sense of uncertainty. This relatively greater isolation left Protestants without the group of believers and the authority of priests in times of stress.

Altruistic suicide occurs in a completely different type of group setting. When groups are highly cohesive, the individual member of such a collectivity tends to be group oriented. Such a group might expect its members to kill themselves for the good of the group under certain conditions. Soldiers may be expected to leave the relative safety of their foxholes and attack a strategic hill even though the odds are against them. The strong allegiance to one's group may force an act that would otherwise seem irrational. The kamikaze attacks by Japanese pilots during World War II were suicide missions in which the pilot guided his ammunition-laden plane into a target. These pilots gave their lives because of their ultimate allegiance to a social group—clearly an example of altruistic suicide. So, too, are the Muslim suicide bombers in the Middle East, young men (and occasionally women) who die for the cause of their group.

The third type of suicide—**anomic suicide**—is also related to the individual's attachment to a group. It differs from the other two types in that it refers especially to the condition in which the expectations of a group are ambiguous or they conflict with other sets of expectations. Typically, behavior is regulated by a clear set of rules (norms). But there are times when these rules lose their clarity and certainty for individuals. This is a condition of anomie (normlessness). Anomie usually occurs in a situation of rapid change. Examples of anomic situations are emigration from one society to another, movement from a rural area to an urban one, rapid loss of status, overnight wealth, widowhood, divorce, and drastic inflation or deflation. In all these cases, people are often not sure how to behave. They are not certain of their goals. Life may appear aimless. Whenever the constraints on behavior are suddenly lifted, the probability of suicide increases. The irony is that we tend to be comfortable under the tyranny of the group and that freedom from such constraints is often intolerable. The sexual freedom of married people in U.S. society, for example, is highly regulated. There is only one legitimate sex partner. The unmarried person is not limited. But even though married people might fantasize that such a life is nirvana, the replacement of regulated sexual behavior with such freedom is a condition of normlessness conducive to higher suicide rates.

The Group Affects Perceptions. The group may affect our perceptions. Apparently, our wish to conform is so great that we often give in to group pressure. Solomon Asch, a social psychologist, has tested this proposition by asking the subjects in an experiment to compare the length of lines on cards (Asch, 1958). The subjects were asked one at a time to identify verbally the longest line. All the subjects but one were confederates of the experimenter, coached to give the same wrong answer, placing the lone subject in the awkward position of having the evidence of her or his senses unanimously contradicted. Each experiment consisted of eighteen trials, with the confederates giving wrong responses on twelve and correct ones on six. For the fifty subjects going through this ordeal, the average number of times they went along with the majority with incorrect judgments was 3.84. Thirteen of the fifty were independent and gave responses in accord with their perceptions, but thirty-seven (74 percent) gave in to the group pressure at least once (twelve did eight or more times). In other experiments in which the confederates were not unanimous in their responses, the subjects were freed from the overwhelming group pressure and generally had confidence enough in their perceptions to give the correct answer.

Muzafer Sherif (1958) also conducted a series of experiments to determine the extent of conformity among individuals. An individual subject was placed in a dark room to observe a pinpoint of light. The subject was asked to describe how many inches the light moved (the light appears to move, even though it is stationary, because of what is called the autokinetic effect). In repeated experiments each subject tended to be consistent as to how far she or he felt the light had moved. When placed in a group, however, individuals modified their observations to make them more consistent with those of the other people in the room. After repeated exposures, the group arrived at a collective judgment. The important point about this experiment is that the group, unlike the one in the Asch experiment, was composed entirely of naive subjects. Therefore, the conclusion about group pressure on individual members is more valid, reflecting natural group processes.

The Group Affects Convictions. Sectarians with group support maintain their conviction despite contrary evidence. Leon Festinger and his associates Riecken and Schachter (1956) at the University of Minnesota carefully studied a group that believed that in 1956 a great flood would submerge the West Coast from Seattle to Chile on December 21 of that year. On the eve of the predicted cataclysm the leader received a message that her group should be ready to leave at midnight in a flying saucer that had been dispatched to save them. The group waited expectantly at midnight for the arrival of the saucer. It did not appear, and finally at 4:45 A.M. the leader announced that she had received another communication. The message was that the world had been spared the disaster because of the force of good found among this small band of believers. Festinger was especially interested in how the group would handle this disconfirmation of prophecy. But this group, like other millennial groups of history, reacted to the disconfirmation by reaffirming their beliefs and doubling their efforts to win converts.

The Group Affects Health and Life. Membership in a group may have an effect on one's health and even on life itself. Pakistan has a caste system; children are destined to occupy the stratum of society into which they are born. Their occupation will be that of their parents with no questions asked. One of the lowest castes is that of beggar. Because the child of a beggar will be a beggar and because the most successful beggars are deformed, the child will be deformed by his or her family (usually by an uncle). Often the method is to break the child's back because the resulting deformity is so wretched. All parents wish success for their children, and the beggar family wishing the same is forced by the constraints of the rigid social system to physically disable their child for life.

Over the past twenty years or so, hundreds of children have died across the United States because their parents belonged to religious sects that do not believe in medical intervention. Eight of these deaths have occurred in Colorado within one sect, the Church of the First Born. One child died of meningitis; others died from pneumonia or other conditions that very likely could have been healed through traditional medical care. A three-year-old boy, for example, whose mother belonged to this sect died of diphtheria. The boy had never been immunized for this disease. Moreover, the mother refused medical treatment for her son after the illness had been diagnosed. The mother knew the consequences of her refusal of medical treatment because her nephew had died of diphtheria, but her faith and the faith of the other members kept her from saving her son's life. This is dramatic evidence for the power of the group to curb what we erroneously call maternal instinct.

Another example of a group demanding hazardous behavior of its members is found among some religious sects of Appalachia that encourage the handling of poisonous snakes (rattlesnakes, water moccasins, and copperheads) as part of worship. Members pick up handfuls of poisonous snakes, throw them on the ground, pick them up again, thrust them under their shirts and blouses, and even cover their heads with clusters of snakes. The ideology of the group thus

A few religious congregations in the United States use snakes in their worship services. Members handle poisonous snakes to show their ultimate faith. Thus, religious ideology takes precedence over rational behavior.

encourages members literally to put their faith to the ultimate test—death. The ideology is especially interesting because it justifies both death by snakebite and being spared the bite or recovering if bitten:

> The serpent-handlers say the Lord causes a snake to strike in order to refute scoffers' claims that the snakes' fangs have been pulled. They see each recovery from snakebite as a miracle wrought by the Lord—and each death as a sign that the Lord "really had to show the scoffers how dangerous it is to obey His commandments." Since adherents believe that death brings one to the throne of God, some express an eagerness to die when He decides they are ready. Those who have been bitten and who have recovered seem to receive special deference from other members of the church. (Gerrard, 1968:23)

The Group Affects Behavior. The group can alter the behavior of members, even behaviors that involve basic human drives. Human beings are biologically programmed to eat, drink, sleep, and engage in sexual activity; but human groups significantly shape how these biological drives are met. How we eat, when we eat, and what we eat are all greatly influenced by social groups. Some groups have rigid rules that require periods of fasting. Others have festivals at which huge quantities of food and drink are consumed. Sexual behavior is also controlled. Although the sex drive is universal, mating is not a universal activity among adults. Some people, because of their group membership, take vows of chastity. Some people, because they have certain physical or mental traits, are often labeled by groups as undesirable and are therefore involuntarily chaste. Some societies are obsessed with sex; others are not. An example of the latter is the Dani tribe of New Guinea. Sexual intercourse is delayed between marriage partners until exactly two years after the ceremony. After the birth of a child there is a five-year period of abstinence.

These dramatic examples of the power of groups over individuals should not keep us from recognizing the everyday and continual constraints on behavior. Our everyday activities, our perceptions and interpretations, and our attitudes are the products of our group memberships. The constraints, however, are for the most part subtle and go unrecognized as such. In short, what we think of as autonomous behavior is generally not autonomous at all.

In summary, social groups undergo a universal process—the process of social organization. Through enduring social interaction, a matrix of social expectations emerges that guides behavior in prescribed channels, making social life patterned and therefore predictable. Thus, social organizations tend to be stable. But this is also a process, as Figure 2.1 indicates.

Interaction among the social actors in a social organization is constant and continuous, reinforcing stability but also bringing about change. Social organizations are never static. New ideas and new expectations emerge over time. Social change, however, is generally gradual. This is because, as shown in Figure 2.1, while social organizations are human-made, the creation, like Frankenstein's monster, to an important degree controls the creator. The culture that emerges takes on a sacred quality (the sanctity of tradition) that is difficult to question. This quality profoundly affects the attitudes and behaviors of the social actors in the social organization and the organization itself. As Wilbert Moore (1969), the distinguished sociologist, puts it,

> [M]an is an inevitably social animal, and one whose social behavior is scarcely guided by instinct. He learns social behavior, well or poorly of one sort or another. As a member of social groups he invents values for himself and his collectivities, rules for his conduct, knowledge to aid him in predicting and controlling his envi-

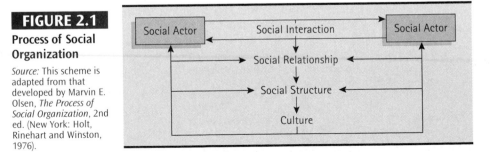

FIGURE 2.1

Process of Social Organization

Source: This scheme is adapted from that developed by Marvin E. Olsen, *The Process of Social Organization*, 2nd ed. (New York: Holt, Rinehart and Winston, 1976).

ronment, gods to reward and punish him, and other ingenious elements of the human condition. . . . Once [the products of this activity] are established in the human consciousness, they become, in turn, guides to behavior. (283)

The Societal or Macro Level

Primary and secondary groups illustrate nicely the process and the components of social organization. But each of these groups exists in a larger social setting—a context that is also structured with norms, statuses, roles, and mechanisms of social control. These are the components of social structure through which society affects our attitudes and behaviors regardless of our other group memberships.

A **society** is the largest social organization to which people owe their allegiance. It is an aggregate of people, united by a common culture, who are relatively autonomous and self-sufficient and who live in a definite geographical location. It is difficult to imagine a society undergoing the same processes as other, smaller, social organizations because societies are typically composed of so many different people and groups, none of whom were present at the beginning of the society. But the conceptual scheme for the process of social organization shown in Figure 2.1 is also applicable at the societal level. Continuing interaction among the members reinforces stability but also is a source of change. At any given time, the actors in the society are constrained by the norms, values, and roles that are the results of hundreds of years of evolution.

Society as a Social System

A society is a **social system**, composed of interdependent parts that are linked together into a boundary-maintaining whole. This concept of system implies that there is order and predictability within. Moreover, there are clear boundaries to a system in terms of membership and territory. Finally, the parts are independent.

The U.S. economy illustrates this interdependence nicely. There is a division of labor in society that provides a wide range of products and services meeting the needs of society's members. The presence of economic booms and depressions further illustrates the interdependence in society. For example, a depression comes about (in overly simplistic terms) when the flow of money is restricted by high taxes, high interest rates, high unemployment, and restricted buying practices by individuals. When large numbers of people delay buying items such as a new car or refrigerator because they are uncertain of the future, the sales of these items decline dramatically. This decrease itself is a source of further pessimism, thereby further dampening sales. The price of stocks in these companies will, of course, plummet under these conditions, causing further alarm. Moreover, many workers in these industries will be laid off. These newly unemployed people, in turn, will purchase only necessities, thereby throwing other industries into panic as their sales decline. A depression, then, is the result of actions by individual consumers, boards of directors of corporations, banks and savings and loan associations, individual and institutional investors, and the government. Additionally, the actions of the United States and the actions of other nations greatly affect the economic conditions of each other because nations, too, form an interdependent network.

The Culture of Society

Culture explains much individual and group behavior, as well as the persistence of most aspects of social life. Social scientists studying a society foreign to them must spend months, perhaps years, learning the culture of that group. They must learn the meanings for the symbols (written and spoken language, gestures, and rituals) used by the individuals in that society. They must know the feelings people share as to what is appropriate or inappropriate behavior. Additionally, they need to know the rules of the society: which activities are considered important, the skills members have in making and using tools, and the knowledge members need to exist in that society. In short, analysts must discover all the knowledge that people share—that is, they must know the culture. Culture and its transmission are discussed fully in Chapters 4 through 7.

Social Classes

A structural component of societies is **social stratification**, the hierarchical arrangement of people in terms of power, prestige, and resources. This universal phenomenon of social inequality is so important for the understanding of individual behavior and the structure of society that Chapters 9 through 12 are devoted to it. At the individual level, one's placement in the hierarchy directly affects self-perception, motivation, political attitudes, and the degree of advantage or disadvantage in school, in the economy, in the courts, and even in life itself. At the societal level, the extent of inequality affects the types and magnitude of social problems, societal stability, and economic growth.

Social Institutions

One distinguishing characteristic of societies is the existence of a set of *institutions*. The popular usages of this term are imprecise and omit some important sociological considerations. An institution is not any one or any thing that is established and traditional (for example, a janitor who has worked at the same school for forty-five years). An institution is not limited to specific organizations, such as a school or a prison or a hospital. An institution is much broader in scope and importance than a person, a custom, or a social organization.

Institutions are social arrangements that channel behavior in prescribed ways in the important areas of social life. They are interrelated sets of normative elements— norms, values, and role expectations—that the people making up the society have devised and passed on to succeeding generations in order to provide permanent solutions to society's perpetually unfinished business. Institutions are cultural imperatives. They serve as regulatory agencies, channeling behavior in culturally prescribed ways. "Institutions provide procedures through which human conduct is patterned, compelled to go, in grooves deemed desirable by society. And this trick is performed by making the grooves appear to the individual as the only possible ones" (Berger, 1963:87).

For example, a society instills in its members predetermined channels for marriage. Instead of allowing the sexual partners a host of options, it is expected in U.S. society that the couple, composed of a man and a woman, will marry and set up a conjugal household. Although the actual options are many, the partners choose what

Gay Marriage?

Canada, the Netherlands, Belgium, and Spain are the only countries to legalize gay marriage nationwide. Other nations have granted same-sex couples rights equal to those of heterosexual couples. The response by politicians in the United States is different—much different. As of 2005, eighteen states have constitutional amendments against same-sex marriage (three more will decide in 2006 and 13 more are weighing similar amendments). Only Massachusetts allows same-sex marriages and Vermont and Connecticut allow civil unions. A variety of court decisions have affirmed and denied gay marriages. Judges in California, New York, and Washington have ruled that prohibiting same-sex marriage violates their state constitutions. The Supreme Court in Oregon, on the other hand has ruled that 3,000 same-sex marriages performed in 2004 were illegal.

In 1996, a conservative Congress and a centrist president signed the so-called Defense of Marriage Act, which allowed states to deny recognition to same-sex marriages that might be accorded full legal status in other states. This is in direct opposition to the "full faith and credit" clause of the Constitution, which requires that each state recognize "the public acts, records, and judicial proceedings of every other state" (Tribe, 1996:E11).

Public opinion in the United States opposes same-sex marriage. Most Christian religious leaders and denominations resist homosexual marriage because they believe that it violates biblical commands for sex to be heterosexual and within marriages, with procreation as the goal. Most politicians, whether Republican or Democrat, favor a ban on same-sex marriages. Conservative, pro-family advocates oppose gay marriage, even though it would promote stable, monogamous relationships among couples who seek to have their loving and committed relationships legitimated by the state. They oppose homosexual marriage because it will change the American family as we know it (Rotello, 1996). The institution of the family is by definition conservative, holding to the traditional demands of heterosexual unions only. Seen in this light, same-sex marriage is considered by some as subversive and therefore an intolerable idea that must be stopped.

society demands. In fact, they do not consider the other options as valid (for example, polygamy, polyandry, or group marriage). The result is a patterned arrangement that regulates sexual behavior and attempts to ensure a stable environment for the care of dependent children. The current demand by state legislatures that gay partners should not be allowed to marry illustrates the strict institutional demands of society over individual behavior (see the panel titled "Diversity: Gay Marriage?").

Institutions arise from the uncoordinated actions of multitudes of individuals over time. These actions, procedures, and rules evolve into a set of expectations that appear to have a design, because the consequences of these expectations provide solutions that help maintain social stability. The design is accidental, however; it is a product of cultural evolution.

All societies face problems in common. Although the variety of solutions is almost infinite, there is a functional similarity in their consequence, which is stability and maintenance of the system. Table 2.1 cites a number of common societal problems and the resulting institutions. This partial list of institutions shows the type of societal problems for which solutions are continually sought. All societies, for instance, have some form of the family, education, polity, economy, and religion. The variations on each theme that are found in societies are almost beyond imagination. These variations, while most interesting, are beyond the scope of this book. By looking at the interrelated norms, values, and role expectations that provide pat solutions to fundamental societal problems we can begin to understand U.S. society.

TABLE 2.1

Common Societal Problems and Their Institutions

Societal Problems	*Institution*
Sexual regulation; maintenance of stable units that ensure continued births and care of dependent children	Family
Socialization of the newcomers to the society	Education
Maintenance of order, the distribution of power	Polity
Production and distribution of goods and services; ownership of property	Economy
Understanding the transcendental; the search for meaning of life and death and the place of humankind in the world	Religion
Understanding the physical and social realms of nature	Science
Providing for physical and emotional health care	Medicine

Institutions are, by definition, conservative. They are the answers of custom and tradition to questions of survival. Although absolutely necessary for unity and stability, institutions in contemporary U.S. society are often outmoded, inefficient, and unresponsive to the incredibly swift changes brought about by technological advances, population shifts, and increasing worldwide interdependence.

As we look at the institutions of U.S. society, we must not forget that institutions are made by people and can therefore be changed. We should be guided by the insight that even though institutions appear to have the quality of being sacred, they are not. They can be changed, but critical examination is imperative. Social scientists must look behind the facades. They must not accept the patterned ways as the only correct ways. This is in the U.S. heritage—as found in the Declaration of Independence. As Skolnick and Currie (1970) put it,

> Democratic conceptions of society have always held that institutions exist to serve man, and that, therefore, they must be accountable to men. Where they fail to meet the test imposed on them, democratic theory holds that they ought to be changed. Authoritarian governments, religious regimes, and reformatories, among other social systems, hold the opposite: in case of misalignment between individuals or groups and the "system," the individuals and groups are to be changed or otherwise made unproblematic. (15)

○ Chapter Review

1. Social organization refers to the observed regularities in the behavior of people that are due to social conditions rather than the physiology or psychology of individuals.

2. Social organization includes both social structure and culture. These emerge through enduring social interaction.

3. Social structure involves the linkages and networks that transform individuals into a group. It includes the patterns of interaction that emerge, the division of labor, and the links and hierarchy of positions.

4. Culture, the shared beliefs of a group's members, guides conduct. The elements of culture include

the norms (rules), roles (behavioral expectations for the occupants of the various positions), and values (the criteria for judging people, things, and actions).

5. Norms are rules specifying appropriate and inappropriate behaviors. The important norms are called mores; the less important ones, folkways.

6. Each of us belongs to a number of social organizations, and in each we occupy a position (status). These statuses are a major source of identity for individuals.

7. The behavior expected of a person occupying a status in a social organization is the role. The pressures to conform to role demands ensure that there is stability and predictability in social groups even though member turnover occurs.

8. There are three reasons, however, that role expectations do not make behavior totally predictable: (a) personality differences, (b) inconsistent messages as to what behavior is expected, and (c) multiple group memberships resulting in conflicting demands.

9. Social organizations use positive sanctions (rewards) and negative sanctions (punishments) to enforce conformity to the norms, values, and roles of the group.

10. Two ways to classify social groups are on the basis of size and the quality of interaction. Primary groups are those whose members are involved in intimate, face-to-face interaction, with strong emotional attachments. The organization is informal and long-lasting. The members identify strongly with each other and with the group. In contrast, secondary groups are large, impersonal, and formally organized. The individual member is relatively unimportant.

11. Primary groups often emerge within secondary groups.

12. Bureaucracies are complex organizations designed to increase efficiency by dividing work into small tasks performed by specialists, by having a chain of command in which each position has clearly defined responsibilities, by making decisions based on technical knowledge, and by judging performance by proficiency.

13. Positively, bureaucracies accomplish coordination, reliability, efficiency, stability, and continuity. Negatively, they create inefficiency through blind obedience to the rules and authority, stifling creativity, and too many regulations. Also, bureaucracies can be dehumanizing (Weber's iron cage of rationality).

14. Social groups have enormous power over their members and affect their beliefs, behaviors, perceptions, and even health.

15. A society is the largest social organization to which people owe their allegiance. The society provides the social context for primary and secondary groups. Society places constraints on these groups and their members through its own norms, values, roles, and mechanisms for social control.

16. A society is a social system composed of interdependent parts that are linked together in a boundary-maintaining whole. There is order and predictability within. There is a division of labor providing for self-sufficiency.

17. A society, like other social organizations, has a culture involving norms, roles, values, symbols, and technical knowledge.

18. Unlike other social organizations, a society has a set of institutions. These are social arrangements that channel behavior in prescribed ways in the important areas of social life.

19. Institutions are conservative, providing the answers of custom and tradition to questions of social survival. Even though they are absolutely necessary for unity and stability, institutions can be outmoded, inefficient, and unresponsive to the swift changes of contemporary life.

Key Terms

Social organization	Social roles	Bureaucracy
Social structure	Folkways	McDonaldization
Culture	Mores	"Iron cage" of rationality
Aggregate	Status	Egoistic suicide
Group	Hierarchy	Altruistic suicide
Social interaction	Master status	Anomic suicide
Social relationship	Role	Society
Realist position	Sanctions	Social system
Nominalist position	Social group	Social stratification
Norms	Primary groups	Institutions
Values	Secondary groups	

Study Questions

1. What is meant by social organization? Describe the social organization of a group to which you belong, using the appropriate sociological concepts.
2. How has recent technology affected interaction patterns? Consider, for example, the effects of television, the Internet, cell phones, and cyberspace games on the number and quality of interactions for children and adults.
3. Define the related concepts of status and role. What do they have to do with social organization?
4. Illustrate McDonaldization with some bureaucracy with which you are familiar.
5. Emile Durkheim made a sociological analysis of the most private of acts—suicide. Describe this sociological analysis. How would psychologists differ from sociologists in their explanations of this phenomenon?
6. What are social institutions? Explain the apparent anomaly that they are both sources of stability in society as well as sources of social problems.

For Further Reading

The Process of Social Organization

Robert K. Merton, *Social Theory and Social Structure* (New York: Free Press, 1968).

S. F. Nadel, *The Theory of Social Structure* (New York: Free Press, 1957).

Marvin E. Olsen, *The Process of Social Organization*, 2nd ed. (New York: Holt, Rinehart and Winston, 1976).

Charles Perrow, *Complex Organizations: A Critical Essay*, 3rd ed. (New York: Random House, 1986).

George Ritzer, *The McDonaldization of Society: An Investigation into the Changing Character of Social Life*, rev. ed. (Thousand Oaks, CA: Pine Forge Press, 1996).

Max Weber, *The Theory of Social and Economic Organization*, A. M. Henderson and Talcott Parsons, trans. (New York: Free Press, 1947).

Micro Structure

Elijah Anderson, *Streetwise: Race, Class, and Change in an Urban Community* (Chicago: University of Chicago Press, 1990).

Harold Garfinkel, *Studies in Ethnomethodology* (Upper Saddle River, NJ: Prentice Hall, 1967).

Erving Goffman, *The Presentation of Self in Everyday Life* (Garden City, NY: Doubleday, 1957).

A. Paul Hare, Robert F. Bales, and Edward Borgatta (eds.), *Small Groups* (New York: Knopf, 1965).

John L. Locke, *The De-Voicing of Society: Why We Don't Talk to Each Other Anymore* (New York: Simon & Schuster, 1998).

William Ian Miller, *The Anatomy of Disgust* (Cambridge, MA: Harvard University Press, 1997).

Macro Structure

Gerhard Lenski and Jean Lenski, *Human Societies: An Introduction to Macrosociology*, 5th ed. (New York: McGraw-Hill, 1987).

Michael Parenti, *Power and the Powerless* (New York: St. Martin's Press, 1978).

Stephen K. Sanderson, *Macrosociology: An Introduction to Human Societies* (New York: Harper & Row, 1988).

Robin M. Williams, Jr., *American Society: A Sociological Interpretation*, 3rd ed. (New York: Knopf, 1970).

Web Resources

http://www.mcdonaldization.com/main.shtml

This site provides information on the *McDonaldization* of society and the different dimensions of it outlined by the sociologist who coined the term, George Ritzer.

http://www.uiowa.edu/~grpproc/

Part of the Sociology Department at the University of Iowa, the Center for the Study of Group Processes online contains an electronic journal with research related to the study of groups. Included in the group studies are formal organizations, political groups, families, intimates, social categories, and societies.

http://www-slis.lib.indiana.edu/CSI/

The Center for Social Informatics does research on the relationship between technology and social change. The site has information on papers, conferences, and other related resources.

http://sun.soci.niu.edu/~sssi/

The Society for the Study of Symbolic Interaction is an "international social science professional organization of scholars interested in qualitative, especially interactionist research."

The Duality of Social Life: Order and Conflict

What is violence? The answer depends on one's vantage point in the power structure, because violence is defined as such if the act threatens the power structure. Protesting Blacks in South Africa, for example, are perceived by Whites as violent, whereas the actions of the police to maintain order are seen as violent by the protestors. Similarly, in the spring of 1989, the students in Tiananmen Square in Beijing who demonstrated for increased freedoms were viewed by the Chinese government as a threat and were forcibly defeated. The students' actions were depicted on government television as being illegitimate (violent), whereas the actions to maintain order were defined as legitimate. From the perspective of the victimized group, however, the actions of the police were illegitimate and, therefore, amounted to police brutality.

Violence always refers to a disruption of some condition of order; but order, like violence, is also politically defined. Order itself can be destructive to some categories of people. In South Africa the normal way that society is organized does harm to Blacks (poor health care, low wages, segregated facilities, unfair system of justice, inferior education). Somehow, the term violence is not applied to high infant mortality and rates of preventable diseases that prevail among the poor and powerless in every society. Critics of this type of societal violence might call such harmful outcomes "institutional violence," to imply that the system itself injures and destroys (Skolnick, 1969:3–8).

Violence is also defined politically through the selection process. Some acts of force (to injure people or to destroy property) are not always forbidden or condemned in U.S. society. Property damaged during celebrations (winning the crucial football game, on Halloween, or during Mardi Gras) is often overlooked. Even thousands of drunken, noisy, and sometimes destructive college students on the Texas beaches of Padre Island during spring break are usually tolerated because they are just boisterous youth on a binge (and the money they spend helps the local economy). But if these same thousands of students were to destroy the same amount of property in a demonstration of which the goal was to change the system, then the acts would be defined as violent and the police would be called to restore order by force if necessary (which, of course, would not be defined as violence by the authorities). Thus, violence is condoned or condemned through political pressures and decisions. The basic criterion is whether the acts are in approved channels or are supportive of existing social and political arrangements. If not supportive, then the acts are, by definition, to be condemned and punished.

In sum, there is a relationship between the power structure and violence. The perception of how violence is defined provides insight toward a greater understanding of the role of conflict and order in society.

Social Systems: Order and Conflict

The analysis of society begins with a mental picture of its structure. This image (or **model**) influences what scientists look for, what they see, and how they explain the phenomena that occur within the society.

One of the characteristics of societies—the existence of segmentation—is the basis for the two prevailing models of society. Every society is composed of parts. This differentiation may result from differences in age, race, sex, physical prowess, wisdom, family background, wealth, organizational membership, type of work, or any other characteristic considered salient by the members. The fundamental question concerning differentiation is this: What is the basic relationship among the parts of society? The two contradictory answers to this question provide the rationale for the two models of society—order and conflict.

One answer is that the parts of society are in harmony. They cooperate because of similar or complementary interests and because they need each other to accomplish those things beneficial to all (examples are the production and distribution of

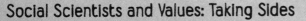

Research Methods

Social Scientists and Values: Taking Sides

Social scientists are not value neutral. Whether they admit it or not, they take sides by adopting a way of perceiving and interpreting the social world. This does not render social science useless, as the late Michael Harrington (1985), a highly esteemed social scientist and political activist, argues in the following excerpt:

Truths about society can be discovered only if one takes sides. . . . You must stand somewhere in order to see social reality, and where you stand will determine much of what you see and how you see it. The data of society are, for all practical purposes, infinite. You need criteria that will provisionally permit you to bring some order into that chaos of data and to distinguish between relevant and irrelevant factors or, for that matter, to establish that there are facts in the first place. These criteria cannot be based upon the data for they are the precondition of the data. They represent—and the connotations of the phrase should be savored—a "point of view." That involves intuitive

choices, a value-laden sense of what is meaningful and what is not. . . .

The poor, I suggest, see a different social world from the rich—and so do those who think, whether consciously or not, from the vantage point of the poor or the rich. I was born into and have lived my life in the middle class. But I have tried to write from the point of view of the poor and excluded, those in the United States and elsewhere. I am therefore a deeply biased man, a taker of sides; but that is not really distinctive at all. Everyone else is as biased as I am, including the most "objective" social scientist. The difference between us is that I am frank about my values while many other analysts fool both themselves and their audiences with the illusion that they have found an intellectual perch that is free of Earth's social field of gravity.

Source: Taking Sides by Michael Harrington © 1985 by Michael Harrington. Reprinted by permission of Henry Holt and Company, LLC, pp. 1–2.

goods and services, and protection). Another answer is that the subunits of society are basically in competition with each other. This view is based on the assumption that the things people desire most (wealth, power, autonomy, resources, high status) are always in short supply; hence, competition and conflict are universal social phenomena. (See the panel titled "Research Methods: Social Scientists and Values: Taking Sides.")

The Order Model

The **order model** (sometimes referred to as **functionalism**) attributes to societies the characteristics of cohesion, consensus, cooperation, reciprocity, stability, and persistence. Societies are viewed as social systems, composed of interdependent parts that are linked together into a boundary-maintaining whole. The parts of the system are basically in harmony with each other. The high degree of cooperation (and societal integration) is accomplished because there is a high degree of consensus on societal goals and on cultural values. Moreover, the different parts of the system are assumed to need each other because of complementary interests. Because the primary social process is cooperation and the system is highly integrated, all social change is gradual, adjustive, and reforming. Societies are therefore basically stable units.

For order theorists, the central issue is: What is the nature of the social bond? What holds groups together? This was the focus of Emile Durkheim, the French social theorist of the early 1900s (see Chapter 1). The various forms of integration were used by Durkheim to explain differences in suicide rates (see Chapter 2), social change, and the universality of religion (Durkheim, 1951; 1960; 1965).

For Durkheim, there are two types of societies, based on the way the members are bonded. In smaller, less complex societies, solidarity among the members occurs through the collective holding of beliefs (ideologies, values, moral sentiments, traditions). Social integration, therefore, occurs because the members are alike. Modern, complex societies, in contrast, achieve social integration through differentiation. Society is based on the division of labor, in which the members involved in specialized tasks are united by their dependence on others.

One way to focus on integration is to determine the manifest and latent consequences of social structures, norms, and social activities. Do these consequences contribute to the integration (cohesion) of the social system? Durkheim, for example, noted that the punishment of crime has the **manifest consequence** (intended)

GREGORY

"Sure, I follow the herd—not out of brainless obedience, mind you, but out of a deep and abiding respect for the concept of community."

of punishing and deterring the criminal. The **latent consequence** (unintended) of punishment, however, is the societal reaffirmation of what is to be considered moral. The society is thereby integrated through belief in the same rules (Durkheim, 1958).

Taking Durkheim's lead, sociologists of the order persuasion have made many penetrating and insightful analyses of various aspects of society. By focusing on all the consequences of social structures and activities—intended and unintended, as well as negative (malintegrative functions or dysfunctions)—we can see behind the facades and thereby understand more fully such disparate social arrangements and activities as ceremonials (from rain dances to sporting events), social stratification, fashion, propaganda, and even political machines.

The Conflict Model

The assumptions of the **conflict model** (the view of society that posits conflict as a normal feature of social life, influencing the distribution of power and the direction and magnitude of social change) are opposite from those of the order model. The basic form of interaction is not cooperation but competition, which often leads to conflict. Because the individuals and groups of society compete for advantage, the degree of social integration is minimal and tenuous. Social change results from the conflict among competing groups and therefore tends to be drastic and revolutionary. The ubiquitousness of conflict results from the dissimilar goals and interests of social groups. It is, moreover, a result of social organization itself. The most famous conflict theorist was Karl Marx. He theorized that there exists in every society (except, Marx believed, in the last historical stage of communism) a dynamic tension between two groups—those who own the means of production and those who work for the owners. Contrary to Durkheim, who saw modern industry and its required division of labor as promoting social solidarity, Marx viewed these groups as the sources of division and exploitation (Walton, 1990:20). Marx focused on inequality—the oppressors and the oppressed, the dominant and the dominated, the powerful and the powerless. For him, the powerful protect their privileges by supporting the status quo. The laws, religion, education, and the mass media all work for the advantage of the advantaged. The powerful use and abuse the powerless, thereby sowing the seeds of their own destruction. The destruction of the elite is accomplished when the dominated people unite and overthrow the dominants.

Ralf Dahrendorf, a contemporary conflict theorist, has also viewed conflict as a ubiquitous phenomenon, not because of economic factors as Marx believed, but because of other aspects of social organization. Organization means, among other things, that power will be distributed unequally. The population will therefore be separated into the haves and the have-nots with respect to power. Because organization also means constraint, there will be a situation in all societies in which the constraints are determined by the powerful, thereby further ensuring that the have-nots will be in conflict with the haves—thus, the important insight that conflict is endemic to social organization.*

One other emphasis of conflict theorists is that the unity present in society is superficial, because it results not from consensus but from coercion. The powerful, it

---

*This description is a very superficial account of a complex process that has been fully described by Ralf Dahrendorf (1959).

TABLE 3.1

Duality of Social Life: Assumptions of the Order and Conflict Models of Society

	Order Model	Conflict Model
Question: What is the fundamental relationship among the parts of society?		
Answer:	Harmony and cooperation.	Competition, conflict, domination, and subordination.
Why:	The parts have complementary interests. Basic consensus on societal norms and values.	The things people want are always in short supply. Basic dissent on societal norms and values.
Degree of integration:	Highly integrated.	Loosely integrated. Whatever integration is achieved is the result of force and fraud.
Type of social change:	Gradual, adjustive, and reforming.	Abrupt and revolutionary.
Degree of stability:	Stable.	Unstable.

is asserted, use force and fraud to keep society running smoothly, with benefits mostly accruing to those in power.

The Duality of Social Life

The basic duality of social life can be seen by summarizing the opposite ways in which order and conflict theorists view the nature of society. If asked, "What is the fundamental relationship among the parts of society?" the answers of order and conflict theorists would disagree. This disagreement leads to and is based on a number of related assumptions about society. These assumptions are summarized in Table 3.1.

One interesting but puzzling aspect of Table 3.1 is that these two models are held by different scientific observers of the same phenomenon. How can such different assumptions be derived by experts on society? The answer is that both models are partially correct. Each model focuses on reality—but on only part of that reality. Scientists have tended to accept one or the other of these models, thereby focusing on only part of social reality, for at least two reasons: (1) one model or the other was in vogue at the time of the scientist's intellectual development; or (2) one model or the other made the most sense for the analysis of the particular problems of interest—for example, the interest of Emile Durkheim, who devoted his intellectual energies to determining what holds society together, or the fundamental concern of Karl Marx, who explored the causes of revolutionary social change.

The analyses of sport and of social problems are two important areas in which sociologists have been influenced by the order and the conflict models. Let us turn to these contrary ways to view these two social phenomena before examining a synthesis of the two models.

Sport from the Order and Conflict Perspectives. Order theorists examining any aspect of society emphasize the contribution that aspect makes to the stability of society (this section is dependent on Coakley, 2005; and Eitzen and Sage, 2003). Sport, from this perspective, preserves the existing social order in several ways. To begin, sport symbolizes the American way of life—competition, individualism, achievement, and fair play. Not only is sport compatible with basic U.S. values, but it also is a powerful mechanism for socializing youth to adopt desirable character traits, such as the acceptance of authority, obeying rules, and striving for excellence.

Sport also supports the status quo by promoting the unity of society's members through patriotism (for example, the national anthem, militaristic displays, and other nationalistic rituals accompanying sports events). Can you imagine, for example, a team that espouses anti-establishment values in its name, logo, mascot, and pageantry? Would Americans, for example, tolerate a major league team called the Atlanta Atheists? the Boston Bigamists? the Pasadena Pacifists? or the Sacramento Socialists? Finally, sport inspires us through the excellent and heroic achievements of athletes, the magical moments in sport when the seemingly impossible happens, and the feelings of unity in purpose and of loyalty of fans.

Clearly, then, sport from the order perspective is good. Sport socializes youth into proper channels; sport unites; and sport inspires. Thus, to challenge or to criticize sport is to challenge the foundation of our society's social order.

Conflict theorists argue that the social order reflects the interests of the powerful. Sport is organized at every level—youth, high school, college, professional, and Olympic—to exploit athletes and meet the goals of the powerful (for example, public relations, prestige, and profits).

Sport inhibits the potential for revolution by society's have-nots in three ways. First, sport validates the prevailing myths of capitalism, such as anyone can succeed if he or she works hard enough. If a person fails, it's his or her fault and not that of the system. Second, sport serves as an opiate of the masses by diverting attention away from the harsh realities of poverty, unemployment, and dismal life chances by giving them a "high" (Hoch, 1972). And, third, sport gives false hope to African Americans and other oppressed members of society, because they see sport as a realistic avenue of upward social mobility. The high visibility of wealthy athletes provides proof that athletic ability translates into monetary success. The reality, of course, is that only an extremely small percentage of aspiring athletes ever achieve professional status. In basketball, for example, there are about 500,000 male high school players and about 4,000 college seniors playing in any one year, and only about 50 of them will play as rookies at the professional level. The chances of upward mobility for women through sport are even less (Eitzen, 2006).

Conflict theorists agree with order theorists on many of the facts but differ significantly in interpretation. Both agree that sport socializes youth, but conflict theorists view this socialization negatively, because they see sport as a mechanism to get youth to follow orders, work hard, and fit into a system that is not necessarily beneficial to them. Both agree that sport maintains the status quo. But instead of this being interpreted as good, as the order theorists maintain, conflict theorists view this as bad because it reflects and reinforces the unequal distribution of power and resources in society.

Social Problems from the Order and Conflict Perspectives. Social problems are societally induced conditions that harm any segment of the population, or acts or conditions that violate the norms and values of society (Eitzen and Baca Zinn, 2006a). Under this rubric fall such phenomena as poverty, homelessness, crime, gender inequality, and discrimination.

The order and conflict perspectives constrain their adherents to view the causes, consequences, and remedies of social problems in opposing ways. The order perspective focuses on deviants themselves. This approach (which has been the conventional way of studying social problems) asks, Who are the deviants? What are their social and psychological backgrounds? With whom do they associate? Deviants somehow do not conform to the standards of the dominant group; they are assumed to be out of phase with conventional behavior. This is believed to occur most often as a result of inadequate socialization. In other words, deviants have not internalized the norms and values of society because they either are brought up in an environment of conflicting value systems (as are children of immigrants or the poor in a middle-class school) or are under the influence of a deviant subculture such as a gang. Because the order theorist uses the prevailing standards to define and label deviants, the existing practices and structures of society are accepted implicitly. The remedy is to rehabilitate the deviants so that they conform to the societal norms.

The conflict theorist takes a different approach to social problems. The adherents of this perspective criticize order theorists for blaming the victim (Ryan, 1976). To focus on the individual deviant locates the symptom, not the disease. Deviants are a manifestation of a failure of society to meet the needs of individuals. The sources of crime, poverty, drug addiction, and racism are found in the laws, the customs, the quality of life, the distribution of wealth and power, and the accepted practices of schools, governmental units, and corporations. In this view, then, the schools are the problem, not the dropouts; the quality of life, not the mentally ill; the maldistribution of wealth, not the poor; the roadblocks to success for minority-group members, not apathy on their part. The established system, in this view, is not sacred. Because the system is the primary source of social problems, it, not the individual deviant, must be restructured.

Although most of this book attempts to strike a balance between the order and conflict perspectives, the conflict model is clearly favored when social problems are brought into focus. This is done explicitly for two reasons. The subject matter of sociology is not individuals, who are the special province of psychology, but society. If sociologists do not make a critical analysis of the social structure, who will? Also, we are convinced that the source of social problems is found within the institutional framework of society (Eitzen and Baca Zinn, 2006a). Thus, a recurrent theme of this book is that social problems are societal in origin and not the exclusive function of individual pathologies.

Synthesis of the Order and Conflict Models

The assumptions of both models are contradictory for each comparison shown in Table 3.1, and their contradictions highlight the duality of social life. Social interaction can be harmonious or acrimonious. Societies are integrated or divided, stable or unstable. Social change can be fast or slow, revolutionary or evolutionary.

Taken alone, each of these perspectives fosters a faulty perception and interpretation of society, but taken together, they complement each other and present a complete and realistic model. A synthesis that combines the best of each model would appear, therefore, to be the best perspective for understanding the structure and process of society (see Lenski, 1966; van den Berghe, 1967).

The initial assumption of a synthesis approach is that *the processes of stability and change are properties of all societies*. There is an essential paradox to human societies: They are always ordered; they are always changing. These two elemental properties of social life must be recognized by the observer of society. Within any society there are forces providing impetus for change, and there are forces insisting on rooted permanence. Allen Wheelis (1958) has labeled these two contrary tendencies as the instrumental process and the institutional process, respectively.

The **instrumental process** is based on the desire for technological change—to find new and more efficient techniques to achieve goals. The **institutional process**, on the other hand, designates all those activities that are dominated by the quest for certainty. We are bound in our activities, often by customs, traditions, myths, and religious beliefs. So, there are rites, taboos, and mores that people obey without thinking. There also are modern institutions such as monotheism, monogamy, private property, and the sovereign state, all of which are coercive in that they limit freedom of choice, but they are assumed proper by almost all individuals in U.S. society.

These two processes constitute the **dialectic** (opposing forces) of society. As contrary tendencies, they generate tension because the instrumental forces are constantly prodding the institutions to change when it is not their nature to do so.

The second assumption is that *societies are organized, but the process of organization generates conflict*. Organization implies, among other things, the differential allocation of power. Inequalities in power are manifested in at least two conflict-generating ways: differentials in decision making, and inequalities in the system of social stratification (social classes and minority groups). Scarce resources can never be distributed equally to all people and groups in society. The powerful are always differentially rewarded and make the key decisions as to the allocation of scarce resources.

A third basic assumption for a synthesis model is that *society is a social system*. The term social system has three important implications: (1) that there is not chaos but some semblance of order—that action within the unit is, in a general way, predictable; (2) that boundaries exist that may be in terms of geographical space or membership; and (3) that there are parts that are interdependent—thus conveying the reality of differentiation and unity. A society is a system made up of many subsystems (for example, groups, organizations, and communities). Although these subsystems are all related in some way, some are strongly linked to others, whereas others have only a remote linkage. The interdependence of the parts implies further that events and decisions in one sector may have a profound influence on the entire system. The terrorist attacks on the World Trade Center and the Pentagon in 2001, for example, had profound effects throughout U.S. society (e.g., the airline and leisure industries suffered financial setbacks resulting in layoffs; airlines received government subsidies while workers put out of work were denied; the stock market declined; screening procedures in airports were revamped causing long delays in airports; and the Justice Department instituted new rules that invaded privacy). Some events, however, have little or no effect on all of U.S. society. Most important for the synthesis approach is the recognition that the parts of the system may have complementary interests with other parts but may also have exclusive, incompatible interests and goals. There is generally some degree of cooperation and harmony found in society because of consensus over common goals and because of similar interests (for example, defense against external threats). Some degree of competition and dissent is also present because of incompatible interests, scarcity of resources, and unequal rewards. Societies, then, are imperfect social systems.

A fourth assumption is that *societies are held together by complementary interests, by consensus on cultural values, and also by coercion*. Societies do cohere. There are forces that bind diverse groups together into a single entity. The emphasis of both order and conflict models provides twin bases for such integration—consensus and coercion.

Finally, *social change is a ubiquitous phenomenon in all societies. It may be gradual or abrupt, reforming or revolutionary.* All social systems change. Order theorists have tended to view change as a gradual phenomenon occurring either because of innovation or because of differentiation (for example, dividing units into subunits to separate activities and make the total operation more efficient). This view of change is partially correct. Change can also be abrupt; it can come about because of internal violence, or it can result from forces outside the society (that is, as a reaction to events outside the system, or an acceptance of the innovations of others).

To summarize, a synthesis of the order and the conflict models views society as having "two faces of equal reality—one of stability, harmony, and consensus and one of change, conflict, and constraint" (Dahrendorf, 1968:127).

The remainder of this chapter illustrates the duality of social life by examining the society of the United States from the perspectives of the conflict and order theorists. We consider the sources of disunity in the United States and the major instances of violence that have occurred throughout U.S. history. Despite the existence of division and violence, the United States is unified, at least minimally. We therefore also consider the factors that work to unify.

Division and Violence

Societies are integrated, but disunity and disharmony also exist to some degree in all societies. It is especially important to examine the segmenting influences in U.S. society, for they aid in explaining contemporary conflict and social change (see "A Closer Look: Deepening Divides in U.S. Society" for the dimensions that have the potential to fragment the United States).

Social scientists studying the divisive forces in U.S. society have found that in small groups, the more heterogeneous the group, the more likely cliques will form. A group composed of members of one religion, for example, cannot form cliques on the basis of religion, but one with three religions represented has the potential of subdividing into three parts (Davies, 1966). This principle applies to larger organizations as well, including societies. The United States, then, has the potential of many, many subgroups because it is so diverse. The United States is, in effect, a mosaic of different groups—different on a number of dimensions, such as occupation, racial and ethnic backgrounds, education, and economic circumstances. Let us briefly examine these and other dimensions and the manner in which they bring about segmentation in U.S. society.

Size. The United States is large in size, in both number of people and expanse of land. Both of these facts have a segmenting influence in U.S. society. With respect to population size, an accepted sociological proposition states: "As the population of a social organization increases, the number of its parts and the degree of their specialization also increases" (Mott, 1965:50). If, as in the United States, there is not only a large population (about 300 million) but also a high level of technology, then the division of labor becomes very refined. This division is so refined that more than 30,000 different occupations are recognized and catalogued by the Bureau of the Census.

Deepening Divides in U.S. Society

The terrorist attacks on the World Trade Center and the Pentagon on September 11, 2001, killing about 3,000, unified Americans in a common cause and a keen sense of patriotism. But beneath this united front there were fissures that eventually divided the nation (most of this essay draws from Eitzen, 2000a). While there are many indicators of reduced societal cohesion, let's consider four—excessive individualism, declining trust, the widening inequality gap, and the deepening racial/ethnic/religious/sexuality divide.

Excessive Individualism

Americans celebrate individualism. It fits with their economic system of capitalism. They value the freedom to make their own choices and to be self-reliant. At its extreme, the individualistic credo says that it is their duty to be selfish, to take care of themselves and let others "sink or swim" on their own. This belief in rugged individualism, however, promotes inequality and the tolerance of inferior housing, schools, and services for "others." As a consequence, the United States has the lowest tax rates in the Western world, thus providing a minimum of resources for the common good (public schools, welfare, parks, health care). In effect, our emphasis on individualism keeps us from feeling obligated to others. Instead of being connected we are atomized individuals.

Diminished Trust

An important ingredient in the glue that holds society together is trust in society's institutions. Today this trust is diminished by scandal after scandal. Honor and trust falter because of the philandering of political leaders, the ineffectiveness of the FBI, the influence peddling by politicians whose votes are given to the highest bidder, the child molestations by priests and the subsequent cover-up by the Catholic hierarchy, and the plundering of the public by corporate executives with the assistance of brokerage and accounting firms. Let's consider the dark side of

corporate America. Street crimes (murder, robbery, assault, and property crimes) have declined in recent years, but crimes such as fraud in health care, government procurement and bankruptcy, identity theft, illegal corporate espionage, and intellectual property piracy have risen sharply (Labaton, 2002). Just in the first half of 2002, scandals involving fraud at Adelphia, Enron, Global Crossing, Kmart, Qwest Communications, Schering-Plough, WorldCom, Tyco, Rite Aid, ImClone Systems, Dynegy, and Xerox, plus accounting firms (e.g., Andersen LLP) and brokerage houses (Merrill Lynch) have rocked commonly held beliefs about the integrity of U.S. corporations. Corrupt executives in these and other corporations have used subterfuge and manipulation of financial statements for huge gains, while their stockholders and lower-level employees lost huge amounts. In the case of Merrill Lynch, there was a huge conflict of interest as one set of employees was making "buy" recommendations to investors (even though, it turns out, in some cases the company knew the recommended companies were actually failing companies) because Merrill Lynch had a stake in these companies. Summing this up, Robert Sheer (2002) asks: "Is there any doubt that the chicanery of Enron executives and that of a growing Who's Who of top CEOs had done more long-term damage to the U.S. Economy than the efforts of anti-American terrorists?"

In short, the scandals in the business world, religion, and politics increase the cynicism in citizens and thereby diminish the trust required to make markets and society cohere.

The Widening Inequality Gap

Compared to other developed nations, the chasm between the rich and the poor in the United States is the widest, and steadily increasing. The earnings gap, as measured by comparing the top 5 percent of the earnings distribution by the bottom 20 percent, was the greatest since the Census Bureau began keeping

If they have specialized occupations, the people will probably interact most often with people like themselves. Because of similar interests, they will tend to cooperate with each other and perhaps compete with other groups for advantage. An important social theorist of the early 1900s, Robert Michels, wrote about this tendency for exclusion and conflict as a universal tendency in all social organizations:

track in 1947. The average salary of a chief executive officer exceeds 500 times the pay of a typical factory worker. In 1980, the difference was only forty-two times as much. At the bottom end of wealth and income, more than 35 million Americans live below the government's official poverty line. The safety net for them is weak and getting weaker. We do not have universal health insurance. Funds for Head Start are so inadequate that only 40 percent of children who are eligible are enrolled in the program. The numbers of homeless and hungry are rising. It's not just the gap between the rich and the poor, but between the rich average workers. "What's happening [according to *Business Week*] is that a new class of left-behind workers is being created, encompassing a large portion of the workforce" (quoted in Phillips, 2002:129).

The data on inequality show clearly that the United States is moving toward a two-tiered society. This has at least three implications for society. First, it divides people into the "deserving" and the "undeserving." This, in turn, justifies not providing a generous safety net. Third, the larger the gap, the more destabilized society becomes. Former Secretary of Labor Robert Reich has put it this way: "At some point, if trends are not reversed, we cease being a society at all. The stability of the country eventually is treated. No country can endure a massive gap between people at the top and people at the bottom" (quoted in Eitzen, 2000a:565). Put another way, again by Reich, "Global terrorism now poses the largest threat to our survival. But the widening split between our have-mores and have-lesses poses the largest single threat to our strength as a society" (Reich, 2002:20).

The Deepening Racial/Ethnic/Religious/Sexuality Divide

The civil rights gains of the previous generation are in jeopardy as U.S. society becomes more diverse. Currently, the racial composition in the United States is 72 percent White and 28 percent non-White. In fifty years, it will be 50 percent non-White. An indicator of fragmentation along racial lines is the "White flight" from high-immigration areas, which is leading to the "Balkanization of America." The trends toward gated neighborhoods, the rise of private schools, and home schooling are manifestations of exclusiveness rather than inclusiveness and are motivated by the increasing number of non-Whites in society.

Along with increasing racial and ethnic diversity, there is religious diversity with about 7 million Jews, 6 million Muslims, and millions of other non-Christians, including Buddhists and Hindus, as well as atheists. Religious differences also are sources of fragmentation. Among Christians, fundamentalists and liberals clash on religious views. Some groups, most notably Muslims, are often victims of hate crimes.

There is also widespread intolerance of and discrimination toward those whose sexual orientation differs from the majority. The behaviors of gay men and lesbian women are defined and stigmatized by many members of society as sinful; their activities are judged by the courts as illegal; and their jobs and advancement within those jobs are often restricted because of their being different sexually.

In sum, diversity and ever-increasing diversity are facts of life in U.S. society. If we do not find ways to accept the differences among us, we will fragment into class, race, ethnic, and sexual enclaves. The challenge is to shift from building walls to building bridges.

Sources: D. Stanley Eitzen, 2000a. "The Fragmentation of Social Life," *Vital Speeches* 66 (July 1):563–566; Bruce Nussbaum, 2002. "Can You Trust Anybody Anymore?" *Business Week* (January 28): 31–32; Stephen Labaton, 2002. "Fraud Becomes the Crime of Choice," *Denver Post* (June 2):3A; Robert Scheer, 2002. "Bush Overplays the Terror Card," *Los Angeles Times* (June 25):1–2. Online: http://www.latimes.com/news/opinion/commentary/la-000044306jun25.column?coll=la%Dne; Robert B. Reich, 2002. *I'll Be Short: Essentials for a Decent Working Society.* Boston: Beacon Press; and Kevin Phillips, 2002. *Wealth and Democracy.* New York: Broadway Books.

By a universally applicable social law, every organ of the collectivity, brought into existence through the need for the division of labor, creates for itself, as soon as it becomes consolidated, interests peculiar to itself. The existence of these special interests involves a necessary conflict with the interests of collectivity. (1966:389, originally published in 1915)

A second segmenting factor related to size has to do with land rather than population. The United States, excluding Alaska and Hawaii, has an area of 3,615,123 square miles. Found within this large territory is a wide range in topography and climate. Some areas are sparsely settled; others, densely populated. Some regions are attracting new residents at a much faster rate than others; some are declining in population. Some areas are rich in natural resources while others are not.

Traditionally, there have been pronounced regional differences (and sometimes rivalries), because each region had its own economic specialization (that is, its own industry and agriculture) and each was relatively isolated from the influences of the others. The revolutions in manufacturing, transportation, and communication have helped to break down this regionalism.

Although regionalism has been declining, it remains a force that sometimes divides peoples. As evidence of this, many votes in Congress show that regional considerations often outweigh national ones, and many nonsoutherners have stereotyped ideas of southerners. Consequently, communication within U.S. society is often blocked and interaction stifled because people from one region feel not only physically separate from but also superior to people from other regions. The residents of some states feel divided from each other in economic function, geography, and power. Northern California, for example, is making a serious attempt to become a separate state because many residents feel that they are different from Californians from the south and because the California legislature is dominated by southern Californians who vote against the interests of the north.

Social Class. Economic differences provide important sources of division in U.S. society. There is a natural resentment of people without the necessities of life toward those with a bountiful supply of not only the necessities but luxuries as well. There is also hostility toward a system that provides excessive benefits (or excessive hurdles) to people not on the basis of demonstrated skills but on family background.

The United States has the most unequal distribution of wealth and income in the industrialized world. Moreover, the rate of growth in inequality is faster than in any other industrialized country. The facts concerning **economic inequality** (the gap between the rich and the poor) are elaborated on in later chapters. For now, consider this: In sharp contrast to the 312 billionaires in the United States in 2003 (*Forbes*, 2004), there were 35.9 million people living below the poverty line.

Status (prestige) differentials also divide. Organizations, residential areas, and social clubs sometimes exclude certain people and groups because of their supposed social inferiority.

Race. Throughout human history, race has been used as a criterion for differentiation. If any factor makes a difference in the United States, it is race. African Americans, Native Americans, Latinos, Asian Americans, and other minority racial groups have often been systematically excluded from residential areas, occupations, and organizations and even sometimes denied equal rights under the law. Although the overt system of racial discrimination has changed, racist acts by individuals and organizations continue in the United States, with the result that members of these disadvantaged groups continue to be treated as second-class citizens.

Racial strife has occurred throughout American history. Slave revolts, Indian battles, race riots, and lynchings have occurred with regularity. Racial conflict continues today not only in the ghettos of large cities but also in most neighborhoods where the minority group is large enough to be perceived by the majority as a threat, in universities and secondary schools, in factories and other places of work, and in the armed forces.

Many members of racial minorities want justice now. It is equally clear that many majority-group members will do virtually anything to keep the status quo (that is, to retain an advantageous position for themselves). Some minority-group members seeking to shake the status quo may participate in various acts of violence. This violence brings repression by the powerful, which further angers and frustrates the minority—thus creating a treadmill of violence and division.

The racial composition of the United States is changing, and this change will likely lead to increased tension and conflict. The two largest racial minorities are increasing in number faster than the rest of the population. The Census Bureau estimated that in 2004 there were 41.3 million Latinos (one out of 7 people in the United States) and 39.2 million African Americans. Also, in recent years legal and illegal (undocumented) immigrants, mostly from Latin America and Asia, have entered the United States in great numbers. About 1 million immigrants enter the United States legally each year. Another estimated 300,000 unauthorized aliens enter and stay (an estimated 1.5 million to 2.5 million enter illegally each year, but most return to their native countries), for a net gain of U.S. immigrants of about 1.3 million. These refugees have brought problems that have led to growing hostility. Jobs are in short supply (hostility toward immigrants rises and falls with the availability of jobs). Taxes are already high, and these groups require large amounts of aid, especially for health services and education. The poor people fear that these new refugees will take jobs, increase demands on cheap housing, and decrease welfare currently allocated to themselves. Schools and other public agencies cannot meet the demands of these new groups.

Ethnicity. The United States is inhabited by a multitude of ethnic groups that migrated to this country in different waves and that continue to do so. Currently about 34 million people in the United States (almost one in eight) were born in another country. These groups have distinctive lifestyles and customs. One reason for this is that they have retained a cultural heritage brought to this country from another society. Another important reason for their continued distinctiveness is the structure of U.S. society. The persistence of subordination, discriminatory housing and work patterns, and other forms of structured inequality encourages solidarity among the disadvantaged. The uniqueness and strong ethnic identification of immigrant groups are sources of internal strength for them but cause resentment, negative stereotypes, competition, hatred, and conflict as other ethnic groups or members of the dominant majority question their loyalty, resent their success, fear being displaced by them in the job market, and worry about maintaining the integrity of their schools and neighborhoods. There is plenty of evidence for increasing racial tensions, including "immigrant bashing" by politicians, websites on the Internet devoted to overt racial and ethnic hostility (405 in 2001; SPLC, 2002), vandalism and arson directed at Muslim mosques and businesses, Jewish synagogues, and African American churches.

Sexual Orientation. Estimates vary, but approximately 2 to 5 percent of the U.S. population is gay or lesbian. This small minority, however, is the object of considerable hostility from the dominant heterosexual population. For example, the Republican

Gays and lesbians are subject to various forms of discrimination—from physical acts of violence to denial of equal right by legislatures and employers.

Party during the 1992, 1994, 1996, 1998, 2000, and 2004 election campaigns made thinly veiled attacks on homosexuals in their "family values" rhetoric.

Religion. A wide variety of religious beliefs abound in the United States. Although 59 percent of Americans are Protestants, the variations among them include snake handlers in Appalachia; the Amish, who refuse to use modern conveniences; sects that refuse medical help; literalists who are dogmatic in their narrow views of the Scriptures; and other groups that accept religious pluralism. Among the 28 percent of the U.S. population who are Roman Catholics, great differences exist in beliefs and lifestyles. The same is true when comparing Orthodox, Conservative, and Reformed Jews. Outside the Judeo-Christian tradition are Muslims (an estimated 6 million), Buddhists, and many other religious organizations and faiths. Religion, like race and ethnicity, evokes an emotional response in individuals. It is difficult to be neutral about religion. It is almost impossible to accept the idea that religious beliefs other than one's own are equally legitimate. Religion also has a polarizing effect because it is often the basis for selecting (or rejecting) mates, friends, neighbors, schools, and employees. Therefore, religious differences in the United States not only differentiate people but also may provide the basis for conflict.

Religious intolerance is not unknown in U.S. history. Although the nation was founded on the principle of religious freedom, at various times and places Jews, Catholics, Quakers, Mennonites, and atheists have been targets of religious bigotry. There have been political parties (Know-Nothing Party), organizations (Ku Klux Klan, American Nazi Party), and demagogues who have been anti-Catholic, anti-Semitic, and anti-Muslim. Their moderate success in attracting followers demonstrates that some people in the United States are susceptible to such appeals. The effects of their success have been to lessen the probability of interfaith cooperation and enhance the likelihood of conflict. Moreover, the religion-based conflicts world-wide (e.g., Israel and its Muslim neighbors, Protestants and Catholics in Ireland, Catholics and Muslims in the Philippines, and Muslims and Christians in the Sudan) often inflame their followers in the United States.

These segmenting factors create some groups in society that are advantaged and others that are disadvantaged. The former work to perpetuate their advantages, while the latter sometimes organize to protest and change the system they consider unfair. But how can these people change the system if they are self-defined as powerless? A first step is legitimate, polite protest, which usually takes the form of voting, petitions, or writing to public officials. A second option is to use impolite, yet legitimate forms of protest (for example, peaceful demonstrations, picket lines, boycotts, and marches). The third alternative, used when others fail, is to use illegitimate forms of protest (for example, civil disobedience, riots, bombings, and guerrilla warfare).

Dissident groups select illegitimate protest because of the intransigence of the people in power toward change. The dissident groups consider their actions legitimate because they are for a just cause ("the ends justify the means"), but these protests are perceived as illegitimate by those in power. The people in authority resort to force, often intensifying the zeal and purpose of the protesters and frequently rallying previously uncommitted people to the cause of the dissidents.

Implicit in this section is the notion that highly differentiated social systems, like that in the United States, must cope with the realities of disharmony, conflict of interest, and even violence. There is no alternative to conflict because of the diverse conditions of the U.S. social structure. This is not to say that conflict is altogether bad. There can be positive consequences of conflict for both parties to the conflict and for society as well (Coser, 1966).

All societies have the potential for cleavage and conflict because of the differential allocation of power. Concomitant with having power is the holding of other advantages (prestige, privilege, and economic benefits). People with advantage almost invariably wish to keep it, and those without typically want to change the reward system.

Coupled with the stratification system (the structured inequality of categories of people; see Chapter 9) in the United States are other aspects of social structure that increase the probability of conflict. The United States, perhaps more than any other society, is populated by a multitude of ethnic groups, racial groups, and religious groups. (For a similar situation in India, see the panel titled "A Closer Look: Violence and Division in India.") The diversity is further increased by the existence of regional differences and by a generation gap. Although assimilation has occurred to some degree, the different groups and categories have not blended into a homogeneous mass but continue to remain separate—often with a pride that makes assimilation unlikely and conflict inevitable.

Violence and the Myth of Peaceful Progress

Two beliefs held typically by U.S. Americans combine to make the **myth of peaceful progress**—the incorrect belief that throughout U.S. history disadvantaged groups have gained their share of power, prosperity, and respectability without violence (Graham and Gurr, 1969; Rubenstein, 1970; Skolnick, 1969). First, there is a widely

Violence and Division in India

Although well known for a strong socioreligious tradition of nonviolence, India has been beset by many forms of collective violence stemming from the many divisions that characterize that society.

1. *Religious violence.* The formation of India and Pakistan in 1947 into predominantly Hindu and Muslim states, respectively, was accompanied by numerous riots between both communities and a bloody, massive exchange of population. In recent times, Hindu-Muslim riots have taken place centering on issues such as the conversion of lower-caste Hindus to Islam, processions on the holy days of each faith, and over mosques that some Hindus claim were built on the sites of preexisting temples and places holy to Hinduism. Religious connotations are also evident in the violence and terrorism that has wracked three states: Punjab through much of the 1980s, based on demands by followers of the Sikh religion, as well as Kashmir and Gujarat more recently, by and against Muslims.

2. *Caste violence.* Caste is a form of social stratification that determines one's position at birth and narrows one's choices with regard to occupation, marriage, and social interaction while rigidly controlling mobility. In an effort to do away with the resulting discriminatory and degrading treatment of the lower castes, government policies provide for preferential treatment in education and employment of some of these groups. Caste violence was traditionally, and continues to be, a rural phenomenon pitting members of the upper castes against those of the lower castes. Such violence has also been seen in urban areas, often as a result of the opposition of upper castes to the extension of these preferential policies.

3. *Partisan violence.* For about thirty years following independence, the major political party in India was the Indian National Congress (known as the Congress). However, the dominance of the Congress has declined in parliament, where it is now an opposition party, and in some state legislatures, where it shares power with other regional parties or is in the opposition. Given the proliferation of parties with narrow and conflicting agendas, collective violence over political issues has taken place regularly. Demands for increased autonomy to particular areas, governmental assistance to certain groups and not others, subsidies, demarcation of state borders, disputes over water and other resources, and elections have all been issues that have generated political violence.

4. *Linguistic violence.* India has fifteen officially recognized languages (including Hindi, the "national" language) along with English, which is used for a number of official and business purposes. Recent

held notion that the United States is made up of diverse groups that have learned to compromise differences in a peaceful manner. Second, there is the belief that any group in the United States can gain its share of power, prosperity, and respectability merely by playing the game according to the rules. Hence, there is no need for political violence in the United States because the system works for the advantage of all.

Because these beliefs are widely shared, most people in the United States do not understand dissent by minority groups. Their opinions are believed to be aberrations and are explained away by saying that they are communist-inspired, or that some groups are exceptions to the rule because they are basically immoral and irrational. Perhaps the most prevalent explanation locates the source of all violence in the individual psyches of the people involved.

These explanations are incomplete because they locate the blame outside the system itself. U.S. history shows that, with few exceptions, powerless and downtrodden groups seeking power have not achieved it without a struggle. U.S. institutions, Rubenstein (1970) notes, are better designed to facilitate the upward mobility of talented individuals than of oppressed groups. "Most groups which have engaged in censuses have enumerated thirty-three languages that are spoken by at least 100,000 people each. Although often unrecognized outside India, the language issue is a potent divisive factor in Indian life and complicates educational, media, and governmental policies. State borders in India were redrawn according to linguistic criteria in the late 1950s. This has enabled, for example, political parties in these "linguistic" states to be formed around and to claim to represent the interests of speakers of those languages. While the number of incidents of linguistic violence has dwindled, demands for and against the recognition of particular languages as "official" or as a medium of educational instruction crop up from time to time.

5. *Ethnic violence.* Race/ethnicity has not been considered a major factor in collective violence in India. Most of India's population represents an intermingling of various racial groups. However, perceived differences between the "Aryan"-dominated north and the "Dravidian"-dominated south resulted in a number of riots, primarily in the southern state of Tamil Nadu in the early 1960s. More recently, the northeastern states of India have witnessed separatist violence based on "pan-Mongolism," a professed identification with similar ethnic groups in Nagaland, Mizoram, Manipur (bordering states in India), and Myanmar (Burma), as well as among various tribal groups.

6. *Economic violence.* Two forms of collective violence, rural and urban, can be traced to the economic structure. Around 70 percent of India's population lives in rural areas, where caste norms still hold sway and economic violence in these settings is often confounded with intercaste violence. Violent confrontations between peasants and landowners (or their hired thugs) on issues related to inadequate pay, debts, putative land ownership reforms and other work-related conditions typify rural economic violence. These result from the structured inequality of traditional village life in India.

Urban economic violence also revolves around a number of issues such as union strikes, lockouts, price rises, job terminations of fellow employees, or it is instigated by factional disputes. Nearly 30 percent of India's population lives below the official poverty line, which in 1990 was set at an annual income of $370. In terms of both absolute and relative deprivation, there is a large segment of the rural and urban population that has not shared in the fruits of economic development and more recent economic liberalization. This segment is consequently willing to engage in the violence of protest to highlight its members' conditions. This, in turn, provokes counterviolence from those whose interests are threatened.

Source: Reprinted by permission of N. Prabha Unnithan, Colorado State University.

---

mass violence have done so only after a long period of fruitless, relatively nonviolent struggle in which established procedures have been tried and found wanting" (8). The problem is that the United States, like all other societies, has not allowed and does not allow for the nonviolent transfer of power.

Throughout the history of the United States, groups that were oppressed resorted to various legitimate and illegitimate means to secure rights and privileges that they believed to be rightfully theirs. Those in power typically reacted either by doing nothing or by repression—the choice depending on the degree to which the minority groups' actions were perceived as a real threat. The following discussion is a partial list of groups that at various times in U.S. history have resorted to violence to achieve social, economic, or political objectives.

Revolutionary Colonists. A notable case of violence by a minority in the New World was the American Revolutionary War. The United States was born through violence. The colonists first petitioned the king of England to redress grievances, and when this failed, they turned to acts of civil disobedience and finally to eight years of war.

The Declaration of Independence, clearly a revolutionary document, provided the rationale for mass violence:

> We hold these truths to be self-evident, that all men are created equal, that they are endowed by their Creator with certain unalienable Rights, that among these are Life, Liberty, and the pursuit of Happiness. That to secure these rights, Governments are instituted among Men, deriving their just powers from the consent of the governed. That whenever any Form of Government becomes destructive of these ends, it is the Right of the People to alter or to abolish it, and to institute new Government, laying its foundation on such principles and organizing its powers in such form, as to them shall seem most likely to effect their Safety and Happiness. Prudence, indeed, will dictate that Governments long established should not be changed for light and transient causes; and accordingly all experiences hath shewn that mankind are more disposed to suffer, while evils are sufferable, than to right themselves by abolishing the forms to which they are accustomed. But when a long train of abuses and usurpations, pursuing invariably the same Object evinces a design to reduce them under absolute Despotism, it is their right, it is their duty, to throw off such Government, and to provide new Guards for their future security.

This document, a cornerstone of the heritage of the United States, legitimates the use of violence by oppressed peoples. It could have been written by a modern-day revolutionary. While still revered, its content is no longer taken literally by the bulk of U.S. citizenry.

Native Americans. Long before the Revolutionary War and continuing to the present day, Native Americans attempted to change the order established by Whites.

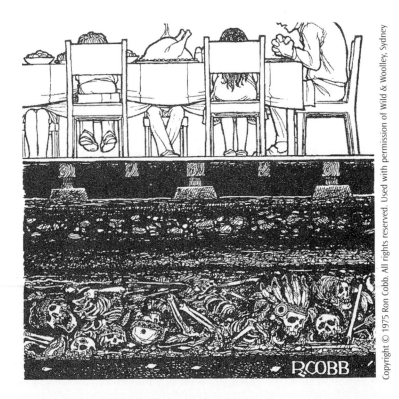

When White settlers took their land, ruined their hunting, and imprisoned them on reservations, the Native Americans fought these occurrences and were systematically suppressed by the U.S. government (Brown, 1971). In recent years, Native Americans have occasionally boycotted, used violence, or used legal offensives to regain former Indian lands. The last tactic has become especially popular. More than half of the 266 federally recognized tribes have claims in various federal courts.

Exploited Farmers. Farmers have used violence on occasion to fight economic exploitation. Between the Revolutionary War and 1800, for example, three such revolts took place—Shays's Rebellion, the Whiskey Rebellion, and Fries's Rebellion. Protesting farmers have used various forms of violence (destruction of property, looting, and killing) throughout U.S. history. Some modern farmers have resorted to acts of violence to publicize their demands and to terrorize other farmers in order to present a united front against their opponents.

Slaveholders. Feeling the threat of the abolitionist movement, White Southerners beginning in about 1820 used violent means to preserve slavery. In the early stages this amounted to civil disobedience, and later it burst out into fighting in places like "bleeding Kansas." Eventually the South seceded, and the Civil War was waged—a classic example of a minority group using violence to force a change and being suppressed by the power of the majority.

WASP Supremacists. Following the Civil War and continuing to the present day, some Whites have engaged in guerrilla warfare, arson, terrorism, and lynching in order to maintain the subjugation of Blacks. From 1882 to 1903, for example, 1,985 Blacks were killed by southern lynch mobs (Cutler, 1905:177).

Riots, lynchings, and mob actions are not solely southern phenomena. Many people from other sections of the United States have used these techniques against various alien groups (usually Catholics and immigrants from non-Teutonic Europe) in order to maintain their superiority. U.S. history is rife with examples of this phenomenon: "native" Americans tore apart the Irish section of Philadelphia in 1844; a Roman Catholic Church and homes of Irish Catholics were destroyed in Boston in 1854; Chinese and Japanese immigrants were victims of both riots and discrimination, particularly on the West Coast; Japanese, even those who were U.S. citizens, were put in concentration camps during World War II because their patriotism was suspect; and Jews have been the objects of physical attack, boycotts, intimidation, and discrimination throughout U.S. history.

Contemporary examples of mob violence against intruders can be seen in some communities where an all-White neighborhood is faced with one or more Haitian or Vietnamese families moving in. Threats, burning crosses, ostracism, and occasional physical violence have occurred with alarming regularity where Blacks have moved into previously all-White areas. This is not a southern phenomenon, but one that is found throughout the United States. So, too, are incidents of violence directed at Muslims and their places of worship.

Ethnic Minorities. Immigrant groups (that is, those groups most recently immigrant), as well as racial groups, because they have been the target of discrimination, threats, and physical violence, have themselves participated in violence. Sometimes gangs have attacked the groups responsible for their deprived condition. Most often, however, hostility by immigrants has been aimed at groups with less power, either toward Blacks or toward more recently arrived immigrants. Violence by Blacks has occurred throughout U.S. history. Always the victims, they have sometimes responded to violence in kind. During the years of slavery, more than 250 insurrections took place. Mass Black violence has occurred in many major cities (for example, Chicago and Washington, DC, in 1919; Detroit in 1943 and again in 1967; Los Angeles in 1965 and again in 1992; Newark in 1967; and Miami in 1987).

The rage that racial minorities feel against Whites has surfaced sporadically in small and diffuse ways as well. Most commonly, it has been manifested in individual crimes (murder, theft, and rape) or in gang assaults on Whites or in destruction of property owned by Whites.

Labor Disputants. Another relatively powerless group resorting to violence to achieve its aims has been organized labor. In the 1870s, workers attempted to organize for collective action against unfair policies of the industrialists. Unions formed, such as the Knights of Labor, American Federation of Labor, and the Industrial Workers of the World. Their primary tactic was the strike, which in itself is nonviolent. But strikers often used force to keep people from crossing the picket lines. Nor were the owners blameless. Their refusal to change existing wages, hours, and working conditions was the source of grievance. They sometimes turned to violence themselves to suppress the unions (for example, hiring people to physically break up picket lines). The intransigent refusal of the owners to change the awful conditions of nineteenth-century workers resulted in considerable violence in many industries, particularly in the coal-mining, steel, timber, and railroad industries. Labor violence, as in other cases mentioned previously, was ultimately effective. Working conditions, wages, and security of the workers improved. Legislation was passed providing for arbitration of differences and recognition of unions. Clearly, the use of force was necessary to gain advances for laboring men and women.

Given the evidence just cited, it is remarkable that people still believe in the myth of peaceful progress. Violence was necessary to give birth to the United States. Violence was used both to keep the Blacks in servitude and to free them. Violence was used to defeat rebellious Native Americans and to keep them on reservations. Additionally, violence has been a necessary means for many groups in the United States to achieve equality or something approaching parity in power and in the rights that all citizens and residents are supposed to enjoy.

The powerful have not been munificent in giving a break to the powerless. To the contrary, much effort has been expended by the powerful to keep the powerless in that condition. Many times in the history of the United States, violence has been the only catalyst for change. Relatively powerless groups in the United States (for example, African Americans, women, and farmers) have repeatedly gone outside existing law. To these groups, the use of force was justified because of the need to right insufferable wrongs—the reason the colonists gave for breaking from England.

We should note, however, that violence does not always work. The revolts of Native Americans were not beneficial in any way to their people. Moreover, some groups, such as the Jews, have advanced with comparatively little violence. Historically, however, violence is as American as apple pie. The Presidential Commissions on Civil Disorders and Violence have laid bare the inaccuracies of the "peaceful progress" idea held by so many people. The uniform remedy suggested by these commissions for minimizing violence is to eliminate the causes of social unrest and perceived injustice. It cannot be a surprise that minority groups occasionally use violence because they are reacting against a system that systematically disadvantages them with little hope for change through peaceful means.

The Integrative Forces in Society

Order theorists recognize that conflict, disharmony, and division occur within societies, particularly in complex, heterogeneous societies. They stress, however, the opposite societal characteristics of cooperation, harmony, and solidarity. They see U.S. society as "We the people of the United States" rather than as a conglomerate of sometimes hostile groups. In particular, order theorists focus on what holds society together. What are the forces that somehow keep anarchy from becoming a reality— or as the English philosopher Thomas Hobbes asked long ago, "Why is there not a war of all against all?" The answer to this fundamental question is found in the combined effects of a number of factors.

Functional Integration. Probably the most important unifying factor is the phenomenon of **functional integration** (the unity among divergent elements of society resulting from a specialized division of labor, noted by Durkheim). In a highly differentiated society such as the United States, with its specialized division of labor, interaction among different segments occurs with some regularity. Interdependence often results because no group is entirely self-sufficient. The farmer needs the miller, the processor, and retail agents, as well as the fertilizer manufacturer and the agricultural experimenters. Manufacturers need raw materials, on one hand, and customers, on the other. Management needs workers, and the workers need management.

These groups, because they need each other, because each gains from the interaction, work to perpetuate a social framework that maximizes benefits to both parties and minimizes conflict or the breaking of the relationship. Written and unwritten rules emerge to govern these relationships, usually leading to cooperation rather than either isolation or conflict and to linkages between different (and potentially conflicting) groups.

Consensus on Societal Values. A second basis for the unification of diverse groups in the United States is that almost all people hold certain fundamental values in common. Order theorists assume that commonly held values are like social glue binding otherwise diverse people in a cohesive societal unit. Unlike functional integration, unity is achieved here through similarity rather than through difference.

Most of us believe that democracy is the best possible government. We accept the wishes of the majority on election day. Defeated candidates, for example, do not go off into the hills with their followers to blow up bridges and otherwise harass the government. Most people are patriotic. They revere the heritage of the United States and believe strongly in individualism and free enterprise and in the Judeo-Christian ethic.

Many symbols epitomize the consensus of people in the United States with respect to basic values. One such unifying symbol is the national flag. Although a mere piece of cloth, the flag clearly symbolizes something approaching the sacred. Reverence for the flag is evidenced by the shock shown when it is defiled and by the punishment given to defilers. The choice of the flag as an object to spit on or burn is a calculated one by dissident groups. They choose to defile it precisely because of what it represents and because most citizens revere it so strongly. In 1989, the Supreme Court ruled that an individual who had desecrated the flag was guaranteed the right to do so because the Constitution protects the freedom of political expression. This decision outraged the majority of citizens, and politicians seized the opportunity to pass legislation making flag desecration an illegal act.

Similarly, such documents as the Declaration of Independence and the Constitution are held in high esteem and serve to unify citizens. The heritage of the United States is also revered through holidays such as Thanksgiving and Independence Day. Consensus is also achieved through the collective reverence for such leaders as George Washington, Abraham Lincoln, and John F. Kennedy.

The Social Order. A third factor that unifies people in the United States, at least minimally, is that they are all subject to similar influences and rules of the game. U.S. inhabitants are answerable to the same body of law (at the national level), and they are under the same government. Additionally, they use the same system of monetary exchange, the same standards for measurement, and so on. The order in society is evidenced by our taking for granted such assorted practices as obeying traffic lights, the use of credit, and the acceptance of checks in lieu of money.

Group Membership. A source of unity (as well as of cleavage) is group memberships. Some groups are exclusive because they limit membership to people of a particular race, ethnic group, income category, religion, or other characteristic. The existence of exclusive organizations creates tension if people are excluded who want to be included, because exclusiveness generally implies feelings of superiority. Country clubs, fraternities, some churches, and some neighborhoods are based on the twin foundations of exclusiveness and superiority. There are other groups, however, whose membership consists of people from varying backgrounds (that is, the membership includes rich and poor, or Black and White). Consequently, heterogeneous organizations such as political parties, religious denominations or churches, and veterans' organizations allow members the chance not only to interact with people unlike themselves but also to join together in a common cause.

Many, if not most, Americans who belong to several organizations belong to organizations with different compositions by race, religion, or other salient characteristics. To the extent that these cross-cutting memberships and allegiances exist, they tend to cancel out potential cleavages along social class, race, or other lines. Individuals belonging to several different organizations will probably feel some cross pressures (that is, pulls in opposite directions), thereby preventing polarization.

Additionally, most people belong to at least one organization such as a school, church, or civic group with norms that support those of the total society. These organizations support the government and what it stands for, and they expect their members to do the same.

International Competition and Conflict. External threats to the society's existence unifies us. The advice Machiavelli gave his prince is a regrettable truth: "If the Prince is in trouble, he should promote a war." This was the advice that Secretary of State William Seward gave to President Lincoln prior to the Civil War. Although expedient advice from the standpoint of preserving unity, it was, Lincoln noted, only a short-term solution.

A real threat to security unifies those groups, no matter how diverse, that feel threatened. Thus, a reasonable explanation for the lack of unity in the U.S. involvement in an Indochinese war was that the Vietcong were not perceived by most Americans as a real threat to their security. The Soviet buildup in armaments in the 1980s, on the other hand, was perceived as a real threat, unifying many Americans in a willingness to sacrifice in order to catch up with and surpass the Soviets. Now that the Soviet Union has been dismantled and the Cold War is a thing of the past, we no longer are united by the possible attack by communists. The Persian Gulf War in 1991, however, was an instance when most Americans were unified against a dictator who threatened democracy and stability in the Middle East. Following the September 11, 2001, attacks by terrorists on the World Trade Center and the Pentagon, Americans of all types rallied behind their president in a sense of outrage and a common purpose in reducing as much as possible the threat of terrorism.

The Mass Media. The world is in the midst of a communications revolution. Television, for example, has expanded to encompass virtually every home in the United States. This phenomenon—universal exposure to television—has been blamed, among other things, for rising juvenile delinquency, lower cultural tastes, declining test scores, general moral deterioration, and suppressed creativity. These criticisms are countered by order theorists, who see television and the other forms of mass media as performing several integrative functions. Government officials, for example, can use the media to shape public actions (for example, to unite against an enemy or to sacrifice by paying higher taxes). The media also reinforce the values and norms of society. Newspaper editorials extol certain people and events while decrying others. Soap operas are stories involving moral dilemmas, with virtue winning out. Newspaper and magazine stories under the caption "It Could Only Have Happened in America" abound. The media do not usually rock the boat. The heroes of the United States are praised and its enemies vilified. Our way of life is the right way; the ways of others are considered incorrect or downright immoral. For an

After the September 11, 2001, tragedy, Americans of all types came together in various symbolic acts of unity.

The Media's Selective Perception of Race and Class

From the window that I wake at, most of my city is untouched. Houses stand stately after the 7.1 earthquake.

Everyone knows from watching television that earthquake damage in the Bay Area has been restricted to a relatively few neighborhoods. But not everyone may realize that considerations of race and class shaped the images that Americans saw on their TV screens.

The Marina district of San Francisco is a stately, upper-middle-class neighborhood. Homes sit alongside the Bay. People here lived well, and they faced tragedy with dignity after their neighborhood was devastated. Marina residents on TV were articulate, focused. No wonder television crews set up their cameras at this neighborhood's periphery and interviewed the residents who, even in anger and frustration, remained gentle.

But why have so few of the television crews chosen to go to the Moscone Center where those who lost homes in the city's low-income neighborhoods are now bedded down? Many of those who sleep at Moscone do not speak in tones modulated with good humor. Many of them possessed little to begin with, and they lost that little bit with the earthquake. Some had nothing and now have to redefine what nothing means.

Why were so few of the camera crews talking to people who live in West Oakland's projects, a stone's throw away from the Interstate 880 freeway that collapsed? These people now live under the same sort of stress that affects those of the Marina district.

Despite the fact that the stench of dead bodies permeates the air around the Cypress projects, help was slow in coming to those people. Not until I-880 was threatened with further collapse did the social service system that sheltered the Marina even reach out to those who lived in the midst of the Cypress deaths.

Why didn't Bryant Gumbel and Jane Pauley venture down to Watsonville, where the population is mostly Mexican and poor, where average family income is about $15,000 a year? Are the losses there less painful, the survival tales less moving?

Or do the media value White life over all by ignoring the fact that the lives of far too many people of color were also shattered by the earthquake?

TV's silence about the earthquake's impact on the non-White and the poor is reminiscent of the Depression, when aid was more available to Whites than to Blacks; when the employment expansion resulting from World War II included Blacks only after a march on Washington was threatened.

At every tragedy we are told to pull together and ignore our differences. We should not complain that the Marina was more televised than the Cypress neighborhoods because earthquake relief will finally assist both areas. We must not point out that Hispanics in Watsonville have been largely ignored because they, too, will gain from regional awareness.

But when the urgency abates, we become separate again: Black, White, yellow, brown. Some have the skills to lobby for press attention or emergency aid, while others merely have the fortitude to survive and pray for help.

This is not the time to speak of race and class, a friend of mine cautions. Our television anchors reflect this point with pithy clichés: "We are all in this together." Together or not, it rankles that some people's suffering generates more concern than that of others.

The fact is that the earth shrugged, concrete tumbled, and people lost their lives. But once again, race and class determined the focus of the news and our national concern.

Source: Julianne Malveaux, 1989. "Race and Class Shape TV Images of Earthquake." *Rocky Mountain News* (November 4):57.

example of how the media tend to ignore the realities of race and class, see the panel titled "Diversity: The Media's Selective Perception of Race and Class."

Planned Integration. Charismatic figures or other people of influence may work to unite segmented parts of the system (conversely, they can promote division). Thus, a union leader or the archbishop of a Catholic diocese can, through personal exhortation or by example, persuade group members to cooperate rather than compete, or to open membership requirements rather than maintain exclusiveness.

Public officials on the local, state, and national levels can use their power to integrate the parts of society in three major ways: by passing laws to eliminate barriers among groups, by working to solve the problems that segment the society, and by providing mediators to help negotiate settlements between such feuding groups as management and labor (Mott, 1965:283–284). High officials such as the president use various means of integration. First, there is the technique of **co-optation** (appointing a member of a dissident group to a policy-making body to appease the dissenting group). Second, they can use their executive powers to enforce and interpret the laws in such a way as to unite groups within the society. Finally, the president and other high officials can use the media to persuade the people. The president, for example, can request television time on all networks during prime time, thereby reaching most of the adult population in order to use full presidential powers of persuasion to unite diverse groups.

False Consciousness. Most Americans do not feel oppressed. Even many people who do not have many material blessings tend to believe in the American creed that anyone can be upwardly mobile—if not themselves, then at least their children (Sennett and Cobb, 1973). According to Marxian theory, when oppressed people hold beliefs damaging to their interests, they have false consciousness.

Thus, contrary to Karl Marx's prediction more than a century ago that capitalism would be overthrown by an oppressed majority, most of us today consider ourselves as haves or as could-be haves rather than as have-nots. There has been little polarization along purely economic lines because of a relatively large middle class. This may be changing, however, as more and more of the middle class are moving downward (see Chapter 10).

The Use of the Order and Conflict Models in This Book

There are two contradictory models of society—the order and conflict models. The order model views society as basically cooperative, consensual, and stable. The system works. Any problems are the faults of people, not of society. At the other extreme, the adherents of the conflict model assume that society is fundamentally competitive, conflictual, coercive, and radically changing. Social problems are the faults of society, not of individuals, in this view.

The order and conflict models of society are both significant, and they are used in the remainder of this book. While each model, by itself, is important, a realistic analysis must include both. The order model must be included because there is integration, order, and stability; because the parts are more or less interdependent; and because most social change is gradual and adjustive. The conflict model is equally important because society is not always a harmonious unit. To the contrary, much of social life is based on competition. Societal integration is fragile; it is often based on subtle or blatant coercion.

A crucial difference between the two models is the implicit assumption of each as to the nature of the social structure (rules, customs, institutions, social stratification, and the distribution of power). The order perspective assumes that the social structure is basically right and proper because it serves the fundamental function of maintaining society. There is, therefore, an implicit acceptance of the status quo, assuming that the system works. As we examine the major institutions of society in this book, one task is to determine how each institution aids in societal integration.

Although order theorists also look for the dysfunctions of institutions, rules, organizations, and customs (**dysfunctions** refer to negative consequences), the critical examination of society is the primary thrust of conflict theorists. While this book describes the way the United States is structured and how this arrangement works for society integration, a major consideration centers on the question of who benefits under these arrangements and who does not. Thus, the legitimacy of the system is always doubted.

Chapter Review

1. Sociologists have a mental image (model) of how society is structured, how it changes, and what holds it together. Two prevailing models—order and conflict—provide contradictory images of society.

2. Order model theorists view society as ordered, stable, and harmonious, with a high degree of cooperation and consensus. Change is gradual, adjustive, and reforming. Social problems are seen as the result of problem individuals.

3. Conflict model theorists view society as competitive, fragmented, and unstable. Social integration is minimal and tenuous. Social change, which can be revolutionary, results from clashes among conflicting groups. Social problems are viewed as resulting from society's failure to meet the needs of individuals. Indeed, the structure of society is seen as the problem.

4. The order and conflict models present extreme views of society. Taken alone, each fosters a faulty perception and interpretation of society. A realistic model of society combines the strengths of both models. The assumptions of such a synthesis are that (a) the processes of stability and change are properties of all societies; (b) societies are organized, but the very process of organization generates conflict; (c) society is a social system, with the parts linked through common goals and similar interests, and is competitive because of scarce resources and inequities; (d) societies are held together both by consensus on values and by coercion; and (e) social change may be gradual or abrupt, reforming or revolutionary.

5. The divisive forces bringing about segmentation in U.S. society are size, social class, race, ethnicity, sexual orientation, and religion. Thus, society has the potential for cleavage and conflict.

6. There is a widespread belief in the myth of peaceful progress—that disadvantaged groups throughout history have gained prosperity and equality without violence. The evidence, however, is that oppressed groups have had to use force or the threat of force to achieve gains.

7. The integrative forces in the United States are functional integration, consensus on values, the social order, group memberships, threats from other societies, the mass media, planned integration, and false consciousness.

Key Terms

Model	Conflict model	Economic inequality
Order model (functionalism)	Social problems	Myth of peaceful progress
Manifest consequence	Instrumental process	Functional integration
Latent consequence	Institutional process	Co-optation
Dysfunctions	Dialectic	

Study Questions

1. What is the order model of society? On what kinds of social phenomena does it focus? What social phenomena are neglected from this perspective?

2. What is the conflict model of society? On what kinds of social phenomena does it focus? What social phenomena are neglected from this perspective?

3. What are the potentially divisive forces in society?
4. Contrary to popular belief, throughout much of U.S. history, oppressed groups have used violence to achieve progress. What is the evidence to support this refutation of the myth of peaceful progress?
5. What are the integrative forces of society?

For Further Reading

Sociological Theories: General

Thomas J. Bernard, *The Consensus-Conflict Debate* (New York: Columbia University Press, 1983).

Tom Campbell, *Seven Theories of Human Society* (New York: Oxford University Press, 1981).

Randall Collins, *Three Sociological Traditions* (New York: Oxford University Press, 1985).

R. P. Cuzzort and Edith W. King, *Social Thought into the Twenty-First Century*, 6th ed. (Fort Worth, TX: Harcourt Brace, 2002).

Charles Lemert (ed.), *Social Theory: The Multicultural and Classic Readings* (Boulder, CO: Westview Press, 1993).

The Order Model

Mark Abrahamson, *Functionalism* (Upper Saddle River, NJ: Prentice Hall, 1978).

Kingsley Davis, *Human Society* (New York: Macmillan, 1948).

Robert K. Merton, *Social Theory and Social Structure*, rev. ed. (New York: Free Press, 1968).

Talcott Parsons, *Sociological Theory and Modern Society* (New York: Free Press, 1967).

Jonathan Turner and Alexandra Maryanski, *Functionalism* (Menlo Park, CA: Benjamin Cummings, 1979).

Robin M. Williams, Jr., *American Society: A Sociological Interpretation*, 3rd ed. (New York: Knopf, 1970).

The Conflict Model

Carol Andreas, *Meatpackers and Beef Barons* (Niwot: University Press of Colorado, 1994).

William J. Chambliss (ed.), *Sociological Readings in the Conflict Perspective* (Reading, MA: Addison-Wesley, 1973).

Ralf Dahrendorf, *Class and Class Conflict in Industrial Society* (Stanford, CA: Stanford University Press, 1959).

Karl Marx and Friedrich Engels, *The Communist Manifesto*, Eden Paul and Cedar Paul, trans. (New York: Russell & Russell, 1963).

C. Wright Mills, *The Power Elite* (New York: Oxford University Press, 1956).

Michael Parenti, *Dirty Truths: Reflections on Politics, Media, Ideology, Conspiracy, Ethnic Life and Class Power* (San Francisco: City Lights Books, 1996).

Michael Parenti, *Power and the Powerless*, 2nd ed. (New York: St. Martin's Press, 1978).

John Walton, *Sociology and Critical Inquiry: The Work, Tradition, and Purpose*, 2nd ed. (Belmont, CA: Wadsworth, 1990).

Lenski, Gerhard E. 1966, *Power and Privilege: A Theory of Social Stratification* (New York: McGraw-Hill).

Web Resources

http://www.hewett.norfolk.sch.uk/curric/soc/theory.htm

This site offers a visually effective map of sociological theories. Included in the map are functionalism and conflict theory.

http://odur.let.rug.nl/~usa/usa.htm

Search this site to find out about U.S. history, including information on slaves and the taking of land from Native Americans.

http://www.journale.com/withoutsanctuary/

Without Sanctuary is a powerful site that contains photographs and postcards on lynchings.

http://www.tolerance.org/index.jsp

Tolerance.org has information on hate groups and encourages everyone to fight hate and promote tolerance.

Much was made of the year 2000. It delineated the end of a thousand-year period and the beginning of another millennium. It is believed to mark the 2,000th year after the birth of Jesus. Some cults believed that this date would bring the apocalypse (the end of the present temporal world) because of their interpretation of two books in the Bible—Daniel in the Old Testament and Revelation in the New Testament. Obviously for them, the number 2,000 is of ultimate importance. But is it? Why is a calendar divided into thousand-year epochs meaningful? If it is important, then did the new millennium begin on January 1, 2000, or January 1, 2001? To begin, the calendar we use, beginning with the birth of Jesus, is off by as much as six years. The Christian calendar was computed by a sixth-century monk, Dionysius Exiguus. Scholars now believe that Exiguus was wrong because Herod, ruler of Judea at the time of Jesus' birth, died in 4 B.C. and Jesus was probably born a year or two before that (Zelizer, 1999). So, was the year 2000 really 2005 or 2006?

When the West marked the year 2000, the Chinese celebrated the year 4698. For followers of Zoroastrianism in Iran, the year was 2390; for Muslims, it was 1421, for it had been that many years since the birth of the prophet Muhammad; and for Jews, it was the year 5760. Rabbi Zelizer (1999) asks: "How can there be a global party to which much of the human population will not show up?" (15A). Obviously, the starting date for calendars is an arbitrary decision on which societies differ.

When do centuries or millennia end? When do we celebrate the beginning of a new century or millennium? Exiguus designated the beginning of the Christian calendar as January 1 of year 1—not year 0.

> If we insist that all decades must have ten years, and all centuries one hundred years, then year 10 belongs to the first decade—and, sad to say, year 100 must remain in the first century. Thenceforward, the issue never goes away. Every year with a '00 must count as the hundredth and final year of its century—no matter what common sensibility might prefer: 1900 went with all 1800 years to form the nineteenth century; and 2000 must be the completing year of the twentieth century, not the inception of the new millennium. . . . If our shortsighted monk had only begun with a year zero, then logic and sensibility would coincide, and the wild millennial bells could ring forth but once and resoundingly at the beginning of January 1, 2000. But he didn't. (Gould, 1997:109–110)

So, a calendar that is not universally accepted throughout the world and that is off by as much as six years and one that did not begin with zero was, nevertheless, used by most of the Western world to designate January 1, 2000, as the beginning of a new millennium.

Among the devices human beings use to impose order upon a complicated world is a way to delineate time. Most of the world's inhabitants call each rotation of the earth a day, and seven of these a week. Four weeks, coinciding roughly with the moon's revolution of the earth, make a month. The twelve months corresponding more or less with the earth's revolution around the sun constitute a year (actually 365 days, 5 hours, 48 minutes, and 45.96768 seconds). These definitions, while arbitrary, are accepted by most cultures because of the facts of nature. But nowhere in nature's cycles are there divisions by thousands:

> The intrinsic advantages of decimal mathematics have often been noted, and our Arabic numerology surely gives 1,000 that nice look of evenness. . . . But we also recognize that these advantages do not arise from nature's construction, and we know that several cultures developed entirely functional (and beautifully complex) mathematical systems on bases other than 10—and, therefore, with no special status attached to the number 1,000 at all. (Gould, 1997:20)

Thus, the notion of the beginning of a new millennium and when it occurred are social constructions. But people attach meanings to these social constructions, and these cultural meanings are powerful determinants of human behavior.

An important focus of sociology is on the social influences on human behavior. As people interact over time, two fundamental sources of constraints on individuals emerge—social structure and culture. As noted in Chapter 2, *social structure* refers to the linkages and networks among the members of a social organization. *Culture*, the subject of this chapter, as defined in Chapter 2, is the knowledge that the members of a social organization share. Because this shared knowledge includes ideas about what is right, how one is to behave in various situations, religious beliefs, and communication, culture constrains not only behavior but also how people think about and interpret their world.

This chapter is divided into two sections. The first section describes the nature of culture and its importance for understanding human behavior. The second section focuses on one aspect of culture—values. This discussion is especially vital for understanding the organization and problems of society—in this case, U.S. society.

Culture: The Knowledge That People Share

Characteristics of Culture

Culture Is an Emergent Process. As individuals interact on any kind of sustained basis, they exchange ideas about all sorts of things. In time they develop common ideas, common ways of doing things, and common interpretations for certain actions. In so doing, the participants have created a culture. The emergent quality of culture is an ongoing process; it is built up slowly rather than being present at the beginnings of social organization. The culture of any group is constantly undergoing change because the members are in continuous interaction. Culture, then, is never completely static.

Culture Is Learned. Culture is not instinctive or innate in the human species; it is not part of the biological equipment of human beings. The biological equipment of humans, however, makes culture possible. That is, we are symbol-making creatures capable of attaching meaning to particular objects and actions and communicating these meanings to other people. When a person joins a new social organization, she or he must learn the culture of that group. This is true for the infant born into a society as well as for a college woman joining a sorority, a young man inducted into the armed forces, or immigrants to a new society. This process of learning the culture, called **socialization**, is the subject of the next chapter.

When we learn the culture of a society, or a group within society, we share with others a common understanding of words and symbols; we know the rules, what is appropriate and inappropriate, what is moral and immoral, and what is beautiful and what is ugly. Even the down-deep emotions of disgust, anger, and shame are related to the culture. A food that makes one gag in one society (insects, for example) may be considered a delicacy in another.

Culture Channels Human Behavior. Culture, because it emerges from social interaction, is an inevitable development of human society. More important, it is essential in the maintenance of any social system because it provides two crucial functions—predictability of action and stability. To accomplish these functions, however, culture must restrict human freedom (although, as we shall see, cultural constraints are not normally perceived as such); through cultural patterns, the individual is expected to conform to the expectations of the group.

How does culture work to constrain individuals? Or stated another way, how does culture become internalized in people so that their actions are controlled? Culture operates not only outside individuals but also inside them. Sigmund Freud recognized this process when he conceptualized the superego as the part of the personality structure that internalizes society's morals and thus inhibits people from committing acts considered wrong by their parents, a group, or the society.

The process of **internalization** (during which society's demands become part of the individual, acting to control her or his behavior) is accomplished mainly in three ways. First, culture becomes part of the human makeup through the belief system into which a child is born. This belief system, provided by parents and those people immediately in contact with youngsters, shapes their ideas about the surrounding world and also gives them certain ideas about themselves. The typical child in the United States, for example, is taught to accept Christian beliefs without reservation. These beliefs are literally force-fed, since alternative belief systems are considered unacceptable. It is interesting to note that after Christian beliefs are internalized by the child, they are often used as levers to keep the child in line.

Second, culture is internalized through psychological identification with the groups to which individuals belong (membership groups) or to which they want to belong (**reference groups**). Individuals want to belong; they want to be accepted by other people. Therefore, they tend to conform to the behavior of their immediate group as well as to the wishes of society at large.

Finally, culture is internalized by providing the individual with an identity. People's age, sex, race, religion, and social class have an effect on the way others perceive them and the way they perceive themselves. Berger (1963) states, "[I]n a sociological perspective, identity is socially bestowed, socially sustained, and socially transformed" (98; see also Cuzzort, 1969:203–204).

Culture, then, is not freedom but rather constraint. Of the entire range of possible behaviors (which probably are considered appropriate by some society somewhere), the person of a particular society chooses only from a narrow range of alternatives. The paradox, as Berger has pointed out, is that while society is like a prison to the people trapped in its cultural demands and expectations, it is not perceived as limiting to individual freedom. Berger states this truism well: "For most of us the yoke of society seems easy to bear. Why? . . . [B]ecause most of the time we ourselves desire just what society expects of us. We want to obey the rules. We want the parts that society has assigned to us" (Berger, 1963:93).

Individuals do not see the prison-like qualities of culture because they have internalized the culture of their society. From birth, children are shaped by the culture of the society into which they are born. They retain some individuality because of the configuration of forces unique to their experience (gene structure, peers, parents' social class, religion, and race), but the behavioral alternatives deemed appropriate for them are narrow.

Culture even shapes thought and perception. What we see and how we interpret what we see are determined by culture. Many White Americans believe that Blacks tend toward criminal activity. This stereotype can, therefore, negatively affect the interpretation of a socially acceptable act such as Black males walking down the street or driving an automobile on the interstate.

For a dramatic illustrative case of the kind of mental closure that may be determined by culture, consider the following riddle about a father and son driving down a highway: "There is a terrible accident in which the father is killed, and the son, critically injured, is rushed to a hospital. There, the surgeon approaches the patient and suddenly cries, 'My God, that's my son!'" How is it possible that the critically injured boy is the son of the man in the accident as well as the son of the surgeon? Answers might involve the surgeon being a priest, or a stepfather, or even artificial insemination. The correct answer to this riddle is that the surgeon is the boy's mother. Americans, male and female alike, have been socialized to think of women as occupying roles less important than physician/surgeon. If Russians were given this riddle, they would almost uniformly give the correct answer because approximately three-fourths of Russian physicians are women. Culture thus can be confining, not liberating. It constrains not only actions but also thinking.

Culture Maintains Boundaries. Culture not only limits the range of acceptable behavior and attitudes, it also instills in its adherents a sense of naturalness about the alternatives peculiar to a given society (or other social organization). Thus, there is a universal tendency to deprecate the ways of people from other societies as wrong, old-fashioned, inefficient, or immoral and to think of the ways of one's own group as superior (as the only right way). The concept for this phenomenon is **ethnocentrism**. The word combines the Greek word *ethnikos*, which means "nation" or "people," and the English word *center*. One's own race, religion, or society is the center of all and therefore superior to all.

Ethnocentrism is demonstrated in statements such as "My fraternity is the best," "Reincarnation is a weird belief," "We are God's chosen people," "Polygamy is immoral," or "The Bible is the greatest book ever written." To call the playoff game between the American and National Leagues the "World Series" implies that baseball outside the United States (and Canada) is inferior. Religious missionaries

Is the United States Culturally Superior?

In 1994, the Lake County (Florida) school board enacted a new school policy for the 22,000 children in the district. The policy: Teachers will be required to teach their students that America's political system, its values, and its culture in general are superior to other cultures in every regard. Specifically, it stated:

> Any instruction about other cultures shall also include and instill in our students an appreciation of our American heritage and culture such as: our republican form of government, capitalism, a free enterprise system, patriotism, strong family values, freedom of religion and other basic values that are superior to other foreign or historic cultures. (cited in Buchanan, 1994:B7)

This school policy is clearly ethnocentric. It is a reaction by political conservatives (three members of the five-person school board of Lake County are members of the Christian Coalition) to the Florida law mandating that teaching about other cultures should "eliminate personal and national ethnocentrism so that children understand that a specific culture is not intrinsically superior or inferior to any other" (cited in Buchanan, 1994:B7).

Supporters of the board's decision believe that schools should promote the culture of the United States because it is superior. The country was founded on Christian principles, its economic and political systems are the best possible, and its values are without peer. Thus, to teach that all nations are equal, all life-styles are equal, and that political and economic systems are equal "is to teach children a moral equivalence that amounts to a moral lie" (Buchanan, 1994:B7).

Opponents argue that the blatant teaching of "We're Number One" masks our flaws, mistakes, and immoral acts. To believe in one's superiority is also to believe in the inferiority of others. This has racist overtones, it hinders cooperation among nations, and it fosters exclusionary policies in such areas as immigration, segregation, and school prayer.

Schools in all societies foster a love of country through their teaching of history and other subjects. But, as political observer Dave Rossie (1994) suggests, "forcing teachers to become cheerleaders at best and propagandists at worst to serve the Christian Coalition's agenda is not the way to teach children to appreciate and love their country" (B6).

---

provide a classic example of one among several typical groups convinced that their own faith is the only correct one (see the panel titled "A Closer Look: Is the United States Culturally Superior?" for an egregious example of ethnocentrism).

A resolution passed at a town meeting in Milford, Connecticut, in 1640 is a blatant example of ethnocentrism. It stated the following:

Voted, the earth is the Lord's and the fullness thereof.

Voted, the earth belongs to the saints.

Voted, we are the saints.

Further examples of ethnocentrism from U.S. history are manifest destiny, White man's burden, exclusionary immigration laws such as the Oriental Exclusion Act, and Jim Crow laws. A current illustration of ethnocentrism can be seen in the activities of the United States as it engages in exporting the so-called American way of life because it is believed that democracy and capitalism are necessities for the good life and therefore best for all peoples.

Ethnocentrism, because it implies feelings of superiority, leads to division and conflict among subgroups within a society and among societies, each of which feels superior. Ethnocentric ideas are real because they are believed and they influence perception and behavior. Analysts of U.S. society (whether they are Americans or not) must recognize their own ethnocentric attitudes and the way these attitudes affect their own objectivity.

To summarize, culture emerges from social interaction. The paradox is that although culture is human-made, it exerts a tremendous complex of forces that constrain the actions and thoughts of human beings. The analyst of any society must be cognizant of these two qualities of culture, for they combine to give a society its unique character. Culture explains social change as well as stability; culture explains existing social arrangements (including many social problems); culture explains a good deal of individual behavior because it is internalized by the individual members of society and therefore has an impact (substantial but not total) on their actions and personalities.

Types of Shared Knowledge

The concept of culture refers to knowledge that is shared by the members of a social organization. In analyzing any social organization and, in this case, any society, it is helpful to conceive of culture as combining six types of shared knowledge—symbols, technology, ideologies, societal norms, values, and roles.

Symbols. By definition, language refers to symbols that evoke similar meanings in different people. Communication is possible only if people attribute the same meaning to such stimuli as sounds, gestures, or objects. Language, then, can be written, spoken, or unspoken. A shrug of the shoulders, a pat on the back, the gesturing with a finger (which finger can be very significant), a wink, and a nod are examples of unspoken language and vary in meaning from society to society. Consider the varying meaning for two common gestures:

> When displayed by the Emperor, the upright-thumb gesture spared the lives of gladiators in the Roman Coliseum. Now favored by airline pilots, truck drivers and others who lean out of windows, it means "all right" in the United States and most of Western Europe. In other places, including Sardinia and Northern Greece, it is the insulting "up yours." . . . [The "A-Okay" gesture with the thumb and forefinger making a circle means "everything is fine" in the United States but it] has very different meanings in parts of Europe. In Southern Italy, for instance, it means "you asshole" or signifies that you desire anal sex. It can mean "you're worth nothing" in France and Belgium. (Ekman, Friesen, and Bear, 1984:67–68)

While president, George H. W. Bush on a trip to Australia unknowingly used the wrong symbolic gesture. While riding in his limousine, the president flashed a "V" sign with the back of his hand. In Australia, this does not mean victory—it is the equivalent of flashing the middle finger in the United States.

Technology. Technology refers to the information, techniques, and tools used by people to satisfy their varied needs and desires. For analytic purposes, two types of technology can be distinguished—material and social. Material technology refers to knowledge of how to make and use things. It is important to note that the things produced are not part of the culture. They represent the knowledge that people share and that make it possible to build and use the object. The knowledge is culture, not the object.

Social technology is the knowledge about how to establish, maintain, and operate the technical aspects of social organization. Examples of this are procedures for operating a university, a municipality, or a corporation through such operations as Robert's Rules of Order, accounting, or the kind of specialized knowledge citizens must acquire to function in society (knowing the laws, how to complete income tax forms, how to vote in elections, how to use credit cards and banks) (Lenski, 1970:37–38; Olsen, 1976:60).

Ideologies. Ideologies are shared beliefs about the physical, social, and metaphysical worlds. They may, for example, be statements about the existence of supernatural beings, the best form of government, or racial pride.

Ideologies help individuals interpret events. They also provide the rationale for particular forms of action. They can justify the status quo or demand revolution. A number of competing ideologies exist within U.S. society—for example, fundamentalism and atheism, capitalism and socialism, and White supremacy and Black supremacy. Clearly, ideology unites as well as divides and is therefore a powerful human-made (cultural) force within societies.

Societal Norms. Norms are societal prescriptions for how one is to act in given situations—for example, at a football game, kegger, concert, restaurant, church, park, or classroom. We also learn how to act with members of the opposite sex, with our elders, with social inferiors, and with equals. Thus, behavior is patterned. We know how to behave, and we can anticipate how other people will behave. This knowledge allows interaction to occur smoothly.

Ethnomethodology is a subdiscipline in sociology that is the scientific study of the commonplace activities of daily life. Its goals are to discover and understand the underpinnings of relationships (the shared meanings that implicitly guide social behavior). The assumption is that much of social life is scripted; that is, the players act according to society's rules (the script). The conduct in the family, in the department store between customer and salesperson, between doctor and patient, between boss and secretary, between coach and player is, in a sense, determined by societal scripts.

What happens when people do not play according to the common understandings (the script)? Ethnomethodologist Harold Garfinkel (1967) has used this technique to discover the implicit bases of social interaction. Examples of possible rule breaking include the following: (1) when answering the phone, you remain silent; (2) when selecting a seat in the audience, you ignore the empty seats and choose rather to sit next to a stranger (violating that person's privacy and space); (3) you act as a stranger in your family; (4) in talking with a friend, you insist that he or she clarify the sense of commonplace remarks; and (5) you bargain with clerks over the price of every item of food you wish to purchase. These behaviors violate the rules of interaction in our society. When the rules are violated, the other people in the situation do not know how to respond. Typically, they become confused, anxious, and angry. These behaviors buttress the notion that most of the time social life is very ordered and orderly. We behave in prescribed ways, and we anticipate that other people will do the same. The norms are strong, and we tend to follow them automatically.

FIGURE 4.1
Classification of Norms

		Severity of Punishment: High	Severity of Punishment: Low
Degree of Importance	High	Mores (a)	(b)
	Low	(c)	Folkways (d)

In addition to being necessary for the conduct of behavior in society, societal norms vary in importance, as we saw in our discussion of norms at the micro level. Norms that are less important (the folkways) are not severely punished if violated. Examples of folkways in U.S. society are the following: It is expected that men should rise when a woman enters the room (unless she is the maid); people should not wear curlers to the opera; and a person does not wear a business suit and go barefoot.

Violation of the mores of society is considered important enough by society to merit severe punishment. This type of norm involves morality. Some examples of mores are the following: A person must have only one spouse at a time; thou shalt not kill (unless defending one's country); and one must be loyal to the United States.

There is a problem, however, for many Americans in deciding the degree of importance for some norms. Figure 4.1 shows the criteria for deciding whether norms should be classified as folkways or mores. This figure shows that on the basis of the two defining criteria, there are four possibilities, not just two. It is difficult to imagine cases that would be located in cell (b). The only possibilities are activities that have only recently been designated as very harmful but against which laws have not yet been passed for strict punishment (either because of the natural lag in the courts and legislatures, or because powerful groups have been influential in blocking the necessary legislation). The best current example of cases that would fall in cell (b) is the pollution of lakes, streams, and air by large commercial enterprises. These acts are recognized as having serious consequences for present and future generations, but either go unpunished or receive only minor fines.

Cell (c), on the other hand, is interesting because there are acts not important to the survival of society or the maintenance of its institutions that receive severe punishments (at least relative to the crime). Some examples include a male police officer being suspended for wearing earrings, and people caught smoking marijuana being sentenced to a jail term.

Both criteria used to delineate types of norms—degree of importance and severity of the punishments—are determined by the people in power. Consequently, activities that the powerful people perceive as being disruptive of the power structure or institutional arrangements that benefit some people and not others are viewed as illegitimate and punished severely. For example, if 10,000 young people protest against the political system with marches, speeches, and acts of civil disobedience, they are typically perceived as a threat and are jailed, beaten, gassed, and harassed by the police and the National Guard. Compare the treatment of these young people with another group of 10,000 on the beaches at Padre Island, Texas, during their annual college spring break. These people often drink to excess, are sexually promiscuous, and are destructive of property. Generally, the police consider these behaviors non-threatening to the system and therefore treat them relatively lightly.

Norms are also situational. Behavior expected in one societal setting may be inappropriate for another. Several examples should make this point clear. One may ask for change from a clerk, but one would not put money in a church collection plate and remove change. Clearly, behavior considered acceptable by fans at a football game (yelling, booing authority figures, even destroying property) would be inexcusable behavior at a poetry reading. Behavior allowable in a bar probably would be frowned on in a bank. Or doctors may ask patients to disrobe in the examining room but not in the subway.

Finally, because they are properties of groups, norms vary from society to society and from group to group within societies. Thus, behavior appropriate in one group of society may be absolutely inappropriate in another. Some examples of this include the following:

Body piercings and tattoos are becoming more and more acceptable, especially among the young. Some employers, however, will not allow their employees to have visible piercings and tattoos.

- *Couvade* is a practice surprisingly common throughout the world but in sharp contrast to what occurs in the United States. This refers to the time when a woman is in childbirth. Instead of the wife suffering, the husband moans and groans and is waited on as though he were in greater pain. After his wife has had the baby, she will get up and bring her husband food and comfort. The husband is so incapacitated by the experience that in some societies he stays in bed for as many as forty days.

- Among the Murgin of Australia, a woman giving birth to twins kills one of the babies because it makes her feel like a dog to have a litter instead of one baby. A tribe along the Niger Delta puts both the mother and the twins to death. With the Bankundo of the Congo Valley, on the other hand, the mother of twins is the object of honor and veneration.

- In some Latin American countries, high-status males are expected to have a mistress. This practice is even encouraged by their wives because it implies high status (given the cost of maintaining two households). In the United States, such a practice is grounds for divorce.

- In Pakistan, one never reaches for food with his or her left hand. To do so would make the observers physically sick. The reason is that the left hand is used to clean oneself after a bowel movement. Hence, the right hand is symbolically the only hand worthy of accepting food.

- Unmarried Dinka men of the Sudan gorge themselves on as much as five gallons of milk blended with cow urine daily for more than three months (Davies, 1996). They do as little activity as possible during this period to avoid burning calories, thus maximizing their weight gain. This is considered the way for them to make themselves attractive to women, by showing that their family's cattle herd is large enough to spare the extra milk.

- In the United States, more than 8.7 million people in 2003 underwent cosmetic surgery at a cost of $9.4 billion to enhance their looks according to the cultural ideal. The most popular surgical procedures were rhinoplasty (nose reshaping), liposuction, breast augmentation, eyelid surgery, and face-lift (Shute, 2004).

Values. Another aspect of society's structure is its values, which are the bases for the norms. Values are the criteria used in evaluating objects, acts, feelings, or events as to their relative desirability, merit, or correctness (see Chapter 2). Values are extremely important, for they determine the direction of individual and group behavior, encouraging some activities and impeding others. For example, efforts to get people in the United States to conserve energy and other resources run counter to the long-held values of growth, progress, and individual freedom. Consequently, the prevailing values have thwarted the efforts of various presidents and other people to plan carefully about future needs and to restrict use and the rate of growth now.

Roles. Societies, like other social organizations, have social positions (statuses) and behavioral expectations for the people who occupy these positions (roles). There are family statuses (son, daughter, sibling, parent, husband, wife); age statuses (child, adolescent, adult, aged); sex statuses (male, female); racial/ethnic statuses (African American, Arab American, Latino, Native American, White); and socioeconomic statuses (poor, middle class, wealthy). For each of these statuses, there are societal constraints on behavior. To become sixty-five years old in U.S. society is a traumatic experience for many people. The expectations of society dramatically shift when one reaches this age. The aged are forced into a situation of dependence rather than independence. To be a male or female in U.S. society is to be constrained in a relatively rigid set of expectations. Similarly, African Americans, Latinos, and other minorities, because of their minority status, have been expected to "know their place." The power of the social role is best illustrated, perhaps, by the person who occupies two relevant statuses—for example, the Black physician or the female airline pilot. Although each of these people is a qualified professional, both will doubtless encounter many situations in which other people will expect them to behave according to the dictates of the traditional role expectations of their **ascribed status** (race, sex, age, or other statuses over which the individual has no control) rather than of their **achieved status** (that is, their occupation).

The Social Construction of Reality

How are we to define what we see, feel, and hear? The important sociological insight is that meaning is not inherent in an object. Rather, people learn how to define reality from other people in interaction and by learning the culture. This process is called the **social construction of reality**.

Neurologist Oliver Sacks (1993) tells of a patient, "Virgil," blinded since age three who had his sight restored forty-five years later:

> Virgil told me later that in this first moment he had no idea what he was seeing. There was light, there was movement, there was color, all mixed up, all meaningless, a blur. . . . The rest of us, born sighted, can scarcely imagine such confusion.

For we, born with a full complement of senses, and correlating these, one with the other, create a sight world from the start, a world of visual objects and concepts and meanings. When we open our eyes each morning, it is upon a world we have spent a lifetime learning to see. We are not given the world, we make our world through incessant experience, categorization, memory, reconnection. But when Virgil opened his eyes, after being blind for forty-five years . . . there were no visual memories to support a perception, there was no world of experience and meaning awaiting him. He saw, but what he saw had no coherence. His retina and optic nerve were active, transmitting impulses, but his brain could make no sense of them. (61)

The point is that what we see does not have meaning until we learn from others and our own experiences how to interpret and thus make sense out of our perceptions.

A society's culture determines how the members of that society interpret their environment (Berger and Luckmann, 1967). Language, in particular, influences the ways in which the members of a society perceive reality. Two linguists, Edward Sapir and Benjamin Whorf, have shown this by the way the Hopi and Anglos differ in the way they speak about time (Carroll, 1956). The Hopi language has no verb tenses and no nouns for times, days, or years. Consequently, the Hopi think of time as continuous and without breaks. The English language, in sharp contrast, divides time into seconds, minutes, hours, days, weeks, months, years, decades, centuries, and the like. The use of verb tenses in English clearly informs everyone whether an event occurred in the past, present, or future. (See "A Closer Look: Cultural Time" panel for other examples of how time is conceived of in various societies.) Clearly, precision regarding time is important to English-speaking peoples, whereas it is unimportant to the Hopi.

There is an African tribe that has no word for the color gray. This implies that they do not see gray, even though we know that there is such a color and readily see it in the sky and in hair. The Navajo do not distinguish between blue and green, yet they have two words for different kinds of black.

The Aimore tribe in eastern Brazil has no word for two. The Yancos, an Amazon tribe, cannot count beyond *poettarrarorincoaroac*, their word for three. The Temiar people of West Malaysia also stop at three (McWhirter and McWhirter, 1972:167). Can you imagine how this lack of numbers beyond two or three affects how these people perceive reality?

Our language helps us to make order out of what we experience. As the philosopher Ludwig Wittgenstein has put it "The limits of my language are the limits of my world." Our particular language allows us to perceive differences among things or to recognize a set of things to be alike even when they are not identical. Language permits us to order these unlike things by what we think they have in common. As Bronowski (1978) puts it:

Habit makes us think the likeness obvious: it seems to us obvious that all apples are somehow alike, or all trees, or all matter. Yet there are languages in the Pacific Islands in which every tree on the island has a name, but which have no word for tree. To these islanders, trees are not at all alike; on the contrary, what is important to them is that the trees are different. (21)

Combining ethnocentrism with social construction, the Western world refers to the Arab countries as in the "Middle East." This is "true" only if one views the world from England, which has been the norm for two hundred years or so. As sociologist Jay Coakley (2001) has said, "This is a trivial point to make unless one is concerned

Cultural Time

To find social time it is necessary to look beyond the individual perceptions and attitudes, to the temporal construct of the society or culture. Temporal constructs are not to be found in human experience, but rather in the cultural symbols and institutions through which human experience is construed. Our own Indo-European language imposes the concept of time on us at a very early age, so it is difficult to identify with the concept of timelessness. Societies do exist without a consciousness of time. But most societies possess a concept of time.

Conceptualizations of time are as varied as the cultures, but most can be categorized by one of three images. Time in the broad sense is viewed as a line (linear), a wheel (cyclical), or as a pendulum (alternating phenomenon). But within these central images, numerous other distinctions must be made. One is tense. Is there a past or present or future, or all three? If more than one, to which is the society oriented and in what way? Another is continuity. Is time continuous or discontinuous? Does the continuity or hiatus have regularity? Another is progressiveness. Is evolutionary transformation expected with the passage of time? Still another is use. Is time used for measuring duration or is it for punctuality? The metaphysical distinctions are numerous. Is there a mode for measuring time? Is it reversible or irreversible? subjective or objective, or both? unidirectional? rectilinear?

These distinctions come into focus when one studies various cultures. The Pawnee Indians, for example, have no past in a temporal sense; they instead have a timeless storehouse of tradition, not a historical record. To them, life has a rhythm but not a progression. To the Hopi, time is a dynamic process without past, present, or future. Instead, time is divided vertically between subjective and objective time. Although Indo-European languages are laden with tensed verbs and temporal adjectives indicating past, present, and future, the Hopi have no such verbs, adjectives, or any other similar linguistic device. The Trobriander is forever in the present. For the Trobriander and the Tiv, time is not continuous throughout the day. Advanced methods of calculating sun positions exist for morning and evening, but time does not exist for the remainder of the day. For the Balinese, time is conceived in a punctual rather than a durational sense. The Balinese calendar is marked off, not by even duration intervals, but rather by self-sufficient periods that indicate coincidence with a period of life. Their descriptive calendar indicates the kind of time, rather than what time it is. The Maya had probably the most complicated system of time yet discovered. Their time divisions were regarded as burdens carried by relays of divine carriers—some benevolent, some malevolent. They would succeed each other, and it was very important to determine who was currently carrying in order to know whether it was a good time or a bad time.

Source: From "A Critical Analysis of Time Stream Discounting for Social Program Evaluation," by F. Gregory Hayden in *The Social Science Journal*, vol. 17 (January 1980):26–27. Reprinted with the permission of the Western Social Science Association.

with how various forms of culturally constructed concepts and terminology have been used as a basis for assumed truth."

The social interpretation of reality is not limited to language. For example, some people believe that there is such a thing as holy water. There is no chemical difference between water and holy water, but some people believe that the differences in properties and potential are enormous. To understand holy water, we must examine priests and parishioners, not water (Szasz, 1974:17). Similarly, consider the difference between saliva and spit (Brouillette and Turner, 1992). There is no chemical difference between them; the only difference is that in one case the substance is inside the mouth and in the other it is outside. We swallow saliva continuously and think nothing about it, yet one would not gather his or her spit in a container and then drink it. Saliva is defined positively and spit negatively, yet the only difference is a social definition. Our bodies produce fluids and substances continuously (urine, feces, mucus, phlegm, saliva, blood). How these are dealt with appropriately by individuals varies from society to society, as is the definition of which practices are disgusting and which ones are not (Miller, William, 1997). The standards also, typically, vary within society by age, social class, and gender. For example, in the United States, "[w]omen are held up to different standards in the realm of the disgusting. A woman picking her nose, a belching or a flatulent woman, a spitting woman—all qualify as rather more revolting than men happily engrossed in the same activities" (Epstein, 1997:80).

There is a debate in philosophy and sociology on this issue of reality. One position—**ontology**—accepts the reality of things because their nature cannot be denied (a chair, a tree, the wind, a society). The opposite side—**epistemology**—argues that all reality is socially constructed. In this view, all meaning is created out of a world that generates no meanings of its own (Edgley and Turner, 1975:6). The world is absurd, and human beings make sense out of it to fit their situation. Two sociologists express this extreme position in the following quote:

> Fundamental to our view is the assumption that the universe has no intrinsic meaning—it is, at bottom, absurd—and that the task of the sociologist is to discover the various imputed or fabricated meanings constructed by [people] in society. Or, to put it another way, the sociologist's job is to find out by what illusions people live. Without these artifacts, these delicately poised fantasies, most of us would not survive. Society, as we know it, could not exist. Meaninglessness produces terror. And terror must be dissipated by participating in, and believing in, collective fictions. They constitute society's "noble lie," the lie that there is some sort of inherent significance in the universe. It is the job of sociology to understand how people impute meaning to the various aspects of life. (Farberman and Goode, 1973:2)

Cultural Relativity. This chapter has so far described a number of customs from around the world. They may seem to us to be weird, cruel, or stupid. Anthropologists, though, have helped us to understand that in the cultural context of a given society, the practice may make considerable sense. For example, anthropologist Marvin Harris (1974) has explained why sacred cattle are allowed to roam the countryside in India while the people may be starving. Outsiders see cow worship as the primary cause of India's hunger and poverty—cattle do not contribute meat, but they do eat crops that would otherwise go to human beings. Harris, however, argues that cattle must not be killed for food because they are the most efficient producers of fuel and food. To kill them would cause the economy to collapse. Cattle contribute to the Indian economy in a number of significant ways. They are the source of oxen, which are the principal traction animals for farming. Their milk helps to meet the nutritional needs of many poor families. India's cattle annually excrete 700 million tons of recoverable manure, half of which is used for fertilizer and the rest for fuel. Cow dung is also used as a household flooring material. If cows were slaughtered during times of famine, the economy would not recover in good times. To Western experts it looks as if Indians would rather starve to death than eat their cows. But as Harris argues, "They don't realize that the farmer would rather eat his cow than starve, but that he will starve if he does eat it" (Harris, 1974:21).

The practice of cow worship also allows for a crude redistribution of wealth. The cattle owned by the poor are allowed to roam freely. In this way, the poor are able to let their cows graze the crops of the rich and come home at night to be milked. As Harris concludes:

> The sacredness of the cow is not just an ignorant belief that stands in the way of progress. Like all concepts of the sacred and the profane, this one affects the physical world; it defines the relationships that are important for the maintenance of Indian society.
>
> Indians have the sacred cow; we have the "sacred" car and the "sacred" dog. It would not occur to us to propose the elimination of automobiles and dogs from our society without carefully considering the consequences, and we should not propose the elimination of zebu cattle without first understanding their place in the social order of India.
>
> Human society is neither random nor capricious. The regularities of thought and behavior called culture are the principal mechanisms by which we human beings adapt to the world around us. Practices and beliefs can be rational or irrational, but a society that fails to adapt to its environment is doomed to extinction. Only those societies that draw the necessities of life from their surroundings, inherit the earth. The West has much to learn from the great antiquity of Indian civilization, and the sacred cow is an important part of that lesson. (Harris, 1978:36)

This extended example is used to convey the idea that the customs of a society should be evaluated in the light of the culture and their functions for that society. These customs should not be evaluated by our standards, but by theirs. This is called **cultural relativity**. The problem with cultural relativity, of course, is ethnocentrism—the tendency for the members of each society to assume the rightness of their own customs and practices and the inferiority, immorality, or irrationality of those found in other societies.

The Globalization of Culture?

Using the conventional view of culture, there should be no global equivalencies to global myths, legends, and symbols that unite the world's people. However, Western culture, especially the commercialized culture of the United States, is marketed worldwide. As a consequence, the popular culture of the United States as manifested in rock music, film, television, video, advertising, fast-food chains, soda pop drinks, and fashion is found in urban centers throughout the world. The English language has become the world's dominant language of commerce (see the panel titled "Globalization: The Downside to English as a Universal Language"). The global economy is becoming more and more unified with multinational corporations organized in various countries to manufacture and sell goods usually compatible with a Western lifestyle. These organizations, regardless of geographic location, are structured along similar Western-style bureaucratic lines and their managers "spend as much time in the air criss-crossing the globe as they do at home, identifying with a global, cosmopolitan culture rather than that of their own nations" (Appelbaum and Chambliss, 1995:73). The Internet increases the likelihood of a global culture as people interact across political boundaries and have access to the same databases and other sources of information (Eitzen and Baca Zinn, 2006b).

The Downside to English as a Universal Language

There are two fundamental trends regarding language use globally. First, the number of languages spoken is decreasing rapidly (Sampat, 2001; *Time*, 2002; *World Watch*, 2001:33):

- There are 6,800 languages that exist today. In A.D. 1400, at least 15,000 languages were spoken. By 2050, the number may be as low as 3,000.
- Only 250 languages are spoken by more than 1 million people. Around 3,000 languages are spoken by less than 2,500 people.
- The world's speech is increasingly homogenized, with about half the world's people using the fifteen most common languages. The top one hundred languages are used by 90 percent of humanity. The ten most common first languages (in order) are (1) Mandarin Chinese, (2) Spanish, (3) English, (4) Arabic, and (5) Bengali.

The second trend is that while English ranks third in the number of people using it as a first language, it is rapidly gaining ground as the primary international medium of science, commerce, and popular culture. Most of the world's books, newspapers, and e-mails are written in English, which is now spoken by more people as a second language (350 million) than as a native tongue (322 million). According to one estimate, English is used in some form by 1.6 billion people every day (Sampat, 2001:34–35).

This homogenization of language with English at the core is significant. First, it means the loss of the richness from language diversity. The extinction of a language is a form of cultural impoverishment. A distinct language provides the nuances of that group's history, which is lost as another language supersedes it. It means the loss of elaborate vocabularies used to describe the natural world. As Payal Sampat (2001) puts it: "No language is an exact map of any other; each is, in a sense, its own world. By allowing so many of these worlds to slip away, we may be forfeiting a lot more than just words" (40).

Second, the ever greater usage and acceptance of English worldwide signifies a form of cultural imperialism. Since language creates and conveys the culture, the users of English, because of the language, will implicitly be using words that convey a way of seeing and a way of understanding.

Summing up these two consequences of the homogenization of language (and culture):

> The loss of tradition or the demise of culture reduces the richness of expression, perspective, and point of view that make human beings so diverse and so interesting. When the world loses something like the stories and music of the Blasket Islands or the poetry of the Gaelic language, social life everywhere is diminished. (Bradshaw, Healey, and Smith, 2001:143)

This spread of one society's cultural characteristics to another is called **cultural diffusion**. This process has existed throughout human history, as people have been influenced by strangers from other societies because of trade, conquest, migration, and other forms of contact. This diffusion of cultures has been slow, but since World War II the process has increased rapidly. Where travel from Europe to the United States used to take months, it now takes a few hours. Today, many millions of people travel back and forth across political boundaries, some to stay permanently. Corporations move their business activities to societies where labor is cheap and regulations minimal (outsourcing). Because of computers and satellites, messages can be sent and money transferred instantaneously across national boundaries. Plagues (e.g., AIDS) and organized crime (drugs, sex trade) spread across the globe. In short, national boundaries and traditional institutions are becoming increasingly obsolete, as eminent political scientist Benjamin Barber (2002) suggests:

By the end of the twentieth century, irresistible interdependence was a leitmotif of every ecological, technological and economic event. It could hardly escape even casual observers that global warming recognizes no sovereign territory, that AIDS carries no passport, that technology renders national boundaries increasingly meaningless, that the Internet defies national regulation, that oil and cocaine addiction circle the planet like twin plagues and that financial capital and labor resources, like their anarchic cousins crime and terror, move from country to country with "wilding" abandon without regard for formal or legal arrangements—acting informally and illegally whenever traditional institutions stand in the way. (12)

All of this diffusion works toward a common homogeneous culture, what we might call **global culture**.

While the forces of globalization are relentless, the opposite forces of localism and parochialism are also at work. Benjamin Barber (1995) calls these contradictory forces "Jihad vs. McDonaldization." He argues that the trivializing, commercialized McWorld ethos associated with the economic power and culture of the West (especially the United States) has led to an ethnic, religious, or nationalistic resurgence or jihad in various parts of the world (Kennedy, 2001:15). This resistance to globalization is found not only in the Islamic world but also among warring factions in places like the Sudan, Croatia, Macedonia, and the Philippines. At the same time that many women across the globe accept the fashions of the West, others willingly cover their bodies completely in public. When leaders attempt to negotiate compromise, others refuse to "water down" their principles, and sometimes they use force to make their case. While science and rationality dominate Western culture, many, including many in the West, reject the findings of science in favor of ancient "truths."

Thus, while the world moves toward a secular Western culture, there are ethnic and religious enclaves that reject the secular modernity of the West. The driving force of division is fundamentalist religion, which is adamantly opposed to many of the most positive values of modern society. Fundamentalists have no time for democracy, pluralism, religious toleration, peacekeeping, free speech, or the separation of church and state. Christian fundamentalists reject the discoveries of biology and physics about the origins of life and insist that the Book of Genesis is scientifically sound in every detail. At a time when many are throwing off the shackles of the past, Jewish fundamentalists observe their revealed Law more stringently than ever before, and Muslim women, repudiating the freedoms of Western women, shroud themselves in veils and chadors. Muslim and Jewish fundamentalists both interpret the Arab-Israeli conflict, which began as defiantly secularist, in an exclusively religious way.

Fundamentalism, moreover, is not confined to the great monotheisms. There are Buddhist, Hindu, and even Confucian fundamentalism, which also cast aside many of the painfully acquired insights of liberal culture, which fight and kill in the name of religion and strive to bring the sacred into the realm of politics and national struggle (Armstrong, 2000:xi).

Thus, the world at the beginning of the twenty-first century is faced with contradictory trends. One is toward convergence—toward a common language, acceptance of science and rationality, and a sense of pluralism and inclusion. But the processes of globalization trigger movements that create localized, cultural-specific identities (Kloos, 2000), emphasizing difference and exclusion. Local folk cultures remain a force in rural areas. At the same time that there is a move to diminish the importance of political boundaries, the importance of tribes is paramount for many. So, it is too facile to say that there is a global culture. As Cohen and Kennedy (2000) put it: "On occasions, some inhabitants of Lagos or Kuala Lumpur may drink Cokes, wear Levi 501 jeans and listen to Madonna records. But that does not mean they are about to abandon their customs, family and religious obligations or national identities wholesale even if they could afford to do so, which most cannot" (243).

Values

Because all the components of culture are essential for an understanding of the constraints on human behavior, perhaps the quickest way to reach this understanding is to focus on its values. These are the criteria the members of society use to evaluate objects, ideas, acts, feelings, or events as to their relative desirability, merit, or correctness.

Human beings are valuing beings. They continually evaluate themselves and other people. What objects are worth owning? What makes people successful? What activities are rewarding? What is beauty? Of course, different societies have distinctive criteria (values) for evaluating. People are considered successful in the United States, for example, if they accumulate many material things as a result of hard work. In other societies people are considered to be successful if they attain total mastery of their emotions or if they totally reject materialism.

One objective common to any social science course is the hope that students will become aware of the various aspects of social life in an analytical way. For people studying their own society, this means that while immersed in the subject matter, they also become participant observers. This implies an objective detachment (as much as possible) so that one may understand better the forces that in large measure affect human behavior, both individually and in groups.

The primary task for the participant observer interested in societal values is to determine what the values are. A number of clues are helpful for such a task (Williams, 1970:444–446). The first clue is to determine what most preoccupies people in their conversations and actions. One might ask: Toward what do people most often direct their action? Is it, for example, contemplation and meditation, or physical fitness, or acquisition of material wealth? In other words, what gives individuals high status in the eyes of their fellows?

A second technique that might help delineate the values is to determine the choices that people make consistently. The participant observer should ascertain what choices tend to be made in similar situations. For example, how do individuals dispose of surplus wealth? Do they spend it for self-aggrandizement or for altruistic reasons? Is there a tendency to spend it for the pleasure of the present, to save it for security in the future, or to spend it on other people?

A third procedure is used typically by social scientists—to find out through interviews or written questionnaires what people say is good, bad, moral, immoral, desirable, or undesirable. There often is a difference between what people say and what people do. A problem in the study of values exists because there are sometimes discrepancies between values and actual behavior. Even if there is a difference between what they write on a questionnaire or say in an interview and their actual behavior, people will probably say or write those responses they feel are appropriate, and this response by itself is a valid indicator of what the values of the society are.

One may also observe the reward-punishment system of the society. What behavior is rewarded with a medal, or a bonus, or public praise? Alternatively, what behavior brings condemnation, ridicule, public censure, or imprisonment? The greater the reward or the punishment, the greater the likelihood that important societal values are involved. Consider, for example, the extraordinary punishment in the United States given to people who willfully destroy or steal the private property of others (for example, a cattle rustler, a thief, a looter, or a pyromaniac). Closely related to the reward-punishment system are the actions that cause individuals to feel guilt or shame (losing a job, living on welfare, declaring bankruptcy) or actions that bring about ego enhancement (getting a better-paying job, receiving an educational degree, owning a business). Individuals feel guilt or shame because they have internalized the norms and values of society. When values and behavior are not congruent, feelings of guilt are a typical response.

Another technique is to examine the principles that are held as part of the so-called American way of life. These principles are enunciated in historical documents such as the Constitution, the Declaration of Independence, and the Bible. We are continually reminded of these principles in speeches by elected officials, by editorials in the mass media, and from religious pulpits. The United States has gone to war to defend such principles as democracy, equality, freedom, and the free enterprise system. One question the analyst of values should ask, therefore, is, For what principles will the people fight? The remainder of this chapter describes the system of values prevalent in the United States. Understanding these values is essential to the analysis of society, for they provide the basis for this country's uniqueness as well as the source of many of its social problems.

Values as Sources of Societal Integration and Social Problems

U.S. society, while similar in some respects to other advanced industrial societies, is also fundamentally different. Given the combination of geographic, historical, and religious factors found in the United States, it is not surprising that the cultural values found there are unique. Geographically, the United States has remained relatively isolated from other societies for most of its history. The United States has also been blessed with an abundance of rich and varied resources (land, minerals, and water). Until only recently, the inhabitants of the United States were unconcerned with conservation and the careful use of resources (as many societies must be to survive) because there was no need. The country provided a vast storehouse of resources so rich that they were often used wastefully.

Historically, the United States was founded by a revolution that grew out of opposition to tyranny and aristocracy. Hence, people in the United States have verbally supported such principles as freedom, capitalism, democracy, equality, and impersonal justice. Another historical factor that has led to the particular nature of the culture in the United States is that the society has been peopled largely by immigrants. This has led, on one hand, to a blending of many cultural traits, such as language, dress, and customs, and on the other hand to the existence of ethnic enclaves that resist assimilation.

A final set of forces that have affected the culture of the United States stem from its religious heritage. First is the Judeo-Christian ethic that has prevailed throughout U.S. history. The strong emphases on humanitarianism, the inherent worth of all individuals, a morality based on the Ten Commandments, and even the biblical injunction to "have dominion over all living things" have had a profound effect on how Americans evaluate each other. Another aspect of religious heritage, the **Protestant ethic**, has been an important determinant of the values believed to typify most people in the

United States (see Weber, 1958). (The Protestant ethic is the religious belief emphasizing hard work and continual striving to prove that one is saved.) The majority of early European settlers in the New World tended to believe in a particular set of religious beliefs that can be traced back to two individuals, Martin Luther and John Calvin. Luther's contribution was essentially twofold: Each person was considered to be his or her own priest (stressing the person's individuality and worth), and each person was to accept his or her work as a calling. To be called by God to do a job, no matter how humble, was to give dignity to the job and to the individual. It also encouraged everyone to work very hard to be successful in that job.

The contribution of John Calvin was based on his belief in predestination. God, because He is all-knowing, knows who will be saved. Unfortunately, individuals do not know whether they are saved or not, and this is very anxiety-producing. Calvinists came to believe that God would look with more favor on people who were preordained to be saved than on people who were not. Consequently, success in one's work became a sign that one was saved, and this was therefore anxiety-reducing. Calvinists worked very hard to be successful. As they prospered, the capital they accumulated could be spent only on necessities, for to spend on luxuries was wasteful and therefore scorned by God. The surplus capital was therefore invested in the enterprise (purchasing more property or better machinery, or hiring a larger workforce, for example).

Luther's and Calvin's beliefs led to an ethic that flourished in the United States. This ethic stressed the traits of self-sacrifice, diligence, and hard work. It stressed achievement, and most important, it stressed a self-orientation rather than a collectivity orientation. Indirectly, this ethic emphasized private property, capitalism, rationality, and growth.

Thus, geography, religious heritage, and history have combined to provide a distinctive set of values for Americans. However, before we describe these dominant values, several caveats should be mentioned. First, the tremendous diversity of the United States precludes any universal holding of values. The country has people and groups that reject the dominant values. Moreover, there are differences in emphasis for the dominant values by region, social class, age, and religion. Second, the system of American values is not always consistent with behavior. Third, the values themselves are not always consistent. How does one reconcile the coexistence of individualism with conformity? or competition and cooperation? Robin Williams (1970), an eminent analyst of U.S. society, concludes:

> [W]e do not find a neatly unified "ethos" or an irresistible "strain toward consistency." Rather, the total society is characterized by diversity and change in values. Complex division of labor, regional variations, ethnic heterogeneity, and the proliferation of specialized institutions and organizations all tend to insulate differing values from one another. (451)

To minimize the problem with inconsistencies, this section examines, in turn, only the most dominant of American values.

Success (Individual Achievement). The highly valued individual in U.S. society is the self-made person, the person who has achieved money and status through personal efforts in a highly competitive system. Our cultural heroes are people like Abraham Lincoln, John D. Rockefeller, Sam Walton, Bill Gates, and Oprah Winfrey, each of whom rose from relatively humble origins to the top of his or her profession.

Success can be achieved, obviously, by outdoing all other people, but it is often difficult to know exactly the extent of one's success. Hence, economic success (one's income, personal wealth, and type of possessions) is the most commonly used measurement. Economic success, moreover, is often used to measure personal worth. As sociologist Robin Williams (1970) states, "The comparatively striking feature of American culture is its tendency to identify standards of personal excellence with competitive occupational achievement" (454–455).

There is evidence that today's parents are putting more and more pressure on their children to succeed. A 1997 University of Michigan study of children under age thirteen found that they had only 25 percent of their day for leisure time, compared to the 40 percent that same age category enjoyed in 1981 (reported in Labi, 1998). Parents today are involving their children in much more structured activities to develop sport, musical, artistic, and cognitive skills than did parents in earlier generations. There are piano and ballet lessons, sessions with tutors, beauty pageants, sports practice and games, and specialized summer camps. Consider this example of a young athlete:

> Joseph [Lorenzetti] recently turned 12. With his slender limbs and unblemished skin, he looks like a boy. But he is really a hockey machine, one as dedicated to the sport as any man-sized player. When he started playing at $3\frac{1}{2}$, he was so small he couldn't hold a stick. He now trains 300 days a year, attends seven summer hockey camps, and travels 4,500 miles a year to compete, while his parents spend $6,000 a year on equipment, ice time, and hotels. (Tye, 1997:30A; see also Eitzen, 2006)

This young man and his parents are pursuing the American dream. Their efforts can be characterized positively as dedicated and achievement-oriented or negatively as fanatical and one-dimensional. But they and countless others are bent on being successful.

While the push by parents toward structured activities for their children is due in part to both parents in the labor force and the need for adult supervision of their children outside of school, the other and more important reason is that parents want their children to find their niche and specialize early so that they can get a college scholarship and get on the narrow road to success in the ever more competitive society where corporate downsizing is commonplace and wages are stagnant (see Chapter 8).

Competition. Competition is highly valued in U.S. society. Most people believe it is the one quality that has made the United States great because it motivates individuals and groups to be discontented with the status quo and with being second best. Motivated by the hope of being victorious in competition, or put another way, by fear of failure, Americans must not lose a war or the Olympics or be the second nation to land its citizens on the moon.

Competition pervades almost all aspects of U.S. society. The work world, sports, courtship, organizations such as the Cub Scouts, and schools all thrive on competition. The pervasiveness of competition in schools is seen in how athletic teams, cheerleading squads, debate teams, choruses, bands, and casts are composed. Competition among classmates is used as the criterion for selection. Of course, the grading system is also often based on the competition of individuals.

The Cub Scouts, because of their reliance on competition, are an all-American organization. In the first place, individual status in the den or pack is determined by the level one has achieved through the attainment of merit badges. Although all boys can theoretically attain all merit badges, there is competition as the boys are pitted against each other to see who can obtain the most. Another example of how the Cub Scouts use competition is their annual event—the Pinewood Derby. Each boy in a Cub pack is given a small block of wood and four wheels that he is to shape into a racing car. The race is held at a pack meeting, and one boy eventually is the winner. The event is rarely questioned, even though nearly all the boys go home disappointed losers. Why is such a practice accepted and publicized? The answer is that it is symbolic of how things are done in virtually all aspects of American life.

An important consequence of this emphasis on the survival of the fittest is that some people take advantage of their fellows to compete successfully. In the business world, we find some people who use theft, fraud, interlocking directorates, and price fixing to get ahead dishonestly. A related problem, abuse of nature for profit, while not a form of cheating, nevertheless takes advantage of other people, while one person pursues economic success. The current ecology crisis is caused by individuals, corporations, and communities that find pollution solutions too expensive. Thus, in looking out for themselves, they ignore the short- and long-range effects on social and biological life. In other words, competition, while a constant spur for individuals and groups to succeed, is also the source of some illegal activities and hence of social problems in U.S. society.

Similar scandals are also found in the sports world. The most visible type of illegal activity in sports is illegal recruiting of athletes by colleges and universities. In the quest to succeed (that is, to win), some coaches have violated NCAA regulations by altering transcripts to ensure an athlete's eligibility, allowing substitutes to take admissions tests for athletes of marginal educational ability, paying athletes for nonexistent jobs, illegally using government work-study monies for athletes, and offering money, cars, and clothing to entice athletes to their schools (Eitzen and Sage, 2003). For other negative consequences of competition in sport, see the panel titled "A Closer Look: Triumph's Great Failure."

The Valued Means to Achieve. There are three related highly valued ways to succeed in U.S. society. The first is through hard work. Americans, from the early Puritans to the present day, have elevated people who were industrious and denigrated those who were not. Most Americans, therefore, assume that poor people deserve to be poor because they are allegedly unwilling to work as hard as people in the middle and upper classes. This type of explanation places the blame on the victim rather than on the social system that systematically thwarts efforts by the poor. Their hopelessness, brought on by their lack of education, or by their being a racial minority, or by their lack of experience, is interpreted as their fault and not as a function of the economic system. The two remaining valued means to success are continual striving and deferred gratification. Continual striving has meaning for both the successful and the not-so-successful. For the former, a person should never be content with what she or he has; there is always more land to own, more money to make, or more books to write. For the poor, continual striving means a never-give-up attitude, a belief that economic success is always possible through hard work, if not for yourself, at least for your children.

Deferred gratification refers to the willingness to deny immediate pleasure for later rewards. The hallmark of the successful person in U.S. society is just such a willingness—to stay in school, to have a second job, or to go to night school. One

Triumph's Great Failure

When winning is the primary standard for evaluation, several negative outcomes result. Let me [D. Stanley Eitzen] enumerate these, using sport for examples. First, in a competitive society there is a tendency to evaluate people by their accomplishments rather than their character, personality, and other human qualities. When "winning is everything," then losers are considered just that. One successful university basketball coach once counseled prospective coaches that if they wanted to be winners, then they should associate only with winners. Is this an appropriate guiding principle for conducting our lives?

Second, when winning is paramount, schools and communities organize sports for the already gifted. This elitist approach means that the few will be given the best equipment, the best coaching, and prime time reserved for their participation, while the less able will be denied participation altogether or given

observer has asserted that the difference between the poor and the nonpoor in this society is whether they are future- or present-oriented (Banfield, 1974). Superficially, this assessment appears accurate, but we argue that this lack of a future-time orientation among the poor is not a subcultural trait (see Chapters 7 and 9) but basically a consequence of their hopeless situation.

Progress. Societies differ in their emphasis on the past, the present, and the future. U. S. society, while giving some attention to each time dimension, stresses the future. Americans neither make the past sacred nor are they content with the present. They place a central value on progress—on a brighter tomorrow, a better job, a bigger home, a move

Triumph's Great Failure continued

very little attention. If sports participation is a useful activity, then it should be for the many, not the few, in my view.

A third problem with the emphasis on winning is that parents may push their children beyond the normal to succeed. . . . In 1972 the national record for one-year-olds in the mile run was established by Steve Parsons of Normal, Illinois (the time was 24:16.16). [Is this an example] of child abuse or what?

A fourth problem with the primacy of winning is that coaches may push their charges too hard. Coaches may be physically or emotionally abusive. They may limit their players' civil rights. And, they may play their injured athletes by using painkillers without regard for their long-term physical well-being.

Fifth, when the desire to win is so great, the "end may justify the means." Coaches and players may use illegal tactics. Athletes may use performance-enhancing drugs such as steroids and amphetamines to achieve a "competitive edge" or, more subtly but nonetheless unethical, they may use such means as blood doping or getting pregnant to get positive hormonal changes and then having an abortion. Both of these practices occur among endurance athletes. So much, I would argue, for the myth that "sport builds character."

Sixth, when winning is all-important, there may be a tendency to crush the opposition. This was the case when the Riverside Poly High School girls basketball team played Norte Vista several years ago. Riverside won by a score of 179 to 15 with one player, Cheryl Miller, scoring a California record of 105 points. Was the Riverside coach ethical? . . . Will Norte Vista girls be motivated to improve their performance or will this humiliating experience crush their spirit?

Seven, many people in a competitive society have difficulty with coming in second. . . . [For example, a few years back, a football team composed of fifth-graders in Florida was] undefeated going into the state finals but lost there in a close game. At a banquet following that season each player on this team was given a plaque on which was inscribed a quote from Vince Lombardi: "There is no room for second place. I have finished second twice at Green Bay and I never want to finish second again. There is a second place bowl game but it is a game for losers played by losers. It is and always will be an American zeal to be first in anything we do and to win and to win and to win."

In other words, the parents and coaches of these boys wanted them to never be satisfied with being second. Second is losing. The only acceptable placement is first.

Finally, when "winning is the only thing" the joy in participation is lost. I have observed that organized sport from youth programs to the professional level is mostly devoid of playfulness. When the object is to win, then the primacy of the activity is lost. In other words, it's the process that is primary, not the outcome. Whitewater rafters and mountain climbers understand this. So, too, do players in a pickup touch football game. Why can't the rest of us figure out this fundamental truth?

Source: Excerpted from D. Stanley Eitzen, 1990. "The Dark Side of Competition in American Society." *Vital Speeches* 56 (January 1): 185–186.

---

to the suburbs, college education for their children, and self-improvement. People in the United States are not satisfied with the status quo; they want growth (new buildings, faster planes, bigger airports, more business moving into the community, larger profits, and new world's records). They want to change and conquer nature (dam rivers, clear forests, rechannel rivers, seed clouds, and spray insecticides).

Although the implicit belief in progress is that change is good, some things are not to be changed, for they have a sacred quality (the political system, the economic system, American values, and the nation-state). Thus, Americans, while valuing technological change, do not favor changing the system (revolution).

100

PART TWO
The Individual
in Society:
Society in
the Individual

"Maybe they didn't try hard enough."

The commonly held value of progress has also had a negative effect on contemporary life in the United States. Progress is typically defined to mean either growth or new technology. Every city wants to grow. Chambers of commerce want more industry and more people (and more consumers). No industry can afford to keep sales at last year's figures. Everyone agrees that the gross national product (GNP) must increase each year. If all these things are to grow as people wish, then concomitant with such growth must be increased population, more products turned out (using natural resources), more electricity, more highways, and more waste. Continued growth will inevitably throw the tight ecological system out of balance because there are limited supplies of air, water, and places to dump waste materials. Not only are these resources limited, but they also diminish as the population increases.

Progress also means faith in technology. Typically, Americans believe that scientific knowledge will solve problems. Scientific breakthroughs and new technology have solved some problems and do aid in saving labor. But new technology often creates problems that were unanticipated.* Although the automobile is of fantastic help to humankind, it has polluted the air, and each year it kills about 60,000 people in the United States in accidents. It is difficult to imagine life without electricity, but the creation of electricity pollutes the air and causes the thermal pollution of rivers. Insecticides and chemical fertilizers have performed miracles in agriculture, but they have polluted food and streams (and even killed some lakes).

Material Progress. A belief of people in the United States holds that work pays off. The payoff is not only success in one's profession but also in economic terms—income and the acquisition and consumption of goods and services that go beyond

---

*Sociologists call this phenomenon *latent functions*, which means, in effect, unintended consequences. The intended consequences of an activity or social arrangement are called *manifest functions*.

Ed Stein. Reprinted by permission of Newspaper Enterprise Association, Inc.

adequate nutrition, medical care, shelter, and transportation. The superfluous things that we accumulate or strive to accumulate, such as country club memberships, jewelry, stylish clothes, lavish homes, boats, second homes, pool tables, electric toothbrushes, and season tickets to the games of our favorite teams or orchestras, are symbols of success in the competitive struggle. But these acquisitions have more than symbolic value because they are elements of what people in the United States consider the good life and, therefore, a right.

This emphasis on having things has long been a facet of U.S. life (Kulman, 2004). This country, the energy crisis notwithstanding, has always been a land of opportunity and abundance. Although many people are blocked from full participation in this abundance, the goal for most people is to accumulate things that bring status and that provide for a better way of life by saving labor or enhancing pleasure in our leisure.

Individual Freedom. Americans value individualism. They believe that people should generally be free from government interference in their lives and businesses and free to make their own choices. Implied in this value is the responsibility of each individual for personal development. The focus on individualism places responsibility on the individual for his or her acts—not on society or its institutions. Being poor is blamed on the individual, not on the maldistribution of wealth and other socially perpetuated disadvantages that blight many families generation after generation. The aggressive behavior of minority youth is blamed on them, not on the limits placed on their social mobility by the social system. Dropping out of high school before graduation is blamed on individual students, not on the educational system that fails to meet their needs. This attitude helps explain the reluctance by people in authority to provide adequate welfare, health care, and compensatory programs to

102

PART TWO
The Individual
in Society:
Society in
the Individual

help the disadvantaged. This common tendency of individuals to focus on the deviant (blaming the victim) rather than on the system that produces deviants has also been true of U.S. social scientists analyzing social problems.

Individual freedom is, of course, related to capitalism and private property. The economy is supposed to be competitive. Individuals, through their own efforts, business acumen, and luck can (if successful) own property and pyramid profits.

The belief that private property and capitalism are not to be restricted has led to several social problems: (1) unfair competition (monopolies, price fixing); (2) a philosophy held by many entrepreneurs of caveat emptor (let the buyer beware), whereby the aim is profit with total disregard for the welfare of the consumer; and (3) the current ecology crisis, which is due in great measure to the standard policy of many people and most corporations in the United States to do whatever is profitable—and thus neglect conservation of natural resources.

These practices have led the federal and state governments to enact and enforce regulatory controls. Clearly, Americans have always tended to abuse nature and their fellows in the name of profit. Freedom, if so abused, must be curtailed, and the government (albeit somewhat reluctantly, given the pressures from various interest groups) has done this.

The related values of capitalism, private property, and self-aggrandizement (individualism) have also led to an environmental crisis. Industries fouling the air and water with refuse and farmers spraying pesticides that kill weeds and harm animal and human life are two examples of how individuals and corporations look out for themselves with an almost total disregard for the short- and long-range effects of their actions on life.

As long as people in the United States hold a narrow self-orientation rather than a collectivity orientation, this crisis will continue and steadily worsen. The use people make of the land (and the water on it or running through it, and the air above it) has traditionally been theirs to decide because of the belief in private property. This belief in private property has meant, in effect, that individuals have had the right to pave a pasture for a parking lot, tear up a lemon grove for a housing development, put down artificial turf for a football field, and dump waste products into the air and water. Consequently, individual decisions have had the collective effect of taking millions of acres of arable land out of production permanently, polluting the air and water, covering land where vegetation once grew with asphalt, concrete buildings, and AstroTurf even though green plants are the only source of oxygen.

Values and Behavior

The discrepancy between values and behavior has probably always existed in the United States. Inconsistencies have always existed, for example, between the Christian ethic of love, brotherhood, and humanitarianism, on one hand, and the realities of religious bigotry, the maximization of self-interest, and property rights over human rights, on the other. The gap may be widening because of the tremendous rate of social change taking place (the rush toward urbanization and the increased bureaucratization in all spheres of social life). Values do not change as rapidly as do other elements of the culture. Although values often differ from behavior, they remain the criteria for evaluating objects, people, and events. It is important, however, to mention behaviors that often contradict values because they demonstrate the hypocrisy prevalent in U.S. society that so often upsets young people (and others) who, in turn, develop countercultures (a topic that we discuss later in this chapter).

Perhaps the best example of the inconsistency between values and behavior is the belief in the American creed held by most people in the United States—generally assumed to encompass equality of all people, freedom of speech and religion, and the guarantees of life, liberty, and prosperity—compared to the injustices perpetuated by the system and individuals in the system on members of minority groups.

Americans glorify individualism and self-reliance. These related traits, however, are not found in bureaucracies, where the watchword is that to get along you have to go along. Rather than individualism, the way to get ahead in corporations and other large bureaucracies is to be a team player.

There is a myth that successful people in the United States have always been self-made. Of course, some individuals have achieved wealth, fame, and power through their own achievements, but many have inherited their advantages. The irony is that the wealthy are considered successful whether they made the money or not. People in the United States tend to give great weight to the opinions expressed by wealthy people, as evidenced by the voters' tendency to elect them to public office.

Americans have always placed high value on the equality of all people (in the courts or in getting a job). This value is impossible to reconcile with the racist, sexist, homophobic, and superiority theories held by some individuals and groups. It is also impossible to reconcile the value on equality with many of the formal and informal practices in workplaces, in the schools, in the lending procedures of banks, and in the courts.

Related to the stated belief in equality are the other fundamental beliefs enunciated by the Founding Fathers: the freedoms guaranteed in the Bill of Rights and the Declaration of Independence. Ironically, although the United States was founded by a revolution, the same behavior (called for by the Declaration of Independence) by dissident groups is now squelched (in much the same way as by King George III). As elaborated in Chapter 6, individual rights and freedoms have become more and more curtailed by the necessity of security following the September 11, 2001, terrorist attacks on the United States.

In the United States, people value law and order. This reverence for the law has been overlooked throughout North American history whenever law-abiding groups, such as vigilante groups, took the law in their own hands (by threatening that anyone who disobeys vigilante law will be lynched). Currently, the groups that make the loudest demands for law and order are ones who disobey certain laws—for example, southern politicians blocking federal court orders to integrate schools; American Legion posts that notoriously ignore local, state, and federal laws about gambling and liquor; and school administrators allowing prayer in public school functions despite Supreme Court rulings to the contrary.

A final example of disparity between values and behavior in the United States involves the pride people have in solving difficult problems. Americans are inclined to be realists. They are pragmatic, down-to-earth problem solvers ready to apply scientific knowledge and expertise to handle such technical problems as getting human beings to and from the moon safely. This realism tends to be replaced by mere gestures, however, when it comes to social problems. In the United States, people have a compulsive tendency to avoid confrontation with chronic social problems. They tend to think that social problems will be solved either by the marketplace or by popular

104

PART TWO
The Individual
in Society:
Society in
the Individual

sayings such as "Just say no" or "Just don't do it." The verbal level is mistaken for action. If we hear our favorite television personality end the program with a statement against pollution or crime, we think the problem will somehow be solved. This is evidenced at another level by proclaiming a war on drugs or by setting up a commission to study stock-market fraud, cost overruns in the Pentagon, or youth gangs. Philip Slater (1970) has said that the typical U.S. approach to social problems is to decrease their visibility—out of sight, out of mind:

> When these discarded problems rise to the surface again—a riot, a protest, an exposé, in the mass media—we react as if a sewer has backed up. We are shocked, disgusted, and angered. We immediately call for the emergency plumber (the special commission, the crash program) to ensure that the problem is once again removed from consciousness. (15)

The examples just presented make clear that while people in the United States express some values, they often behave differently. The values do, however, still provide the standards by which individuals are evaluated. These inconsistencies are sometimes important in explaining individual behavior (guilt, shame, aggression) and the emergence of insulating personal and social mechanisms such as compartmentalization and racial segregation.

Not only is there an inconsistency between values and behavior, but there is also a lack of unity among some of the values themselves. Some examples of this phenomenon, which has been called ethical schizophrenia, are individualism versus humanitarianism, materialism versus idealism, and pragmatism versus utopianism (Record and Record, 1965).

Cultural Diversity

In the United States, people are far from unanimous on a number of public issues (for example, gun control, abortion, the death penalty, or prayer in schools). Despite inconsistencies and ambiguities, Americans as a whole do tend to believe in certain things—for example, that democracy is the best form of government; that capitalism is the best economic system; that success can be defined in terms of hard work, initiative, and the amassing of wealth and property; that Christianity should be the country's dominant religion; and that there should be equality of opportunity and equal justice before the law. But even though these values are held generally by the U.S. populace, there is never total agreement on any of them. The primary reason for this is the tremendous diversity found within the United States.

The United States is composed of many people who differ on important social dimensions: age, sex, race, region, social class, ethnicity, religion, geography, and so on. These variables suggest that groups and categories will differ in values and behavior because certain salient social characteristics imply differential experiences and expectations. These are noted often in the remainder of this book.

Let us examine a few differences held by various groups and categories to illustrate the lack of consistency among people in the United States. Values are the criteria used to determine, among other things, morality. Public opinion polls show that the vast majority accept the legality of abortion, at least under certain circumstances. When these data are examined according to the age, income, and education of the respondents, we find systematic differences. The older the individual and the lower a person's income or education, the more likely the person is to be anti-abortion.

The rural–urban differences in U.S. society are well known. An interesting example is the probability that rural people are more humanitarian, yet more intolerant of deviance among their neighbors, than are urban dwellers. There also are variations among rural communities, as there are among urban places, on these and other differences.

Region of the country accounts for some variation in values held. But the generalizations made about Southerners, Easterners, and Midwesterners, while having some validity, gloss over many real differences. Within any one region there are differences among rural and urban people, among different religious groups, and among different ethnic groups.

The concept of **subculture** has been defined typically as a relatively cohesive cultural system that varies in form and substance from the dominant culture. Under the rubric subculture, then, there are ethnic groups, delinquent gangs, and religious sects (for a technique to study subculture, see the panel titled "Research Methods: The Researcher as Participant"). Milton Yinger (1962) has proposed that the concept of subculture be defined more precisely. He suggests that it be used for one type of group and *counterculture* for another type that has been previously called a subculture.

For Yinger, the concept of subculture should be limited to relatively cohesive cultural systems that differ from the dominant culture in such things as language, values, religion, and style of life. Typically, a group that is a subculture differs from the larger group because it has emigrated from another society and, because of physical

Research Methods

The Researcher as Participant

A common method of data collection is participant observation—the direct observation of social phenomena in natural settings. One way to accomplish this is for the researcher to become part of what he or she is studying. There are several roles that observers may take in this regard. One is to hide the fact that one is a researcher and participate as a member of the group being studied. Another is to let the subjects know that you are a scientist but remain separate and detached from the group. A third option is to identify oneself as a researcher and become friends with those being studied. Each of these alternatives has its problems, such as the ethics of deceiving subjects and the fundamental problem of subjects altering their behavior if they know they are being investigated.

Elliot Liebow—a White, Jewish, middle-class researcher—investigated the subculture of poor Black males in one section of the Washington, DC, ghetto. From the beginning, Liebow identified himself as a researcher. He became deeply involved with his subjects. He partied with them, visited in their homes, gave them legal advice, and just generally hung around with them in their leisure hours. As the research progressed, he became more and more a part of the street-corner life he was investigating. As a White, though, he never escaped completely being an outsider.

At first Liebow's field notes concentrated on individuals: what they said, what they did, and the contexts in which they said or did them. Through this beginning, he ultimately saw the patterns of behavior and how the subjects perceived and understood themselves. He was able to understand the social structure of street-corner life. More important, his research enabled him to see the complexity of the social network of society's losers and how they continuously slip back and forth between the values and beliefs of the larger society and those of their own social system.

Source: Elliot Liebow, 1967. *Tally's Corner* (Boston: Little, Brown).

106

PART TWO
The Individual
in Society:
Society in
the Individual

or social isolation, has not been fully assimilated. The cultural differences, then, are usually based on ethnicity. Tradition keeps the culture of this group somewhat unique from the dominant culture. Examples of such subcultures in the United States include the Amish, the Hutterites, some Orthodox Jewish sects, many Native American tribes, Appalachian snake handlers, and Polish, Croatian, Hungarian, Italian, Greek, and Irish groups at one time or another in U.S. history. Recent immigrants often cluster together for mutual benefit but also to maintain their traditions. The existence of numerous subcultures within the United States explains much of the lack of consistency with respect to U.S. values.

A **counterculture**, as defined by Yinger, is a culturally homogeneous group that has developed values and norms that differ from the larger society because the group opposes the larger society. This type of group is in conflict with the dominant culture. The particular values and norms can be understood only by reference to the dominant group.

The values held by delinquent gangs such as the Crips and the Bloods are commonly believed to be a reaction against the values held by the larger society (and hence would represent a counterculture). Albert K. Cohen (1955) has noted, for example, that lower-class juvenile gangs not only reject the dominant value system, but also exalt opposite values. These boys, Cohen argues, are ill-equipped because of their lower-class origins and other related drawbacks to be successful in "the game" as it is defined by the dominant society. They therefore repudiate the commonly held values for new values that have meaning for them and under which they can perform satisfactorily. These values differ from the values of the larger culture because the delinquents actually want the larger values but cannot attain them. If Cohen's thesis is correct, then delinquent gangs form a counterculture (although Cohen specifically names them subcultures).

Values from the Order and Conflict Perspectives

Values are sources of both societal integration and social problems. Order theorists assume that sharing values solves the most fundamental problem of societal integration. The values are symbolic representations of the existing society and therefore promote unity and consensus among Americans. They must, therefore, be preserved.

Conflict theorists, on the other hand, view the mass acceptance of values as a form of cultural tyranny that promotes political conservatism, inhibits creativity, and gets people to accept their lot because they believe in the system, rather than joining with others to try and change it. Thus, conflict theorists believe that slavish devotion to society's values inhibits necessary social change. Moreover, conflict theorists assume that U.S. values are the actual source of social problems such as crime, conspicuous consumption, planned obsolescence, the energy crisis, pollution, and the artificial creation of winners and losers.

Regardless of which side one may take on the consequences of U.S. values, most people would agree that the traditional values of individual freedom, capitalism, competition, and progress have made the United States relatively affluent. The future, however, will probably be very different from the past, requiring a fundamental change in these values. The future of slow growth or no growth, lower levels of affluence, and resource shortages will require that people adapt by adopting values that support cooperation rather than competition, group goals over individual goals, and a mode of making do rather than purchasing unnecessary products and relentlessly searching for technological solutions.

Chapter Review

1. Culture, the knowledge the members of society or other social organizations share, constrains behavior and how people think about and interpret their world.

2. Culture emerges as a result of continued social interaction.

3. Culture is learned behavior. The process of learning the culture is called socialization.

4. Through the socialization process, individuals internalize the culture. Thus, the control that culture has over individuals is seen as natural.

5. Culture channels behavior by providing the rules for behavior and the criteria for judging.

6. Culture is boundary-maintaining. One's own culture seems right and natural. Other cultures are considered inferior, wrong, or immoral. This tendency to consider the ways of one's own group superior is called ethnocentrism.

7. Six types of shared knowledge constitute the culture—symbols, technology, ideologies, norms, values, and roles.

8. Norms are divided into two types by degree of importance and severity of punishment for their violation. Folkways are less important. Mores are considered more vital and therefore are more severely punished if violated.

9. Roles are the behavioral expectations of people who occupy the statuses in a social organization.

10. Through language and other symbols, culture determines how the members of a society will interpret their environment. The important point is that through this construction of reality, the members of a society make sense out of a world that may have no inherent meaning.

11. The variety of customs found throughout the world is staggering. The members of one society typically view the customs found elsewhere as weird, cruel, and immoral. If we understand the cultural context of a given society, however, their practices generally make sense. This is called cultural relativity.

12. There are two contradictory forces at work in today's world. One is toward a global culture based on the customs and values of the West, especially the United States. At the same time opposite forces of localism and parochialism are at work, fueled by resistance to the ways of the secular West. These tribal identities openly oppose the new and reinforce tradition.

13. Knowing the values (the criteria for evaluation) of a society is an excellent way of understanding that society.

14. Values in the United States are the result of three major factors: (a) geographic isolation and being blessed with abundant resources; (b) founding of the nation in opposition to tyranny and aristocracy and supporting freedom, democracy, equality, and impersonal justice; and (c) a religious heritage based on the Judeo-Christian ethic and the Protestant work ethic.

15. The dominant U.S. values are success through individual achievement, competition, hard work, progress through growth and new technology, material progress, and individual freedom.

16. These values are the sources of societal integration as well as social problems.

17. Despite the power of culture and U.S. values over individual conduct, the diversity present in U.S. society means that for many people there are inconsistencies between values and actual behavior. There are clear variations in how people feel on public issues based on their different social situations.

18. A major source of cultural variation in the United States is the existence of subcultures. Because of different religions and ethnicity, some groups retain a culture different from the dominant one. Other groups form a culture because they oppose the larger society. The latter are called countercultures.

19. Order theorists assume that sharing values promotes unity among the members of society. The values therefore must be preserved.

20. Conflict theorists view the mass acceptance of values as a form of cultural tyranny that promotes political conservatism, inhibits creativity, and encourages false consciousness.

Key Terms

Socialization
Internalization
Reference groups
Ethnocentrism
Material technology
Social technology
Ethnomethodology

Ascribed status
Achieved status
Social construction of reality
Ontology
Epistemology
Cultural relativity
Cultural diffusion

Global culture
Protestant ethic
Deferred gratification
Subculture
Participant observation
Counterculture

Study Questions

1. Because individuals internalize the culture, they tend to assume that its control over one's behavior is not an external force, but a natural one. Assess your ideas and behaviors to determine which of them, if any, are culture-free.

2. What is meant by the social construction of reality? Provide examples.

3. How are U.S. values sources of both societal integration and social problems?

4. How do order theorists and conflict theorists differ in their interpretation of values?

For Further Reading

Culture: General

Ruth Benedict, *Patterns of Culture* (Baltimore: Penguin, 1946).

Peter L. Berger and Thomas Luckmann, *The Social Construction of Reality* (Garden City, NY: Doubleday, 1967).

Stephen Jay Gould, *Time's Arrow Time's Cycle* (Cambridge, MA: Harvard University Press, 1987).

Marvin Harris, *Cows, Pigs, Wars, and Witches: The Riddles of Culture* (New York: Random House, 1974).

Jane Holtz Kay, *Asphalt Nation: How the Automobile Took Over America and How We Can Take It Back* (New York: Random House, 1997).

Charles Kimball, *When Religion Becomes Evil* (New York: HarperCollins, 2002).

William Ian Miller, *The Anatomy of Disgust* (Cambridge, MA: Harvard University Press, 1997).

Jeremy Rifkin, *Time Wars: The Primary Conflict in Human History* (New York: Henry Holt, 1987).

American Values

Robert N. Bellah et al., *Habits of the Heart: Individualism and Commitment in American Life,* updated ed. (Berkeley: University of California Press, 1996).

Charles Derber, *The Wilding of America: How Greed and Violence Are Eroding Our Nation's Character* (New York: St. Martin's Press, 1996).

Robert H. Frank and Philip J. Cook, *The Winner-Take-All Society* (New York: Free Press, 1995).

Stephen Jay Gould, *Questioning the Millennium: A Rationalist's Guide to a Precisely Arbitrary Countdown* (New York: Harmony Books, 1997).

Andrew Hacker, *Money: Who Has How Much and Why* (New York: Scribner, 1997).

Marvin Harris, *America Now: The Anthropology of a Changing Culture* (New York: Simon & Schuster, 1981).

Seymour Martin Lipset, *American Exceptionalism: A Double-Edged Sword* (New York: W. W. Norton, 1996).

Philip Slater, *Wealth Addiction* (New York: Dutton, 1980).

Ben J. Wattenberg, *Values Matter Most: How Republicans or Democrats or a Third Party Can Win and Renew the American Way of Life* (New York: Free Press, 1995).

Robin M. Williams, Jr., *American Society: A Sociological Interpretation,* 3rd ed. (New York: Knopf, 1970).

Subcultures

Sue Bender, *Plain and Simple: A Woman's Journey to the Amish* (San Francisco: Harper & Row, 1989).

Martin Sanchez Jankowski, *Islands in the Street: Gangs and American Urban Society* (Berkeley: University of California Press, 1990).

William M. Kephart and William W. Zellner, *Extraordinary Groups: The Sociology of Unconventional Life-Styles*, 4th ed. (New York: St. Martin's Press, 1991).

Elliot Liebow, *Tally's Corner* (Boston: Little, Brown, 1967).

Jay MacLeod, *Ain't No Makin' It: Aspirations and Attainment in a Low-Income Neighborhood*, rev. ed. (Boulder, CO: Westview Press, 1995).

J. Milton Yinger, *Countercultures: The Promise and Peril of a World Turned Upside Down* (New York: Free Press, 1982).

William W. Zellner, *Countercultures: A Sociological Analysis* (New York: St. Martin's Press, 1995).

Global Culture

D. Stanley Eitzen and Maxine Baca Zinn (eds.), *Globalization: The Transformation of Social Worlds* (Belmont, CA: Wadsworth, 2006).

Mike Featherstone (ed.), *Global Culture: Nationalization, Globalization, and Modernity* (Newbury Park, CA: Sage, 1990).

David Held and Anthony McGrew (eds.), *The Global Transformations Reader*, 2nd ed. (Malden, MA: Blackwell, 2002).

Don Kalb, Marco van der Land, Richard Staring, Bart van Steenbergen, and Nico Wilterdink (eds.), *The Ends of Globalization: Bringing Society Back In* (Lanham, MD: Rowman & Littlefield, 2000).

Robert K. Schaeffer, *Understanding Globalization: The Social Consequences of Political, Economic, and Environmental Change*, 2nd ed. (Lanham, MD: Rowman & Littlefield, 2002).

Web Resources

http://www.hewett.norfolk.sch.uk/curric/soc/ethno/intro.htm

This site offers a thorough explanation of what ethnomethodology is and how it differs from other sociological perspectives.

http://dmoz.org/Society/Subcultures/

This site provides a list of some common and some not-so-common subcultures. Each category offers links to sites related to the subculture.

http://dir.yahoo.com/Society_and_Culture/cultures_and_groups/cultures/

The Yahoo! directory of culture provides a list of different cultural groups. Each group contains links to other sites for information on that culture.

http://www.culturalsurvival.org/newpage/index.cfm

Cultural Survival is a site "promoting the rights, voices, and visions of indigenous peoples since 1972." The site offers links and information on different indigenous cultures in various parts of the world.

http://www.chcp.org/

The Chinese Historical and Cultural Project (CHCP) was founded in 1987. CHCP's goal is to promote and preserve Chinese American culture and history through community outreach activities.

http://www.jewishculture.org/

Founded by the Council of Jewish Federations, the National Foundation for Jewish Culture is a "leading advocate for Jewish cultural preservation."

Socialization

Northern Ireland is rigidly divided between pro-British Protestants and pro-Irish Catholics. The hatred between the members of these two groups is intense, as evidenced by the number of violent incidents. The elementary schoolchildren of Northern Ireland are educated in segregated schools. But even before these children go to school they have been taught to fear and loathe the other side.

Research conducted by the University of Ulster surveyed children at forty-four elementary schools and nurseries throughout Northern Ireland (reported in Pogatchnik, 2002). The children were shown pictures and objects such as Irish and British flags, Protestant and Catholic parades, and different soccer teams' uniforms. The research found that girls and boys from the British Protestant and Irish Catholic sides of Northern Ireland society absorbed their communities' prejudices by age five. They expressed preferences for the symbols that represented their side. And they made comments such as, "I like the people who are ours. I don't like those ones because they are Orangemen [Protestants]. They're bad people," and, "Catholics are the same as masked men. They smash windows."

In June 2001, the Hotari family in Jordan held a party to celebrate the killing of twenty-one Israelis by their son, a suicide bomber. To them, it was a heroic act that they were proud of. As one eleven-year-old boy stated, "I will make my body a bomb that will blast the flesh of Zionists, the sons of pigs and monkeys. I will tear their bodies into little pieces and cause them more pain than they will ever know" (reported in Kelley, 2001).

These children were not born with these prejudices. They had been taught to hate by their families and communities. In this chapter we examine the process of socialization that is so powerful in shaping human thought and behavior as to make children hate.

Every day thousands of newborns arrive in U.S. society. How do these newborns become members of society? How do they become what we term human? The answer to these questions is that they learn to be human by acquiring the meanings, ideas, and actions appropriate for that society. This process of learning cultural values, norms, and expectations is called **socialization**.

Socialization is a lifelong process from infancy to death, where at each stage of the life-cycle individuals are continually socialized into different institutions and

Kelly Eitzen Smith, University of Arizona, is a co-author of this chapter.

112

PART TWO
The Individual
in Society:
Society in
the Individual

expected behaviors. For example, when an individual enters the institution of marriage, he or she must learn the expected behaviors as a married person in that culture. This includes norms regarding gender roles as well as society's rules regarding taxes and other laws. Even though socialization is a lifelong process, the focus of this chapter is on the most critical time of socialization—childhood.

Children are born with the limits and potential established by their unique genetic compositions. Their physical features, size and shape, rate of physical development, and even temperament unfold within predetermined boundaries (Franklin, 1989). The limits of their intellectual capabilities are also influenced by biological heritage. But even though children are biologically human, they do not have the instincts or the innate drives that will make them human. They acquire their humanness through social interaction. Their concepts of themselves, personality, love, freedom, justice, right and wrong, and reality are all products of social interaction. In other words, human beings are essentially the social creations of society.

Evidence for this assertion is found by examining the traits and behaviors of children raised without much human contact. There have been approximately 100 documented cases of **feral children** throughout history—children alleged to have been raised by animals or raised in severe isolation. When found, they may look human but act like the animals with whom they have had contact. One case involved a Tarzan-like child reported to have been raised by monkeys in the jungles of central Africa. The boy was discovered in 1974 at about age six with a troop of gray monkeys. Two years later, after painstaking efforts to rehabilitate him, he remained more monkey than human. "He is unable to talk and communicates by 'monkey' grunts and chattering. He will eat only fruit and vegetables, and when excited or scared jumps up and down uttering threatening monkey cries" (Associated Press, 1976). If a child's personality were largely determined by biological heritage, this child would have been much more human than simian. But there is a consistent finding in all cases that feral children are not normal. They cannot talk and have great difficulty in learning human speech patterns. They do not walk or eat like human beings. They express anger differently. In essence, the behavior that arises in the absence of human contact is not what we associate with human beings.

While the reported cases of feral children should be viewed with considerable skepticism, the cases of children living in human settings but kept isolated from most human contact reveal much about the importance of human interaction in becoming human. The most famous case of a child who was raised with only minimal human contact was a girl named Anna (Davis, 1940; 1948). Anna was an illegitimate child. Her grandfather refused to acknowledge her existence, and to escape his ire, the mother put the child in an attic room and, except for minimal feeding, ignored her. Anna was discovered by a social worker at about age six, and she was placed in a special school. When found, Anna could not sit up or walk. She could not talk and was believed to be deaf. She was immobile and completely indifferent to the people around her. She did not laugh, show anger, or smile. Staff members worked with Anna (during one year, a single staff member had to receive medical attention more than a dozen times for bites she received from Anna). Eventually, Anna learned to take care of herself and to walk, talk, and play with other children:

> By the time Anna died of hemorrhagic jaundice approximately four and a half years [after she was found], she had made considerable progress as compared with her con-

dition when found. She could follow directions, string beads, identify a few colors, build with blocks, and differentiate between attractive and unattractive pictures. She had a good sense of rhythm and loved a doll. She talked mainly in phrases but would repeat words and try to carry on a conversation. She was clean about clothing. She habitually washed her hands and brushed her teeth. She would try to help other children. She walked well and could run fairly well, though clumsily. Although easily excited, she had a pleasant disposition. Her involvement showed that socialization, even when started at the late age of six, could still do a great deal toward making her a person. Even though her development was no more than that of a normal child of two or three years, she had made noteworthy progress. (Davis, 1948:205)

The conclusion from observers of Anna and other cases of isolated children is that being deprived of social interaction during one's formative years deprives individuals of their humanness. Thanks to modern science and studies of the brain, we now know that in cases of extreme child neglect, the brains of these children are smaller than nonneglected children, with obvious atrophy (Perry, 2002). In other words, the very makeup of their brains is altered by lack of human contact.

In addition to social contact, the second essential to socialization is language. Language is the vehicle through which socialization occurs. In Anna's case, what little human contact she had during her first six years was physical and not communicative interaction. As Kingsley Davis has noted, Anna's case illustrates "that communicative contact is the core of socialization" (Davis, 1948:205). This principle is also illustrated by Helen Keller. This remarkable person became deaf and blind as a result of illness during infancy. She was locked into her own world until her teacher, Anne Sullivan, was able to communicate to her that the symbols she traced on Helen's hand represented water. That was the beginning of language for Helen Keller and the beginning of her understanding of who she was and the meaning of the world and society in which she was immersed (Keller, 1954).

Learning language has profound effects on how individuals think and perceive the world. Through their languages, societies differ in how they conceive of time, space, distance, velocity, action, and specificity. To illustrate this last dimension specifically, let us consider the Navajo language. With respect to rain, the Navajo language makes much finer distinctions than English speakers who generally say, "It has started to rain," "It is raining," and "It has stopped raining." When the Navajo reports personal experiences,

> he uses one verb form if he himself is aware of the actual inception of the rain storm, another if he has reason to believe that the rain has been falling for some time in his locality before the occurrence struck his attention. One form must be employed if rain is generally found about within the range of vision; another if, though it is raining about, the storm is plainly on the move. Similarly, the Navaho must invariably distinguish between the ceasing of rainfall (generally), and the stopping of rain in a particular vicinity because the rain clouds have been driven off by the wind. The people take the consistent noticing and reporting of such differences . . . as much for granted as the rising of the sun. (Kluckhohn and Leighton, 1946:194)

In short, the languages of different societies are not parallel methods for expressing the same reality. Our perception of reality depends on our language (this is the social construction of reality, as discussed in the previous chapter). In this way experience itself is a function of language. As the distinguished linguist B. L. Whorf (1956) puts it,

114

PART TWO
The Individual
in Society:
Society in
the Individual

"no individual is free to describe nature with absolute impartiality but is constrained to certain modes of interpretation even while he thinks himself most free" (1).

In learning language, we discover the meaning of symbols not only for words but also for objects such as the cross, the flag, and traffic lights. Through language we can think about the past and the future. Language symbolizes the values and norms of the society, thus enabling the user to label and evaluate objects, acts, individuals, and groups. Often, the description of the same act can portray a positive or a pejorative image. This can be seen in the sports world, as reported by syndicated columnist Jim Murray:

- On our side, a guy is "colorful." On their side, a "hotdog."
- Our team is "resourceful." Theirs is "lucky."
- Our guys are "trusted associates." Theirs are "henchmen."
- Our team gives "rewards." Theirs, "bribes."
- Our team plays "spirited" football. Theirs plays "dirty."
- Our team is "opportunistic." Theirs gets all the "breaks."
- Our guy is "confident." Theirs is ["cocky"] (Murray, 1976:150).

Thus, language is a powerful labeling tool, clearly delineating who is in and who is out.

Finally, children learn who they are by using words to describe themselves. Most societies have particular traits and behaviors that are associated with masculinity and femininity (for more on gender roles, see Chapter 12). In the United States, the stereotypes and language surrounding masculinity and femininity often indicate opposite traits; for example, aggressive/passive, independent/dependent, strong/weak, objective/subjective, provider/nurturer, rational/emotional, to name a few. Nilsen (2000) argues that language reveals much about society and gender expectations. She demonstrates this in a telling look at the military, noting:

> Once the [male] recruits are enlisted, they find themselves doing much of the work that has been traditionally thought of as 'women's work.' The solution to getting the work done and not insulting anyone's masculinity was to change the titles as shown below:
>
> | | |
> |---|---|
> | waitress | orderly |
> | nurse | medic or corpsman |
> | secretary | clerk-typist |
> | assistant | adjutant |
> | dishwasher or kitchen helper | KP (kitchen police) (310) |

Language is a powerful medium of socialization, and through language, children absorb subtle messages regarding societal expectations.

The Personality as a Social Product

Chapter 2 notes the dialectic character of society. Society is at once a product of social interaction, yet that product continuously acts back on its producers. Scientists have long argued as to what extent humans are the product of nature versus nurture. Bruce Perry (2002) writes:

Are we born evil—natural born killers or the most creative and compassionate of all animals? Are we both? Does our best and our worst come from our genes or from our learning? Nature or nurture?. . . We now know more about our genes and more about the influence of experience on shaping biological systems than ever before. What do these advances tell us about the nature or nurture debate? Simply, they tell us that this is a foolish argument. Humans are the product of nature and nurture. Genes and experience are interdependent (p.1).

Matt Ridley, a zoologist and science writer, agrees. Ridley argues that genes are not just the carriers of heredity. They are constantly active, switching on and off as a response to one's environment (2003).

While it is clear that we are all products of nature *and* nurture, in this section the emphasis is on this second process—human beings as a product of society. In particular, we examine the emergence of the human personality as a social product.

We develop a sense of **self** (our personality) in interaction with other people. Newly born infants have no sense of self-awareness. They are unable to distinguish between themselves and their surroundings. They cry spontaneously when uncomfortable. They eventually become aware that crying can be controlled and that its use can bring a response from other people. In time, and especially with the use of language, the child begins to distinguish between "I" and "you" and "mine" and "yours"—signs of self-awareness. But this is just the beginning of the personality formation process. Let us look now at several classical theories of how children develop personalities and how they learn what is expected of them in the community and society.

Charles H. Cooley (1864–1929): The Looking-Glass Self

Charles Cooley (1922) believed that children's conceptions of themselves arise through interaction with other people. He used the metaphor of a **looking-glass self** to convey the idea that all people understand themselves through the way in which other people act toward them. They judge themselves on how they think others judge them. Cooley believed that each of us imagines how we look to others and what their judgment of us is. Robert Bierstedt (1974) summarizes this process: "I am not what I think I am and I am not what you think I am. I am what I think you think I am" (197).

The critical process in Cooley's theory of personality development, then, is the feedback the individual receives from other people. Others behave in particular ways with regard to an individual. The individual interprets these behaviors positively or negatively. When the behaviors of other people are perceived as consistent, the individual accepts this definition of self, which in turn has consequences for her or his behavior. In sum, there is a self-fulfilling prophecy—the individual is as defined by other people. Suppose, for example, that whenever you entered a room and approached a small knot of people conversing with each other, they promptly melted away with lame excuses. This experience, repeated many times, would affect your feelings about yourself. Or, if wherever you appeared, a conversational group quickly formed around you, would not such attention tend to give you self-confidence and ego strength?

Cooley's insight that our self-concepts are a product of how other people react to us is important in understanding behavior. Why are some categories of people more likely to be school dropouts or criminals or malcontents or depressed, while others fit in? As we see in Chapter 7, deviance is the result of the successful application of a

The Looking-Glass Self and Body Image

According to Charles Cooley (1922), the looking-glass self involves three elements: the *imagination* of one's appearance or behavior to another person; the *imagination* of their judgment of that appearance or behavior; and resulting feelings of pride or mortification. Where does this imagination come from? In terms of body appearance, is it possible that the beauty ideals put forth in the media might have a profound impact on how we imagine others view or judge us? If that is indeed the case, what do we learn from the media?

Recent "reality" television has put average citizens in the spotlight, usually competing for some kind of monetary reward. Unfortunately, much of this programming involves transforming those individuals into people other than their normal selves. For example, shows like MTV's *I Want a Famous Face, America's Next Top Model, Extreme Makeover, Ambush Makeover, The Biggest Loser,* and *Sports Illustrated Swimsuit Model Search* all emphasize beauty and outward appearance. Shows like *The Swan* advocate the complete transformation of a person from head to toe, with painful cosmetic surgery required as part of the transformation from "ugly duckling" to swan.

While reality television is a more recent phenomenon, famous actors have always set the standards for beauty ideals. Media analysts argue that while the Miss Americas, Playboy models, Barbie dolls, and famous actresses have become increasingly thin over time, young boys are assaulted with an ever-muscular, increasingly larger male ideal. In *The Adonis Complex,* Pope et al. argue that men are becoming more affected by the muscular images they see in the media and are increasingly dissatisfied with their own bodies, leading to steroid abuse, eating disorders, weightlifting compulsion, and body obsession (2000).

Although it is impossible to make a direct causal argument between the media and behavior, the numbers of both surgical and nonsurgical cosmetic procedures are up drastically for both women and men. According to the American Society for Aesthetic Plastic Surgery, the numbers of procedures are up from over 2 million in 1997 to over 11.9 million in 2004 (a 465 percent increase in the total numbers of procedures done) (2005). Furthermore, Americans spent over $12.5 billion on cosmetic procedures in 2004, with women receiving 90 percent of the procedures. Is the media to blame? Recall Cooley's looking-glass self. "I am not what I think I am, and I am not what you think I am. I am what I think you think I am" (Bierstedt, 1974; 197).

---

social label, a process akin to the looking-glass self. For more on the impact of the media and the looking-glass self, see "A Closer Look: The Looking-Glass Self and Body Image."

George Herbert Mead (1863–1931): Taking the Role of the Other

George Mead (1934) theorized about the relationship of self and society. In essence, he believed that children find out who they are as they learn about society and society's expectations. This occurs in several important stages, the first being the imitation stage. Infants learn to distinguish between themselves and others from the actions of their parents. By age two or so, children have become self-conscious. By this Mead meant that the children are able to react to themselves as others will react to them. For example, they will tell themselves "no-no," as they have been told many times by their parents, and not touch the hot stove. The importance of this stage is

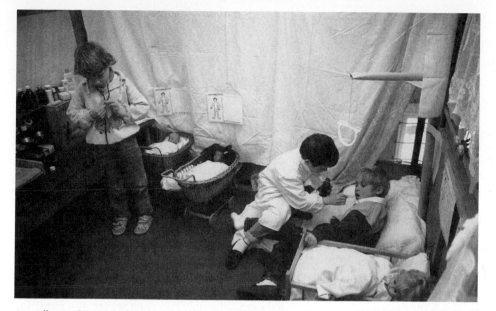

According to George Herbert Mead, during the play stage (ages four to seven), children spend much of their free time pretending to be mothers, fathers, teachers, police officers, ministers, and playing other adult roles. As they "take the role of others," children act out the behavior associated with these social positions and thus develop a rudimentary understanding of adult roles.

that the children have internalized the feelings of other people. What others expect has become a part of them. They have become conscious of themselves by incorporating the way other people are conscious of them.

The next stage is the play stage. Children from ages four to seven spend many hours a day in a world of play. Much of this time is spent in pretending to be mothers, teachers, doctors, police officers, ministers, grocers, and other roles. Mead called this form of play "taking the role of the other." As they play at a variety of social roles, children act out the behavior associated with these social positions and thus develop a rudimentary understanding of adult roles and why people in those positions act the way they do. They also see how people in these roles interact with children. Thus, children learn to look at themselves as other people see them. As Reece McGee (1975) puts it, "he learns who he is by 'being' who he is not" (74–75). The play stage, then, accomplishes two things. It provides further clues for children as to who they are, and it prepares them for later life. Furthermore, this stage is crucial to the development of gender roles. If the child sees the adult roles of "mommy" or "daddy" in a certain way, or if in playacting adult roles the child sees work occupations as masculine or feminine, this may affect the way that she or he learns gender.

The game stage, which occurs at about age eight, is the final stage of personality development in Mead's scheme. In the play stage, the children's activities are fluid and spontaneous. The game stage, in contrast, involves activities that are structured. There are rules that define, limit, and constrain the participants. Mead used baseball to illustrate what occurs in the game stage. In baseball, children must understand and abide by the rules. They must also understand the entire game—that is, when playing second base, what they and the other players must do if there

118

PART TWO
The Individual
in Society:
Society in
the Individual

is a player on first, one out, and the batter bunts down the first baseline. In other words, the various individuals in a game must know the roles of all the players and adjust their behavior to that of the others. The assessment of the entire situation is what Mead called the discovery of the "generalized other." In the play stage, children learn what is expected of them by **significant others** (parents, relatives, teachers). The game stage provides children with constraints from many other people, including people they do not know. In this way children incorporate and understand the pressures of society—what Mead called the **generalized other**. By passing through these stages, children have finally developed a social life from the expectations of parents, friends, and society. The important insight of Mead is that the self emerges as the result of social experience. Thus, the self does not exist at birth but is a social creation.

Albert Bandura (1925–   ): Social Cognitive Theory

According to social cognitive theorist Albert Bandura (1977; 1986) human behavior is the result of the continuous interaction between cognitive, behavioral, and environmental influences. In this way, people both produce and are produced by their environment. In its simplest form, children observe the behavior of others and the feedback (positive and/or negative) for such behavior. This then serves as a guide for their actions as they model after others. According to Bandura, children will use their cognitive skills to predict the outcomes of their behavior, and thus exercise personal control over their thoughts and actions. They will also adopt a behavior if it results in outcomes that they value.

These ideas are in fact the backbone of the advertising industry, where advertisers display products and the positive outcomes of using those products in the hopes that consumers will buy them. So, for example, consumers who desire the outcome of happiness will choose one particular brand of diet soda over another.

In terms of socialization, children then learn appropriate and inappropriate behavior by observing and modeling others in society. If, for example, a young boy never observes other boys playing with Barbie dolls and receives negative feedback from adults and peers by playing with them, he will be less likely to adopt such behavior. Instead, if he receives positive rewards for playing with trucks and army toys, he will be more likely to pursue them in order to receive the desirable outcome. In this way, he has learned the expectations of society for his gender.

Sigmund Freud (1856–1939): The Psychoanalytic View

While in recent years Sigmund Freud has fallen out of favor with many academics, it is impossible to overlook his significant contributions to the field of psychology. Freud (1946) emphasized the biological dimension along with social factors in personality development. For Freud, the infant's first years are totally egocentric, with all energies directed toward pleasure. This is an expression of a primitive biological force—the **id** that dominates the infant. The id, although a force throughout life, is gradually stifled by society. Parents, as the agents of society, hamper children's pleasure-seeking by imposing schedules for eating, punishing them for messy behavior and masturbation, forcing them to control their bowels, and the like.

The process of socialization is, in Freud's view, the process of society controlling the id. Through this process, children develop egos. The **ego** is the rational part of the personality that controls the id's basic urges, finding realistic ways of satisfying these biological cravings. The individual also develops a **superego** (conscience) (Chapter 4), which regulates both the id and ego. The superego is the consequence of the child's internalizing the parents' morals. A strong superego represses the id and channels behavior in socially acceptable ways. Freud saw the individual as being pulled by two contradictory forces—the natural impulses of biology and the constraints of society—resulting in the imperfection and discontent of human beings.

Society's Socialization Agents

Two themes stand out in this section. First, the personality of the child is, to a large degree, socially created and sustained. Second, through the process of socialization, the child internalizes the norms and values of society. In a sense, the child learns a script for acting, feeling, and thinking that is in tune with the wishes of society. Before we leave this topic, let us look briefly at the special transmitters of the cultural patterns—the family, the schools, and the media.

The Family. Aside from the obvious function of providing the child with the physical needs of food, clothing, and shelter, the family is the primary agent of socialization. The family indoctrinates the child in the ways of society. The parents equip the child with the information, etiquette, norms, and values necessary to be a functioning member of society. In blatant and subtle ways, parents emit messages of what is important, appropriate, moral, beautiful, and correct—and what is not. There is no option for young children. They must accept the messages of their parents of what is and what ought to be. As Everett Wilson (1966) puts it:

> But when [the child] enters the human group, he is quite at the mercy of parents and siblings. They determine both what and when he shall eat and wear, when he shall sleep and wake, what he shall think and feel, how he shall express his thoughts and feelings (what language he shall speak and how he shall do it), what his political and religious commitments shall be, what sort of vocation he shall aspire to. Not that parents are ogres. They give what they have to give: their own limited knowledge, their prejudices and passions. There is no alternative to this giving of themselves; nor for the receiver is there any option. Neither can withhold the messages conveyed to the other. (92)

Thus, the children learn from their parents. They learn from them the meaning of physical symbols such as the cross, the poison sign, and the police officer's badge. They also learn the relative worth of social groups such as Jews or Arab Americans or African Americans. The panel titled "A Closer Look: Learning to Hate" provides an example of how two young men were raised to hate Blacks.

The Schools. In contrast to families who may differ somewhat in their attitudes, interests, and emphases, the schools provide a more uniform indoctrination of youth in the culturally prescribed ways. The formal curriculum provides children with the education needed to take on adult roles: reading, math, science, and so on. In addition to the formal curriculum, young people are also exposed to the hidden curriculum—expectations about appropriate skills, character traits, and attitudes (such as patriotism) that pay off. In the United States, some valued character traits are competitiveness, ambition, and conformity.

Learning to Hate

What follows are two examples of children raised to hate.

Don Black created the Web's first hate site in 1995 (there are now more than 2,500 extremist and hate sites). That site, *Stormfront,* is visited by about 5,000 visitors daily (McKelvey, 2001). Don Black's twelve-year-old son, Derek, runs a children's website that, like his Dad's, promotes White supremacy and racial hate. Was Derek born a hater? He learned to hate from his parents. In addition to the obvious hate lessons given by his father, Derek was home-schooled since the third grade by his mother, Chloe, who is the ex-wife of David Duke, former grand wizard of the Ku Klux Klan. When confronted by people who object to the way he has raised his son, Don Black says: "People say, 'You're teaching your son Satan,' but I think anyone who is critical of me for instilling in my son my worldview has lost track of how a society should function" (quoted in McKelvey, 2001:3D).

In July 1993, eight skinheads from three subgroups (the Fourth Reich Skins, the White Youth Alliance, and the White Aryan Resistance) were arrested for conspiring to kill several well-known African American leaders and plotting to blow up the First African Methodist Episcopal Church in Los Angeles and gun down its parishioners in the hope of starting a race war. Greg Withrow is widely acknowledged as the founder of the U.S. version of the so-called skinhead movement in 1978. Since then this White supremacy organization has grown to an active membership of 3,500 in forty states, doubling since 1988. The motivation to become a member is extreme hatred for minorities. In addition to physical assaults on racial and ethnic minorities, these groups print and distribute thousands of pieces of hate literature, blaming racial minorities and Jews for all manner of social problems.

What makes one a candidate for skinhead membership? Why would one hate others so fiercely? In the case of its founder, Greg Withrow, he was brought up to be a racist. In his words, "Some fathers raise their sons to be doctors, some fathers raise their sons to be lawyers. I

Don Black is proud that his son Derek, age 12, runs a White supremacy website for kids.

was raised to be the Fuhrer" (quoted in Mulvaney, 1993:22A). His father made him study the life of Hitler and read hate literature. At age fourteen, he joined the Ku Klux Klan. Later, he was arrested for heading a group that mugged Japanese tourists and homosexuals. While in college, he formed the White Students Union and the Aryan Youth Movement. From these roots came the hatred of one individual for racial minorities and the founding of the skinhead movement.

As we see in Chapter 16, the formal system of education is conservative; it transmits the attitudes, values, and training necessary for the maintenance of society. Thus, schools are preoccupied with order and control. This emphasis on order teaches the norms and prepares youth for the organizational life they are expected to experience as adults. Unlike the family, in which the child is part of a loving relationship, the school is impersonal. The rules are to be obeyed. Activities are regimented rather than spontaneous. Thus, the child learns how to function in the larger society by learning the formal prescriptions of society and by learning that to get along one must go along.

The Media. The mass media, consisting of newspapers, magazines, movies, radio, and television, play a vital role in promoting the existing values and practices of society. For example, the mass media provide us with most of the information that helps us to define sociopolitical reality. As Michael Parenti (1993) suggests,

> [F]or many people, an issue does not exist until it appears in the news media. Indeed, what we even define as an issue or event, what we see and hear, and what we do not see and hear are greatly determined by those who control the communications world. . . . Even when we don't believe what the media say, we are still hearing or reading their viewpoints rather than some other. They are still setting the agenda, defining what it is we must believe or disbelieve, accept, or reject. The media exert a subtle, persistent influence in defining the scope of respectable political discourse. (1)

In this way, the media have a profound influence on the way we view the world and what is seen as important. For example, in the spring and summer of 2005, Americans were bombarded with report after report about famous pop singer Michael Jackson's criminal trial. Analysts spent countless hours discussing his behavior, what he wore to court, and whether he did or did not commit the crime of child molestation. His trial dominated news programs night after night. Was this news? Or was this entertainment? Unfortunately, the line between news and entertainment has become increasingly more blurry.

The hard news side of the media also has a class, race, and gender bias, which serves the privileged and the powerful. In 2001, a study (reported in Howard, 2002) of *ABC World News Tonight*, *NBC Nightly News*, and *CBS Evening News* found that:

> Instead of a liberal bias, . . . source selection favored the elite interests that the corporate owners of these shows depend on for advertising revenue, regulatory support and access to information. Network news demonstrated a clear tendency to showcase the opinions of the most powerful political and economic actors, while giving limited access to those voices that would be most likely to challenge them.

The study coded news reports from January 1 to December 31, 2001. Researchers found that of news sources with an identifiable party affiliation, 75 percent of the sources were Republican, 24 percent were Democrat, and 1 percent were third party or Independent. In addition, only 9 percent of all professional/political sources were women, reflecting the male bias in news media. Furthermore, among the U.S. source where race was determinable, 92 percent of the sources were White, 7 percent were Black; .6 percent were Latino; and .2 percent were Asian.

Television, through its entertainment shows, also functions to promote the status quo. Stereotypes of the aged, of women, gays, and minorities are promoted on these

122

PART TWO
The Individual
in Society:
Society in
the Individual

programs. Many analysts argue that media content is largely driven by the advertising industry. "Through the medium of television, corporations have a captive audience to mass market their goods and services to people who neither want nor need them, but buy them because they are psychologically manipulated into doing so" (Miller, 2005).

The messages children receive are consistent: They are bombarded with materialism and consumerism, what it takes to be a success, with sex, violence, and the value of law and order. In short, the media have tremendous power to influence us all, but particularly young people (see "A Closer Look: What Is the Impact of Media Violence on Youth?").

What Is the Impact of Media Violence on Youth?

Let's consider another possible socialization impact of the media—the bombardment of violence and violent themes in the movies, television, video games, and rap music. By the time a child in the United States graduates from high school, he or she will have spent more time in front of the tube than in class. This means that "by the age of eighteen, the average American child will have seen 200,000 violent acts on television, including 40,000 murders" (Plagens, 1991:51). Or put another way, a study by *TV Guide* in 1992 recorded 1,846 acts of violence during a single day of television, with WTBS (a Turner Broadcasting superstation) averaging 18 an hour; HBO, 14 an hour; USA Network, 12 an hour; 11 an hour on MTV; and 10 an hour on Fox and CBS (reported in the *Wall Street Journal*, 1992:B6).

In terms of video games, even E-rated games (E for "everyone") contain violent content. Harvard researchers found that two-thirds of E-rated games contained intentional violence, where injuring or killing characters is rewarded or required to advance in the game (reported in Bowman, 2001). Does watching violence explain the high rate of teenage violence? Does

playing violent video games result in violent youth? There are conflicting views on this.

Politicians are fond of blaming Hollywood for violence. The American Medical Association has demanded tighter movie regulations concerning violence. The American Psychological Association lists four experiences crucial to the development of violent behavior: access to guns, involvement with alcohol or other drugs, involvement in antisocial groups, and exposure to violence in the mass media (American Psychological Association, 1993). Similarly, various news magazines and politicians have often pointed to various forms of music that teenagers listen to and watch (MTV), such as rap music, rock and roll, and heavy metal, as responsible for youth violence.

But this argument does not hold up, as Mike Males (1996) argues forcefully. If the media are a significant cause of youth violence, then we should find similar levels of violence among different subgroups of youth, since they are all exposed to similar amounts of media influence. But, as Males points out, youth violence levels are extremely dissimilar: African American youths

© Rockstar Games/Handout/Reuters/Corbis

Popular video games frequently incorporate violence into game strategy. Often, killing or wounding an opponent is necessary to advance to the next level of the game. Some researchers argue that this encourages violence and aggression among youth.

What Is the Impact of Media Violence on Youth? continued

are twelve times more likely to commit murders than White youths; males are nine times more violent than females; teens from Washington, DC, are twenty-two times more likely to be arrested for homicide than teens from Washington State; inner-city youth are much more violent than youth from the suburbs. Mike Males (1996) presents the following compelling argument:

> Thirty-one suburban and rural California counties with a population of 2.5 million, in which a quarter-million teenagers reside, experienced zero murders in 1993. Zero. . . . Same rock'n'roll furies, same rap concerts, same TV barbarism (worse, since suburban and rural families are more likely to subscribe to graphic cable channels), same guns on every block (more in rural towns), no shortage of drug and alcohol involvement, no lack of opportunity to form anti-social groups for youths who so desire, the same teenagers bearing whatever innate "high risk" teenage qualities and "crises" of growing up experts offer as all-purpose explanations. But no killings. Yet central Los Angeles census tracts with the same youth population as these 31 counties experienced more than 200 murders. (127)

What are the reasons for this dramatic difference for two categories of youth from the same state? Clearly, the media, which are full of gratuitous violence, sexual degradation, and bad taste, are not to blame, since both the violent and the nonviolent watch them. Males points to the different conditions in which youth grow up. The Los Angeles census tracts with 200 teenage murders have high concentrations of poverty, compared to the more affluent suburban and rural counties where no youth murders occurred. Growing up in poverty is brutalizing. Children in such situations see real shootings, not just the make-believe violence on television. Again, Males (1996) argues:

> [The media devote] far more attention to the oft-repeated assertion that "the average American child sees 8,000 murders and 10,000 acts of violence on television before he or she is out of grammar school" than to the rarely examined fact that millions of American children experience real rapes and beatings before they are old enough to get out of grammar school. (123)

124

PART TWO
The Individual
in Society:
Society in
the Individual

The media, whatever the source, tend to present a similar message. This is because the media are controlled by fewer and fewer corporations. Consider the following:

- Ten great multinational corporations—AOL Time Warner, Disney, General Electric, News Corporation, Viacom, Vivendi, Sony, Bertelsmann, AT&T, and Liberty Media—comprise a media cartel (The Nation, 2002); that is, they effectively control television, radio, movies, books, magazines, and the Internet in the United States.
- Until the 1980s, one company could legally own no more than seven AM and seven FM radio stations. In 2002, one company, Clear Channel, owned more than 1,200 (Donahue, 2002:24).
- About 80 percent of the daily newspaper circulation in the United States belongs to a few giant chains (Gannett, Knight-Ridder, New York Times, Washington Post, and the Tribune Company). Less than 2 percent of U.S. cities have competing newspapers under separate ownership (Parenti, Michael, 2002:178).
- Six major companies distribute almost all the magazines sold on newsstands, and eight corporate conglomerates control most of the book-sales revenues (Parenti, Michael, 2002:178).

This ever greater concentration of the media in the hands of a few has several important consequences. First, it results in an ideological monopoly, that is, newspapers, magazines, television, and radio offer little variety in perspective and editorial policy, ranging from centrist to moderately conservative. There is an unquestioned acceptance of the foundations of society. Consider the treatment of capitalism, for example:

> News reports on business rely almost entirely on business sources. The workings of the capitalist political economy remain virtually unmentioned. The tendency toward chronic instability, recession, inflation, and underemployment; the transference of corporate diseconomies onto the public—these and other such problems are treated superficially, if at all, by pundits who have neither the inclination nor the freedom to offer critical observations about our capitalist paradise. (Parenti, Michael, 2002:182)

A second consequence of the media consolidation is that, since the media conglomerates are profit-seeking organizations, they emphasize entertainment over news. This results, often in broadcast dissemination that does not distinguish well between the trivial and the momentous, and "thus we become obsessed with the O. J. Simpson trial while ignoring things like genocide in Rwanda" (McCleary, 2002:22). The result, as one observer puts it, is that the media cartel "keeps us fully entertained and permanently half-informed" (Miller, 2002:18). Third, and related to the profit emphasis: "When a media outlet is a cog in a wheel that must help maximize corporate profits, not part of an information-gathering entity, then containing costs, not providing information, is a priority" (Malveaux, 2002:34). And, fourth, the decision makers in these conglomerates are located in the large urban centers of the United States and Europe. Thus, the focus is away from local issues and toward what is believed of interest to the widest audience nationwide.

Similarities and Differences among the Members of Society

Modal Personality Type

Chapter 2 describes the condition that Durkheim called *anomie*. This refers to a situation in which an individual is unsure of his or her social world—the norms are ambiguous or conflicting. In other words, an anomic situation lacks consistency, predictability, and order. Because this condition is upsetting, individuals and groups seek order. Every society provides a common **nomos** (meaningful order) for its members (Berger and Luckmann, 1967). "Every society has its specific way of defining and perceiving reality—its world, the universe, its overarching organization of symbols" (Berger and Kellner, 1975:219). Through the socialization process, the newcomer to society is provided a reality that makes sense. By learning the language and the ready-made definitions of society, the individual is given a consistent way to perceive the world. We take for granted the order that is created for each of us; it is the only world that we can conceive of; it is the only system in which we feel comfortable. "This order, by which the individual comes to perceive and define his world, is thus not chosen by him, except perhaps for very small modifications. Rather it is discovered by him as an external datum, a ready-made world that simply is there for him to go ahead and live in, though he modifies it continually in the process of living in it" (Berger and Kellner, 1975:220).

Each society has its unique way of perceiving, interpreting, and evaluating reality. This common culture, and nomos, is internalized by the members of society through the process of socialization—thus, people are a product of their culture. It follows, then, that the members of a society will be similar in many fundamental respects. Although there are individual exceptions and subcultural variations, we can say that Americans differ fundamentally from Mexicans, Germans, the French, Malaysians, and others. Let us illustrate how people in a society develop similarly by briefly characterizing two categories of Native Americans of North America (taken from Barnouw, 1979:59–75).

- **The Pueblo of the Southwest**. The Zuni and Hopi are submissive and gentle peoples. Children are treated with warmth and affection. They live in highly cooperative social structures where individualism is discouraged. One who thirsts for power is ridiculed. Life in these societies is highly structured. The rules are extremely important, and order is highly valued. They never brew intoxicants and reject the use of drugs. In these orderly and cooperative settings, people are trusted. Life is pleasant and relatively free from hatred. The kind of person that develops in these societies tends to be confident, trusting, generous, polite, cooperative, and emotionally controlled.

- **The Northern Plains**. The Native Americans of this area are aggressive peoples. They are fierce warriors exhibiting almost suicidal bravado in battle. They stress individuality with fierce competition for prestige. They boast of their exploits. They stress individual ecstasy in their religious experiences, brought about by fasting, self-torture, and the use of drugs (peyote and alcohol). The Plains

126

PART TWO
The Individual
in Society:
Society in
the Individual

tribes, in contrast to the Pueblo, are more individualistic, competitive, and aggressive. They are more expressive as individuals and less orderly in group life.

These examples show that each society tends to produce a certain type of individual—a **modal personality** type. The individual growing up in the United States, with its set of values, tends to be individualistic, competitive, materialistic, and oriented toward work, progress, and the future. Even though this characterization is generally correct, there are some problems with the assumption that socialization into a culture is all-powerful. First, the power of socialization can vary by the type of society. Small, **homogeneous** societies like those of Native American tribes provide the individual member of society with a consistent message, whereas in a large, **heterogeneous** society like the United States, individuals are confronted with a number of contradictory themes and expectations.

Why We Are Not All Alike

Even though individuals within societies are socialized and generally comply with the demands of their society, every society has its deviants. Given the power of society through the socialization process, what are the forces that allow for differences in people in the United States? We begin with a discussion of the major agents of socialization.

The Family. We have said that the family is the ultimate societal agency for socialization. Families teach their children the language, etiquette, and skills that enable the child to find her or his niche in society. But families differ in a variety of important ways (for example, in religion, political views, optimism, and affluence). Some parents tend to be authoritarian, demanding control of their youngsters and providing punishment for failure to comply. Authority figures are to be obeyed without question. In contrast, other parents allow their children to explore, experiment, and question. The family is democratic. Rules are not necessarily absolute. Clearly, children growing up in authoritarian and permissive families differ in their acceptance of authority, political proclivities, and views of the world.

The family may have little influence on the child if the parents disagree on politics, religion, and/or values. Or, if they are consistent, the parents' views may be neutralized by contrary values held by friends. This neutralization process is facilitated by the decreasing amount of time that parents spend with their children compared to the time spent in previous generations. According to 2003 Census statistics, 22.4 percent of families constitute a married couple with children under age 18, and another 12.6 percent of families with children under age 18 are female-headed with no husband present (American Community Survey, 2003). With changing family forms and the increasing need for dual incomes, parents spend less and less time raising and influencing their children while their youngsters are influenced more and more not only by their peers but also by day care centers, schools, and television.

Some families may have little or negative influence on their children because they are hopelessly disorganized. One or both parents may be absent, alcoholic, unstable, or uncommunicative. In sum, although children raised in the United States are affected by a common culture, family experiences and emphases can vary enough to result in behavioral and attitudinal differences. That children and families can be fundamentally different is seen in the occasional value conflicts between parents and school authorities on sex education, the use of certain literature, rules, and the proper way to enforce rules. But the schools themselves also vary, resulting in different products by type of school.

The Schools. U.S. schools, as are schools in all societies, are conservative. But there are differences that have a substantial impact on students. According to the National Center for Education Statistics (2004), in 2003, 73.9 percent of American students attended the public school in their neighborhood, while another 15.4 percent attended a public school of their choosing. An estimated 10.8 percent of American students attended a private school, the majority of which were church-related. In some schools, for example, the curriculum, schedule, and philosophy are very rigid. Children sit in straight rows, may talk only with permission, wear the prescribed clothing, and accept without question the authority of the teacher. In other schools, however, the curriculum, schedules, teachers, and rules are flexible. The products of these two types of schools are likely to differ in much the same way as do the children of autocratic or permissive homes.

The Religion. In general, organized religion in the United States reinforces U.S. values and the policies of the government (see Chapter 17). But significant differences exist among and within the various religious bodies. There are religious disagreements on morality, birth control, sex education, abortion, gay rights, capital punishment, evolution, and other volatile issues. Moreover, religious ideas can conflict with those of one's peers and with what is taught in school. The more salient one's religion, then the more likely one will differ from people who do not share one's religious views.

The Social Location. Each of us is located in society, not only geographically, but also socially. Depending on our wealth, occupation, education, ethnic or racial heritage, gender, and family background, we see ourselves (and other people see us) as being superior to some people and inferior to others. According to census figures, in 2003 roughly 15 million households had incomes over $100,000. On the other side of the spectrum, roughly 30 million households had incomes less than $24,999 (American Community Survey, 2003). Our varying positions in this hierarchy have an effect on our attitudes and perceptions. In particular, people who are highly placed tend to support the status quo, whereas those who are less advantaged are likely to be more antagonistic to the way things are and to desire changes beneficial to them.

The Generation Cohort. An **age cohort** is a category of people of the same age. The life experiences of people typically vary depending on when they were born. In other words, people of the same age tend in a general way to be alike in behavior and attitudes, because they were influenced by the same major events such as the Great Depression, World War II, or the antiwar protests of the 1960s. Similarly, the members of age cohorts such as the baby boomers (born 1946–1964), the post–baby boomers ("Generation X" born 1965–1976), and the "Millennial Generation" (those born 1977–1995 a generation larger than the baby boom generation) differ from each other because of differing opportunities, changing economic realities, and the circumstances of their parents. According to Strauss and Howe (1991), each generation cohort can be characterized by some typical traits and behaviors. Generation Xers are often seen as individualistic, resistant to authority, and skeptical about politics.

128

PART TWO
The Individual
in Society:
Society in
the Individual

They are the first generation of "latch-key" children, whose mothers were more likely to work outside the home. The Millennial Generation is often characterized as affluent, protected, educated, and technologically savvy. This generation has grown up with highly structured lives and does not know a life without seatbelts, bike helmets, computer technology, and cable television. These generation differences can often cause conflict and disagreement over things like politics and even parenting styles.

Contradictory Influences and Role Conflicts. We have seen that youngsters may experience pulls in opposite directions from family, church, and school. Other sources of contradictory attractions are peer groups and the media. Parents may insist, for instance, that their children not fight. Yet, the children's peers might demand such behavior. Moreover, children are bombarded by violence (much of which is considered appropriate) in the movies and on television. How are these children to behave, faced with such opposing and powerful stimuli? In addition to violence, teenagers are also bombarded with sexual images and themes in the media, at the same time they are not given consistent sex education and messages about sexual behavior. In many states they receive abstinence-only education, yet are assaulted by images of teenagers engaging in sexual activity on television and in movies. How are they to behave? Some will follow their parents' dictates or their religion; others will succumb to other pressures.

Some societies are clear and consistent in their expectations for members' behavior. There is no such consensus in the United States. An examination of a few fundamental social roles illustrates the disagreement on the expectations of the occupants. Adolescents are often unsure of what is expected of them. The law sometimes defines them as children and at other times as adults. For example, at age eighteen they are able to vote in political elections, but they are not old enough to drink alcohol legally.

Gender roles provide another example of varying expectations depending on the individual, audience, and community. Traditional masculine and feminine roles are in flux. What precisely is expected of a man and woman as they enter a building? Does the man open the door for the woman? This was appropriate behavior in the past and it may be now, but one is never sure, for some women find such behavior offensive. What are the expectations of a newly married husband and wife? How will they divide the household chores? Who is to be the breadwinner? And later, if there is a divorce, who will take the children? Twenty years ago, or even five years ago, the answers to these questions were much more certain.

To conclude, the emphasis of this chapter is on how the individual is shaped by powerful social forces, but we must remember that people are not utterly predictable. Moreover, human beings are actively involved in shaping the social landscape. In sum, the person is, as Kenneth Westhues (1982) says, "a two-sided being, at once created and creating, predictable and surprising" (viii).

Both order and conflict theorists acknowledge the power of the socialization process. They differ, however, in their interpretation of this universal process. The order theorists view this process as necessary to promote stability and law-abiding citizens. Children must be socialized into the values, morals, and expectations of society in order to keep balance and harmony. Conflict theorists, on the other hand, view the process as one in which people are led to accept the customs, laws, and values of society uncritically and therefore become willing participants in a society that may be in need of change. In other words, the members of society are taught to accept the way things are, even though the social order benefits some people and disadvantages others. This process is so powerful that most of the powerless and disadvantaged in our society do not rebel because they actually believe in the system that systematically keeps them down. Karl Marx explained this irony through the concept of *false consciousness*. What is undeniable to both order and conflict theorists is that the socialization process is inevitable, powerful, and necessary.

Chapter Review

1. Socialization is the process of learning the culture. Children must learn the culture of the society in which they are born. Socialization, however, is a lifelong process and occurs in all social groups.

2. Infants become human only through learning the culture.

3. The socialization of youth requires social interaction.

4. Another essential to socialization is language, which has profound effects on how individuals think and perceive the world.

5. The personality emerges as a social product. We develop a sense of self only through interaction with other people.

6. One theory of how personality develops is Cooley's "looking-glass self." Through interaction, children define themselves according to how they interpret how other people think of them.

7. Mead's theory of self-development involves several stages. Through interaction with their parents, infants are able to distinguish between themselves and other people. By age two, they are able to react to themselves as others react to them. In the play stage (from ages four to seven), children pretend to be in a variety of adult roles (taking the role of the other). In the game stage (about age eight), children play at games with rigid rules. They begin to understand the structure of the entire game with the expectations for everyone involved. This understanding of the entire situation is called the "generalized other."

8. According to Bandura's social cognitive theory, children observe the behavior of others and the feedback (positive and/or negative) for such behavior. This then serves as a guide for their actions as they model after others.

9. According to Freud's theory, socialization is the process by which society controls the id (the biological needs for pleasure). Through this process, children develop egos (the control of the id by finding appropriate ways to satisfy biological urges). A super-

ego also emerges, which is the internalization of the morals of the parents, further channeling behavior in socially acceptable ways.

10. Through interaction, children internalize the norms and values of society. Three special transmitters of the cultural patterns are the family, the schools, and the media.

11. Ten multinational corporations control television, radio, movies, books, magazines, and the Internet in the United States. This concentration of the media in the hands of a few results in: (a) an ideological monopoly that supports the status quo; (b) an emphasis of entertainment over news; (c) an emphasis on profit-making over information gathering, and (d) news of local interest being sacrificed for what the media moguls consider of interest to the widest audience nationwide.

12. Because the socialization agents of society present a relatively consistent picture, the members of a society tend to be alike in fundamental ways (modal personality type). The smaller and more homogeneous the society, the more alike the members of that society will be.

13. Despite the tendency for the members to be alike, people, especially in large, heterogeneous societies, are not all similar. The sources of deviation are the differences found in families (social class, religion, ethnic background), schools with differing philosophies (rigid or flexible, public or sectarian), religions, social locations, age cohorts, contradictory influences, and conflicts in role definitions.

14. Both order and conflict theorists acknowledge the power of the socialization process, but differ in their interpretation of it. Order theorists view socialization as necessary to promote stability and the development of law-abiding citizens. Conflict theorists, in contrast, view the process as one in which people are led to accept the customs, laws, and values of society uncritically. This process is so powerful that disadvantaged people may accept the system that disadvantages them (false consciousness).

Key Terms

Socialization
Feral children
Self
Looking-glass self

Significant others
Generalized other
Id
Ego

Superego
Nomos
Modal personality type
Age cohort

Study Questions

1. To what extent is "humanness" a social product rather than instinctual?
2. What is meant by the assertion that "human beings are social animals"?
3. How do order and conflict theorists differ in their evaluation and interpretation of the role of the media in the socialization process?
4. The forces that socialize us are powerful, but they are not totally deterministic. Why not?

For Further Reading

The Socialization Process

Albert Bandura, *Social Learning Theory* (New York: General Learning Press, 1977).

Bandura, Albert. 1986. *Social Foundations of Thought and Action*. Englewood Cliffs, NJ: Prentice Hall.

Charles Horton Cooley, *Human Nature and the Social Order* (New York: Scribner, 1922).

Erik Erikson, *Childhood and Society* (New York: W. W. Norton, 1950).

Frances FitzGerald, *America Revised: History Schoolbooks in the Twentieth Century* (Boston: Atlantic/Little, Brown, 1979).

Sigmund Freud, *Civilization and Its Discontents*, Joan Riviére, trans. (London: Hogarth Press, 1946).

Herbert J. Gans, *Deciding What's News* (New York: Pantheon, 1979).

Todd Gitlin, *Media Unlimited: How the Torrent of Images and Sounds Overwhelms Our Lives* (New York: Metropolitan Books, 2002).

Erving Goffman, *The Presentation of Self in Everyday Life* (Garden City, NY: Doubleday, 1959).

Mike Males, *Framing Youth: Ten Myths about the Next Generation* (Monroe, ME: Common Courage Press, 1999).

Mike Males, *The Scapegoat Generation: America's War on Adolescents* (Monroe, ME: Common Courage Press, 1996).

George Herbert Mead, *Mind, Self, and Society* (Chicago: University of Chicago Press, 1934).

Michael Parenti, *Inventing Reality: The Politics of the News Media*, 2nd ed. (New York: St. Martin's Press, 1993).

Jean Piaget and Barbara Inhelder, *The Psychology of the Child* (New York: Basic Books, 1969).

Modal Personality

Victor Barnouw, *Culture and Personality*, 3rd ed. (Homewood, IL: Dorsey, 1979).

Ruth Benedict, *Patterns of Culture* (Baltimore: Penguin, 1946).

Urie Bronfenbrenner, *Two Worlds of Childhood: U.S. and U.S.S.R.* (New York: Simon & Schuster, 1973).

Stanley Elkins, *Slavery: A Problem of American Institutional and Intellectual Life* (New York: Universal Library, 1963).

Margaret Mead, *Sex and Temperament in Three Primitive Societies* (New York: Morrow, 1935).

David Riesman, *The Lonely Crowd* (New Haven, CT: Yale University Press, 1950).

William Strauss and Neil Howe, *Generations: The History of America's Future, 1584 to 2069* (New York: Morrow and Co., 1991).

Web Resources

http://www2.pfeiffer.edu/~lridener/DSS/Cooley/LKGLSSLF.html

This site is an excerpt from Charles Cooley's Human Nature and the Social Order, which talks about the looking-glass self.

http://www.honestreporting.com/

Honest Reporting is a media watch group that advocates honesty in news reporting and exposes dishonesty. The site has links to other media watch groups.

http://www.cyfc.umn.edu/

The Children, Youth, and Family Consortium is part of the University of Minnesota. It does studies on children, including those that have implications for socialization.

http://www.feralchildren.org/

This site documents the cases of feral children throughout history.

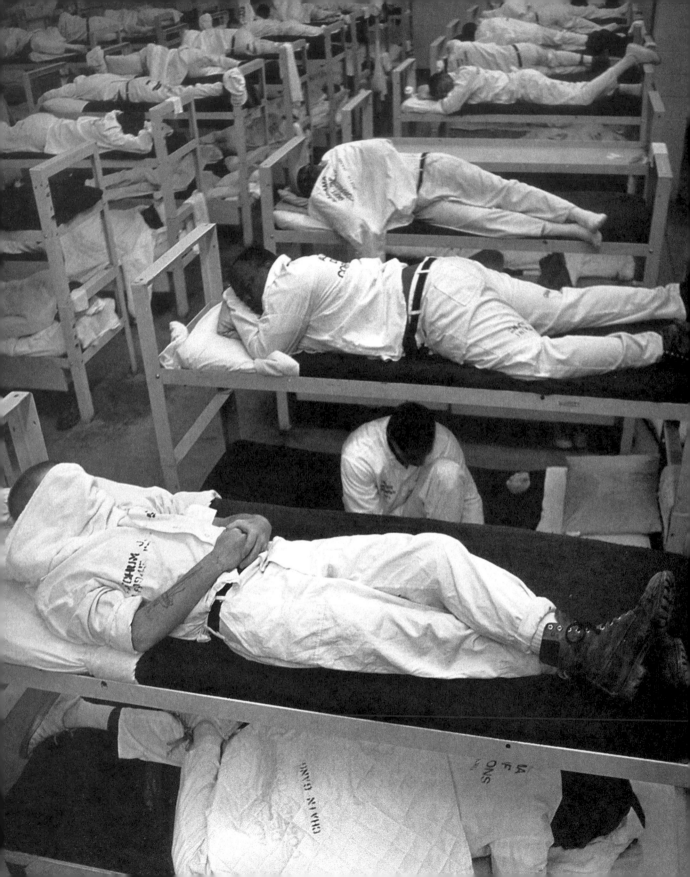

Social Control

At 9:34 P.M. on July 13, 1977, the electricity went out in New York City and in some areas did not work again for twenty-five hours. Under the cover of darkness, many areas of the city were pillaged. More than 2,000 stores were wrecked or looted, over 1,000 fires were set, with property losses estimated at more than $1 billion. The plunderers were of all ages. They stole appliances, jewelry, shoes, groceries, clothes, furniture, liquor, and automobiles (fifty new Pontiacs from one dealer). The atmosphere was a mixture of revenge, greed, and festival. Observers characterized the looting binge as a carnival atmosphere in which the actors had no concept of morality. It was as if they were immune from the law and from guilt. All of society's constraints were removed, resulting in anarchy. When the lights went out, the social controls on behavior left as well for many people.

Social control is a central fact of social organization (Eitzen, 2000b). As Ray Cuzzort (1989) asserts: "A sociocultural system cannot rely on random individual responses to create the structure and the cohesiveness required of organized effort. A society cannot, in other words, rely on people simply 'doing their thing.' A society must, in effect, generate ways that ensure that what gets done is 'society's thing'" (179). Control, then, is essential for social order. Without it, social organizations—whether they are societies, communities, churches, prisons, hospitals, schools, corporations, athletic teams, or families—would be chaotic, fragmented, uncoordinated, unpredictable, and fragile.

All social groups have mechanisms to ensure conformity—mechanisms of **social control**. The socialization process is one of these ways by which individuals internalize the norms and values of the group. People are taught what is proper, moral, and appropriate. This process is generally so powerful that individuals conform, not out of fear of punishment, but because they want to. In other words, group demands that are out there become demands that are inside us. But socialization is never perfect—we are not all robots. As we see in Chapter 7, people deviate. To cope with this, social groups exert external control over their members. These controls are the subject of this chapter.

The focus of this chapter is on social control at the societal level. The dominant modes of socialization vary by type of society. Small, homogeneous societies, for

134

PART TWO
The Individual
in Society:
Society in
the Individual

example, are dominated by tradition, whereas large, modern societies are less affected by the force of tradition. Traditional societies tend to have an overriding consensus on societal values; therefore, the family, religion, and community convey to each individual member a consistent message about which behaviors are appropriate and which ones are not. Although formal punishment of norm violators does occur in traditional societies, informal controls are usually quite effective and more typical.

In a complex society such as the United States, social control is more difficult to attain because of the existence of different groups with values that often compete. Therefore, social control tends to be more formal and appears more repressive (because it is more overt) than that found in traditional societies. It occurs in many forms and disguises. Social control is accomplished in the home and school and through various other institutions. It is attained through the overt and covert activities of political agencies, psychotherapists, and even genetic engineers. Efforts to manipulate the masses through various techniques of persuasion also keep deviance in check.

The remainder of this chapter is devoted to an extensive examination of the various agents of social control in U.S. society. These agents are divided into two types, by the means used to achieve social control: ideological control (belief systems, one of Peter Berger's eight sources of social control, listed in the next section) and direct intervention (the other seven sources). The former aims at control through manipulation of ideas and perceptions; the latter controls the actual behavior of individuals.

Agents Of Ideological Social Control

All social groups have mechanisms to ensure conformity—mechanisms of social control. Peter Berger (1963:68–78) has identified eight sources of social control: (1) force, the use of violence or threats of violence; (2) economic rewards or punishments, the promise or denial of material rewards; (3) ridicule and gossip, fear of being belittled for outside group expectations; (4) ostracism, the threat or actual removal from the group; (5) fraud and deception, actions to manipulate (trick) others to conform; (6) belief systems, the use of ideology to induce individuals to conform; (7) the sphere of intimates, pressures from close friends, peers, and relatives to conform; and (8) the contract, actions controlled by the stipulations of a formal agreement.

Ideological social control (belief systems) is the attempt to manipulate the consciousness of citizens so that they accept the ruling ideology and refuse to be moved by competing ideologies. Other goals are to persuade the members of society to comply willingly with the law and to accept without question the existing distribution of societal power and rewards. These goals are accomplished in at least three ways. First, ideological social control is accomplished through the socialization of youth. Young people, for example, are taught the values of individualism, competition, patriotism, and respect for authority at home, in school, in scouting organizations, in sports, and through the media. The socialization process could be referred to as cultural control, because the individual is given authoritative definitions of what should and should not be done, which make it appear as if there were no choice (Stivers, 1975). Second, ideological conformity occurs by frontal attacks on competing ideologies by politicians, pastors, teachers, and other people in authority. Finally, there are propaganda efforts by political authorities to convince the public of which actions are moral, who the enemies are, and why certain courses of governmental action are required.

Ideological social control is more effective than overt social control measures because individuals impose controls upon themselves (Collins, 1992:63–85). Through the socialization process we learn not only the rules of a social organization but also the supporting ideology. The norms are internalized in this process. To the degree that this process works, individuals are not forced to conform, they want to conform. Let us examine this process by describing the agents of social control that are especially important in accomplishing the goal of ideological conformity.

Family

The primary responsibility of parents is to teach their children the attitudes, values, and behavior considered appropriate by the parents (and society). Parents universally want their children to succeed. Success is measured in terms not only of monetary achievement but also whether the child fits in society. Fitting in requires that the child learns to behave and think in the ways that are deemed proper. Although, as noted in Chapter 5, there is a wide latitude in the actual mode of socialization in the family, most children do behave in acceptable ways.

Education

The formal system of education is an important societal agent for conformity. The school insists that the behavioral standards of the community be maintained in speech, dress, and demeanor. More than this, the schools indoctrinate their pupils

An important function of schools is to promote ideological conformity.

136

PART TWO
The Individual
in Society:
Society in
the Individual

in the correct attitudes about work, respect for authority, and patriotism. The text-books used in schools have typically not provided an accurate account of history, for example, but rather an account that is biased in the direction the authorities wish to perpetuate (Loewen, 1995). The treatment given minorities in these texts is one indicator of the bias. Another indicator is the contrast between descriptions of the behavior of the United States and the behavior of its enemies in wars (see FitzGerald, 1979).

One critic of the schools is concerned with the problem of conformity, which taken to the extreme results in blind obedience to such malevolent authority figures as Adolf Hitler, Charles Manson, Osama bin Laden, and Saddam Hussein. Rather than turning out conformists, the schools should be turning out individuals with the ability to recognize false prophets and the courage to disobey them:

> The power of socialization can conceivably be harnessed so as to develop individuals who are rational and skeptical, capable of independent thought, and who can disobey or disagree at the critical moment. Our society, however, continues systematically to instill exactly the opposite. The educational system pays considerable lip service to the development of self-reliance, and places huge emphasis on lofty concepts of individual differences. Little notice is taken of the legions of overly obedient children in the schools; yet, for every overly disobedient child, there are probably twenty who are obeying too much. There is little motivation to encourage the unsqueaky wheels to develop as noisy, creative, independent thinkers who may become bold enough to disagree. (McCarthy, 1979:34)

Religion

Religious groups are in many ways involved with social control. Most noticeably, they typically have guidelines for the behavior of members and punishments for disobedience. As an extreme example, see the panel titled "Diversity: The Amish and Social Control."

Established religion in the United States tends to reinforce the status quo. Few clergy and their parishioners work actively to change the political and economic system. Instead, they preach sermons extolling the virtues of "the American way of life" and "giving unto Caesar the things which are Caesar's." Directly or indirectly, there has been a strong tendency for religious groups throughout U.S. history to accept existing government policies, whether they are slavery, war, or the conquest of Native Americans.

Religious groups also preserve the status quo by teaching that people should accept an imperfect society (poverty, racism, and war) because they are born sinners. In this way, religion, as Marx suggested, is an opiate of the masses because it persuades them to accept an unjust system rather than work to change it. The downtrodden are advised to accept their lot because they will be rewarded in the next life. Thus, they have no need to change the system from below. As Albert Szymanski (1978) argues:

> The doctrine of the omnipotence of God and total submission to His will pervades the general world views of religious people, and hence is sublimated as submission to political rulers and the upper class. Religion provides a consolation for the suffering of people on earth and a deflection of one's hopes into the future. Combined

The Amish and Social Control

The Amish are a religious sect found mainly in Pennsylvania, Indiana, and Kansas. They are farmers who resist modern technology. They forbid the use of motorcycles, automobiles, and electricity. They wear simple clothes of the nineteenth century. They believe that they are only temporary visitors on earth, and hence remain aloof from it. This explains why they insist on being different. Most important, the Amish insist on conformity within their community.

The Amish descend from Jacob Amman, a Mennonite preacher in Switzerland. The Mennonites and other Anabaptists of that day differed from mainstream Protestants because they believed in the separation of church and state, adult baptism, and refusal to bear arms and take oaths. Amman and his followers split away from the Mennonites in 1700 over an issue of church discipline—the *Meidung*. Amman felt that the Mennonites were too lax in their discipline of deviants and that the *Meidung* must be enforced in severe cases. The *Meidung* is one of the most potent of all social control mechanisms. The following is a description by William M. Kephart and William W. Zellner (1990):

> The ultimate sanction is imposition of the *Meidung*, also known as the "shunning" or "ban," but because of its severity, it is used only as a last resort. The followers of Jacob Amman have a strong religious orientation and a finely honed conscience—and the Amish community relies on this fact. Actions such as gossip, reprimand, and the employment of confession are usually sufficient to bring about conformity. The *Meidung* would be imposed only if a member were to leave the church, or marry an outsider, or break a major rule (such as buying an auto) without full repentance.

Although the *Meidung* is imposed by the bishop, he will not act without the near unanimous vote of the congregation. Generally speaking, however, the ban is total. No one in the district is permitted to associate with the errant party, including members of his or her own family. Even normal marital relations are forbidden. Should any member of the community ignore the *Meidung*, that person would also be placed under the ban. In fact, the *Meidung* is honored by all Amish districts, including those that are not in full fellowship with the district in question. There is no doubt that the ban is a mighty weapon that Jacob Amman intended it to be.

On the other hand, the ban is not irrevocable. If the shunned member admits the error of his or her ways—and asks forgiveness of the congregation—the *Meidung* will be lifted and the transgressor readmitted to the fold. No matter how serious the offense, the Amish never look upon someone under the ban as an enemy, but only as one who has erred. And while they are firm in their enforcement of the *Meidung*, the congregation will pray for the errant member to rectify his or her mistake.

Although imposition of the ban is infrequent, it is far from rare. Males are involved much more often than females, the younger more frequently than the old. The *Meidung* would probably be imposed on young males more often were it not for the fact that baptism does not take place until the late teens. Prior to this time, young males are expected to be—and often are—somewhat on the wild side, and allowances are made for this fact.

Baptism changes things, however, for this is the rite whereby the young person officially joins the church and makes the pledge of obedience. Once the pledge is made, the limits of tolerance are substantially reduced. More than one Amish youth has been subjected to the *Meidung* for behavior that, prior to his baptism, had been tolerated.

Source: From *Extraordinary Groups: An Examination of Unconventional Life-Styles,* 4th ed. by William Kephart and William Zellner, p. 25. © 1990 by St. Martin's Press. Used with permission of W. H. Freeman and Company/Worth Publishers.

with its advocacy of the earthly status quo, religion thus typically serves as a powerful legitimatizing force for upper-class rule. Further, most religions, especially the religions of the working class and the poor-Baptism, Methodism, the Messianic sects, and Catholicism-in their sermons typically condemn radical political movements and preach instead either political abstention or submission to government authority. (253)

138

PART TWO
The Individual
in Society:
Society in
the Individual

Sport

School and professional sports work to reinforce conforming attitudes and behaviors in the populace in several ways (Eitzen, 2000b; Eitzen and Sage, 2003). First, there is the strong relationship between sport and nationalism. Success in international sports competition tends to trigger pride among that nation's citizens. The Olympics and other international games tend to promote an us-versus-them feeling among athletes, coaches, politicians, the press, and fans. It can be argued, then, that the Olympic games are a political contest, a symbolic world war in which nations win or lose. Because this interpretation is commonly held, citizens of the nations involved unite behind their flag and their athletes.

The integral interrelationship of sport and nationalism is easily seen in the blatantly militaristic pageantry that surrounds sports contests. The playing of the national anthem, the presentation of the colors, the jet aircraft flyovers, and the band forming a flag or a liberty bell are all political acts supportive of the existing political system.

For whatever reason, sport competition and nationalism are closely intertwined. When U.S. athletes compete against athletes of another country, national unity is the result (for both sides, unless one's athletes do poorly). Citizens take pride in their representatives' accomplishments, viewing them as collective achievements. This identification with athletes and their cause of winning for the nation's glory tends to unite a nation's citizens regardless of social class, race, and regional differences. Thus, sport can be used by political leaders whose nations have problems with divisiveness.

As noted in Chapter 3, sport can serve as an opiate of the masses in several ways. Virtually all homes have television sets, making it possible for almost everyone to participate vicariously in and identify with local and national sports teams. Because of this, the minds and energies of the viewers are deflected away from the hunger and misery that are disproportionately the lot of the lower classes in U.S. society. The status quo is thereby preserved.

Sport also acts as an opiate by perpetuating the belief that people from the lowest classes can achieve upward mobility through success in sports. Clearly this is a myth; for every major leaguer who has come up from poverty, tens of thousands of poor people have not become professional athletes. The point, however, is that most people in the United States believe that sport is a mobility escalator and that it is merely a reflection of the opportunity structure of the society in general. Again, poor youth who might otherwise invest their energies in changing the system work instead on a jump shot. The potential for revolution is thus impeded by sport.

Another way that sport serves to control people ideologically is by reinforcing U.S. values among the participants. Sport is a vehicle by which the values of success in competition, hard work, perseverance, discipline, and order are transmitted. This is the explicit reason given for the existence of Little League programs for youngsters and the tremendous emphasis on sports in U.S. schools. Coaches commonly place signs in locker rooms to inspire certain traits in their athletes. Some examples include the following (Snyder, 1972):

- "The will to win is the will to work."
- "By failing to prepare yourself you are preparing to fail."
- "Winners never quit and quitters never win."
- "United we stand, divided we fall."

One explicit goal of sports is to build character. The assumption is that participation in sports from the Little Leagues through the Big Leagues (professional ranks) provides athletes with American values: achievement in competitive situations through hard work, materialism, progress, and respect for authority. As David Matza (1964b) puts it: "The substance of athletics contains within itself—in its rules, procedures, training, and sentiments—a paradigm of adult expectations regarding youth" (207). Schools want individuals to follow rules, to be disciplined, to work hard, and to fit in; sports accomplish these goals.

Not only do schools insist that athletes behave a certain way during practice and games, but they also strictly monitor the behavior of the athletes in other situations. The athletes must conform to the school's norms in dress, speech, demeanor, and grades if they want to continue to participate. In this way, school administrators use athletes as models of decorum. If other people in the school and community admire athletes, then athletes serve to preserve the community and school norms.

Media

The movies, television, newspapers, and magazines also serve to reinforce the system. There is clearly a conservative bias among the various corporations involved because their financial success depends on whether the public will buy their product and whether advertisers will use their vehicles. As Michael Parenti (1986) argues:

> [A]long with products, the corporations sell themselves. By the 1970s, for the first time since the Great Depression, the legitimacy of big business was being called into question by large sectors of the public. Enduring inflation, unemployment, and a decline in real wages, the American people became increasingly skeptical about the blessings of the corporate economy. In response, corporations intensified their efforts at the kind of "advocacy advertising," designed to sell the entire capitalist system rather than just one of its products. . . . *Today, one-third of all corporate advertising is directed at influencing the public on political and ideological issues as opposed to pushing consumer goods.* (That portion is tax deductible as a "business expense," like all other advertising costs.) Led by the oil, chemical, and steel companies, big business fills the airwaves and printed media with celebrations of the "free market," and warnings of the baneful effects of government regulation. (67)

That the media reinforce the values and norms of society is seen in newspaper editorials that extol certain people and events while decrying others and in stories under the caption, "It Could Only Have Happened in America." Soap operas also accomplish this because they are stories involving moral dilemmas, with virtue winning out. Television, in particular, has had a significant impact on the values of people in the United States. The average two- to eleven-year-old child watches television twenty-five hours a week. What are the consistent messages that television emits?

Parenti's book *Make-Believe Media: The Politics of Entertainment* (1992) demonstrates that films and television programs promote images and ideologies that support imperialism, capitalism, racism, sexism, militarism, authoritarian violence, vigilantism, and anti-working-class attitudes. More specifically, he argues that media dramas teach us the following:

- Individual effort is preferable to collective action.
- Free enterprise is the best economic system in the world.
- Private monetary gain is a central and worthy objective of life.

140

PART TWO
The Individual
in Society:
Society in
the Individual

- Affluent professionals are more interesting than blue-collar or ordinary service workers.
- All Americans are equal, but some (the underprivileged) must prove themselves worthy of equality.
- Women and ethnic minorities are not really as capable, effective, or interesting as White males.
- The police and everyone else should be given a freer hand in combating the large criminal element in the United States, using generous applications of force and violence without too much attention to constitutional rights.
- The ills of society are caused by individual malefactors and not by anything in the socioeconomic system.
- There are some unworthy people in our established institutions, but they usually are dealt with and eventually are deprived of their positions of responsibility.
- United States military force is directed only toward laudable goals, although individuals in the military may sometimes abuse their power.
- Western industrial and military might, especially that of the United States, has been a civilizing force for the benefit of "backward" peoples throughout the Third World.
- The United States and the entire West have long been threatened from abroad by foreign aggressors, such as Russians, communist terrorists, and swarthy hordes of savages, and at home by un-American subversives and conspirators. These threats can be eradicated by vigilant counterintelligence and by sufficient doses of force and violence (Parenti, 1992:2–3).

In short, the media shape how we evaluate ourselves and other people. Just as important, they affect directly the way viewers or readers perceive and interpret events. The media, therefore, have tremendous power to influence us to accept or question the system. Although the media do investigative reporting and occasionally question the system, the overall impact of the media is supportive of it.

Government

Governmental leaders devote a great deal of energy toward ideological social control. One governmental effort is to convince the public that capitalism is good and socialism is bad. That the government (and schools) have been successful is seen in the powerful argument by noted theologian Harvey Cox that in the United States the market is believed to have the same characteristics as God—omnipotent (all-powerful), omniscient (all-knowing), and omnipresent (existing everywhere) (Cox, 1999).

Government ideological control occurs in political speeches, books, and legislation. Sometimes state legislatures have tried to control the ideological content in schools by requiring certain course content (patriotism, pro-capitalism, anticommunism). Another example of ideological control is seen in government agencies such as the Defense Department and the Departments of Agriculture, Commerce, and Education. Each department maintains active public relations programs that spend millions of dollars to convince the public of their views.

The public can also be manipulated by being convinced that their security is threatened by an enemy. The efforts by President George W. Bush and the members of his cabinet following the terrorist attack on September 11, 2001, to convince the public that we must come together against the terrorist threat, that we must spend more to enhance our security, and to inform us who the enemies were (Osama bin Laden and his al Qaeda network, Saddam Hussein of Iraq, and more obliquely, the threat by rogue nations such as Iran and North Korea) were a prime example of this manipulation.

Perhaps the most obvious way that government officials attempt to shape public opinion is through speeches, especially on television. The president can request free prime-time television to speak to the public. These efforts are typically intended to unite the people against an enemy (inflation, the national debt, the energy crisis, Osama bin Laden, Saddam Hussein).

We have described how the various agents of ideological social control operate. Perhaps the best evidence that they are successful is that few of the downtrodden in U.S. society question the legitimacy of the political and economic system. Karl Marx theorized that the have-nots in a capitalist society (the poor, the minority-group members, the workers) would eventually feel their common oppression and unite to overthrow the owners of capital. That this has not happened in the United States on a large scale is due, mainly, to the success of the various agents of ideological social control (Parenti, Michael, 1978).

Agents of Direct Social Control

Direct social control refers to attempts to punish or neutralize (render powerless) organizations or individuals who deviate from society's norms. The deviant targets here are essentially four: the poor, the mentally ill, criminals, and political dissidents.

"So, does anyone else feel that their needs aren't being met?"

142

PART TWO
The Individual
in Society:
Society in
the Individual

This section is devoted to three agents of social control whose efforts are directed at these targets—social welfare, science and medicine, and the government.

Welfare

Piven and Cloward (1993), in their classic study of public welfare, argue that public assistance programs serve a social control function in times of mass unemployment by defusing social unrest. When large numbers of people are suddenly barred from their traditional occupations, the legitimacy of the system itself may be questioned. Crime, riots, looting, and social movements bent on changing the existing social and economic arrangements become more widespread. Under this threat, relief programs are initiated or expanded by the government. Piven and Cloward show how during the Great Depression, for example, the government remained aloof from the needs of the unemployed until there was a great surge of political disorder. The function of social welfare, then, is to defuse social unrest through direct intervention of the government. Added proof for Piven and Cloward's thesis is the contraction or even abolishment of public assistance programs when political stability is restored.*

The conditions of the early 2000s should provide an interesting test of Piven and Cloward's theory. Current trends indicate that the middle class is shrinking, that the gap between the haves and the have-nots is increasing (see Chapters 10, 11, and 13), and the 1996 welfare legislation has caused a drastic shrinkage in those receiving welfare, leaving many poor people poorer than before. As long as these increasing numbers of the deprived are docile, government programs to alleviate their suffering will be meager; but should the outrage of the oppressed be manifested in urban riots (for example, the 1992 Los Angeles riots), acts of terrorism by the disaffected (church burnings, lynchings of minorities), or in social movements aimed at political change, then, if Piven and Cloward are correct, government welfare programs to aid the poor will become more generous.

Science and Medicine

Practitioners and theoreticians in science and medicine (physicians, psychotherapists, geneticists, electrical engineers, and public health officials) have devised a number of techniques for shaping and controlling the behavior of nonconformists. In the words of Michael Parenti (1988):

> In their never-ending campaign to contain the class struggle and control behavior unacceptable to the existing order, authorities have moved beyond clubs, bullets,

---

*The second function of welfare mentioned by Piven and Cloward is more subtle (and fits more logically as an agent of ideological social control). Even in good times some people must live on welfare (the disabled). By having a category of people on welfare who live in wretched conditions and who are continually degraded, work is legitimized. Thus, the poor on welfare serve as an object lesson—keeping even those who work for low wages relatively satisfied with their lot. As Piven and Cloward (1971) conclude: "In sum, market values and market incentives are weakest at the bottom of the social order. To buttress weak market controls and ensure the availability of marginal labor, an outcast class—the dependent poor—is created by the relief system. This class, whose members are of no productive use, is not treated with indifference but with contempt. Its degradation at the hands of relief officials serves to celebrate the virtue of all work and deters actual or potential workers from seeking aid" (52).

and eavesdropping devices and are resorting to such things as electroshock, mind-destroying drugs, and psychosurgery. Since the established powers presume that the present social system is virtuous, then those who are prone to violent or disruptive behavior, or who show themselves to be manifestly disturbed about the conditions under which they live, must be suffering from inner malfunctions that can best be treated by various mind controls. Not only are political and social deviants defined as insane, but sanity itself has a political definition. The sane person is the obedient one who lives in peace and goes to war on cue from his leaders, is not too much troubled by the inhumanities committed against people, is capable of fitting into one of the mindless job slots of a profit-oriented hierarchical organization, and does not challenge the established rules and conventional wisdom. Since authorities accept the present politico-economic system as a good one, then anything that increases its ability to control dissident persons is also seen as good. (150–151)

Psychologists and psychotherapists are clearly agents of social control. Their goal is to aid people who do not follow the expectations of society. In other words, they attempt to treat people considered abnormal in order to make them normal. By focusing on the individual and his or her adjustment, mental health practitioners validate, enforce, and reinforce the established ways of society. The implicit assumption is that the individual is at fault and needs to change, not that society is the root cause of mental suffering.

More generally, the labeling of mental illness works as a system of social control. As Scarpitti and Andersen (1992) argue,

[T]hose who are labeled mentally ill are often the outgroups of society. In fact, labeling groups or individuals as mentally ill can work to contain social and political protest, if those who are disturbed are institutionalized, treated with drug therapy, or otherwise incapacitated. The historic identification of homosexuality with mental illness is a case in point. As long as gay men and women were defined as "sick," then it was less likely that other people in society would challenge the heterosexual privilege characteristic of economic, social, and political institutions. (384)

In short, this application of the medical model to individuals exhibiting certain behaviors personalizes the problem and deflects attention away from the social sources for the behaviors. Another application of the medical model is the control of violent people. The National Institute of Mental Health has considered a National Violence Initiative. Under this plan, researchers would use genetic and biochemical indicators to identify potentially violent children as young as five for biological and behavioral interventions such as drug therapy or even possibly psychosurgery (Horne, 1992–1993). This proposal specifically rejected any examination of social and economic factors such as racism, poverty, or unemployment.

Psychosurgery is another method with important implications for social control. As with drug therapy or psychotherapy, individuals who are considered abnormal are treated to correct the problem, but this time through brain surgery. With modern techniques, surgeons can operate on localized portions of the brain that govern particular behaviors (for example, sex, aggression, appetite, or fear).

Eugenics, the improvement of the human race through control of hereditary factors, is an ultimate form of social control. That is, if society decided that certain types of people should be sterilized, then those types would be eliminated in a generation. This practice was tried in Nazi Germany, where Jews, gypsies, and the so-called

144

PART TWO
The Individual
in Society:
Society in
the Individual

feebleminded were sterilized. It has also occurred in the United States. From 1907 through the mid-1970s, for instance, more than 70,000 people in thirty states were legally sterilized for perceived abnormalities such as drunkenness, criminality, sexual perversion, and feeblemindedness. The Supreme Court ruled that this practice was constitutional in 1924 and it remains the law of the land today (Sinderbrand, 2005).

The potential for eugenics will progress dramatically in the near future through biotechnology. Scientists are now capable of manipulating, recombining, and reorganizing living tissue into new forms and shapes. Cells have been fused from different species. Genes have been isolated and mapped—that is, the genes responsible for various physical traits have been located at specific sites on specific chromosomes. Moreover, scientists have been able to change the heredity of a cell. These breakthroughs have positive consequences. Prospective parents, for example, can have the genes of their unborn fetus checked for abnormalities. If a hereditary disorder such as hemophilia or sickle-cell anemia is found, the fetus could be aborted or the genetic makeup of the fetus could be altered before birth.

Even though this new technology has useful applications, it raises some serious questions. Will parents, doctors, and scientists correct only genetic defects, or will they intervene to make genetic improvements? Should dark skin be eliminated? Should aggression be omitted from the behavior traits of future people? If so, passive subjects could be totally controlled without fear of revolution. The social-political-economic system, whatever its composition, would go unchallenged, and society would be tranquil. The logic of genetic engineering, while positive in the sense of ridding future generations of hereditary diseases, is frightening in its basic assumption that problems arise, not from the faults of society, but from the genes of individuals in society. The Human Genome Project raises a number of fears regarding eugenics and social control.

Similar questions can be raised about the other techniques in this section. The creativity of the scientific community has presented the powerful people in society with unusually effective means to enforce conformity. Aggressive individuals in schools, prisons, mental hospitals, and in society can be anesthetized. But what is aggressive behavior? What is violence?

In 1983, the Justice Department proposed a test of 2,000 boys ages nine to twelve who had already had their first contact with the police. The goal of this test was to identify the chronic offender. Proponents of the proposal argued that chronic offenders have certain characteristics that the tests could identify—such as left-handedness, dry or sweaty palms, below-normal reactions to noise and shocks, high levels of the male hormone testosterone, abnormalities in alpha waves emitted by their brains, and physical anomalies such as malformed ears, a high steepled palate, a furrowed tongue, curved fingers, and a wide gap between the first and second toes (reported in Anderson, 1983).

Such a plan, if implemented, has frightening implications. Would these tests actually separate chronic offenders from one-time offenders? Is criminal behavior actually related to the formation of one's tongue, ears, and toes? And, if the tests do identify potential problem people accurately, should such people be punished for their potential behaviors rather than for their actual behaviors? Most significant, what are the negative effects of being labeled a chronic offender? Such a label would doubtless have a self-fulfilling prophecy effect, as people who interact with labeled people do so on the basis of that label.

Government

The government, as the legitimate holder of power in society, is directly involved in the control of its residents. A primary objective of the government is to provide for the welfare of its citizens. This includes protection of their lives and property. It requires, further, that order be maintained within the society. There is a clear mandate, then, for the government to apprehend and punish criminals. In 2002, at years' end, the various levels of government had incarcerated about 2.17 million people in prison, jail, or juvenile facilities. Millions more were under the jurisdiction of the criminal justice system, either on probation or parole. The number of U.S. prison inmates amounts to 25 percent of the world's prisoners. The incarceration rate in the United States is six times higher than in Canada, England, and France, seven times higher than in Switzerland and Holland, and ten times higher than in Sweden and Finland (Street, 2001). For an example of a society tightly controlled by its government, see the panel titled "A Closer Look: The Iron Fist in the Land of Order."

Less clear, however, is the legitimacy of a government in a democracy to stifle dissent, which is done in the interests of preserving order. The U.S. heritage, best summed up in the Declaration of Independence, provides a clear rationale for dissent:

> Governments are instituted among Men, deriving their just powers from the consent of the governed. That whenever any Form of Government becomes destructive of these ends, it is the Right of the People to alter or to abolish it, and to institute new Government, laying its foundation on such principles and organizing its powers in such form, as to them shall seem most likely to effect their Safety and Happiness.

The U.S. government, then, is faced with a dilemma. American tradition and values affirm that dissent is appropriate. Two facts of political life work against this principle, however. First, for social order to prevail, a society needs to ensure that existing power relationships are maintained over time (otherwise, anarchy will result). Second, the well-off in society benefit from the existing power arrangements, so they use their influence (which is considerable, as noted in Chapter 14) to encourage the repression of challenges to the government. The evidence is strong that the U.S. government has opted for repression of dissent. Let us examine this evidence.

To begin, we must peruse the processes of law enactment and law enforcement. These two processes are both directly related to political authority. Some level of government determines what the law will be (that is, which behaviors are to be allowed and which ones are to be forbidden). The agents of political authorities then apprehend and punish violators. Clearly, the law is employed to control behaviors that might otherwise endanger the general welfare (for example, the crimes of murder, rape, and theft). But laws also promote certain points of view at the expense of others (for example, the majority instead of the minority, or the status quo rather than change). With this in mind, let us turn to the two schools of thought on the function of the law—the prevailing liberal view and the Marxist interpretation (Quinney, 1970:18–25; 1973).

The dominant view in U.S. society is based on liberal democratic theory and is congruent with the order model. The state exists to maintain order and stability. Law is a body of rules enacted by representatives of the people in the interests of the people. The state and law, therefore, are essentially neutral, dispensing rewards and punishments without bias. A basic assumption of this view is that the political system

The Iron Fist in the Land of Order

Singapore is a small country (244 square miles) with 2,700,000 residents. The population is culturally diverse (76 percent Chinese, 15 percent Malay, and 7 percent Indian). It is a prosperous nation known for its efficiency and cleanliness. There is a very strict security system, with the largest army per capita in Asia, a relatively large police force, and the Internal Security Department. Since Singapore gained its independence from Great Britain in 1959, it has been ruled by Lee Kuan Yew and now Goh Chok Tong "in much the way a strict father might rear what he feels are errant children" (Sesser, 1992:37). The authoritarian government has many rules for its citizens and strict punishments if they are broken. Some examples:

- There is censorship, with magazines such as *Cosmopolitan* and *Playboy* banned, as well as the monitoring and censorship of newspapers, books, movies, music, and television.
- Anyone caught littering must pay a fine of up to $620 and undergo counseling.
- Eating or drinking on the subway costs the equivalent of $310.
- Smoking is illegal in public buses, elevators, restaurants, theaters, cinemas, and government offices ($300 fine).
- Videogame centers are outlawed because they allegedly harm children.
- Driving without a seatbelt costs $120.
- Jaywalkers are fined $30.
- Beginning in 1988, a law required the flushing of toilets and urinals, with violators fined.
- At the end of 1991, the government banned the import of chewing gum because it is a "perennial nuisance" in public facilities.
- Trucks and commercial vans are required to install a yellow roof light that flashes when the vehicle exceeds the speed limit.

- Cameras mounted above stop lights at intersections photograph the license plates of cars that pass through a red light, with the drivers receiving bills for the offense in the mail (fine of $150).
- Illegal immigrants, burglars, and car thieves are subject to imprisonment and lashes with a cane. As described by the Bar Association, "When the rattan hits the bared buttocks, the skin disintegrates, leaving initially a white line and then a flow of blood. The victim must lie on his front for three weeks to a month because the buttocks are so sore" (reported in Sesser, 1992:56).
- Anyone trafficking a controlled drug receives ten years in prison and five lashes with a cane. Anyone caught with more than fifteen grams of heroin or thirty grams of morphine is hanged.
- During the Vietnam War, when long hair was believed to be linked to drug use and political dissent, Singapore police would detain long-haired male youths and give them involuntary haircuts. There is still a regulation that hair must not reach below an ordinary shirt collar.
- Except for social gatherings, assemblies of more than five people in public must have police permission.
- In 1990, Parliament passed the Religious Harmony Act, which gave the government the power to arrest religious workers who it believed were engaged in politics. This act barred judicial review of these cases (that is, the courts cannot rule on the government's actions).
- Renewal of appointments and tenure in the universities are refused to academics whose work deviates from government views.
- Political dissidents, as a condition for release from detention, must make a public confession.

is pluralistic—that is, made up of the existence of a number of interest groups of more-or-less equal power. The laws, then, reflect compromise and consensus among these various interest groups. In this way the interests of all people are protected.

Contrary to the prevailing view of law based on consensus for the common good is the view of the radical criminologists, which is based on conflict theory. The assumptions of this model are that (1) the state exists to serve the ruling class (the owners of large corporations and financial institutions), (2) the law and the legal system reflect and serve the needs of the ruling class, and (3) the interests of the ruling class are served by the law when domestic order prevails and challenges to changing the economic and political system are successfully thwarted. In other words, the law does not serve society as a whole, but the interests of the ruling class.

Closely related to the Marxian view of the role of law in capitalist societies is the interest group theory of Richard Quinney (1970:29–42). The essence of this theory is that a crime is behavior that conflicts with the interests of the segments of society that have the power to shape criminal policy: "Law is made by men, representing special interests, who have the power to translate their interests into public policy. Unlike the pluralist conception of politics, law does not represent a compromise of the diverse interests of society, but supports some interests at the expense of others" (Quinney, 1970:35).

Quinney's view is in the conflict-model tradition. Society is held together by some segments coercing other segments. Interest groups are unequal in power. The conflict among interest groups results in the powerful getting their way in determining public policy. Evidence for this position is seen in the successful efforts of certain interest groups to get favorable laws passed: the segregation laws imposed by Whites on Blacks, the repression of political dissidents whose goal is to transform society, and the passage of income tax laws that benefit the rich at the expense of wage earners.

Quinney's model makes a good deal of sense. The model is not universally applicable, however, because certain crimes—burglary, murder, and rape—would be regarded as crimes no matter which interest group was in power. A very important part of his theory that does fit almost universally is this proposition: "The probability that criminal definitions will be applied varies according to the extent to which the behaviors of the powerless conflict with the interests of the power segments" (Quinney, 1970:18).

The Repression of Dissent Prior to September 11, 2001. All governments are interested in maintaining the existing structure of power. Thus, the resources of the government are used to control political dissent.

Government agencies have a long history of surveillance of people in the United States. The pace quickened in the 1930s and increased further with the communist threat in the 1950s. The FBI's concern with internal security, for example, dates back to 1936, when President Franklin Roosevelt directed J. Edgar Hoover to investigate domestic communist and fascist organizations in the United States. In 1939, as World War II began in Europe, President Roosevelt issued a proclamation that the FBI would be in charge of investigating subversive activities, espionage, and sabotage, and he directed that all law enforcement offices should give the FBI any relevant information on suspected activities. These directives began a pattern followed by the FBI under the administrations of Presidents Harry Truman, Dwight Eisenhower, John Kennedy, Lyndon Johnson, Richard Nixon, Gerald Ford, Jimmy Carter, Ronald Reagan, George H. W. Bush, Bill Clinton, and George W. Bush.

Surveillance reached its peak during the height of antiwar and civil rights protests of the late 1960s and early 1970s. The scope of these abuses by the FBI and other government agencies such as the CIA, the National Security Agency, and the Internal Revenue Service is enormous. We focus here on what occurred under the FBI domestic

148

PART TWO
The Individual
in Society:
Society in
the Individual

surveillance program (COINTELPRO) begun in 1956. The mission of this program, according to FBI director J. Edgar Hoover, was to "neutralize the effectiveness of civil rights, New Left, anti-war and black liberation groups" (quoted in Rosen, Ruth, 2000:18). Thus, in the name of national security, the FBI "used forged documents, illegal break-ins, false charges, intercepted mailings, telephone taps, and undercover provocateurs and informants" to disrupt and subvert political dissent (Parenti, Michael, 2002:141). Consider a few examples of actions by the FBI against U.S. citizens:

- The FBI over the years conducted about 1,500 break-ins of foreign embassies and missions, mob hangouts, and the headquarters of such organizations as the Ku Klux Klan and the American Communist Party.
- Beginning in 1957, the FBI monitored the activities of civil rights leader Martin Luther King, Jr. The efforts included physical and photographic surveillance and the placement of electronic listening devices in his living quarters. Using the information gathered, the FBI actually made a serious effort to blackmail Dr. King into committing suicide.
- The FBI consistently monitored the activities of hundreds of U.S. writers, including Nelson Algren, Pearl S. Buck, Truman Capote, William Faulkner, Ernest Hemingway, Sinclair Lewis, Archibald MacLeish, Carl Sandburg, John Steinbeck, Thornton Wilder, Tennessee Williams, James Baldwin, and Thomas Wolfe (Robins, 1992). The question is, Why? Was it because the most acclaimed writers in the United States were part of a conspiracy or were individual lawbreakers, or was it, as has been suggested by Natalie Robins, "an unconscious effort on the FBI's part to control writers with a chilling effect that really adds up to intimidation?" (Robins, 1987:367)
- Beginning in late 1981, the FBI conducted a massive investigation of 1,330 organizations and individuals who were opposed to President Reagan's South American policy. The main target was the Committee in Solidarity with the People of El Salvador (CISPES). For just that one organization, "although no terrorist connection was found, hundreds of people were surveilled and photographed, their meetings infiltrated, their families, friends, and employers questioned, their trash and financial and telephone records examined" (Gentry, 1991:759; Weisbrot, 2002).
- An organization of progressive lawyers, the National Lawyers Guild, was under FBI surveillance for fifty years, yet was never found to engage in illegal activity (Parenti, Michael, 1995:153).
- During the 1970s, the FBI paid informants to infiltrate the Feminist Movement. Director J. Edgar Hoover told his agents that feminists "should be viewed as part of the enemy, a challenge to American values" (quoted in Rosen, Ruth, 2000:20).
- During the1960s and the 1970s, the FBI investigated 6,000 University of California, Berkeley, faculty members and top administrators and a number of students as Hoover wanted to squelch the student protest movement (Associated Press, 2002).

These examples are just for the FBI. Actually, the extent of the government's monitoring of the country's residents is much greater than these examples indicate. As examples, the Internal Revenue Service (IRS) monitored the activities of 99 political organizations and 11,539 individuals from 1969 to 1973; and the CIA opened and photographed nearly 250,000 first-class letters in the United States between 1953 and 1973.

Today, the techniques of surveillance by government agencies are much more sophisticated. A survey of 142 federal agencies by the Office of Technology found that one-fourth of them conducted some form of electronic surveillance. The Drug Enforcement Administration, for example, uses ten separate surveillance technologies, and the FBI uses seventeen. Moreover, various federal and state agencies use computerized record systems used for law enforcement, investigative, and intelligence purposes. Government officials in Washington, DC, plan to link a thousand cameras to watch streets, public schools, the DC Metro transit system, and federal facilities. The cameras will feed a command center where surveillance images are recorded and logged by the police, Secret Service, and FBI (Parenti, Christian, 2002). An early version of this surveillance network was used to monitor activists protesting NATO's fiftieth-anniversary summit in 1999 and the monitoring of crowds during mass protests against the joint World Bank and International Monetary Fund meeting in 2000. The FBI has an eavesdropping device called Carnivore that is an Internet wiretap. It is intended to sift through the Internet traffic of potential criminals, but the tool gives the FBI the ability to track not just the individual named in the court order, but also everyone who uses the same server at the Internet service provider (*USA Today*, 2000). The FBI has another computer-bugging device called a key logger system that registers every keystroke typed as it is made on a computer terminal's keyboard.

Another snooping operation, called Echelon, is conducted by the National Security Agency. Using a combination of spy satellites and listening stations, this system eavesdrops on just about every electronic communication that crosses a national border—phone calls, faxes, e-mail, radio signals—and domestic long-distance calls and local cell-phone calls. Supercomputers screen these communications for key words related to possible terrorist plots, drug smuggling, and political unrest. When target words are found, the intercept goes to humans for analysis. John E. Pike, a military analyst at the Federation of American Scientists, says, "Americans should know that every time they place an international call, the NSA is listening. Just get used to the fact—Big Brother is listening. . . . Surveillance technology is becoming so competent that snooping systems soon may outstrip the wildest dreams of George Orwell" (quoted in Port, 1999:110–111).

U.S. Army Military Police escort a detainee to his cell at Guantanamo Bay, Cuba. Alleged terrorists imprisoned there are denied the protections of the Bill of Rights given to other prisoners.

Government efforts, especially since the 1950s, have been aimed at squelching political protest, which counters the belief of Thomas Jefferson that protest is the hallmark of a democracy. The implication of government control of dissidents is that the government is beyond questioning—the dissidents are the problem. This problem became especially acute after September 11, 2001, when government officials labeled any questioning of their actions in the war on terrorism as unpatriotic.

Government Control after September 11, 2001. Because of the excesses of the FBI and other government agencies during the 1960s and 1970s, President Ford issued an executive order placing greater controls over these agencies. The FBI, for example, was required to show evidence of a crime before engaging in domestic spying. These limited constraints were lifted following the terrorist attacks on September 11, 2001. Given the choice between security and constitutional guarantees, government officials chose increased security. President George W. Bush signed executive orders and Congress passed the USA Patriot Act of 2001, which unleashed the FBI and other agencies to spy on speech, behaviors, and ideas of citizens and noncitizens. Under the new guidelines, FBI agents are able to monitor what you say in Web chatrooms, or in religious and political meetings, without any court order, without any evidence of a potential crime, even without approval from FBI headquarters. For the first time, the FBI also is able to use commercial databases to monitor the books you buy, the publications you subscribe to, where you travel, your credit profile, and a wide swath of other data (Ireland, 2002:12).

To further thwart terrorism, the new government guidelines also suspended many guarantees in the Constitution. The Fourteenth Amendment states, "Nor shall any state deprive any person of life, liberty, or property, without due process of law; nor deny to any person within its jurisdiction the equal protection of the laws." These laws, including the Bill of Rights, guarantee that those suspected of crimes must be informed of the charges against them, be able to confront their accusers, consult a lawyer, and have a speedy and open trial. But by labeling a suspected terrorist, whether a U.S. citizen or not, as a combatant, the government denies these guarantees to any person suspected of terrorist activity.

The Sixth Amendment provides that all citizens and noncitizens in this country are assured in all criminal prosecutions of a speedy and public trial by an impartial jury. This was overturned in an executive order by President Bush, which created military tribunals for all those noncitizens suspected of links to terrorism. Military trials, unlike those in the criminal justice system, are held in secret, before officers who are subordinate to officials bringing the charges, defendants are not able to choose their own lawyers, and, if two-thirds of the judges concur, those found guilty

"Look, you've got to accept some curtailment of your freedom in exchange for increased security."

can be executed. Under Bush's edict, he can substitute a military trial for a criminal trial for any noncitizen accused of terrorism. As one critic puts it: "We cannot know whether someone is a 'foreign terrorist' until those charges are proven in a fair proceeding. The military tribunals eliminate virtually every procedural check designed to protect the innocent and accurately identify the guilty" (Cole, David, 2001:5).

In direct violation of the right of habeas corpus, under the new guidelines aliens can be incarcerated, potentially indefinitely, on mere suspicion, without any hearing. Nine months after the terrorist attacks, some 1,200 aliens were incarcerated without specific charges.

Another executive order permits the monitoring of attorney-client conversations without a warrant. Before the terrorist attacks, these were considered privileged conversations.

The law allows secret searches of any home or business by federal agents, with no deadline to notify the owners or occupants that a search has taken place. This "sneak and peek" provision is contrary to the strong American tradition that the government must announce when it is entering a home. Another law, the Foreign Intelligence Surveillance Act, allows for the government to never reveal that is has conducted a search (*New York Times*, 2005).

Finally, the government made ethnic profiling explicit. The Justice Department instructed law enforcement agents across the United States to interrogate more than 5,000 immigrants based not on any evidence of terrorism but on only their age, gender, and country of origin (in other words, young adult Arab men).

One should remember that the government must exert some control over its population. There must be a minimum of control if the fabric of society is to remain

152

PART TWO
The Individual
in Society;
Society in
the Individual

intact, and, in times of crisis, such as the very real threat of terrorist acts, the need for vigilance and social control is magnified. But in exerting control, serious problems surface. First, there is the problem of the violation of individual rights as guaranteed in the Constitution. Under what conditions can these rights be violated by the government—if ever? A closely related problem can be framed in the form of a question: Who monitors the monitors? The problem inherent in this question is not only the tactics of the monitors but also the criteria used to assess who should be controlled or who should not. Finally, there is the ultimate irony that the United States is waging a war to defend its free society but in doing so it restricts those very freedoms it seeks to defend. As Salim Muwakkil (2002) points out: "Soon after 9/11, Bush said the people who perpetuated the terrorist murders hate America because of 'our freedoms.' After a few more executive orders and congressional capitulations, they won't have much left to hate" (18). This argument is countered by then Attorney General John Ashcroft who, when asked if his policies were jeopardizing the very liberties we are fighting for, said: "The security we are fighting for is not security for nothing. We're not destroying rights. We're protecting rights. I believe the American people deserve to have their rights protected, and that is the job of the Justice Department" (quoted in Klein, 2002:6).

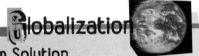

Terrorism: If It's a Muslim Problem, It Needs a Muslim Solution

Yesterday's bombings in downtown London [July 7, 2005] are profoundly disturbing. In part, that is because a bombing in our mother country and closest ally, England, is almost like a bombing in our own country. In part, it's because one assault may have involved a suicide bomber, bringing this terrible jihadist weapon into the heart of a major Western capital. That would be deeply troubling because open societies depend on trust—on trusting that the person sitting next to you on the bus or subway is not wearing dynamite.

The attacks are also deeply disturbing because when jihadist bombers take their madness into the heart of our open societies, our societies are never again quite as open. Indeed, we all just lost a little freedom yesterday.

But maybe the most important aspect of the London bombings is this: When jihadist-style bombings happen in Riyadh, that is a Muslim–Muslim problem. That is a police problem for Saudi Arabia. But when Al-Qaeda-like bombings come to the London Underground, that becomes a civilizational problem. Every Muslim living in a Western society suddenly becomes a suspect, becomes a potential walking bomb. And when that

happens, it means Western countries are going to be tempted to crack down even harder on their own Muslim populations.

That, too, is deeply troubling. The more Western societies—particularly the big European societies, which have much larger Muslim populations than America—look on their own Muslims with suspicion, the more internal tensions this creates, and the more alienated their already alienated Muslim youth become. This is exactly what Osama bin Laden dreamed of with 9/11: to create a great gulf between the Muslim world and the globalizing West.

So this is a critical moment. We must do all we can to limit the civilizational fallout from this bombing. But this is not going to be easy. Why? Because unlike after 9/11, there is no obvious, easy target to retaliate against for bombings like those in London. There are no obvious terrorist headquarters and training camps in Afghanistan that we can hit with cruise missiles. The Al Qaeda threat has metastasized and become franchised. It is no longer vertical, something that we can punch in the face. It is now horizontal, flat and widely distributed, operating through the Internet and tiny cells.

The ultimate social control issue after September 11 was how to control international terror. The solution chosen by the United States policymakers was to initiate war on Afghanistan (where al Queda leaders were located and Iraq where, it was argued, the real threat to U.S. security was to be found). This two-pronged war, however, has not stopped terrorist acts. The globalization panel offers a different tactic for solving this problem a day after the suicide bombers hit the mass transit trains in London.

Social Control in the Private Sector: Implications for Contemporary Social Life

In 1949, George Orwell wrote a novel about life as he envisioned it to be in the year 1984. The essence of his prediction was that every word, every thought, and every facial expression of citizens would be monitored by the government using sophisticated electronic devices. We have already noted the government's surveillance of private citizens, and with the new technology there is the very real possibility of realizing Orwell's prediction. The private sector helps to fulfill, at least in part, Orwell's

Terrorism: If It's a Muslim Problem, It Needs a Muslim Solution continued

Because there is no obvious target to retaliate against, and because there are not enough police to police every opening in an open society, either the Muslim world begins to really restrain, inhibit and denounce its own extremists—if it turns out that they are behind the London bombings—or the West is going to do it for them. And the West will do it in a rough, crude way—by simply shutting them out, denying them visas and making every Muslim in its midst guilty until proven innocent.

And because I think that would be a disaster, it is essential that the Muslim world wake up to the fact that it has a jihadist death cult in its midst. If it does not fight that death cult, that cancer, within its own body politic, it is going to infect Muslim-Western relations everywhere. Only the Muslim world can root out that death cult. It takes a village.

What do I mean? I mean that the greatest restraint on human behavior is never a policeman or a border guard. The greatest restraint on human behavior is what a culture and a religion deem shameful. It is what the village and its religious and political elders say is wrong or not allowed. Many people said Palestinian suicide bombing was the spontaneous reaction of frustrated Palestinian

youth. But when Palestinians decided that it was in their interest to have a cease-fire with Israel, those bombings stopped cold. The village said enough was enough.

The Muslim village has been derelict in condemning the madness of jihadist attacks. When Salman Rushdie wrote a controversial novel involving the prophet Muhammad, he was sentenced to death by the leader of Iran. To this day—to this day—no major Muslim cleric or religious body has ever issued a fatwa condemning Osama bin Laden.

Some Muslim leaders have taken up this challenge. This past week in Jordan, King Abdullah II hosted an impressive conference in Amman for moderate Muslim thinkers and clerics who want to take back their faith from those who have tried to hijack it. But this has to go further and wider.

The double-decker buses of London and the subways of Paris, as well as the covered markets of Riyadh, Bali and Cairo, will never be secure as long as the Muslim village and elders do not take on, delegitimize, condemn and isolate the extremists in their midst.

Source: Thomas L. Friedman, "If it's a Muslim Problem, It needs a Muslim Solution," *New York Times* (July 8, 2005). Copyright © 2005 by the New York Times Co. Reprinted with permission.

154

PART TWO
The Individual
in Society:
Society in
the Individual

prophecy, as well. Whenever we put a bank card in an ATM machine or drive through an E-ZPass lane on the highway, our whereabouts is registered. Customers in banks, 7-11s, and other stores are routinely photographed by surveillance cameras (an average of twenty times a day if you live or work in New York City). For example, the faces of the 72,000 attendees at the 2001 Super Bowl ("Snooper Bowl") were secretly scanned and checked against a database of potential troublemakers (Slevin, 2001). When travelers pass through an EntryScan detector, air jets dislodge microscopic particles from the skin and clothing. These particles are then analyzed for traces of explosives, chemicals, or drugs (Snider, 2001). Along the 100 miles of interstates linking Washington, DC, to its suburbs there are remote control cameras every mile or so capable of reading license plates or peering inside vehicles (there are similar systems in Chicago, Seattle, and Los Angeles) (Zuckerman, 2000). Whenever we purchase goods over the Internet or shop by mail order, our purchasing habits are recorded. Whenever we inform the postal service of a change of address, that fact is not only registered with the government but transferred to private data warehouses (money spent on building and maintaining these storehouses of information was estimated at more than $10 billion in 2000, up from $2 billion in 1995). There are over a thousand of these data warehouses.

The privacy of workers is also violated routinely. As of 2000, 81 percent of large companies required some form of drug testing, up from 21 percent in 1987 (Ehrenreich, 2000). Some employers require prospective employees to be given psychological tests that ask about, among other things, sexual behavior, religious beliefs, and political

a Closer Look

The Internet's Private Eye

The Internet is a digital revolution on a global scale, connecting computers, businesses, and people instantaneously around the world. "Few technologies have developed so quickly, captured our imagination so completely, or impacted our world as much as the Internet. In a few short years it has become the backbone of research, the lifeblood of business and finance, and the promise of education" (Rain, 1999:1). This online communication is transforming society in many important ways, affecting, among other things, commerce, the knowledge explosion, and even relationships. This transformation through Internet technology is, on one hand, terrific. It is important, useful, convenient, rapid, fascinating, and almost universally available. But there is an important downside—the Internet can be and is used as a surveillance tool—and thus is a significant and new way to invade the privacy of individuals. And, as such, it is a form of social control.

In the workplace some but not all employers use software to track their employees' use of the Internet at work. The assumption is that workers may be using company time to write personal messages on e-mail, track stocks, check sports scores, visit sexually explicit websites, or otherwise use computers to reduce their work productivity. Employers can even retrieve the results of an employee's search through Internet directories such as Yahoo! and Excite.

E-mail messages sent long ago are never lost; they can always be retrieved. Employers wishing to get rid of an employee can dredge up all his or her e-mail messages sent and received in search of a rationale for the dismissal. E-mail messages can be subpoenaed as evidence in court cases. In the recent Microsoft antitrust trial, for example, the prosecutors, ironically, used e-mail messages sent between Microsoft employees and even e-mail messages that were stored on the attitudes. Many large corporations regularly review health information before making hiring decisions. Workers using telephones and computers may find their work watched, measured, and analyzed in detail by supervisors. According to an American Management Association survey, 80 percent of corporations do one or more of the following: use video surveillance to monitor their employees, look at employees' e-mail, listen to employees' phone calls, or open employees' computer files (Parenti, Christian, 2001) (see the panel titled "A Closer Look: The Internet's Private Eye"). Workers can be issued cell phones equipped with a GPS (global positioning system) that pinpoints their locations to computers in the main office (Levy, 2004).

This computer-stored knowledge, especially from centralized and increasingly interrelated databases (credit bureaus, banks, marketing companies, stock brokerage firms, health insurers and other insurance companies, and governments), is a threat to privacy. Jeffrey Rosen, in his book *The Unwanted Gaze: The Destruction of Privacy in America* (2000), concludes that nothing is private (see also O'Harrow, 2005). Added to this loss of privacy is the danger that employers, banks, and government agencies will use databases to make decisions about our lives without our knowing about it. Most especially, if the government has access to these data, it can use modern technology to monitor closely the activities of those people who threaten it. And, as we have seen in this chapter, the government is strongly inclined to do so.

But the political dissident is not the only person whose freedoms are being threatened; all of us are threatened by the power of large organizations. As Jeffrey Rothfeder (1992) says:

The Internet's Private Eye continued

user's hard drive but never sent to support their case against Microsoft.

In effect, then, when we are alone in our cubicles using the Internet, we are being "watched by computers whenever we visit websites; by the mere act of 'browsing' (it sounds so passive!) [and by simply sending an e-mail message] we're going public in a way that was unimaginable a decade ago" (Quittner, 1997:30). Jane Bryant Quinn (2000) says that "it's risky to view, or say, anthing on the WEB that you're not willing to announce on live TV" (63). Simson Garfinkel, author of *Database Nation*, argues that we are seeing the dawn of absolute accountability. "Anything that can be known will be known, and it will be known to a greater degree of precision than was ever thought possible" (quoted in Quinn, 2000:63).

Consider, for example, a software tool for spying on employees. An advertisement by Spectorsoft in the June 2005 issue of *PC World* was titled "Record Everything Your Employees Do On the Internet." The software ("Spector CNE") on a company's network provides at the touch of a button an immediate and accurate record of every employee's:

- E-mails sent and received
- Chats/instant messages
- Keystrokes typed
- Websites visited
- Files downloaded
- Programs run

And, unlike many filtering and blocking tools, Spector CNE records everything an employee does on the Internet in exact visual detail, providing absolute proof of every activity.

156

PART TWO
The Individual
in Society:
Society in
the Individual

Increasingly people are at the whim of . . . large organizations—direct marketers, credit bureaus, the government, and the entire information economy—that view individuals as nothing but lifeless data floating like microscopic entities in vast electronic chambers, data that exist to be captured, examined, collated and sold, regardless of the individual's desire to choose what should be concealed and what should be made public. (30)

Our privacy is invaded even when we drive. About two-thirds of the new cars sold in the United States—and about 30 million cars already on the road—contain a 4-inch square device called an "event data recorder." This box constantly records information about the driver such as speed, acceleration, braking, and seat belt use. In the event of an accident, the police and insurance company can access the information, even without the owner's knowledge. This raises issues of privacy. Most important, who owns the information—the car owner, the government, the insurance company, or the car manufacturer? Even more serious, if this device is coupled with a wireless transmitter, it could record conversations in the car (Kiser, 2005).

The technology for the futuristic novel *1984* exists in drugs, human genome mapping, DNA data banks, psychosurgery, telecommunications, cyberspace, telemetry, and other high-tech devices. Currently, various arms of the government have used some of these techniques in their battle to fight crime, recidivism, political dissidence, terrorism, and other forms of nonconformity. But at what point does the government go too far in its control of nonconformity? The critical question, as stated earlier, is, Who monitors the monitors? One can easily envision a future when the government, faced with anarchy or political revolution, might justify ultimate control of its citizens—in the name of national security. If this were to take place, then, obviously, the freedoms rooted in more than 200 years of history will have been washed away.

So, too, is there a danger from the private sector. In 1984, George Orwell imagined a future in which a totalitarian state used spies, video surveillance, historical revisionism and control over the media to maintain its power. . . . Orwell thought the Communist system represented the ultimate threat to individual liberty. Over the next fifty years, we will see new kinds of threats to privacy that find their roots not in Communism but in capitalism, the free market, advanced technology and the unbridled exchange of electronic information. (Garfinkel, 2000a:11)

But are there situations when the rights of privacy ought to be curtailed for the good of society? Esteemed social scientist Amitai Etzioni argues that excessive protection of privacy in certain areas (for example, parents need to know whether one of their neighbors is a child molester, and there should be mandatory HIV testing of infants) undermines public safety and health. And, of course, the threat of terrorist acts requires government scrutiny of its citizens and noncitizens. Etzioni's communitarian philosophy holds that a good society seeks "a carefully crafted balance between individual rights and social responsibilities, between liberty and the common good" (Etzioni, 1999:5; see also Etzioni, 2000).

This raises the fundamental question: Are there situations in which society must/should place limits on individual behaviors to ensure safety, maintain clear air, preserve natural resources, and the like? But who decides what is the common good? And do we want an authoritarian government that controls us for this common good?

Social Control from the Order and Conflict Perspectives

A perennial question for many sociologists is: How is social order possible? Order theorists and conflict theorists answer this question quite differently. For order theorists, the answer to this question is that the vast majority of members of any social organization share a consensus on the norms, laws, and values. In premodern societies, social order occurs because the norms and values are shared and legitimized by deeply held religious authority. In modern complex societies, social order is maintained as citizens accept the legal order and the state, which are believed to serve the common good.

Conflict theorists, on the other hand, reject the assumption of normative consensus, arguing rather that social order is the result of government force or the threat of force, economic dominants using the law, the media, or other institutions to hold power over the relatively powerless.

Chapter Review

1. The socialization process through which the demands of the group become internalized is a fundamental mechanism of social control. This process is never complete, however; otherwise, we would be robots.

2. Ideological social control is the attempt to manipulate the consciousness of citizens so they accept the status quo and ruling ideology.

3. The agents of ideological social control are the family, education, religion, sport, and the media.

4. Direct social control refers to attempts to punish or neutralize organizations or individuals who deviate from society's norms, especially the poor, the mentally ill, criminals, and political dissidents.

5. According to Piven and Cloward, public assistance programs serve a direct social control function in times of mass unemployment by defusing social unrest.

6. Science and medicine provide the techniques for shaping and controlling the behavior of nonconformists. Drugs, psychosurgery, and genetic engineering are three such techniques.

7. The government is directly involved in the control of its citizens. It apprehends and punishes criminals. It is also involved in the suppression of dissent, which, while important for preserving order, runs counter to the U.S. democratic heritage. Following the terrorist attacks in 2001, the government instituted a number of new rules restricting freedoms.

8. Privacy is threatened by the private sector as personal information on purchases, websites visited, and demographics is stored in huge databases. Employers can invade the personal space of employees through surveillance, intercepting e-mail messages, and psychological testing.

9. Order theorists argue that social order results from a shared consensus on the norms, laws, and values. In modern complex societies, citizens accept the legal order and the state because they are believed to serve the common good. In this view, the state and the law are neutral, dispensing rewards and punishments without bias. Conflict theorists, however, believe that the state and the law (as well as the other institutions) exist to serve the ruling class. Squelching political dissent, therefore, benefits the powerful.

Key Terms

Social control   Direct social control
Ideological social control   Eugenics

Study Questions

1. How do order and conflict theorists differ in their interpretation of the role of sport and social control?
2. What is the relationship of ideological social control to what we learned about socialization in the previous chapter?
3. What is Piven and Cloward's thesis concerning the social control function of welfare assistance programs?
4. Make the argument, as *Consumer Reports* (2002) did, that biometrics, automated identification gadgetry such as iris scans, thumbprints, hand maps, and other computer technologies may make us safer, but they also make us more vulnerable at the same time.
5. How do order theorists and conflict theorists differ in their views of the state and the law?

For Further Reading

Ideological Social Control

Martin Carnoy, *Education as Cultural Imperialism* (New York: Longman, 1974).

Jules Henry, *Culture against Man* (New York: Random House, 1963).

Donald B. Kraybill, *Our Star-Spangled Faith* (Scottsdale, PA: Herald Press, 1976).

James W. Loewen, *Lies My Teacher Told Me: Everything Your American History Textbook Got Wrong* (New York: Simon & Schuster, 1995).

Michael Parenti, *Inventing Reality: The Politics of the News Media*, 2nd ed. (New York: St. Martin's Press, 1993).

Michael Parenti, *Make-Believe Media: The Politics of Entertainment* (New York: St. Martin's Press, 1992).

Direct Social Control

Daniel Burton-Rose (ed.), *The Celling of America: An Inside Look at the U.S. Prison Industry* (Monroe, ME: Common Courage Press, 1998).

Ward Churchill and Jim Vander Wall, *Agents of Repression: The FBI's Secret Wars against the Black Panther Party and the American Indian Movement* (Boston: South End Press, 1988).

Steven R. Donziger (ed.), *The Real War on Crime: The Report of the National Criminal Justice Commission* (New York: HarperPerennial, 1996).

Amitai Etzioni, *The Limits of Privacy* (New York: Basic Books, 1999).

Jerome G. Miller, *Search and Destroy: African-American Males in the Criminal Justice System* (New York: Cambridge University Press, 1996).

Robert O'Harrow, Jr., *No Place to Hide* (New York: Free Press, 2005).

Frances Fox Piven and Richard A. Cloward, *The Breaking of the American Social Compact* (New York: New Press, 1997).

Frances Fox Piven and Richard A. Cloward, *Regulating the Poor: The Functions of Public Welfare*, updated ed. (New York: Random House, 1993).

Richard Quinney, *Critique of Legal Order: Crime Control in Capitalist Society* (Boston: Little, Brown, 1973).

George Ritzer, *Expressing America: A Critique of the Global Credit Card Society* (Thousand Oaks, CA: Pine Forge Press, 1995).

B. F. Skinner, *Beyond Freedom and Dignity* (New York: Knopf, 1972).

Thomas Szasz, *The Manufacture of Madness* (New York: Harper & Row, 1970).

Web Resources

http://www.eugenicsarchive.org/html/eugenics/agreement.html

The Eugenics Archive website has information on the history of eugenics in America. The site contains textual information, as well as reports, charts, articles, and pedigrees made by the scientists involved with eugenics.

http://www.fbi.gov/

The Federal Bureau of Investigation has information on arrests and crime.

http://www.projectfreedom.cng1.com/part_6.html

Project Freedom explores the issue of government and how it serves as social control.

http://www.bop.gov/

The Federal Bureau of Prisons contains information on inmates and prisons. Race and gender makeup in the prison and other quick facts are available.

The previous three chapters analyzed the ways in which human beings, as members of society, are constrained to conform. We have seen how society is not only outside us, coercing us to conform, but also inside us, making us want to behave in the culturally prescribed ways. But despite these powerful forces, people deviate from the norms. These acts and actors are the subjects of this chapter. Who are the deviants in U.S. society? There is considerable evidence that most of us at one time or another break the laws. For example:

- Surveys by the Internal Revenue Service consistently find that three out of ten people cheat on their income taxes. This does not include the monies received from the selling of goods or services for cash and tips received that go unreported to the government. An estimated 25 percent of the total labor force does not report all or part of its income from these otherwise legal practices.
- Otherwise law-abiding citizens routinely copy computer software, videos, and music and photocopy copyrighted sheet music, even though these activities are against the law.
- Employees embezzle and pilfer an estimated $10 billion from their employers. Time theft by employees (for example, faked illnesses, excessive breaks, and long lunches) costs U.S. business as much as $200 billion annually.
- Theft by guests costs U.S. hotels and motels more than $100 million annually (cited in Yancey, 1999).
- About 75 percent of high school students admit to "serious test cheating" (*U.S. News & World Report*, 2002).
- More than four out of ten job applicants misrepresent their education or employment history on their resumes (cited in Armour, 2002).
- Marijuana is the most commonly used illegal substance in the United States, and may be the country's largest cash crop, with annual harvests valued at anywhere between $10 billion and $33 billion. The Justice Department's Drug Enforcement Agency (DEA) estimates the number of commercial growers at between 90,000 and 150,000, with another million people growing marijuana for their personal use. In addition, 45.7 percent of twelfth graders in 2004 admitted to marijuana use at least once in their lifetime (National Institute on Drug Abuse, 2005).

Kelly Eitzen Smith, University of Arizona, is a co-author of this chapter.

162

PART TWO
The Individual
in Society:
Society in
the Individual

- The Internet has provided a venue for sexually deviant material to be disseminated widely. Some statistics show that 40 million adults regularly visit Internet pornographic sites; there are approximately 68 million pornographic search engine requests daily and 1.5 billion pornographic downloads per month. Furthermore, there are over 100,000 websites offering illegal child pornography, and 20 percent of youth have received sexual solicitations in chat rooms (*Internet Filter Review*, 2005).

These illustrations indicate that many of us are guilty of cheating, stealing, and other behaviors clearly considered wrong. But are those of us who commit these illegal or immoral acts deviant?

Deviance is behavior that does not conform to social expectations. It violates the rules of a group (custom, law, role, or moral code). Deviance, then, *is socially created* (Becker, 1963:8–9). Social organizations create right and wrong by originating norms, the infraction of which constitutes deviance. This means that nothing inherent in a particular act makes it deviant. Whether an act is deviant depends on how other people react to it. As Kai Erikson (1966) puts it, "Deviance is not a property inherent in any particular kind of behavior; it is a property *conferred upon* that behavior by the people who come into direct or indirect contact with it" (6). This means that *deviance is a relative, not an absolute, notion*. Evidence for this is found in two sources: inconsistencies among societies as to what is deviance, and inconsistencies in the labeling of behavior as deviant within a single society.

There is abundant anthropological evidence that what is right or wrong varies from society to society. Consider the following:

- The Ila of Africa encourage sexual promiscuity among their adolescents. After age ten, girls are given houses of their own during harvest time, where they can play at being a wife with boys of their choice. In contrast, the Tepoztlan Indians of Mexico do not allow girls to speak to or encourage a boy after the time of the girl's first menstruation.
- Egyptian royalty were required to marry their siblings, whereas this was prohibited as incestuous and sinful for European royalty.
- Young men of certain Native American tribes are expected, after fasting, to have a vision. This vision is interpreted by the tribal elders to decide that young man's future occupation and status in the tribe. If an Anglo youth were to tell his elders that he had such a vision, it would likely be considered a hallucination.
- Experts estimate the average age of weaning a child from breast-feeding is around age three worldwide, and in some developing countries it is not unusual to breast-feed until age five or later. In contrast, in the United States more than two-thirds of mothers breast-feed for six months or less, and mothers who choose to breast-feed for longer than a year or more are often stigmatized. For example, in July 2000, in Champaign, Illinois, a five-year-old boy was removed from his mother's custody when a babysitter found out that he was still being breast-fed (Corbett, 2001).

Differential treatment for similar behavior by different categories of people within a single society provides further proof that deviance is not a property of the act but depends on the reaction of the particular audience. Several examples illustrate that it is not the act but the situation that determines whether behavior is interpreted by others as deviant:

- Sexual intercourse between consenting adults is not deviant except when one partner pays another for his or her services, and then the deviant is the recipient of the money, not the giver. Participants in pornographic films are paid for engaging in explicit sexual activities but they are not considered prostitutes.
- Murder is a deviant act, but the killing of an enemy during wartime is rewarded with praise and medals.
- Marriage is applauded and encouraged . . . but is considered by many to be deviant when two consenting adults of the same sex desire marriage.
- A father would be considered a deviant if he removed his bathing suit at a public beach, but his two-year-old son could do this with impunity. The father can smoke a cigar and drink a martini every night, but if his young son did, the boy (and his parents, if they permitted the act) would be considered deviant (Weinstein and Weinstein, 1974:271).
- Smoking tobacco, long considered appropriate for adult males and only in recent decades for females, is now considered deviant by more and more people.

In a heterogeneous society there is often widespread disagreement on what the rules are and therefore on what constitutes deviance. For example, there are differences over sexual activities between consenting adults (regardless of sex or marital status); over smoking marijuana and drinking alcohol; over public nudism and pornography; over remaining seated during the national anthem; and refusing to fight in a war.

This point leads to a further insight about deviance: *The majority determines who is a deviant.* If most people believe that Iraqis are the enemy, then bombing their villages is appropriate and refusing to do so is deviant. If most people believe there is a God you may talk to, then such a belief is not deviance (in fact, refusing to believe in God may be deviant). But if the majority is atheists, then those few who believe in God would be deviant and subject to ridicule, job discrimination, and treatment for mental problems.

Kai Erikson (1966) summarizes how deviance is a relative rather than an absolute notion in the following statement:

> Definitions of deviance vary widely as we range over the various classes found in a single society or across the various cultures into which mankind is divided, and it soon becomes apparent that there are no objective properties which all deviant acts can be said to share in common—even within the confines of a given group. *Behavior which qualifies one man for prison may qualify another for sainthood, since the quality of the act itself depends so much on the circumstances under which it was performed and the temper of the audience which witnessed it.* (5–6; italics added)

Durkheim said that by punishing the deviant publicly, society expresses its collective indignation and reaffirms its commitment to society's rules.

An insight of the order theorists is important to note. Deviance is an integral part of all healthy societies (Dentler and Erikson, 1959; Durkheim, 1958; 1960). Deviant

164

PART TWO
The Individual
in Society:
Society in
the Individual

behavior, according to Durkheim, actually has positive consequences for society because it gives nondeviants a sense of solidarity. By punishing the deviant, the group expresses its collective indignation and reaffirms its commitments to the rules:

> Crime brings together upright consciences and concentrates them. We have only to notice what happens, particularly in a small town, when some moral scandal has just been committed. They stop each other on the street, they visit each other, they seek to come together to talk of the event and to wax indignant in common. From all the similar expressions which are exchanged, for all the temper that gets itself expressed, there emerges a unique temper . . . which is everybody's without being anybody's in particular. That is the public temper. (Durkheim, 1960:102)

Durkheim believed that the true function of punishment was not the prevention of future crimes. He asserted, rather, that the basic function of punishment is to reassert the importance of the rule being violated. It is not that a murderer is caught and put in the electric chair to keep potential murderers in line. That argument assumes people to be more rational than they really are. Instead, the extreme punishment of a murderer reminds each of us that murder is wrong. In other words, the punishment of crimes serves to strengthen our belief as individuals and as members of a collectivity in the legitimacy of society's norms. This enhances the solidarity of society as we unite in opposition to the deviant.

Crime, seen from this view, has positive functions for society. In addition to reaffirming the legitimacy of the society, defining certain acts as crimes creates the boundaries for what is acceptable behavior in the society.

The conflict theorists have pointed out that all views of rule violations have political implications (Becker, 1963:4). When persons mistreat rule breakers, they are saying, in effect, that the norms are legitimate. Thus, the bias is conservative, serving to preserve the status quo, which includes the current distribution of power. The opposite view, that the norms of society are wrong and should be rejected, is also political. When people and groups flout the laws and customs (for example, the draft, racial segregation, and marijuana smoking), they not only are rejecting the status quo but also are questioning the legitimacy of those in power. As Edwin Schur (1980) argues: "[D]eviance issues are inherently political. They revolve around some people's assessments of other people's behavior. And power is a crucial factor in determining which and whose assessments gain an ascendancy. Deviance policies, likewise, affect the distribution of power and always have some broad political significance" (xi).

Traditional Theories for the Causes of Deviance

The Individual as the Source of Deviance

Biological, psychological, and even some sociological theories have assumed that the fundamental reason for deviance is a fatal flaw in certain people. From this perspective, the criminal, the dropout, the addict, and the schizophrenic have something "wrong" with them. These theories are deterministic, arguing that the individual ultimately has no choice but to be different.

Biological Theories. Biological explanations for deviance have focused on physiognomy (the determination of character by facial features), phrenology (the determination of mental abilities and character traits from the configuration of the skull), somatology (the determination of character by physique), genetic anomalies (for example, XYY chromosomes in males), and brain malfunctions. Some of these theories have been discredited, (as, for example, the theory of Caesare Lombroso (1835–1909) that criminals were physically different—with low foreheads, protruding ears, long arms, and hairy bodies. (These distinct characteristics suggested that criminals were throwbacks to an earlier stage of human development—closer to the ape stage than were nondeviants.) Other biological theories have shown a statistical link between certain physical characteristics and deviant behavior. Chances are, though, that when such a relationship is found, it also will be related to social factors. For example, the learning disability known as dyslexia is related to school failure, emotional disturbance, and juvenile delinquency. This disability is a brain malfunction in which visual signs are scrambled. Average skills in reading, spelling, and arithmetic are impossible to attain if the malady remains undiagnosed. Teachers and parents often are unaware that the child is dyslexic and assume, rather, that she or he is mentally challenged, lazy, or belligerent. The child (who actually may be very bright—Thomas Edison and Woodrow Wilson were dyslexic) finds school frustrating. Such a child is therefore much more likely than those not affected to be a troublemaker, to be alienated, to be either pushed out of school or to drop out and never reach full intellectual potential.

Similarly, XYY Syndrome (where a male is born with an extra Y chromosome) is another biological trait that has been unfairly linked to crime. In the 1960s and seventies, papers were published that indicated there was a slightly higher incarceration rate for XYY males, and the assumption was that the extra Y chromosome somehow caused aggressive behavior. However, later studies pointed to low intelligence and low socioeconomic status that placed XYY males at a higher risk of being caught committing crime (Nuffield Council on Bioethics, 2005).

Psychological Theories. These theories also consider the source of deviance to reside within the individual, but they differ from the biological theories in that they assume conditions of the mind or personality to be the fault. Deviant individuals, depending on the particular psychological theory, are psychopaths (asocial, aggressive, impulsive), resulting from a lack of affection during childhood, an Oedipal conflict, a psychosexual trauma, or another traumatic early life experience (Cohen, Albert, 1966:41–45). Using Freudian assumptions, the deviant is a person who has not developed an adequate *ego* to control deviant impulses (the *id*). Alternatively, deviance can result from a dominating *superego*. People with this condition are so repulsed by their own feelings (such as sexual fantasies or ambivalence toward parents and siblings) that they may commit deviant acts in order to receive the punishment they deserve. Freudians, therefore, place great stress on the relationship between children and their parents. The parents, in this view, can be too harsh, too lenient, or too inconsistent in their treatment of the child. Each situation leads to inadequately socialized children and immature, infantile behavior by adolescents and adults.

Because the fundamental assumption of the biological and psychological theories of deviance is that the fault lies within the individual, solutions are aimed at chang-

166

PART TWO
The Individual
in Society:
Society in
the Individual

ing the individual. Screening of the population for individuals with presumed flaws is considered the best preventive approach. Doctors could routinely determine which boys have the XYY chromosome pattern. Psychological testing in the schools could find out which students are unusually aggressive, guilt-ridden, or fantasy-oriented. Although the screening for potential problem people may make some sense (to detect dyslexics, for example), there are some fundamental problems with this type of solution. First, the screening devices likely will not be perfect, thereby mislabeling some people. Second, screening is based on the assumption that there is a direct link between certain characteristics and deviance. If a person is identified as a predeviant by these methods, the subsequent treatment of that individual, who has a new definition of self, would likely lead to a self-fulfilling prophecy and a false validation of the screening procedures, increasing their use and acceptability.

A related problem with these screening procedures is the tendency to overpredict. In one attempt to identify predelinquents, a panel of experts examined a sample of youths already in the early stages of troublemaking and made predictions regarding future delinquency. Approximately 60 percent of the cases were judged to be predelinquents. A follow-up twenty years later revealed, however, that less than one-third actually became involved in difficulties with the law (Powers and Witmer, 1951).

For people identified as potential deviants or who are actually deviants, the kinds-of-people theorists advocate solutions aimed at changing the individuals: drug therapy, electrical stimulation of the brain, electronic monitoring, surgery, operant conditioning, counseling, psychotherapy, probation with guidance of a psychiatric social worker, or incarceration. The assumption is clearly that deviants are troubled and sick people who must be changed to conform to the norms of society.

The Sociological Approach. A number of sociological theories are also kinds-of-people explanations for deviance. Instead of individual characteristics distinguishing the deviant from the nondeviant, these theories focus on differing objective social and economic conditions. These theories are based on the empirical observations that crime and mental illness rates, to name two forms of deviance, vary by social location—that is, by social class, ethnicity, race, place of residence, and sex: "From these gross differences, the sociologist infers that something beyond the intimacy of family surroundings is operative in the emergence of delinquent patterns; something in the cultural and social atmosphere apparent in certain sectors of society" (Matza, 1964a:17).

Let us look at some of these theories, which emphasize that certain social conditions are conducive to the internalization of values that encourage deviance.

Cultural Transmission. Edwin Sutherland's theory of differential association sought to explain why some people are criminals while others are not, even though both may share certain social characteristics, such as social class position (Sutherland and Cressey, 1966:81–82). Sutherland believed that through interaction, one learns to be a criminal. If our close associates are deviants, there is a strong probability that we will learn the techniques and the deviant values that make criminal acts possible: "The significant feature of Sutherland's theory is his claim that procriminal sentiments are acquired, as are all others, by association with other individuals in a process of social interaction. Criminal orientations do not, thus, stem from faulty metabolism, inadequate superego development, or even poverty" (Hartjen, 1974:51).

Societal Goals and Differential Opportunities. Robert Merton (1957) presented an explanation for why the lower classes disproportionately commit criminal acts. In Merton's view, societal values determine both what are the appropriate goals (success through the acquisition of wealth) and the approved means for achieving these goals. The problem, however, is that some people are denied access to the legitimate means of achieving these goals. The poor, especially those from certain racial and ethnic groups, in addition to the roadblocks presented by negative stereotypes, often receive a second-class education or must drop out of school prematurely because of financial exigencies, all of which effectively exclude them from high-paying and prestigious occupations. Because legitimate means to success are inaccessible to them, they often resort to certain forms of deviant behavior to attain success. Viewed from this perspective, deviance is a result of social structure and not the consequence of individual pathology. Reece McGee (1975) makes this point in his analysis of Merton's scheme:

> [T]he individuals are behaving as they have been taught by their societies. They are not sinful or weak individuals who choose to deviate. They are, in fact, doing what they have learned they are supposed to do in order to earn the rewards which their society purports to offer its members. But either because their positions in the social structure do not permit them access to the means through which to seek the rewards they have learned to want, or because the means do not in fact guarantee goal attainment, they become frustrated and experience loss of self-esteem. In a final attempt to do and be what they have been taught they must, they engage in what is called deviant behavior. Such behavior is simply an attempt to gain the same self-esteem which others are presumed to have and which the society has made it intolerable to be without. (211–212)

Although Merton's analysis provides many important insights, the emphasis is on the adjustments people make to the circumstances of society. Deviance is a property of people because they cannot adapt to the discrepancy between the goals and the means of society. The problem is that Merton accepts the U.S. success ethic. In the words of Doyle and Schindler (1974):

> What is missing is the perspective that the winner, firster, money mentality could be a pathology rather than a [positive] value in America, a pathology that so powerfully corrupts our economy, polity, and way of life that it precludes any possibility of a cohesive, healthy community. Certainly it is valid and worthwhile to explore the situation of the deprived in a success-oriented society, but it is also valid to question the viability of a social system with such a "value" at its core. The sociology of deviance has turned too quickly and too exclusively to hypotheses about "bad" people. The analysis of "bad" societies has been neglected. (2)

Subcultural Differences by Social Class. We explore the culture-of-poverty hypothesis in Chapter 9. (The **culture of poverty** is the view that the poor are qualitatively different in values and lifestyles from the rest of society and that these cultural differences explain their poverty.) Because it has special relevance for explaining differ-

168

PART TWO
The Individual
in Society:
Society in
the Individual

ential crime rates, we briefly characterize it here with that emphasis. The argument is that people, because of their social class position, differ in resources, power, and prestige and hence have different experiences, lifestyles, and ways of life. The lower-class culture has its own values, many of which run counter to the values of the middle and upper classes. A unique morality (a right action is one that works and can be gotten away with) and a unique set of criteria make a person successful in the lower-class community (Banfield, 1974; Miller, 1958).

Edward Banfield (1974) argues, for example, that lower-class individuals have a propensity toward criminal behavior. He asserts that a person in the lower class does not have a strong sense of morality and thus is not constrained by legal rules. These people, according to Banfield, have weak ego strength, a present-time orientation (i.e., they live for the moment rather than the future), a propensity for taking risks, and a willingness to inflict injury. Many scholars accept Banfield's assertions about the "lower-class culture," but there is strong evidence that it is incorrect (see Chapter 9). Even if Banfield's characterization of the lower-class propensity to crime is correct, the critical question is whether these differences are durable. Will a change in monetary status or peer groups make a difference because the individual has a dual value system—one that is a reaction to his or her deprived situation and one that is middle class? This is a key research question because the answer determines whether to attack the problem—at the individual or the societal level.

Kenneth Lay, Chief Executive Officer of Enron, testifies before Congress. We tend to assume crimes are usually committed by those in the lower social classes but the corporate scandals of 2002, led by Enron, revealed crimes by wealthy executives in U.S. corporations.

Also, this approach focuses on the presumed disproportionate deviance by those in the lower social classes. This ignores the facts about criminality (recall the facts at the beginning of this chapter regarding the number of citizens who cheat on their income taxes or resumes—acts committed by the middle and upper classes).

Most telling, consider also the criminality of individuals within major corporations revealed in the scandals involving Enron, Bristol-Myers-Squibb, and Worldcom, to name a few. In these cases, executives and their accountants "cooked the books" to make company profits seem much greater than they actually were and the value of their stocks increase. These crimes, of course, are crimes by economic elites, and thus cannot be explained by "lower-class culture."

The Blaming-the-Victim Critique

Although socialization theories focus on forces external to individuals that push them toward deviant behavior, they, like the biological and psychological theories, are kinds-of-people theories that find the fault within the individual. The deviant has an acquired trait—the internalization of values and beliefs favorable to deviance—that is social in origin. The problem is that this results in *blaming the victims*, as William Ryan (1976) forcefully argues:

> The new ideology attributes defect and inadequacy to the malignant nature of poverty, injustice, slum life, and racial difficulties. The stigma that marks the victim and accounts for his victimization is acquired stigma, a stigma of social, rather than genetic origin. But the stigma, the defect, the fatal difference—though derived in the past from environmental forces—is still located within the victim, inside his skin. With such an elegant formulation, the humanitarian can have it both ways. He can, all at the same time, concentrate his charitable interest on the defects of the victim, condemn the vague social and environmental stresses that produced the defect (some time ago), and ignore the continuing effect of victimizing social forces (right now). It is a brilliant ideology for justifying a perverse form of social action designed to change, not society, as one might expect, but rather society's victim. (7)

There are two ways to look at deviance—blaming the victim or blaming society. The fundamental difference between these two approaches is whether the problems emanate from the pathologies of individuals or because of the situation in which deviants are immersed. The answer is doubtless somewhere between these two extremes; but because the individual blamers have held sway, let us look carefully at the critique of this approach (Caplan and Nelson, 1973; Ryan, William, 1976).

We begin by considering some victims. One group of victims is composed of children in slum schools who are failures. Why do they fail? Victim blamers point to

"We find that all of us, as a society, are to blame, but only the defendant is guilty."

170

PART TWO
The Individual
in Society:
Society in
the Individual

the children's **cultural deprivation**.* They do not do well in school because their families speak a different dialect, because their parents are uneducated, because they have not been exposed to all the education experiences of middle-class children (for example, visits to the zoo, extensive travel, attendance at cultural events, exposure to books, exposure to correct English usage). In other words, the defect is in the children and their families. System blamers, however, look elsewhere for the sources of failure. They ask, What is there about the schools that make slum children more likely to fail? The answer for them is found in the irrelevant curriculum, the class-biased IQ tests, the tracking system, the overcrowded classrooms, the differential allocation of resources within the school district, and insensitive teachers whose low expectations for poor children comprise a prophecy that is continually fulfilled.

Another victim is the criminal. Why is the **recidivism** rate (reinvolvement in crime) of criminals so high? In a study of prisoners in fifteen different states, over two-thirds of released prisoners were re-arrested within three years (Bureau of Justice Statistics, 2002). The individual blamer would point to the faults of the individual criminals: their greed, feelings of aggression, weak impulse control, and lack of a conscience (superego). The system blamers' attention is directed to very different sources for this problem. They would look, rather, at the penal system, the employment situation for ex-criminals, and the schools. For example, studies have shown that 20 to 30 percent of inmates are functionally illiterate. This means they cannot meet minimum reading and writing demands in U.S. society, such as filling out job applications. Yet these people are expected to leave prison, find a job, and stay out of trouble. Because they are illiterate and ex-criminals, they face unemployment or at best the most menial jobs (for which there are low wages, no job security, and no fringe benefits). The system blamer would argue that these people are not to blame for their illiteracy, but rather that first the schools and later the penal institutions have failed to provide the minimum requirements for productive membership in society. Moreover, the lack of employment and the unwillingness of potential employers to train functional illiterates force many to return to crime in order to survive.

African Americans (and other racial minorities) constitute another set of victims in U.S. society. What accounts for the greater probability for Blacks than Whites to be failures in school, to be unemployed, and to be criminals? The individualistic approach places the blame on the Blacks themselves. They are culturally deprived, they have high rates of illegitimacy and a high proportion of transient males, and a relatively high proportion of Black families have a matriarchal structure. This approach neglects the pervasive effects of racism in the United States, which limits the opportunities for African Americans, provides them with a second-class education, renders them powerless to change the system through approved channels, and limits their opportunities.

---

*The term *cultural deprivation* is a loaded ethnocentric term. It implies that the culture of the group in question is not only deficient but also inferior. This label is applied by members of the majority to the culture of the minority group. Not only is it a malicious putting-down of the minority, but the concept itself also is patently false because no culture can be inferior to another; it is only different. The concept does remind us, however, that people can and do make invidious distinctions about cultures and subcultures. Furthermore, they act on these definitions as if they were true, resulting, often, in a self-fulfilling prophecy.

Why is there a strong tendency to place the blame for deviance on individuals rather than on the social system? The answer lies in the way that people tend to define deviance. Most people define deviance as behavior that deviates from the norms and standards of society. Because people do not ordinarily question the norms or the way things are done in society, they tend to question the exceptions. The system is not only taken for granted, but it also has, for most people, an aura of sacredness because of the traditions and customs behind it. Logically, then, the people who deviate are the source of trouble. The obvious question, then, is, Why do these people deviate from the norms? Because most people abide by society's norms, the deviation of the exceptions must be the result of some kind of unusual circumstance—accident, illness, personal defect, character flaw, or maladjustment (Ryan, William, 1976:10–18). The key to this approach, then, is that the flaw is within the deviant and not a function of societal arrangements.

The position taken in this debate has important consequences. Let us briefly examine the effects of interpreting social problems solely within a person-blame framework (Caplan and Nelson, 1973). First, this interpretation of social problems frees the government, the economy, the system of stratification, the system of justice, and the educational system from any blame. The established order is protected against criticism, thereby increasing the difficulty encountered in trying to change the dominant economic, social, and political institutions. A good example is found in the strategy of social scientists studying the origins of poverty. Because the person blamer studies the poor rather than the nonpoor, the system of inequality (buttressed by the tax laws, welfare rules, and employment practices) goes unchallenged. A related consequence of the person-blame approach, then, is that the relatively advantaged segments of society retain their advantages.

Not only is the established order protected from criticism by the person-blame approach, but the authorities also can control dissidents under the guise of being helpful. Caplan and Nelson (1973) provide an excellent illustration of this in the following quote:

> Normally, one would not expect the Government to cooperate with "problem groups" who oppose the system. But if a person-blame rather than system-blame action program can be negotiated, cooperation becomes possible. In this way, the problem-defining process remains in the control of the would-be benefactors, who provide "help" so long as their diagnosis goes unchallenged.
>
> In 1970, for example, while a group of American Indians still occupied Alcatraz Island in San Francisco Bay, a group of blacks took over Ellis Island in New York Harbor. Both groups attempted to take back lands no longer used by the Federal Government. The Government solved the Ellis Island problem by getting the blacks to help establish a drug-rehabilitation center on it. They solved the Alcatraz problem by forcibly removing the Indians. Had the Indians been willing to settle for an alcoholism-treatment center on Alcatraz, thereby acknowledging that what they need are remedies for their personal problems, we suspect the Government would have "cooperated" again. (104)

Another social control function of the person-blame approach is that troublesome individuals and groups are controlled in a publicly acceptable manner. Deviants, whether they be criminals or social protesters, are controlled by incarceration in prisons or mental hospitals, by drugs, or by other forms of therapy. In this

172

PART TWO
The Individual
in Society:
Society in
the Individual

manner, not only is blame directed at individuals and away from the system, but the problems (problem individuals) are in a sense also eliminated.

A related consequence is how the problem is to be treated. A person-blame approach demands a person-change treatment program. If the cause of delinquency, for example, is defined as the result of personal pathology, then the solution lies clearly in counseling, behavior modification, psychotherapy, drugs, or some other technique aimed at changing the individual deviant. Such an interpretation of social problems provides and legitimates the right to initiate person-change rather than system-change treatment programs. Under such a scheme, norms that are racist or sexist, for example, go unchallenged.

The person-blame ideology invites not only person-change treatment programs but also programs for person control. The typical result is that the overwhelming emphasis of government programs is on more police, courts, and prisons, rather than on changing criminogenic social conditions (that is, those that cause crime).

A final consequence of person-blame interpretations is that they reinforce social myths about the degree of control we have over our fate. Such interpretations provide justification for a form of **social Darwinism**—that is, a person's placement in the stratification system is a function of ability and effort. By this logic, the poor are poor because they are the dregs of society. In short, they deserve their fate, as do the successful in society. Thus, there is little sympathy for governmental programs to increase welfare to the poor.

We should recognize, however, that the contrasting position—the system-blame orientation—also has its dangers. First, it is only part of the truth. Social problems and deviance are highly complex phenomena that have both individual and systemic origins. Individuals, obviously, can be malicious and aggressive for purely psychological reasons. Perhaps only a psychologist can explain why a particular parent is a child abuser, or why a sniper shoots at cars passing on the freeway. Clearly, society needs to be protected from some individuals. Moreover, some people require particular forms of therapy, remedial help, or special programs on an individual basis if they are to participate in society. But much that is labeled deviant is the end product of social conditions.

A second danger in a dogmatic system-blame orientation is that it presents a rigidly deterministic explanation for social problems. Taken too far, this position views individuals as robots controlled totally by their social environment. A balanced view of people is needed, because human beings have autonomy most of the time to choose between alternative courses of action. This raises the related question as to the degree to which people are responsible for their behavior. An excessive system-blame approach absolves individuals from the responsibility for their actions. To take such a stance argues that society should never restrict deviants. This extreme view invites anarchy.

Despite the problems just noted, the system-blame approach is emphasized in this chapter. The rationale for this is, first, that the contrasting view (individual blame) is the prevailing view in U.S. society. Because average citizens, police personnel, legislators, judges, and social scientists tend to interpret social problems from an individualistic perspective, a balance is needed. Moreover, as noted earlier in this section, to hold a strict person-blame perspective has many negative consequences, and citizens must realize the effects of their ideology.

A second basis for the use of the society-blaming perspective is that the subject matter of sociology is not the individual, who is the special province of psychology, but society. If sociologists do not emphasize the social determinants of behavior, and if they do not make a critical analysis of the social structure, then who will? As noted in Chapter 1, an important ingredient of the sociological perspective is the development of a critical stance toward societal arrangements. The job of the sociologist is to look behind the facade to determine the positive and negative consequences of societal arrangements. The persistent question is, Who benefits under these arrangements and who does not? This is why there should be such a close fit between the sociological approach and the society-blaming perspective. Unfortunately, this has not always been the case.

Society as the Source of Deviance

We have seen that the traditional explanations for deviance, whether biological, psychological, or sociological, have located the source of deviance in individual deviants, their families, or their immediate social settings. The basic assumption of these theories is that because deviants do not fit in society, something is wrong with them. This section provides an antidote to the medical analogy implicit in those theories by focusing instead on two theories that place the blame for deviance on the role of society—labeling theory and conflict theory.

Labeling Theory

All the explanations for deviance described so far assume that deviants differ from nondeviants in behavior, attitude, and motivation. This assumption is buttressed by the commonly held belief that deviance is the actions of a few people who are either criminals, insane, or both. In reality, however, most people break the rules of society at one time or another. The evidence is that members of all social classes commit thefts and assaults and use illegal drugs. Summarizing a number of studies on the relationship between socioeconomic class and crime, Travis Hirschi (1969) says, "While the prisons bulge with the socioeconomic dregs of society, careful quantitative research shows again and again that the relation between socioeconomic status and the commission of delinquent acts is small, or nonexistent" (66).

These studies do not mesh with our perceptions and the apparent facts. Crime statistics do show that the lower classes are more likely to be criminals. Even data on mental illness demonstrate that the lower classes are more likely than the middle classes to have serious mental problems (Hudson, Christopher, 2005). The difference is that most people break the rules at one time or another, even serious rules for which they could be placed in jail (for example, theft, statutory rape, vandalism, violation of drug or alcohol laws, fraud, violations of the Internal Revenue Service), but only some get the label of deviant (Becker, 1963:14). As one adult analyzed his ornery but normal youth:

> I recall my high school and college days, participating in vandalism, entering locked buildings at night, drinking while under age—even while I made top grades and won athletic letters. I was normal and did these things with guys who now are preachers, professors, and businessmen. A few school friends of poorer families

174

PART TWO
The Individual
in Society:
Society in
the Individual

somehow tended to get caught and we didn't. They were failing in class, and we all
believed they were too dumb not to know when to have fun and when to run.
Some of them did time in jail and reformatories. They were "delinquents" and we
weren't. (Janzen, 1974:390; see also Chambliss, 1973)

This chapter begins with the statement that society creates deviance by creating
rules, the violation of which constitutes deviance. But rule breaking itself does not
make a deviant. The successful application of the label deviant is crucial (Schur,
1971). This is the essence of **labeling theory**, the view of deviant behavior that
stresses the importance of the society in defining what is illegal and in assigning
deviant status to particular individuals, which in turn dominates their identities and
behaviors.

Who gets labeled as a deviant (thug, psycho, faggot, or junkie) is not just a matter of luck or random selection but the result of a systematic societal bias against
the powerless. William Chambliss (1969) summarizes the empirical evidence for
criminals:

> The lower-class person is (1) more likely to be scrutinized and therefore to be
> observed in any violation of the law, (2) more likely to be arrested if discovered
> under suspicious circumstances, (3) more likely to spend the time between arrest
> and trial in jail, (4) more likely to come to trial, (5) more likely to be found guilty,
> and (6) if found guilty, more likely to receive harsh punishment than his middle-
> or upper-class counterpart. (86)

That there is a bias is beyond dispute (see the panel titled "Diversity: The Criminal
Justice System: Unreasonable Stops and Searches by Race"), because the studies
compare defendants by socioeconomic status or race, *controlling* for type of crime,
number of previous arrests, type of counsel, and the like. In short, the well-to-do are
much more likely to avoid the label of *criminal*. If they are found guilty, they are
much less likely to receive a punishment of imprisonment, and those who are
imprisoned receive advantages over lower-class and minority inmates.

The most blatant example of this is found by examining what type of person
actually receives the death penalty and, even more particularly, those who are executed by the state. The data on capital punishment show consistently that people
from disadvantaged categories (racial minorities, the poor, the illiterate) are disproportionately given the death penalty as well as disproportionately executed by the
state. A good example is the difference in sentence when a White person is found
guilty of killing a Black person, compared to when a Black person is the perpetrator
and a White person the victim. The behavior is the same, one individual found guilty
of killing another, yet juries and judges make a difference—Blacks receive the
harsher sentence and punishment. To date, in cases resulting in a death row execu-
tion, over 80 percent of the murder victims were White compared to 14 percent
Black and 4 percent Hispanic. Nationally, only 50 percent of murder victims generally are White (Death Penalty Information Center, 2005). Furthermore, since 1976,
202 Black defendants have been executed for the murder of a White victim, compared to 12 White defendants executed for the murder of a Black victim. See Figure
7.1 on page 176 for more data on death row and race.

Who gets paroled is another indicator of a bias in the system. Parole is a condi-
tional release from prison that allows prisoners to return to their communities under
the supervision of a parole officer before the completion of their maximum sentence.

The Criminal Justice System: Unreasonable Stops and Searches by Race

Cornel West (1992), the highly esteemed African American philosopher and theologian at Princeton, has noted several incidents where he was stopped by the police because of his race:

> Years ago, while driving from New York to teach at Williams College, I was stopped on fake charges of trafficking cocaine. When I told the police officer I was a professor of religion, he replied, "Yeh, and I'm the Flying Nun. Let's go, nigger!" I was stopped three times in my first ten days in Princeton for driving too slowly on a residential street with a speed limit of twenty-five miles per hour. . . . Needless to say, these incidents are dwarfed by those like Rodney King's beating or the abuse of black targets of the FBI's COINTELPRO efforts in the 1960s and 1970s. Yet the memories cut like a merciless knife at my soul. (x–xi)

Similarly, an African American dentist, Elmo Randolph, has been pulled over by state troopers on the New Jersey Turnpike more than fifty times since 1991, yet has never been issued a ticket. Each time he was asked, "Do you have any drugs or weapons in your car?" (Hosenball, 1999). The harassing of Cornel West and Elmo Randolph was a consequence of "racial profiling," the police practice of stopping African American and Latino drivers for routine traffic violations and then searching them for evidence of criminal activity (for example, drugs or guns). This practice, known as stopping people for DWB (Driving While Black) is widespread.

- A study of traffic stops in Florida found that while 5 percent of the drivers on the road were African American or Latino, nearly 70 percent of those stopped and 80 percent of those searched were Black or Latino (Cole, 1999).
- A Temple University study of one stretch of Interstate 95 found that while 75 percent of the motorists and traffic violations were by Whites, 80 percent of the searches were of minorities (Cannon, 1999).
- An ACLU study of traffic stops in Rhode Island found that minority drivers were more than twice as likely to be stopped as White drivers (American Civil Liberties Union, 2005).
- On Interstate 95 in Maryland, Blacks were 17 percent of the motorists but 73 percent of those stopped and searched (USA Today, 1999c).
- The authorities also use suspect "profiles" to question and search "questionable people" in airline, train, and bus terminals. A study involving federal cases involving bus and train sweeps found that nearly 90 percent of those targeted were people of color (Cole, 1999).

This disproportionate targeting of minorities reflects a pattern of stereotyping by police. It results in a self-fulfilling prophecy: When the police look for minorities, it is minorities that they will arrest. Thus, while African Americans compose only about 12 percent of the population, they are half of the prison population. Put another way, "the per capita incarceration rate among Blacks is seven times that among Whites" (Cole, 1999:24). Ironically, these statistics are used by the authorities to justify their racial profiling strategy.

The American Civil Liberties Union argues that the practice of racial profiling also threatens the legitimacy of the criminal justice system. It does so by deterring "people of color from cooperating with the police in criminal investigations. And in the courtroom, it causes jurors of all races and ethnicity to doubt testimony of police officers when they serve as witnesses, making criminal cases more difficult to win" (quoted in Johnson, Kevin, 1999:3A).

Typically, parole is granted by a parole board set up for the correctional institution or for the state. Often, the parole board members are political appointees without training. The parole board reviews a prisoner's social history, past offenses, and behavior in prison and makes its judgment. The decision is rarely subject to review and can be made arbitrarily.

176

PART TWO
The Individual
in Society:
Society in
the Individual

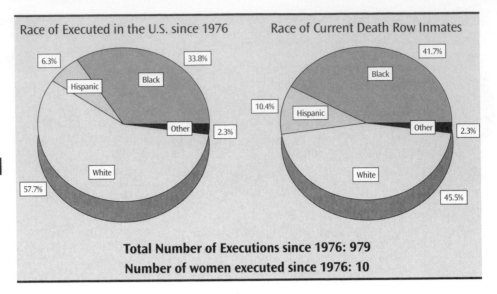

FIGURE 7.1

**Death Penalty
Facts.**[2]

[2]Information taken
from the Death Penalty
Information Center,
2005. 1001 Vermont
Avenue NW, Suite 701,
Washington, DC 2005.
www.deathpenaltyinfo.
org.

Race of Executed in the U.S. since 1976 — Race of Current Death Row Inmates

6.3% Hispanic — 33.8% Black — Other 2.3% — White 57.7%

41.7% Black — 10.4% Hispanic — Other 2.3% — White 45.5%

**Total Number of Executions since 1976: 979
Number of women executed since 1976: 10**

The bias that disadvantages minorities and the poor throughout the system of justice continues as parole board members, corrections officers, and others make judgments that often reflect stereotypes. What type of prisoner represents the safest risk, a Latino or a White? an uneducated or an educated person? an Enron executive or a chronically unemployed unskilled worker? The evidence is overwhelming and consistent—the parole system, like the rest of the criminal justice system, is biased against people of color and those of low socioeconomic status. As Jeffrey Reiman (2001) says, "The criminal justice system is sometimes thought of as a kind of sieve in which the innocent are progressively sifted out from the guilty, who end up behind bars. . . . [T]he sieve works another way as well. It sifts the affluent out from the poor, so it is not merely the guilty who end up behind bars, but the *guilty poor*" (144).

In 2004, the state and federal prisons and local jails held about 2.1 million inmates. Even more striking, an estimated 12.6 percent of all Black males in their late twenties were inmates, compared to 3.6 percent Hispanic males and 1.7 percent White males (Bureau of Justice Statistics, 2005). In fact, nearly one in three Black males in the United States between the ages of twenty and twenty-nine is either incarcerated, on probation, or on parole. This statistic shows that the underdogs in society (the poor and the minorities) are disproportionately represented in the prison population. An important consequence of this representation is that it reinforces the negative stereotypes already present in the majority of the population. The large number of Blacks and the poor in prison "prove" that they have criminal tendencies. This belief is reinforced further by the high recidivism rate of 67.5 percent of ex-prisoners (Bureau of Justice Statistics, 2002).

At least four factors relative to the prison experience operate to fulfill the prophecy that the poor and racial minorities are likely to behave criminally. The first is that the entire criminal justice system is viewed by the underdogs as unjust. There is a growing belief among prisoners that because the system is biased against them, all prisoners are, in fact, political. This consciousness raising increases the bitterness and anger among them.

A second reason for the high rate of crime among those processed through the system of criminal justice is the accepted fact that prison is a brutal, degrading, and altogether dehumanizing experience. Mistreatment by guards, sexual assaults by fellow prisoners, overcrowding, and unsanitary conditions are commonplace in U.S. jails and prisons. Prisoners cannot escape the humiliation, anger, and frustration. These feelings, coupled with the knowledge that the entire system of justice is unjustly directed at certain categories of people, creates within many ex-cons the desire for revenge.

A third factor is that prisons provide learning experiences for prisoners in the art of crime. Through inmate interaction, individuals learn the techniques of crime from the masters and develop contacts that can be used later.

Finally, the ex-con faces the problems of finding a job and being accepted again in society. Long-termers face problems of adjusting to life without regimentation. More important, since good paying jobs, particularly in times of economic recession, are difficult for anyone to find, the ex-con, who is automatically assumed to be untrustworthy, is faced with either unemployment or those jobs nobody else will take. Even the law works to his or her disadvantage by prohibiting certain jobs to ex-cons.

The result of nonacceptance by society is often a return to crime. Previous offenders, on the average, are arrested for crime within six weeks after leaving prison. This, of course, justifies the beliefs by police officers, judges, parole boards, and other authorities that certain categories of people should receive punishment whereas others should not.

The Consequences of Labeling. We have just seen that the labeling process is a crucial factor in the formulation of a deviant career. In other words, the stigma of the label leads to subsequent deviance. This is what Lemert (1951) meant by the concept of secondary deviance. **Primary deviance** is the rule breaking that occurs before labeling. **Secondary deviance** is behavior that results from the labeling process. Being labeled a criminal means being rejected by society, employers, friends, and even relatives. There is a high probability that such a person will turn to behavior that fulfills the prophecies of others. Put another way, people labeled as deviants tend to become locked into a deviant behavior pattern (deviant career). Looking at deviance this way turns the tables on conventional thought:

Instead of assuming that it is the deviant's difference which needs explanation, [the labeling perspective] asks why the majority responds to this difference as it does. This shift of the question reverses the normal conception of causation; the labeling school suggests that the other person's peculiarity has not caused us to regard him as different so much as our labeling hypothesis has caused his peculiarity. (Nettler, 1974:203)

178

PART TWO
The Individual
in Society:
Society in
the Individual

Ex-mental patients, like ex-convicts, usually have difficulty in finding employment and establishing close relationships because of the stigma of the label. This difficulty, of course, leads to frustration, anger, low self-esteem, and other symptoms of mental illness. Moreover, the consistent messages from other people (recall Cooley's looking-glass self) that one is sick are likely to lead the individual to behavior in accord with these expectations. Even while a patient is in a mental hospital, the actions of the staff may actually foster in the person a self-concept of deviant behavior consistent with that definition. Patients who show insight about their illness confirm the medical and societal diagnosis and are positively rewarded by psychiatrists and other personnel (see Scheff, 1966). The opposite also occurs, as illustrated so vividly by the character R. P. McMurphy in the novel *One Flew Over the Cuckoo's Nest* (Kesey, 1962). Although the fictitious McMurphy fought this tendency to confirm the expectations of powerful others, the pressures to conform were great. Stephen Cole (1975) summarizes this process of how the deviant role is sustained:

> After someone is labeled as deviant, he often finds it rewarding to accept the label and act deviant. Consider, for example, a patient in a mental hospital who has been diagnosed as a schizophrenic. If the patient refuses to accept the diagnosis, claims that he is not mentally ill, and demands to be immediately released, the staff will consider him to be hostile and uncooperative. He may be denied privileges and treated as hopelessly insane. After all, the person who cannot even recognize that he is ill must be in a mental state in which he has no perception of reality! On the other hand, if the patient accepts the validity of the diagnosis, admits his illness, and tries to cooperate with the staff in effecting a cure, he will be rewarded. He will be defined as a good cooperative patient who is sincerely trying to get better. Any weird or unusual behavior he engages in will be ignored; after all, he is mentally ill, and such types of behavior should be expected from a person in his mental state. He may even be rewarded for engaging in behavior which is considered to be characteristic of schizophrenia. Such behavior serves to reassure the staff that the patient is indeed mentally ill and that the social organization of the mental hospital makes sense. (141–142)

The labeling perspective is especially helpful in understanding the bias of the criminal justice system. It shows, in summary, that when society's underdogs are disproportionately singled out for the criminal label, the subsequent problems of stigmatization and segregation they face result in a tendency toward further deviance, thereby justifying the society's original negative response to them. This tendency for secondary deviance is especially strong when the imposition of the label is accompanied by a sense of injustice. Lemert (1967) argues that a stronger commitment to a deviant identity is greatest when the negative label (stigma) is believed by the individual to be inconsistently applied by society. The evidence of such inconsistency is overwhelming.

From this perspective, then, the situations showing that society's underdogs engage in more deviance than do people from the middle and upper classes are invalid because they reflect the differential response of society to deviance at every phase in the process of criminal justice. Hartjen (1974) provides an excellent statement that summarizes this process:

> Criminal sanctions are supposedly directed toward a person's behavior—what he does, not what kind of person he is. Yet, the research on the administration of criminal justice . . . reveals that just the opposite occurs. A person is likely to

acquire a social identity as a criminal precisely because of what he is—because of the kind of personal or social characteristics he has the misfortune to possess. Being black, poor, migrant, uneducated, and the like increases a person's chances of being defined as a criminal. . . . What I am suggesting here is that the very structure and operation of the judicial system, which was created to deal with the problem called crime, are not only grounded in an unstated image of the criminal but also—merely because the system exists—serve to produce and perpetuate the "thing" it was created to handle. That is to say, the criminal court (and especially the juvenile court) does not exist in its present form because the people it deals with are what they are. Rather, the criminals and delinquents become the way they are characterized by others as being because the court (and the world view it embodies) exists in the form that it does. *The criminal, thus, is a "product" of the structural and procedural characteristics of the judicial system.* (120–121)

"Solutions" for Deviance from the Labeling Perspective. The labeling theorist's approach to deviance leads to unconventional solutions (Schur, 1971). The assumption is that deviants are not basically different—except that they have been processed (and labeled) by official sources (judges and courts, psychiatrists and mental hospitals). The primary target for policy, then, should be neither the individual nor the local community setting, but the process by which some people are singled out for the negative label. From this approach, organizations produce deviants. Speaking specifically about juvenile delinquency, Schur (1973) argues that the solution should be what he has called **radical nonintervention** (the strategy of leaving juvenile delinquents alone as much as possible rather than giving them a negative label):

> We can now begin to see some of the meanings of the term "radical nonintervention." For one thing, it breaks radically with conventional thinking about delinquency and its causes. Basically, radical nonintervention implies policies that accommodate society to the widest possible diversity of behaviors and attitudes, rather than focusing on as many individuals as possible to "adjust" to supposedly common societal standards. This does not mean that anything goes, that all behavior is socially acceptable. But traditional delinquency policy has proscribed youthful behavior well beyond what is required to maintain a smooth-running society or to protect others from youthful depredations.
>
> Thus, the basic injunction for public policy becomes: leave kids alone wherever possible. This effort partly involves mechanisms to divert children away from the courts but it goes further to include opposing various kinds of intervention by diverse social control and socializing agencies. . . . Subsidiary policies would favor collective action programs instead of those that single out specific individuals; and voluntary programs instead of compulsory ones. Finally, this approach is radical in asserting that major and intentional sociocultural change will help reduce our delinquency problems. Piecemeal socioeconomic reform will not greatly affect delinquency; there must be thorough-going changes in the structure and the values of our society. If the choice is between changing youth and changing society (including some of its laws), the radical noninterventionist opts for changing the society. (154–155)

One way to accomplish this "leave the deviants alone whenever possible" philosophy would be to treat fewer acts as criminal or deviant. For adults, this could be accomplished by decriminalizing victimless crimes, such as gambling, drug posses-

180

PART TWO
The Individual
in Society:
Society in
the Individual

sion, prostitution, and homosexual acts by consenting adults. Youth should not be treated as criminals for behavior that is legal if one is old enough. Truancy, running away from home, curfew violations, and purchasing alcohol are acts for which people below the legal age can receive the label *delinquent*, yet they are not crimes for adults. Is there any wonder, then, why so many youthful rule breakers outgrow their so-called delinquency, becoming law-abiding citizens as adults?

Acts dangerous to society do occur, and they must be handled through legal mechanisms. But when a legal approach is required, justice must be applied evenly. Currently, the criminal label is disproportionately applied to individuals from the other side of the tracks. This procedure increases the probability of secondary deviance and justifies further stern punishment for this category. This unfair cycle must be broken. The panel titled "Human Agency: The Gay Rights Movement" provides an example of one effort to break that cycle.

The strengths of labeling theory are that it (1) concentrates on the role of societal reactions in the creation of deviance, (2) realizes that the label is applied disproportionately to the powerless, and (3) explains how deviant careers are established and perpetuated. There are problems with the theory, however (see Davis, Nanette, 1975; Gibbs, 1966; Liazos, 1972; Warren and Johnson, 1973). First, it avoids the question of causation (primary deviance). Labeling, by definition, occurs after the fact. It disregards undetected deviance. As Charles McCaghy (1976) argues:

> [B]y minimizing the importance of explaining initial (primary) deviance, whatever meaning the behavior originally had for the deviant is ignored as a contributor to subsequent behavior. Although societal reaction may become a crucial factor in behavior, it is questionable that whatever purpose or reward the behavior first held is invariably replaced. For example, if a person first steals for thrills, do thrills fail to be a factor once societal reaction has taken its toll? (87)

Another problem with labeling theory involves the assumption that deviants are really normal—because we are all rule breakers. Thus, it overlooks the possibility that some people are unable to cope with the pressures of their situation. Some people are dangerous. Individuals who are disadvantaged tend to be more angry, frustrated, and alienated than the more fortunate. The result may be differences in quantity and quality of primary deviance.

This perspective also relieves the individual deviant from blame. The underdog is seen as victimized by the powerful labelers. Further, individuals enmeshed in the labeling process are so constrained by the forces of society that they are incapable of choice. Once again, McCaghy (1976) puts it well: "Although it is true that deviants may be pawns of the powerful, this does not mean that deviants are powerless to resist, to alter their behavior, or to acquire power themselves" (88).

Perhaps its most serious deficiency, though, is that labeling theory focuses on certain types of deviance but ignores others. The attention is directed at society's underdogs, which is good. But the forms of deviance emanating from the social structure or from the powerful are not considered a very serious omission. As Liazos (1972) puts it, the themes of labeling theory focus attention on people who have been successfully labeled as deviants ("nuts, sluts, and perverts"), the deviant subculture, and the self-fulfilling prophecy that perpetuates their deviant patterns. Even though this is appropriate and necessary, it concentrates on the powerless. The impression is that deviance is an exclusive property of the poor in the slums, the

The Gay Rights Movement

The forces of society converge to restrict the behavior of individuals to those activities considered socially acceptable. But occasionally, some individuals who find these demands too confining organize to change society. One contemporary example is the gay rights movement. Although homosexuals have been accepted by some societies (for example, ancient Greece and Rome), they have never been accepted in the United States. Sexual attraction and behaviors between members of the same sex have always been severely sanctioned in Western society. Formal laws forbidding such behaviors have been enacted. For example, laws regarding private sexual behavior, child adoption, and marriage have clearly defined homosexuals as deviants with fewer rights than heterosexuals. Because of discrimination against them, fear of social ostracism, and other forms of rejection even by friends and family, many homosexuals have felt it necessary to conceal their sexual preference.

These compelling fears have kept homosexuals in most periods of American history from organizing to change a repressive situation. A few homosexual organizations were formed (the first in 1925 and others in the 1950s) for mutual support, but a relatively few homosexuals were willing at these times to declare publicly their deviance from the norm of society.

The 1960s provided a better climate for change as youths, Blacks, women, pacifists, and other groups questioned the norms and ideologies of the dominant society. This time clearly was one of heightened awareness among the oppressed of their oppression and of the possibility that through collective efforts they could change what seemed before unchangeable.

The precipitating event for homosexual unity occurred at 3 A.M. on June 28, 1969, when police raided the Stonewall Inn in New York's Greenwich Village. Instead of dispersing, the 200 homosexual patrons, who had never collectively resisted the police before, threw objects at the police and set fire to the bar. The riot lasted forty-five minutes, but it gave impetus to a number of collective efforts by gays to publicize police harassment of the gay community, job discrimination, and other indignities that homosexuals face. Gay liberation groups emerged in numerous cities and on university campuses. By 1980,

more than 4,000 homosexual organizations existed in the United States. Many neighborhoods in major cities became openly homosexual—most notably the Castro district in San Francisco, New Town in Chicago, and Greenwich Village in New York City. Gay organizations now include churches, associations of professionals, health clinics, and networks of gay-owned businesses to supply the gay community's needs. The proliferation of these organizations for homosexuals has provided a supportive climate, allowing many of them to come out of the closet.

The increased numbers of public homosexuals have provided the political base for changing the various forms of oppression that homosexuals experience. A Gay Media Task Force promotes accurate and positive images of gays in television, films, and advertising; a Gay Rights National Lobby promotes favorable legislation; and a National Gay Task Force furthers gay interests by attacking the minority-group status of homosexuals in a variety of political and ideological arenas.

The positive results of these political activities, although limited, have been encouraging to the gay community. Since 1983, the state of Wisconsin and most of the larger cities in the United States have enacted gay rights laws. The Civil Service Reform Act of 1978 prohibits federal agencies from discriminating against gays in employment practices. And, although openly gay politicians are still rare, a few avowed homosexuals have been elected to public office.

The successes of gay rights political activists have not yet achieved their ultimate goal—the full acceptance of homosexuality as an alternative lifestyle. Homosexuals are still not allowed to marry in all but a very few cities. Discrimination in housing and jobs still occurs. Gays are allowed in the military as long as they "stay in the closet," that is, live a lie. Polls show that only about one-third of people in the United States consider it an acceptable lifestyle. Gay rights movements also have met fierce resistance by fundamentalist religious groups who believe homosexuality to be morally offensive and dangerous. But clearly during the past twenty years, the collective efforts of homosexuals and their supporters have had an enormous and positive impact for homosexuals (see Kopkind, 1993).

182

PART TWO
The Individual
in Society:
Society in
the Individual

minorities, and street gangs. But what of the deviance of the powerful members of society, and even of society itself? Liazos (1972) chronicles these acts for us:

1. The unethical, illegal, and destructive actions found in the corporate world, such as robbery through price fixing, low wages, pollution, inferior and dangerous products, deception, and outright lies in advertising.
2. The covert institutional violence committed against the poor by the institutions of society: schools, hospitals, corporations, and the government.
3. The political manipulators who pass laws that protect the interests of the powerful and disadvantage the powerless.
4. The power of the powerful is used to deflect criticism, labeling, and punishment even when deserved.

In short, labeling overlooks the deviant qualities of the society and its powerful members. Although social structure should be central to sociologists, the labeling theorists have minimized its impact on deviance. Liazos (1972) summarizes the problem this way:

> We should banish the concept of "deviance" and speak of oppression, conflict, persecution, and suffering. By focusing on the dramatic forms, as we do now, we perpetuate most people's beliefs and impressions that such "deviance" is the basic cause of many of our troubles, that these people (criminals, drug addicts, political dissenters, and others) are the real "troublemakers"; and, necessarily, we neglect conditions of inequality, powerlessness, institutional violence, and so on, which lie at the bases of our tortured society. (119)

Another way to explain deviance—conflict theory—extends labeling theory by focusing on social structure, thereby overcoming the fundamental criticisms of Liazos and others.

Conflict Theory

Why is certain behavior defined as deviant? The answer, according to conflict theorists, is that powerful economic interest groups are able to get laws passed and enforced that protect their interests (Quinney, 1970; 1974). They begin, then, with the law.

Of all the requirements for a just system, the most fundamental is the foundation of nondiscriminatory laws. Many criminal laws are the result of a consensus among the public as to what kinds of behaviors are a menace and should be punished (for example, murder, rape, theft). The laws devised to make these acts illegal and the extent of punishment for violators are nondiscriminatory (although, as we have seen, the administration of these laws is discriminatory), because they do not single out a particular social category as the target.

There are laws, however, that do discriminate, because they result from special interests using their power to translate their interests into public policy. These laws may be discriminatory in that some segments of society (for example, the poor, minorities, youth, renters, debtors) rarely have access to the lawmaking process and therefore often find the laws unfairly aimed at them. Vagrancy, for example, is really a crime that only the poor can commit.

Not only is the formation of the law political, but so, too, is the administration of the law. This is true because at every stage in the processing of criminals, authorities make choices based on personal bias, pressures from the powerful, and the constraints of the status quo. Some examples of the political character of law administration are these: (1) The powerful attempt to coerce other people to adopt their view of morality, hence laws against homosexuality, pornography, drug use, and gambling; (2) the powerful may exert pressure on the authorities to crack down on certain kinds of violators, especially individuals and groups who are disruptive (protesters); (3) there may be political pressure exerted to keep certain crimes from public view (embezzlement, stock fraud, accounting tricks that make losses appear to be gains); (4) there may be pressure to protect the party in power, the elected officials, the police, the CIA, and the FBI; and (5) any effort to protect and preserve the status quo is a political act. Hartjen (1974) summarizes why the administration of justice is inherently political:

> Unless one is willing to assume that law-enforcement agents can apply some magic formula to gauge the opinions of the public they serve, unless one is willing to assume that citizens unanimously agree on what laws are to be enforced and how enforcement is to be carried out, unless one is willing to assume that blacks, the poor, urbanites, and the young are actually more criminalistic than everyone else, it must be concluded, at least, that discriminatory law enforcement is a result of differences in power and that actual decisions as to which and whose behavior is criminal are expressions of this power. One need only ask himself why some laws, such as those protecting the consumer from fraud, go largely unenforced while the drug addict, for example, is pursued with a paranoiac passion. (11)

The conflict approach is critical of the kinds-of-people explanations of order theorists and the focus of labeling theorists because both explanations center on individual deviants and their crimes. Order theorists and labeling theorists tend to emphasize street crimes and ignore the crimes of the rich and powerful, such as corporate crimes (which go largely unpoliced) and crimes by governments (which are not even considered crimes, unless they are committed by enemy governments). Conflict theorists, in contrast, emphasize corporate and political crimes, which cause many times more economic damage and harm to people than do street crimes. **Corporate crime** refers to the "illegal and/or socially harmful behaviors that result from deliberate decision making by corporate executives in accordance with the operative goals of their organizations" (Kramer, 1982:75). This definition focuses attention on corporations, rather than on individuals, as perpetrators, and it goes beyond the criminal law to include "socially harmful behaviors."

Both of these elements are critical to conflict theorists. First, deviance is not limited to troubled individuals, as is the traditional focus in sociology. Organizations, too, can be deviant. Moreover, research has shown that corporations have a higher criminality rate than do individuals (and the law does not define most harmful corporate behavior as illegal) (Simon and Eitzen, 1993:358).

The second part of the definition of corporate crime stresses "socially harmful behaviors," whether criminal or not. This means that conflict theorists ask such questions as these: "What about selling proven dangerous products (e.g., pesticides, drugs, or food) overseas, when it is illegal to do so within the United States? What about promoting an unsafely designed automobile such as the Ford Pinto? Or, what about being excessively slow to promote a safe work environment for workers?" (Timmer and Eitzen, 1989:85). See the panel titled "A Closer Look: Corporate Perjury and Obstruction of Justice."

Corporate Perjury and Obstruction of Justice

For what seems an eternity, Washington, DC, has been abuzz with talk of perjury and obstruction of justice.

Not so surprisingly, the politicians and talking heads have failed to broaden their discussion to cover the category of perjury and obstruction of justice with important consequences—rampant corporate lying under oath and interference with law enforcement.

The most prominent example occurred four and a half years ago, when tobacco company executives appeared before a committee of the House of Representatives and mocked the members of Congress by testifying under oath that they did not believe that nicotine is addictive. Documents since made public show that the companies have known of nicotine's addictiveness for decades—and have based marketing strategies on tobacco's addictive quality.

More important is Big Tobacco's decades'-long conspiracy to lie to federal and state agencies about cigarette's health effects and addictiveness. That has interfered with and prevented efforts to regulate the tobacco industry, at a potential cost of perhaps hundreds of thousands of lives. Unfortunately, lying and obstruction of justice is not limited to the pariah tobacco industry.

Consider the coal industry. In 1991, then-Secretary of Labor Lynn Martin announced a stunning pattern and practice of coal company cheating on dust sampling tests. More than 500 mine operators had submitted coal dust monitoring cassettes that

displayed "abnormal white centers," suggesting they had been vacuumed. These tests are designed to ensure that miners are not exposed to unsafe levels of coal dust, the cause of debilitating and deadly black lung disease. Efforts to prosecute the companies floundered, because in each individual case the companies were able to argue that the abnormal white centers may have been the result of mishandling of the cassettes—but no one was really fooled as to what took place.

Then, in April 1998, in a stunning series in the *Louisville Courier-Journal*, reporter Gardiner Harris documented even more conclusively that cheating on the tests continues. The paper examined coal dust sampling records and found that, in fiscal year 1997, 80 percent of the nation's underground mines submitted air samples that were impossibly clean. Harris supplemented the statistical analysis with interviews with foremen and workers who described how the coal companies cheated on the dust sampling tests. "I was told by the superintendent or the owner to see to it that the dust pumps was turned off," one typical foreman told Harris. "I turned off the machines myself when I was a foreman."

There are countless other examples of known corporate lying and obstruction of justice. To mention only a few prominent U.S. cases from 1998:

- Hudson Foods (now owned by Tyson Foods) was indicted in December for lying to the U.S. Department of Agriculture in an effort to delay recall of

The definition of **political crime** separates order and conflict theorists. Because order theorists assume that the law and the state are neutral, they perceive political crimes as activities against the government, such as acts of dissent and violence whose purpose is to challenge and change the existing political order. Conflict theorists, in sharp contrast, assume that the law and the state are often tools of the powerful used to keep them in power. Thus, the political order itself may be criminal because it can be unjust. Moreover, government, like a corporation, may follow policies that go against democratic principles and that do harm. Examples of political crimes from this perspective are CIA interventions in the domestic affairs of other nations, Watergate, the Iran-contra affair, war crimes, slavery, imperialism (such as forcibly taking the land from the Indians), police brutality, and using citizens experimentally without their knowledge and consent.

Corporate Perjury and Obstruction of Justice continued

25 million pounds of hamburger meat, some of it infected by E. coli, in 1997.

- Seven heavy-duty diesel engine makers entered into a $1 billion civil settlement in October to resolve Justice Department allegations that they equipped their engines with software that allowed the engines to pass emissions tests but turned off pollution control equipment under normal driving conditions. The engine makers still proclaim their innocence.
- Even the seemingly harmless company Royal Caribbean Cruise Lines has recently been caught in a web of lies. Not only did the company illegally dump oil waste in the Gulf of Mexico, it destroyed physical evidence related to the crime and presented a doctored log book to conceal the discharges.

For two reasons, no one knows how extensive is corporate lying and obstruction of justice. Relatively few law enforcement resources in the United States are directed to investigating and prosecuting corporate crime, so corporate perjury and obstruction of justice is massively underprosecuted. And there is no U.S. national collection of corporate crime data, no analogue to the federal crime database for street crime, which generates reams of data and enables police to check quickly on prior convictions of criminal suspects.

These shortcomings point the way to a citizens' agenda for cracking down on corporate crime:

- First, beef up the budgets and strengthen the authority of the cops on the corporate crime beat—regulatory agencies and federal, state, and local prosecutors. Along with bigger budgets, these agencies need stronger sanctions—higher fines, plus the ability to impose innovative terms of probation, the authority to withdraw corporate lawbreakers' right to bid for government contracts, and other creative sanctions.
- Second, the federal government should immediately establish a centralized federal database on corporate crime and violence.
- Third, citizens should demand new statutes and rules that empower citizens themselves to take on perjury and obstruction and other corporate crimes. Citizens should have standing to enforce health, safety, environmental, and financial laws against corporate wrongdoers; and bounties should reward those who provide information about corporate lying and obstruction, and those who successfully bring cases against corporate lawbreakers. Unfortunately, there is no faction in Congress nor an independent counsel to press the agenda for redress of corporate perjury and obstruction of justice. Only a mobilized citizenry can place it on the congressional dockets.

Source: Multinational Monitor, 1998. "Corporate Perjury and Obstruction of Justice." Vol. 19 (December):5. Reprinted by permission.

An extreme example of using human subjects as guinea pigs is a study begun in 1932 by the U.S. Public Health Service. The subjects were 400 African American male syphilis patients in Macon County, Alabama. The patients did not know that they had syphilis and were never informed of that fact. Because the purpose of the study was to assess the consequences of not treating the disease, the men were not treated, nor were their wives—and when their children were born with congenital syphilis, they, too, were not treated. The experiment lasted forty years, until 1972 (Jones, J. H., 1981).

In sum, the focus of the conflict perspective is on the political and economic setting in society. The power of certain interests determines what gets defined as deviance (and who, then, is a deviant) and how this "problem" is to be solved. Because the powerful benefit from the status quo, they vigorously thwart efforts to reform society. The

186

PART TWO
The Individual
in Society:
Society in
the Individual

solution, from the conflict theorists, however, requires not only reform of society but also its radical transformation. The structure of society is the problem.

The strengths of the conflict perspective on deviance are (1) its emphasis on the relationship between political order and nonconformity; (2) the understanding that the most powerful groups use the political order to protect their interests; (3) that it emphasizes how the system of justice is unjust and the distribution of rewards in society is skewed; and (4) the realization that the institutional framework of society is the source of so many social problems (for example, racism, sexism, pollution, unequal distribution of health care, poverty, and economic cycles) (Sykes, 1974).

There are some problems with this perspective, also. First, there is the tendency to assume a conspiracy by the well-to-do. Because the empirical evidence is overwhelming that the poor, the uneducated, and the members of minority groups are singled out for the deviant label, some persons make the too-facile imputation of motive.

Second, the answer of the conflict theorists is too utopian. The following quotation by Quinney (1974) is representative of this naivete:

> The alternative to the contradictions of capitalism is a truly democratic society, a socialist society in which human beings no longer suffer the alienation inherent in capitalism. When there is no longer the need for one class to dominate another, when there is no longer the need for a legal system to secure the interests of a capitalist ruling class, then there will no longer be the need for crime. (25)

But would crime and other forms of deviance disappear under such a socialist system? This, like Marx's final stage of history, is a statement of faith rather than one based on proof.

Deviance from the Order and Conflict Perspectives

The two contrasting theoretical perspectives in sociology—the order model and the conflict model—constrain their adherents to view the causes, consequences, and remedies of deviance in opposing ways. The order perspective focuses on deviants themselves. This approach (which has been the conventional way of studying social problems) asks, Who are the deviants? What are their social and psychological backgrounds? With whom do they associate? Deviants somehow do not conform to the standards of the dominant group; they are assumed to be out of phase with conventional behavior. This is believed to occur most often as a result of inadequate socialization. In other words, deviants have not internalized the norms and values of society because they are either brought up in an environment of conflicting value systems (as are children of immigrants or the poor in a middle-class school) or are under the influence of a deviant subculture, such as a gang. Because the order theorist uses the prevailing standards to define and label deviants, the existing practices and structures of society are accepted implicitly. The remedy is to rehabilitate deviants so that they conform to the societal norms.

The conflict theorist takes a different approach to social problems. The adherents of this perspective criticize order theorists for blaming the victim. To focus on the individual deviant is to locate the symptom, not the disease. Individual deviants are a manifestation of a failure of society to meet the needs of individuals. The sources of crime, poverty, drug addiction, and racism are found in the laws, the customs, the quality of life, the distribution of wealth and power, and the accepted practices of schools, governmental units, and corporations. The established system, in this view, is not sacred. Because it is the primary source of social problems, it, not the individual deviant, must be restructured.

Because this is a text on society, we emphasize the conflict approach. The insights of this approach are clarified further in the remainder of this book as we examine the structure and consequences of social inequality in the next five chapters, followed by six chapters describing the positive and negative effects of institutions.

Chapter Review

1. Deviance is behavior that violates the laws and expectations of a group. This means that deviance is not a property inherent in a behavior but a property conferred on that behavior by other people. In short, deviance is socially created.

2. What is deviant varies from society to society, and within a society the same behavior may be interpreted differently when it is done by different categories of people.

3. The norms of the majority determine what behaviors are considered deviant.

4. Order theorists point out that deviant behavior has positive consequences for society, because it gives nondeviants a sense of solidarity and reaffirms the importance of society's rules.

5. Conflict theorists argue that all views of rule violations have political implications. Punishment of deviants reflects a conservative bias by legitimating the norms and the current distribution of power. Support of the deviant behavior is also political, because it rejects the legitimacy of the people in power and their rules.

6. Several traditional theories for the causes of deviance assume the source as a fatal flaw in certain people. These theories focus on physical or psychological reasons for deviant behavior.

7. Kinds-of-people explanations for deviance also apply to some theories by sociologists. One theory argues that crime results from the conditions of city life. Another theory blames the influences of peers. A third focuses on the propensity of the poor to be deviants because of the gap between the goal of success and the lack of the means for these people to attain it. A fourth theory argues that people deviate when their internal or external controls are weak.

Finally, some people have argued that lower-class culture is responsible.

8. These kinds-of-people theories have been criticized for blaming the victim. Because they blame the victim, the society (government, system of justice, education) is freed from blame. Since the established order is thus protected from criticism, necessary social change is thwarted.

9. An alternative to person-blame theories is labeling theory. This approach argues that even though most people break the rules on occasion, the crucial factor in establishing a deviant career is the successful application of the label deviant.

10. Who gets labeled as a deviant is not a matter of luck but the result of a systematic societal bias against the powerless.

11. Primary deviance is the rule breaking that occurs prior to labeling. Secondary deviance is behavior resulting from the labeling process.

12. Labeling theorists argue that because deviants are not much different from nondeviants, the problem lies in organizations that label. Thus, these organizations should (a) leave deviants alone whenever possible and (b) apply justice fairly when the legal approach is required.

13. Labeling theory has been criticized because it (a) disregards undetected deviance, (b) assumes that deviants are really normal because we are all rule breakers, (c) relieves the individual from blame, and (d) focuses on certain types of deviance but ignores deviance by the powerful.

14. Conflict theory focuses on social structure as the source of deviance. There is a historical bias in the law that favors the powerful. The administration of justice is also biased. In short, the state is a politi-

cal organization controlled by the ruling class for its own advantage. The power of powerful interests in society determines what and who are deviant.

15. From the conflict perspective, the only real and lasting solution to deviance is the radical transformation of society.

16. Order theorists focus on individual deviants. Because this perspective uses the prevailing standards to define and label deviants, the existing practices and structures of society are accepted implicitly. The remedy is to rehabilitate deviants so they conform to the societal norms.

Key Terms

Deviance
Culture of poverty
Cultural deprivation
Recidivism

Social Darwinism
Labeling theory
Primary deviance
Secondary deviance

Radical nonintervention
Corporate crime
Political crime

Study Questions

1. Are there universal criteria that determine what is deviant at all times and places? Explain.
2. Most of us at one time or another behave in deviant ways. Why, then, aren't we considered deviants?
3. Explain how deviant behavior has positive social consequences for the group.

4. What is labeling theory? What are its strengths and weaknesses in understanding deviant behavior?
5. Contrast the order and conflict interpretations of deviance.

For Further Reading

Analyses of Deviance

David Cole, *No Equal Justice: Race and Class in the American Criminal Justice System* (New York: New Press, 1999).

James William Coleman, *The Criminal Elite: The Sociology of White-Collar Crime*, 3rd ed. (New York: St. Martin's Press, 1994).

Elliott Currie, *Crime and Punishment in America* (New York: Metropolitan Books, 1998).

Charles Derber, *Corporation Nation* (New York: St. Martin's Press, 1998).

Steven R. Donziger (ed.), *The Real War on Crime: The Report of the National Criminal Justice Commission* (New York: HarperPerennial, 1996).

M. David Ermann and Richard J. Lundman, *Corporate and Governmental Deviance: Problems of Organizational Behavior in Contemporary Society*, 5th ed. (New York: Oxford University Press, 1996).

Frank E. Hagan, *Political Crime: Ideology and Criminality* (Boston: Allyn and Bacon, 1997).

Jerome G. Miller, *Search and Destroy: African-American Males in the Criminal Justice System* (New York: Cambridge University Press, 1996).

Jeffrey H. Reiman, *The Rich Get Richer and the Poor Get Prison: Ideology, Class, and Criminal Justice*, 6th ed. (Boston: Allyn and Bacon, 2001).

Edwin Schur, *The Politics of Deviance* (Upper Saddle River, NJ: Prentice Hall, 1980).

Theories of Deviance

Howard S. Becker, *The Outsiders: Studies in the Sociology of Deviance*, 2nd ed. (New York: Free Press, 1973).

Kai Erikson, *Wayward Puritans: A Study in the Sociology of Deviance* (New York: Wiley, 1966).

Erving Goffman, *Stigma: Notes on the Management of Spoiled Identity* (Upper Saddle River, NJ: Prentice Hall, 1963).

Travis Hirschi, *Causes of Delinquency* (Berkeley, CA: University of California Press, 1969).

Robert K. Merton, *Social Theory and Social Structure*, rev. and enlarged ed. (Glencoe, IL: Free Press, 1957).

Richard Quinney, *The Social Reality of Crime* (Boston: Little, Brown, 1970).

Earl Rubington and Martin S. Weinberg, *The Study of Social Problems. Six Perspectives*, 4th ed. (New York: Oxford University Press, 1989).

William Ryan, *Blaming the Victim*, rev. ed. (New York: Vintage Books, 1976).

Edwin M. Schur, *Radical Non-Intervention: Rethinking the Delinquency Problem* (Upper Saddle River, NJ: Prentice Hall, 1973).

Nathan Caplan, and Stephen D. Nelson. 1973. "On Being Useful: The Nature and Consequences of Psychological Research on Social Problems," *American Psychologist* 28 (March):199–211.

Web Resources

http://www.ojp.usdoj.gov/bjs/

The Bureau of Justice Statistics is a branch of the government that provides information on crime and deviance. Among the subjects on the site are criminal offenders, courts and sentencing, and key facts at a glance.

http://crimespider.com/

Crime Spider provides a list of crime and law enforcement sites arranged by topic. Topics include homicide, cybercrime, and crime studies.

http://www.asc41.com/

The American Society of Criminology is "an international organization concerned with criminology, embracing scholarly, scientific, and professional knowledge concerning the etiology, prevention, control and treatment of crime and delinquency. This includes the measurement and detection of crime, legislation and practice of criminal law, as well as the law enforcement, judicial and correctional systems."

http://www.fas.org/sgp/

Part of the Federation of American Scientists, the Project on Government Secrecy "works to challenge excessive government secrecy and to promote public oversight."

http://www.truthinjustice.org/

Truth in Justice is an organization whose goal is to free innocent people convicted of crimes they didn't commit.

http://www.deathpenaltyinfo.org

The Death Penalty Information Center provides statistics and information regarding all aspects of capital punishment.

http://www.hewett.norfolk.sch.uk/curric/soc/crime/crim.htm

This site has links to information on deviance, crime, and criminological theory. There is a useful map that outlines the different theories on deviance and how they relate and differ.

http://www.civilrights.org/

This site provides information on hate crimes and other issues of civil rights.

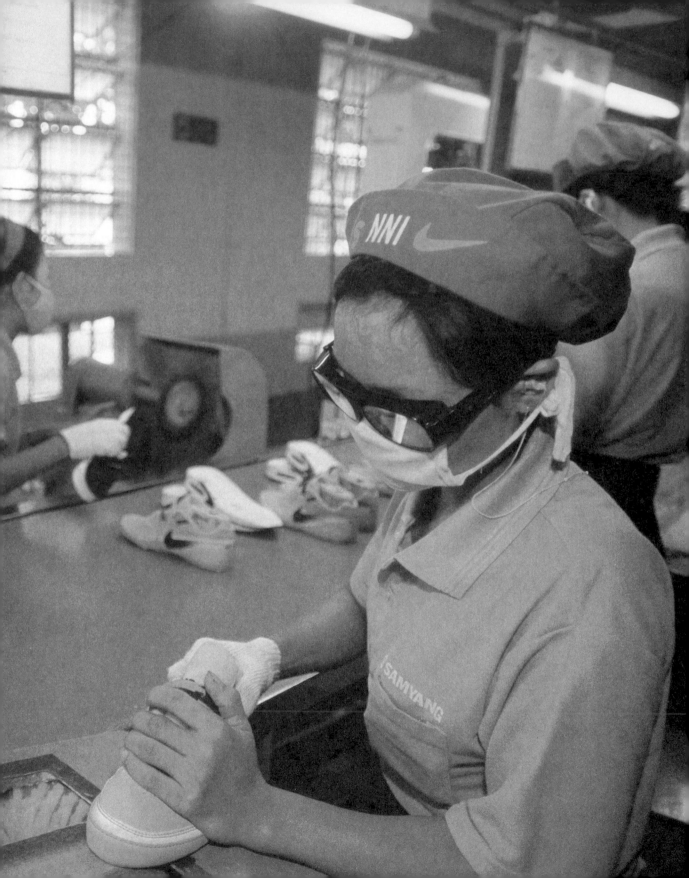

Structural Sources of Societal Change: Economic and Demographic

We are in the midst of three societal "earthquakes." For most of the twentieth century, the U.S. economy was primarily based on domestic production and consumption and its population was overwhelmingly young, White, and of European heritage. Now three massive changes are in progress: (1) the globalization of the U.S. economy, which has a profound effect on jobs and security here and abroad; (2) the "new immigration," which is changing the racial composition of the United States, as Latino and Asian American populations increase dramatically; and (3) the aging of the population, which is transforming families, politics, work, and public policies. These social changes are more far-reaching and are occurring more rapidly than at any other time in human history. The purpose of this chapter is to understand these three macro social trends and the important ways that they affect individuals, families, communities, and the institutions of society.

Globalization and the Structural Transformation of the Economy

There have been two fundamental turning points in human history. The Neolithic agricultural revolution began about 8000 B.C., marking the transition from nomadic pastoral life, during which the animal and vegetable sources of food were hunted and gathered, to life in settlements based on agriculture. During this phase of human existence, tools were created and used; animals were domesticated; language, numbers, and other symbols became more sophisticated; and mining and metalworking were developed.

The second fundamental change, the Industrial Revolution, began in Great Britain in the 1780s. With the application of steam power and later oil and electricity as energy sources for industry, mining, manufacturing, and transportation came fundamental changes to the economy, the nature of work, family organization, and a transition from rural to urban life. In effect, societies are transformed with each surge in invention and technological growth. Peter F. Drucker (1993) describes the historical import of such transformations:

Every few hundred years in Western history there occurs a sharp transformation. We cross . . . a "divide." Within a few short decades, society rearranges itself—its worldview; its basic values; its social and political structure; its arts; its key institutions. Fifty years later, there is a new world. And the people born then cannot even imagine the world in which their grandparents lived and into which their own parents were born. We are currently living through just such a transformation. (1)

Technological innovations and applications are expanding ever more rapidly (e.g., superfast computers, the Internet, fiber optics, biotechnology, the decoding of the human genome, and cell telephony). The amazing scientific breakthroughs have had and will continue to have immense implications for commerce, international trade, global politics, and, at the individual level, work opportunities (as some businesses thrive while others become outmoded). In Drucker's (1999) words: "The next two or three decades are likely to see even greater technological change than has occurred in the decades since the emergence of the computer, and also even greater change in industry structures, in the economic landscape, and probably in the social landscape as well" (54).

Among other changes, the new technologies have, most significantly, magnified the connections among all peoples across the globe. The Internet makes worldwide communication instantaneous. Money moves across political boundaries with a few keystrokes. Low wages in one country affect wages elsewhere. A drought in one part of the world drives prices up for commodities everywhere, while overproduction of a product in one region brings down the prices of that product everywhere else. A collapse in the stock market of one country has ramifications for financial markets in other countries. Movies, television, and advertising from one society affect the tastes, interests, and styles in other societies. Polluted air and water cross national borders. Deforestation in the Third World, which has a major effect on climate change, occurs because of the greed of developers, the desperation of poor peasants, and the shortsighted efforts by governments to pay off debt to wealthy nations. Global warming caused by the burning of fossil fuels also changes climates, generates megastorms, and increases the spread of tropical diseases around the world. A disease such as HIV/AIDS left Africa forty years ago and now infects about 40 million people worldwide. There has been a dramatic increase in migration flows, especially from poorer to richer nations. With sophisticated weapons systems, no nation is immune from assault from other nations or terrorist acts by revolutionary groups.

Each of these is an example of **globalization**, which involves the processes by which everyone on Earth becomes increasingly interconnected economically, politically, culturally, and environmentally. Connections among peoples outside their tribes or political units are not new but the linkages now are increasing geometrically, with few if any groups not affected. We concentrate here on economic globalization.

Most significant in the emergence of the globalization of the economy was the development of new technologies associated with production, transportation, and communications. Three technological developments—jumbo jet aircraft, the container ship, and computer/satellite-based telecommunications—were vitally important to the interconnectedness of all peoples. The rapid changes in information and communications technology (satellites, computers, cell phones) have made it possible to have instantaneous communication worldwide. Whole databases can be transferred in seconds. Money can be transferred anywhere in the world twenty-four hours a day. The Internet makes an integrated economy possible.

193

CHAPTER 8
Structural Sources
of Societal Change:
Economic and
Demographic

"Look, I've got nothing against globalization, just as long as it's not in my backyard."

Although trade between and among nations is not new, global trade entered a new phase after World War II. What has evolved is a global trade network, the integration of peoples and nations, and a global economy, with a common ideology—capitalism. Former colonies have established local industries and sell their raw materials, products, and labor on the global market. The United States emerged as the strongest economic and military power in the world, with U.S. corporations vitally interested in expanding their operations and markets to other societies for profit. The shift to a global economy has been accelerated by the tearing down of tariff barriers. The North American Free Trade Agreement (NAFTA) and the General Agreement on Tariffs and Trade (GATT), both passed in 1994, are two examples of agreements that increased the flow of goods across national boundaries. In 2005 Congress passed and President Bush signed the Central American Free Trade Agreement (CAFTA), which institutes a Western hemisphere–wide version of NAFTA (Rasmus, 2005).

The globalization of the economy is not a neutral process. Decisions are based on what will maximize profits, thus serving the owners of capital not necessarily workers or the communities where U.S. operations are located. In this regard, private businesses, in their search for profit, make crucial investment decisions that change the dynamics of families and communities. Most significant are the corporate decisions regarding the movement of corporate moneys from one investment to another (called **capital flight**). This shift of capital takes several forms: investment in plants located in other nations, plant relocation within the United States, and mergers. While these investment decisions may be positive for corporations, they also take away investment (disinvestment) from others (workers and their families, communities, and suppliers). See the panel titled "Globalization: Boxing Up U.S. Jobs and Sending Them Overseas."

Globalization has meant the migration of manufacturing jobs to low-wage economies. It has also affected white-collar jobs as they, too, are done by cheaper labor in other countries as U.S. corporations seek to improve their profits. This migration of jobs takes two forms: offshoring and outsourcing (Friedman, 2005).

Boxing Up U.S. Jobs and Sending Them Overseas

Following the September 11, 2001, terrorist attacks, Boeing, the giant aerospace corporation, laid off nearly 30,000 workers due to many airlines canceling or delaying plane orders (the following is mostly from Holmes, Stanley, 2002). A year later, Boeing announced that it would not hire back these workers but instead would shift most of its work to lower-cost suppliers in the United States, and would move the advanced design and engineering tasks to Russia and China (the Russian engineers, for example, make about $10,000 a year, compared to $72,000 that the average Boeing engineers make). Specifically, the company has already moved many of its operations outside the United States:

- 500 engineers and technicians from the Moscow Design Center design parts for the 777 and other commercial jetliners.
- Xian Aircraft in central China builds tail sections for the 737.
- WZK-Mielec of Poland makes aircraft doors for the 757.
- Shanghai Aircraft manufactures components for several types of Boeing planes.

- Mexmil in Mexicali, Mexico, makes fuselage-insulation blankets for all of Boeing's commercial planes.

These are examples of outsourcing by Boeing. Outsourcing is the practice of subcontracting work outside the company and its relatively well-paid (usually unionized) workers to companies inside and outside the United States where the costs are cheaper. As the head of the engineers' union affected by Boeing's moves, the Society of Professional Engineering Employees in Aerospace (SPEEA), puts it, "They have to stop boxing up our work and sending it to Moscow" (quoted in Holmes, 2002:75).

Boeing executives see globalization as a way to both expand sales to nations that sign on as manufacturing partners and to tap into cheaper labor markets. Philip M. Condit, the chief executive officer of Boeing, used the massive layoffs after September 11 as a window of opportunity to transform Boeing into a "global enterprise that's much less dependent on the U.S. For both brawn and brains" (quoted in Holmes, 2002:74).

Offshoring is when a company moves its production to another country, producing the same products in the same way, but with cheaper labor, lower taxes, and lower benefits to workers. **Outsourcing** refers to taking some specific task that a company was doing in-house—such as research, call centers, accounting, or transcribing—and transferring it to an overseas company to save money and then reintegrating that work back into the overall operation.

Out of this economic mix transnational corporations have emerged as economic and political powers, sometimes eclipsing the wealth of nation-states, which compare the gross domestic product of countries with the revenues of the largest corporations. The United States dominates this global corporate network with U.S. transnational corporations in 2002 accounting for more than half the capitalization of the top 1,000 global companies and with General Electric, Microsoft, Exxon Mobil, Wal-Mart, and Citigroup taking the top five places (*Business Week*, 2002). Strengthening the corporate linkages across political boundaries, transnational corporations often own stakes in each other. In the automobile industry, for example, Chrysler is now owned by German automaker Daimler Chrysler, which also owns a controlling stake in Mitsubishi Motors and 10 percent of Hyundai; General Motors owns Saab and has stakes in Isuzu, Suzuki, Suburu, Fiat, and Daewoo; Ford owns Mazda, Volvo, Jaguar, Land Rover, and Aston Martin (Muller, 2002). Moreover, foreign companies such as Honda, Toyota, Mercedes, and BMW have built automobile-manufacturing plants in the United States (usually in the South where wages are lower and unions weaker). Similarly, Ford and General Motors have automobile assembly plants in Europe, Latin America, and Australia. Takeovers, mergers, and expansion to other countries have resulted in only five major surviving automobile companies. The important point is that economic power in the worldwide economy is concentrated in the boardrooms of an ever-decreasing number of transnational corporations.

Global investment worldwide has potential for improving the lot of billions of people. The rise of market capitalism around the world has increased economic growth by transferring nearly $2 trillion from rich countries to poor through investments and loans and by creating millions of jobs. But there is a downside. *Business Week* argues that the multinational corporations have contributed to labor, environmental, and human-rights abuses.

Outsourcing refers to taking some specific task that a company was doing in-house—such as research, call centers, accounting, or transcribing—and transferring it to an overseas company to do it for less money, and then reintegrating that work back into the overall operation.

The extremes of global capitalism are astonishing. While the economies of East Asia have achieved rapid growth, there has been little overall progress in much of the rest of the developing world. Income in Latin America grew by only 6 percent in the past two decades, when the continent was opening up. Average incomes in sub-Saharan Africa and the old Eastern bloc have actually contracted. The World Bank figures the number of people living on $1 a day increased, to 1.3 billion, over the past decade. The downside of global capitalism is the disruption of whole societies. While the industrialized countries have enacted all sorts of worker and environmental safeguards since the turn of the century, the *global economy is pretty much still in the robber-baron age.* (Engardio and Belton, 2000:74. Italics added)

Structural Changes in the U.S. Economy Resulting from Globalization

From Manufacturing to Services. The U.S. economy was once dominated by agriculture, but in the twentieth century, while agricultural productivity increased, the number employed in agriculture declined precipitously. Manufacturing replaced agriculture, representing a **structural transformation of the economy**. Now we are undergoing another shift—from an economy dominated by manufacturing to one now characterized by service occupations and the collection, storage, and dissemination of information.

In a special issue devoted to the twenty-first-century corporation, *Business Week* notes the profound transformation of corporations occurring now.

For nearly all of its life, the modern corporation has made money by making things. It has done so by amassing fixed assets, organizing large workforces, and managing hierarchically. The 21st century corporation will do little of that. It will make money by producing knowledge created by talented people working with partners all over the world. So fundamental will the changes be that the corporation as we know it will likely exist only on the margins of the economy. . . . We are just in the beginning of the beginning. The 21st century is going to be hard on corporations, governments, and all the rest of us. But the changes the century will bring will be nothing short of astonishing. (*Business Week*, 2001:278)

The United States is shifting to an economy based on ideas rather than physical capital. Most of the manufacturing by U.S. transnational corporations is now done in foreign countries. Corporate capital is invested overseas because manufacturing overseas is profitable, mainly because of cheap, nonunionized labor and the relative lack of government regulations over corporations' operations. The companies believe that U.S. regulations—on pollution and worker safety, for instance—are excessive and expensive.

The fundamental reason for foreign location of production, though, is greater profit from lower wages. Corporate executives, seeking to maximize profits, may decide to move their business to another locality. Such decisions involve what is called plant migration or, more pejoratively, "runaway shops." The decision may be to move the plant to Mexico, to the Caribbean, to Central America (all baseballs for Major League Baseball, for example, are manufactured in Costa Rica), or to the Far East, where many U.S. plants involved in textiles, electronics assembly, and other labor-intensive industries are located.

U.S. corporations are also moving some of their operations to other English-speaking countries such as Ireland, Barbados, Jamaica, the Philippines, and Singapore, where cheap labor does such tasks as data entry for accounting, medical transcription, airline and hotel reservations, and telemarketing.

As manufacturing jobs shift to low-wage economies, transnationals move their operations from place to place in search of ever lower wages. In this "race to the bottom," countries such as Mexico, which once benefited, are now losing jobs to even lower wage countries such as China. "Globalization promotes a destructive competition in which workers, communities, and entire countries are forced to cut labor, social, and environmental costs to attract mobile capital. When many countries each do so, the result is a disastrous 'race to the bottom'" (Brecher, Costello, and Smith, 2000:5).

Capital is also moved within the United States as corporations shut down operations in one locality and start up elsewhere. Profit is the motivation for investment in a new place and disinvestment in another. Corporations move their plants into communities and regions where wages are lower, unions are weaker or nonexistent, and the business climate is more receptive (i.e., there are lower taxes and greater government subsidies to the business community).

Obviously, the corporations profit greatly from such arrangements; U.S. workers do not. In the United States, corporations have threatened to move their operations to another part of the United States or to a foreign country, resulting in workers accepting lower wages and fewer benefits. Similarly, workers everywhere have lost

all rights except the right to sell their labor power. All over the world, employers have downsized, outsourced, and made permanent jobs into contingent ones. Employers have attacked job security requirements, work rules, worker representation, healthcare, pensions, and other social benefits, and anything else that defined workers as human beings and employers as partners in a social relationship, rather than simply as buyers and sellers of labor power. (Brecher et al., 2000:3)

197

CHAPTER 8
Structural Sources
of Societal Change:
Economic and
Demographic

Another source of downward pressure on wages is the use of subcontractors. In a domestic form of outsourcing, corporations hire domestic firms to do facets of their work. An airline, for example, may hire subcontractors to handle baggage, do janitorial services, or do clerical work. A local cable company may subcontract for workers to lay cable or install new lines. By hiring subcontractors for such tasks, the company avoids paying its employees, who would do that work, union wages and benefits.

The Changing Nature of Jobs in the United States. Every new era poses new problems of adjustment, but this one differs from the agricultural and industrial eras. The earlier transformations were gradual enough for adaptation to take place over several decades, but conditions are significantly different now (see the panel titled "A Closer Look: Capitalism's Changing Job Market: A Process of Creative Destruction"). The rate of change is phenomenal and unprecedented. In today's global economy, communication is instantaneous and capital is incredibly mobile. The types of work and the characteristics of the workforce in the United States are changing. These factors result in considerable discontinuity and disequilibrium, especially job loss.

The demand for workers has shifted from physical labor to cognitive abilities in the United States, meaning that the best educated and trained will benefit with good jobs, benefits, and opportunities. The less educated do not benefit in such a climate. When workers had strong union industrialized jobs, their wages and benefits were enough for a middle-class lifestyle. Now, typically, their work provides the services that are poorly paid, and some jobs have few if any benefits; for example, working as clerks, cashiers, custodians, nurses' aides, security guards, waiters, retail salespersons, and telemarketers. As a result, the Census Bureau estimates that someone whose education does not go beyond high school but who works full time can expect to earn about $1.2 million between the ages of twenty-five and sixty-four. A college graduate, in contrast, can expect to earn $2.1 million, and those with professional degrees, $4.4 million (Armas, 2002).

Technological change has meant the loss of jobs. Production jobs have also been lost to automation. Robots have replaced humans doing routine work such as picking fruit, shearing sheep, welding, painting, and scanning products for defects. Similarly, many white-collar jobs are being lost because of new technologies. The Internet, for example, allows people to make their own travel arrangements, reducing or eliminating the need for travel agents, or to buy and sell stocks, making stock brokers unnecessary. Within firms, computer programs take care of payrolls, inventory, and delivery schedules, reducing the need for accountants. Primarily because of voice mail, laser printers, and word processors, hundreds of thousands of secretarial and clerical jobs have been eliminated.

The organization of work is being reshaped. The Internet is revolutionizing how business is transacted. Consumers can now purchase goods over the Internet, reducing the need for sales clerks and allowing warehouses to replace retail stores. Most significant, about 30 million U.S. workers function in temporary, contracted, self-employed, leased, part-time, and other "nonstandard" arrangements. These **contingent workers** typically lack an explicit contract for ongoing employment and thus receive sporadic wages. This trend represents a dramatic change in work. Businesses argue that they need this arrangement for flexibility in a

Capitalism's Changing Job Market: A Process of Creative Destruction

Societies experience periodic sharp economic transformations, each having dramatic effects on jobs—creating new ones and destroying others. Let's consider, briefly, two economic transformations in the United States during the twentieth century—the fall of agriculture and the rise and fall of manufacturing.

Agriculture

In 1850, 60 percent of workers were employed in agriculture. Now, less than 2.7 percent are engaged in farming (Rifkin, 1995:109–110). This dramatic shift was caused by the new technologies (for example, tractors replaced horses; trucks displaced wagons; combines deposed threshing machines; mechanized cotton, tomato, and corn pickers made field workers obsolete; and herbicides took the place of people with hoes). In effect, the combustion engine replaced oxen, mules, horses, and all but a few people. The result was that many millions of farmers changed jobs. Many occupations (harnessmakers, those who made handcrafted wood plows, farriers) became obsolete while others flourished (for example, the manufacture of farm implements, giving rise to the John Deere Company and Ford, which specialized in tractors and trucks). The science of farming also created new jobs with the need for more effective fertilizers, herbicides, and insecticides, as well as the development of new plant-breeding techniques designed to produce varieties and strains that were more uniform and easier to manipulate with machines.

Manufacturing Products

During the twentieth century, the great job growth machine was in manufacturing. Workers, many of whom formerly worked on farms or in the mines, moved to industrial centers, where work was plentiful in the steel mills, automobile plants, and other places of manufacture. With the help of unions and increased government programs (for example, Social Security), these blue-collar workers prospered.

There is no parallel in history to the rise of the working man in the developed countries during this century. Eighty years ago American blue-collar workers, toiling 60 hours a week, made $250 a year at most . . . and they had no "fringes," no seniority, no unemployment insurance, no Social Security, no paid holidays, no overtime, no pension—nothing but a cash wage of less than one dollar a day. Today's employed blue-collar worker in a unionized mass-production industry (steel, automotive, electrical machinery, paper, rubber, petroleum) working 40 hours a week earns about $50,000 a year—half in cash wages, half in benefits. . . . And now it is suddenly over. There is no parallel in history to the abrupt decline of the blue-collar worker during the past 15 years. As a proportion of the working population, blue-collar workers in manufacturing have decreased to [16 percent] of the American labor force from more than a third. By the year 2010 . . . they will constitute no larger a proportion of the labor force of every developed country than farmers do today—that is, a 20th of the total. . . . Yesterday's blue-collar workers in manufacturing were society's darlings; they are fast becoming stepchildren. (Drucker, 1989:81–82)

These workers are being displaced by automation and the flight of capital. In 1980, for example, U.S. Steel employed 120,000 people in steel production. Ten years later, it employed 20,000, yet maintained the same steel tonnage (Drucker, 1993:72). Even with the dramatic decline of workers in the entire manufacturing industry, U.S. companies have continued to increase output and overall production, with more and more automation, including the use of robots. "Automated technologies have been reducing the need for human labor in every manufacturing category. . . . Over the next quarter-century we will see the virtual elimination of the blue-collar, mass assembly-line worker from the production process" (Rifkin, 1996:11). These two transformations show that capitalism is a process of creative destruction. This is to say that with technological change, new opportunities emerge just as the old ways are destroyed. The present transformation from the industrial age to an information age presents just such a situation with winners and losers.

rapidly changing competitive economy. These growing numbers of workers are not tied to an employer, which makes them free to choose from available work options. The downside of this trend is that most of the jobs (60 percent) pay, on average, 40 percent less than regular full-time jobs held by similar workers. In short, this trend has meant the proliferation of marginal jobs, with employers now shifting the burden of fringe benefits to individual workers. About three-fourths of those working in contingent work arrangements are women, many of whom work out of their homes.

199
CHAPTER 8
Structural Sources
of Societal Change:
Economic and
Demographic

Job Insecurity. From 2001 through 2003 some 9.86 million workers lost their jobs. Forty-five percent of them—4.4 million—had new full-time jobs by the end of 2003, but over half of them were earning less than before (Bureau of Labor Statistics, reported in Reuteman, 2004). In June 2004 more than one-fifth of the jobless were unemployed long term, that is 27 weeks or more (Mishel, Bernstein, and Allegretto, 2004) (see Figure 8.1).

Even during the economic boom of the late 1990s when the unemployment rate was the lowest in thirty years, about one-third of the nation's 140-million-strong workforce feared losing their jobs (Leonhardt, 2000). Then the economic climate changed with the bursting of the technology speculation bubble on Wall Street and the September 11 terrorist attacks. With declining profits, companies downsized. Mergers brought more downsizing. The movement of capital and jobs to other countries caused a further decline in jobs. Those who kept their jobs found that their employers often reduced their benefits.

The least secure are minorities, women, and the working poor. The median African American family income in 2003 was about $30,000, which was 62 percent of the median White family income ($48,000), and their rate of joblessness is consistently at least twice that of Whites (see Table 8.1). The median hourly wage of

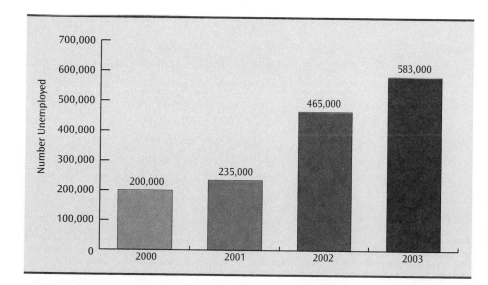

FIGURE 8.1

The Number of Parents Experiencing Long-Term Unemployment Nearly Tripled between 2000 and 2003 (Parents Unemployed Longer than 26 Weeks, Annual Averages)

Source: U.S. Department of Commerce, Bureau of the Census, *Current Population Survey,* January 2000–December 2003. Calculation by Children's Defense Fund.

Sure, jobs are lost through downsizing, but new jobs are created to take their place.

PART TEMP

PART TIME TEMP INC

© Kirk Anderson. Reprinted by permission.

Black men was about 73 percent that of White men in 2003 and the median wage for Latino men was about 64 percent of the White median wage rate. Women are much less secure than men. They earn less money (about 76 cents for every dollar a man made in 2003). Compared with White women workers, the percentages for Blacks and Latinas in 2003 were 86 and 75 percent respectively (Yates, 2005). Women are easy targets when downsizing occurs because they usually have less

TABLE 8.1

U.S. Unemployment Rates

Years	Overall Rate	White Rate	Black Rate	Hispanic Rate
1973–79	6.5%	6.8%	12.5%	9.5%
1979–89	7.1	5.5	14.7	10.3
1989–2000	5.6	4.2	10.8	8.6
1995	5.6	4.9	10.4	9.3
1996	5.4	4.7	10.5	8.9
1997	4.9	4.2	10.0	7.7
1998	4.5	3.9	8.9	7.2
1999	4.2	3.7	8.0	6.9
2000	4.0	3.5	7.6	5.7
2001	4.7	4.2	8.6	6.6
2002	5.8	5.1	10.2	7.5
2003	6.0	5.2	10.8	7.7
2004	5.5	4.8	10.4	7.0

Sources: Bureau of Labor Statistics (BLS), http://www.bls.gov. These are official unemployment rates, derived from a monthly survey of households. They include only those who are without jobs but are actively seeking work. They exclude so-called "discouraged workers," those who have given up looking for work for market-related reasons. They also exclude "involuntary part-time" workers, those who desire full-time work but cannot find it.

seniority than men. More women than men are contingent workers, and therefore they have no guarantees of work. And almost six out of ten minimum-wage workers are women, for which not only the pay is weak ($5.15 an hour) but benefits are virtually nonexistent. The 2.5 million people who left welfare for work since the 1996 welfare reform laws are especially vulnerable in the declining economy. Since they are only recently hired, they will be the first fired. Moreover, they tend to work in the very industries hit hardest by the September 11 fallout—hotel, restaurant, travel, tourism, and retail (Leondar-Wright, 2001). More fundamentally, there are not enough jobs for the poor, even during boom times. Economist Timothy Bartik (2002) estimates that the United States is 5 to 9 million jobs short of jobs for the poor. A surplus of workers over jobs means high rates of unemployment, low wages, and no impetus for the government to raise the minimum wage. Thus, the poor, even the working poor, remain poor.

Job insecurity is heightened further by mergers. Mergers reduce the number of jobs (for example, after Qwest merged with US West in 2000, the new corporate entity cut 11,000 jobs and 1,800 contractor positions).

What happens to displaced workers? Some become permanently unemployed while others find work. For those who become employed again, many will be downwardly mobile, taking lower paying jobs with fewer if any benefits. This trend toward downward mobility has occurred at the very time when the government "safety net" has decreased.

Benefits Insecurity. Workers in the major sectors of the economy (steel, automobile manufacturing, airlines, and the like) have benefited in the past from union contracts whereby employers subsidized health care plans and provided Defined Benefit Pension plans (a promise of a specified monthly benefit at retirement). Today's workers, however, are increasingly insecure about their health benefits and pensions. With relatively weak unions and competition from low-wage economies, U.S. corporations have been reducing their benefits to workers. Some have quit providing health insurance while others have required the workers to pay for a larger portion of their insurance.

In 2005 a federal court allowed United Airlines to renege on its pension promises to 134,000 employees and retirees (saving United $9.8 billion in total pension liabilities). Part of the shortfall will be paid by the Pension Benefit Guarantee Corporation, but that federal agency has a deficit of $23 billion. This may have a snowball effect as pension underfunding for U.S. companies is an estimated $450 billion. A major trend is for corporations to shift from Defined Benefit Pension plans to 401(k) plans and individual health savings accounts. These shift the risks of old age and ill health off the corporate ledger and onto the worker. "The premise behind the plotline is that workers must accept whatever cuts corporate titans choose to impose—wage reductions, pension terminations, health insurance that is ended or eroded through higher co-payments—as the price of holding onto their jobs." (Cocco, 2005:A32).

Declining Middle Class. As we have seen, technological changes, the global economy, and the shift from manufacturing to service jobs have reduced labor's bargaining power, lowered wages and workers' benefits, and increased job insecurity. In effect, these powerful forces are shifting the income distribution of people in the United States so that the middle class is declining and the gap between the haves and the have-nots is expanding.

201

CHAPTER 8
Structural Sources
of Societal Change:
Economic and
Demographic

One reason for a declining middle class is the loss of jobs in the relatively well-paid industrial sector. The jobs created to replace them in services, information, and high technology are at the extremes, with few in the middle. There are top jobs (about 20 percent of jobs) with advancement potential, high pay, and prestige, such as in banking, finance, and engineering. These jobs require considerable education and specialized training. Jobs at the low end of the services industry offer low pay, few benefits, low prestige, and no bridge to upward mobility. Workers who have been downsized from their middle-income manufacturing jobs are not suited for the top-tier jobs, and, if they find jobs, are paid, on average, 20 percent less than they were paid for the jobs they lost.

Many communities have been devastated when companies located in them moved to new localities. When U.S. Steel or some other corporation closes its plants, permanently laying off thousands in a community, individuals and families suffer but so, too, do the communities, with declining real estate values, diminished retail sales, plummeting tax revenues, and severely reduced bank assets. Thus, the standard of living for entire communities is negatively affected.

Finally, even workers who remain in the declining manufacturing industries experience a decline in their standard of living. Given the triple threats of employers moving plants to the Sun Belt or to foreign countries, heightened international competition for their products, and more layoffs, the unions have accepted steep concessions to stem further job losses, but this reduces further the middle-class lifestyle once enjoyed by these workers.

The Increase in the Working Poor. Having a job is not necessarily a path out of poverty. About one-seventh of all poor people work full-time for the entire year. Despite working, these people remain poor because they hold menial, dead-end jobs that have no benefits and pay the minimum wage or below. In 2003 almost one-fourth of workers worked at or below the poverty wage (see Table 8.2). The federal minimum wage of $5.15 an hour adds up to only $10,712 for full-time work ($8,267 short of what a family of four needed to exceed the poverty line in 2003). Just above the minimum wage are more than 2 million Americans working in nursing homes, as child care workers, janitors, health care aides, hospital orderlies, and retail sales clerks (Reich, 2000).

Those working at poverty wages are disproportionately women and racial/ethnic minorities. One in three women earns poverty-level wages, compared with one out of five men. Similarly, one in three African American men, two out of five African American women and Latino men, and slightly more than half of Latina women work at jobs that pay poverty wages.

The New Poor. Millions of blue-collar workers have lost their jobs when companies closed, as companies moved in search of cheaper labor, and when they were replaced by robots or other forms of automation. Many of these displaced workers find other work, but usually at lower-paying jobs. They are poorer but not poor. Many others, though, especially those who are over forty, find gaining employment difficult because their skills are outmoded and they are considered too old to retrain.

These **new poor** are quite different from the "old poor." The old poor—that is, the poor of other generations—had hopes of breaking out of poverty; if they did not break out themselves, at least they believed their children would. This hope was

203

CHAPTER 8
Structural Sources
of Societal Change:
Economic and
Demographic

TABLE 8.2

Poverty-Level Employment, 2003

Workers	Percent of Employment at or below the Poverty Wage
All workers	24.3%
Men	19.6
Women	29.4
Whites	20.4
Men	15.1
Women	26.0
Blacks	30.4
Men	26.2
Women	33.9
Hispanics	39.8
Men	35.7
Women	45.8

From "A Statistical Portrait of the U.S. Working Class," by Michael D. Yates, *Monthly Review* (2005), 56 (April), p.17. Copyright © 2005 by Monthly Review Press.

based on a rapidly expanding economy. There were jobs for immigrants, farmers, and grade-school dropouts because of the needs of mass production. The new poor, however, are much more trapped in poverty. A generation ago, those who were unskilled and uneducated could usually find work and could even do quite well financially if the workplace was unionized. But now these people are displaced or misplaced. Hard physical labor is rarely needed in a high-tech society. This phenomenon undercuts the efforts of the working class, especially African Americans, Latinos, and other minorities who face the additional burden of institutional racism.

Government data reveal the contours of the new poor. Tens of millions of Americans have lost their jobs in the past two or three decades because of plant closings and layoffs. Almost half of these newly unemployed were longtime workers (workers who had held their previous jobs at least three years), and seven out of ten of them found new jobs. Of those reemployed full-time, slightly less than half make less money than before. These workers were downwardly mobile but likely not poor. About 14 percent, however, did not find employment, and they constitute the new poor. Michael Parenti (1995) summarizes the bleak picture:

> We [are] witnessing the gradual Third-Worldization of the United States, involving the abolition of high-wage jobs, a growth of low-wage and part-time employment, an increase in permanent unemployment, a shrinking middle-income population, a growing number of mortgage delinquencies, greater concentrations of wealth for the few and more poverty and privation for the many. (24)

In summary, the problems associated with the economy and work in U.S. society are structural in origin. To understand the economy and work setting in our society, we must understand the nature of capitalism, for which profit rather than the human consequences guides managerial decisions. Transnational corporations make decisions based on global markets and where the cost of labor and doing business worldwide are the cheapest. While the transnationals prosper, U.S. labor is negatively impacted. This is a profound transformation, causing many dislocations for workers, their families, communities, and society.

The New Immigration and the Changing Racial Landscape

Immigration, the movement of people across political boundaries, is one manifestation of globalization. Since the Pilgrims left Europe and arrived in what is now New England for permanent residence, this process has had important consequences for what has become the United States. The latest wave of immigration—the new immigration—is shaking up society. This change in **demography** challenges the cultural hegemony of the White European tradition; creating incredible diversity in race, ethnicity, language, religion, and culture; and leading, often, to division and hostility.

This **new immigration** represents two trends that set it apart from past immigration. First, the volume of immigration is relatively large. For example, in the ten years from 1963 to 1972, there were about 3.5 million legal immigrants; from 1973 to 1982, there were slightly fewer than 5 million; 9 million were added in the next ten years; and nearly a million have entered the United States every year since 1992 (Spain, 1999:3). As a result, the foreign-born population has risen from 19.8 million in 1990 to 34 million in 2004 (see Figure 8.2). Second, the racial landscape and rate of population growth are greatly affected, as approximately 1 million immigrants annually set up permanent residence in the United States. These new residents are primarily Latino and Asian, not European as was the case in earlier immi-

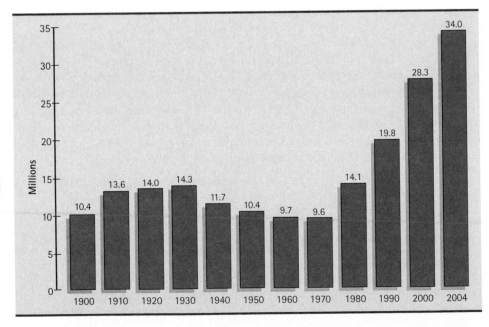

FIGURE 8.2

Foreign-Born Population: 1900 to 2004 (millions)

Sources: U.S. Bureau of the Census, 1993. *We the American . . . Foreign Born* (September):2; Genaro C. Armas, 2000, and El Nassar, 2005:1A.

gration eras. This demographic transition has significant implications for U.S. society, communities, families, and individuals. The facts, myths, and consequences of these two demographic changes are the subjects of this section.

Immigration Patterns

Historically, there have been four major waves of immigration, which were major sources of population growth and ethnic diversity in the United States (Martin and Widgren, 2002:12–13). The first wave of immigrants arrived between 1790 and 1820 and consisted mainly of English-speaking Britons. The second wave, mostly Irish and German, came in the 1840s and 1850s and challenged the dominance of Protestantism, which led to a backlash against Catholics. The third wave, between 1880 and 1914, brought over 20 million, mostly Southern and Eastern Europeans who found factory jobs in large cities. In the 1920s, the United States placed limits on the number of immigrants it would accept, the operating principle being that the new immigrants should resemble the old ones. The "national origins" rules were designed to limit severely the immigration of Eastern Europeans and to deny the entry of Asians.

The fourth immigration wave began in 1965 and continues. The Immigration Act amendments of 1965 abandoned the quota system that had preserved the European character of the United States for nearly half a century. The new law encouraged a new wave of immigrants, only this time the migrants arrived not from northern Europe but from the Third World, especially Asia and Latin America. Put another way, a hundred years ago Europeans were 90 percent of the immigrants to the United States; now, 90 percent of immigrants are from non-European countries. The result, obviously, is a dramatic alteration of the ethnic composition of the U.S. population (see Figure 8.3). And the size of the contemporary immigrant wave has

FIGURE 8.3

U.S. Population by Race, 1980, 1990, 2000, and Projected 2050

Sources: U.S. Bureau of the Census, 1996. *Current Population Reports,* Series P25–1130. Washington, DC: U.S. Government Printing Office; U.S. Bureau of the Census, 2000. Available online: www.census.gov/ population/www/ cen2000.

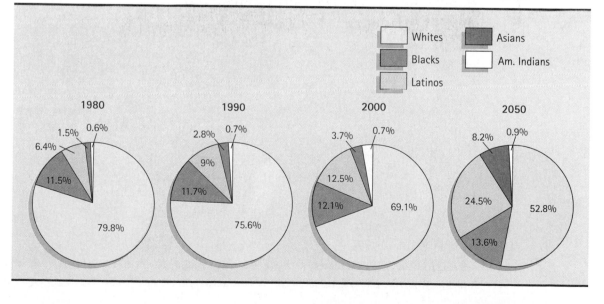

resulted in a visible and significant number of U.S. residents who are foreign-born (slightly more than 12.5 percent in 2004, compared to 5 percent in 1970 and 8 percent in 1990).

In addition to the legal migrants (about 1 million each year), an estimated 300,000 unauthorized aliens enter and stay (an estimated 1.5 million to 2.5 million people enter the United States illegally each year, but most return to their native countries) for a net gain of U.S. immigrants of about 1.3 million annually. Although the number who enters clandestinely is impossible to determine, the best estimate is that approximately 11 million unauthorized foreign nationals resided in the United States in 2005 (Passel, 2005). Roughly 81 percent of these undocumented immigrants are Latino (and about 60 percent of Latinos are Mexicans).

The settlement patterns of this new migration differ from previous flows into the United States. Whereas previous immigrants settled primarily in the industrial states of the Northeast and Middle Atlantic regions, or in the farming areas of the Midwest, recent immigrants have tended to locate on the two coasts and in the Southwest. Asians have tended to settle on the West Coast, Mexicans in the Southwest, with other Latinos scattered (for example, Cubans in Florida and Puerto Ricans and Dominicans in New York).

California is a harbinger of the demographic future of the United States. As recently as 1970, California was 80 percent White, but since then it has been uniquely affected by immigration. The result is that Whites now are a numerical minority (47 percent in 2000, with 32 percent being Latino, 11 percent Asian, and 7 percent African American) (Werner, 2001), and by 2025, only one-third of California's population will be White (Chideya, 1999). Less than 38 percent of California's current public school students are White (Verdin, 2000). Los Angeles

New immigrants are changing the racial/ethnic composition of the United States.

has the largest population of Koreans outside of Korea, the biggest concentration of Iranians in the Western world, and a huge Mexican population. The diverse population of southern California speaks eighty-eight languages and dialects. The Los Angeles metropolitan area has more than fifty foreign-language newspapers, and there are television shows that broadcast in Spanish, Mandarin, Armenian, Japanese, Korean, and Vietnamese. For example, in one ZIP code—90706—lies Bellflower, where 38 languages are spoken (Mohan and Simmons, 2004).

207

CHAPTER 8
Structural Sources
of Societal Change:
Economic and
Demographic

For all this diversity, though, California, most notably southern California, is becoming more and more Latino. California holds nearly half of the U.S. Latino population and well over half of the Mexican-origin population. Latinos are expected to surpass Whites in total California population by 2025 and to become an absolute majority by 2040 (Purdum, 2000).

Similar concentrations of Latinos are found in Arizona and Texas. Historian David Kennedy (1996) argues that there is no precedent in U.S. history for one immigrant group to have the size and concentration that the Mexican immigrant group has in the Southwest today:

> If we seek historical guidance, the closest example we have in hand is the diagonally opposite corner of the North American continent, in Quebec. The possibility looms that in the next generation or so we will see a kind of Chicano Quebec take shape in the American Southwest, as a group emerges with strong cultural cohesiveness and sufficient economic and political strength to insist on changes in the overall society's ways of organizing itself and conducting its affairs. (68)

The Consequences of the New Immigration

Although there are many consequences of the new immigration, we concentrate on three: (1) increasing diversity; (2) the reaction of the hosts to the new immigrants; and (3) the effects of immigration on the immigrants.

Immigration and Increasing Diversity. The United States is shifting from an Anglo-White society rooted in Western culture to a society with three large racial-ethnic minorities, each of them growing in size while the White majority declines in population. Five facts show the magnitude of this demographic transformation.

- *More than one-fourth of the people in the United States are African American, Latino, Asian, or Native American.* The non-White population is numerically significant, comprising 31 percent of the population in 2000 (up from 15 percent in 1960) and more than one-third of all children in the United States are non-White. Three states have non-White majorities (California, New Mexico, and Hawaii). Minorities make up the majority in six of the eight U.S. cities with more than a million people—New York, Los Angeles, Chicago, Houston, Detroit, and Dallas.
- *Racial minorities are increasing faster than the majority population.* While almost 30 percent of Americans are non-Whites, by 2030 a majority of children (under eighteen) will be from a minority background (Chideya, 1999:37), and between 2050 and 2060, Whites will be the numerical minority (Riche, 2000). (See Figure 8.4.)
- *African Americans have lost their position as the most numerous racial minority.* In 1990, for the first time, African Americans were less than half of all minorities. By 2004, Latinos outnumbered African Americans 41.3 million to 36.0 million.

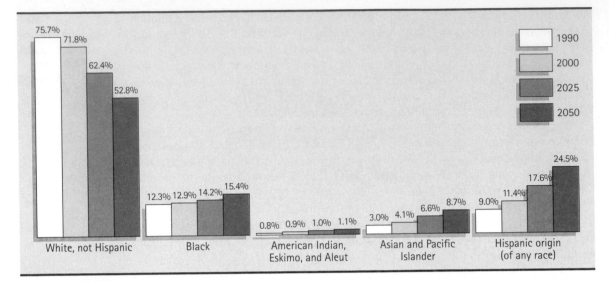

White, not Hispanic: 75.7% (1990), 71.8% (2000), 62.4% (2025), 52.8% (2050)

Black: 12.3% (1990), 12.9% (2000), 14.2% (2025), 15.4% (2050)

American Indian, Eskimo, and Aleut: 0.8% (1990), 0.9% (2000), 1.0% (2025), 1.1% (2050)

Asian and Pacific Islander: 3.0% (1990), 4.1% (2000), 6.6% (2025), 8.7% (2050)

Hispanic origin (of any race): 9.0% (1990), 11.4% (2000), 17.6% (2025), 24.5% (2050)

FIGURE 8.4

U.S. Population by Race and Hispanic Origin, 1990, 2000, 2025, and 2050 (Percent)

Source: U.S. Bureau of the Census, 1998. "1997 Population Profile of the United States." *Current Population Reports,* Special Studies P23–194 (September):9.

By 2050, Latinos are estimated to comprise about one-fourth of the U.S. population with African Americans at about 14 percent. This demographic transformation will make two common assumptions about race obsolete: that "race" is a "Black-and-White" issue, and that the United States is a "White" society (Chideya, 1999).

- *Immigration now accounts for a large share of the nation's population growth.* Today, 12.5 percent of current U.S. residents are foreign-born. Since 1970 the number of foreign-born people has more than tripled from 9.6 million to 34 million. This growth far outpaces the growth of the native-born population. Immigration accounts for over a third of the current population growth directly and adds more indirectly as first- and second-generation Americans have more children on average than the rest of the population (Chideya, 1999).

- *New patterns of immigration are changing the racial composition of society.* Among the expanded population of first-generation immigrants, the Asian-born now outnumber the European-born and those from Latin America, especially Mexicans, outnumber both. This contrasts sharply with what occurred as recently as the 1950s, when two-thirds of legal immigrants were from Europe and Canada.

These trends signal a transformation from a White majority to a multiracial/multicultural society:

Sometime before the year 2060, Whites will become a "minority." This is uncharted territory in this country and this demographic change will affect everything. Alliances between the races are bound to shift. Political and social power will be reapportioned. Our neighborhoods, our schools and workplaces, even racial categories will be altered. (Chideya, 1999:35)

The pace of these changes is quickening. During the 1990s, while the White population increased by 2 percent, the African American population rose by 12 percent, and the Native American numbers increased by 15 percent, the Asian and Latino populations each increased by 58 percent. One consequence of this is that across the United States, there were 47 million people ages 5 and older who spoke a language other than English in 2000. This translates into nearly one in five, compared with one in seven 10 years earlier (U.S. Bureau of the Census, cited in Associated Press, 2003).

209

CHAPTER 8
Structural Sources
of Societal Change:
Economic and
Demographic

The Reaction of the Hosts to the New Immigrants

We consider three questions raised by the new immigration: (1) Do immigrants take jobs away from Americans? (2) Are immigrants a drain on society's resources? (3) Will the increasing proportion of non-Whites, fueled by immigration, lead to a blurring of racial lines or a heightening of tensions among the races/ethnic groups? (Much of the following is taken from a major report by the National Academy of Sciences/National Research Council, reported by Cassidy, 1997.)

Do Immigrants Take Jobs from U.S. Citizens? Immigrants do not have negative effects on the wages of most Americans, but they do for the low-wage/poorly skilled segment of workers (20 percent of all low-wage workers are immigrants). The wages of the lowest 15 percent of the workforce (typically, those with less than a high school degree) receive about 5 percent less in their paychecks because of competition from a large number of immigrants who are relatively uneducated, unskilled, and eager to work. This problem will increase in the future as the federal and state governments no longer provide welfare benefits to legal immigrants and most nonimmigrant welfare recipients are required to leave welfare and find work, adding several million workers to compete for relatively few jobs at the low end of the occupational scale.

On the positive side, immigrants are more likely than the rest of the population to be self-employed and start their own businesses, which in turn creates jobs (Defreitas, 1994) and adds strength to local economies. For example, five years after

the 1992 Los Angeles riots there was an unexpected rebirth in some of the riot-torn areas, led largely by Asian and Latino entrepreneurs, many of whom are first-generation immigrants. These people invested locally and hired locals who spent much of the wages locally. Similar patterns of a migrant-based economy led by entrepreneurs from Jamaica, Mexico, Korea, Taiwan, and India have led to the resurgence in parts of Brooklyn and Queens in New York City and in Houston (Kotkin, 1997).

Immigrants (legal and undocumented) also provide a service to society by doing society's dirty work (stoop labor in the fields, working in sweatshops), work that many poor U.S. citizens are unwilling to do. The panel titled "Human Agency: Low-Wage Immigrant Workers Fight Back" describes the immigrant laborers and their attempt to secure better working conditions.

Are Immigrants a Drain on Society's Resources? Immigrants are found at the top and bottom educational levels. About 30 percent of recent foreign-born arrivals over age twenty-four had an undergraduate, professional, or graduate degree. These immigrants generally find good jobs in the United States. At the other end of the distribution, about 34 percent of the immigrants have not finished high school. Many of these foreign-born arrivals also have difficulties with English. Thus, their employment, generally, is marginal in pay and benefits.

The majority of immigrants require more resources from the state than nonimmigrant families for two reasons. First, they have relatively large families, and these children go to public schools. Second, they pay less in taxes because they tend to earn low wages and have relatively little discretionary income. However, an estimated 7 million undocumented workers pay $7 billion into Social Security and Medicare and are not eligible to receive the benefits, thus, subsidizing these two programs (Porter, 2005).

Immigration policies are federal policies, yet the cost of providing services to immigrants (education, health care) are typically the responsibility of the individual states. This places an unfair burden on states such as California, New York, Texas, and Florida, which have the largest immigrant populations. In California, for example, households headed by U.S.-born persons paid, on average, $2,700 more in federal taxes than they received in federal benefits in 1996. Immigrant households, in contrast, received $2,700 more in federal benefits than they paid in federal taxes. The deficit accrued largely because immigrant households had below-average incomes and thus paid lower taxes than the average household, but they had more children attending public schools than households headed by U.S.-born Californians. The average native-born household paid $1,200 more in taxes to cover the deficit in California. The deficit is less in states with relatively few immigrants. Using the entire U.S. population, households headed by a U.S.-born person paid an extra $200 each in 1996 to cover the gap between taxes paid and services used by immigrant-headed households (Martin and Midgley, 1999:31).

In the long run, however, immigrants are a good investment for society. The Academy of Sciences study reported in Cassidy (1997) found that by the time a typical immigrant with a family dies, that person and his or her children will have paid $80,000 more in taxes than they received in government benefits. The evidence is that immigrants are a fiscal burden for the first twenty-two years, mainly because of educational costs. After that, the society benefits monetarily.

Research also shows that legal and illegal immigration add $1 billion to $10 billion per year to the U.S. gross domestic product, "largely because immigration holds

Low-Wage Immigrant Workers Fight Back

They have the invisibility blues, these low-wage workers in New York's black market labor. On Long Island, they are Central American women who work as maids, or men who wait on the street corners to be picked up for day jobs as gardeners or in construction. In New York City, they are Mexican workers laboring behind deli and pizza counters, delivery men dropping off takeout food, or sweatshop workers competing with low-wage garment factories abroad. Even working long hours, their weekly pay may reach only $150. Sometimes a boss doesn't pay them at all.

Workers in the growing unregulated economy have been invisible to the labor department inspectors who are supposed to enforce minimum wage and hour laws for all, documented and undocumented workers alike. They are largely invisible to the unions. It seems that the only government agency eager to find them is the Immigration and Naturalization Service (INS), which won extra funding from President Clinton and Congress last year to conduct workplace sweeps in search of undocumented— "illegal"—workers to deport. The INS gets help, of course, as it did from Albany-area construction workers who called its agents in this summer to deport nonunion workers removing asbestos from schools.

For the past fifteen years, though, these workers have been visible to workers centers. The organizers and fast-growing membership of these centers reach out to low-income immigrants and native-born Americans to build campaigns for fair and legal working conditions and sometimes for affordable housing. While small, with handfuls of paid staff and at most 1,000 members each, the centers are on the front lines of a battle against harmful, sub-minimum-wage work that depresses the labor conditions of all workers—a battle that most other combatants, from unions to labor investigators, have not been effectively fighting.

It is hard to pinpoint what makes four workers centers in the New York area—and the hundreds elsewhere in the country—distinctive from other organizing. Their tactics are not new, but are particularly suited to reaching the low-wage workers most abused by the system. Campaigns target one high-profile employer for years and build upon ethnic or racial solidarity. Women organize women. Pickets, education, media zaps; these time-worn tactics have an impact because members deploy them in long community-based campaigns and not just workplace struggles.

In a storefront office in Brooklyn, you can see the impact as the women's committee of New York's oldest workers center, Chinese Staff and Workers Association (CSWA) campaign for safety on the job. "Occupational health and safety" is not a bureaucratic turn of phrase for the women, but a need to live without crippling back pain, or without the tips of their fingers peeling off from contact with toxic dyes. One evening in June, they photographed each other's injuries earned working 60 or 70 hours a week in Brooklyn or Manhattan sweatshops. Glued on plasterboard, the photos would soon be displayed on a sidewalk information table and at a neighborhood meeting called to challenge garment bosses.

"We're adopting the older models to new circumstances," says Jennifer Gordon, a Harvard-trained lawyer who four years ago helped found a Long Island workers center, the Workplace Project. "You can't pretend we're making this up."

In some cases, the workers centers' community-based tactics have challenged unions to become more active in organizing or promoting to leadership people they were neglecting. And unions are finding workers centers' innovations worth borrowing. Five years ago the International Ladies Garment Workers Union (ILGWU) began establishing its own workplace justice centers to reach out to undocumented or unorganized workers, and the Service Employees International Union will soon follow with its own in New York.

The workers centers' impact can also be seen in the news every day, as exploitative labor conditions receive more attention. This year, designer Jessica McClintock bowed to the four-year campaign of Oakland's Asian Immigrant Women's Advocates and agreed to subcontract only to bonded manufacturers obeying labor law. Restaurants in Manhattan's Chinatown now pay overtime (even though most still confiscate waiters' tips) as a result of Chinese Staffs' decade-long campaign targeting Silver Palace, the largest restaurant in the neighborhood.

Now the question is: Can the isolated, tiny offices, staffed by three or four activists, help build a widespread movement?

Source: Excerpted from Abby Scher, 1996. "Immigrants Fight Back: Workers Centers Lead Where Others Don't." *Dollars and Sense,* no. 207 (September/October):30–35.

down wages for some jobs, and thus prices, and increases the efficiency of the economy" (Martin and Midgley, 1999:24).

There is also a global dimension to the economic benefits derived from immigrants. Most undocumented immigrants are young, male, and Mexican. They leave their families in Mexico and work for months at a time as manual laborers in the United States. Typically, they send some of their earnings back to their families in Mexico—an aggregate of about $15 billion annually. "As a source of foreign capital [to Mexico], migrant remittances trail only oil, tourism, and illegal drugs. They provide basic support for nearly 1.2 million Mexican households, about 5 percent of the total, according to Mexico's National Population Council" (Smith, 2001:9A).

Will the Increasing Proportion of Non-Whites, Fueled by Immigration, Lead to a Blurring of Racial Lines or a Heightening of Tensions among the Races/Ethnic Groups? The latest wave of immigration has taken place in a historical context that includes the restructuring of the U.S. economy and an increasingly conservative political climate. New immigrants have always been seen as a threat to those already in place. The typical belief is that immigrants, because they will work for lower wages, drive down wages and take jobs away from those already settled here. These fears increase during economic hard times. That is the problem now as businesses downsize and replace workers with technology as they adapt to global competition and the economic transformation.

Previous immigration waves were White, coming mostly from Ireland, England, Germany, Italy, and Eastern Europe. Today's immigrants, in sharp contrast, are coming from Latin America and Asia. They are non-White and have distinctly non-European cultures. When these racial and ethnic differences are added to economic fears, the mix is very volatile.

The situation is worsened further by where the new migrants locate. Typically, they situate where migrants like themselves are already established. For example, 20 percent of the 90,000 Hmong living in the United States live in Minnesota, mostly around Minneapolis–St. Paul. One in twelve Asian Indians lives in Illinois, primarily in the Chicago area. Approximately 40 percent of all Asian Americans live in California. This tendency of migrants to cluster geographically by race/ethnicity provides them with a network of friends and relatives who provide them with support. This pattern of clustering in certain areas tends to increase the fear of nonmigrants toward them. They fear that wages will be depressed and taxes greater because the new neighbors are relatively poor, tend to have children with special needs in school, and they likely do not have health insurance.

A second tendency is for new migrants to locate where other poor people live for the obvious advantages such as cheaper housing. A problem sometimes arises when poor Whites live side by side with one or more racial minorities. Despite their common condition, tensions in such a situation are heightened as groups disadvantaged by society often fight each other for relative advantage. The tensions between African Americans and Asian immigrants was evidenced, for example, during the South Los Angeles riots in 1992, when roughly 2,000 Korean-owned businesses were looted or damaged by fire.

The result of these factors is often an anti-immigrant backlash. Opinion polls taken over the past fifty years report consistently that Americans want to reduce immigration. Typically, these polls report that immigration in the past was a good thing for the country but that it no longer is.

The states with the most immigrants have the highest levels of anti-immigrant feeling. Several states have filed suit against the federal government, seeking reimbursement for the services provided to immigrants. Some twenty-two states have made English the official state language. The voters in California have passed two propositions recently that indicate anti-immigrant feelings. In 1994, they denied public welfare such as nonemergency medical care, prenatal clinics, and public schools to undocumented immigrants. Californians in 1998 also passed a proposition eliminating bilingual education in public schools.

If present immigration patterns continue, by 2050 about one-third of the U.S. population will be post-1970 immigrants and their descendants. As noted earlier, by then neither Whites nor non-Whites will be the numerical majority. Under these circumstances of racial diversity, will the social meaning of ethnic and racial lines become increasingly blurred or more starkly defined? Will people be pulling together or pulling apart? Will the gulf between affluent Whites and the disproportionately poor non-Whites be narrowed or widened? Will there be a de facto segregation as Whites who once lived and worked together with non-Whites move to White gated enclaves, send their children to private schools, and play at private clubs? The noted demographer William Frey describes the current "White flight" from high-immigration areas, a trend that he fears may lead to the "Balkanization of America" (cited in Cassidy, 1997:43). Is this what the future holds? For how one rural Colorado town is coping with a wave of immigration, see the panel titled "Diversity: Newcomers Bring Diversity but Fuel Fears."

Immigration and Agency

Immigration can be forced (e.g., the slave trade) or freely chosen. Immigration in this latter sense is clearly an act of human agency (rather than passively accepting structural constraints, people cope with, adapt to, and change their social situations to meet their needs). Most people in developing countries do not move. Others move, breaking with their extended family and leaving neighborhood and community ties, most to improve their economic situation or to flee repression.

Typically, new immigrants face hostility from their hosts, who, as we have seen, fear them as competitors or hate them because they are "different" or because they suspect that they are terrorists. In this latter instance, immigrants from Islamic countries have had to confront considerable hostility and suspicion since September 11, 2001. Moreover, they face language barriers as they seek jobs. Often, most especially for undocumented immigrants, their initial jobs are demeaning, poorly paid, and without benefits. How do they adapt to these often very difficult circumstances? Most commonly, immigrants move to a destination area where there is already a network of friends and relatives. These networks connect new immigrants with housing (often doubling up in very crowded, but inexpensive, conditions), jobs, and an informal welfare system (health care, pooling resources in difficult times). These mutual aid efforts by immigrant communities have been used by immigrant networks throughout U.S. history, whether by Swedish settlers in Minnesota, Mennonite settlers in Kansas, Irish settlers in Boston, or Mexican or Vietnamese settlers today (Martin and Midgley, 1999).

213

CHAPTER 8
Structural Sources
of Societal Change:
Economic and
Demographic

Newcomers Bring Diversity but Fuel Fears

The seventh- and eighth-graders of Yuma [Colorado] Middle School file into lunch amid the same cacophony of giggles and horseplay that clatters through school lunchrooms everywhere.

But taking their seats with trays of the regular Wednesday fried chicken, these teenagers unconsciously divide the cafeteria in two—white students sit exclusively on one side, brown on the other.

Mixing English and Spanish, the school's growing number of Hispanic students chat about Colombian pop star Shakira or Spanish-language soap operas. Across the room, their classmates gab about Britney Spears' breakup and the Olsen twins.

"We just feel more comfortable in our own group," said Guadalupe Hermosillo, a seventh-grader with big, dark eyes who moved here with her parents from Mexico six years ago.

The same invisible line that divides the lunchroom stretches out across a community that in the last five years has seen a dramatic growth in its Hispanic population, fed mostly by workers from Mexico, many of them undocumented. Hispanics now make up nearly a quarter of the 3,200 residents of this farming town on Colorado's eastern prairie, up from just 4 percent at the beginning of the 1990s, census figures show.

In many cases, the line is little more than a conspicuous absence. At the Beacon cafe on U.S. 34, farmers in stained baseball caps chat over steaming cups of coffee. Their faces are weathered and covered with at least a day's growth of whiskers, but not one of them is Hispanic.

"I have mixed feelings about all these changes," said Ken Custer, 57, who was born and raised in Yuma, but now complains that he can't understand the language many of his neighbors speak.

Occasionally, the tensions bubble up beneath the pleasantries of a small-town main street, like the day Sylvia Castillo went into the hardware store and waited as customer after white customer was served before her.

"It felt like racism," said Castillo, 31, whose parents came from Mexico, but who was born and raised in Colorado. "It doesn't seem to matter if you speak English or not."

But Yuma, like other Colorado towns hit by a wave of immigration over the last decade, is also beginning to come to terms with its new identity.

From a mostly white dairy town that a decade ago was in decline, Yuma now finds itself a center of industrial hog farming and sprawling feedlots, brimming with immigrant passion and a newfound prosperity.

Alliance Farms and Central Plains, the two big corporate-owned pig farms in the area, together employ 220 workers, between 65 and 75 percent of them Hispanic.

Those jobs, in turn, have fed a boom in such things as consumer loans and car sales. Rents and housing prices have started to rise. And everybody from the hospital to the First National Bank is hiring bilingual employees.

"I think most people realize that if these workers weren't here, many businesses wouldn't be here either," said Tom Holtorf, who manages a feedlot east of Yuma that employs mostly Hispanics.

Paychecks in hand, the newcomers are peeling away the old face of Yuma and remaking it in their own image.

To overcome low wages, all able family members may work in the family enterprise or at different jobs, combining family resources. To overcome various manifestations of hostility by others, the immigrant community may become closer (the pejorative word is "clannish"), having as little interaction with outsiders as possible. Some may become involved in gangs for protection. Still others may move to assimilate as quickly as possible.

The Effects of Migration on Immigrants: Ethnic Identity or Assimilation? Martin and Midgley (1999) sum up the universal dilemma for immigrants: "There is always

Newcomers Bring Diversity but Fuel Fears continued

Mustain's Grocery on Main Street now stocks Mexican sweets and soda. Visitors to the Yuma County Hospital are directed by signs in both Spanish and English. And the sprawling trailer court north of town has been re-christened "Little Mexico." . . .

Old-time residents complain about loud music and cluttered yards—or that the newcomers are taking jobs that would otherwise go to locals.

"People see that the way of life they've always known is going to change forever," Brewster-Willeke said. "It's when people feel threatened that racism is always worst."

While Yuma's older generation may have a hard time adjusting, many here say that it's in the schools where those attitudes can change.

When middle school principal Dave Wells arrived here five years ago, his student body was 5 percent Hispanic; now it's more than 30 percent. And many new students come without speaking a word of English.

The heavy load of foreign students initially slowed the pace in classrooms, residents say, prompting complaints among English-speaking parents who believed their children's education was suffering.

But Wells said that with time, the school has learned to cope. When Spanish speakers arrive, they're paired with one of the growing number of bilingual students who have now been in the school for several years.

And the middle school now has a new group, the Rainbow Tribe, to try to attune students to the complex themes of race and diversity. Whites join Hispanics and other minority children to talk about issues that might be nuanced as "respect" or as simple as why it's wrong to use the epithet "beaner."

"A young man has to leave the class and complains that he's being made to leave because he's Mexican,"

Wells said. "We have to talk a long time about why he was asked to leave. Was it because he's Mexican or because he keeps talking?"

Still, the differences are often gaping—and go far beyond language.

After a spate of recent immigration arrests in Yuma, many of the school's Spanish-speaking students disappeared for more than a week. Some had parents arrested; others simply went into hiding.

And even as new students master English, they remain in a world distant from the average American teenager's. They listen to Latin pop, watch Spanish-language cable, and gossip about the towns and villages they came from in Mexico, the students said.

"Last year, I tried sitting with my American friends a couple times, but they were talking about stuff that I didn't get," said Hermosillo, the seventh-grader who comes from Chihuahua, the same northern Mexican state as many of her friends.

"If a Mexican starts hanging out with [Americans], they're not Mexican anymore. That's what the other kids think," she said.

But school officials say they are determined.

The middle school tracks suspension rates to make sure bias isn't creeping into disciplinary actions. And teachers are counseled about the difficulties of managing a multi-ethnic classroom.

"The diversity is enriching the community, even though some people are really having a hard time about it," said Liz Felker, the middle school counselor. "They just have to open up and let it happen."

Source: Michael Riley, "Newcomers Bring Diversity but Fuel Fears," *Denver Post* (April 14, 2002):excerpts from 1A, 16A. Reprinted by permission of *The Denver Post.*

a tension between the newcomers' desires to keep alive the culture and language of the community they left behind, and their need and wish to adapt to new surroundings and a different society" (35–36).

Assimilation is the process in which individuals or groups adopt the culture of another group, losing their original identity. A principal indicator of assimilation is language. Many recent immigrants speak a language other than English at home. For earlier immigrants to the United States, the shift to English usage took three generations—from almost exclusive use by newcomers of their traditional language, to their children being bilingual, to their children's children (third-generation immigrants) being monolingual English speakers (Martin and Midgley, 1999).

If the past is a guide, the new immigrants will assimilate. "Our society exerts tremendous pressure to conform, and cultural separatism rarely survives more than a generation" (Cole, 1994:412). But conditions now are different.

An argument countering the assumption that the new immigrants will assimilate as did previous generations of immigrants is that the new immigrants are racial/ethnics, not Whites. As such, they face individual and institutional racism that excludes them from full participation, just as it has excluded African Americans and Native Americans (O'Hare, 1993:2). The current political mood is to eliminate affirmative action (as did California in 1997), thus eliminating a policy aimed at leveling the playing field so that minorities would have a fair chance to succeed. Moveover, new immigrants, different in physical characteristics, language, and culture, will likely be used as scapegoats for the difficulties that the White nonimmigrant majority faces.

Another negative factor facing this generation of immigrants is that they enter the United States during a critical economic transformation, in which the middle class is shrinking and the working class faces difficult economic hurdles. In the past, the industrial economy had jobs for low-skilled workers. Non-English-speaking people even had opportunities on assembly lines where the pay and benefits were often quite good. Now, the available jobs for the unskilled are limited to dead-end jobs with low pay and benefits. Sociologist Herbert Gans (1990) argues, for example, that the second generation of post-1965 immigrants will experience downward mobility compared to their parents because of the changing opportunity structure in the U.S. economy.

The issue of immigrant adaptation to the host society is complex, depending on a number of variables. Min Zhou (1997) describes a number of these critical variables, including the immigrant generation (for example, first or second), their level in the ethnic hierarchy at the point of arrival, what stratum of U.S. society absorbs them, the degree to which they are part of a family network, and the like.

Immigrants who move to the United States permanently have four options regarding assimilation. Many try to blend into the United States as quickly as possible. Others resist the new ways, either by developing an adversarial stance toward the dominant society or by focusing more intensely on the social capital (that is, social networks) created through ethnic ties (Portes and Zhou, 1993). The fourth alternative is to move toward a bicultural pattern (Buriel and De Ment, 1997); that is, immigrants adopt some patterns similar to those found in the host society and retain some from their heritage. While this concept of biculturalism appears to focus on culture, retention or abandonment of the ethnic ways depends on structural variables (Kibria, 1997:207). These variables include the socioeconomic resources of the ethnic community, the extent of continued immigration from the sending society, the links between the ethnic community and the sending society, and the obstacles to obtaining equal opportunity in the new society.

In sum, the new immigration, occurring at a time of economic uncertainty and reduced governmental services, has three pronounced effects that will accelerate in the foreseeable future: (1) an increased bifurcation between the haves and the have-nots; (2) increased racial diversity; and (3) heightened tension among the races.

The Aging Society

217
CHAPTER 8
Structural Sources
of Societal Change:
Economic and
Demographic

Peter Drucker (2001), writing an article titled "The Next Society" in a special issue of *The Economist*, says:

> In the developed countries, the dominant factor in the next society will be something to which most people are only just beginning to pay attention: the rapid growth in the older population and the rapid shrinking of the younger generation. Politicians everywhere still promise to save the existing pensions system, but they—and their constituents—know perfectly well that in another 25 years people will have to keep working until their mid-70s, health permitting. (1)

During the twentieth century, the population of the United States experienced a pronounced change—it has become older, much older. In 1900, about one in twenty-five residents of the United States was sixty-five years and older. By 1950, it was about one in twelve. In 2000, one in eight was sixty-five and older, and, by 2030, it will likely be around one in five. (See Figure 8.5.) In effect, by 2030, when most of today's college students will be around fifty, there will be more grandparents than grandchildren. "The Senior Boom is coming, and it will transform our homes, our schools, our politics, our lives and our deaths. And not just for older people. For everybody" (Peyser, 1999:50).

The Demographics of an Aging Society

In 1900, there were about 3 million Americans age sixty-five and older. Now there are more than 35 million. Two forces—falling birth rate (3.7 children, on average, per family in 1900 compared to 2.1 in 2000) and advances in medicine (life expectancy has increased from 49 in 1900 to 77 in 2000)—have joined to generate this tenfold increase. Figure 8.6 shows the increasing population numbers of the elderly from 1900 to the projected number in 2050.

Not only are the numbers in the elderly category rising, so, too, are the numbers of the old-old (those eighty-five and older). In 2000, 4.3 million people in the United States were eighty-five and older (12 percent of the elderly). By 2050, this number is expected to be 19 million (or 23 percent of all elderly Americans). Children born today have a 50/50 chance of reaching 100 years of age.

The elderly population is disproportionately composed of women. Older women outnumber older men by a ratio of 3 to 2. As age increases, the disparity becomes greater—for those age eighty-five and older, there are about five women to every two men. And, by age one hundred and older, four in five are women.

A combination of biological advantages for women and social reasons explains this difference. Traditionally, men have had the more dangerous occupations (e.g., military combat, miners, police, firefighters). It will be interesting to note whether there are any effects on female longevity as women receive a more equal share of all types of jobs. Meanwhile, though, the current situation creates problems for the majority of elderly women. Because of pensions through work and the traditional bias of Social Security toward women who have not worked outside the home, elderly women are much more likely than elderly men to be poor. Elderly women are much more likely to be

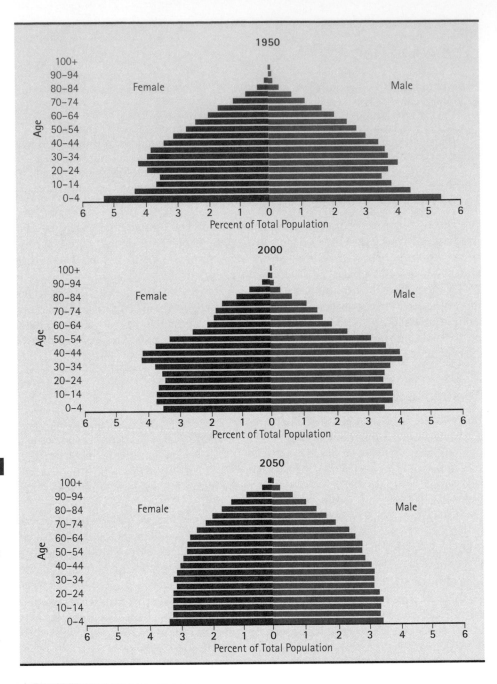

FIGURE 8.5

Population Aging Is a Long-Term Trend

Source: U.S. Bureau of the Census. Projections for 2050 are from U.S. Census middle-series projections of U.S. population. Reprinted from "Government Spending in an Older America." *Reports on America* 3. Washington, DC: Population Reference Bureau, p. 2.

widowed and to live alone. This is the result of the greater longevity of women and the social norm for men to marry younger women. Thus, to the extent that isolation is a problem of the aged, it is overwhelmingly a problem for elderly women.

Racial/ethnic minorities are underrepresented among the elderly. Latinos, for example, while 12.5 percent of the U.S. population in 2000, were only 5 percent of the elderly population in that year. Similarly, African Americans were 12.1 percent

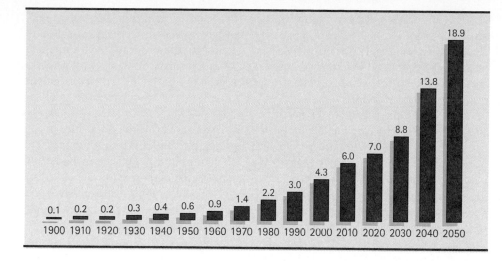

FIGURE 8.6

U.S. Population Age 85 and Older, 1900 to 2050 (in Millions)

Source: Frank B. Hobbs with Bonnie L Damon, 1996. "65+ in the United States." *Current Population Reports,* P23-290:2–8.

of the population but only 8 percent of the elderly population. There are two reasons for these discrepancies. The gap for Latinos is explained in part by immigration, because most immigrants are young adults. But the primary reason for the relatively low proportion of minorities among the elderly, compared to Whites, is that they do not live as long because large numbers do not have health insurance, they receive poor health care, and they work at physically demanding and sometimes dangerous jobs. Most important, the elderly who are members of a racial or ethnic minority are disproportionately poor. In 2000, for example, about 22 percent of Blacks and 19 percent of Latinos were poor compared to only 8 percent of Whites age sixty-five and older (Dalaker, 2001:23–25). This greater likelihood of poverty for racial minorities occurs throughout the life cycle, during which unemployment rates are typically twice as high and average incomes only 60 percent those of Whites. Because of low incomes while working, minorities are doubly disadvantaged when they are old. Not only do they have less chance than those who are better off building a financial reserve to supplement Social Security, their Social Security benefits will be lower, because they are based on lifetime income.

Problems of an Aging Society

Although there are several problems brought about by an aging society, we focus on two: (1) inadequate income from pensions or Social Security; and (2) the high cost of elderly health care.

Social Security. "One out of three seniors depends on Social Security for 90 to 100 percent of their income. Two out of three seniors depend on it for more than half their income" (Sklar, 2004). Since the introduction of Social Security in the 1930s, this program has been a significant aid to the elderly. Social Security has reduced poverty significantly among the elderly—from 35.2 percent in 1959 to 9.8 percent in 2004. "Without Social Security income, 54 percent of America's elderly would live in poverty" (Wellstone, 1998:5).

Despite its considerable strengths, the Social Security program has several serious problems that place a disproportionate burden on certain categories of the elderly and on some portions of the workers paying into the program. An immediate problem is that not all workers are covered by Social Security. Some groups of workers are unable to participate because they work for states with alternative retirement programs. Also, legislation has specifically exempted certain occupations such as agricultural workers from Social Security.

For workers who are eligible for Social Security, there are wide disparities in the benefits received. The amount of benefits depends on the length of time workers have paid into the Social Security program and the amount of wages on which they paid a Social Security tax. In other words, low-paid workers receive low benefits during retirement. Thus, 30 percent of the elderly who depend almost exclusively on Social Security benefits are below the poverty line. These elderly typically are people who have been relatively poor during their working years or are widows.

The Social Security system is also biased against women. Some of these disadvantages are:

- Social Security recognizes only paid work. The benefits for spouses (typically wives) who did not work in the labor force are 50 percent of the working spouse's benefits.
- Social Security benefits are based on the number of years in the labor force and the amount earned from wages. Since women are in the workforce fewer years than men (mostly because they take time off to bear and care for children), and because women typically earn less than men, women receive smaller retirement benefits than men (Hinden, 2001).
- A divorced woman receives half of her former husband's benefit if the couple was married at least ten years. If the divorce occurs before being married ten years, then she receives nothing.
- Where wife and husband are both employed, the wife receives Social Security benefits for her work only if her benefits exceed those earned by her husband. If she collects a benefit based on her own wages, she loses the 50 percent spouse's payment for which her husband's payroll taxes paid.
- A woman who is widowed will not receive any Social Security benefits under age sixty unless she has a child under sixteen or an older disabled child or she herself is disabled.
- Retired female workers receive lower monthly Social Security benefits than retired male workers because women are usually paid less than men and they spend more time out of the workforce usually to care for children.

There is an overarching problem facing Social Security—how to finance it in the future. Two demographic factors make financing the program problematic. The first is that more people are living to age sixty-five and, second, after reaching sixty-five, people live much longer than in earlier generations. Average life spans now are fourteen years longer than they were when Social Security was created in 1935. The obvious consequence of this greater longevity is that the Social Security system pays out more and more to an ever-expanding pool of elderly who live longer and longer.

The second demographic factor working against the system is a skewed **dependency ratio** (the proportion of the population who are workers compared to the proportion not working). Social Security is financed by a tax on workers and their employers. In 1950, there were 16 workers for each person on Social Security; in 1970, there were 3.7 workers; in 2000, there are 3.2; and in 2030 there will be 2.1 workers for each person receiving benefits. At present, the Social Security Administration collects more in taxes than it pays out, with the surplus going into a trust fund. But as people live longer and the baby boomers reach retirement, this system as presently funded will fail. Estimates vary, but sometime around 2015 the system will begin paying out more than it collects, and around 2037, just after the last of the baby boomers turn sixty-five, the trust fund will be empty.

221
CHAPTER 8
Structural Sources
of Societal Change:
Economic and
Demographic

Among the options Congress has to deal with this impending crisis in funding Social Security are to cut benefits; to eliminate the Cost of Living Adjustment (COLA), which allows the payments to keep pace with inflation; to raise the age of eligibility; and to raise Social Security taxes. The first two choices hurt the elderly population, and the other two options place an extraordinary burden on the workers who finance the system. In either case, there will likely be increasing hostility between the generations.

Paying for Health Care. Of all age groups, the elderly are the most affected by ill health. These problems escalate especially from age seventy-five onward, as the degenerative processes of aging accelerate. Consider the following facts:

- Although the elderly comprise only about 13 percent of the population presently, they consume more than one-third of all health care in the United States.
- Elderly people make more than twice as many doctor visits, on average, than younger people age fifteen to forty-four.
- The elderly are four times as likely as the nonold to be hospitalized. When hospitalized, they stay an average of about three days longer than the nonold.
- The medical expenses of the old are three times greater than those of middle-aged adults, yet their incomes are typically much less.
- The elderly account for more than one-third of all spending for prescription drugs.
- The incidence of Alzheimer's disease, the leading cause of dementia in old age, rises sharply with advancing age—from less than 4 percent of those age sixty-five to seventy-four to nearly half (48 percent) of those age eighty-five and older.
- The cost of long-term care is prohibitive, with the average yearly cost in 1999 for nursing home care at $46,000. Since Medicare does not pay for most long-term care, long-term care insurance is expensive, and Medicaid will help only after the patient's resources are exhausted, the result is that many elderly will end their lives impoverished (*USA Today*, 1999c).
- The rapid rise in the numbers of old-old (those eighty-five and older) exacerbates the health needs that society must supply. For example, about 4 million Americans now have Alzheimer's disease, a number expected to rise to 16 million by 2050 because of the ever-increasing number of old-old, according to the U.S. Centers for Disease Control and Prevention (reported in *USA Today*, 2002a). This will put an enormous strain on the families of those impaired who must provide round-the-clock care. Most will end up in nursing homes, which are in short supply now. In 2050, the number of old-old will be almost five times the number now, and society has difficulty supplying nursing needs now.

Medicare is the health insurance program begun in 1965 for almost everyone age sixty-five and older. Everyone is automatically entitled to hospital insurance, home health care, and hospice care through this program. For an additional modest fee, Medicare offers supplemental medical insurance that helps pay for doctors' bills, outpatient services, diagnostic tests, physical therapy, and medical supplies. Overall, Medicare is financed by payroll taxes, premiums paid by recipients, and a government subsidy.

There are three major problems with Medicare. First, it is insufficiently financed by the government. Second, from the perspective of the elderly, only about half of their health care bills are paid through the program, leaving them with substantial costs. The affluent elderly are not hurt because they can afford supplemental health insurance. The poor are not hurt because they are also covered by Medicaid (a government program that is also in financial difficulty), a separate program financed by federal and state taxes that pays for the health care of indigent people. The near poor, however, do not qualify for Medicaid and cannot afford additional health insurance. A third problem with Medicare is that physicians feel that the program pays them too little for their services. As a result many physicians limit the number of Medicare patients they will serve, some even refusing to serve any Medicare patients. Thus, some elderly have difficulty in finding a physician.

Responses by the Elderly: Human Agency

Being old is a difficult stage in life for many. People who were once attractive, active, and powerful may no longer be so. They must live on restricted incomes that become more constricted by inflation. They must face health problems, pain, and impending death. Many are isolated because they have lost a spouse and their children live at a distance. Some elderly, especially the poor and those in many nursing homes, live lives of desperation and hopelessness.

After studying the aged for fifteen years, Bernice Neugarten and her associates delineated four major personality types among people age seventy and older (Neugarten, 1980). The majority of the elderly retain integrated personalities. They function well, are intellectually able, and have competent egos. Another category, the defended, are achievement-oriented people who continue to work hard. They fight the aging process by not giving in to it and by remaining very active. Passive-dependent people, in contrast, have essentially given in to the inevitability of aging. They become inactive and depend on others. Finally, a relatively small proportion are the disinterested (disorganized) elderly. These people have experienced a deterioration of their thought processes. They may be confused, disoriented, forgetful, childish, and paranoid.

These personality types reflect responses to being old, a devalued status in the United States. Being considered old by society and by oneself is a catalyst that provokes the individual to respond in characteristic ways. But—and this is the crucial sociological point—the elderly are reacting to socially structured inequalities and socially constructed definitions, not to age as such. In a different cultural setting in which status increased with age, observers would likely find different personality types and responses.

Some researchers have argued that senior citizens respond to the aging process by retreating from relationships, organizations, and society (called **disengagement**). This behavior is considered normal and even satisfying for the individual, because withdrawal brings a release from societal pressures to compete and conform. Other researchers have quarreled with the disengagement theory, arguing that many elderly people are involved in a wide range of activities.

223

CHAPTER 8
Structural Sources
of Societal Change:
Economic and
Demographic

The majority of the elderly does remain active until health problems curtail their mobility and mental acuity. A striking number of them become politically active in an attempt to change some of the social conditions especially damaging to them. Faced with common problems, many join in collective efforts both locally and nationally. Several national organizations are dedicated to political action to benefit the elderly. Most significant is the American Association of Retired Persons (AARP), with more than 35 million members. Representative other groups are the National Committee to Preserve Social Security and Medicare, the National Council of Senior Citizens, the National Council on Aging, the National Caucus of Black Aged, and the Gerontological Society. These organizations work through lobbyists, mailing campaigns, advertising, and other processes to improve the lot of the elderly in the United States.

As the elderly increase in numbers, their sphere of influence increases as well (Confessore, 2002). In 2000, the elderly accounted for 22 percent of the voting public; in 2038, it is estimated that they will make up 34 percent of the electorate. Thus, there will be strong and coordinated efforts by the elderly for more generous Social Security and Medicare systems. Seniors, if history is a guide, will likely oppose higher taxes and school bond elections. Future politics, then, will be characterized by generational tensions, with the younger generations fighting against higher taxes to fund the elderly and fighting for school taxes for the children's education, and seniors resisting them on both fronts. The tensions will be not only generational but also racial (Peyser, 1999). This is because the younger generation, which is asked to pay the bills for the elderly, is increasingly multiracial and multiethnic, while the sixty-five-plus population is overwhelmingly White (85 percent).

The Three Structural Transformations of Society

This chapter focuses on three major transformations in U.S. society and worldwide. These macro forces have huge consequences for societies, for communities, for families, and for individuals and the nature of work. The global economy, networked through new technologies in communications and transportation and the emergence of a relatively few large transnational corporations, moves capital and jobs around the world and within the United States to where wages are the lowest and the regulatory rules the most lenient. This phenomenon, coupled with the shift within the United States from a manufacturing to a service economy, has profoundly affected the distribution and type of jobs. Fewer and fewer workers are engaged in mass assembly-line production, jobs that paid well and had good benefits. Many assumed that new jobs in the service sector, along the information superhighway, and in cyberspace would absorb those downsized from changing industries. This occurred only to a limited extent, since the skills required are very different from those in the industrial age, and high-tech corporations also downsize their workers as they automate and use low-cost labor worldwide. As a result, only 35 percent of displaced workers have found work that equaled or surpassed their previous wages and benefits. In effect, the economic transformation has caused millions of workers to transfer from high-wage jobs to lower-wage jobs, to temporary or contingent work, or to no work at all. Also, unskilled and semiskilled workers have been either left out or left to work at low-wage jobs with few, if any, benefits.

Thus, wages have stagnated or declined for many millions. The results, among others, are a declining middle class and an ever greater gap between the haves and the have-nots.

One aspect of the global economy is the movement of people (immigration) generally from poor societies to rich societies. The consequence for the United States is a racial transformation as most of the recent immigrants are from Latin America and Asia. Most of these immigrants arrive without the work and language skills to fit into a knowledge society. Past immigrants have succeeded economically, but the realities of the economic transformation increase the likelihood that they will be left on the margins. Moreover, the political climate fosters the elimination of affirmative action and other compensatory programs to aid minorities, as well as the downsizing of public supports to the poor and the neglect of urban blight and inner-city schools. All of these occur as racial minorities move toward becoming the numerical majority by the mid-twenty-first century.

In addition to immigration, another demographic change—the growing proportion of the elderly—is having and will increasingly have dramatic effects on U.S. society. This increase in the dependent population places pressure on workers and families to provide for them. Their growing political power will affect public policies, the politics of elections, and the political dynamics of certain states and regions.

The consequences for U.S. society, then, of the convergence of these three powerful macro social forces are (1) a dislocation for many workers as some jobs become obsolete, their skills are no longer needed in a service/knowledge economy, their jobs have been replaced by automation, or their jobs have moved to a lower-wage environment; (2) an increasing wealth/income gap; (3) the downward economic spiral for racial minorities; (4) an increased proportion of people on the economic margins; (5) growing social unrest by the have-nots but also by workers who fear for their economic future; (6) an increase in scapegoating as animosities intensify because of economic tough times and a revival of racism; and (7) an increasing economic burden on the working population who must finance pension plans and other assistance for an ever larger elderly population.

Chapter Review

1. Globalization refers to the processes by which the world's peoples become increasingly interconnected economically, politically, culturally, and environmentally.

2. The powerful forces affecting the U.S. economy are (a) the globalization of the economy; (b) technological change; (c) capital flight; and (d) the shift from an industrial economy to a service/information economy.

3. These forces combine to create considerable discontinuity and disequilibrium in society. In particular, low-wage labor outside the United States and the movement of business activity to low-wage areas within the United States have depressed wages and

weakened unions. The result is a declining middle class, downward social mobility for many, and the creation of the new poor.

4. The nature of work is shifting as employers downsize their workforce and use more part-time or temporary workers. Two-thirds of these contingent workers are women.

5. The economic transformation has expanded the numbers of the working poor. This growth is a result of unemployment and underemployment (wages that do not lift a family above the poverty line).

6. The new poor are those blue-collar workers who lost manufacturing jobs with good pay and benefits because their companies closed or moved

elsewhere, or who were replaced by automation. These "new poor" are much more trapped in poverty than were the "old poor" of other generations.

7. The second societal upheaval that is shaking up society and families is massive immigration. This wave of immigration differs from previous waves because the immigrants come primarily from Latin America and Asia rather than Europe.

8. Racial and ethnic diversity ("the browning of America") is increasing, with the influx of immigrants and differential fertility. The two fastest-growing minorities are Latinos and Asian Americans.

9. The reaction of Americans to the new immigrants is typically negative. This is based on two myths: (a) that immigrants take jobs away from those already here, and (b) that immigrants are a drain on society's resources.

10. Immigrants face a dilemma: Do they fit into their new society or do they retain the traditions of the society they left? Immigrants in the past, for the most part, assimilated. But conditions are different for the new immigrants: (a) They are racial/ethnics, not Whites; (b) the current political mood is to eliminate affirmative action programs and welfare programs; and (c) they have entered during difficult economic times brought about by the economic transformation.

11. The proportion of the U.S. population age sixty-five and older is growing. In this age category, women outnumber men and minorities are underrepresented. Although the elderly are not disproportionately poor, the elderly who are women, are minorities, or live alone are disproportionately poor.

12. The Social Security program is the only source of income for about one-half of retired people and a major source of income for 80 percent of the elderly. Medicare is the universal health insurance program for the elderly. The key problem for both Social Security and Medicare is how they will be financed in the future.

13. The elderly may respond to their devalued status in several characteristic ways. They may withdraw from social relationships; they may continue to act as they have throughout their adult lives; or they may become politically active to change the laws, customs, and social structures that disadvantage them.

14. The numbers and proportion of the elderly in the U.S. population will increase. This aging population will create a difficult burden for the young, who, through taxes, are required to finance pension plans and other assistance for the elderly. Thus, there likely will be increased tensions between the generations in the future. This tension will also be racial, as the younger generation will be multiracial and multiethnic, while the elderly will be overwhelmingly White.

15. The consequences of the convergence of these three powerful forces—the structural transformation of the economy, the changing racial composition of society because of immigration, and the aging of society—are (a) an increasing wealth/income gap; (b) the downward spiral for racial minorities; (c) an increased proportion of people on the economic margins; (d) growing social unrest; and (e) an increase in scapegoating.

Key Terms

Globalization	Contingent workers	New immigration
Capital flight	New poor	Assimilation
Offshoring	Immigration	Dependency ratio
Outsourcing	Demographics	Disengagement
Structural transformation of the economy		

Study Questions

1. What are the consequences of globalization on individuals, communities, and the nature of work in U.S. society?

2. The U.S. economy has been transformed as it moved from one dominated by manufacturing to one based on services/knowledge. What social

categories are most disadvantaged by these changes? Why?

3. A common argument is that unemployment is the consequence of individuals lacking the proper values of initiative, hard work, and a success orientation. Write an essay making the opposite case, that the fundamental reasons for unemployment are structural.

4. Compare the immigrants entering the United States in the late nineteenth century with the immigrants today. In your comparison, consider personal characteristics, where they are located, the jobs available to them, and their chances for upward mobility.

5. Are the fears toward immigrants warranted?

6. What are the sociological reasons for the contemporary rise in the numbers in such groups as "skinheads," self-appointed state militias, and other "hate" groups?

7. Why is the analysis of these two macro social forces—economic transformation and immigration—important sociologically?

For Further Reading

Globalization and the Structural Transformation of the Economy

Sarah Anderson and John Cavanagh with Thea Lee and the Institute for Policy Studies, *Field Guide to the Global Economy* (New York: New Press, 1999).

Jeremy Brecher, Tim Costello, and Brendan Smith, *Globalization from Below: The Power of Solidarity* (Cambridge, MA: South End Press, 2000).

Jefferson Cowie, *Capital Moves: RCA's 70-Year Quest for Cheap Labor* (Ithaca, NY: Cornell University Press, 1999).

Peter F. Drucker, "The Next Society," *The Economist* (November 3, 2001):1–20.

Thomas L. Friedman, *The World Is Flat* (New York: Farrar, Straus and Giroux, 2005).

Miriam Ching Yoon Louie, *Sweatshop Warriors: Immigrant Women Workers Take on the Global Factory* (Cambridge, MA: South End Press, 2001).

Richard H. Robbins, *Global Problems and the Culture of Capitalism*, 2nd ed. (Boston: Allyn and Bacon, 2002).

William K. Tabb, *Unequal Partners: A Primer on Globalization* (New York: New Press, 2002).

The New Immigration and the Changing Racial Landscape

Stephen Castles and Mark J. Miller, *The Age of Migration*, 2nd ed. (New York: Guilford Press, 1998).

David Heer, *Immigration in America's Future: Social Science Findings and the Policy Debate* (Boulder, CO: Westview Press, 1996).

Pierrette Hondagneu-Sotelo, *Gendered Transitions: Mexican Experiences of Immigration* (Berkeley: University of California Press, 1994).

Philip Martin and Jonas Widgren, "International Migration: Facing the Challenge," *Population Bulletin* 57 (March 2002):entire issue.

Ruben Martinez, *Crossing Over: A Mexican Family on the Migrant Trail* (New York: Metropolitan Books, 2001).

Douglas S. Massey, Jorge Durand, and Nolan J. Malone, *Beyond Smoke and Mirrors: Mexican Immigration in an Era of Economic Integration* (New York: Russell Sage, 2002).

Douglas Massey et al., *Worlds in Motion: Understanding International Migration at the End of the Millennium* (New York: Oxford University Press, 1999).

Min Zhou and Carl L. Bankston, III, *How Vietnamese Children Adapt to Life in the United States* (New York: Sage, 1999).

The Aging Society

Simone de Beauvoir, *The Coming of Age* (New York: Warner Paperback Library, 1973).

Federal Interagency Forum on Aging-Related Statistics, *Older Americans 2000: Key Indicators of Well-Being* (Washington, DC: U.S. Government Printing Office, 2000).

Christine L. Himes, "Elderly Americans," *Population Bulletin* 56 (December 2001):entire issue.

Ronald Lee and John Haaga, *Government Spending in an Older America* (Washington, DC: Population Reference Bureau, 2002).

http://www.ifg.org/

"The International Forum on Globalization (IFG) is an alliance of sixty leading activists, scholars, economists, researchers and writers formed to stimulate new thinking, joint activity, and public education in response to economic globalization."

http://www.guerrillanews.com/

Guerrilla News is an alternative media source that explores issues such as globalization and corporate crime. It includes information not found in mainstream news.

http://www.michaelmoore.com/

Michael Moore is an author and filmmaker from Flint, Michigan. His site contains information on his books and movies that address issues on downsizing and actions of corporations. The site also provides up-to-date information on current legislation.

http://stats.bls.gov/opub/cwc/cwcwelc.htm

Part of the Bureau of Labor Statistics, Compensation and Working Conditions Online provides articles on different labor-related topics.

http://www.usasnet.org/

United Students against Sweatshops is an international movement "that supports the struggles of working people and challenges corporate power."

http://www.helpage.org/

HelpAge International is a "global network of not-for-profit organizations with a mission to work with and for disadvantaged older people worldwide to achieve a lasting improvement in the quality of their lives."

http://www.who.int/hpr/ageing/index.htm

This site is part of the World Health Organization and deals specifically with aging and the life course. The site has news, current events, links, and publications dealing with these issues.

http://www.nia.nih.gov/

The National Institute on Aging is one center at the National Institutes of Health that seeks to "understand the nature of aging and to extend the healthy, active years of life."

http://www.ins.usdoj.gov/graphics/index.htm

The Immigration and Naturalization Services site provides various information related to immigration. The site subjects include law enforcement and border management and immigration services and benefits.

http://opr.princeton.edu/

The Office of Population Research is part of Princeton University and has a "distinguished history of contributions in formal demography and the study of fertility change."

http://cmd.princeton.edu/

The Center for Migration and Development, a center at Princeton University, is concerned with international migration and national development.

http://www.familiesusa.org/index.htm

Families USA is focused on making health care more affordable for everyone. There are sections on the site devoted to children, Medicaid, and Medicare.

http://www.umass.edu/complit/aclanet/USMigrat.html

This site describes some of the major migration and immigration laws from U.S. history.

http://www.ameristat.org/

This is the website of the Population Reference Bureau In partnership with the Social Science Data Analysis Network. It provides the latest statistics on foreign-born populations, immigration, and the elderly.

http://www.caasf.org/

Chinese for Affirmative Action has a mission "to defend and promote the civil and political rights of Chinese and Asian Americans within the context of, and in the interest of, advancing multiracial democracy in the United States."

http://www.americandemographics.com

This is the website for *American Demographics* magazine. It includes data and articles on various population issues.

http://globalissues.org

This site has information on "global issues that affect everyone," including trade-related, environmental, and human rights issues.

$ocial $tratification

Inequality is a fact of social life. All known societies have some system of ranking individuals and groups along a superiority-inferiority scale. Consider the following examples:

In India, birth into a particular family often determines one's caste position, which in turn establishes one's social position, work, and range of marriage partners. At the bottom of this system is one group—the untouchables—that is so low that its members are not even part of the caste system. The untouchables do society's dirty work: sweeping floors, collecting garbage, and washing the latrines. Traditional Hindus of the upper castes believe untouchables pollute everything they touch (Crossette, 1996). But there is even a hierarchy among the untouchables, with one category so sullied that they cannot be seen by others during the daylight hours. (See the panel titled "A Closer Look: Birth as Destiny: India's Caste System.")

In South Africa there is an unofficial caste system based on race (just a decade ago it was the official state policy). There are four racial castes: Whites, Blacks, Coloureds (mixed races), and Asians. The conditions for housing, work, pay, and schooling in this apartheid system are decidedly unequal by race.

In Saudi Arabia men have higher status than women. By law, custom, and religious beliefs, women are restricted from certain jobs, from driving automobiles, and from positions of authority.

Brazil was the last nation in the Western Hemisphere to abolish slavery (1888). However, a form of slavery continues as workers in some situations are virtually imprisoned by their employers, working for food and shelter with no hope of paying off their debts.

These examples indicate a range of patterned social inequality in various societies. (See the panel titled "Globalization: Inequality among Nations" for stratification across societies.) Variations on these themes are also found in the United States, where people are divided and ranked by family of origin, race, gender, and economic position.

The pattern of structured inequities is called social stratification, the subject of this and the following three chapters. This chapter examines these ranking systems. These structured systems of inequality are crucial to the understanding of human

Birth as Destiny: India's Caste System

The caste system in India was outlawed in 1950. Modern commerce and transportation diminished its force in urban India. It remains in force, however, in many rural villages and regions where tradition retains a powerful grip.

A **caste system** is a system of social stratification based on ascription. In such a system, birth into a particular family determines one's destiny—social position, type of work, and range of marriage partners—for life. In principle there is no social mobility, and each subcaste is identified with an occupation, such as priests, barbers, sweepers, or leatherworkers.

There are four major castes (varnas) in hierarchical order (and thousands of subcastes—jatis—within them). One category—the untouchables—is considered so low that it is below the caste system; thus, its members are outcasts. Untouchables do society's "unclean work." Their work involves physical contact with blood, excrement, and other bodily "defilements" as defined by Hindu law. "Untouchables cremate the dead, clean latrines, cut umbilical cords, remove dead animals from the roads, tan hides, sweep gutters. These jobs, and the status of Untouchability, are passed down for generations" (O'Neill, 2003:13).

Because the family transmits social position from one generation to the next, a rigid system requires that marriage occur only between social equals. Thus, a caste system mandates endogamous marriage (within one's group).

An integral part of the Indian caste system is the concern for ritual purity. Because it is believed that the higher the caste, the more pure the members, there are elaborate rules of etiquette governing social distance between the castes. Untouchables, for example, pollute their superiors by their smell, touch, or even their presence. They are required to hide whenever anyone from a higher caste is present or, if this is not possible, they must bow with their faces turned downward. Highborns must not take food or water from an untouchable because it pollutes them. Untouchables must take water only from their own well because to draw water from the same well as the other castes pollutes all others. If polluted, there are a number of practices used for ritual purification (fire, bathing, family shrine, or temple).

The caste system is supported by powerful cultural beliefs. The Hindu religion emphasizes a strong concern for duty (dharma). This involves one's duty to family, caste, age, and sex. In effect, there is a moral duty to accept one's fate. Moreover, if one does not fulfill the requirements of his or her particular caste position, there are dire consequences. Central to the Hindu religion is the belief in reincarnation—that souls are reborn after death. Thus, for people who do not observe the moral laws of their particular caste, after death their souls will be reborn in a lower caste. Conversely, faithful obedience to caste duties will result in rebirth into a higher caste. Brahmins (the highest caste), then, are being rewarded for excellence in previous lives while untouchables are being punished. This belief system provides a very strong mechanism for maintaining the rigid stratification system. "No one wants to be reborn as an untouchable, least of all the untouchables, who best know the miseries of this position. Furthermore, we can understand the contempt received by untouchables: they are those believed to have sinned most in a previous life" (Kerbo, 1983:20).

groups because they are important determinants of human behavior and because they have significant consequences for society and its members.

This chapter is divided into three sections. First, the important concepts are introduced. Second, the three major hierarchies—class, race, and gender—are described briefly. The third section describes and critiques the theories used to explain the universality of stratification systems and how hierarchies of dominant and subordinate groups are established and maintained.

Inequality among Nations

There is a huge inequality gap worldwide. Here are some representative facts:

- In 1900, people in the 10 richest nations earned 9 times as much per capita as did people in the 10 poorest nations. This gap increased to 30 to 1 in 1960 and to 72 to 1 in 2001 (Gergen, 2001).
- The top fifth of nations possess 86 percent of the world's gross domestic product, 68 percent of direct foreign investment, and 74 percent of the world's telephone lines (Street, 2001).
- The richest 20 percent of the world's people receive at least 150 times more income than the poorest 20 percent (Street, 2001b).
- The top 20 percent consume 86 percent of the world's goods and services, while the poorest fifth consumes but 1 percent (Williamson, 2001).
- In 2001, there were 497 billionaires worldwide with a combined wealth of $1.54 trillion. Their collective wealth is greater than the combined incomes of the poorest half of humanity (Mokhiber and Weissman, 2002).
- In annual spending for education, the developed countries spend $4,636 per child, compared to $165 in developing countries, and $49 in sub-Saharan Africa (Briscoe, 1999).

The causes of world poverty are many. First, the poorest nations were once colonies of the richer nations and this legacy of exploitation has left them behind (in leadership and in economies that are based on a single agricultural crop or other commodity). Second, the governments that formed following independence from colonial rule were typically corrupt and unable to control the lawlessness of criminals or warlords. Third, many poor countries are located in extreme climates where droughts or floods or earthquakes or other natural disasters are commonplace. Fourth, as their economies crumble, many of these governments have borrowed heavily from lenders such as the World Bank and the International Monetary Fund. As a condition of these loans, the poor nations are, typically, required to reduce government spending on human services. Fifth, the global economic system with free-trade policies makes it difficult for nations with a limited number of crops/commodities to cope with plunging world markets due to recessions, oversupply, and wildly fluctuating prices. The results in these countries are economic chaos, widespread unemployment, declining wages, and government instability. And, sixth, many transnational corporations continue the tradition of exploitation by using the cheap labor and cheap resources of the poor countries to their advantage.

To amplify this last point, when transnational corporations locate in poor countries, the local economies and workers should, in theory, benefit by gaining a higher standard of living and because of access to modern technology. They have not for several reasons. One reason is that the profits generated in these countries are channeled back to the home nation of the transnational corporation, not the host economy. Moreover, the assembly plants in these poor companies tend to hire young women (because they will work for lower wages than men and they are more docile in the workplace), replacing them with other young women after a few years. This pattern disrupts family arrangements, and the benefits of relatively high wages (for that economy) are short lived.

So, the global economic system does not distribute wealth ever more fairly. What we have is a situation in which about half of the world's people live on less than $2 a day (the poverty line) (Gergen, 2001), and more than 1.3 billion people earn less than $1 a day. Meanwhile, the wealthy nations and the wealthy in those nations are doing very well indeed.

Major Concepts

People differ in age, physical attributes, and what they do for a living. The process of categorizing people by age, height, occupation, or some other personal attribute is called **social differentiation**. When people are ranked in a vertical arrangement (hierarchy) that differentiates them as superior or inferior, we have **social stratification**. The key difference between differentiation and stratification is that the process of ranking or evaluation occurs only in the latter. What is ranked and how it is ranked are dependent on the values of the society.

Social stratification refers, in essence, to structured social inequality. The term structured refers to stratification being socially patterned. This implies that inequalities are not caused by biological differences such as sex or race. Biological traits do not become relevant in patterns of social superiority or inferiority until they are socially recognized and given importance by being incorporated into the beliefs, attitudes, and values of the people in the society. People in the United States, for example, tend to believe that gender and racial characteristics make a difference—therefore, they do.

The social patterning of stratification is also found in the distribution of rewards in any community or society, because that distribution is governed by social norms. In the United States few individuals seriously question the income differential between medical doctors and nurses or college professors and primary school teachers because the norms and values of society dictate that such inequalities are just.

Patterned behavior is also achieved through the socialization process. Each generation is taught the norms and values of the society and of its social class. The children of slaves and the children of the ruling family in a society are each taught the behavior proper for people of their station in life.

Finally, the system of stratification is always connected with other aspects of the society. The existing stratification arrangements are affected by and have effects on such matters as politics, marriage, economics, education, and religion. Harold Kerbo (1983) summarizes what is meant by social stratification:

> Social stratification means that inequality has been hardened or institutionalized, and there is a system of social relationships that determines who gets what, and why. When we say institutionalized we mean that a system of layered hierarchy has been established. People have come to expect that individuals and groups with certain positions will be able to demand more influence and respect and accumulate a greater share of goods and services. Such inequality may or may not be accepted equally by a majority in the society, but it is recognized as the way things are. (11)

The hierarchies of stratification—class, race, and gender—place groups, individuals, and families in the larger society. The crucial consequence of this so-called placement is that the rewards and resources of society such as wealth, power, and privilege are unequally distributed. And, crucially, differential access to these societal resources and rewards produces different life experiences and different life chances. **Life chances** refer to the chances throughout one's life cycle to live and to experience the good things in life. Life chances are most significant because they are those things that "(1) . . . better-off people can purchase (good education, good medical care, comfortable homes, fine vacations, expert services of all kinds, safe and satisfying occupations) and which poor people would also purchase if they had the money; and (2) . . . make life easier, longer, healthier, and more enjoyable" (Tumin, 1973:104). The converse, of course, is that people at the low end of the stratification hierarchies will have inadequate health care, shelter, and diets. Their lives will be more miserable and they will die sooner.

To understand U.S. society we must understand the hierarchies of class, race, and gender. Class, race, and gender are macro structures of inequality that shape our micro worlds. These structures organize society as a whole and create varied environments for individuals and families through their unequal distribution of social opportunities.

These structures of inequality array the resources and advantages of society in patterned ways. These hierarchies are also structured systems of exploitation and discrimination in which the affluent dominate the poor, men dominate women, and Whites dominate people of color (Feagin and Feagin, 1997:26–27).

Traditionally, the family has been viewed as the principal unit in the class system because it passes on privilege (or the lack thereof) in wealth and resources from generation to generation. Even though the family is basic in maintaining stratification, life chances are affected by race and gender inequalities as well as by social class. In most families, men have greater socioeconomic resources and more power and privileges than do women, even though all family members are viewed as members of the same social class. While a family's placement in the class hierarchy does determine rewards and resources, hierarchies based on sex create different conditions for women and men even within the same family (Acker, 1973). Systems of sex stratification cut across class and racial divisions to distribute resources differently to men and women (Baca Zinn and Eitzen, 2005:chapter 5).

Class

When a number of people occupy the same relative economic rank in the stratification system, they form a **social class**. Social class "implies having or not having the following: individual rights, privileges, power, rights over others, authority, life style choices, self-determination, status, wealth, access to services, comfort, leisure, etc." (Comer, 1978:171). People are socially located in a class position on the basis of income, occupation, and education, either alone or in combination. In the past, the occupation, income, and education of the husband determined the class location of the family. But family behavior is better explained by locating families according to the more prestigious occupation, regardless of whether it is the husband's or the wife's (Yorburg, 1983:189). Occupations are part of the larger opportunity structure of society. Those that are highly valued and carry high income rewards are unevenly distributed. The amount of income determines how well a given household can acquire the resources needed for survival and perhaps for luxury. The job or occupation that is the source of the paycheck connects families with the opportunity structure in different ways. This connection generates different kinds of class privileges for families. **Privilege** refers to the distribution of goods and services, situations, and experiences that are highly valued and beneficial (Jeffries and Ransford, 1980:68). Class privileges are those advantages, prerogatives, and options that are available to those in the middle and upper classes. They involve help from the system: banks, credit unions, medical facilities, schools, and voluntary associations. Class privileges are based on the systematic linkages between families and society. Class privilege creates many differences in family patterns.

Race and Ethnicity

Racial and ethnic stratification refers to systems of inequality in which some fixed group membership, such as race, religion, or national origin, is a major criterion for ranking social positions and their differential rewards. Like the class system, this

"We should consider ourselves fortunate. At least we have food and shelter."

hierarchy represents institutionalized power, privilege, and prestige. Racial and ethnic hierarchies generate domination and subordination, often referred to as majority-minority relations. Minority groups are those that are dominated by a more powerful group, stigmatized, and singled out for differential treatment.

Race is socially defined on the basis of a presumed common genetic heritage resulting in distinguishing physical characteristics. **Ethnicity** refers to the condition of being culturally rather than physically distinctive. Ethnic peoples are bound together by virtue of a common ancestry and a common cultural background.

A racial group that has a distinctive culture or subculture, shares a common heritage, and has developed a common identity is also an ethnic group. Both race and ethnicity are traditional bases for systems of inequality, although there are historical and contemporary differences in the societal placement of racial ethnics and White ethnics in this society. We examine how racial stratification deprives people of color of equal access to society's resources and thereby creates family patterns that are different from the idealized family model.

The most important feature of racial stratification is the exclusion of people of color from equal access to society's valued resources. People of color or racial ethnics have less power, wealth, and social status than do other people in the United States. African Americans, Latinos, and Asian Americans constitute the largest of the racial minorities in the United States.

Gender

Gender, like race and class, is a basic organizing principle of society. From the macro level of the societal economy, through the institutions of society, to interpersonal relations, gender shapes activities, perceptions, roles, and rewards. Gender is the patterning of difference and domination through distinctions between women and men (Acker, 1992:565).

The stratification system that assigns women's and men's roles unequally is the **sex-gender system**. It consists of two complementary yet mutually exclusive categories into which all human beings are placed. The sex-gender system combines biologically based sex roles with socially created gender roles. In everyday life, the terms *sex role* and *gender role* are used interchangeably. This use obscures important differences and underlying issues in the study of women's and men's experiences. **Sex roles** refer to behaviors determined by an individual's biological sex. **Gender roles** are social constructions; they contain self-concepts and psychological traits, as well as family, occupational, and political roles assigned dichotomously to each sex. For example, the traditional female gender role includes expectations for females to be passive, nurturant, and dependent. The standard male gender role incorporates alternative expectations—behaviors that are aggressive, competitive, and independent (Lipman-Blumen, 1984:1–2).

Patriarchy is the term for forms of social organization in which men are dominant over women. As described in Chapter 12, patriarchy is infused throughout U.S. society. Generally, men have more power than women, and, generally, they also have greater power over women. Even though there is considerable class and racial variation here, men in general gain some privilege at the expense of women. In sum, the sex-gender system distributes power, resources, prestige, and privilege unequally.

The Intersection of Class, Race, and Gender

The hierarchies of class, race, and gender do not stand alone. They are interrelated systems of stratification. Economic resources, the bases of class, are not randomly distributed but vary systematically by race and sex. For example, people of color and women have fewer occupational choices than do White males. People of color and women often experience separate and unequal education and receive less income for the work they do, resulting in different life chances.

These systems of inequality form what sociologist Patricia Hill Collins (1990) calls a **matrix of domination** in which each of us exists. The existence of these intersections has several important implications (Baca Zinn and Dill, 1996). First, people experience race, class, gender, and sexuality differently depending upon their social location in these structures of inequality. For example, people of the same race will experience race differently depending upon their location in the class structure as poor, working class, professional/managerial class, or unemployed, their location in the gender structure as female or male, and their location in the sexuality system as heterosexual or homosexual.

Second, class, race, and gender are components of both social structure and social interaction. As a result, individuals, because of their social locations, experience different forms of privilege and subordination. In short, these intersecting forms of inequality produce both oppression and opportunity.

A third implication of the inequality matrix has to do with the relational nature of dominance and subordination. Power is embedded in each system of stratification, determining whether one is dominant or subordinate. The intersectional nature of hierarchies means that power differentials are linked in systematic ways, reinforcing power differentials across hierarchies.

Theories of Stratification

Sociologists and other observers of society have pondered two fundamental questions about stratification. The first is, Why are societies stratified? The second is, Within stratified societies, why are certain categories ranked as superior while others are considered inferior? There are alternative theoretical explanations for each question, and each explanation has important implications. Let's begin with the two sociological theories for the more general and logically prior question.

All societies have some form of stratification. How is this universal phenomenon to be explained? Sociologists answer this question from either the order or the conflict perspective. The position of the order theorists is basically supportive of inequality, because the unequal distribution of rewards is assumed to be not only inevitable but also necessary. Conflict theorists, on the other hand, tend to denounce the distributive system as basically unjust, unnecessary, and the source of many social problems.

Order Theory

Adherents of the order model begin with the fact that social inequality is a ubiquitous and apparently unavoidable phenomenon. They reason that inequality must, therefore, serve a useful function for society. The argument, as presented in the classic statement by Kingsley Davis and Wilbert Moore (1945), is as follows. The smooth functioning of society requires that various tasks be accomplished through a division of labor. There is a universal problem, then, of allocation—of getting the most important tasks done by the most talented people. Some jobs are more important for societal survival than are others (typically those involved in decision making, medicine, religion, teaching, and the military). The societal problem is how to get the most talented people motivated to go through the required long periods of training and to do these important tasks well. The universally found answer, according to Davis and Moore, is differential rewards. Society must provide suitable rewards (money, prestige, and power) to induce individuals to fill these positions. The rewards must, it is argued, be distributed unevenly to various positions because the positions are not equally pleasant or equally important. Thus, a differential reward system guarantees that the important societal functions are fulfilled, thereby ensuring the maintenance of society. In this way, differential ranks actually serve to unify society through a division of labor (functional integration) and through the socialization of people to accept their positions in the system.

Although there probably is some truth to this argument, the analysts of society must also ask: Is inequality primarily integrative or divisive? Is it necessary? Must the poor always be with us (see Huaco, 1966; Tumin, 1953)?

Conflict Theory

Conflict theorists view stratification in a wholly different manner from the order theorists. Rather than accepting stratification as a source of societal integration, the conflict perspective assumes that stratification reflects the distribution of power in society and is therefore a major source of discord and coercion. It is a source of discord because groups compete for scarce resources and because the powerless, under certain conditions, resent their lowly position and lack of rewards. Coercion results from stratification as the powerful (who are coincidentally male, White, and wealthy) prey on the weak. From this view, then, the unequal distribution of rewards reflects the interests of the powerful and not the basic survival needs of society, as the order theorists contend.

A major contention of the conflict theorists is that the powerful people use ideology to make their value system paramount. Karl Marx argued that the dominant ideology in any society is always the ideology of the ruling class. The ruling class uses the media, schools, religion, and other institutions to legitimate systems of inequality. So powerful is this socialization process that even oppressed peoples tend to accept their low status as natural. Marx called this tendency of the oppressed to accept their oppression false consciousness (see Marx and Engels, 1959; Parenti, Michael, 1978:15–18). The working class and the poor in the United States, for example, tend to accept their lack of monetary rewards, power, and prestige because they believe that the system is truly meritocratic—and that they lack the skills and brains to do the better-rewarded tasks in society. In short, they believe that they deserve their fate (see Sennett and Cobb, 1973). Consequently, they accept a differential reward system and the need to leave supervision and decision making to experts. False consciousness thus inhibits efforts by the disadvantaged to change an oppressive system. Marx argued, however, that when the oppressed become aware of their common oppression and that they have been manipulated by the powerful to serve the interests of the powerful, they will develop a class consciousness—an objective awareness of their common exploitation—thus becoming unified in a cause to advance their class interests.

Even though it is true that social stratification is an important source of societal friction, conflict theorists have not answered the important question as to its necessity (neither have the order theorists, for that matter, although they address themselves directly to that question). Both theoretical perspectives have important insights that must be considered. The order theorists see stratification serving the useful function of societal maintenance by providing a mechanism (differential rewards) to ensure that all the slots in the division of labor are filled. Conflict theorists are equally valid in their contention that stratification is unjust, divisive, and a source of social instability or change.

Deficiency Theories

Some categories of people are systematically disadvantaged in the United States, most especially the poor, non-Whites, and women. Is there some flaw within these groups—perhaps biological or cultural—that explains their inferiority? Or, is it the structure of society that blocks their progress while encouraging the advancement of others? To answer these questions, we examine the various explanations for poverty. The specific explanations for inequities by race and gender are addressed in detail in Chapters 11 and 12, using the same explanatory categories used to understand poverty.

Who or what is to blame for poverty? There are two very different answers to these questions (Barrera, 1979:174–219). One is that the poor are in that condition because of some deficiency: Either they are biologically inferior or their culture fails them by promoting character traits that impede their progress in society. The other response places the blame on the structure of society: Some people are poor because society has failed to provide equality in educational opportunity, because institutions discriminate against minorities, because private industry has failed to provide enough jobs, because automation has made some jobs obsolete, and so forth. In this view, society has worked in such a way as to trap certain people and their offspring in a condition of poverty.

Biological Inferiority

In 1882, the British philosopher and sociologist Herbert Spencer came to the United States to promote a theory later known as social Darwinism. He argued that the poor were poor because they were unfit. Poverty was nature's way of "excreting . . . unhealthy, imbecile, slow, vacillating, faithless members of society in order to make room for the 'fit,' who were duly entitled to the rewards of wealth. Spencer preached that the poor should not be helped through state or private charity, because such acts would interfere with nature's way of getting rid of the weak" (*The Progressive*, 1980).

Social Darwinism has generally lacked support in the scientific community, although it has continued to provide a rationale for the thinking of many individuals. Recently, however, the concept has resurfaced in the work of three scientists. They suggest that the poor are in that condition because they do not measure up to the more well-to-do in intellectual endowment.

Arthur Jensen, professor of educational psychology at the University of California, has argued that there is a strong possibility that Blacks are less well endowed mentally than are Whites. From his review of the research on IQ, he claimed that approximately 80 percent of IQ is inherited, while the remaining 20 percent is attributable to environment. Because Blacks differ significantly from Whites in achievement on IQ tests and in school, Jensen claims that it is reasonable to hypothesize that the sources of these differences are genetic as well as environmental (Jensen, 1969; 1980).

The late Richard Herrnstein, a Harvard psychologist, agrees with Jensen that intelligence is largely inherited. He goes one step further, positing the formation of hereditary castes based on intelligence (Herrnstein, 1971; 1973). For Herrnstein, social stratification by inborn differences occurs because (1) mental ability is inherited and (2) success (prestige of job and earnings) depends on mental ability. Thus, a **meritocracy** (social stratification by ability) develops through the sorting process. This reasoning assumes that people close in mental ability are more likely to marry and reproduce, thereby ensuring castes by level of intelligence. According to this thesis, "in times to come, as technology advances, the tendency to be unemployed may run in the genes of a family about as certainly as bad teeth do now" (Herrnstein, 1971:63). This is another way of saying that the bright people are in the upper classes and the dregs are at the bottom. Inequality is justified, just as it was years ago by the social Darwinists.

Charles Murray, along with Herrnstein, wrote *The Bell Curve* (Herrnstein and Murray, 1994), the latest revival of social Darwinism. Their claim, an update of Herrnstein's earlier work, is that the economic and social hierarchies reflect a single dimension—cognitive ability, as measured by IQ tests.

Notwithstanding the flaws in the logic and in the evidence used by Jensen, Herrnstein, and Murray (for excellent critiques of the Herrnstein and Murray work, see Gould, 1994; Hermann, 1994; Reed, 1994; the symposium appearing in *Contemporary Sociology*, 1995; and Fischer et al., 1996), we must consider the implications of their biological determinism for dealing with the problem of poverty.

Jensen and Herrnstein have argued that dispassionate study is required to determine whether intelligence is inherited to the degree that they state. Objectivity is the sine qua non of scientific inquiry, and one cannot argue with its merits, although science, all science, is tainted (see the panel titled "Research Methods: The Political Climate and Scientific Ideas"). We should recognize, however, the important social consequences implied by the Jensen-Herrnstein argument. First, biological determinism is a classic example of blaming the victim. The individual poor person is blamed instead of inferior schools, culturally biased IQ tests, low wages, corporate downsizing, or social barriers of race, religion, or nationality. By blaming the victim, this thesis claims a relationship between lack of success and lack of intelligence. This relationship is spurious because it ignores the advantages and disadvantages of ascribed status (statuses of individuals assigned without reference to abilities or efforts but rather on the basis of age, sex, race, ethnicity, and family background). According to William Ryan (1972), "Arthur Jensen and Richard Herrnstein confirm regretfully that Black folks and poor folks are born stupid, that little rich kids grow up rich adults, not because they inherited Daddy's stock portfolio, but rather because they inherited his brains" (54).

The Jensen-Herrnstein-Murray thesis divides people in the United States further by appealing to bigots. It provides "scientific justification" for their beliefs in the racial superiority of some groups and the inferiority of others. By implication, it legitimates the segregation and unequal treatment of so-called inferiors. The goal of integration and the fragile principle of egalitarianism are seriously threatened to the degree that members of the scientific community give this thesis credence or prominence.

Another serious implication of the biological determinism argument is the explicit validation of the IQ test as a legitimate measure of intelligence. The IQ test attempts to measure innate potential, but to do this is impossible, because the testing process must inevitably reflect some of the skills that develop during the individual's lifetime. For the most part, intelligence tests measure educability—that is, the prediction of conventional school achievement. Achievement in school is, of course, also associated with a cluster of other social and motivational factors, as Joanna Ryan (1972) observes:

> The test as a whole is usually validated, if at all, against the external criterion of school performance. It therefore comes as no surprise to find that IQ scores do in fact correlate highly with educational success. IQ scores are also found to correlate positively with socio-economic status, those in the upper social classes tending to have the highest IQs. Since social class, and all that this implies, is both an important determinant and also an important consequence of educational performance, this association is to be expected. (54)

The Political Climate and Scientific Ideas

The following essay is by the late Stephen Jay Gould, Harvard professor of evolutionary biology. Gould argues that scientists—all scientists—are enmeshed in a web of personal and social circumstances that affect their science. Leftist geneticists, for example, are more likely to combat biological determinism just as politically conservative geneticists favor interpretations of inequality as the reflection of genetic inadequacies of people.

Social Disparities as "A Product of Nature"

The rise and fall in popularity of scientific theories correlates with changes in the political and social climate. That's why, as the nation moves to the right politically, arguments for biological determinism are bound to become popular. The determinists' message is that existing inequalities in society are a reflection of the intrinsic character of people and are not the fault of social institutions. Determinists are saying that disparities are a product of nature and therefore cannot be alleviated by very expensive social programs.

Similarly, the hereditarian version of IQ, which holds that you are measuring something that's inherited and unchangeable, flourished in the 1920s, the age of Sacco and Vanzetti and of jingoism inspired by World War I. The hereditarians argued that the single number called IQ could capture the multifarious complexities of the concept of intelligence and that you could rank races, classes, and sexes on the basis of their average scores. To think that a whole host of abilities could be encompassed in a meaningful way by a single number is fundamentally fallacious. An approach that recognizes that intelligence is a word we give to an irreducible set of multifarious abilities might lead to a more adequate assessment.

The "Grievous Consequences" of IQ Testing

I don't deny there is biology involved in some human abilities. I'd never be a marathon runner no matter how hard I trained, and I'll certainly never be a basketball player, because I am too short. But it is one thing to acknowledge that there is biology behind a lot of what we do; it is quite another to say that abilities are the result of intrinsic and unalterable heredity.

Yet today there are still many people, including some scientists, who think in their heart of hearts, that IQ tests are measuring something intrinsic and permanent. That kind of thinking has had grievous social consequences for many groups in American society.

"Scientists Reflect the Prejudices of Their Lives." In evaluating these and other arguments by scientists, it is important that people be wary of the claim that science stands apart from other human institutions because its methodology leads to objective knowledge. People need to realize that scientists are human beings like everybody else and that their pronouncements may arise from their social prejudices, as any of our pronouncements might. The public should avoid being snowed by the scientist's line: "Don't think about this for yourself because it's all too complicated."

I wish scientists scrutinized more rigidly the sources of justification for their beliefs. If they did, they might realize that some of their findings do not derive from a direct investigation of nature but are rooted in assumptions growing out of experience and beliefs.

But don't draw from what I have said the negative implication that science is a pack of lies—that it's merely social prejudice. On the one hand, science is embedded in society, and scientists reflect the social prejudices of their own lives and those of their class and culture. On the other hand, I believe that there are correct answers to questions, and science, in its own bumbling, socially conditioned manner, stumbles toward those answers.

Gauging "the Truth Value of an Idea." In evaluating science, a distinction has to be drawn between where an idea comes from and how worthy it is. The truth value of an idea is independent of its source, but when you know its source, you might get more suspicious about its potential truth value.

Darwin's theory of natural selection, for example, came directly out of a social context: It was essentially Adam Smith's economics read into nature. Without Adam Smith and the whole school of Scottish economics, I doubt that Darwin would ever have thought of it. Yet Darwin was right, in large measure. So social conditioning doesn't make an idea wrong; it does mean you have to scrutinize it.

Thus, the Jensen-Herrnstein-Murray thesis overlooks the important contribution of social class to achievement on IQ tests. This oversight is crucial, because most social scientists feel that these tests are biased in favor of people who have had middle- and upper-class environments and experiences. IQ tests discriminate against the poor in many ways. They discriminate obviously in the language that is used, in the instructions that are given, and in the experiences they assume the subjects have had. The discrimination can also be more subtle. For minority-group examinees, the race of the person administering the test influences the results. Another, less well-known fact about IQ tests is that in many cases they provide a self-fulfilling prophecy, as Joanna Ryan (1972) notes: "IQ scores obtained at one age often determine how an individual is subsequently treated, and, in particular, what kind of education he receives as a consequence of IQ testing will in turn contribute to his future IQ, and it is notorious that those of low and high IQ do not get equally good education" (44).

Another implication is the belief that poverty is inevitable. The "survival of the fittest" capitalist ideology is reinforced, justifying both discrimination against the poor and continued privilege for the advantaged. Inequality is rationalized so that little will be done to aid its victims. Herrnstein and Murray argue that public policies to ameliorate poverty are a waste of time and resources. "Programs designed to alter the natural dominance of the 'cognitive elite' are useless, the book argues, because the genes of the subordinate castes invariably doom them to failure" (Muwakkil, 1994:22). The acceptance of this thesis, then, has obvious consequences for what policy decisions will be made or not made in dealing with poverty. If their view prevails, then welfare programs will be abolished, as will programs such as Head Start.

This raises the serious question: Is intelligence immutable or is there the possibility of boosting cognitive development? A number of studies have shown that Head Start–type programs raise scores among poor children by as much as nine points. These results, however, fade out entirely by the sixth grade. Yet this rise and fall of IQ scores makes the case for the role of environmental factors in cognitive development. As Beth Maschinot (1995) argues:

> [The critics of Head Start] ignore the obvious fact that once they leave Head Start, poor students typically attend substandard schools from the first grade onward. The fact that IQ scores drop again after this experience should lead one logically to conclude that intelligence as defined by IQ tests is highly responsive to environmental manipulations, not the reverse. (33)

Research on programs other than Head Start makes the same point. The Abecedarian Project conducted by the University of North Carolina studied high-risk children from 120 families. The conclusion:

> The most important policy implication of these findings is that early educational intervention for impoverished children can have long-lasting benefits, in terms of improved cognitive performance. This underscores the critical importance of good early environments and suggests that the focus of debate should now be shifted from whether government should play a role in encouraging good early environments to how these environments can be assured. (Campbell and Ramey, 1994:694–695)

Research shows that students in Head Start programs improve in IQ scores. This positive result tends to fade, however, if the children go to substandard schools after Head Start.

Another study, by the Robert Wood Johnson Foundation, of low-birthweight infants followed their development for three years. The researchers found that the infants who had stimulating day care environments had, on average, a thirteen-point higher IQ score than the babies who did not have those experiences (reported in Richmond, 1994).

As a final example, high-risk African American children in Ypsilanti, Michigan, were randomly divided into two groups. One group received a high-quality active learning program as three- and four-year-olds. The other groups received no preschool education. The two groups were compared at age twenty-seven, with these results:

> By age 27, those who had received the preschool education had half as many arrests as the comparison group. Four times as many were earning $2,000 or more a month. Three times as many owned their own homes. One-third more had graduated from high school on schedule. One-fourth fewer of them needed welfare as adults. And they had one-third fewer children born out of wedlock. (Beck, 1995:7B)

The Jensen-Herrnstein-Murray thesis also provides justification for unequal schooling. Why should school boards allot comparable sums of money for similar programs in middle-class and lower-class schools if the natural endowments of children in each type of school are so radically different? Why should teachers expect the same performance from poor children as from children from the more well-to-do? Why spend extra money on disadvantaged children in Head Start programs if these children are doomed by genetic inferiority? The result of such beliefs is, of course, a self-fulfilling prophecy. Low expectations beget low achievement.

Finally, the Jensen-Herrnstein-Murray thesis encourages policymakers either to ignore poverty or to attack its effects rather than its causes in the structure of society itself.

Cultural Inferiority

The *culture-of-poverty* hypothesis (see Chapter 7) contends that the poor are qualitatively different in values and lifestyles from the rest of society *and that these cultural differences explain continued poverty.* In other words, the poor, in adapting to their deprived condition, are found to be more permissive in raising their children, less verbal, more fatalistic, less apt to defer gratification, and less likely to be interested in formal education than are the more well-to-do. Most important is the contention that this deviant cultural pattern is transmitted from generation to generation. Thus, there is a strong implication that poverty is perpetuated by defects in the lifeways of the poor. If poverty itself were to be eliminated, the former poor would probably continue to prefer instant gratification, be immoral by middle-class standards, and so on. This reasoning blames the victim. From this view, the poor have a subculture with values that differ radically from the values of the other social classes. And this explains their poverty.

Edward Banfield, an eminent political scientist and advisor to Republican presidents, has argued that the difference between the poor and the nonpoor is cultural—the former have a present-time orientation, while the nonpoor have a future-time orientation (Banfield, 1974). He does not see the present-time orientation of the poor as a function of the hopelessness of their situation. Yet it seems highly unlikely that the poor see little reason to complain about the slums: What about the filth, the rats, the overcrowded living conditions, the high infant mortality? What about the lack of jobs and opportunity for upward mobility? This feeling of being trapped seems to be the primary cause of hedonistic present-time orientation. If the structure were changed so that the poor could see that hard work and deferred gratification really paid off, they could adopt a future-time orientation.

Critics of the culture-of-poverty hypothesis argue that the poor are an integral part of U.S. society; they do not abandon the dominant values of the society, but rather, retain them while simultaneously holding an alternative set of values. This alternative set is a result of adaptation to the conditions of poverty. Elliot Liebow (1967), in his classic study of lower-class Black men, has taken this view. For him, street corner men strive to live by American values but are continually frustrated by externally imposed failure:

> From this perspective, the street corner man does not appear as a carrier of an independent cultural tradition. His behavior appears not so much as a way of realizing the distinctive goals and values of his own subculture, or of conforming to its models, but rather as his way of trying to achieve many of the goals and values of the larger society, of failing to do this and of concealing his failure from others and from himself as best he can. (222)

Most people in the United States, however, believe that poverty is a combination of biological and cultural factors. Judith Chafel (1997) reviewed a number of studies on the beliefs of Americans and found that they "view economic privation as a self-inflicted condition, emanating more from personal factors (e.g., effort and ability) than the external-structural ones (e.g., an unfavorable labor market, institutional racism). Poverty is seen as inevitable, necessary, and just" (434).

Current research shows that this prevailing view is a myth. If there were a culture of poverty, then there would be a relatively large proportion of the poor that would constitute a permanent underclass. The deviant values and resulting behaviors of the poor would doom them and their children to continuous poverty. But the University of Michigan's Panel Study of Income Dynamics (Duncan, 1984) followed 5,000 representative households for ten years and found that only 2.6 percent fit the stereotype of permanent poverty. Contrary to common belief, most poor people are poor only temporarily; their financial fortunes rise and fall with widowhood, divorce, remarriage, acquiring a job with decent pay or losing one, or other changes affecting economic status. The 2.6 percent who are persistently poor are different from the temporarily poor: 62 percent are Black, compared with 19 percent of the temporarily poor; 39 percent are disabled, compared with 17 percent; one-third are elderly, compared with 14 percent; and 61 percent were female heads of households, compared with 28 percent of the temporarily poor. Examining just the two-thirds of the persistently poor who are not elderly, 65 percent live in households headed by women and almost three-quarters of these women are Black (Duncan, 1984:48–52). These facts show once again the interconnections of race and gender in understanding inequality in U.S. society and, as discussed in the next section, how inequality is structured by race and gender. The other important implication of these findings is that inequality negates the culture of poverty. Duncan and his colleagues find little evidence that poverty is a consequence of the way poor people think. Economic success is not a function of "good" values and behaviors, and failure the result of "bad" ones. Thus, the solution to poverty is not to change the attitudes of "flawed persons" but to change the opportunity structures in society (Duncan, 1984:65).

Structural Theories

In contrast to blaming the biological or cultural deficiencies of the poor, there is the view that how society is organized creates poverty and makes certain kinds of people especially vulnerable to being poor.

Institutional Discrimination

Michael Harrington (1963), whose book *The Other America* was instrumental in sparking the federal government's war on poverty, says, "The real explanation of why the poor are where they are is that they made the mistake of being born to the wrong parents, in the wrong section of the country, in the wrong industry, or in the wrong racial or ethnic group" (21). This is another way of saying that the structural conditions of society are to blame for poverty, not the poor. When the customary ways of doing things, prevailing attitudes and expectations, and accepted structural arrangements work to the disadvantage of the poor, it is called **institutional discrimination**. Let us look at several examples of how the poor are trapped by this type of discrimination.

Most good jobs require a college degree, but the poor cannot afford to send their children to college. Scholarships go to the best-performing students. Children of the poor usually do not perform well in school, primarily because of low expectations for them among teachers and administrators. This is reflected in the system of tracking by ability as measured on class-biased examinations. Further evidence is found in the disproportionately low amounts of money given to schools in impoverished neighborhoods. All of these acts result in a self-fulfilling prophecy—the poor are not expected to do well in school, and they do not. Because they are failures as measured by so-called objective indicators (such as the disproportionately high number of dropouts and discipline problems and the very small proportion who desire to go to college), the school feels justified in its discrimination toward the children of the poor.

The poor also are trapped because they get sick more often and stay sick longer than do the more well-to-do. The reasons, of course, are that they cannot afford preventive medicine, proper diets, and proper medical attention when ill. The high incidence of sickness among the poor means either that they will be fired from their jobs or that they will not receive money for the days missed from work (unlike the more well-to-do, who usually have jobs with such fringe benefits as sick leave and paid-up medical insurance). Not receiving a paycheck for extended periods means that the poor will have even less money for proper health care—thereby ensuring an even higher incidence of sickness. Thus, there is a vicious cycle of poverty. The poor will tend to remain poor, and their children tend to perpetuate the cycle.

The traditional organization of schools and jobs in the United States has limited the opportunities of racial minorities and women. Chapters 11 and 12 describe at length how these social categories are systematically disadvantaged by the prevailing laws, customs, and expectations of society. Suffice it to say in this context that

- Racial minorities are deprived of equal opportunities for education, jobs, and income.
- Women typically work at less prestigious jobs than do men, and when working at equal-status jobs receive less pay and fewer chances for advancement.

The Political Economy of Society

The basic tenet of capitalism—that who gets what is determined by private profit rather than by collective need—explains the persistence of poverty. The primacy of maximizing profit works to promote poverty in several ways. First, employers are constrained to pay their workers the least possible in wages and benefits. Only a portion of the wealth created by the laborers is distributed to them; the rest goes to the owners for investment and profit. Therefore, employers must keep wages low. That they are successful in this is demonstrated by the more than *2 million people who work full-time but remain under the poverty level.*

A second way that the primacy of profit induces poverty is by maintaining a surplus of laborers, because a surplus depresses wages. Especially important for employers is to have a supply of undereducated and desperate people who will work for very low wages. A large supply of these marginal people (such as minorities, women, and undocumented workers) aids the ownership class by depressing the wages for all workers in good times and provides the obvious category of people to be laid off from work in economic downturns.

More than 2.2 million people who work full time remain under the poverty level.

A third impact of the primacy of profits in capitalism is that employers make investment decisions without regard for their employees (potential or actual). If costs can be reduced, employers will purchase new technologies to replace workers (such as robots to replace assembly-line workers and word processors to replace secretaries). Similarly, owners may shut down a plant and shift their operations to a foreign country where wages are significantly lower.

To reiterate, the fundamental assumption of capitalism is individual gain without regard for what the resulting behaviors may mean for other people. The capitalist system, then, should not be accepted as a neutral framework within which goods and services are produced and distributed, but rather as an economic system that perpetuates inequality.

A number of political factors complement the workings of the economy to perpetuate poverty. Political decisions to fight inflation with high interest rates, for example, hurt several industries, particularly automobiles and home construction, causing high unemployment.

The powerful in society also use their political clout to keep society unequal. Clearly, the affluent in a capitalist society will resist efforts to redistribute their wealth to the disadvantaged. Their political efforts are, rather, to increase their benefits at the expense of the poor and the powerless (see the panel titled "Diversity: Who Benefits from Poverty?"). In short, they work for laws beneficial to them, sympathetic elected and appointed officials, policies based on trickle-down economics, and favorable tax laws such as low capital-gains taxes and regressive taxes.

In sum, this chapter has examined three stratification systems—the social class system, the system based on race and ethnicity, and the sex-gender system. By

Who Benefits from Poverty?

Herbert Gans, a sociologist, has some interesting insights about the benefits of poverty. He begins with the assumption that if some social arrangement persists, it must be accomplishing something important (at least in the view of the powerful in society). What, then, does the existence of a relatively large number of people in a condition of poverty accomplish that is beneficial to the powerful?

1. Poverty provides a low-wage labor pool that is willing (or unable to be unwilling) to do society's necessary "dirty work." The middle and upper classes are subsidized by the existence of economic activities that depend on the poor (low wages to many workers in restaurants, hospitals, and truck farming).

2. The poor also subsidize a variety of economic activities for the affluent by supporting, for example, innovations in medicine (as patients in research hospitals or as guinea pigs in medical experiments) and providing servants, gardeners, and house cleaners who make life easier for the more well-to-do.

3. The existence of poverty creates jobs for a number of occupations and professions that serve the poor or protect the rest of society from them (penologists, social workers, police, pawnshop owners, numbers racketeers, and owners of liquor stores). The presence of poor people also provides incomes for doctors, lawyers, teachers, and others who are too old, poorly trained, or incompetent to attract more affluent clients.

4. Poor people subsidize merchants by purchasing products that others do not want (seconds; dilapidated cars; deteriorated housing; day-old bread, fruit, and vegetables) and that otherwise would have little or no value.

5. The poor serve as a group to be punished in order to uphold the legitimacy of conventional values (hard work, thrift, honesty, and monogamy). The poor provide living proof that moral deviance does not pay, and thus an indirect rationale for blaming the victim.

6. Poverty guarantees the status of those who are not poor. The poor, by occupying a position at the bottom of the status hierarchy, provide a reliable and relatively permanent measuring rod for status comparison, particularly by those just above them (that is, the working class, whose politics, for example, are

often influenced by the need to maintain social distance between themselves and the poor).

7. The poor aid in the upward mobility of others. A number of people have entered the middle class through the profits earned from providing goods and services in the slums (pawnshops, secondhand clothing and furniture stores, gambling, prostitution, and drugs).

8. The poor, being powerless, can be made to absorb the costs of change in society. In the nineteenth century they did the backbreaking work that built the railroads and the cities. Today they are the ones pushed out of their homes by urban renewal and the building of expressways, parks, and stadiums. Many economists assume that a degree of unemployment is necessary to fight inflation. The poor, who are "first to be fired and the last to be hired," are the ones who make the sacrifice for the economy.

Gans notes:

This analysis is not intended to suggest that because it is often functional, poverty should exist, or that it must exist. For one thing, poverty has many more dysfunctions than functions; for another, it is possible to suggest functional alternatives. For example, society's dirty work could be done without poverty, either by automation or by paying "dirty workers" decent wages. Nor is it necessary for the poor to subsidize the many activities they support through their low-wage jobs. This would, however, drive up the costs of these activities, which would result in higher prices to their customers and clients. . . .

In sum, then, many of the functions served by the poor could be replaced if poverty were eliminated, but almost always at higher costs to others, particularly more affluent others. Consequently a functional analysis equivalent to the order model must conclude that poverty persists not only because many of the functional alternatives to poverty would be quite dysfunctional for the affluent members of society. . . . Poverty can be eliminated only when they become dysfunctional for the affluent or powerful, or when the powerless can obtain enough power to change society. (Gans, 1971:24)

From "The Uses of Power: The Poor Pay All," by Herbert J. Gans, Robert S. Lynd Professor of Sociology at Columbia University, as appeared in *Social Policy 2* (July–August 1971):20–24. Used by permission of the author.

TABLE 9.1

Varying Explanations of Inequality by Class, Race, and Gender

Explanations for Inequality	Structures of Inequality		
	Class	Race	Gender
Biological inferiority	Social Darwinism: The poor are unfit.	Jensen-Herrnstein: Blacks are less endowed mentally than Whites.	Women are biologically different from men: weaker, less aggressive, more nurturant, less able in mathematics and spatial relationships but better in language.
Cultural inferiority	Culture of poverty: The poor have a maladaptive value system that dooms them and their children.	Blacks have loose morals, have unstable families, do not value education, and lack motivation.	Gender-role socialization leads females to accept society's devalued roles, to be passive, and to be secondary to males.
Structural descrimination	The dominant use their power to maintain advantage. The poor are trapped by segmented labor markets, tracking in schools, and other structural arrangements.	Institutional racism blocks opportunities via segmented labor markets, use of biased tests for jobs, school placement, and residential segregation.	Institutional sexism limits women's chances in the legal system, job markets, wages, etc. Patriarchy occurs where men are dominant over women through organizational norms.

definition, in each stratification system certain categories of people are considered inferior and treated unfairly. Various theories have provided the rationales for this alleged inferiority. A review of these explanations is found in Table 9.1, which summarizes the theories used to explain why the poor are poor as discussed in this chapter and which anticipates the discussion of racial and gender inequalities found in Chapters 11 and 12.

1. The process of categorizing people on some dimension(s) is called social differentiation.

2. When people are ranked in a hierarchy that differentiates them as superior or inferior, this is called social stratification.

3. The three hierarchies of stratification—class, race, and gender—place groups, families, and individuals in the larger society. The rewards and resources of society are unequally distributed according to this placement. Most crucially, this social location determines for people the chances for a longer, healthier, and more enjoyable life.

4. Order model theorists accept social inequality as universal and natural. They believe that inequality serves a basic function by motivating the most talented people to perform the most important tasks.

5. Conflict theorists tend to denounce social inequality as basically unjust, unnecessary, and the source of many social problems. The irony is that the oppressed often accept their deprivation. Conflict theorists view this as the result of false consciousness—the acceptance through the socialization process of an untrue belief that works to one's disadvantage.

6. The explanations for why some categories of people are ranked at the bottom of the various hierarchies of stratification are biological, cultural, or structural.

7. The biological explanation for poverty is that the poor are innately inferior. Arthur Jensen, Richard Herrnstein, and Charles Murray, for example, have argued that certain categories of people are disadvantaged because they are less well endowed mentally (a theoretical variation of social Darwinism).

8. Another explanation that blames the poor for their poverty is the culture-of-poverty hypothesis. This theory contends that the poor are qualitatively different in values and lifestyles from the successful and that these differences explain the persistence of poverty from generation to generation.

9. Critics of innate inferiority and culture-of-poverty explanations charge that, in blaming the victim, both theories ignore how social conditions trap individuals and groups in poverty. The source of the problem lies not in the victims but in the way society is organized to advantage some and disadvantage others.

Key Terms

Caste system
Social differentiation
Social stratification
Life chances
Social class
Privilege

Race
Ethnicity
Gender
Sex-gender system
Sex roles

Gender roles
Patriarchy
Matrix of domination
Meritocracy
Institutional discrimination

Study Questions

1. Explain what is meant by this statement: "The structures of inequality—class, race, and gender—array the resources and advantages of society in patterned ways."

2. Within your college community, is there a system of stratification? What appear to be the criteria used in this ranking of individuals and groups on your campus?

3. Contrast the views of order theorists and conflict theorists on social stratification.

4. What are the sociological criticisms of the deficiency theories of social inequality? How do structural theories of inequality meet these criticisms?

5. Summarize Gans's argument in the panel titled "Diversity: Who Benefits from Poverty?" on page 247. Is this analysis from the order or the conflict perspective? Elaborate.

For Further Reading

General

Margaret L. Andersen and Patricia Hill Collins (eds.), *Race, Class, and Gender: An Anthology*, 5th ed. (Belmont, CA: Wadsworth, 2004).

Maxine Baca Zinn and D. Stanley Eitzen, *Diversity in Families*, 7th ed. (Boston: Allyn and Bacon, 2005).

Harold R. Kerbo, *Social Stratification and Inequality*, 5th ed. (New York: McGraw- Hill, 2003).

Martin N. Marger, *Social Inequality: Patterns and Processes*, 2nd ed. (New York: McGraw-Hill, 2002).

Sam Pizzigati, *Greed and Good: Understanding and Overcoming the Inequality That Limits Our Lives* (New York: Apex Press, 2004).

Jeffrey Reiman, *The Rich Get Richer and the Poor Get Prison*, 7th ed. (Boston: Allyn and Bacon, 2004).

Stratification Theory

Kingsley Davis and Wilbert E. Moore, "Some Principles of Stratification," *American Sociological Review* 10 (April 1945):242–249.

Claude S. Fischer, Michael Hout, Martin Sanchez Jankowski, Samuel R. Lucas, Ann Swidler, and Kim Voss, *Inequality by Design: Cracking the Bell Curve Myth* (Princeton, NJ: Princeton University Press, 1996).

Stephen Jay Gould, *The Mismeasure of Man* (New York: W. W. Norton, 1981).

Richard Herrnstein and Charles Murray, *The Bell Curve: Intelligence and Class Structure in American Life* (New York: Free Press, 1994).

Gerhard E. Lenski, *Power and Privilege: A Theory of Social Stratification* (New York: McGraw-Hill, 1966).

R. C. Lewontin, Steven Rose, and Leon J. Kamin, *Not in Our Genes: Biology, Ideology, and Human Nature* (New York: Pantheon, 1984).

Amartya Sen, *Inequality Reexamined* (Cambridge, MA: Harvard University Press, 1992).

Melvin M. Tumin, "Some Principles of Stratification," *American Sociological Review* 18 (August 1953): 387–393.

Empirical Studies of Stratification

Kathryn Edin and Laura Lein, *Making Ends Meet: How Single Mothers Survive Welfare and Low-Wage Work* (New York: Russell Sage, 1997).

Barbara Ehrenreich, *Nickel and Dimed: On (Not) Getting By in America* (New York: Metropolitan, 2001).

D. Stanley Eitzen and Kelly Eitzen Smith (eds.), *Experiencing Poverty: Voices from the Bottom* (Belmont, CA: Wadsworth, 2003).

Jonathan Kozol, *Rachel and Her Children: Homeless Families in America* (New York: Crown, 1988).

Jay MacLeod, *Ain't No Makin' It: Aspirations and Attainment in a Low-Income Neighborhood* (Boulder, CO: Westview Press, 1995).

Katherine S. Newman, *No Shame in My Game: The Working Poor in the Inner City* (New York: Knopf and the Russell Sage Foundation, 1999).

Kevin Phillips, *Wealth and Democracy: A Political History of the American Rich* (New York: Broadway Books, 2002).

Web Resources

http://www.census.gov/

This is the home of the Census Bureau, which has statistics on poverty, income, and other topics.

http://www.trinity.edu/mkearl/strat.html

This site has a comprehensive list of links related to social inequality and stratification. Topics include race, class, gender, and age stratification.

http://www.dollarsandsense.org/

A magazine of economic justice, this site offers articles that talk about current news issues from the political left. The site also has an archive with articles starting in 1996.

http://dir.yahoo.com/Social_Science/Sociology/Social_Class_and_Stratification/

Go to this site for links to other sites containing information on class and stratification.

http://www.hewett.norfolk.sch.uk/curric/soc/class/class.htm

This site contains general information and definitions on social class and social stratification.

http://www.worldbank.org/poverty/data/index.htm

The World Bank provides data on global inequality.

CHAPTER 10

Ten days after the terrorist attacks on the World Trade Center and the Pentagon, Congress created the Victim Compensation Fund to compensate the families of the 3,000 who died. The total government outlay was nearly $7 billion, with the individual compensation ranging from $250,000 to $7.1 million (tax-free). The variation depended on the age, estimated lifetime earnings, and family obligations of the victim. If the victim's age was forty-five, for example, the family would receive $788,109 if the income at the time of death was $30,000; $1,023,196 if the income was $50,000; $1,536,662 if the income was $100,000; and $2,682,827 if the income level was $225,000 (U.S. Department of Justice, reported in Savage, 2001:A38). Is that fair? As Frank Keating, then governor of Oklahoma, said: "The government authors official inequity when it compensates a dishwasher at the World Trade Center differently from the way it compensates the person whose dishes were washed" (Keating, 2002:A10). The counterargument is that the government's compensation plan was to provide for the victims' families with a safety net to ensure that they maintain their current standard of living. In short, to allow them to remain in the same economic strata in the stratification system. So, what is a life worth? Apparently, it depends on one's social class.

The democratic ideology that "all men are created equal" has been a central value throughout U.S. history. We are often reminded by politicians, editorial writers, and teachers that ours is a society in which the equality of every person is highly valued. This prevailing ideology, however, does not mesh with reality. Slavery was once legal, and racial discrimination against African Americans was legal until the 1960s. Women were not permitted to vote until the early 1900s. Native Americans had their land taken from them and were then forced to locate on reservations. Japanese Americans were interned against their will during World War II. Or, consider the following facts about the United States now:

- At a time (2003) when 313 people in the United States were billionaires (*Forbes*, 2004), 35.9 million people were living below the official poverty line.
- In a society with the best medical technology, hospitals, and physicians, some 45 million Americans had no health insurance.
- In 2003, one in five children under six lived in poverty, the highest rate of any developed nation.

- In the 1970s, young women and men from the top 25 percent economically were four times more likely to go to college than everyone else. Now they are ten times more likely to attend college.
- Executive pay at the top U.S. corporations climbed 571 percent from 1990 to 2000, while average wages in the United States are at or below the wage rate of 1973 (Mokhiber and Weissman, 2002).
- "In this, the wealthiest country in the world, 36 million people go hungry every day and two million are homeless for at least part of the year" (McIsaac, 2002:6).
- In 2000, a full quarter of the U.S. population earned poverty-level wages (Mokhiber and Weissman, 2002).

Clearly, as George Orwell wrote in his classic *Animal Farm*, "all . . . are equal but some are more equal than others" (1946:123).

The previous chapter considered some general principles and theories of social stratification. This chapter focuses on one hierarchy of stratification—the social class system, which is the ranking based primarily by economic resources. The chapter is divided into several parts, which describe (1) the dimensions of socioeconomic inequality, (2) the class structure in the United States, (3) the consequences of class position, (4) the degree to which people can move from one class to another—social mobility, and (5) poverty in the midst of plenty.

Dimensions of Inequality

People in the United States rank differently from one another on a number of socio-economic dimensions: wealth, income, education, and occupation.

Wealth

Wealth is unquestionably maldistributed in the United States. There exists unbelievable wealth in the hands of a few and wretched poverty for millions. At the top in 2004, the 400 richest people in the United States had a total net worth of $1 trillion (an average of $2.5 billion).

The concentration of wealth is greatly skewed:

- The top 1 percent of wealth holders controlled 29.5 percent of total household wealth while the bottom 50 percent had just 5.6 percent of the wealth (Federal Reserve data reported in Mandel, 2004).
- Personal wealth is badly skewed by race. In 2001, White households had a median net worth of $120,900, about seven times that of households of color ($17,000) (Federal Reserve data reported in United for a Fair Economy, 2004).

Income

The data on wealth always show more concentration than do income statistics, but the convergence of money among the few is still very dramatic when considering income. The share of the national income by the richest 20 percent of households was 49.8 percent, while the bottom 20 percent received only 3.4 percent of the nation's income in 2003. The data in Table 10.1 show that income inequality is increasing in U.S. society. Especially noteworthy is the sharp gain in the Gini index, which measured the magnitude of income concentration from 1970 to 2003. The Gini index of 0.464 in 2003 is the highest (indicating the greatest degree of inequality) of any other rich country. Great Britain's is 0.346, Germany's 0.300, Canada's 0.286, and Sweden's 0.222 (Murphy, 2000).

Another way to see the increasing gap between the rich and the rest of society is to look at the growth in income for various categories in the population. Using data from the Congressional Budget Office, the Economic Policy Institute calculated the average real annual income in 2001 dollars, finding that the income of the lowest fifth in households rose from $14,100 in 1979 to $14,900 in 2001. The income for the top 1 percent, on the other hand, rose from $466,800 to $1,050,100 (reported in Mott, 2005). This gap will increase further since more than half of the tax cuts enacted during President George W. Bush's first term go to the wealthiest 1 percent of all U.S. taxpayers (Mokhiber and Weissman, n.d.).

Bill Gates, the co-founder of Microsoft, is the world's richest individual.

Another measure of this increasing gap is the difference in earnings between the heads of corporations and the workers in those corporations. In 1980, the average chief executive officer (CEO) of a corporation was paid forty-two times more than the average worker. In 1990, the CEOs made 96 times as much. By 2001, the average CEO at the big corporations was paid 411 times more than the average production and nonsupervisory worker (Sklar, 2001). Also, the average CEO compensation of Fortune 500 companies was $37.5 million, while the average worker's salary of all companies was $38,000, or a ratio of 1,000 to 1 (Americans for Democratic Action, 2004). Put another way,

> average Chief Executive Officer (CEO) pay in 2002 was $7.4 million. It would take 241 years for an average worker paid $30,722 to make that amount. Since 1980, average CEO pay has skyrocketed 442 percent, adjusting for inflation, from $1,364,524. Average worker pay has inched up just 1.6 percent from an inflation-adjusted $30,244 in 1980. If CEO pay had grown at the average worker pace since 1980, it would be $1,386,065. If average worker pay had grown at the CEO pace, it would be $164,018. (Sklar, 2003:1)

Clearly, wealth and income disparities in the United States are great and growing. Robert Reich (2002), former Secretary of Labor, warns that this widening gap may lead to trouble: "Inequality has widened and the rich have grown richer while the poorer members of our society have been losing ground. . . . Global terrorism now poses the largest threat to our survival. But the widening split between our have-mores and have-lesses poses the largest threat to our strength as a society" (20).

Education

In the United States, people also vary considerably in educational attainment. The amount of formal education an individual achieves is a major determinant of her or

TABLE 10.1

Share of Aggregate Income by Each Fifth of Households, 1970, 1980, 1990, 2000, 2003

	Percentage Distribution of Aggregate Income					
Year	Lowest Fifth	Second Fifth	Third Fifth	Fourth Fifth	Highest Fifth	Gini* Index
2003	3.4	8.7	14.8	23.4	49.8	0.464
2000	3.6	8.9	14.9	23.0	49.6	0.460
1990	3.9	9.6	15.9	24.0	46.6	0.428
1980	4.3	10.3	16.9	24.9	43.7	0.403
1970	4.1	10.8	17.4	24.5	43.3	0.394

*The income inequality of a population group is commonly measured using the Gini index. The Gini index ranges from 0, indicating perfect equality (i.e., all persons having equal shares of the aggregate income), to 1, indicating perfect inequality (i.e., where all of the income is received by only one recipient or one group of recipients and the rest have none). The increase in the Gini index for household income between 1970 and 2000 indicates a significant in income inequality.

Sources: U.S. Bureau of the Census, 2001, *Current Population Surveys.* Available online: www.census.gov/hhes/income/histinc/ie3.html. U.S. Bureau of the Census, 2004. "Income, Poverty, and Health Insurance Coverage in the United States: 2003." *Current Population Reports,* P60–226 (August).

his occupation, income, and prestige. Despite the standard belief by people in the United States in free mass education and the almost uniform requirement that citizens complete at least eight years of formal schooling, real differences in educational attainment exist (see Table 10.2).

"The poor are getting poorer, but with the rich getting richer it all averages out in the long run."

TABLE 10.2

Education Attainment of People Age Twenty-Five and Older, 2000

Highest Level Attained	Percent
Less than ninth grade	6.9
Some high school (no diploma)	11.4
High school graduate	29.5
Some college (no degree)	20.5
Associate's degree	6.4
Bachelor's degree	16.1
Graduate of professional degree	9.0

Source: U.S. Bureau of the Census, 2001. Available online: http://factfinder.census.gov/.

There is an obvious correspondence between being inadequately educated and receiving little or no income. Census data from 1999 indicate that the average estimated lifetime earnings for full-time workers ranged from $1 million for those with less than a high school education to $2.1 million for those with a college degree, and $4.4 million for those with a professional degree (reported in Armas, 2002). The difference in income is compounded when race is considered, as revealed in Figure 10.1.

There is not only a generational correlation between education and income but an intergenerational one as well. The children of the poor and uneducated tend not to do well in school and eventually drop out (regardless of ability), while the children of the educated well-to-do tend to continue in school (regardless of ability). Thus, the cycle of inequality is maintained.

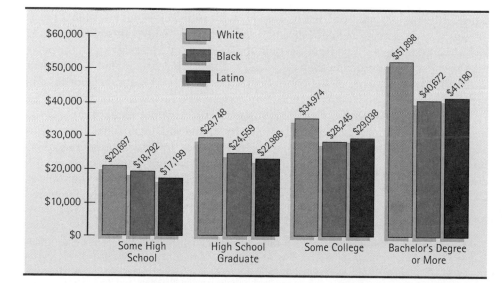

FIGURE 10.1

Median Annual Income for Full-Time Workers by Educational Attainment for People 25 Years Old and Over by Race and Hispanic Origin: 2000

Source: U.S. Bureau of the Census, 2000. "Educational Attainment in the United States: March 2000." *Current Population Reports.* Series P20–536. Washington, DC: U.S. Government Printing Office.

Occupation

Another demonstration that people diverge in status is that occupations vary systematically in prestige. The degree of prestige and difference accorded to occupations is variable. A justice of the Supreme Court obviously enjoys more prestige than a bartender. But society makes much more subtle prestige distinctions. There is a rather uniform tendency to rate physicians slightly higher than college professors, who in turn are somewhat higher in rank than dentists. Further down the prestige scale, mail carriers outrank carpenters, who in turn have higher prestige than do automobile mechanics (see Table 10.3).*

The culture provides a ready-made, well-understood, relatively uniform ranking system based on several related factors: (1) the importance of the task performed (that is, how vital the consequences of the task are for the society), (2) the degree of authority and responsibility inherent in the job, (3) the native intelligence required, (4) the knowledge and skills required, (5) the dignity of the job, and (6) the financial rewards of the occupation.

But society also presents us with warped images of occupations, which leads to the acceptance of stereotypes. The media, for example, through advertisements, television, and movie portrayals, evoke positive images for middle- and upper-class occupations and negative ones for lower-prestige occupations. Professional and business leaders are White, male, cultured, and physically attractive. They are decisive, intelligent, and authoritative. At the other end of the occupational spectrum, workers are often portrayed as ethnic, bigoted, and ignorant.

Occupation, then, is a very important variable that sorts people into hierarchically arranged categories. It is highly correlated with income level, but the gender of the worker makes a tremendous difference. Regardless of the occupational category, women make considerably less, on average, than do men employed in the same category.

The Consequences of Increasing Inequality for Society

This inequality gap in the United States is the highest in the industrialized world. Considering the gap between CEOs and workers, the ratio in Japan is less than 25 to 1; in France and Germany, the compensation ratio for CEOs and workers is less than 35 to 1. If we compare the income of the richest 20 percent of Americans with the poorest, the gap is not only greater than elsewhere in the developed world but is equivalent to the inequality in some of the poorest countries such as Honduras, Jamaica, and Kenya, and twice as bad as Japan, India, Bangladesh, and Rwanda (Food First, 1998).

The divide between the wealthy and the nonaffluent, let alone the poor; the highly skilled and the unskilled; and the educated and the uneducated grows. This gap is manifested in a number of ways. The very rich live in exclusive neighborhoods, belong to exclusive private clubs, play at exclusive resorts, and send their children to private schools. In each instance they interact with people like themselves. Even the less-than-rich but still affluent make major attempts to segregate them-

*There is a strong correlation in these rankings over time. The National Opinion Research Center's findings in 1994 are quite similar to those found by sociologists C. C. North and Paul K. Hatt (1947) and by Hodge, Seigel, and Rossi (1964). Also noteworthy, sociologists have found a high correlation in the rating for occupations for a number of industrialized nations (Hodge, Treiman, and Rossi, 1966).

TABLE 10.3

Prestige Rankings of Selected Occupation

Occupation	Prestige Ranking
Physician	86
College professor	74
Aerospace engineer	72
Dentist	72
Clergy	69
Secondary school teacher	66
Accountant	65
Elementary school teacher	64
Computer programmer	61
Sociologist	61
Police officer	60
Librarian	54
Firefighter	53
Electrician	51
Machinist	47
Mail carrier	47
Bank teller	43
Carpenter	39
Hairdresser	36
Truck driver	30
Garbage collector	28
Janitor	22

Source: National Opinion Research Center, 1994. *General Social Surveys, 1972–1994: Cumulative Codebook.* Chicago: National Opinion Research Center, pp. 881–889.

selves from those they consider below them. They, too, often send their children to private schools or home school them, and they move from the central cities to the suburbs. Many millions of Americans live in gated communities, and millions more live in locked apartment buildings.

The ever-increasing wealth and income inequality has implications for democracy, crime, and civil unrest. The greater the wealth and income inequality in society, the greater the economic and social fragmentation. As economist Lester Thurow (1995b) asks: "How much inequality can a democracy take? The income gap in America is eroding the social contract. If the promise of a higher standard of living is limited to a few at the top, the rest of the citizenry, as history shows, is likely to grow disaffected, or worse" (78). Or, as economist James K. Galbraith (1998) puts it: "[Inequality] is now so wide it threatens, as it did in the Great Depression, the social stability of the country. It has come to undermine our sense of ourselves as a nation of equals. Economic inequality, in this way, challenges the essential unifying myth of American national life" (24).

Evidence for this is found in our political discourse. As Galbraith (1998) says: "A high degree of inequality causes the comfortable to disavow the needy. It increases the psychological distance separating these groups, making it easier to imagine that defects of character or differences of culture, rather than an unpleasant turn in the larger schemes of economic history, lie behind the separation" (24). Since politicians represent the monied interests (see Chapter 13), the wealthy get their way, as seen in the decline in welfare programs for the poor, the demise of affirmative action, and tax breaks that benefit them disproportionately. Most telling, the inequality gap is not part of the political debate, nor is the plight of those with no effective access to health care (Nichol, 1999a).

The United States, compared to other advanced industrial societies, has the highest proportion of its population below the poverty line, a withering bond among those of different social classes, a growing racial divide, and an alarming move toward a two-tiered society. The consequences of an extreme bipolar society are seen in the following description by James Fallows:

> If you had a million dollars, where would you want to live, Switzerland or the Philippines? Think about all the extra costs, monetary and otherwise, if you chose a vastly unequal country like the Philippines? Maybe you'd pay less in taxes, but you'd wind up shuttling between little fenced-in enclaves. You'd have private security guards. You'd socialize only in private clubs. You'd visit only private parks and beaches. Your kids would go to private schools. They'd study in private libraries. (quoted in Carville, 1996:87)

The United States is not the Philippines, but we are seeing a dramatic rise in private schooling (about 12 percent of students), home schooling (about 2 percent), and in the number of walled and gated affluent neighborhood enclaves on the one hand, and ever greater concentration of the poor and especially poor racial minorities in segregated and deteriorating neighborhoods and inferior schools on the other. Finally, democracy is on the wane as more and more people opt out of the electoral process. The affluent are more likely to vote, because the politicians of both parties are in tune with their wishes. The poor, near-poor, and working classes, in contrast, are not likely to vote, presumably because they are not connected to either political party and the political process works against their interests. As a result, the United States has the lowest voter turnout among the industrialized nations, further evidence of the inequality gap and the erosion of social solidarity in society.

Social Classes

Social class is a complex concept that centers on the distribution of economic resources. That is, when a number of individuals occupy the same relative economic rank in the stratification system, they form a social class. A significant question is, Does economic ranking place people in an identifiable class, in which they identify with and share common interests with the other members, or is the designation a fuzzy one? The dominant view is that there are no clear class boundaries, except perhaps those delineating the highest and lowest classes. A social class is not a homogeneous group, given the diversity within it, yet there is some degree of identification with other people in similar economic situations. Also, people have a sense of who is superior, equal, and inferior to them. This is evidenced in patterns of deference and feelings of comfort or uneasiness during interaction. Similarly, there tend to be commonalities in lifestyles and tastes (for example, consumption patterns, child-raising patterns, the role of women) among people in a similar economic position. But even though we can make fairly accurate generalizations about people in a social class, the heterogeneity within it precludes accurate predictions about each person included. In the words of Barbara Ehrenreich (1989):

> Class is a notion that is inherently fuzzy at the edges. When we talk about class, we are making a generalization about large groups of people, and about how they live and make their livings. Since there are so many borderline situations, and since people do move up and down between classes, a description like middle class may mean very little when applied to a particular individual. But it should tell us something about the broad terrain of inequality, and about how people are clustered, very roughly, at different levels of comfort, status, and control over their lives. (13)

Sociologists agree that social classes exist and that money is a central criterion for classification, but they disagree on the meaning of social classes for people. For example, in contrast to the prevailing view that social classes are generally correlated with the society's income distribution and that their boundaries are inherently fuzzy, there is the opposing view that society is divided into conflicting classes with definite boundaries, each of which has a common interest. These two models of social class represent the views of the order model and the conflict model. Although this oversimplifies the debate, we examine these two theoretical ways to conceptualize social class. Let's examine these two positions and the resulting social class structure that results from each approach (the following discussion is dependent on Liazos, 1985:228–234; Lucal, 1994; Sanderson, 1988:191–195; Vanneman and Cannon, 1987; and Wright et al., 1982).

The Order Model's Conception of Social Class

Order theorists use the terms income, occupation, and education as the fundamental indicators of social class, with occupation as central. Occupational placement determines income, interaction patterns, opportunity, and lifestyle. Lifestyle is the key dependent variable. Each social class is viewed as having its distinct culture. There are believed to be class-specific values, attitudes, and motives that distinguish its members from other classes. These orientations stem from income level and especially from occupational experiences (Collins, 1988:29). From this perspective, "how people get the money and what they do with it is as important (perhaps even more important than) as how much they have" (Liazos, 1985:230).

The typical class system from the order perspective has these classes, distributed in an income and status hierarchy.

1. *Upper-Upper Class.* Sometimes referred to as the *old rich*, the members of this class are wealthy, and because they have held this wealth for several generations, they have a strong ingroup solidarity. They belong to exclusive clubs and attend equally exclusive boarding schools. Their children intermarry, and the members vacation together in posh, exclusive resorts around the world (Baltzell, 1958; Domhoff, 1970; Mills, 1959).

2. *Lower-Upper Class.* The wealth of the members is of relatively recent origin (hence, the term *new rich*). The new rich differ from the old rich in prestige, but not necessarily in wealth. Great wealth alone does not ensure acceptance by the elite as a social equal. The new rich are not accepted because they differ from the old rich in behaviors and lifestyles. The new rich is composed of the self-made wealthy. These families have amassed fortunes typically through business ventures or because of special talent in music, sport, or other form of entertainment. Additionally, some professionals (doctors, lawyers) may become wealthy because of their practice and/or investments. Finally, a few people may become very wealthy by working their way to the top executive positions in corporations, where high salaries and lucrative stock options are common.

3. *Upper-Middle Class.* The key distinguishing feature of this class is high-prestige (but not necessarily high-income) jobs that require considerable formal education and have a high degree of autonomy and responsibility. This stratum is composed largely of professional people, executives, and businesspeople. They are self-made, having accomplished their relatively high status through personal education and occupational accomplishments.

4. *Lower-Middle Class.* These are white-collar workers (as opposed to manual workers) who work primarily in minor jobs in bureaucracies. They work, for example, as secretaries, clerks, salespeople, police officers, and teachers.

5. *Upper-Lower Class.* These people work at repetitive jobs with little autonomy that require no creativity. They are blue-collar workers who, typically, have no education beyond high school. They are severely blocked from upward mobility.

6. *Lower-Lower Class.* This class is composed of unskilled laborers whose formal education is often less than high school. The chronically unemployed are in this class. When they do work, it is for low wages, no fringe benefits, and no job security. Minority-group members—African Americans, Puerto Ricans, Mexican Americans, Native Americans—are disproportionately found in this category. These people are looked down on by all others in the community. They live on the other side of the tracks. They are considered by other people to be undesirable as playmates, friends, organization members, or marriage partners. Lower-lowers are thought to have a culture of poverty—that is, their presumed traits of laziness, dependence, and immorality, which, because they are the opposite of good middle-class virtues, lock them into their inferiority.

The Conflict Model's Conception of Social Class

The conception of social class presented by the order theorists has important insights. As Liazos (1985), a conflict theorist, puts it: "Only a fool would deny that occupation, education, and the various 'life-style' qualities (speech, dress, leisure activities, etc.) define a person's class. They do matter to people, and we do distinguish one person or family from another by the kind of work they do, where they went to school, and so on" (230–231).

Conflict theorists, however, argue that order theorists understate the centrality of money in determining where people fall in the class system. "Where people live, how much education they receive, what they do to earn an income (or if they do not need to earn an income), who they associate with, and so forth, depend on how much money their families earn or have" (Liazos, 1985:231). Conflict theorists, in contrast to order theorists, focus on money and power, rather than on lifestyle. Again, turning to Liazos (1985):

> In capitalist societies, the greatest class division is between the few who own and run corporations . . . and the rest of the people. This is not to say that all other people belong to one class; obviously they do not. But it is to say that the one million or so people who belong to the families that own, control, and profit by the largest corporations differ fundamentally from the rest of us. It is their power and wealth that essentially distinguish them from the rest of society, not their speech, dress, education, leisure activities, and so on. (231)

Conflict theorists also differ from order theorists in how they view occupation as a criterion for social class. A social class, in this view, is not a cluster of similar occupations but, rather, a number of individuals who occupy a similar position within the social relations of economic production (Wright et al., 1982). In other words, what is important about social classes is that they involve relationships of domination and subordination that are made possible by the systematic control of society's scarce resources. The key, then, is not the occupation itself but the control one has over one's own work, the work of others, decision making, and investments. People who own, manage, oppress, and control must be distinguished from those who are managed, oppressed, and controlled (Eshleman, 1988:216).

Using these three criteria—money, relation to the means of production, and power—conflict theorists tend to distinguish five classes.

1. *Ruling Class*. The people in this class hold most of the wealth and power in society. The richest 1 percent own as much as or more than the bottom 90 percent of the population. But the ruling class is smaller than the richest 1 percent. These are the few who control the corporations, banks, media, and politics. They are the very rich and the very powerful. The key is that the families and individuals in the ruling class own, control, govern, and rule the society. They control capital, markets, labor, and politics. In Marxist terms, the great wealth held by the ruling class is extracted from the labor of others.

2. *Professional-Managerial Class*. Four categories of people are included in this class—managers, supervisors, professionals in business firms, and professionals outside business but whose mental work aids business.

The most powerful managers are those near the top of the organizational charts who have broad decision-making powers and responsibilities. They have considerable power over the workers below them. In the words of sociologists Vanneman and Cannon (1987):

> As firms grew, an army of managers, professionals, and white-collar employees took over some of the managerial functions previously reserved for capitalists alone. These salaried officials work for owners of productive property, just as blue-collar workers do, but earn generous incomes and enjoy substantial prestige. And—what is crucial for a class analysis—the new middle class also shares in some of the power that capital has exercised over workers. (53)

There are also lower-level managers, forepersons, and other supervisors. They have less training than do the organizational managers, have limited authority, and are extensively controlled by top and middle managers. These people hold a contradictory class position. They have some control over others, which places them in this category, but their limited supervision of the routine work of others puts them close to the working class. The key for inclusion in this class, though, is that the role of supervisor places the individual with the interests of management in opposition to the working class (Vanneman and Cannon, 1987:55; see also Poulantzas, 1974:14). As Randall Collins (1988) argues: "The more one gives orders, the more one identifies with the organizational ideals in whose name one justifies the orders, and the more one identifies with one's formal position, the more opposed they are to the interests of the working class" (31).

Another social category within this class includes professionals employed by business enterprises. These professionals (doctors, lawyers, engineers, accountants, inspectors) have obtained their position through educational attainment, expertise, and intellect. Unlike the ruling class, these professionals do not own the major means of production, but rather they work for the ruling class. They do not have supervisory authority, but they influence how workers are organized and treated within the organization. They are dominated by the ruling class, although this is mediated somewhat by the dependence of the elite on their specialized knowledge and expertise (for an extended discussion of this growing class, see Ehrenreich, 1989).

Finally, there are professionals who have substantial control over workers' lives but who are not part of business enterprises. Their mental labor exists outside the corporation, but nonetheless their services control workers. Included in this category are social workers, who are responsible for ensuring that the unemployed and poor do not disrupt the status quo (Piven and Cloward, 1993). Educators serve as gatekeepers, sifting and sorting people for good and bad jobs, which gives them enormous power over workers and their children (Vanneman and Cannon, 1987:76). Doctors keep workers healthy, and psychologists provide help for troubled people and seek to bring deviants back into the mainstream where they can function normally. Vanneman and Cannon (1987) argue that these professionals outside business belong in the same social class as those professionals working directly for business:

> If [this class] is defined by the control it exerts over other people, then, it necessarily incorporates the social worker, teacher, and doctor as well as the first-line supervisor and plant manager. What the social worker, teacher, and doctor share with the engineer, accountant, and personnel officer is a specialization of mental labor: they all plan, design, and analyze, but their plans, designs, and analyses are largely executed by others. (76)

3. *Small-Business Owners.* The members of this class are entrepreneurs who own businesses that are not major corporations. They may employ no workers (thus, exploiting no labor power) or a relative few. The income and power over others possessed by members of this class vary considerably.

4. *Working Class.* The members of this class are the workers in factories, restaurants, offices, and stores. They include both white-collar and blue-collar workers. White-collar workers are included because they, like blue-collar workers, do not have control over other workers or even over their own lives (Vanneman and Cannon, 1987:11). The distinguishing feature of this class is that they sell their labor power to capitalists and earn their income through wages. Their economic well-being depends on decisions made in corporate boardrooms and by managers and supervi-

"Carpe diem."

sors. They are closely supervised by other people. They take orders. This is a crucial criterion for inclusion in the working class, because "the more one takes orders, the more one is alienated from organizational ideals" (Collins, Randall, 1988:31). Thus, they are clearly differentiated from classes whose members identify with the business firms for which they work.

5. *Poor.* These people work for minimum wages and/or are unemployed. They do society's dirty work for low wages. At the bottom in income, security, and authority, they are society's ultimate victims of oppression and domination.

Wright and his colleagues (1982) made an empirical investigation of the U.S. class structure using the conflict approach. Among their results are several interesting findings. First, it is incorrect to rank occupations, as order theorists do, because within the various occupational categories there are managers/supervisors and workers. In other words, workers in white-collar jobs can be divided into managers and workers (proletariat). So, too, can we categorize jobs for laborers, operatives, and unskilled services:

> There is a long tradition in sociology of arguing over whether or not lower white-collar jobs should be considered in the working-class or the "middle-class." Usually it is assumed in such debates that occupations as such can appropriately be grouped into classes, the issue being where a specific occupation ought to be located. . . . [I]f classes are conceptualized in relational terms, this is not even the correct way to pose the problem. Instead, the empirical question is the extent of proletarianization within different occupational categories. (Wright et al., 1982:720)

Second, social class is closely related to gender and race. Wright and his associates found that women are more proletarianized, regardless of occupational category, than are men (54 percent occupy working-class locations, compared with only 40 percent for men). Similarly, 64 percent of all African Americans are in the working class, compared with only 44 percent of Whites. "If we examine the combined race-sex-class distributions, we see that black women are the most proletarianized of all: 65 percent of black women in the labor force are in the working class, compared to 64 percent of black men, 52 percent for white women, and only 38 percent for white men" (Wright et al., 1982:724).

Summary: Class from the Order and Conflict Perspectives

Vanneman and Cannon (1987) have summarized the fundamental differences between the order and the conflict views of social class:

> In the [conflict] vision, class divides society into two conflicting camps that contend for control: workers and bosses, labor and capital, proletariat workers and bourgeoisie [middle class]; in this dichotomous image, classes are bounded, identifiable collectivities, each one having a common interest in the struggle over control of society. In the [order] vision, class sorts out positions in society along a many-runged ladder of economic success and social prestige; in this continuous image, classes are merely relative rankings along the ladder: upper class, lower class, upper-middle class, "the Toyota set," "the BMW set," "Brahmins," and the dregs "from the other side of the tracks." People are busy climbing up (or slipping down) these social class ladders, but there is no collective conflict organized around the control of society. (39)

These radically different views on social class should not obscure the insights that both views provide for the understanding of this complex phenomenon. Occupation is critical to both, but for very different reasons. For the order theorist, occupations vary in how people evaluate them; some occupations are clearly superior to others in status. Thus, the perceptions of occupations within a population indicate clearly that there is a prestige hierarchy among them and the individuals identified with them.

The conflict theorist also focuses on occupations, but without reference to prestige. Where a person is located in the work process determines the degree of control that individual has over others and himself or herself. The key to determining class position is whether one gives orders or takes orders. Moreover, this placement determines one's fundamental interests, because one is either advantaged (living off the labor of others) or disadvantaged (oppressed). Empirically, both of these views mesh with reality.

Second, order theorists focus on commonalities in lifestyles among individuals and families similar in education, income, and occupation. These varying lifestyles are real. There are differences in language use, tastes for music and art, interior decorating, dress, child-rearing practices, and the like (see Fussell, 1983). Although real, the emphasis on lifestyle misses the essential point, according to conflict theorists. For them, lifestyle is not central to social class; giving or taking orders is. This is why there is disagreement on where, for example, to place lower-level white-collar workers, such as clerks and secretaries. Order theorists place them in the middle class because the prestige of their occupations is higher than that of blue-collar workers and because their work is mental rather than manual. Conflict theorists, on the other hand, place them with workers who take orders, that is, in the worker class.

Conflict theorists also point to two important implications of the emphasis on lifestyle. First, although culture is a dependent variable (that is, it is a consequence of occupation, income, and education), the culture of a social class is assumed to have a power over its members that tends to bind them to their social class (for example, the culture of poverty is believed to keep the poor, poor—see Chapters 7, 9, and 11). A second implication is the implicit assumption that these cultures are themselves ranked, with the culture of the higher classes being more valued. Conflict theorists have the opposite bias—they view the denigration of society's losers as blaming the victim. From this perspective, the higher the class, the more its members are guilty of oppressing and exploiting the labor of those below. In short, there is a strong tendency among conflict theorists to identify with the plight of underdogs and to label pejoratively the behaviors of top dogs.

Finally, each view of social class is useful for understanding social phenomena. The order model's understanding of inequality in terms of prestige and lifestyle differences has led to research that has found interesting patterns of behaviors by social location, which is one emphasis of sociology. Similarly, the focus of the order model has resulted in considerable research on mobility, mobility aspirations, and the like, which is helpful for the understanding of human motivation as well as the constraints on human behavior. The conflict model, on the other hand, examines inequality from differences in control—control over society, community, markets, labor, others, and oneself. The resulting class division is useful for understanding conflict in society—strikes, lockouts, political repression, social movements, and revolutions.

The Consequences of Social Class Positions

Regardless of the theoretical position, there is no disagreement on the proposition that one's wealth is the determining factor in a number of crucial areas, including the chance to live and the chance to obtain those things (for example, possessions or education) that are highly valued in society. As discussed in Chapter 9, life chances refer to the chances throughout one's life cycle to live and to experience the good things in life. These chances are dependent almost exclusively on the economic circumstances of the family into which one is born. Gerth and Mills (1953) contend that life chances refer to "everything from the chance to stay alive during the first year after birth to the chance to view fine art, the chance to remain healthy and grow tall, and if sick to get well again quickly, the chance to avoid becoming a juvenile delinquent—and very crucially, the chance to complete an intermediary or higher educational grade" (313).

Physical Health

Economic position has a great effect on how long one will live, or, in a crisis, who will be the last to die. For instance, the official casualty lists of the transatlantic luxury liner *Titanic*, which rammed an iceberg in 1912, listed 3 percent of the first-class female passengers as lost, 16 percent of the second-class female passengers, and 45 percent of the third-class female passengers (Lord, 1955:107). Apparently, even in a disaster, socioeconomic position makes a real difference—the higher the economic status of the individual, the greater the probability of survival.

The greater advantage toward longer life by the well-to-do is not limited to disasters such as the *Titanic*. A consistent research finding is that health and death are influenced greatly by social class.

Economic disadvantage is closely associated with health disadvantages. Put another way: "How people live, get sick, and die depends not only on their race and gender, but primarily on the class to which they belong" (Navarro, 1991:2). The poor are more likely than the affluent to suffer from certain forms of cancer (cancers of the lung, cervix, and esophagus), hypertension, infant mortality, disabilities, and infectious diseases (especially influenza and tuberculosis). The affluent live longer, and when stricken with a disease they are more likely to survive than are the poor. For example, women with family incomes below $10,000 are more than three times as likely to die of heart disease, compared to those with family incomes above $25,000 (Reuss, 2001). Using education as an indicator of social class, men with less than twelve years of education are more than twice as likely to die of heart disease, and more than three times as likely to die as a result of injury, compared to those with thirteen or more years of education (Reuss, 2001). For the consequences of social class on the health of children, see Table 10.4.

An obvious health advantage of the affluent is access to health-promoting and health-protecting resources and, when needed, access to medical services, paid for, at least in part, typically, with health insurance. Health insurance in the United States is typically tied to employment, with employers and employees splitting the cost. Structural changes in the U.S. economy (see Chapter 8)—the shift of employment from manufacturing to services, the rise in contingent and part-time employment, and the decline of union membership—have resulted in a decline in employment-related health insurance coverage. And the lower the prestige and the lower the wages in the job, the less likely the pay will include a health benefits package.

TABLE 10.4

Poverty Matters

Outcomes	Low-Income Children's Higher Risk
Health	
Death in infancy	1.6 times as likely
Premature birth (under 37 weeks)	1.8 times as likely
Low birthweight	1.9 times as likely
No regular source of health care	2.7 times as likely
Inadequate prenatal care	2.8 times as likely
Family had too little food sometime in the last 4 months	8 times as likely
Education	
Math scores at ages 7 to 8	5 test points lower
Reading scores at ages 7 to 8	4 test points lower
Repeated a grade	2.0 times as likely
Expelled from school	3.4 times as likely
Being a dropout at ages 16 to 24	3.5 times as likely
Finishing a four-year college	half as likely

Source: Children's Defense Fund, 2004. *The State of America's Children, 2004.* Washington, DC. Reprinted by permission of the Children's Defense Fund.

Currently about 45 million people in the United States, mostly the near-poor younger than age sixty-five, have no medical insurance, including an estimated 500,000 pregnant women, who as a result often do not receive prenatal and post-natal health care. The consequences are a high maternal death rate (typically from hemorrhage and infection) and a relatively high infant mortality rate. Of the twenty industrialized countries, eighteen have lower infant mortality rates than the United States.

The common belief is that the poor are accountable for their health deficiencies; that is, their lack of education and knowledge may lead to poor health practices. Research shows, for example, that those with lower incomes are more likely to smoke and be overweight. They are also less likely to exercise and engage in preventive health care. The essence of this argument is that the problems of ill health that beset the poor disproportionately are a consequence of their different lifestyle. This approach, however, ignores the fundamental realities of social class—that is, privilege in the social stratification system translates both directly and indirectly into better health in several major ways (Williams, David, 1990).

1. The privileged live in home, neighborhood, and work environments that are less stressful. The disadvantaged are more subject to stresses (and resulting ill health) from high crime rates, financial insecurity, marital instability, death of loved ones, spells of unemployment, unhealthy work conditions, and exposure to pollution and toxic materials in their neighborhoods.
2. Children of privilege have healthier environments in the crucial first five years of life.
3. The privileged have better access to and make better use of the health care system. The fewer the economic resources, the less likely a person will receive preventive care and early treatment.
4. The privileged have health insurance to pay for a major portion of their physician, hospital, diagnostic test, and pharmaceutical needs. Many people in the United States, however, cannot afford health insurance and/or their employers do not provide medical insurance, resulting in some 45 million uninsured people, about 10 million of whom are children.

In a series on social class by the *New York Times*, one essay was titled "Life at the Top in America Isn't Just Better, It's Longer." Janny Scott (2005), the author, summarized the importance of social class on health:

> Class is a potent force in health and longevity in the United States. The more education and income people have, the less likely they are to have and die of heart disease, strokes, diabetes and many types of cancer. Upper-middle-class Americans live longer and in better health than middle-class Americans, who live longer and better than those at the bottom. And the gaps are widening, say people who have researched social factors in health. (1)

Family Instability

Research relating socioeconomic status to family discord and marital disruption has found an inverse relationship—the lower the status, the greater the proportion of divorce or desertion.

The lack of adequate resources places a burden on intimate relationships. . . . Poor two-parent families are twice as likely to break up as are two-parent families not in poverty. . . . Moreover, the likelihood of marital breakup increases when a husband does not work, and it is even greater when neither spouse works. Sudden financial difficulties such as unexpected unemployment also increase the possibility of marital breakdown. (Baca Zinn and Eitzen, 2005:400)

The Draft

Involuntary conscription into the U.S. Army—the draft system—works to the disadvantage of the uneducated. In 1969, during the Vietnam War, only 10 percent of the men drafted were college men. The Supreme Court has further helped the educated by ruling that a person can be a conscientious objector on a basis of either religion or philosophy. Young intellectuals can use their knowledge of history, philosophy, and even sociology to argue that they should not serve. The uneducated will not have the necessary knowledge to make such a case.

Educated young men who end up in the armed services are more likely to serve in noncombat supply and administrative jobs than are non-college-educated men. People who can type, do bookkeeping, or know computer programming will generally be selected to do jobs in which their skills can be used. Conversely, the nonskilled will generally end up in the most hazardous jobs. The chances for getting killed while in the service are greater, therefore, for the less educated than for the college educated.

When the draft is not used, as is the case at present in the war in Afghanistan and Iraq, the personnel in the lower ranks of the military come disproportionately from the disadvantaged segments of society. This occurs because the military offers a job and stability for young people who find little or no opportunity in the job market. The downside, of course, is that they risk injury and even death during combat. Without a draft, the privileged can avoid these risks.

Justice

The administration of justice is unequal in the United States. Low-income people are more likely to be arrested, to be found guilty, and to serve longer sentences for a given violation than are people in the middle and upper classes.

The casket of a U.S. soldier killed in Iraq. Deaths in battle are not randomly distributed by social class—youth from lower strata are the most likely to die.

Why is the system of justice unjust? The affluent can afford the services of the best lawyers for their defense, detectives to gather supporting evidence, and expert witnesses such as psychiatrists. The rich can afford to appeal the decision to a series of appellate courts. The poor, on the other hand, cannot afford bail and must await trial in jail, and they must rely on court-appointed lawyers, who are usually among the least experienced lawyers in the community and who often have heavy case-loads. All the evidence points to the regrettable truth that a defendant's wealth makes a significant difference in the administration of justice.

A class bias held by most citizens, including arresting officers, prosecuting attorneys, judges, and jury members, affects the administration of justice. This bias is revealed in a set of assumptions about people according to their socioeconomic status. The typical belief is that the affluent or the children of the affluent, if law-breakers, are basically good people whose deviance is an aberration, a momentary act of immaturity. Thus, a warning will suffice or, if the crime is serious, a short sentence is presumed to cause enough humiliation to bring back their naturally con-forming ways. Lawbreaking by the poor, on the other hand, is more troublesome and must be punished harshly, because these are essentially bad people and their deviance will persist if tolerated or mildly punished by the authorities.

Education

In general, life chances depend on wealth—they are purchased. The level of educa-tional attainment (except for the children of the elite, where the best in life is a birthright) is the crucial determinant of one's chances of income.

Inequality of educational opportunity exists in all educational levels in many subtle and not-so-subtle forms (see Chapter 16). It occurs in the quality of education when schools are compared by district. Districts with a better tax base have superior facilities, better-motivated teachers (because those districts can pay more), and better techniques than do the poorer districts. Within each school, regardless of the type of district, children are given standardized tests that have a middle-class bias. Armed with these data, educators place children in tracks according to ability. These tracks thus become discriminatory, because the lowest track is composed disproportionately of the lower socioeconomic category. These tracks are especially harmful in that they structure the expectations of the teacher.

Consider these facts concerning college—the gateway to upward mobility (Symonds, 2003):

- 35 percent of students from families with incomes of less than $25,000 enroll, compared to 80 percent of those from families with incomes of more than $75,000. Of those who enroll, 55 percent of those in the bottom quartile of socio-economic status graduate and 73 percent of those in the top quartile graduate.
- Only 78 percent of students from low-income families who rank as top achievers attend college—about the same as the 77 percent of affluent students who rank at the bottom academically.
- Although 28 percent of all 18-year-olds are African American or Latino, only 12 percent of the freshman classes at the top 146 colleges are African American or Latino.
- For students in the top 146 colleges only 3 percent come from families in the bottom socioeconomic quartile and just 10 percent are from families in the bottom half.

These economic disparities have serious implications for American society. Tom Mortensen of the Pell Institute for the Study of Opportunity in Higher Education says that "the trajectory we're on suggests we will become a poorer, more unequal, and less homogeneous country" (quoted in Symonds, 2003:66).

Social Mobility

This section analyzes the degree of social mobility in society. This emphasis fits with the order model. It assumes that status (as opposed to class) differences are grada-tions, corresponding with occupation. Moreover, there is the assumption that a high degree of social mobility exists in U.S. society, with a growing middle mass of work-ers enjoying a high standard of living (Knottnerus, 1987).

Societies vary in the degree to which individuals may move up in status. Proba-bly the most rigid stratification system ever devised was the **caste system** of India. In brief, this system, as noted in the previous chapter, (1) determines status by hered-ity, (2) allows marriage to occur only within one's status group (endogamy), (3) determines occupation by heredity, and (4) restricts interaction among the status groups. Even the Indian caste system, however, is not totally rigid, for some mobility has been allowed under certain conditions.

In contrast to this closed stratification system, the United States has a relatively open system. Social mobility is not only permitted, but is also part of the U.S. value system that upward mobility is good and should be the goal of all people in the United States.

The United States, however, is not a totally open system. All U.S. children have the social rank of their parents while they are youths, which in turn has a tremendous influence on whether the child can be mobile (either upward or downward).

Social mobility refers to an individual's movement within the class structure of society. **Vertical mobility** is movement upward or downward in social class. **Horizontal mobility** is the change from one position to another of about equal prestige. A shift in occupation from electrician to plumber is an example of horizontal mobility.

Social mobility occurs in two ways. **Intergenerational mobility** refers to vertical movement comparing a daughter with her mother or a son with his father. **Intragenerational mobility** is the vertical movement of the individual through his or her adult life.

Some societal factors increase the likelihood of people's vertical mobility regardless of their individual efforts. The availability of cheap and fertile land with abundant resources gave many thousands of Americans in the nineteenth century opportunities for advancement no longer present. Similarly, the arrival of new immigrants to the United States from 1880 to 1920 provided a status boost for the people already here. Economic booms and depressions obviously affect individuals' economic success. Technological changes also can provide increased chances for success as well as diminish the possibilities for those trained in occupations newly obsolete. Finally, the size of one's age cohort can limit or expand opportunities for success.

Sociological research leads to several conclusions about social mobility in the United States (from Blau and Duncan, 1967; De Lone, 1979; Duncan et al., 1998; and Scott and Leonhardt, 2005):

- Few children of white-collar workers become blue-collar workers.
- Most mobility moves are short in distance.
- Occupational inheritance is highest for children of professionals (physicians, lawyers, professors).
- The opportunities for the children of nonprofessionals to become professionals are very small.
- The long-term trend in social mobility has been upward, but since the 1970s (with the globalization of the economy and the shift from a manufacturing to a service/ knowledge economy) this trend has reversed.
- Social mobility is the least likely at the extremes of wealth and poverty.
- While there are many individual exceptions, the overall trend by race/ethnicity is that the gap in wealth/income between African Americans and Latinos and the more privileged Whites has remained about the same.
- Women, historically, have been blocked in their occupational aspirations (being limited to low-prestige, low-paying jobs). There has been a gradual lifting of these barriers since the 1970s, but women working full-time still earn only 76 cents for each dollar as men working full-time. Moreover, while there are more and more exceptions, barriers still remain for full equality for women as they compete for the best jobs.

In sum the commonly accepted belief of people in the United States that ours is a meritocratic society is largely a myth. Equality of opportunity does not exist because (1) employers may discriminate on the basis of age, race, sex, ethnicity, or sexuality of their employees or prospective employees; (2) educational and job training opportunities are unequal; and (3) the family has great power to enhance or retard a child's aspirations, motivation, and cognitive skills.

Education and Social Mobility

The schools play a major part in both perpetuating the meritocratic myth and legitimizing it by giving and denying educational credentials on the basis of open and objective mechanisms that sift and sort on merit. The use of IQ tests and tracking, two common devices to segregate students by cognitive abilities, are highly suspect because they label children, resulting in a positive self-fulfilling prophecy for some children and a negative one for others. Moreover, the results of the tests and the placement of children in tracks because of the tests are biased toward middle- and upper-class experiences.

Educational attainment, especially receiving a college degree, is the most important predictor of success in the United States. But a college education is becoming more difficult to attain for the less-than-affluent.

- After accounting for inflation, tuition at four-year public institutions is up 128 percent since 1980–1981; private tuition is up 131 percent. This hits low-income students the hardest. In 2000, tuition at public four-year institutions represented 25 percent of income for low-income families in 2000, up from 13 percent in 1980 (Marklein, 2002).
- Federal grant programs have failed to keep up with college costs. Pell grants were instituted by the government to help students from poor families attend college. In 1986, a Pell grant covered 98 percent of tuition at a public four-year college; in 2003 it covered only 42 percent (Symonds, 2003). Moreover, the amount of money appropriated by Congress for Pell grants has declined.

"Actually, Lou, I think it was more than just my being in the right place at the right time. I think it was my being the right race, the right religion, the right sex, the right socioeconomic group, having the right accent, the right clothes, going to the right schools . . . "

- The majority (70 percent) of government aid to students takes the form of loans. Families of low-income students borrow to pay an average of $7,500 a year for a public four-year college, which is about one-third of their income (Briggs, Tracey, 2002).

- Institutional scholarships have shifted their emphasis from awards based on financial need to aid based on academic achievement.

- More and more four-year schools are raising admissions standards and limiting remediation programs that help those from disadvantaged school backgrounds to attend college and overcome their academic deficiencies.

- Affirmative action programs are being challenged successfully in both the political and judicial arenas. With the loss of affirmative action, minority children, who are disproportionately poor, will be increasingly denied access to higher education. This trend is occurring at the very time that racial minorities are increasing in size.

- A study by an advisory committee to Congress and the Secretary of Education reported that in 2002, 406,000 college-qualified high school graduates were not able to go to college because they could not afford it (reported in Briggs, Tracey, 2002).

To conclude, money provides access to a higher education, which in turn increases one's life chances throughout life.

Christopher Jencks and his associates provide the most methodologically sophisticated analysis of the determinants of upward mobility in their book *Who Gets Ahead?* (Jencks et al., 1979). Their findings, summarized, show the following as the most important factors leading to success.

1. Family background is the most important factor. Children coming from families in the top 20 percent in income will, as adults, have incomes of 150 to 186 percent of the national average, whereas those from the bottom 20 percent will earn 56 to 67 percent of the national average.

2. Educational attainment—especially graduating from college—is very important to later success. It is not so much what one learns in school but obtaining the credentials that counts. The probability of high educational attainment is closely tied to family background.

3. Scores from intelligence tests are by themselves poor predictors of economic success. Intelligence test scores are related to family background and educational attainment. The key remains the college degree. If people with a high IQ do not go to college, they will tend not to succeed economically.

4. Personality traits of high school students, more than grades and IQ, have an impact on economic success. No single trait emerges as the decisive determinant of economic success, but rather the combined effects of many different traits are found to be important. These are self-concept, industriousness (as rated by teachers), and the social skills or motivations that lead students to see themselves as leaders and to hold positions of leadership in high school.

Let's add another generalization to the list by Jencks. Not only are the financial, educational, and demographic assets of one's family important to success, but so, too, are the assets of one's social environment. As Fischer and his associates (1996) assert:

The immediate neighborhood [affects] people's ways of life, whatever the family's own resources. . . . It is one thing to come from a low-income family but live in a pleasant suburb with parks, low crime, and quality schools, and another thing altogether to live in an inner-city neighborhood that lacks those supports. . . . The concentration of the disadvantaged in particular communities and particular schools undermines the fortunes of otherwise able youth. Schools in low-income and minority neighborhoods tend to lack resources and quality instruction. . . . In the local neighborhoods, similar effects occur. Low-income areas have fewer jobs, fewer resources, and poorer-quality services than do affluent ones. (83)

The picture drawn by Jencks and other experts on social mobility in the United States is of a relatively rigid society in which being born to the right family has a profound impact, especially on the probability of graduating from college. There are opportunities for advancement in society, but they are clustered among the already advantaged. If the stratification system were open with equality of opportunity, it would make sense that people, even the disadvantaged, would support it. The irony is that although the chances of the poor being successful are small, the poor tend to support the inequality generated by capitalism—truly a case of false consciousness. This irony becomes clearer as we see the consequences of inequality for individuals.

Poverty in the United States

The United States, arguably the richest nation on earth, has the highest proportion of its population living in poverty (Smeeding and Gottschalk, 1998).* Consider the following international comparisons, where the United States does not fare well:

- U.S. Women Connect compiled a report card on the U.S. government's efforts to improve equality for women and gave it an F for its attempts to reduce poverty among American women (reported in Winfield, 2000).
- Among the industrialized nations, the United States has the highest rate of child poverty (one in five for children under age 6 and one in six for children under 18).
- Compared with Canada and the nations of Western Europe and Scandinavia, the United States eliminates much less poverty through welfare subsidies than any of the other fourteen nations (Solow, 2000).

What separates the poor from the nonpoor? In a continuum, there is no absolute standard for wealth. The line separating the poor from the nonpoor is necessarily arbitrary. The Social Security Administration (SSA) sets the official poverty line based on what it considers the minimal amount of money required for a subsistence level of life. To determine the poverty line, the SSA computes the cost of a basic nutritionally adequate diet and multiplies that figure by three. This figure is based on a government research finding that poor people spend one-third of their income on food. Thereafter, the poverty level was readjusted annually using the consumer price index to account for inflation. If we use this official standard ($8,5734 for

---

*This section on poverty relies heavily on Eitzen and Eitzen Smith (2003:1–12).

one person under age sixty-five, $14,680 for a nonfarm family of three, and $18,810 for a nonfarm family of four) from 2003, 12.5 percent of the population (35.9 million people) were defined as living in poverty (the data on poverty in this section were taken from the DeNavas-Walt, Protor, and Mills, U.S. Bureau of the Census, 2004). See Figure 10.2 for the poverty trend from 1959 to 2003.

The following discussion considers the poor as people below this arbitrary line, realizing that it actually minimizes the extent of poverty in the United States. Critics of the measure argue that it does not keep up with inflation, that housing now requires a much larger portion of the family budget than food, that there is a wide variation in the cost of living by locality, and that the poverty line ignores differences in medical care needs of individual families. Were a more realistic formula used, the number of poor would likely be at least 50 percent higher than the current official number (i.e., 17 percent or 46.6 million impoverished Americans; see the panel titled "Human Agency: Coping Strategies among the Poor").

Also, the official number of poor people is minimized because government census takers miss many poor people, an estimated 3.4 million in the 2000 Census. Those most likely to be overlooked in a census live in high-density urban areas where several families may be crowded into one apartment or in rural areas where some homes are inaccessible. Some workers and their families follow a harvest from place to place and have no permanent home, as is the case for transients and homeless people. This underestimate of the poor has important consequences, because U.S. Census data are the basis for political representation in Congress, for the distribution of welfare, and for instituting new governmental programs or abandoning old ones. Needless to say, an accurate count of the total population is necessary if the census is so used.

Despite these difficulties and the understanding of actual poverty by the government's poverty line, we do know some facts about the poor.

Number in Poverty and Poverty Rate: 1959 to 2003

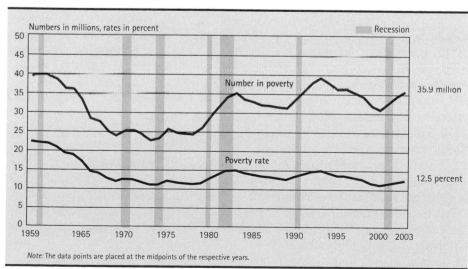

FIGURE 10.2

Sources: U.S. Bureau of the Census, Current Population Survey, 1960 to 2004 Annual Social and Economic Supplements; U.S. Bureau of the Census "Income, Poverty, and Health Insurance Coverage in the United State 2003," *Current Population Reports*, P60–226 (August 2004):9.

Coping Strategies among the Poor

The lot of poor people is difficult, to say the least. If the poor receive welfare, the benefits are insufficient to meet minimal needs of food, clothing, and shelter. Suitable housing in cities is especially difficult to obtain because rents are, typically, beyond the reach of the poor. Food, clothing, banking, and other purchases/ services are more expensive in the inner cities than elsewhere. How do poor people deal with the lack of money to deal with exigencies of living?

Some do not do well at all. Some are forced to live in housing that is dangerous (exposure to the cold, lead, rats, and sewage; unsafe structures that defy city building codes). Some cannot even afford those dangerous places and must live on the streets or in homeless shelters. Some are malnourished because they cannot afford enough nutritious food. Many go without visits to doctors and dentists because the cost is beyond their means or the services are unavailable.

Other poor people do better through various coping strategies. Those with family or close friendship networks may share housing costs by doubling or tripling up. They may share child care to free parents to work. Families may go together to buy food in bulk at cheaper prices. And they pool their resources in many other creative ways to manage the stresses and strains of poverty.

A few organized networks have also emerged in various inner cities (St. Louis; Miami; Chicago; New York City; Cleveland; and Norfolk, Virginia). In the case of inner-city St. Louis, several thousand people are engaged in a barter economy where people short of cash can exchange their labor/expertise for that of others without using money. Individuals earn credit ("time dollars") by cleaning, painting, providing child care, delivering goods, or repairing appliances, which can be exchanged for other services or even goods (food, clothing) that have been donated to the network. This plan has two major benefits: (1) It cushions the harshness of poverty by getting goods and services to the people who need them; and (2) it creates a sense of community among the powerless, which may ultimately lead to power, as those in the network work together for common goals.

Sources: Peter T. Kilborn, 1996. "Build a Better Welfare System, and the World . . .," *Denver Post* (September 29):17A; Michael Hudson, 1996. *Merchants of Misery.* Monroe, ME: Common Courage Press; and Doug A. Timmer, D. Stanley Eitzen, and Kathryn D. Talley, 1994. *Paths to Homelessness: Extreme Poverty and the Urban Housing Crisis.* Boulder, CO: Westview Press.

Racial Minorities

Income in the United States, as we have discussed, is maldistributed by race. In 2003, the median family income for Asian American households was about $55,500, compared with $48,000 for White households, $33,000 for Native American and Alaskan Native households, $33,000 for Latino households, and $30,000 for African American households. Not surprisingly, then, 8.2 percent of Whites were officially poor, compared with 11.8 percent of Asian Americans, 22.5 percent of Latinos, 24.4 percent of African Americans, and 23.2 percent of Native American and Alaskan Natives.

These summary statistics mask the differences within each racial/ethnic category. For example, Latinos of Cuban descent, many of whom were middle-class professional in Cuba, have relatively low poverty rates, whereas Puerto Ricans, Mexicans, and Central Americans have disproportionately high poverty rates. Similarly, Japanese Americans are much less likely to be poor than Asians from Cambodia, Laos, and Vietnam.

Nativity

In 2003, 5.9 million foreign-born individuals in the United States (17.2 percent of the foreign-born) were poor. Of these poor foreign-born, 1.3 million were naturalized citizens and 4.6 million were noncitizens, for poverty rates of 10.0 and 21.7 percent, respectively. These official statistics do not include the 11 million undocumented workers and their families who enter the United States illegally.

Gender

Women are more likely to be poor than men. For example, for female householders with no husband present the official poverty rate was 28.0 percent in 2003, compared to 13.5 percent of male householders with no wife present. This is the consequence of the prevailing institutional sexism in society that, with few exceptions, provides poor job and earnings opportunities for women. This gender disparity, combined with the high frequency of marital disruption and the number of never-married women with children, results in the high probability of women who head families being poor.

This trend, termed the **feminization of poverty**, implies that the relatively large proportion of poor women is a new phenomenon in U.S. society. Thus, the term obscures the fact that women have always been more economically vulnerable than men, especially older women and women of color. But when women's poverty was mainly limited to these groups, their economic deprivation was mostly invisible. The plight of women's poverty became a visible problem when the numbers of poor White women increased rapidly in the past decade or so with rising marital disruption. Even with the growing numbers of poor White women, the term *feminization of*

Two out of three impoverished adults in the United States are women.

poverty implies that all women are at risk, when actually the probability of economic deprivation is much greater for certain categories of women. The issue, then, is not only gender but class and race as well.

Race and gender combine to increase the probability of poverty. An African American woman is almost two and a half times more likely to be poor as a White woman and a Latino woman is almost twice as likely to be poor as a White woman.

Children

The nation's poverty rate was 12.5 percent in 2003, but the rate for children was 17.6 percent for those under age eighteen (12.9 million children). For those under age six, the rate was 19.8 percent. Related children under age six living in families with a female head of household, no husband present, had a poverty rate of 52.9 percent, a rate more than five times that for their counterparts in married-couple families (9.6 percent). Although there are more White children in poverty, children of color are disproportionately poor: In 2000, the rate for White children under age eighteen was 13.5 percent, compared to 33.1 percent of African American children and 30.3 percent of Latino children. Especially noteworthy is that the United States has the highest youth poverty rate of any Western nation.

The consequences of childhood poverty are grave. Children in poverty are more likely than their more fortunate peers to suffer from stunted growth, score lower on tests and be held back in school, suffer from lead poisoning which may lead to mental retardation, and suffer a host of other problems.

The Elderly

Contrary to popular belief, the elderly as a category (age sixty-five and older) have a lower poverty rate (10.2 percent in 2003) than the general population (12.5 percent). Actually, there are four times as many children as elderly people living in poverty in the United States. This seeming anomaly is the result of government programs for the elderly being indexed for inflation, whereas many welfare programs targeted for the young have been reduced or eliminated since 1980.

While the elderly are underrepresented in the poverty population, the rate increases with age. This is likely because as the age increases, the proportion of women in that category increases. Gender and race combine once again to make the economic situation especially difficult for elderly African Americans (a rate of 29.0 percent for women seventy-five and older) and Latino women (27.4 percent), compared with 12.1 percent of elderly White women.

The Geography of Poverty

Poverty is not randomly distributed geographically; it tends to cluster in certain places. Regionally, the area with highest poverty is the South (14.1 percent), compared with 12.6 percent in the West, 11.3 percent in the Northeast, and 10.7 percent in the Midwest. The South and West have the highest poverty rates because they have large minority populations and relatively high concentrations of recent immigrants. The three states with the highest poverty rates in 2003 were (in order) New Mexico, Arkansas, and Mississippi. The states with the lowest poverty rates were New Hampshire, Minnesota, and Maryland.

In metropolitan areas, the poverty rate in 2003 was higher in the central cities (17.5 percent) than in suburban areas (9.1 percent). For those living outside metropolitan areas, the poverty rate was 14.2 percent. With respect to central cities, two trends are significant: The proportion who are poor is increasing in the central cities; and increasingly, the poverty is more and more concentrated (i.e., the poor are more and more likely to be living in already poor neighborhoods) (Massey, 1996). This spatial concentration of poverty means that the poor have poor neighbors, and the area has a low tax base to finance public schools, and a shrinking number of businesses because they tend to move to areas where the local residents have more discretionary income. These factors mean a reduction in services and the elimination of local jobs. Moreover:

> Just as poverty is concentrated spatially, anything correlated with poverty is also concentrated. Therefore, as the density of poverty increases in cities . . . so will the density of joblessness, crime, family dissolution, drug abuse, alcoholism, disease, and violence. Not only will the poor have to grapple with the manifold problems due to their own lack of increase; increasingly they also will have to confront the social effects of living in an environment where most of their neighbors are also poor. (Massey, 1996:407)

Although poverty is generally more concentrated in cities, the highest concentrations exist in four rural regions (Grunwald, 1999): the Mississippi Delta, which extends across seven states, where the poor are mostly African American; the Rio Grande Valley/Texas Gulf Coast/U.S.-Mexico border, a four-state region where the poor are largely Latino; the Native American reservations of the Southwest and Plains states; and Appalachia, a twelve-state region characterized by marginal farmland and a declining mining industry where the poor are predominantly White.

There are important differences between the rural and the urban poor. The rural poor have some advantages (low-cost housing, raising their own food) and many disadvantages (low-paid work, higher prices for many products, fewer social services, fewer welfare benefits) as compared with the urban poor.

Poverty is greatest among those who do not have an established residence. People in this classification are typically the homeless and migrant workers. The homeless, estimated between half a million and 3 million, are those in extreme poverty—they are the poorest of the poor (see Timmer, Eitzen, and Talley, 1994). The other category, migrant workers, is believed to be about 3 million adults and children who are seasonal farm laborers working sporadically for low wages and no benefits. It is estimated that about 50 percent of all farm workers live below the official poverty line; this percentage has not changed since the 1960s. Latinos are overrepresented in this occupation.

Finally, as noted earlier, the United States, when compared to other major industrialized democracies, has more poverty, has more severe poverty, and supports its poor people least.

The Severely Poor

Use of the official poverty line designates all people below it as poor whether they are a few dollars short of the threshold or far below it. Most impoverished individuals and families have incomes considerably below the poverty threshold. In 2003, for example, the average deficit (the dollar amount below the poverty line) was $7,627 for all families. An estimated 5.3 percent of the population (15.3 million Americans) were **severely poor** (i.e., those people living at or below half the poverty line). Typically, the severely poor must use 50 percent or more of their meager income for housing.

This category of the severely poor has almost doubled since 1979. This upsurge in the truly destitute occurred because (1) many of them live in rural areas that have prospered less than other regions; (2) a decline in marriage (and a rise in divorce) resulted in a substantial increase in single mothers and unattached men; and (3) public assistance benefits, especially in the South, have steadily declined since 1980.

Myths about Poverty

What should be the government's role in caring for its less fortunate residents? Much of the debate on this important issue among politicians and citizens is based on erroneous assumptions and misperceptions.

Refusal to Work

Several facts belie the faulty assumption that poor people refuse to work. First, about 90 percent of poor households contained at least one worker in 2002. In 2003, almost one in four workers worked at or below the poverty wage (see Table 10.5). They hold menial, dead-end jobs that have no benefits and pay the minimum wage or less. Low wages are the problem: Today, about 2.1 million workers make the minimum wage ($5.15 an hour) or less, which will not get them above the poverty line. A full-time minimum-wage worker earns only 76 percent of the poverty level for a family of three (in 1968 a family of three with one minimum-wage earner had a standard of living 17 percent *above* the poverty line). Second, many of the poor who do not work are too young (under age eighteen), are too old (sixty-five and older), or have a work disability. Third, people of color are more likely to be poor than Whites in the same working category—that is, unemployed, having worked less than full-time, and worked full-time. Fourth, the main increase in the number of poor since 1979 has been among the working poor. This is the result of declining wages, an increase in working women who head households, and a very low minimum hourly wage of $5.15 that has not kept up with inflation. The lot of the working poor is similar to that of the nonworking poor on some dimensions and worse on others. They do society's dirty work for low pay and no benefits. Like the poor, they live in substandard housing and their children go to underfinanced schools. They are poor but, unlike the nonworking poor, they are not eligible for many government supports such as subsidized housing, medical care, and food stamps.

Economist Marlene Kim (1998) analyzed census data on a sample of 57,000 U.S. households and concludes:

> Most of the working poor would remain poor even if they worked 40 hours a week, 52 weeks a year. In addition, of those who could climb out of poverty if they worked such hours, two out of five are either disabled or elderly or unable to find full-time

TABLE 10.5
Poverty-Level Employment, 2003

Workers	Percent of Employment at or below the Poverty Wage
All workers	24.3%
Men	19.6
Women	29.4
Whites	20.4
Men	15.1
Women	26.0
Blacks	30.4
Men	26.2
Women	33.9
Hispanics	39.8
Men	35.7
Women	45.8

Source: Michael D. Yates, "A Statistical Portrait of the U.S. Working Class," *Monthly Review* 56 (April 2005):17. Copyright © 2005 by Monthly Review Press. Reprinted by permission.

or full-year employment. Thus it appears that most of the working poor are doing all they can to support themselves. (97)

For those poor not officially in the labor force, many work (either for money or for the exchange of goods or services) in the informal economy by cleaning, painting, providing child care, repairing automobiles or appliances, or other activities. Clearly, these people are workers, they just are not in the official economy.

Welfare Dependency

In 1996, Congress passed the Personal Responsibility and Work Opportunity Reconciliation Act, which reformed the welfare system (the following is from Eitzen and Baca Zinn, 1998). This new law shifted the Aid to Families with Dependent Children (AFDC) welfare program from the federal government to the states, mandated that welfare recipients find work within two years, limited welfare assistance to five years, and cut various federal assistance programs targeted for the poor by $54.5 billion over six years. Thus, the law made assistance to poor families temporary and cut monies to supplemental programs such as food stamps and child nutrition. The assumption by policymakers was that welfare was too generous, making it easier to stay on welfare than leave for work, and welfare was believed to encourage unmarried women to have children (see the panel titled "A Closer Look: The New Welfare Policy: A Critique").

We should recognize some facts about government welfare before the 1996 welfare reform (O'Hare, 1996). First, welfare accounted for about one-fourth of the income of poor adults; nearly half of the income received by poor adults came from some form of work activity. Second, about three-fourths of the poor received some type of noncash benefit (Medicaid, food stamps, or housing assistance), but only

The New Welfare Policy: A Critique

During the Great Depression, President Franklin Roosevelt's New Deal programs changed the fundamental relationship between the federal government and the needy. Among these programs were Social Security, unemployment insurance, and Aid to Families with Dependent Children (AFDC). In the 1960s, President Lyndon Johnson initiated the War on Poverty to help poor families with programs such as Medicaid, food stamps, and Head Start.

During the 1980s, under Presidents Reagan and Bush, various poverty programs were gradually reduced. This erosion of welfare benefits accelerated with the election of President Clinton in 1992 and a Republican-controlled Congress in 1994. There was general agreement among the Republicans and Democrats that welfare needed to be changed dramatically. Their aim was not directed at programs for the elderly (Social Security and Medicare) nor at "wealth-fare" for corporations and well-off individuals, but rather at programs for the weakest and neediest.

The rationale for dismantling the welfare state is that government efforts to reduce poverty actually cause poverty and other social problems. Welfare dependency, in this view, is the source of poverty, illegitimacy, laziness, crime, unemployment, and other social pathologies. If people were forced to go to work, there might be some hardships along the way, but this is the only way to make individuals moral and self-reliant.

Three of the major provisions of the resulting legislation were as follows:

- *Devolution.* The new law decentralizes welfare policy through federal grants to state governments that are free (except for a few federal restrictions) to organize and run their own programs. State-run programs will likely have several problems: (1) The poor will generally receive less assistance than before; (2) the states will be uneven in their programs—some generous, some not (under the old plan, a family of four received $660 a month in New York but just $220 in Mississippi), some enlightened, some not; (3) some states may deliberately keep their benefits low to discourage poor people from settling there; (4) if the past is any guide, some states and localities will use their power to promote racial injustice; and (5) if a recession hits or there is a surge in poor families, the states, limited for the most part to their own resources, will provide less for the poor.

- *Time limits.* The new law states that welfare recipients must give up most benefits unless the family head begins to work within two years. Also established was a lifelong time limit of 60 months (not necessarily consecutive) on receiving assistance. The problem with time limits is that people will be pushed off welfare without receiving help for child care, job training, and jobs as well as a minimum wage that would get the disadvantaged above the

about 40 percent received cash welfare payments. Third, the poverty population changes—that is, people move in and out of poverty every year. The average welfare recipient stayed on welfare less than two years (Sklar, 1992). Only 12 percent of the poor remain poor for five or more consecutive years (O'Hare, 1996). Fourth, although the prereform welfare system was much more generous than now, it was inadequate to meet the needs of the poor, falling far short. The average poor family of three on welfare had an annual income much below the poverty line.

> Many poor families manage by cutting back on food, jeopardizing their health and the development of their children, or by living in substandard and sometimes dangerous housing. Some do without heat, electricity, telephone service, or plumbing for months or years. Many do without health insurance, health care, safe child care, or reliable transportation to take them to or from work. (Children's Defense Fund, cited in Sklar, 1992:10)

The New Welfare Policy: A Critique continued

poverty line. Moreover, there are no federal plans to expand health care to low-wage workers.

- *Ineligibility of legal immigrants.* Legal immigrants are denied most welfare benefits until they have been here five years. This is exceptionally problematic since these people are especially vulnerable to discrimination by not knowing English and the American culture.

The 1996 welfare legislation embarks U.S. society on a huge social experiment. Will it work? Will society be safer or more dangerous? Will poverty be reduced when the pool of unskilled workers is expanded but there is no effort to create jobs for them? Will the lot of the children of the poor be improved or harmed? What happens to the previous welfare recipients when the economy turns sour as it did in 2000–2003? And, the big question: Will the former welfare recipients have jobs that will lift them above the poverty line? Lawrence Aber, director of Columbia University's Center for Children in Poverty, says, "Welfare reform has done better at moving families off the rolls than it has at moving families out of poverty" (cited in Meckler, 1999:23).

Evidence from other societies and sociological research suggests that in the long run, the poor and society will be worse off by reducing welfare. The number of people on the economic margins will rise. Unemployment will surge, especially in inner-city neighborhoods, where the rate was 30 to 50 percent before the welfare legislation. Homelessness will increase. Crime rates will swell. Public safety will become more problematic. The racial divide will widen. Civil unrest will intensify.

Contrary to what our politicians tell us, these grim predictions appear to be our future. They will be exacerbated even more as policymakers make further cutbacks in Medicaid, housing, legal aid, and other social services to the poor. The United States has the most meager safety net of any of the major industrialized countries. We have chosen to reduce that net even further. This decision takes us down a path where all of us, poor and nonpoor, are increasingly in peril.

Sources: William P. O'Hare, 1996. "A New Look at Poverty in America." *Population Bulletin* 51 (September):3–5; Frances Fox Piven, 1996. "Welfare and the Transformation of Electoral Politics." *Dissent* 43 (Fall):61–67; Randy Albelda, 1996. "Farewell to Welfare." *Dollars & Sense* no. 208 (November/December):16–19; D. Stanley Eitzen, 1996. "Is Dismantling the Welfare State the Solution to America's Social Problems?" *Vital Speeches of the Day* (June 15):532–536; Laura Meckler, 1999. "Poor Going from Welfare to Low-Paying Jobs." *Rocky Mountain News* (June 18):23, and D. Stanley Eitzen and Maxine Baca Zinn, 1998. "The Shrinking Welfare State: The New Welfare Legislation and Families." Paper presented at the annual meeting of the American Sociological Association, San Francisco (August 21–25).

Fifth, contrary to the common assertion that welfare mothers keep having babies to get more welfare benefits and thereby escape working, research from a number of studies shows that most welfare recipients bring in extra money from various activities such as house cleaning, laundry, repairing clothing, child care, and selling items they have made. For example, sociologist Kathleen Harris (1996), summarizing her findings from a nationally representative sample of single mothers who received welfare, says:

> I found exclusive dependence on welfare to be rare. More than half of the single mothers whom I studied worked while they were on welfare, and two-thirds left welfare rolls when they could support themselves with jobs. However, more than half (57 percent) of the women who worked their way off public assistance later returned because their jobs ended or they still could not make ends meet. (B7)

Concerning the larger picture about government welfare programs, there is a fundamental misunderstanding by the U.S. public about where most governmental benefits are directed. We tend to assume that government monies and services go mostly to the poor (**welfare**, the receipt of financial aid and/or services from the government), when in fact the greatest government aid goes to the nonpoor ("**wealthfare**," the receipt by the nonpoor of financial aid and/or services from the government). Most (about three-fourths) of the federal outlays for human resources go to the nonpoor, such as to all children in public education programs and to most of the elderly through Social Security retirement and Medicare payments.

The upside-down welfare system, with aid mainly helping the already affluent, is accomplished by two hidden welfare systems. The first is through tax loopholes (called **tax expenditures**). Through these legal mechanisms, the government officially permits certain individuals and corporations to pay lower taxes or no taxes at all. For illustration, one of the biggest tax expenditure programs is the money that homeowners deduct from their taxes for real estate taxes and interest on their mortgages (mortgage interest is deductible on mortgages up to $1 million). In a telling irony, government tax breaks to homeowners ($32.1 billion). Ironically, while fewer than one-fourth of low-income Americans receive federal housing subsidies, more than three-quarters of Americans, many living in mansions, get housing aid from Washington.

The second hidden welfare system to the nonpoor is in the form of direct subsidies and credit to assist corporations, banks, agribusiness, defense industries, and the like. Some examples are:

- Tax avoidance by transnational corporations ($137.2 billion a year).
- Lower taxes on capital gains ($89.8 billion a year).
- Insurance loopholes ($23.5 billion a year).
- Tax-free municipals bonds ($6.4 billion a year).
- The Savings and Loan Bailout ($32 billion a year).
- Agribusiness subsidies ($30.5 billion a year).
- Aviation subsidies ($4.7 billion a year) (Zepezauer, 2004).

Totaling all of the subsidies (wealthfare) amounts to $815 billion a year. This is more than *four times the amount we spend on welfare for the poor ($193 billion a year)* (Zepezauer, 2004:1).

Finally, an assessment of the 1996 welfare reform five years after it was passed reveals premature, mixed, and uncertain results. Positively, the number of people on welfare has fallen by half to 6 million. Many of the former recipients, including single mothers, have found at least part-time employment. Research by sociologists William Julius Wilson and Andrew J. Cherlin (2001) in Boston, Chicago, and San Antonio reveals that while work has improved the sense of self-worth for former welfare recipients, three-fourths of the women who had been off welfare for two years or less had incomes below the federal poverty line. They were meeting basic expenses with government help such as food stamps. But the longer these women had been off welfare, the less likely they were to have health insurance for themselves and their children. The women facing the greatest difficulties after welfare were those with less education, poorer health, and younger children.

The first five years were extraordinary, with historically low unemployment, low inflation, and a booming economy. In 2001–2002, two powerful forces—the September 11 attacks on the World Trade Center and the Pentagon and a severe and prolonged economic downturn—combined to wreak havoc on the poor, especially those who had left welfare for work, as the 1996 Welfare Reform dictated. Rising unemployment rates hit former welfare recipients hard because, as recently hired employees, they were the most likely to be fired when the companies they worked for reduced their workforces. Moreover, the lower end of the service sector of the economy (sales clerks, janitors, restaurant workers, hotel workers), where former welfare recipients were most likely to find jobs, were especially hard hit in those difficult times. Moreover, this recession was the first since the 1930s in which the "safety net" for the poor was almost nonexistent. As a result, the number of people seeking emergency food aid and the number without shelter rose significantly.

The Poor Get Special Advantages

The common belief is that the poor get a number of handouts for commodities for which other Americans have to work—food stamps, Medicaid, housing subsidies, and the like. As we have seen, these subsidies amount to much less than the more affluent receive, and recent legislation has reduced them more and more. Most significant, *the poor pay more than the nonpoor for many services*. This, along with low wages and paying a large proportion of their income for housing, explains why some have such difficulty getting out of poverty.

The urban poor find that their money does not go as far in the inner city. Food and commodities, for example, cost more since supermarkets, discount stores, outlet malls, and warehouse clubs have bypassed inner-city neighborhoods. Since many inner-city residents do not have transportation to get to the supermarkets and warehouse stores, they must buy from nearby stores, giving the store owners monopoly powers. As a result, the poor pay more. Consider the following:

- Hospitals routinely charge more for services to patients without health insurance, compared to those covered by a health plan (Ehrenreich, 2004).
- Check-cashing centers, largely located in poor neighborhoods, prey on customers without bank accounts, often charging 10 percent of the check's value (Curtis, 2000).
- There are some WIC-only grocery stores (Women, Infants, Children). They accept just WIC vouchers as payment, not cash. Prices are 10 to 20 percent higher in these WIC-only stores (Pear, 2004).
- The "payday loan" industry offers an advance on a person's paycheck, with interest rates ranging from 500 to 2,000 percent, a devastating financial obligation for those strapped for cash (Lydersen, 2002).

The conclusion is obvious: The poor pay more for commodities and services in absolute terms, and they pay a much larger proportion of their incomes than the nonpoor for comparable items. Similarly, when the poor pay sales taxes on the items they purchase, the tax takes more of their resources than it does from the nonpoor, making it a **regressive tax**. Thus, efforts to move federal programs to the states will cost the poor more, since state and local taxes tend to be regressive (sales taxes), while federal taxation tends to be progressive.

tHe WeLfaRe LiNe

Welfare Is an African American and Latino Program

The myth is that most welfare monies go primarily to African Americans and Latinos. While poverty rates are higher for Blacks and Hispanics than for other racial/ethnic groups, they do not make up the majority of the poor. In 2003, non-Hispanic Whites were the most numerous racial/ethnic group (44.3 percent of the poor are White) among the poverty population. Thus, almost 16 million Whites are in poverty, compared to just over 9 million African Americans and 9 million Latinos in poverty. Barbara Ehrenreich (1991) states:

> [W]hite folks have been gobbling up the welfare budget while blaming someone else. But it's worse than that. If we look at Social Security, which is another form of welfare, although it is often mistaken for an individual insurance program, then whites are the ones who are crowding the trough. We receive almost twice as much per capita, for an aggregate advantage to our race of $10 billion a year— much more than the $3.9 billion advantage African Americans gain from their disproportionate share of welfare. One sad reason: whites live an average of six years longer than African Americans, meaning that young black workers help subsidize a huge and growing "overclass" of white retirees. (84)

1. People in the United States vary greatly on a number of socioeconomic dimensions. Wealth and income are maldistributed. Educational attainment varies. Occupations differ greatly in prestige and pay.

2. Order theorists place individuals into social classes according to occupation. Each social class is composed of social equals who share a similar lifestyle. Each class-specific culture is assumed to have power over its members.

3. Conflict theorists focus on money, relation to the means of production, and power as the determinants of class position. Crucial to this placement is not occupational prestige as the order theorists posit, but whether one gives orders or takes orders in the work process.

4. The consequences of one's socioeconomic status are best expressed in the concept of life chances, which refer to the chances to obtain the things highly valued in society. The data show that the higher one's economic position, the longer one's life, the healthier (physically and mentally) one will be, the more stable one's family, the less likely one will be drafted, the less likely one will be processed by the criminal justice system, and the higher one's educational attainment.

5. Societies vary in the degree to which individuals may move up in status. The most rigid societies are called caste systems. They are essentially closed hereditary groups. Class systems are more open, permitting vertical mobility.

6. Although the United States is a relatively open class system, the extent of intergenerational mobility (a son or daughter surpassing his or her parents) is limited.

7. Graduation from college is the most important predictor of upward social mobility. However, a college education is becoming more difficult to attain for the less than affluent.

8. According to the government's arbitrary line, which minimizes the actual extent of poverty, in 2003, 12.5 percent (35.9 million) of the U.S. population was officially poor. Disproportionately represented in the poor category are African Americans, Latinos, women, and children.

9. The poor are not poor because they refuse to work. Most adult poor either work at low wages, cannot find work, work part-time, are homemakers, are ill or disabled, or are in school.

10. Government assistance to the poor is not sufficient to eliminate their economic deprivation. Less than half of the poor actually receive any federal assistance. When compared with the nonpoor, their life chances are negative, with a higher incidence of health problems, malnutrition, social pathologies, and homelessness.

11. Most government assistance is targeted to the affluent rather than the poor. The nonpoor receive three-fourths of the federal monies allocated to human services. Tax expenditures and other subsidies provide enormous economic benefits to the already affluent, which further redistributes the nation's wealth upward.

12. The poor pay more than the nonpoor for services and commodities, which helps to trap them in poverty.

13. Contrary to popular belief, Whites receive more welfare than do African Americans and Latinos.

Key Terms

Social mobility	Intragenerational mobility	Wealthfare
Vertical mobility	Feminization of poverty	Tax expenditures
Horizontal mobility	Severely poor	Regressive tax
Intergenerational mobility	Welfare	

Study Questions

1. What are the key differences in the conception of social class by order-model and conflict-model theorists?
2. What are the consequences of social class position in terms of life chances?
3. What is the evidence that the gap between the haves and the have-nots is increasing in the United States?
4. To what extent is upward social mobility difficult for poor youth?
5. Which social categories are most likely to be poor? Referring to the discussion in Chapter 9, what are the fundamental reasons for the over-representation of these categories in the poor classification?
6. Write an essay titled "The Poor Pay More."

For Further Reading

Social Class in the United States

Bruce Ackerman and Anne Alstott, *The Stakeholder Society* (New Haven, CT: Yale University Press, 1999).

Adalberto Aguirre, Jr., and David V. Baker, *Structured Inequality in the United States* (Upper Saddle River, NJ: Prentice Hall, 2000).

Chuck Collins, Betsy Leondar-Wright, and Holly Sklar, *Shifting Fortunes: The Perils of the Growing American Wealth Gap* (Boston: United for a Fair Economy, 1999).

Nancy Folbre and the Center for Popular Economics, *The New Field Guide to the U.S. Economy*, rev. ed. (New York: New Press, 1999).

Robert H. Frank, *Luxury Fever: Why Money Fails to Satisfy in an Era of Excess* (New York: Free Press, 1999).

Robert H. Frank and Philip J. Cook, *The Winner-Take-All Society* (New York: Free Press, 1995).

James K. Galbraith, *Created Unequal: The Crisis in American Pay* (New York: Free Press/Century Fund, 1998).

Lisa A. Keister, *Wealth in America: Trends in Wealth Inequality* (Cambridge, UK: Cambridge University Press, 2000).

Kevin Phillips, *Wealth and Democracy: A Political History of the American Rich* (New York: Broadway Books, 2002).

Sam Pizzigati, *Greed and Good: Understanding and Overcoming the Inequality That Limits Our Lives* (New York: Apex Press, 2004).

Edward N. Wolff, *Top Heavy: The Increasing Inequality of Wealth in America and What Can Be Done about It*, updated and expanded ed. (New York: New Press, 2002).

Social Mobility

Peter Blau and Otis Dudley Duncan, *The American Occupational Structure* (New York: Wiley, 1967).

Robert L. Featherman and Robert M. Hauser, *Opportunity and Change* (New York: Academic Press, 1978).

Dennis Gilbert and Joseph A. Kahl, *The American Class Structure*, 4th ed. (Belmont, CA: Wadsworth, 1994).

Christopher Jencks, Marshall Smith, Henry Ackland, Mary Jo Bane, David Cohen, Herbert Gintis, Barbara Heyns, and Stephen Michelson, *Inequality: A Reassessment of the Effects of Family and Schooling in America* (New York: Harper & Row, 1973).

Poverty

Kathryn Edin and Laura Lein, *Making Ends Meet: How Single Mothers Survive Welfare and Low-Wage Work* (New York: Russell Sage, 1997).

D. Stanley Eitzen and Kelly Eitzen Smith (eds.), *Experiencing Poverty: Voices from the Bottom* (Belmont, CA: Wadsworth, 2003).

Alex Kotlowitz, *There Are No Children Here: The Story of Two Boys Growing Up in the Other America* (New York: Doubleday/Anchor, 1991).

Jonathan Kozol, *Savage Inequalities: Children in America's Schools* (New York: Crown, 1991).

Elliot Liebow, *Tell Them Who I Am: The Lives of Homeless Women* (New York: Free Press, 1993).

Katherine S. Newman, *No Shame in My Game: The Working Poor in the Inner City* (New York: Knopf, 1999).

Reiman, Jeffrey, *The Rich Get Richer and the Poor Get Prison*, 7th ed. (Boston: Allyn and Bacon, 2003).

Doug A. Timmer, D. Stanley Eitzen, and Kathryn D. Talley, *Paths to Homelessness: Extreme Poverty and the Urban Housing Crisis* (Boulder, CO: Westview Press, 1994).

U.S. Bureau of the Census, "Income, Poverty, and Health Insurance Coverage in the United States: 2003," *Current Population Reports*, P60–226 (August 2004).

Web Resources

http://www.as.ysu.edu/~cwcs/
The Center for Working-Class Studies at Youngstown State University studies working-class life and culture. The site also has links to other class-related sites.

http://www.secondharvest.org/
Home of America's Second Harvest, a hunger relief program, this site contains facts on hunger in America and policies related to hunger. The site follows the search of Hunger in America 2001, which provides "a comprehensive profile of the incidence and nature of hunger and food insecurity in the U.S."

http://www.inequality.org/
This is a site that contains extensive information on class inequality and "news, information and expertise on the divide in income, wealth, and health." Among the topics on Incquality.org are links, quotes, and the overclass.

http://www.forbes.com/people/lists/
Search the home of *Forbes* magazine to see a list of the wealthiest people in America and in the world.

http://www.ufenet.org/
United for a Fair Economy is a group that is dedicated to building a fair economy movement centered on decreasing the income gap.

http://www.pscw.uva.nl/sociosite/CLASS/bibA.html
Go to this site for a bibliography on class.

http://www.pbs.org/peoplelikeus/
This site is one that is a supplement to a PBS documentary called *People Like Us*. The site has games, resources, and information to show how class works in America and to test preconceptions people have about class.

http://www.nationalhomeless.org/
Through work in housing justice, economic justice, health care justice, and civil rights, the National Coalition for the Homeless seeks to end homelessness.

http://www.aflcio.org/paywatch/
PayWatch is part of the AFL-CIO, and it tracks earnings of CEOs. Among the features of the site is the ability of the visitor to compare her or his salary or wage to that of CEOs of various companies.

http://www.isr.umich.edu/src/psid/
The Panel Study of Income Dynamics is a "longitudinal survey of a representative sample of U.S. individuals and the families in which they reside." It emphasizes economic and demographic behaviors.

http://www.jcpr.org/
The Joint Center for Poverty Research is a research center that "seeks to advance our understanding of what it means to be poor in America."

http://www.welfareinfo.org
The Welfare Information Network provides information on government welfare programs, housing, homelessness, immigrants, food stamps, and family formation.

Racial Inequality CHAPTER 11

Since its beginning, the United States has been a nation divided by race. Today, racial divisions are changing, but they are not disappearing. Instead of fading into an integrated social order, new color lines prevent equal opportunities for all. As this society moves from being predominantly White to being a global society of diverse racial and ethnic peoples, old forms of discrimination thrive alongside new patterns of inequality. Such inequalities are found around the world. Racial disparities continue to shape social relations even as many societies are being recast in a multiracial light.

Why are some groups dominant and others subordinate? The basic reason is power—power derived from superior numbers, technology, weapons, property, or economic resources. Those holding superior power in a society—**the majority group**—establish a system of inequality by dominating less powerful groups. This system of inequality is then maintained by power. The terms *majority* and *minority* describe power differences.

Racial inequalities produce opportunities for some and oppression for others. This is accomplished by the distribution of privilege based on race. Racial privilege reaches far back into the past of the United States. The racial hierarchy with White groups of European origin at the top and people of color at the bottom serves important functions for society and for certain categories of people. For example, it ensures that some people are available to do society's dirty work at low wages. The racial hierarchy reinforces the status quo. It enables the powerful to retain their control and their advantages.

Racial stratification offers better occupational opportunities, income, and education to White people. These patterns are found throughout the world. Today, many racially defined people are becoming even more marginalized by global restructuring (discussed in Chapter 8), which includes sweatshops that employ people of color, new fiscal policies imposed on developing countries, and disruptions of national and local economies that force people to migrate in search of jobs and better lives.

This chapter examines racial inequality from several vantage points. First, we outline the important features of race and of racial and ethnic groups in the United States. We then profile four racial minority groups: African Americans, Latinos, Asian Americans, and Native Americans. Next, we examine explanations of racial inequality. We look, then, at how the racial hierarchy affects Blacks and Hispanics in

293

"Would you mind if I told some offensive racist jokes?"

terms of income, jobs, education, and health. Finally, the chapter turns to current trends in racial and ethnic relations.

The theme of the chapter is that racial oppression has structural foundations. This framework challenges common misperceptions about race and race relations. Many people think that multicultural attitudes and a "color-blind" climate have replaced old-fashioned racism. We show that racial inequalities persist in today's multiracial world. Racially defined groups lack the same opportunities as everyone else. Yet, they are not to blame for these social realities. Instead, the cause lies in the racial foundation of society. Our emphasis on persistent racial divisions does not mean that minorities are passive victims of oppression. Minority histories are filled with human agency—both individual and collective oppositions to racist practices.

Racial and Ethnic Minorities

Racial categories are a basis of power relations and group position. Because race relations are power relations, conflict (or at least the potential for conflict) is always present. Overt conflict is most likely when dominated groups try to change the distribution of power. Size is not crucial in determining whether a group is the most powerful. A numerical minority may in fact have more political representation than the majority, as is the case in South Africa. Thus, the most important characteristic of a **minority group** is that it is dominated by a more powerful group.

Determining who is a minority is largely a matter of history, politics, and judgment—both social and political. Population characteristics other than race and ethnicity—such as age, gender, sexual orientation, or religious preference—are sometimes used to designate minority status. However, race and ethnicity are the characteristics used most often to define the minority and majority populations in contemporary U.S. society (O'Hare, 1992:5).

Race is a subjective category and racial criteria are inconsistently applied. Races are a social invention. They do not exist biologically. What does exist is the *idea* that races are distinct biological categories. But despite the common belief, social scientists now reject the biological concept of race. Scientific examination of the human genome finds no genetic differences between the so-called races. Fossil and DNA evidence show that humans are all one race, evolved in the last 100,000 years from the same small number of tribes that migrated out of Africa and colonized the world (American Sociological Association, 2003; Angier, 2000; Bean et al., 2004; Mukhopadhyay and Henze, 2003). Although there is no such thing as biological race, races are real insofar as they are *socially defined*. In other words, racial categories *operate* as if they are real.

Racial classification in the United States is based on a Black/White dichotomy—that is, two opposing categories into which all people fit. However, social definitions of race have changed throughout the nation's history. At different points in the past, "race has taken on different meanings. Many of the people considered White and thought of as the majority group are descendants of immigrants who at one time were believed to be racially distinct from native-born White Americans, the majority of whom were Protestants" (Higginbotham and Anderson, 2005:3). Racial categories vary in different regions of the country and around the world. Someone classified as "Black" in the United States might be considered "White" in Brazil and "Coloured" (a category distinguished from both "Black" and "White") in South Africa (Bamshad and Olson, 2003:80). In the United States, a Black/White color line has always been complicated by regional racial divides. Today, those divides are taking on new meanings with "the arrival of unprecedented numbers of Asians and Latinos" (Lee and Bean, 2004:224). Global events also complicate the color lines. Since the terrorist attacks on the World Trade Center and the Pentagon, Arab Americans, Muslims, and people of Middle Eastern descent (viewed by many as a single entity) are stereotyped as different and possibly dangerous.

Racial Categories

In Chapter 8, we discussed present immigration patterns that are reshaping the U.S. racial landscape. Immigration from Asia, Latin America, and the Caribbean are also changing the character of race and ethnic relations. Sociologists Michael Omi and Howard Winant (1994:55) call this **racial formation**, meaning that society is continually creating and transforming racial categories. Groups once self-defined by their ethnic backgrounds (such as Mexican Americans and Japanese Americans) are now racialized as "Hispanics" and "Asian Americans."

Even "official" racial categories in the United States have changed over time. The U.S. Census Bureau, which measures race on the basis of self-identification, revised its racial categories for the 2000 Census.

People may now identify themselves as members of more that one racial group on the census and other federal forms.

For the first time, people were allowed to record themselves in 2 or more racial categories. Of the U.S. population, 2.4 percent, or 7 million people, identified themselves as multiracial, reporting that they were of two races. The option of choosing more than one race provides a more accurate and visible portrait of the multiracial population in the United States. We can expect that the use of the multiracial option will grow, especially among the younger population. Marrying across racial lines is on the increase, as attitudes toward interracial unions become more tolerant. Thirteen percent of U.S. marriages now involve someone of a different race (Lee and Bean, 2004:228). Already, children are much more likely to identify themselves as multiracial than adults. Four percent of the population under age eighteen were identified in more than one racial category in the 2000 Census, twice the percentage for adults (Kent et al., 2001:6; Prewitt, 2003:39). (See the Diversity panel: "Growing Difficulty of Defining Race.")

Although the 2000 Census has begun to capture the complex mix of racial groups in the United States, it uses a confusing classification for Hispanics. According to the U.S. guidelines, Hispanics are an ethnic group, not a race. A person who identified their ethnicity as Hispanic could also indicate a racial background. But despite this murky classification, Hispanics *are racialized* in the United States. Although classified as an ethnic group, "Hispanic" encompasses a range of ethnic groups. At the same time, although Hispanics are not officially defined as a race, they are socially defined in racial terms. In other words, Hispanics are treated as a racial group and many identify themselves as belonging to a distinctive racial category.

Despite the past and present racialization of different groups, we tend to see race through a Black/White lens. At the same time, Whites as the dominant group are usually seen as raceless, or having no race at all (McIntosh, 1992). In this view, whiteness is the natural or normal condition. It is racially unmarked and immune to investigation. This is a false picture of race. In reality, the racial order shapes the lives of all people, even Whites who are advantaged by the system. Just as social classes exist in relation to each other, "races" are labeled and judged *in relation to other races*. The categories "Black" and "Hispanic" are meaningful only insofar as they are set apart from and in distinction to "White." This point is particularly obvious when people are referred to as "non-White" (a word that ignores the differences in experiences among people of color) (Lucal, 1996:246). Race is not simply a matter of two opposite categories of people but a range of power relations among dominant and subordinate groups (Weber, 2001).

Whereas race is an invention used for socially marking groups based on presumed physical differences, **ethnicity** is a social category that allows for a broader range of affiliation. Ethnic groups are distinctive on the basis of national origin, language, religion, and culture. Today's world is replete with examples of socially constructed ethnicities. At the same time that the world is becoming throughly globalized, it is also being transformed by new ethnic diversities. As European countries struggle with political and economic integration, people may no longer identify as Italian, but as Lombardians or Sicilians (Wali, 1992). Immigration is also changing European societies that were once characterized as White and Christian. "The arrival of large numbers of people from the Middle East, East Asia, and Africa—many European countries now have minority ethnic populations of around 10 percent—is pushing aside old concepts of what it means to be French, or German, or Swedish" (Richburg, 2004:17). Expanding communications networks and the increased social interaction that have resulted from immigration have not suppressed ethnic conflicts. During the last decade of the twentieth century, ethnic and religious differences have led to massacres of ethnic Tutsis by Hutus in Rwanda; full-scale war involving Serb, Bosnian,

The Growing Difficulty of Defining Race

The 2000 Census was the first U.S. Census that allowed people to mark more than one race. The Census Bureau added this option because of increasing rates of interracial marriage and the growing population of children and minorities who identify with more than one race. Of the 281.4 million people counted in the census, about 6.8 million (2 percent) identified with two or more races. The most common multiracial combinations in the 2000 Census were White and "some other race" (32 percent), White and American Indian/Alaska Native (16 percent), White and Asian (13 percent), and White and Black/African American (11 percent). There are 63 possible combinations of racial categories, but these four combinations alone account for 72 percent of those who selected more than one race.

The growing number of interracial marriages means that there are more children being born to parents of different races. Data from the 2000 Census show that 4 percent of American children under 18 years old are multiracial, compared with 2 percent of adults.

There are also distinct regional differences in multiracial identity. In the country's most multiracial state, Hawaii (21 percent multiracial), the most frequent combinations were Asian and Native Hawaiian/Other Pacific Islander, followed by White and Asian. In Oklahoma (5 percent multiracial), by contrast, two-thirds of the multiracial population considered themselves White and American Indian. In famously diverse California (5 percent multiracial), the most frequent multiple-race selection was White and "some other race," followed by White and Asian, and White and American Indian/Alaska Native. Among Hispanics/Latinos who selected more than one race, two-thirds (66 percent) marked White and "some other race."

With so many new categories, defining race is more complicated than ever. In the past, race was understood as a biological concept. Census enumerators were instructed to report a person's race based on observation. Today, there is general agreement that race is a social construct. But to what extent are respondents' choices influenced by their physical characteristics? by their ancestries? by the families or communities in which they live?

If the meaning of race is ambiguous, why does the federal government continue to expend large amounts of time and money to collect racial data? The answer is not simple, but the most important reason is that race continues to be a social reality in U.S. society, shaping the experiences of many individuals from childhood to old age. Upholding laws that seek to prevent racial discrimination, such as the civil rights laws of the 1960s, depends on the collection of data on race.

Source: Ameristat. "Who Marked More Than One Race in the 2000 Census?" Population Reference Bureau. Reprinted by permission. Available online: http://AmeristatTemplate.cfm?Section=RaceandEthnicity&Template=/Conten (accessed June 22, 2002).

States in Rank Order, by Percent Multiracial, 2000

		2000 Population	*Multiracial Population*	*Percent*
1	Hawaii	1,211,537	259,343	21.4
2	Alaska	626,932	34,146	5.4
3	California	33,871,648	1,607,646	4.7
4	Oklahoma	3,450,654	155,685	4.5
5	Nevada	1,998,257	76,428	3.8
6	New Mexico	1,819,046	66,327	3.6
7	Washington	5,894,121	213,519	3.6
8	New York	18,976,457	590,182	3.1
9	Oregon	3,421,399	104,745	3.1
10	Arizona	5,130,632	146,526	2.9

Source: U.S. Bureau of the Census.

Albanian, and other ethnic groups in the Balkans; and violence against ethnic Chinese in Indonesia (Pollard and O'Hare, 1999:5). Across Europe today, anti-immigrant racism is on the rise. Growing fears of a mounting foreign influx are fueling political movements to stop immigration. (See the panel titled "Globalization: The Changing Face of Sweden")

In the United States, race and ethnicity both serve to mark groups as different. Groups *labeled as races* by the wider society are bound together by their common social and economic conditions. As a result, they develop distinctive cultural or ethnic characteristics. Today, we often refer to them as racial-ethnic groups (or racially defined ethnic groups). The term **racial ethnic group** refers to groups that are socially subordinated and remain culturally distinct within U.S. society. It includes (1) the systematic discrimination of socially constructed racial groups and (2) their distinctive cultural arrangements. The categories of **African American**, **Latino**, **Asian American**, and **Native American** have been constructed as both racially and culturally distinct. Each group has a distinctive culture, shares a common heritage, and has a common identity within a larger society that subordinates it. The racial characteristics of these groups have become meaningful in a society that continues to change (Baca Zinn and Dill, 1994).

Terms of reference are also changing, and the changes are contested within groups and between them. For example, *Blacks* continue to debate the merits of the term *African American*, while *Latinos* disagree on the label *Hispanic*. In this chapter, we use such interchangeable terms because they are currently used in both popular and scholarly discourse.

Differences among Racial and Ethnic Groups

Both race and ethnicity are historical bases for inequality, although they have differed in how they incorporated groups into society. Race was the social construction setting people of color apart from European immigrant groups (Takaki, 1993:10). Groups identified as races came into contact with the dominant majority through force, in work that was unfree, low in pay, and low in status, and that offered little opportunity for upward mobility. In contrast, European ethnics migrated to the United States voluntarily, to enhance their status or to market their skills in a land of opportunity. They came with hope and sometimes with resources to provide a foundation for their upward mobility. Unlike racial groups, most had the option of returning if they found the conditions here unsatisfactory. The voluntary immigrants came to the United States and suffered discrimination in employment, housing, and other areas. Clashes among Germans, Irish, Italians, Poles, and other European groups during the nineteenth and early twentieth centuries are well documented. But most European immigrants and their descendants—who accounted for four-fifths of the U.S. population in 1900—eventually achieved full participation in U.S. society (Pollard and O'Hare, 1999:5).

While European ethnics have moved into the mainstream of society, racially defined peoples have remained in a subordinate status. Native Americans, African Americans, Latinos, and Asian Americans have not been assimilated. Continuing racial discrimination sets them apart from others.

African Americans. By 2003, African Americans (38 million) were 13.3 percent of the population (U.S. Bureau of the Census, 2004). Before 1990, virtually all descended from people who were brought involuntarily to the United States before the slave trade ended in the nineteenth century. They entered the southern states to provide free labor to plantations, and as late as 1890, 90 percent of all Blacks lived in the South, 80 percent as rural dwellers. In the South, they endured harsh, violent, and arbitrary conditions under slavery, an institution that would have consequences for centuries to come. During the nineteenth century, the political storm over slavery almost destroyed the nation. Although Blacks left the South in large numbers after 1890, within northern cities they also encountered discrimination and an extreme level of segregation that exposed them to unusually high concentrations of poverty and other social problems (Massey, 1993:7; Takaki, 1993:7). African Americans have a distinctive history of slavery and oppression.

Since 1990, the "Black" population in the U.S. has changed. More Blacks are coming from Africa than during the slave trade. About 50,000 legal immigrants arrive annually and more have migrated here than in nearly the entire preceding centuries (Roberts, 2005:A1). This demographic shift in the Black population has sparked a new debate about the "African American" label. It ignores the enormous linguistic, physical, and cultural diversity of the peoples of Africa. The term "Black" is also problematic in that it risks conflating people of African descent who were brought here as slaves with recent immigrants from Africa and the Caribbean (Mukhopadhyay and Henze, 2003:675). (See the panel titled "A Closer Look: Diverging Paths for Foreign-Born Blacks and African Americans.")

Latinos. As we saw in Chapter 8, the size of the U.S. Latino population has now surpassed the African American population to become the nation's largest minority. In many respects, the Latino population is the driving force of this society's racial and ethnic transformation (Saenz, 2004:29). In 2003, Hispanics or Latinos numbered 39.9 million, or 13.7 percent of the total U.S. population. Two thirds (66 percent) of all Latinos are Chicanos or Mexican Americans, 8.6 percent are Puerto Ricans, 3.7 percent are Cubans, 14.3 percent are Central Americans and South Americans, and 6 percent are "other Hispanic" (U.S. Bureau of the Census, 2003). (See Figure 11.1 for Hispanic growth and population projections through 2030.)

The category "Hispanic" was created by the federal government to provide data on people of Mexican, Cuban, Puerto Rican, and other Hispanic origins in the United States. The term was chosen as a label that could be applied to all people from the Spanish-speaking countries of Latin America and from Spain. Since the population is highly heterogeneous, there is no precise definition of group membership. Even the term *Latino*, which many prefer, is a new invention.

Immigration is a thread that unifies much of the Latino experience in the United States. The vast majority of Latinos are immigrants or children of immigrants (Suarez-Orozco and Paez, 2002). However, the national origins of Latinos are diverse, and so is the timing of their arrival in the United States. As a result, Mexicans, Puerto Ricans, Cubans, and other Latino groups have varied histories that set them apart from each other. Cubans arrived largely in the period between 1960 and 1980; a group of Mexicans indigenous to the Southwest was forcibly annexed into the United States in 1848, and another has been migrating continuously since around 1890. Puerto Ricans came under U.S. control in 1898 and obtained citizenship in 1917; Salvadorans and Guatemalans have been migrating to the United States in substantial numbers during the past two decades.

The Changing Face of Sweden: Dark Skin and Brown Eyes

In one of his most popular songs, Swedish hip-hop artist Timbuktu sings of two strangers warily eyeing each other on a Stockholm subway, one a white Swede, the other an immigrant, each with his own thoughts and prejudices.

"I wonder why he's eyeing me like this," the white Swede asks himself. "Maybe he's planning to follow me and rob me at knife tip. I bet he's a drug user that beats his kids, forces his wife to wear a veil."

Timbuktu knows something about racial prejudice—as a black man born in Lund, Sweden, whose first language is Swedish, but who for most of his life has had to deal with the stares, the taunts, the curiosity and the inevitable question: "But where are you really from?"

From first grade through sixth, he recalls, he fought frequently during recess with a group of three boys who taunted him with racial insults. Even though he's a celebrity in Malmo, which he calls home, he says he is still followed by security guards when he enters a department store. And while his DJ sessions can pack the house, he finds he is denied entry to some clubs.

"I'm Swedish, definitely, and more and more so now," says Timbuktu, whose real name is Jason Diakité. He is the son of a black American man from Harlem and a white American woman from Scranton, Pa. "But Sweden still has a very clear picture of what a Swede is. That no longer exists—the blond, blue-eyed physical traits. That's changing. But it still exists in the minds of some people."

Across Europe, societies that were once solidly white and Christian are being recast in a multicultural light. The arrival of large numbers of people from the Middle East, East Asia and Africa—many European countries now have minority populations of around 10 percent—is pushing aside old concepts of what it means to be French or German or Swedish.

In Sweden, nowhere is the change happening faster than in Malmo, the country's third-largest city behind Stockholm and Goteborg. It is a gritty shipyard town of about 265,000 people. Once a major industrial center that drew people from abroad with the prospect of jobs, Malmo has lately fallen on hard times as factories have closed.

About 40 percent of Malmo's population is foreign-born or has at least one foreign-born parent. The bulk of foreign-born people come from the former Yugoslavia, Iran, Iraq and the Horn of Africa. Among school-age children, 50 percent have at least one foreign-born parent, and analysts project that the number will soon reach 60 percent.

The city's official Web site boasts that its inhabitants come from 164 countries and speak 100 languages.

A walk through the Mollevangstorget area of Malmo, where Timbuktu lives, shows how much immigration has changed this city. The Middle East restaurant sits across the street from a falafel shop, down the road from an Indian shop and the Tehran Supermarket, which is filled with nuts, dates, dried fruits and banana-flavored tobacco imported fresh from Iran.

"Immigrants like being here, because they can find things from their own country," said a man working behind the supermarket counter, who gave his name only as Rahim. "Four thousand Iranians live here. But there are Swedes shopping here as well."

The ethnic diversity is part of what drew Timbuktu, 29, here to make his music. "Malmo is a quite interesting town for the way Sweden may look in the future," he said in an interview over coffee at the city's Hilton Hotel, as two female fans ogled him from a table nearby.

Almost 12 percent of the roughly 9 million people living in Sweden as of this past summer were foreign-born, government statistics show. Sweden has long hosted white immigrants from Finland and the Baltic countries. But according to the later figures, about 7 percent of the population comes from outside Europe, most of them nonwhite.

Though immigrants here frequently experience prejudice and rejection, it appears to be less institutionalized than in other European countries; an anti-immigrant party in Sweden got just 1.4 percent of the vote in elections two years ago.

That result occurred partly because the Swedish majority populace has gone about the business of absorbing the newcomers with the famous Scandinavian seriousness of purpose. There are programs to help new arrivals learn Swedish. There are programs to

The Changing Face of Sweden: Dark Skin and Brown Eyes continued

help them find housing. And there are generous subsidies for those who aren't working.

In France, black and brown faces are largely nonexistent in politics, government, the news media and the top echelons of business—anywhere outside of sports and music. But in Sweden, immigrants have assumed a much higher profile.

Foreign-born Swedes hold a significant number of parliamentary seats. The top Swedish chef, Marcus Samuelsson, is an ethnic Ethiopian. Some of the most popular comedians on television are foreign-born, including Ozz Nujen and Shan Atci, both Kurds. One of Sweden's top filmmakers, Josef Fares, came to Sweden from Lebanon. And Sweden's silver medal–winning Olympic wrestler, Ara Abrahamian, was born in Armenia.

But Sweden's quiet transformation has not been without problems. In Malmo, the biggest problem is unemployment. In Rosengard, the most heavily immigrant district of Malmo, the unemployment rate is around 65 percent.

But the biggest problem in Malmo, and in other parts of Sweden, is what people here call "ghettoization": White Swedes typically live in certain areas, in this case the city center, while immigrants are increasingly clustered on the outskirts in their own communities.

Ghettoization is a problem that also unsettles Timbuktu. "Will it be like the United States," he asks rhetorically, "where all the Somalis live in one part of town, and all the Koreans in another?" He adds, "I get the feeling that tension is going to increase in Sweden over the next 25 years."

Country of Immigrants

The image of Sweden as a country of Nordic people no longer fits the nation, as thousands of immigrants from all over the world are being admitted each year to a country of 9 million people.

Number of legal immigrants
In thousands, 1973-2003

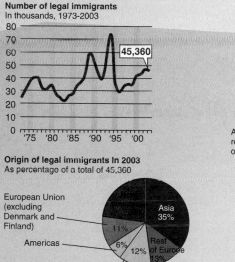

Origin of legal immigrants In 2003
As percentage of a total of 45,360

European Union (excluding Denmark and Finland) 11%

Asia 35%

Americas 6%

Others (of which Africa 9%)

12% Rest of Europe 13%

SOURCES: Swedish Migration Board, City of Malmo

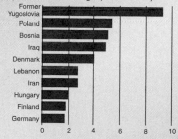

As of Jan. 1, 2002, almost a quarter of **Malmo's** 265,000 residents were born in another country. Here is a breakdown of the top 10 countries of origin (in thousands):

Former Yugoslavia
Poland
Bosnia
Iraq
Denmark
Lebanon
Iran
Hungary
Finland
Germany

Source: Keith B. Richburg, 2004. "A Smorgasbord of Cultures." *The Washington Post National Weekly Edition* (Nov. 1–7):17. © 2004, The Washington Post, reprinted by permission.

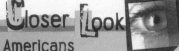

a Closer Look

Diverging Paths for Foreign-Born Blacks and African Americans

More Africans have immigrated to the United States in the past fifteen years than the total number of slaves brought to the United States during the slave trade period. Africans now represent 6 percent of all the immigrants of the United States. As the number of Black immigrants continues to rise, two important questions must be considered. First, how are the identities of Black Americans different from or similar to twentieth- and twenty-first-century African immigrants and the children of African immigrants? Second, if these identities are different, how will this affect the future of the Black community politically, economically, and socially?

African immigrants are the most educated group in the nation with almost half holding bachelor's or advanced degrees, compared to 23 percent of native-born Americans and less than 17 percent of African Americans. Ninety-eight percent of African immigrants are high school graduates compared to 80 percent of African Americans. More than 40 percent of Black students currently enrolled in the nation's most selective colleges and universities identify themselves as immigrants, children of immigrants, or as mixed race. Comparatively only 9 percent of 18- to 25-year-old Blacks nationally identify as African or West Indian ancestry. These data have raised concern that native-born Blacks with soon be eclipsed by Black immigrants and have led some to question whether these two groups can, or should, claim the same identity of African American.

The educational attainment of African immigrants and their children indicate that this population has access to far greater resources and opportunities than most native-born Blacks. Further, they indicate that the experiences of African immigrants may be markedly different from those who have descended from slaves. Because educational attainment often leads to increased mobility, it is useful to consider how the experiences of African immigrants with discrimination compare to those of native-born Blacks. In her research on West Indian immigrants, Mary Waters (1999) found that first-generation Black immigrants typically encounter less prejudice and discrimination than native-born Blacks because Americans tend to have a more positive view of immigrants as "hard working" and, when compared with native Blacks, many Whites see immigrant Blacks as being free of the "chip on their shoulder." In his research on Haitian immigrants, however, Alex Stepick (1997) found that regardless

of education and job experience, discrimination and structural barriers prevent the advancement of many Black immigrants. How will the mobility of African immigrants compare of that of other Black immigrants and to native-born Blacks?

Both Waters and Stepick found that Black immigrants prefer to distinguish themselves from the native-Black population, particularly in the middle class. Research on African immigrants suggests that Africans tend to identify as African first and members of a national group second. If this is the case, how will the declining Black American community respond to a growing population of Blacks who do not want to be associated with them?

With rapidly increasing numbers of foreign-born Blacks, it is important to consider what it will mean to have "black skin." Those Blacks who are most likely to be stuck in concentrated poverty, with limited access to quality education and employment opportunities, are those who have been here for generations. They are in direct competition with other Blacks for admissions to schools and job hires—but they are not in a position to compete with the resources that Black immigrants bring with them. When we consider this, the declining proportion of Blacks with slave descent is surely going to comprise an even more rapidly declining proportion of middle-class Blacks.

How will this affect the relationship between native and immigrant Blacks? Waters suggests that by the second generation, once the language accent is lost, immigrant Blacks are more likely to identify as African American and Whites are more likely to view them as such. But the initial access to greater resources and opportunity may be all the impetus needed to leave native-born Blacks behind. What will become of the ever-shrinking population of slave descendents? What will this division mean for the Black community, both socially and politically?

References

A. Stepick, *Pride against Prejudice: Haitians in the United States*. (Boston, MA: Allyn & Bacon, 1997).

M. C. Waters, *Black Identities: West Indian Immigrant Dreams and American Realities*. (New York: Russel Sage Foundation, 1999).

Source: "African Immigration Produces Dramatic Change in U. S. Population," by Jessica C. Mills, Department of Sociology, Michigan State University, 2005. Reprinted by permission.

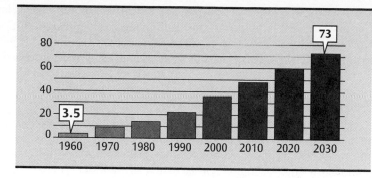

FIGURE 11.1

Hispanic Growth in Population (in millions)

Hispanics now comprise 12.5 percent of the U.S. population, making them the largest minority racial/ethnic group. How the Hispanic population has risen and is projected to grow in (millions).

Source: Martin Kinsdorf, 2004. "Hispanic Voters Paint a New Picture." *USA Today*, November 11, 2004. Reprinted with permission.

As a result of these varied histories, Hispanics are found in many legal and social statuses—from fifth-generation to new immigrants, from affluent and well educated to poor and unschooled. Such diversity means that there is no unified "Hispanic" population. Hispanics neither have a common history, nor do they compose a single, coherent community. Rather, they are a collection of national-origin groups with heterogeneous experiences of settlement, immigration, political participation, and economic incorporation into the United States. Saying that someone is "Hispanic" or "Latino" reveals little about likely attitudes, behaviors, beliefs, race, religion, class, or legal situation in the United States (Massey, 1993).

Despite these differences, Latinos in the United States have endured a long history of discrimination. Mexican Americans in the Southwest lost property and political rights as Anglos moved into the region in the 1800s. As late as the 1940s, local ordinances in some Texas cities blocked Mexican Americans from owning real estate or voting. Also, Mexican Americans were required to attend segregated public schools in many jurisdictions before 1950 (Pollard and O'Hare, 1999:6).

Asian Americans. Asian Americans are another rapidly growing minority group in the country. By 2005, Asians Americans accounted for 5 percent of the U.S. population (U.S. Bureau of the Census, 2004). The nation's 13.5 million Asians now make up 25 percent of the nation's immigrants.

Like the Latino population, the Asian population in the United States is extremely diverse, giving rise to the term *Pan-Asian*, which encompasses immigrants from Asian and Pacific Island countries and native-born citizens descended from those ethnic groups (Lott and Felt, 1991:6). Until recently, immigrants who arrived in the United States from Asian countries did not think of themselves as "Asians," or even as Chinese, Japanese, Korean, and so forth, but rather people from Toisan, Hoeping, or some other district in Guangdong Province in China, or from Hiroshima, Yamaguchi, or some other place. It was not until the late 1960s, with the advent of the Asian American movement, that a Pan-Asian consciousness was formed (Espiritu, 1996:51).

The largest Asian American groups are Chinese (23 percent), Filipinos (18 percent), Japanese (9.2 percent), Vietnamese (10 percent), Koreans (10 percent), and Asian Indians (16 percent) (U.S. Bureau of the Census, 2004). There also are Laotians, Kampucheans, Thais, Pakistanis, Indonesians, Hmongs, and Samoans (Lee, 1998:15).

The characteristics of Asians vary widely according to their national origins and time of entry into the United States. Most come from recent immigrant families, but many Asian Americans can trace their family's history in the United States more than 150 years. Much of this period was marked by anti-Asian laws and discrimination. The 1879 California constitution barred the hiring of Chinese workers, and the federal Chinese Exclusion Act of 1882 halted the entry of most Chinese immigrants until 1943. Americans of Japanese ancestry were interned in camps during World War II by an executive order signed by President Franklin D. Roosevelt. Not until 1952 were Japanese immigrants granted the right to become naturalized U.S. citizens (Pollard and O'Hare, 1999:6–7).

Whereas most of the pre–World War II Asian immigrants were peasants, the recent immigrants vary considerably by education and social class. On one hand, many arrived as educated middle-class professionals with highly valued skills and some knowledge of English. Others, such as the Indochinese, arrived as uneducated, impoverished refugees. These differences are reflected in the differences in income and poverty level by ethnic category. Asian Americans taken together have higher average incomes than do other groups in the United States. Although a large segment of this population is financially well off, many are poor. Given this diversity in social classes among the immigrants, most Asian American leaders say the "model minority" label is misleading. Even the term *Asian American* masks great diversity.

Native Americans. Once thought to be destined for extinction, the Native American or American Indian population today is larger than it has been for centuries. Now at 1.5 percent of the total U.S. population (Kent et al., 2001:6), Native Americans have more autonomy and are more self-sufficient than at any time since the last century (Snipp, 1996:390). Nevertheless, the population remains barred from full participation in U.S. society.

The tribes located in North America were and are extremely heterogeneous, with major differences in physical characteristics, language, and social organization. As many as 7 million indigenous people lived in North America when the Europeans arrived. However, disease, warfare, and in some cases genocide reduced the Indian population to less than 250,000 by 1890. In the first half of the nineteenth century, the U.S. government forced Indians from their homelands. Those forced migrations accelerated after President Andrew Jackson signed the Indian Removal Act of 1830. Many tribes then lived on marginal land that was reserved for them.

The current political and economic status of American Indians stems from the process that forced them into U.S. society. "This amounts to a long history of efforts aimed at subordinating an otherwise self-governing and self-sufficient people that eventually culminated in widespread economic dependency" (Snipp, 1996:390).

Important changes have occurred in the social and economic well-being of the Native American population from 1960 to the present. At the time of the 1970 Census, American Indians were the poorest group in the United States, with incomes well below those of the Black population. By 1980, despite poverty rates as high as 60 percent on many Indian reservations, poverty among American Indians had declined. As the twentieth century drew to a close, Native Americans were better off than they were in the 1900s. Today, 20 percent live below the poverty line. This rate is lower than the poverty rates for Blacks and Hispanics (U.S. Bureau of the Census, 2004). Nevertheless, native peoples ranked at the bottom of most U.S. socioeconomic indicators, with low levels of life expectancy, per capita income, employment, and education (Harjo, 1996; Pollard and O'Hare, 1999; Thornton, 1996).

Although Third World conditions prevail on many reservations, a renaissance has occurred in American Indian communities. In cities, modern pan-Indian organizations have been successful in making the presence of American Indians known to the larger community and have mobilized to meet the needs of their people (Snipp, 1996:390). A college-educated Indian middle class has emerged, American Indian business ownership has increased, and some tribes are creating good jobs for their members (Fost, 1991:26).

To summarize this section, the combined population of the four racial minority groups accounts for 30 percent of the total U.S. population. New waves of immigration from non-European countries, high birth rates among these groups, and a relatively young age structure account for the rapid increase in minorities. By the middle of the twenty-first century, today's minorities will comprise nearly one-half of the U.S. population. (See Figure 11.2 for population projections through 2050.) African Americans, Latinos, Asian Americans, and Native Americans are different in many respects. Each group encounters different forms of exclusion. Nevertheless, as racial minorities they remain at the lowest rungs of society.

Explanations of Racial and Ethnic Inequality

Why have some racial and ethnic groups been consistently disadvantaged? Some ethnic groups, such as the Irish and the Jews, have experienced discrimination but moved up from the bottom economic rungs. However, African Americans, Latinos, Asian Americans, and Native Americans have not been able to cast off their secondary

FIGURE 11.2

Percent of the Population, by Race and Hispanic Origin: 1990, 2000, 2025, and 2050 (Middle-Series Projection)

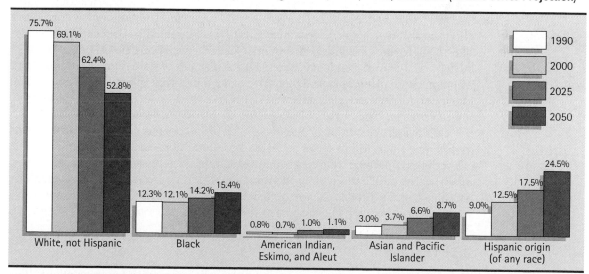

Source: U.S. Bureau of the Census, 1997. "Population Profile of the United States: 1997." *Current Population Reports,* Series P23–194. Washington, DC: U.S. Government Printing Office, p. 9.

status. Three types of theories have been used to explain why some groups are treated differently: deficiency theories, bias theories, and structural discrimination theories.

Deficiency Theories

A number of analysts have argued that some groups are disadvantaged because they *are* inferior. That is, when compared with the majority, they are deficient in some important way. There are two variations of **deficiency theories**, biological and cultural.

Biological Deficiency. This classical explanation for racial inferiority maintains that group inferiority is the result of flawed genetic—and, therefore, hereditary—traits. This is the position of Arthur Jensen, Richard Herrnstein, and Charles Murray (as discussed in Chapter 7). *The Bell Curve* (Herrnstein and Murray, 1994) is the latest in a long series of works claiming that Blacks are genetically inferior to Whites and this explains differences in the success of racial groups. Despite the media attention given the work of these and other theorists, there is no definitive evidence for the thesis that racial groups differ in intelligence. Biological deficiency theories are generally not accepted in the scientific community (see *Contemporary Sociology*, 1995).

Cultural Deficiency. Many explanations of racial subordination center on group-specific cultural traits handed down from generation to generation. According to this explanation, the cultural beliefs and practices of minority groups are deficient when compared to those of the majority. Cultural differences (including motivation, moral background, and behavior) are the reason some groups remain at the bottom. Cultural explanations argue that flawed minority lifestyles account for each group's secondary status.

From this perspective, minorities are disadvantaged because of their cultural heritage and customs. Cultural deficiency was the basis for Daniel Patrick Moynihan's famous 1967 report, which charged that the "tangle of pathology" within Black ghettos was rooted in the deterioration of the Negro family (U.S. Department of Labor, 1965). High rates of marital dissolution, female-headed households, out-of-wedlock births, and welfare dependency were said to be residues of slavery and discrimination, a complex web of pathological patterns passed down through the generations. The Moynihan report was widely criticized for being a classic case of "blaming the victim." It locates the problem within Blacks, not in the structure of society.

Cultural-deficiency theorists ignore the social opportunities that affect groups in different ways. Many social scientists have long opposed cultural explanations. Nevertheless, this approach is still found in scholarship and popular thought. Today, much of the public discussion about race and poverty rests on false assumptions about minorities (Bonilla-Silva, 2003; di Leonardo, 1992; Reed, Adolph, 1990). We return to this theme in the last part of this chapter.

Bias Theories

The deficiency theories just discussed blame the minorities for their plight. Bias theories, on the other hand, blame the members of the majority. They blame individuals who hold *prejudiced attitudes* toward minorities. Gunnar Myrdal (1944), for example, argues in his classic book *An American Dilemma* that prejudiced attitudes toward an entire group of people are the problem. This reduces racism to a set of ideas or beliefs that cause individuals to discriminate (Bonilla-Silva, 1996:466).

Many sociologists have argued that prejudiced attitudes are not the essence of racism. For example, David Wellman (1977) challenged the notion that the hostile attitudes of White Americans, especially lower-class Whites, are the major cause of racism. Instead, he shows that prejudiced beliefs do not explain the behaviors of unprejudiced Whites who defend the traditional arrangements that negatively affect minorities. Unbiased people fight to preserve the status quo by favoring, for example, the seniority system in occupations, or they oppose affirmative action, quota systems, busing to achieve racial balance, and open enrollment in higher education.

These people defend institutional arrangements, but strictly speaking, they are not examples of racial prejudice. Nevertheless, their sentiments maintain the status quo, and in this way keep Blacks in subordinate positions (Wellman, 1977).

To focus strictly on prejudice is to take too narrow a view. This view is inaccurate because it concentrates on the bigots and ignores the structural foundation of racism. The determining feature of majority-minority relations is not prejudice, but differential systems of privilege and disadvantage. "The subordination of people of color is functional to the operation of American society as we know it and the color of one's skin is a primary determinant of people's position in the social structure" (Wellman, 1977:35). Thus, institutional and individual racism generate privilege for Whites. Discrimination provides the privileged with disproportionate advantages in the social, economic, and political spheres. Racist acts, in this view, are based not only on stereotypes, hatred, or prejudgment, but are also rational responses to the struggle over scarce resources by individuals acting to preserve their own advantage.

Structural Discrimination Theories

Deficiency and bias theories focus, incorrectly, on individuals: the first on minority flaws, and the second on the flawed attitudes of the majority. Both kinds of theory ignore the social organization that oppresses minorities. Michael Parenti criticizes those who ignore the system as victim blamers. "Focusing on the poor and ignoring the system of power, privilege, and profit which makes them poor, is a little like blaming the corpse for the murder" (1978:24). The alternative view is that racial inequality is not fundamentally a matter of what is in people's heads, not a matter of their private individual intentions, but rather a matter of public institutions and practices that create racism or keep it alive. **Structural discrimination theories** move away from thinking about "racism in the head" toward understanding "racism in the world" (Lichtenberg, 1992:5).

Many sociologists have examined race as a structural force that permeates every aspect of life. Those who use this framework make a distinction between **individual racism** and **institutionalized racism** (Carmichael and Hamilton, 1967). Individual racism is related to prejudice. It consists of overt acts by individuals that harm other individuals or their property. Institutional racism is structural. It refers to processes that, intentionally or not, protect the advantages of the dominant group while maintaining the unequal position of the subordinate group (Miles, 1989:50). Institutional racism views inequality as part of society's structure. Therefore, individuals and groups discriminate whether they are bigots or not. These individuals and groups operate within a social milieu that ensures racial dominance. The social milieu includes laws, customs, religious beliefs, and the stable arrangements and practices through which things get done in society.

Social institutions have great power to reward and penalize. Therefore, the term *institutional discrimination* is a useful one for understanding racial inequality. There are four basic themes of institutional discrimination (Benokraitis and Feagin, 1974). First is the importance of history in determining present conditions and affecting resistance to change. Historically, institutions defined and enforced norms and role relationships that were racially distinct. The United States was founded and its institutions established when Blacks were slaves, uneducated, and different culturally from the dominant Whites. From the beginning, Blacks were considered inferior (the original Constitution, for example, counted a slave as three-fifths of a person). Religious beliefs buttressed this notion of the inferiority of Blacks and justified the differential allocation of privileges and sanctions in society.

The second theme of institutional discrimination is that discrimination can occur without conscious bigotry. Everyday practices reinforce racial discrimination and deprivation. Although actions by the Ku Klux Klan have an unmistakable racial tone, many other actions (choosing to live in a suburban neighborhood, sending one's children to a private school, or opposing government intervention in hiring policies) also maintain racial dominance (Bonilla-Silva, 1996:475). With or without malicious intent, racial discrimination is the "normal" outcome of the system. Even if "racism in the head" disappeared, "racism in the world" would not, because it is the *system* that disadvantages (Lichtenberg, 1992).

Finally, institutional discrimination is reinforced because institutions are interrelated. The exclusion of minorities from the upper levels of education, for example, is likely to affect their opportunities in other institutions (type of job, level of remuneration). Similarly, poor children will probably receive an inferior education, be propertyless, suffer from bad health, and be treated unjustly by the criminal justice system. These inequities are cumulative.

Institutional derogation occurs when minority groups and their members are made to seem inferior or to possess negative stereotypes through legitimate means by the powerful in society. The portrayal of minority-group members in the media (movies, television, newspapers, and magazines) is often derogatory. A study of prime-time network programming by the advocacy group Children Now found that minorities are still shortchanged. In 2003–2004, Blacks made up 16 percent of prime-time characters, while Latinos made up 6 percent, and Asian Americans made up 3 percent. No Native American characters were represented in any episodes in the study's sample (Children Now, 2004). According to another study, Black men are also depicted disproportionately as drug users, criminals, lower-class, and "pathological" (Muwakkil, 1998b:18). If we based our perceptions of certain minority populations on media images, we would have considerably skewed views.

Why is the United States structured along racist lines? Sociologists have a long-standing debate over the relative importance of race and class in shaping racial stratification. Those emphasizing class contend that the economy and the class system are what produce racial inequality. (See the discussion of the underclass later in the chapter.) Some scholars argue that modern race relations are produced by world capitalism. Using the labor of non-White peoples began as a means for White owners to accumulate profits. This perspective contends that capitalism as a system of class exploitation has shaped race and racism in the United States and the world (Bonacich, 1992a).

Other theories point to race itself as a primary shaper of inequality. For example, racial-formation theory proposes that the United States is organized along racial lines from top to bottom—a racial state, composed of institutions and policies to support and justify racial stratification (Omi and Winant, 1986; 1994). Another theory, called *systematic racism*, also argues that race is paramount in explaining inequality. Systematic racism includes a diverse assortment of racist practices; the unjustly gained economic and political power of Whites; the continuing resource inequalities; and the White-racist ideologies, attitudes, and institutions created to preserve White advantages and power. Systematic racism is both structural and interpersonal. "At the macro level, large-scale institutions . . . routinely perpetuate racial subordination and inequalities. These institutions are created and recreated by routine actions at the micro level by individuals" (Feagin, 2000:16).

Racial Stratification from the Order and Conflict Perspectives

Order perspectives of race and ethnic relations have assumed that the United States is a land of opportunity and that all groups—ethnic and racial—would eventually assimilate or blend into the country's social melting pot. This was the experience of the European immigrants who came to the United States in the nineteenth and early twentieth centuries and who were absorbed into the broader society a few genera tions after they arrived (Pollard and O'Hare, 1999:44). Order theories accent patterns of inclusion, orderly integration, and the assimilation of racial and ethnic groups. The word assimilate comes from the Latin word *assimulare*, meaning "to make similar" (Feagin and Feagin, 1993:27). Order theories are concerned with how minorities adapt to the core society. These theories see the situations of Blacks and non-Whites as similar to those of earlier White immigrants. Just as White ethnics made a place for themselves in the land of opportunity, so should racial minorities. With the right motivation and behaviors, minorities can lift themselves up and succeed in the U.S. mainstream.

Conflict (or power-conflict) theories are critical of assimilation theories for ignoring social conditions that exclude racial minorities from full participation in U.S. society. Most conflict theories emphasize the deep-lying roots of racial and ethnic inequalities in the U.S. economy. Social institutions, not group culture, keep minorities stuck on the bottom rungs of society. Conflict theories argue that racial-ethnics were never meant to assimilate. Racial stratification exists because certain segments of society benefit from it. Racial-ethnics are located in the larger society in ways that prevent their assimilation. The melting pot does not apply to people of color. Differences between Whites and people of color produce conflict, not consensus, across race lines.

Neither the conflict nor the order model captures the complexity of today's multiracial society. While some minorities remain at the bottom, racially defined immigrants are entering a U.S. society that is unlike the country that absorbed the

European immigrants. New theories are needed to illuminate the experiences of different racial groups and their connections to global transformations.

Discrimination against Blacks and Hispanics: Continuity and Change

The treatment of Blacks and Hispanics has been disgraceful throughout American history. Through public policies and everyday practices, they have been denied the opportunities that should be open to all people. Since World War II, however, under pressure from civil rights advocates, the government has led the way in breaking down these discriminatory practices. The 1960s civil rights movement overturned segregation laws, opened voting booths, created new job opportunities, and renewed hope for racial equality. By the close of the twentieth century, many well-educated people of color had climbed into the middle class.

In 2003, 33 percent of African Americans and 32 percent of Latino families had incomes of $50,000 or more compared with 59 percent of White families (U.S. Bureau of the Census, 2004). They have taken advantage of fair-housing legislation and moved to the suburbs looking for better schools, safer streets, and better services. Yet having "made it" in the United States does not shield African Americans from discriminatory treatment. Studies of public accommodation have found that in stores, bars, restaurants, and theaters, middle-class Blacks are ignored or treated with hostility (Feagin and Sikes, 1994). No matter how affluent or influential, Black people are vulnerable to "micro-insults" such as being followed around in stores (Bonilla-Silva, 2003, Muwakkil, 1998a:11).

The minority middle class has not erased the problem of segregation. A class divide now characterizes minority communities across the country. As some successful people of color have become richer, many more unsuccessful ones have been marginalized. As much as some things have changed, others have remained the same. The present segregation of African Americans cannot be dismissed as wrongs committed in the past. U.S. neighborhoods were sharply segregated in the 1900s (Massey and Denton, 1993). Today, they are just as segregated. The 2000 Census data show high levels of racial segregation in residential areas. Whites tend to live in neighborhoods that are overwhelmingly White, while minorities live in neighborhoods with other minorities. The average Black person lives in a neighborhood that is 33 percent White and 51 percent Black. Compared with 1990, Blacks were more likely to have Hispanic and Asian neighbors, but they were no more likely to have White neighbors. Asian and Hispanic populations—which include large numbers of recent immigrants—were somewhat more isolated from other racial groups in 2000 than they were in 1990 (Kent et al., 2001:24). (See Figure 11.3 for data on the segregation of Asians, Blacks, and Hispanics.)

Income

The average income for White families and households is greater than the average income for those of Blacks and Hispanics. Racial income disparities have remained unchanged over time. In 2003, the median income of Black households was about $30,000, the median income of White households was about $48,000, and the

Separation of Asians			...and of Blacks			...and of Hispanics		

Of the 50 metropolitan areas with the largest percentage of Asians, here are the 10 areas where Asians and Whites are most segregated:

Of the 50 metropolitan areas with the largest percentage of Blacks, here are the 10 areas where Blacks and Whites are most segregated:

Of the 50 metropolitan areas with the largest percentage of Hispanics, here are the 10 areas where Hispanics and non-Hispanic Whites are most segregated:

Area Name	2000 Rank	1990 Rank	Area Name	2000 Rank	1990 Rank	Area Name	2000 Rank	1990 Rank
New York	1	7	Detroit	1	1	New York	1	2
Stockton, Calif.	2	1	Milwaukee–Waukesha, Wisc.	2	4	Newark, NJ	2	1
Houston	3	8	New York	3	7	Los Angeles–Long Beach	3	5
Sacramento	4	6	Chicago	4	2	Chicago	4	4
San Francisco	5	4	Newark, N.J.	5	3	Philadelphia	5	3
Los Angeles	6	15	Cleveland	6	5	Salinas, Calif.	6	7
Vallejo, Calif.	7	16	Cincinnati	7	6	Boston	7	8
San Diego	8	10	Nassau–Suffolk, NY	8	9	Bergen, NJ	8	6
Detroit	9	9	St. Louis	9	8	Ventura, Calif.	9	11
Atlanta	10	17	Miami	10	15	Orange County, Calif.	10	14

For the complete segregation report, go to www.albany.edu/mumford/census.

FIGURE 11.3

Segregation Still Touches Minorities Where They Live

Source: Haya El Nasser, 2000. "Segregation Still Touches Minorities Where They Live." USA Today (April 4):2A.

median income of Hispanic households was about $33,000. Even though the median household income for Blacks is still below that of Hispanics, per-person income for Hispanics is actually lower because Hispanics tend to have larger households.

Although the racial income gap is wide, the racial *wealth gap* is even wider. White families are generally wealthier than Black or Latino families (Collins et al., 1999). In their book *White Wealth/Black Wealth*, Melvin Oliver and Thomas Shapiro (1995) define wealth as the sum of important assets a family owns. This includes home ownership, pension funds, savings accounts, and investments. Many of these are inherited across generations. White families generally have greater resources for their children and bequeath them as assets at death. Oliver and Shapiro call this "the cost of being Black." According to this line of thought the African American disadvantage will persist until the wealth divide is closed (Shapiro, 2004).

One important indicator of a family's wealth is home ownership. Paying off a home mortgage is the way most people build net worth over their lifetimes. More minorities are buying homes, but because of discrimination in employment, housing, and insurance, a great race gap remains. Fewer than half of Blacks and Latinos and fewer than 60 percent of Asians and American Indians own their own homes, compared to 3 quarters of Whites (see Figure 11.4). Rampant racial discrimination prevails in the housing market, even after forty years of federal fair housing laws (Crowley, 2002:25; Leondar-Wright et al., 2005:11).

Poverty rates for all minority groups are higher than those of Whites. The percentage of Blacks, Hispanics, and Native Americans in poverty is about three times that of Whites. Even Asian Americans, who have a higher average income than Whites, are more likely to live in families with incomes below the poverty line (O'Hare, 1992:37). Although most poor people are White, Blacks remain dispro-

FIGURE 11.4

Homeownership
Rates by Race and
Ethnicity of
Householder,
1994–2003

Sources: Betsy Leondar-
Wright, Meizhu Lui,
Gloribell Mota, Dedrick
Muhammad, and Mara
Voukydis, 2005. *State of
the Dream 2005:
Disowned in the Owner-
ship Society.* Boston:
United for a Fair
Economy, p. 11.
www.faireconomy.com.
Reprinted by
permission.

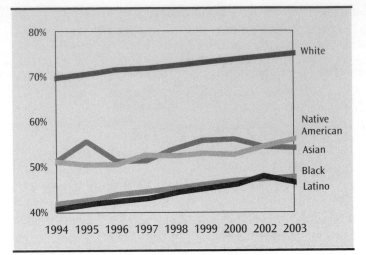

portionately poor, followed by Hispanics and then Whites. The 2001–2003 aver-
aged poverty rate was 8 percent, compared with 23 percent for Blacks and 21 percent for Hispanics (U.S. Bureau of the Census, 2004). (See Figure 11.5 for Family
Poverty Rates by Race.) In recent years, the poverty rate of Hispanics rose more rapidly than that of Whites or Blacks. However, poverty rates differ greatly among Hispanic groups. Puerto Rican and Mexican families are most likely to be poor, while
Cubans are least likely (del Pinal and Singer, 1997:39). Economic conditions in
some areas where Hispanics are concentrated account for the differences. Puerto
Ricans are concentrated in major cities of the eastern end of the Snow Belt, where
larger economic changes have affected unskilled workers (Aponte, 1991).

Many factors explain the difference in White and minority earnings. Racial-
ethnics are concentrated in the South and Southwest, where incomes are lower for
everyone. Another part of the explanation is the differing age structure of minorities.
They are younger, on average, than is the White population. A group with a higher
proportion of young people of working age will have a lower average earning level,
higher rates of unemployment, and lower rates of labor-force participation.

FIGURE 11.5

Family Poverty
Rates by Race,
1988–2003

Source: Betsy Leondar-
Wright, Meizhu Lui,
Gloribell Mota, Dedrick
Muhammad, and Mara
Voukydis, 2005. *State
of the Dream 2005:
Disowned in the
Ownership Society.*
Boston: United for a
Fair Economy, p. 10.
www.faireconomy.com.
Reprinted by
permission.

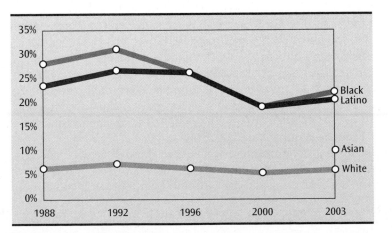

Looking at racial inequalities by age reveals another disturbing pattern. The degree of inequality increases after the teenage years. Racial disparities become greater in peak earning years. This suggests that another part of the explanation for racial inequalities in earnings lies in the lack of education and skill levels required to move out of poor-paying jobs. All of these explanations leave a substantial amount of inequality unexplained. Minorities at all levels of unemployment and education still earn less than do Whites as we see in Chapter 13. (See Table 11.1 for average earnings by race, sex, and Hispanic origin.)

Education

In 1954, the Supreme Court outlawed segregation in the schools. Yet the landmark *Brown* v. *Board of Education* ruling did not end segregation. In 2004, on the fiftieth anniversary of the historic ruling, U.S. schools were becoming increasingly segregated. "Minority" schools have limited access to important resources and African Americans and Latinos trail Whites in educational achievement.

Among young adults, Hispanics have the lowest educational attainment, while Whites and Asians have the highest. The 2004 high school graduation rates for Whites were 90 percent compared with 86 for Asian Americans, 80 percent for African Americans, and 58 percent for Hispanics (U.S. Bureau of the Census, 2005). This is a growing problem, since most new jobs in the new century will require education beyond high school (Pollard and O'Hare, 1999:30).

The minority education gap is the result of several factors, including language differences, different educational opportunities, and lack of family support for education. Yet many of the problems have less to do with minority students themselves and more to do with the failure of schools to retain minority students and pro-

TABLE 11.1

Average Earnings in 2002 by Educational Attainment, Sex, Race, and Hispanic Origin for All Workers, 18 Years and Over

Characteristic	Total	Not a High School Graduate	High School Graduate	Some College or Associate's Degree	Bachelor's Degree	Advanced Degree
Total	$36,308	$18,826	$27,280	$31,046	$51,194	$72,824
Men	$44,310	$22,091	$32,673	$38,377	$63,503	$90,761
Women	$27,271	$13,459	$21,141	$23,905	$37,909	$50,756
White alone	$37,376	$19,264	$28,145	$31,878	$52,479	$73,870
Non-Hispanic						
White alone	$39,220	$19,423	$28,756	$32,318	$53,185	$74,122
Black alone	$28,179	$16,516	$22,823	$27,626	$42,285	$59,944
Asian alone	$40,793	$16,746	$24,900	$27,340	$46,628	$72,852
Hispanic	$25,824	$18,981	$24,163	$27,757	$40,949	$67,679

Source: Nicole Stoops, 2004. "Educational Attainment in the United States: 2003." *Current Population Reports Series,* P20–550. U.S. Bureau of the Census. Washington, DC: U.S. Government Printing Office, (June) p. 7.

vide them with a marketable education. Segregation in schools is due largely to the residential segregation that exists throughout the country. Minority students attend schools with mostly minority students (Sidel, 1994:67). Black students are no longer the most segregated group. In today's public schools, Latino students are even more segregated (Tienda and Simonelli, 2001).

Several additional trends are creating problems for minority students. The general movement against increased taxes hurts public schools. Inner-city schools, where minorities are concentrated and which are already understaffed and underfinanced, face even greater financial pressures because of current reductions in federal programs.

There are large racial gaps in college enrollment. Of the total campus population in 2002, 81 percent were White, 12 percent were African American, and 12 percent were Latino (U.S. Department of Labor, 2003). Although many colleges actively recruit students of color, many factors contribute to low retention rates. Even when they reach college, students of color often confront a range of discriminatory barriers. Studies have consistently found that they are more alienated than White students and drop out more often than White students. Discrimination by Whites on and off campus is a recurring problem (Feagin, 2000:170).

All of these disparities translate into economic inequalities. Yet education alone is not the answer. Even with a college degree, African Americans and Latinos had far higher unemployment rates than their White counterparts. This is compounded by the fact that education does not pay equally. Minority membership, regardless of level of education, is underpaid compared with Whites of similar education. A highly educated White man still makes more money than anyone else. On average, a White man with a college degree earned about $65,500 in 2001. Similarly educated White women made 40 percent less, while Black and Hispanic men earned 30 percent less (Armas, 2003). (See Table 11.1 on the disparities in median income by race and education.)

Unemployment

African Americans and Latinos are more likely than Whites to be unemployed. For the last three decades, unemployment rates among Black workers have been twice that of White workers, with Latinos in between. Unemployment among Latinos is now almost as pervasive as among Blacks. In 2004, the unemployment rate for Latinos was 7 percent, compared with 10 percent for African Americans and 5.0 percent for Whites (U.S. Department of Labor, 2005). The unemployment rate among Black teens was 31 percent, for Latinos it was 20, and for Whites it was 15 percent (U.S. Department of Labor, 2005).

These government rates are misleading because they count as employed the almost 6 million people who work part-time because they cannot find full-time jobs, and they do not count as unemployed the discouraged former workers, numbering more than 1 million, who have given up their search for work.

Type of Employment

African Americans and Latinos have always been an important component of the U.S. labor force. However, their job prospects and the jobs they hold are different from those of other people in the United States. Not only are minorities twice as likely as Whites to be unemployed, they are more likely to work in low-skilled occupations and less likely to work in managerial or professional occupations. Black and Latino workers are more likely to be in jobs with pay too low to lift a family of four above the poverty line (Leondar-Wright et al., 2005:9). Sociological research shows that race is related to workplace recruitment, hiring, firing, and promotion. Seemingly neutral practices can advantage some groups and adversely affect others (American Sociological Association, 2003).

Although Black, Hispanic, and Native American minorities are in the least rewarding jobs, and many face discrimination in hiring and promotion, the occupational status of minorities improved slowly during the last decade. Between 1990 and 2004, the percentage of Blacks in management and professional occupations increased from 17 to 26 percent, while the percentage increased from 13 to 17 to percent for Hispanics (U.S. Department of Labor, 2005; Pollard and O'Hare, 1999:33). Despite these gains, however, a huge gap remains. As more minorities enter high-status work, they are confronting new forms of job discrimination in the form of "job ceilings" that separate them from executive suites and boardrooms (Higginbotham, 1994).

Economic restructuring of the U.S. economy is affecting minority employment patterns in communities across the country. The job crisis in minority communities is linked to globalization and the structural transformation of the economy (see Chapter 8). This transformation is eliminating jobs for unskilled, poorly educated workers. Research in New York City found that only 51 percent of Black men between the ages of 16 through 64 were employed from 2000 to 2003 (Muwakkil, 2004).

Because African Americans and Latinos established successful niches in civil service, they are also being replaced by government downsizing (American Sociological Association, 2003). The new economy will be increasingly made up of people of color. If they continue to be denied equal access to higher-paying jobs, the entire society will be at risk for poverty and other problems associated with economic inequality.

Health

The health of the U.S. population is distributed unevenly across race. Hispanics are the most likely to be without health coverage. Thirty-two percent of Hispanics, 19 percent of African Americans, 18 percent of Asian Americans, and 11 percent of Whites were not covered by private or government medical insurance in 2003 (U.S. Bureau of the Census, 2004). Hispanics born outside the United States were almost twice as likely to lack health insurance as their U.S.-born counterparts. Many are unfamiliar with the U.S. health care system, and a few are illegal immigrants who are afraid to seek medical assistance (del Pinal and Singer, 1997:37; Folbre and the Center for Popular Economics, 2000).

Racial discrimination affects health in other ways as well. **Environmental racism** is the disproportionate exposure of some racial groups to environmental toxic substances. Race is the strongest predictor of hazardous waste facilities in the country, even after adjustment for social class. Minorities receive lower quality health care than Whites even when their insurance and income are the same, due to racial prejudice and difference in the quality of health plans (Stolberg, 2002). On virtually every measure of health, African Americans and Latinos are disadvantaged, as revealed in the following selected facts:

- Compared to the general population, Blacks and Hispanics are less likely to have a consistent source of medical care and more likely to use emergency rooms as a primary source of care. Compared to Whites, Hispanics had a 700 percent higher rate of visits to community health centers, but a 35 percent lower rate of visits to physicians' offices. Compared to Whites, Blacks had a 550 percent higher rate of visits to community health centers, but a 48 percent lower rate of visits to physicians' offices (Forrest and Whelan, 2000).
- Compared to the general population, Blacks and Hispanics are less likely to have a consistent source of medical care and are more likely to use emergency rooms as a primary source of care. Compared to Whites, Hispanics had a 700 percent higher rate of visits to community health centers, but a 35 percent lower rate of visits to physicians offices. Compared to Whites, Blacks had a 550 percent higher rate of visits to community health centers, but a 40 percent lower rate of visits to physicians offices (Forrest and Whelan, 2000).
- Cancer is the leading cause of death for most racial minorities in the United States. Cancer hits African Americans particularly hard: the group is 23 percent more likely to die from all types of cancer than Whites (U.S. Department of Health and Human Services, 2004).
- Hispanics are almost twice as likely to die from diabetes as are Whites. American Indians have a rate of diabetes that is more than twice that for Whites (Office of Minority Health, 2005).
- White men live approximately seven years longer than Black men, and White women live about five years longer than Black women (Kochanek et al., 2001).
- Minority groups are overexposed to occupational respiratory hazards. Occupational lung disease is the number one work-related illness in the United States. African Americans are more likely than Whites to hold "dirty" and dangerous jobs such as in the asbestos, textile, coal, and silica-mining industries, each of which is associated with respiratory disease (American Lung Association State of the Air, 2001).
- Black babies are nearly twice as likely as White babies to die within their first year. Although the infant mortality rate for Hispanic infants is less than the rate for White infants, within the Puerto Rican subgroup, the rate of infant deaths from Sudden Infant Death Syndrome is 1.5 times higher than for Whites (U.S. Department of Health and Human Services, 2004).

Contemporary Trends and Issues in U.S. Racial and Ethnic Relations

Racial diversity presents a host of new social problems that reflects differences in group power and access to social resources. Three major trends reveal new forms of racial inequality: growing racial strife, the economic polarization of minorities, and a national shift in U.S. racial policies. These trends are occurring in a global context, closely associated with macro social forces at work around the world.

Growing Racial Strife

Together with racial impoverishment, the growing immigrant and minority presence is adding tensions in society. Here, and in countries around the world, racial diversity is marked by growing conflicts. Some cities are like racially divided societies where minorities seldom meet Whites as neighbors or as classmates in public schools (Harris and Bennett, 1995:158). Racial tensions often erupt in violence between Whites and minorities, and among minorities themselves, as individuals compete for a shrinking number of jobs and other opportunities. The 1992 Los Angeles riots exhibited rivalries between neighborhood groups and between neighborhoods in Los Angeles that erupted in violence.

Racial violence is often associated with uncertain economic conditions. Lack of jobs, housing, and other resources can add to fear and minority scapegoating on the part of Whites. In Florida and many parts of the West and Southwest, perceptions that Cubans, Mexicans, and other Hispanics are taking jobs from Anglos have touched off racial tensions.

Old-fashioned forms of bigotry and hate crimes are also fueled by misbeliefs about minorities (Blauner, 2001:191). For example, anti-Hispanic incidents increased steadily during the 1990s. The perception that Latinos are "foreign" or "un-American" often translates into hate-related activity. One effect of the increasing anti-immigrant sentiment in the nation is the surge in incidents of vigilantism—unauthorized attempts to enforce immigration laws by ordinary citizens. Some private citizens are increasingly taking the law into their own hands to stem the perceived "flood" of illegal immigrants in the country (National Council of La Raza, 1999). Certain forms of racial strife are on the rise.

More Racially Based Groups and Activities

The Southern Poverty Law Center (SPLC) documented 762 hate groups in forty-eight states and the District of Columbia in 2004, up from 751 the year before (SPLC, 2005). Hate groups include White supremacist groups with such diverse elements as the Ku Klux Klan, Neo-Confederate groups (those describing southern culture as fundamentally White), Nazi-identified parties, and skinheads. Many groups use the Internet to spread their literature to young people. As a result, more than half of all hate crimes are now committed by young people, ages fifteen to twenty-four. In addition to racist websites, cyber extremism flourishes on e-mail and in discussion groups and chat rooms (SPLC, 2001:47). Violence is the driving force of racist music, which is rapidly spreading around the world.

Native Americans Hit Hard by Violent Crime. Native Americans are far more likely to be victims of violent crimes than members of any other racial groups. Between 1992 and 2001, American Indians experienced violence at rates more than twice that of Blacks, two and a half times that of Whites, and four and a half times that of Asians (SPLC, 1999; U.S. Department of Justice, 2005).

Profiling and Maltreatment. Numerous reports testify to the widespread police practice of systematically stopping (and sometimes savagely beating) Black and Latino drivers. Some state troopers illegally target minority drivers. Racial profiling is the use of race and ethnicity as clues to criminality and potential terrorism. Racial profiling on the highways has become so prevalent that a term has emerged to explain it: "driving while Black" (Bonilla-Silva, 2003). Prior to the September 11 terrorist attacks, racial profiling was a state and local law enforcement practice that unfairly targeted Blacks, Native Americans, Asian Americans, and Latinos. Since September 11, Arab Americans, Muslims, and other Middle Easterners have been the targets of threats, gunshots, firebombs, and other forms of vigilante violence (Fahim, 2003). Fear of terrorism has provoked a rash of hate crimes and a national debate about the official use of profiling—that is, the use of race and ethnicity as clues to criminality and potential terrorism.

Campus Racial Tensions. Recent headlines about racism on college campuses have surprised many people because educational institutions are formally integrated. Yet, campus racism is widespread. From MIT to the University of California, Berkeley, and on campuses across the nation, racial attacks on Blacks, Hispanics, and Asians are revealing an extensive problem of intolerance. According to the U.S. Department of Education and watchdog and advocacy groups, every year, more than a half million college students are targets of bias-driven slurs or physical assaults. Every day, at least one hate crime occurs on a college campus and every minute, a college student somewhere sees or hears racist, sexist, homophobic, or otherwise biased words or images. Sixty-four percent of all campus hate crimes in 2003 were racially motivated (U.S. Department of Justice, 2004). These problems are not isolated or unusual events. Instead, they reflect what is occurring in the wider society (Feagin, 2000; Sidel, 1994).

Economic Polarization in U.S. Inner Cities

The notion of a troubled "underclass," locked in U.S. inner cities by a deficient culture, is commonly used to explain racial poverty. According to this reasoning, broken families and bad lifestyles prevent minorities from taking advantage of the opportunities created by antidiscrimination laws. However, like the older cultural-deficiency models we discussed earlier, this explanation is wrong on many counts. It relies too heavily on behavioral traits to explain poverty. It falls back on blaming the victim to explain patterns that are actually rooted in social structure. Economic and technological changes in society have removed jobs and other opportunities from inner-city residents. This is a better explanation of persistent and concentrated poverty among Blacks.

This explanation is detailed in two works by sociologist William J. Wilson. In his compelling book *The Truly Disadvantaged* (1987), he argues that the social problems of the inner city are due to transformations of the larger economy and to the class structure of ghetto neighborhoods. The movement of middle-class Black professionals from the inner city has left behind a concentration of the most disadvantaged segments of the Black urban population. In his more recent book *When Work Disappears* (1996), he shows how crime, family dissolution, and welfare are connected to the structural removal of work from the inner city.

Wilson (1987) examines the relationship between work and marriage, finding that men with higher incomes are more likely to be married than are men with lower incomes. He proposes that inner-city male joblessness encourages nonmarital child-bearing and undermines the foundation of Black families. Structural conditions require that many Black women leave their marriages or forego marriage altogether. Adaptations to structural conditions leave Black women disproportionately divorced and solely responsible for their children. The Black inner city is not destroying itself by its own culture; rather, it is being destroyed by economic forces.

Rising poverty rates among Latinos have led many policymakers and media analysts to conclude that Latinos have joined inner-city African Americans to form a hopeless "underclass." Although changes in the U.S. economy have also hit Latinos hard because of their low educational attainment and their labor market position, structural unemployment has a different effect on the many diverse Latino barrios across the nation (Moore and Pinderhughes, 1994). The loss of jobs in Rust Belt cities has left many Puerto Ricans living in a bleak ghetto economy. Mexicans living in the Southwest, where low-paying jobs remain, have not suffered the same degree of economic dislocation. Despite high levels of poverty, Latino communities do not conform to the conventional portrait of the underclass.

A structural analysis of concentrated poverty does not deny that inner cities are beset with a disproportionate share of social problems. As poverty is more concentrated in inner cities, crime and violence proliferate. The poor may adopt violence as survival strategies. This escalates violence even further (Massey, 1996). A structural analysis, however, focuses on social conditions, not immoral people. Vanishing jobs and many forms of unemployment are related to the worldwide realignment of work that accompanies corporate globalization. According to national Urban League president Hugh Price, "The manufacturing jobs that once enabled blue collar workers to purchase their own homes and occasional new cars have all but vanished from the inner city"; and while racism is still widespread, "the global realignment of work and wealth" is also a culprit (cited in Brecher, Costello, and Smith, 2000).

Racial Policies in the New Century

The 1960s civil rights movement legalized race-specific remedies to end racial bias. Government policies based on race overturned segregation laws, opened voting booths, created new job opportunities, and brought hopes of racial justice for people of color. As long as it appeared that conditions were improving, government policies to end racial justice remained in place.

But by the end of the 1980s, the United States had become a very different society from the one in which civil

Asian and Arab immigrants participate in a rally in conjunction with the National Day of Solidarity in front of the Immigration and Naturalization Services building, February 20, 2002, in New York City. The protesters were demanding an end to the racial profiling, detentions, and deportations that many immigrants have been subjected to since the September 11 attacks on New York City.

rights legislation was enacted. Economic restructuring brought new dislocations to both Whites and minorities. As racial minorities became an ever larger share of the U.S. population, racial anxieties flourished and grew more politicized. Many Whites began to feel uncomfortable with race-conscious policies in schools and the workplace. The social climate fostered an imaginary White disadvantage, said to be caused by affirmative action multiculturalism. Although there is no research evidence for White disadvantage, a powerful conservative movement is producing new debates about the fairness of racial policies and campaigns.

Just as the United States is becoming a multiracial society, we are witnessing a backlash against civil rights reforms. Overt prejudice has diminished, but new forms of racism support White privilege. The ironic view has emerged that we are now in a post-racial, color-blind world (Winant, 2001:1). Despite such claims about color-blindness, contemporary forms of racism continue in all arenas of public life. Higginbotham and Andersen (2005) tell us why race is a still a building block of society. "Race matters because it segregates our neighborhoods, our schools, our churches, and our relationships. Race matters because it is often a matter of heated political debate, and the dynamics of race lie at the heart of the systems of justice and social welfare" (7–8). The demise of the welfare state and the retreat from health care and other forms of social responsibility are important causes of racial inequality in the new century. Finally, international systems of dominance (global capitalism and geopolitical relations) are producing still more racial inequalities in the United States. For example, "model minority" and "illegal aliens" along with new racialized standards in the education and the workplace (e.g., Asian quotas) pit Asians and Latinos against Blacks (Allen and Chung, 2000:802).

Despite the new racial climate, the struggle against racism continues. Rich historical traditions of resistance and creative adaptations that exist today demonstrate the tremendous ingenuity and resourcefulness of people of color. Since the country was founded, antiracist activities have sought to end discrimination. Multiracial organizations composed of racial-ethnic *and* White activists continue to work at national and local levels to fight and eradicate racist beliefs and institutional racism.

1. Racial and ethnic stratification are basic features of U.S. society. They are also found throughout the world and are an important feature of globalization. Patterns of inequality are built into everyday social practices. They exclude people from full and equal participation in social institutions. Racial and ethnic stratification exist because they benefit certain segments of society.

2. The concept of race is a social invention. It is not biologically significant. Racial groups are set apart and singled out for unequal treatment.

3. An ethnic group is culturally distinct in race, religion, or national origin. The group has a distinctive culture. Some ethnic groups such as Jews, Poles, and Italians have distinguishing cultural characteristics that stem from religion and national origin. Because racial groups also have distinctive cultural characteristics, they are referred to as *racial-ethnics*.

4. Minority racial and ethnic groups are systematically disadvantaged by society's institutions. Both race and ethnicity are traditional bases for systems of inequality, although there are historical and contemporary differences in the societal placement of racial-ethnics and White ethnics in this society.

5. Racial-ethnic groups are socially subordinated and remain culturally distinct within U.S. society. African Americans, Latinos, Asian Americans, and Native Americans are constructed as both racially and culturally distinct. Each group has a distinctive culture, shares a common history, and has developed a common identity within a larger society that subordinates it.

6. Deficiency theories view minority-group members as unequal because they lack some important feature common among the majority. These deficiencies may be biological (such as low intelligence) or cultural (such as the culture of poverty).

7. Bias theories place the blame for inequality on the prejudiced attitudes of the dominant group. These theories, however, do not explain the discriminatory acts of the unprejudiced, which are aimed at preserving privilege.

8. Structural theories argue that inequality is the result of external constraints as opposed to internal cultural factors. There are four main features of institutional discrimination: (a) Forces of history shape present conditions; (b) discrimination can occur without conscious bigotry; (c) institutional discrimination is less visible than are individual acts of discrimination; and (d) discrimination is reinforced by the interrelationships among the institutions of society.

9. Civil rights legislation improved the status of some racial-ethnics, yet the overall position of Blacks and Latinos relative to Whites has not improved. Large gaps remain in work, earnings, and education. Global and economic transformations have contributed to the persistent poverty in U.S. urban centers.

10. The racial demography of the United States is changing dramatically. Immigration and high birth rates among minorities are making this a multiracial, multicultural society. These trends are also creating racial anxiety and racial conflict.

11. Public policy has shifted from race-conscious remedies to a color-blind climate that is dismantling historic civil rights reforms.

Key Terms

Majority group	Deficiency theories	Individual racism
Minority group	Bias theories	Institutional racism
Racial formation	Structural discrimination	Environmental racism
Racial-ethnic groups	theories	

Study Questions

1. What constitutes a minority group?
2. What is the key difference between deficiency theories and bias theories as they explain the existence of minorities?
3. Order theories argue that minorities should eventually assimilate. What does this mean, and why does the conflict perspective disagree with this assumption?
4. How do everyday social arrangements work to keep minorities subordinate?
5. What is meant by the changing demography of race? What are the anticipated consequences of this trend for schools, employment, incidents of violence, and life chances?
6. Is the persistent poverty of minorities a consequence of culture or structure?

For Further Reading

Bob Blauner, *Still the Big News, Racial Oppression in America* (Philadelphia: Temple University Press, 2001).

Eduardo Bonilla-Silva, *Racism without Racists: Color Blind Racism and the Persistence of Racial Inequality in the United States* (New York: Rowman and Littlefield Publishers, Inc., 2003).

Joe R. Feagin, *Racist America* (New York: Routledge, 2000).

Elizabeth Higginbotham and Margaret L. Andersen (eds.), *Race and Ethnicity in Society: The Changing Landscape* (Thompson Wadsworth, 2005).

Michael Omi and Howard Winant, *Racial Formation in the United States*, 2nd ed. (New York: Routledge, 1994).

Alejandro Portes and Ruben G. Rumbaut (eds.), *Immigrant America*, 2nd ed. (Berkeley: University of California Press, 1996).

Clara E. Rodriguez, *Changing Race: Latinos, The Census, and the History of Ethnicity in the United States* (New York: New York University Press, 2000).

Marcelo M. Suarez-Orozco and Mariela M. Paez (eds.), *Latinos Remaking America* (Berkeley: University of California Press, 2002).

Ronald Takaki, *A Different Mirror: A History of Multicultural America* (Boston: Little, Brown, 1993).

Russell Thornton, *Studying Native America: Prospects and Problems* (Madison: University of Wisconsin Press, 1998).

Howard Winant, *The World Is a Ghetto* (New York: Basic Books, 2002).

Web Resources

http://www.census.gov/pubinfo/www/hotlinks.html

This is the U.S. Census Bureau site that contains the most recent census data collected on racial-ethnic groups in the United States.

http://www.usanetwork.com/functions/nohate/erasehate.html

Erase the Hate is affiliated with USA Network and is "dedicated to combating hate and racism while promoting respect and understanding."

http://www.abacon.com/sociology/soclinks/race.html

This site, by Allyn and Bacon, offers sociology links to race, ethnicity, and inequality.

http://www.webcom.com/~intvoice/

Interracial Voice is "an independent, information-oriented, networking newsjournal, serving the mixed-race/interracial community in cyberspace."

http://www.nativeweb.org/

The Native Web offers information about and resources for indigenous cultures around the world.

http://www.hispaniconline.com/

Hispanic Online has a mission "to offer more news, resources, and entertainment options that are relevant to Latinos than any other site."

http://www.asianamerican.net/index.html

Asian American Net "is the first and the only web site whose mission is to serve all Asian American communities and to promote and strengthen cultural, educational, and commercial ties between Asia and North America." The site is for people looking to learn more about Asia and also for "Asian American communities to remind them of their national and cultural origins they can be proud of."

http://www.omhrc.gov/

The Office of Minority Health looks to improve the health of racial and ethnic minorities and to eliminate the racial disparities in health.

http://afroamhistory.about.com/

This site contains information on African American history. Information on influential African Americans and details of important historical events related to African Americans can be found here.

http://usinfo.state.gov/usa/race/hate/homepage.htm

This site has links to and information about hate crimes.

http://www.ctwo.org/

Center for Third World Organizing is "a racial justice organization dedicated to building a social justice movement led by people of color."

http://www.arc.org/

Applied Research Center is "a public policy, educational and research institute whose work emphasizes issues of race and social change."

Gender Inequality

Every society treats women and men differently. Today, there is no nation where women and men are equals. Worldwide, women perform an estimated 60 percent of the work, yet they earn only 10 percent of the income and own only 10 percent of the land. Two-thirds of the world's illiterate are women. Despite massive political changes and economic progress in countries throughout the world, women continue to be the victims of abuse and discrimination. Even where women have made important strides in politics and the professions, women's overall progress remains uneven.

This chapter examines the unequal placement of women and men. We show gender inequality is built into the larger social world we inhabit. From the macro level of the global economy, through the institutions of society, to interpersonal relations, gender is the basis for dividing labor, assigning roles, and allocating social rewards. Until recently, this kind of differentiation seemed natural. However, new research shows that gender is not natural at all. Instead, "women" and "men" are social creations. To emphasize this point, sociologists distinguish between *sex* and *gender*. **Sex** refers to the biological differences between females and males. **Gender** refers to the social and cultural meanings attached to femininity and masculinity. This distinction is a central organizing principle of social life. (See the panel titled "Diversity: Is a Gender-Free World Possible?")

Gender is not only about women. Men often think of themselves as "genderless," as if gender did not matter in the daily experience of their lives. Yet, from birth through old age, men's worlds are deeply **gendered** (Kimmel and Messner, 2004). In the big picture, gender divisions make women and men unequal. Still, we cannot understand the gender system, nor women's and men's experiences, by looking at gender alone; gender is linked with other power systems such as race, class, and sexual orientation. These interconnected inequalities mean that different groups of men exhibit varying degrees of power, while different groups of women exhibit varying levels of inequality. Nevertheless, the gender system denies both women and men the full range of human and social possibilities. This chapter examines gender stratification in U.S. society at both structural and interpersonal levels of organization. Taking a **feminist approach** (one in support of women's equality), the theme of this chapter is that social conditions are responsible for women's inequality.

Is a Gender-Free World Possible?

What can we do to solve the problems produced by gender inequality? Many argue that we must build a gender-free world, that is, a world in which society does not define and organize all people on the basis of gender categories. The Freedom from Gender Society, founded in 1988, is an educational and social organization dedicated to promoting gender research and education, supporting the struggles of gender-free people for acceptance and understanding, and building a world in which the freedoms of belief and self-definition are respected.

The Freedom from Gender Society provides answers to the following commonly asked questions about dismantling gender.

What is a gender-free person?

A gender-free person is a person who does not believe in gender categories because

- gender categories do not reflect the objective reality of human diversity, such as the spectrum of human genotypes, anatomies, and personalities; and,
- gender categories are unrescuably loaded with stereotypes.

Isn't a gender-free person still a man or a woman?

Since the socially constructed categories "man" and "woman" do not reflect the reality of human diversity

and are loaded with stereotypes, gender-free persons do not believe in and thus do not define their identity in terms of them.

Does a gender-free person suffer from gender confusion?

A gender-free person cannot be gender confused because a gender-free person does not believe in the categories that are needed to produce such confusion.

What pronoun is appropriate for a gender-free person?

Most sentences can be rephrased to avoid the use of genderized pronouns such as *he*, *she*, and *s/he*. In those that can't, the simplest solution is to use the person's name, or *they*.

Which locker room or restroom does a gender-free person use?

Affirming a gender-free identity and respecting equal, rather than sexually discriminatory, standards of privacy, a gender-free person claims the right to use any locker room or restroom.

Source: Adapted from "What Is a Gender-Free Person?" n.d. The Freedom from Gender Society, P.O. Box 1551, Brookline, MA 02446. Reprinted by permission.

Women and Men Are Differentiated and Ranked

Gender stratification refers to the ranking of the sexes in such a way that women are unequal in resources, power, and opportunities. Although there is worldwide variation in women's and men's roles, gender inequality exists in most parts of the world. Every society has certain ideas about what women and men should be like as well as ways of producing people who are much like these expectations.

Scientists have competing explanations for gender differences. Biological models argue that innate biological differences between men and women program different social behaviors. Anthropological models look at masculinity and femininity cross-culturally, stressing the variations in women's and men's roles. Sociologists treat gender as a feature of social structure.

Is Gender Biological or Social?

We know that there are biological differences between the two sexes. The key question is whether these "natural" differences in the sexes contribute to gender inequality. Do biological differences explain male domination? To answer this question, let us first review the evidence for each position.

Biological Bases for Gender Roles. Males and females are different from the moment of conception. Chromosomal and hormonal differences make females and males physically different. Hormonal differences in the sexes are also significant. The male hormones (androgens) and female hormones (estrogens) direct the process of sex differentiation from about six weeks after conception throughout life. They make males taller, heavier, and more muscular. At puberty, they trigger the production of secondary sexual characteristics. In males, these include body and facial hair, a deeper voice, broader shoulders, and a muscular body. In females, puberty brings pubic hair, menstruation, the ability to lactate, prominent breasts, and relatively broad hips. Actually, males and females have both sets of hormones. The relative proportion of androgens and estrogens gives a person masculine or feminine physical traits.

These hormonal differences may explain in part why males tend to be more active, aggressive, and dominant than females. However, there are only slight differences in the level of hormones between girls and boys in childhood. Yet, researchers find differences in aggression between young girls and boys (Fausto-Sterling, 1992).

Biological differences that do exist between women and men are only averages. They are often influenced by other factors. For example, although men are on the average larger than women, body size is influenced by diet and physical activity, which in turn may be influenced by culture, class, and race. The all-or-none categorizing of gender traits is misleading because there is considerable overlap in the distribution of traits possessed by women and men. Although most men are stronger than most women, some men are weaker than some women, and vice versa. And although males are on the average more aggressive than females, greater difference may be found among males than among males and females (Basow, 1996:81). Furthermore, gender is constantly changing. Femininity and masculinity are not uniformly shaped from genetic makeup. Instead, they are modeled differently (1) from one culture to another, (2) within any one culture over time, (3) over the course of all men's and women's lives, and (4) between and among different groups of women and men, depending on class, race, ethnicity, and sexuality (Kimmel, 1992:166).

The Social Bases for Gender Roles. Every society transforms biological females and males into socially interacting women and men. Cross-cultural evidence shows a wide variation of behaviors for the sexes. Table 12.1 provides some interesting cross-cultural data from 224 societies on the division of labor by sex. This table shows that for the majority of activities, societies are not uniform in their gendered division of labor. Even activities requiring strength, presumably a male trait, are not strictly apportioned to men. In fact, activities such as burden bearing and water carrying are done by females more than by males. Even an activity such as house building is not exclusively male. Although there is a wide variety in the social roles assigned to women and men, their roles seldom vary "randomly" (O'Kelly, 1980:41). In most societies of the world, domestic and family settings are women's worlds, while public and political settings are men's worlds.

TABLE 12.1

Gender Allocation in Selected Technological Activities in 224 Societies

Activity	Number of Societies in Which the Activity Is Performed by:					
	Males Exclusively	Males Usually	Both Sexes Equally	Females Usually	Females Exclusively	Percent Male
Smelting of ores	37	0	0	0	0	100.0
Hunting	139	5	0	0	0	99.3
Boat building	84	3	3	0	1	96.6
Mining and quarrying	31	1	2	0	1	93.7
Land clearing	95	34	6	3	1	90.5
Fishing	83	45	8	5	2	86.7
Herding	54	24	14	3	3	82.4
House building	105	30	14	9	20	77.4
Generation of fire	40	6	16	4	20	62.3
Preparation of skins	39	4	2	5	31	54.6
Crop planting	27	35	33	26	20	54.4
Manufacture of leather products	35	3	2	5	29	53.2
Crop tending	22	23	24	30	32	44.6
Milking	15	2	8	2	21	43.8
Carrying	18	12	46	34	36	39.3
Loom weaving	24	0	6	8	50	32.5
Fuel gathering	25	12	12	23	94	27.2
Manufacture of clothing	16	4	11	13	78	22.4
Pottery making	14	5	6	6	74	21.1
Dairy production	4	0	0	0	24	14.3
Cooking	0	2	2	63	117	8.3
Preparation of vegetables	3	1	4	21	145	5.7

Source: Adapted from George P. Murdock and Caterina Provost, 1973. "Factors in the Division of Labor by Sex. A Cross-Cultural Analysis." *Ethnology* 12 (April):207. Reprinted by permission.

Gender and Power

Gender differences are social creations that are embedded in society. The term **gendered institutions** means that entire institutions are patterned by gender (Acker, 1992; Lorber, 2005). Everywhere we look—the global economy, politics, religion, education, and family life—men are in power. But men are not uniformly dominant. Some men have great power over other men. In fact, most men do not feel powerful; most feel powerless, trapped in stifling old roles and unable to implement the changes in their lives that they want (Kimmel, 1992:171). Nevertheless, socially defined differences between women and men legitimate **male dominance**, which refers to the beliefs and placement that value men over women and that institutionalize male control of socially valued resources. *Patriarchy* is the term used for forms of social organization in which men are dominant over women.

Gender inequality is tied to other inequalities such as race, class, and sexuality to sort women and men differently. These inequalities also work together to produce differences *among women* and differences *among men*. Some women derive benefits from their race and their class while they are simultaneously restricted by gender. Such women are subordinated by patriarchy, yet race and class intersect to create for them privileged opportunities and ways of living (Baca Zinn, Hondagneu-Sotelo, and Messner, 2005). Men are encouraged to behave in "masculine" fashion to prove that they are not gay (Connell, 1992). In defining masculinity as the negation of homosexuality, **compulsory heterosexuality** is an important component of the gender system. Compulsory heterosexuality imposes negative sanctions on those who are homosexual or bisexual. This system of sexuality shapes the gender order by discouraging attachment with members of the same sex. This enforces the dichotomy of "opposite" sexes. *Sexuality* is also a form of inequality in its own right because it systematically grants privileges to those in heterosexual relationships. Like race, class, and gender, sexual identities are socially constructed categories. **Sexuality** is a way of organizing the social world based on sexual identity and a key linking process in the matrix of domination structured along the lines of race, class, and gender (Messner, 1996:223).

Gender scholars have debated the question of universal male dominance, asking whether it is universal, found in all societies across time and space. Many scholars once claimed that all societies exhibit some forms of patriarchy in marriage and family forms, in division of labor, and in society at large (Ortner, 1974; Rosaldo, 1974). Other scholars have challenged universal patriarchy with cases that serve as counterexamples (Shapiro, Judith, 1981). Current thought follows the latter course. Sexual differentiation, it seems, is found in all societies, but it does not always indicate low female status (Rogers, 1978). Male dominance is not homogeneous. Instead, it varies from society to society.

We should keep in mind that although gender stratification makes women subordinate to men, they are not simply the passive victims of patriarchy. Like other oppressed groups, women find ways to resist domination. Through personal and political struggles, they often change the structures that subordinate them.

Gender Stratification from the Order and Conflict Perspectives

The Order Perspective

From the order perspective, biology, history, and society's needs combine to separate men and women into distinctive gender roles. Biologically, men are stronger, while women bear and nurse children. As a result, men fill the "instrumental" roles in society, while women fill the "expressive" roles. According to this view, role division is "functional" or beneficial for society.

"We'll settle this man to man. I'm calling your husband."

The need for women to nurse their infants and stay near home meant that for most of human history, they have done the domestic work, while men were free to hunt and leave the village for extended periods. Thus, a whole set of customs supporting men as the providers and women as the nurturers established the norms for future generations.

Although modern technology has freed women from the need to stay at home and has allowed them to work at jobs formerly requiring great strength, order theorists believe that distinct and separate roles are good for society. Clear-cut gender roles promote stable institutions and an efficient system in which girls and boys are socialized to take their places in society.

Talcott Parsons, a major order theorist, argued in the 1950s that with industrialization, the family and the role of women as nurturers and caretakers was more important than ever. The husband in the competitive world outside the home needs a place of affection. As women take on the roles of providing affection and emotional support within the family, men perform instrumental roles outside the family that provide economic support. Parsons argued that not only is this division of labor practical, but it is also necessary because it assures that the important societal tasks are accomplished (Parsons and Bales, 1955:3–9).

The Conflict Perspective

A different view of gender emerges from the conflict perspective. Conflict theorists are critical of the order model because it neglects what is most important about gender roles—that they are unequal in resources, power, and opportunities. According to the conflict view, gender roles are not neutral ways of meeting societies' needs but are part of the larger system of power and domination.

There are several conflict explanations for gender inequality. Most of them focus on the divisions of labor and power between women and men, and the different values placed on their work. This idea originated in the work of Friedrich Engles and Karl Marx. They wrote that industrialism and the shift to a capitalist economy widened the gap between the power and value of men and women. As production moved out of the home, the gendered division of labor left men with the greater share of economic and other forms of power (Chafetz, 1997; Sapiro, 1999:67).

Most conflict theories explain gender stratification as an outcome of how women and men are tied to the economic structure of society (Nielson, 1990:215). These theories say that women's economic role in society is a primary determinant of their overall status (Dunn, 1996:60). The division between domestic and public spheres of activity is constraining to women and advantageous to men. Women's reproductive roles and their responsibilities for domestic labor limit their association with the resources that are highly valued (Rosaldo, 1980). Men are freed from these responsibilities. Their economic obligations in the public sphere assure them control of highly valued resources and give rise to male privilege.

In capitalist societies the domestic-public split is even more significant, because highly valued goods and services are exchanged in the public, not the domestic, sphere. Women's domestic labor, although important for survival, ranks low in prestige and power because it does not produce exchangeable commodities (Sacks, Karen, 1974). Because of the connections between the class relations of production (capitalism) and the hierarchical gender relations of its society (patriarchy) (Eisenstein, 1979), the United States is a capitalist patriarchy, where male supremacy keeps women in subordinate roles at work and in the home.

The Implications of the Order and Conflict Perspectives

A point should be made about the implications of the conflict and order perspectives. Each position, with its emphasis on different factors, calls for a different approach to the study of gender. One consequence of the focus on gender roles by the order model has been to treat gender inequality as a problem of roles. Outmoded masculine and feminine roles are thought to be responsible for keeping women from achieving their full potential. This interpretation ignores the ways in which gender roles are rooted in power relations.

The difference between the order and conflict models lies in whether the individual or the society is the primary unit of analysis. The *gender-roles* approach emphasizes traits that individuals acquire during the course of socialization, such as independent or dependent behaviors and ways of relating. The **gender structure** approach emphasizes factors that are external to individuals, such as the social structures and social interactions that reward women and men differently. These approaches differ in how they view the sexes, in how they explain the causes and effects of sexism, and in the solutions they suggest for ending inequality. Understanding sexism requires both the individual and the structural approaches. Though gender roles are learned by individuals and produce differences in the personalities, behaviors, and motivations of women and men, gender stratification essentially is maintained by societal forces. This chapter places primary emphasis on social structure as the cause of inequality.

Learning Gender

The most complex, demanding, and all-involving role that a member of society must learn to play is that of female or male. "Casting" for one's gender role takes place immediately at birth, after a quick biological inspection; and the role of "female" or "male" is assigned. It is an assignment that will last one's entire lifetime and affect virtually everything one ever does. A large part of the next twenty years or so will be spent gradually learning and perfecting one's assigned role (David and Brannon, 1980:117).

Sociologists use the term *gender socialization* to describe how we learn gender. Gender socialization takes place throughout life. From infancy through early childhood and beyond, children learn what is expected of boys and girls, and they learn to behave according to those expectations.

The traits associated with traditional gender roles are those valued by the dominant society. Keep in mind that the gender is not the same in all classes and races. However, most research on gender socialization reflects the experience of White, middle-class people—those who are most often the research subjects of these studies. How gender is learned depends on a variety of social conditions affecting the socialization practices of girls and boys. Still, society molds boys and girls along different lines.

Children at Home

Girls and boys are perceived and treated differently from the moment of birth. Parents and "congratulations" greeting cards describe newborn daughters as "sweet," and "soft," whereas boys are immediately described as "strong," and "hardy." Cards sent to parents depict ribbons, hearts, and flowers for girls, but mobiles, sports equipment, and vehicles for boys. The most striking difference in cards, however, is that expressions of happiness or joy are more often found on cards for boys. People, in a sense, expect parents to be happier about the birth of a boy than about the birth of a girl. Newborn greeting cards thus project a very early gender scheme that introduces two "classes" of babies: one decorative, the other physically active and bringing greater joy (Valian, 1998:19–20).

Children learn at a very early age what it means to be a boy or a girl in our society. One of the strongest influences on gender role development in children occurs within the family setting, with parents passing on, both overtly and covertly, their own beliefs about gender (Witt, 1997:254). From the time their children are babies, parents treat sons and daughters differently, dressing infants in gender-specific colors, giving them gender-differentiated toys, and expecting different behavior from boys and girls (Thorne, 1993; Witt, 1997). While both mothers and fathers contribute to the gender stereotyping of their children, fathers have been found to reinforce gender stereotyping more often than mothers (Campenni, 1999; Idle, Wood, and Desmarias, 1993; Valian, 1998; Witt, 1997).

In addition to the parents' active role in reinforcing society's gender demands, a subtler message is emitted from picture books for preschool children. A classic sociological study of eighteen award-winning children's books conducted over thirty years ago found the following characteristics (Weitzman et al., 1972):

- Females were virtually invisible. The ratio of male pictures to female pictures was 11:1. The ratio of male to female animals was 95:1.
- The activities of boys and girls varied greatly. Boys were active in outdoor activities, while girls were passive and most often found indoors. The activity of the girls typically was that of some service for boys.
- Adult men and women (role models) were very different. Men led, women followed. Females were passive and males active. Not one woman in these books had a job or profession; they were always mothers and wives.

We have seen improvements in how girls and women are portrayed. Females are no longer invisible; they are as likely as males to be included in the books, and they have roles beyond their family roles. In many respects, however, gendered messages in children's books still exist (Crabb and Bielawski, 1994). An update of the classic Weitzman study found that while the proportion of female characters as portrayed as dependent and submissive, male characters were commonly portrayed as being independent and creative (Oskamp, Kaufman, and Wolterbeek, 1996). A subsequent study, which focused on the representation of gender and physical activity level in award-winning books from 1949 through 1999, found that female characters are much less likely to be depicted in active roles than male characters, and that this depiction has not changed significantly over this vast time period (Nilges and Spencer, 2002).

Gendered socialization is found even where gender roles are becoming more flexible or androgynous. **Androgyny** refers to the integration of traditional feminine and masculine characteristics in the same individual. Are girls more androgynous than boys? If so, what explains the difference? And what difference does androgyny make in an individual's overall well-being? Research finds that fathers who display the most traditional attitudes about gender transmit their ideas onto their sons more so than onto their daughters, whereas mothers who tend to have more liberal attitudes do not transmit their attitudes onto their daughters more than their sons. The consequence of this is that "when the sons establish their own families, they will be more likely than the daughters to transmit traditional attitudes to their own sons" (Kulik, 2002:450. Other research finds that while adolescent girls tend to be more supportive of egalitarian gender roles than their parents (especially their fathers), adolescent boys follow their fathers' resistance to changes in traditional male roles. Therefore, it is predictable that males would be less likely than females to develop androgynous characteristics (Burt and Scott, 2002).

Gender identities affect individuals, well-being in various ways. For example

Studies have shown that children construct gender in their daily lives.

Witt (1997) found that parents who foster androgynous attitudes and behaviors in their children ultimately cause their girls and boys to have high self-esteem and self-worth. Androgynous-minded individuals appear to manage stress well and practice good health (Gianakos, 2002; Shifren and Bauserman, 1996, cited in Edwards and Hamilton, 2004), and as college students report having better relationships with their parents (Guastello and Guastello, 2003:664).

Children at Play

Children teach each other to behave according to cultural expectations. Same-sex peers exert a strong influence on how gender is learned. In a classic study of children's play groups, Janet Lever (1976) discovered how children's play groups stress particular social skills and capabilities for boys and others for girls. Her research among fifth graders, most of whom were White and middle class, found that boys, more than girls: (1) played outdoors, (2) played in larger groups, (3) played in age-heterogeneous groups, (4) were less likely to play in games dominated by the opposite sex, (5) played more competitive games, and (6) played in games that lasted longer.

Barrie Thorne's (1993) study of gender play in multiracial school settings found that boys control more space, more often violate girls' activities, and treat girls as contaminating. According to Thorne, these common ritualized interactions reflect larger structures of male dominance. In reality, the fun and games of everyday schoolchildren are *power play*, a complex social process involving both gender separation and togetherness. Children's power play changes with age, ethnicity, race, class, and social context. In her analysis of how children themselves construct gender in their daily play, Thorne (1993) shifts the focus from individuals to *social relations*:

> The social construction of gender is an active and ongoing process. . . . Gender categories, gender identities, gender divisions, gender-based groups, gender meanings—all are produced actively and collaboratively, in everyday life. When kids maneuver to form same-gender groups on the playground or organize a kickball game as "boys-against-the-girls," they produce a sense of gender as dichotomy and opposition. And when girls and boys work cooperatively on a classroom project, they actively undermine a sense of gender as opposition. This emphasis on action and activity, and on everyday social interactions that are sometimes contradictory, provides an antidote to the view of children as passively socialized. Gender is not something one passively "is" or "has." (Thorne, 1993:4–5)

New research on fourth-grade children in schoolyards supports Thorne's conclusions about gendered interaction in schoolyards. Boyle and her colleagues (Boyle, Marshall, and Robeson, 2003), found a great deal of intra gender variation in the schoolyard with girls engaging in many different activities. They also found that boys were more easily accepted into play with girls than was the case when girls tried to play with a group of boys, and that boys tend to use more space in the schoolyard and are more likely to violate girls' space and games than the reverse.

Toys play a major part in gender socialization. Toys entertain children; they also teach particular skills and encourage them to explore a variety of roles they may one day occupy as adults. Today, most toys for sale are gender-linked. Toys for boys tend to encourage exploration, manipulation, invention, construction, competition, and aggression. In contrast, girls' toys typically rate high on manipulability, creativity, nurturance, and attractiveness. Playing with gendered toys may be related to the development of differential cognitive skills and social skills in girls and boys (Renzetti and Curran, 2003:89–92).

As noted in the previous section, parents encourage their sons and daughters to play with gendered toys, including dolls and housekeeping equipment for girls and trucks and sporting equipment for boys. This is reinforced by the resurgence of gender-specific toy marketing. Some Toys R Us outlets have inaugurated separate "Boys World" and "Girls World" sections (Bannon, 2000:7D). The boys' section of toy stores are filled with cars, weapons, and action figures, and since the 1980s, toys that depict men as machines have become popular (Varney, 2002:153). At least one chain of stores, Zany Brainy, which has 104 stores in 26 states, purposefully does not divide the toys into gendered sections. The company only sells nonviolent, nonsexist toys, and therefore does not sell Barbies or G. I. Joe figures (Vascenda, 2000:15–16).

In a study of parents and children in a day care setting, children eagerly accepted most of the toys presented to them by their parents and discarded other available toys in favor of their parents' choices (Idle et al., 1993). When parents discouraged sons from playing with cross-gender toys, their sons learned and adopted this behavior. Campenni (1999) found that adults were most likely to choose gender-specific toys for their children. Toys that adults deemed most appropriate for girls included items pertaining to domestic tasks (such as a vacuum cleaner or kitchen center), child rearing (dollhouse, cradle, stroller), or beauty enhancement (makeup kits, jewelry items). Toys rated "appropriate" for boys included sports gear, male action figures, building items, plastic bugs, and attire for traditional male occupations. Like other research, the Campenni study found that girls are often involved in cross-gender or neutral toy behavior. While girls are often encouraged by both parents to branch out and play with neutral toys some of the time, boys tend not to be given this same encouragement (Campenni, 1999). While we may be seeing some breakdown of traditional play patterns and socialization of girls, the same does not appear true for boys. Studies have also found that messages transmitted to children from advertisements affect their toy use and that the effects are different for boys and girls. Research finds that the messages in commercials have stronger effects on boys than girls (Pike and Jennings, 2005).

Although girls are now encouraged to engage in activities such as playing video games, traditional gender stereotypes still underlie this pastime. A popular video game among girls today is the "Barbie Fashion Designer" game, which made its debut in 1996 (Hafner, 1998). Subsequently, Mattel has produced twenty-nine more "girl games," each carrying Barbie's name. Other companies are following suit with makeover and jewelry software. Feminine toys are certainly not out—in fact, these pink-and-purple-gendered games are doing quite well with little girls all over the world.

Dichotomous gender experiences may be more characteristic among White, middle-class children than among children of other races. An important study on Black adolescent girls by Joyce Ladner (1971) has shown that Black girls develop in a more independent fashion. Other research has also found that among African Americans, both girls and boys are expected to be nurturant and expressive emotionally as well as independent, confident, and assertive (McAdoo, 1988; Stack, 1990). Recent studies examining whether or not the socialization of Black children is more gender-neutral than that in other groups is inconsistent. Most scholars now say there is too much variation in any group to make generalizations (Hill and Sprague, 1999; Smith, 2001).

Formal Education

In 1972, Congress outlawed sex discrimination in public schools through Title IX of the Educational Amendments Act. More than three decades later, girls and boys in the United States are still not receiving the same education. Major reports by the American Association of University Women (AAUW, 1992; 1999) offer compelling evidence that twenty years after the passage of Title IX, discrimination remains pervasive. Schools shortchange girls in every dimension of education. This contradicts a popular view of school as a place in which boys are victims and girls rule. But the idea that girls are "ahead" in school is simply wrong (Sadker, 2002). Let us examine the following areas: course offerings, textbooks, teacher-student interactions, sports, female role models, and counseling.

Curriculum. Schools are charged with the responsibility of equipping students to study subjects (for example, reading, writing, mathematics, and history) known collectively as the formal curriculum. But schools also teach students particular social, political, and economic values that constitute the so-called hidden curriculum operating alongside the more formal one. Both formal and informal curricula are powerful shapers of gender (Renzetti and Curran, 2003:109).

The patterns of courses that high school girls enroll in are increasingly similar to those of boys. Still, there are noticeable gaps. "Female enrollment in science and mathematics courses increased dramatically in recent years. Girls are more likely to take biology and chemistry as well as trigonometry and algebra II. However boys still dominate physics, calculus, and more advanced courses, and boys are more likely to take all three core science courses—biology, chemistry, and physics" (Sadker, 2002:238)

Although girls on the average receive higher grades in high school than boys, they tend to score lower on some standardized tests, which are particularly important because such test scores are used to make decisions on the awarding of scholarships and admissions. Schools ignore topics that matter in students' lives. The "evaded curriculum" is a term coined in the AAUW Report to refer to matters central to students' lives that are touched on only briefly, if at all, in most schools. Students receive inadequate education on sexuality, teen pregnancy, the AIDS crisis, and the increase of sexually transmitted diseases among adolescents. According to the AAUW Report, gender bias also affects males. Three out of four boys currently report that they were the targets to sexual harassment in schools—usually of taunts challenging their masculinity. In addition, while girls receive lower test grades, boys often receive lower overall course grades.

Textbooks. The content of textbooks transmits messages to readers about society, about children, and about what adults are supposed to do. For this reason, individuals and groups concerned about gender bias in schools have looked carefully at how males and females are portrayed in textbooks assigned to students. Their findings provide a consistent message: Textbooks commonly used in U.S. schools are both overtly and covertly sexist. Sexism has become a recent concern of publishers, and a number have created guidelines for creating inclusive images in educational materials.

No doubt these efforts have produced better textbooks. Reading lists are more inclusive and textbooks are more balanced then they used to be. But notable disparities still exist. Girls, for instance, tend to be in needy positions while males are more likely to be portrayed as offering help. Furthermore, girls are often pictured less often, but, if included, they typically maintain supportive rather than lead roles in the stories or pictures. Also, girls are more likely to be the spectators rather than the participants in textbook pictures (Bauer, 2000:23). "Males are more likely to be discussed in the context of their occupational roles, whereas when females are discussed, it is their personality characteristics that get the most attention" (Renzetti and Curran, 2003:109).

Teacher-Student Interactions. Even when girls and boys are in the same classrooms, boys are given preferential treatment. Girls receive less attention and different types of attention from classroom teachers.

Teachers are now being advised to encourage cooperative cross-sex learning, to monitor their own (teacher) behavior, to be sure that they reward male and female students equally, and actively familiarize students with gender-atypical roles by assigning them specific duties as leaders, recording secretary, and so on (Lockheed, 1985, cited in Giele, 1988).

Despite the fact that many teachers are trying to interact with their students in nongendered ways, they nonetheless continue to do so. In her study of third-grade classes, Garrahy (2001) found that while the teachers were claiming to be gender-neutral, they voiced beliefs about gendered differences among students and interacted with their students in gendered ways. Spencer and Toleman (2003), found that teachers spent more time with the male students when they were working independently and in small groups; perhaps most troubling, the students normalized and naturalized these gendered differences. Unfortunately, despite the increasing awareness of gender inequality within schools, new teachers are not adequately being taught about gender equity issues.

Sports. Sports in U.S. high schools and colleges have historically been almost exclusively a male preserve (this section is dependent on Eitzen and Sage, 2003). The truth of this observation is evident if one compares by sex the number of participants, facilities, the support of school administrations, and financial support.

Such disparities have been based on the traditional assumptions that competitive sport is basically a masculine activity and that the proper roles of girls and women are as spectators and cheerleaders. What is the impact on a society that encourages its boys and young men to participate in sports while expecting its girls and young women to be spectators and cheerleaders? Sports reinforce societal expectations

Interest in women's sports is increasing.

for males and females. Males are to be dominant and aggressive—the doers—while females are expected to be passive supporters of men, attaining status through the efforts of their menfolk.

An important consequence of this traditional view is that approximately one-half of the population was denied access to all that sport has to offer (physical conditioning, enjoyment, teamwork, goal attainment, ego enhancement, social status, and competitiveness). School administrators, school boards, and citizens of local communities have long assumed that sports participation has general educational value. If so, then girls and women should also be allowed to receive the benefits.

In 1972, passage of Title IX of the Educational Amendments Act required that schools receiving federal funds must provide equal opportunities for males and females. Despite considerable opposition by school administrators, athletic directors, and school boards, major changes have occurred over time because of this federal legislation. More monies were spent on women's sports; better facilities and equipment were provided; and women were gradually accepted as athletes. The most significant result was an increase in female participation. The number of high school girls participating in interscholastic sports increased from 300,000 in 1971 to 2.8 million in 2001. By 2004, 42 percent of all high school participants were female, and the number of sports available to them was more than twice the number available in 1970. Similar growth patterns have occurred in colleges and universities.

On the positive side, budgets for women's sports have improved dramatically, from less than 1 percent of the men's budgets in 1970 at the college level to approximately 33 percent of the men's budgets in 2004. On the negative side, budgets for women's sports will stay at about the same level because football is so expensive and is exempt from the equation (*USA Today*, 2002b). Thus, women's sports remain and will remain unequal to men's sports. This inequality is reinforced by unequal media attention, the scheduling of games (men's games are always the featured games), and the increasing lack of women in positions of power. One ironic consequence of Title IX has been that as opportunities for female athletes increased and programs expanded, the majority of coaching and administration positions formerly held by women is now held by men. In the early 1970s, most coaches of women's intercollegiate teams were women. But by 2002, the percentage had declined to 45.6, the lowest in the history of intercollegiate athletics. This trend is also true at the high school level. Also, whereas women's athletic associations at the high school and college levels were once controlled by women, they have now been subsumed under male-dominated organizations. Thus, females who aspire to coaching and athletic administration have fewer opportunities; girls see fewer women as role models in such positions, and inequality is reinforced as women are dominated by men in positions of power. Thus, even with federal legislation mandating gender equality, male dominance is maintained.

Despite many obstacles to gender equity in sports, there are many signs of progress. More television time and newspaper space are now devoted to women's sports. Professional female tennis players are at least as popular with crowds as men, and they compete for significant payoffs. The Tennessee-Connecticut women's basketball game was attended by over 26,000 fans in 2002. U.S. female athletes have been incredibly successful in international competition. In the 2000 Olympics, U.S. women captured forty medals, more than women from any other nation. U.S. women also took first place in the 1999 Soccer World Cup before more than 90,000 fans. This last event appears to indicate a sea change. In the words of former professional basketball player Mariah Burton Nelson:

> American sports fans' fascination with female athletes has shifted from skirted skaters . . . and tiny teenage tumblers . . . to rough muscular women in their 20s and 30s who grunt, grimace and heave each other aside with their hips. (Nelson, 1999:55)

Female Role Models. The work that women and men do in the schools supports gender inequality. The pattern is the familiar one found in hospitals, in business offices, and throughout the occupational world: Women occupy the bottom rungs, and men are in the more powerful positions. Women make up a large percentage of the nation's classroom teachers but a much smaller percentage of school district superintendents. In 2003, women comprised 81 percent of all elementary school teachers, more than half of all secondary school teachers (55 percent), and 65 percent of all school administrators (U.S. Bureau of the Census, 2004).

As the level of education increases, the proportion of female teachers declines. In the 2003–2004 academic year (nineteen years after the Office of Civil Rights issued guidelines spelling out the obligations of colleges and universities in the development of affirmative action programs), women represented only 38 percent of full-time faculty. Furthermore, they remained overwhelmingly in the lower faculty ranks, where faculty are much less likely to hold tenure. In 2004, women comprised 23 percent of full professors, 38 percent of associate professors, 46 percent of assistant professors, and 58 percent of instructors/lecturers (American Association of

FIGURE 12.1

Science Is Still A Man's World

Source: Amanda Ripley. 2005. "Who Says a Woman Can't Be Einstein?" *Time* (March 7):52. © 2005 Time Inc. Reprinted by permission.

The great majority of scientists and engineers in the U.S. are men, but that has less to do with differences in the brain than with academic history. The balance is changing, slowly, as more women pursue advanced degrees.

THE DOCTORAL GAP

Three decades ago, women received only 1 of every 10 science and engineering Ph.D.s. Today, women earn one-third of all science doctorates

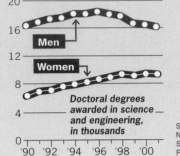

Doctoral degrees awarded in science and engineering, in thousands

Source: National Science Foundation

AT THE TOP OF THE IVORY TOWER

Women occupy 29% of science and engineering positions at U.S. educational institutions. But they fill only 15% of those positions at the top 50 research universities in these fields:

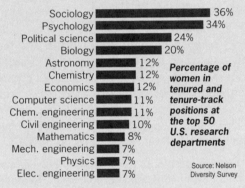

Sociology	36%
Psychology	34%
Political science	24%
Biology	20%
Astronomy	12%
Chemistry	12%
Economics	12%
Computer science	11%
Chem. engineering	11%
Civil engineering	10%
Mathematics	8%
Mech. engineering	7%
Physics	7%
Elec. engineering	7%

Percentage of women in tenured and tenure-track positions at the top 50 U.S. research departments

Source: Nelson Diversity Survey

LIFE OUTSIDE ACADEMIA

In government and the private sector, women occupy just under one-quarter of science and engineering jobs. As in the academic world, men dominate jobs in the physical sciences and engineering

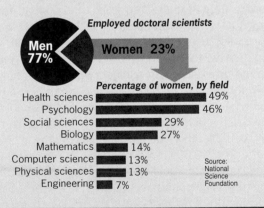

Employed doctoral scientists

Men 77% Women 23%

Percentage of women, by field

Health sciences	49%
Psychology	46%
Social sciences	29%
Biology	27%
Mathematics	14%
Computer science	13%
Physical sciences	13%
Engineering	7%

Source: National Science Foundation

University Professors, 2004) (see Figure 12.1 on Women in Science and Engineering). Since 1986, the percentage of college presidents has doubled—from 9.5 percent to 21 percent in 2002. Although women now hold a greater percentage of the top positions at colleges and universities than ever before, women presidents remain underrepresented in comparison to their share of all faculty and senior staff positions (American Council on Education, 2000).

Counseling. A fundamental task of school guidance personnel is to aid students in their choice of a career. The guidance that students receive on career choice tends to be biased. High school guidance counselors may channel male and female students into different (i.e., gender-stereotyped) fields and activities. There is evidence that gender stereotyping is common among counselors and that they steer female and male students into different fields and activities, and that they discourage female students from pursuing fields requiring mathematics and the sciences (Renzetti and Curran, 2003:116).

In the past, aptitude tests have themselves been sex-biased, listing occupations as either female or male. Despite changes in testing, counselors may inadvertently channel students into traditional gendered choices.

Socialization as Blaming the Victim

The discussion so far demonstrates that gender differences are learned. This does not mean that socialization alone explains women's place in society. In fact, a socialization approach alone can be misused in such a way that it blames women themselves for sex inequality. This is the critique offered by Linda Peterson and Elaine Enarson (1974). They argue that socialization diverts attention from structured inequality: "Misuse of the concept of socialization plays directly into the Blaming the Victim ideology; by focusing on the victim, responsibility for 'the woman problem' rests not in the social system with its sex-structured distribution of inequality, but in socialized sex differences and sex roles" (8).

Not only is the cause of the problem displaced, but so are the solutions: "Rather than directing efforts toward radical social change, the solution seems to be to change women themselves, perhaps through exhortation ('If we want to be liberated, we'll have to act more aggressive . . .') or, for example, changing children's literature and mothers' child rearing practice" (8).

This issue raises a critical question: If the socialization perspective is limited and perhaps biased, what is a better way of analyzing gender inequality? To answer this question, let us look at how male dominance affects our society.

Reinforcing Male Dominance

Male dominance is both a force that socializes and a force that structures the social world. It exists at all levels of society, from interpersonal relations to outside institutions. This section describes the interpersonal and institutional reinforcement of gender inequality.

Language

Language perpetuates male dominance by ignoring, trivializing, and sexualizing women. Use of the pronoun *he* when the sex of the person is unspecified and of the generic term *mankind* to refer to humanity in general are obvious examples of how the English language ignores women. Common sayings such as "that's women's work" (as opposed to "that's men's work!"), jokes about female drivers, and phrases such as *women and children first,* or *wine, women, and song* are trivializing. Women, more than men, are commonly referred to in terms that have sexual connotations. Terms referring to men (*studs, jocks*) that do have sexual meanings imply power and success, whereas terms applied to women (*broads, bimbos, chicks*) imply promiscuity or being dominated. In fact, the term *promiscuous* is usually applied only to women, although its literal meaning applies to either sex (Richmond-Abbott, 1992:93). Research shows that there are many derogatory or at least disrespectful generic terms for women, but few for men (Sapiro, 1999:329). Not only are there fewer derogatory terms that refer to men, but of those that exist, such terms are considered derogatory because they invoke the images of women. "Some of the more common derogatory terms applied to men such as bastard, motherfucker, and son of a bitch actually degrade women in their role as mothers" (Romaine, 1999:999).

Interpersonal Behavior

Gender inequality is different than other forms of inequality because individuals on both sides of the power divide (the divide being between women and men) interact very frequently (in the home, in the workplace, and in other role relations). Consequently, gender inequalities can be reproduced and resisted in everyday interactions (Ridgeway and Smith-Lovin, 1999:191).

Sociologists have done extensive research on the ways in which women and men interact, with particular attention being paid to communication styles. This research finds that in mixed-sex groups men talk more, show more visual dominance, and interrupt more, whereas women display more tentative and polite speech patterns (Ridgeway and Smith-Lovin, 1999). Sociolinguist Deborah Tannen (1990) contends that women and men have different styles of communication and different communication goals. Women and men speak different "genderlects." These differences sometimes lead to miscommunication based on how girls and boys learn to use language differently in their sex-separate peer groups:

> Typically, a girl has a best friend with whom she sits and talks, frequently telling secrets. It's the telling of secrets, the fact and the way that they talk to each other, that makes them best friends. For boys, activities are central: Their best friends are the ones they do things with. Boys also tend to play in larger groups that are hierarchical. High-status boys give orders and push low-status boys around. So boys are expected to use language to seize center stage: by exhibiting their skill, displaying their knowledge, and challenging and resisting challenges. (Tannen, 1991:B3)

More recent studies challenge some of these findings, because they overstate the differences between women and men while overlooking the similarities between groups of women and groups of men (Hannan and Murachver, 1999; McGeorge et al., 2004).

Power is also sustained by various forms of nonverbal communication. Men take up more space than do women and also touch women without permission more than women touch men. Women, on the other hand, engage in more eye contact, smile more, and generally exhibit behavior associated with low status. These behaviors show how gender is continually being created in various kinds of social interaction that occur between women and men. Candace West and Don Zimmerman (1987) call this "doing gender." It involves following the rules and behaviors expected of us as males or females. We "do gender," because if we don't, we are judged incompetent as men and women. Gender is something we create in interaction, not something we are (Risman, 1998:6).

Mass Communications Media

Much of the information we receive about the world around us comes not from direct experience but from the mass media of communication (radio, television, newspapers, and magazines). Although media are often blamed for the problems of modern society, they are not monolithic and do not present us with a simple message. The media have tremendous power. They can distort women's images and they can bring about change as well (Sapiro, 1999:224). In the print media, women's influence has not matched their larger presence in the field. The percentage of women in newsrooms is now at 37 percent. Studies show that women journalists' role in newsrooms is shrinking even though women predominate in undergraduate and graduate journalism programs and have for decades (Lauer, 2002). In magazines, women's portrayal has become less monolithic since the 1980s. With the rise of feminism, many magazines devoted attention to women's achievements. Alongside these new magazines for the new woman, many "ladies'" magazines continue to define the lives of women in terms of men—husbands or lovers.

Women are 52 percent of the population, but you would not know it by reading most newspapers or watching network news. Although they fare better on local newscasts than national ones, they are still underrepresented in television newsrooms. In 2003, women made up 39 percent of the television news workforce, while the percentage of women news directors in television is at 25 percent (Papper, 2004).

Studies have continually demonstrated that highly stereotyped behavior characterizes both children and adult programming as well as commercials. Male role models are provided in greater numbers than are female, with the exception of daytime soap operas, in which men and women are equally represented. Prime-time television is distorted. Although men represent 49 percent of the U.S. population, they represented 59 percent of prime-time television characters in 2002 (National Organization for Women, 2002).

Images of women on entertainment television have changed greatly in recent decades. A report by the National Commission on Working Women has found increasing diversity of characters portraying working women as television's most significant improvement. In many serials, women do play strong and intelligent roles, but in just as many shows, men are still the major characters and women are cast as glamorous objects, scheming villains, or servants. And for every contemporary show that includes positive images of women, there are numerous other shows in which women are sidekicks to men, sexual objects, or helpless imbeciles (Andersen, 2005:60). In response to the imbalances in prime-time television, the National Organization for Women states, "If you are a middle-aged woman, a lesbian, a Latina, a woman with a disability, a women of size, a low-income mom struggling to get by . . . good luck finding programming that even pretends to reflect your life" (National Organization for Women, 2002).

Television commercials have long presented the sexes in stereotyped ways. Women appear less frequently in ads than men, are much more likely to be seen in the home rather than in work settings, and are much more likely to be in ads for food, home products, and beauty/clothing products (Andersen, 2005:61). In the past decade, however, the potential buying power of working women has caused the advertising industry to modify women's image. Working women have become targets of advertising campaigns. But most advertising aimed at women with jobs sends the message that they should be superwomen, managing multiple roles of wife, mother, and career woman, and be glamorous as well. Such multifarious expectations are not imposed on men.

The advertising aimed at the "new woman" places additional stresses on women and at the same time upholds male privilege. Television commercials that show women breezing in from their jobs to sort the laundry or pop dinner in the oven reinforce the notion that it is all right for a woman to pursue a career as long as she can still handle the housework.

Religion

Most U.S. religions follow a typical pattern. The clergy is male, while the vast majority of worshipers is women (Paulson, 2000). Despite important differences in religious doctrines, there are common views about gender. Among these are the beliefs that (1) women and men have different missions and different standards of behavior, and (2) although men and women are equal in the eyes of the deity, women are to some degree subordinate to men (Sapiro, 1999:219). Limiting discussion to the Judeo-Christian heritage, let us examine some teachings from the Old and New Testaments regarding the place of women. The Old Testament established male supremacy in a number of ways. Images of God are male. Females were second to men because Eve was created from Adam's rib. According to the Scriptures, only a man could divorce a spouse. A woman who was not a virgin at marriage could be stoned to death. Girls could be purchased for marriage. Employers were enjoined to pay women only three-fifths the wages of men: "If a male from 20 to 60 years of age, the equivalent is 50 shekels of silver by the sanctuary weight; if it is a female, the equivalent is 30 shekels" (Leviticus 27:4). As Gilman (1971) notes:

> The Old Testament devotes inordinate space to the listing of long lines of male descent to the point where it would seem that for centuries women "begat" nothing but male offspring. Although there are heroines in the Old Testament—Judith, Esther and the like—it's clear that they functioned like the heroines of Greek drama and later of French: as counterweights in the imaginations of certain sensitive men to the degraded position of women in actual life. The true spirit of the tradition was unabashedly revealed in the prayer men recited every day in the synagogue: "Blessed art Thou, O Lord . . . for not making me a woman." (51)

The New Testament retained the tradition of male dominance. Jesus was the son of a male god, not of Mary, who remained a virgin. All the disciples were male. The great leader of the early church, the apostle Paul, was especially adamant in arguing for the primacy of males over females. According to Paul, "the husband is supreme over his wife," "woman was created for man's sake," and "women should not teach nor usurp authority over the man, but to be silent." Contemporary religious thought reflects this heritage. In 1998, the Southern Baptist Convention, the nation's biggest Protestant denomination, amended its statement of beliefs to include a declaration that "a woman shall submit herself graciously to her husband's leadership and a husband should provide for, protect and lead his family." Some denominations limit or even forbid women from any decision making. Others allow women to vote but limit their participation in leadership roles.

There are, however, many indications of change. Throughout the West, women are more involved in churches and religious life (Paulson, 2000; Van Biema, 2004). The National Council of Churches seeks to end sexist language and to use "inclusive language" in the Revised Standard Version of the Bible. Terms such as *man, mankind, brothers, sons, churchmen,* and *laymen* would be replaced by neutral terms that include reference to female gender. But these terms, while helpful, do not address a fundamental theological cause: "When God is perceived as a male, then expecting a male voice interpreting the word of God naturally follows" (Zelizer, 2004:11A).

The percentage of female seminary students has exploded in the past thirty-five years, from 4 percent in 1972 to 31 percent in 2003 (Van Biema, 2004:59). Yet women made up only 13 percent of the nation's clergy in 2003 (U.S. Bureau of the Census, 2004). Across the United States, female clergy are struggling for equal rights, bumping up against what many call a "stained-glass ceiling." Today, half of all religious denominations in the United States ordain women. At the same time, the formal rules and practices discriminate against women. In denominations that ordain women and those that do not, women often fill the same jobs: leading small churches, directing special church programs, preaching and evangelizing (Van Biema, 2004). Despite the opposition of organized religion, many women are making advances within established churches and leaving their mark on the ministerial profession.

The Law

That the law has been discriminatory against women is beyond dispute. We need only recall that women were specifically denied the right to vote prior to the passage of the Nineteenth Amendment.

During the past three decades, legal reforms and public policy changes have attempted to place women and men on more equal footing. Some laws that focus on employment include the 1963 Equal Pay Act, Title VII of the 1964 Civil Rights Act, and the 1978 Pregnancy Discrimination Act. The 1974 Educational Amendments Act calls for gender equality in education. Other reforms have provided the framework for important institutional changes. For example, sexist discrimination in the granting of credit has been ruled illegal, and discrimination against pregnant women in the workforce is now prohibited by the law. Affirmative action (which is now under assault) remedied some kinds of gender discrimination in employment. Sexist discrimination in housing is prohibited, and the differential requirements by gender as traditionally practiced by the airline industry have been eliminated. The force of these new laws, however, depends on their enforcement as well as on the interpretation of the courts when they are disputed.

Legal discrimination remains in a number of areas. There are still hundreds of sections of the U.S. legal code and of state laws that are riddled with sex bias or sex-based terminology, in conflict with the ideal of equal rights for women (Benokraitis and Feagin, 1995:24). State laws vary considerably concerning property ownership by spouses, welfare benefits, and the legal status of homemakers.

Today, many legal reforms are threatened by recent Supreme Court decisions in the areas of abortion and affirmative action. In 1989 and 1992, the Supreme Court narrowed its 1973 landmark *Roe* v. *Wade* decision, which established the right to abortion. *Roe* v. *Wade* was a major breakthrough for women, giving them legal choice to control their bodies. The 1989 and 1992 decisions made it easier for the states to restrict women's reproductive freedoms at any stage of pregnancy, including the first three months. These decisions have steadily chipped away at a women's right to abortion.

By moving the battleground to state legislatures, the Supreme Court has returned the nation to a pre-Roe patchwork of laws and conditions that challenge legalized choice. State restrictions that now make it more difficult for women to obtain abortions include parental notification rules and mandatory waiting periods. In 2004, states enacted nearly 30 new antichoice measures (NARL, 2005). In 2005, the House passed a teen endangerment bill, restricting the ability of young women to obtain an abortion outside of her home state. The bill makes no exception for a medical emergency unless the young woman has complied with her home state's parental involvement laws (National Organization for Women, 2005). Since 1995, more than 4,000 antichoice measure have been enacted.

Politics

Women's political participation has always been different from that of men. Women received the right to vote in 1920, when the Nineteenth Amendment was ratified. Although women make up a very small percentage of officeholders, 1992 was a turning point for women in politics. Controversies such as Anita Hill's harassment allegations, the abortion rights battle, and the lack of representation at all levels of politics propelled women into the political arena. In 1992, Congress experienced the biggest influx of women (and minorities) in history. Subsequent elections have increased the number of women in our national legislature. As of 2005, fourteen U.S. senators are women, and sixty-six women are in the House of Representatives (Center for American Women and Politics, 2005) (see Table 12.2 for the Percentages

TABLE 12.2

Percentages of Women in Elective Offices: 1979–2005

Year	U.S. Congress	Statewide Elective	State Legislatures	Year	U.S. Congress	Statewide Elective	State Legislatures
1979	3%	11%	10%	1993	10.1%	22.2%	20.5%
1981	4%	11%	12%	1995	10.3%	25.9%	20.6%
1983	4%	11%	13%	1997	11.0%	25.4%	21.6%
1985	5%	14%	15%	1999	12.1%	27.6%	22.4%
1987	5%	14%	16%	2001	13.6%	27.6%	22.4%
1989	5%	14%	17%	2003	13.6%	26.0%	22.4%
1991	6%	18%	18%	2004	13.8%	26.0%	22.5%
				2005	15.0%	25.7%	22.5%

Source: Center for American Women and Politics (CAWP). "Women in Elective Office 2005." Eagleton Institute of Politics. Rutgers, The State University of New Jersey, p 2. Reprinted with permission.

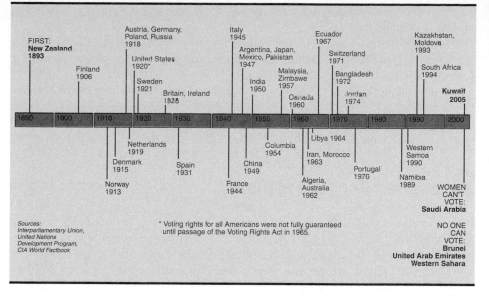

FIGURE 12.2

Women Gain Votes (Some Even Matter)

Source: "Women Gain Votes (Some Even Matter)," by Bill Marsh, *The New York Times,* May 22, 2005 by The New York Times Co. Reprinted by permission.

Kuwait's Parliament granted full voting rights to women last week, a surprising reversal: two weeks earlier, a similar measure was defeated.

Women's suffrage has been entwined with other struggles. Canadian women won the right to vote in 1917—except for native Americans. They (and native men) were denied the vote until 1960. Likewise, Australia gave most women the vote in 1902, but its aboriginal population had to wait six more decades.

New Zealand led the way with universal suffrage in 1893. Here is a timeline showing when some countries—from democracies to dictatorships— granted women the vote, and some others that have yet to do so.

of U.S. Women in Elective Office). If Congress were representative of the nation, the House would have 222 women and the Senate 51 (Sklar, 2004).

Despite this progress, the gender gap in our nation's capital is scandalous. In Washington, DC's, less visible workforce of professional staff employees, women hold 60 percent of the jobs, but they are nowhere equal to men. Congress has two classes of personal staff employees: highly paid men who hold most of the power and lower-paid women who tend to be relegated to clerical and support staff. Many answer the phones and write letters to constituents—invisible labor that is crucial to their bosses' reelection.

Across the world, women are making substantial gains in politics. Figure 12.2 charts women's global progress in gaining full voting rights. And as for female lawmakers, sixty-five countries do better than the United States when it comes to women serving in national legislatures. The United States has just 15 percent female lawmakers in Congress. In 2003, women held 43 percent of the seats in Sweden's parliament, 38 percent of the seats in Denmark, 35 percent in Costa Rica, 31 percent in Germany, 30 percent in South Africa, 27 percent in Spain, and 24 percent in Canada (Sklar, 2004).

In the 200-year history of the United States, there has never been a female president or vice president. Before 1993, there was only one female justice on the Supreme Court.

The gender gap refers to differences in political attitudes and voting patterns of women and men. Voting studies of national elections since 1980 demonstrate that women often vote differently from men, especially on issues of economics, social welfare, and war and peace (Renzetti and Curran, 2003:299).

Structured Gender Inequality

In this section of the chapter, we focus on the contemporary workplace because it is a key arena for inequality. In fact, the United States has one of the highest levels of workplace gender inequality in the industrial world (Kimmel, 2004:186). The workplace distributes women and men in different settings, assigns them different duties, and rewards them unequally.

Occupational Distribution

The new economy discussed in Chapter 8 has changed both women's and men's employment rates. Increasingly, it is viewed as "normal" for adult women and men, regardless of parental status, to be employed (Bianchi, 1995:110). Yet, men's labor-force participation rates have decreased slightly, while women's have increased dramatically. In 2005, 76 percent of all men were in the labor force, compared with 60 percent of all women. Today, women make up nearly half of the workforce. African American women have had a long history of high workforce participation rates. In 2004, they edged ahead of other women, participating in the labor force at a rate of 64 percent; 59 percent of White women were in the labor force in 2004, compared with 57 percent of Hispanic women (Bureau of Labor Statistics, 2005) (see Table 12.3).

Today's working woman may be any age. She may be any race. She may be a nurse or a secretary or a factory worker or a department store clerk or a public schoolteacher. Or she may be—though it is much less likely—a physician or the president of a corporation or the head of a school system. Hers may be the familiar face seen daily behind the counter at the neighborhood coffee shop, or she may work virtually unseen, mopping floors at midnight in an empty office building. The typical female worker is a wage earner in clerical, service, manufacturing, or some technical job that pays poorly and gives her little possibility for advancement and little control over her work. More women work as sales workers, secretaries, and cashiers than in any other line of work. The largest share of women (37 percent), however, work in technical, sales, and administrative support occupations (Bureau of Labor Statistics, 2004).

Economic restructuring has fundamentally altered the gender distribution of many occupations. Since 1980, women have taken 80 percent of the new jobs created in the economy. But the overall degree of gender segregation has not changed much since 1900. Women and men are still concentrated in different occupations

TABLE 12.3

Projected Civilian Labor Force and Participation Rates of Women, by Race

Women	Labor Force (in Thousands)		Change, 1998–2008		Participation Rate	
	1998	2008	Numerical	Percent	1998	2008
All races	63,714	73,444	9,729	15.3	59.8	61.9
Hispanic origin	5,746	8,552	2,806	48.8	55.6	57.9
White	52,380	59,001	6,621	12.6	59.4	61.5
Black	8,441	10,224	1,783	21.1	62.8	64.6
Asian and other	2,895	4,219	1,323	45.7	59.2	60.5

Source: U.S. Department of Labor, Women's Bureau, 2000. *Facts on Working Women: Women of Hispanic Origin in the Labor Force,* no. 00-04 (April 2000, p. 3). Available online: www.dol.gov/dol/wb/public/wb-pubs/hispwom2.htm (accessed September 3, 2000).

(Dubeck and Dunn, 2002). **Gender segregation** refers to the pattern whereby women and men are situated in different jobs throughout the labor force (Andersen, 2005:120). Overall, just 15 percent of women work in jobs typically held by men (engineer, stockbroker, judge), while fewer than 8 percent of men hold female-dominate jobs such as nurse, teacher, or sales clerk (Bernstein, 2004).

In 2004, the six most prevalent occupations for women were, in order of magnitude, (1) secretary and administrative assistant; (2) elementary and middle school teacher; (3) registered nurse; (4) nursing, psychiatric, and home health aide; (5) cashier; and (6) first line supervisors/managers of office and administrative support (U.S. Department of Labor, Women's Bureau, 2004) (see Table 12.4).

Media reports of women's gains in traditionally male jobs are often misleading. In blue-collar work, for example, gains appear dramatic at first glance, with the number of women in blue-collar jobs rising by 80 percent in the 1970s. But the increase was so high because women had been virtually excluded from these occupations until then. Women's entry into skilled blue-collar work such as construction and automaking was limited by the very slow growth in those jobs (Amott, 1993:76). In 2004, only 1.3 percent of automotive service technicians and mechanics, 3 percent of construction workers, and 3 percent of tool and die makers were women (U.S. Department of Labor, Women's Bureau, 2004). However, some women made inroads into historically male jobs in the highly paid primary sector. The years from 1970 to 1990 found more women in the fields of law, medicine, journalism, and higher education. Today, women fill 37 percent of all management positions (up from 19 percent in 1972). Still, there are fewer women in prestige positions than men. In 2003, only 27 percent of lawyers, 30 percent of doctors, and 44 percent of full-time university or college teachers were women (U.S. Bureau of the Census, 2004).

Although women have made inroads in high-paying and high-prestige professions, not all have fared equally. White women were the major beneficiaries of the new opportunities. There has been an occupational "trickle-down" effect, as White women improved the occupational status by moving into male-dominated

TABLE 12.4

20 Leading Occupations of Employed Women Full-Time Wage and Salary Workers 2004 Annual Averages (Employment in Thousands)

Occupation	Total Employed Women	Total Employed (Men and Women)	Percent Women	Women's Median Weekly Earnings
Total, 16 years and older (all employed women, full-time wage and salary workers)	44,223	101,224	43.7	$573
Secretaries and admin. assistants	2,570	2,657	96.7	550
Elementary and middle school teachers	1,772	2,206	96.7	550
Registered nurses	1,651	1,800	91.8	895
Nursing, psychiatric, and home health aides	1,113	1,261	88.3	383
Cashiers	1,016	1,355	75	313
First-line supervisors/managers of office and admin. support	1,001	1,441	69.5	636
First-line supervisors/managers of retail sales workers	985	2,246	43.9	505
Customer service representatives	967	1,379	70.1	504
Bookkeeping, accounting, and auditing clerks	916	1,004	91.2	542
Accountants and auditors	842	1,385	60.8	757
Receptionists and information clerks	795	847	93.9	463
Retail salespersons	766	1,865	41.1	386
Maid and housekeeping cleaners	723	818	89.7	324
Office clerks, general	559	667	83.8	499
Secondary school teachers	555	1,013	54.8	824
Waiters and waitresses	538	799	67.3	327
Financial managers	535	961	55.7	839
Teacher assistants	500	545	91.7	373
Preschool and kindergarten teachers	473	484	97.7	515
Social workers	472	620	76.1	689

Source: U.S. Department of Labor, Women's Bureau, 2005. "Twenty Leading Occupations of Employed Women, Full Time Wage and Salary Workers, 2004 Annual Averages." Available online: http://www.dol.gov/wb/factsheets/20lead2004.htm.

professions such as law and medicine, while African American women moved into the female-dominated jobs, such as social work and teaching, vacated by White women. This improvement for White women was related to federal civil rights legislation, particularly the requirement that firms receiving federal contracts comply with affirmative action guidelines (Amott, 1993:76).

The Earnings Gap

Although women's labor-force participation rates have risen, the gap between women's and men's earnings has remained relatively constant for three decades. Women do not approach earnings parity with men, even when they work in similar occupations and have the same levels of education.

The pay gap between women and men has narrowed. It hovered between 70 and 74 percent throughout the 1990s. In 2004, women who worked full-time, year-round earned 77 cents for every dollar men earned. For every $10,000 men earn, women make $7,700, a loss of $2,300. Closing the wage gap has been slow, amounting to less than half a cent per year! At this rate, 87 more years could go by before women and men reach parity (Sklar, 2004).

For women of color, earnings discrimination is even greater. Women's incomes are lower than men's in every racial group. Among women and men working year-round and full-time in 2003, White women earned 79 percent of White men's earnings; Black women earned 88 percent of Black men's earnings but only 68 percent of White men's earnings; Hispanic women earned 88 percent of Hispanic men's earnings, but only 57 percent of White men's earnings (U.S. Department of Labor, 2004) (see Table 12.4). The earnings gap affects the well-being of women and their families. If women earned the same as men, their annual family incomes would rise by $4,000 and poverty rates would be cut in half. Their lost earnings could have bought a home, educated their children, and been set aside for retirement (Greim, 1998; Love, 1998; The Wage Gap, 2003).

"I feel like a man trapped in a woman's salary."

The earnings gap persists for several reasons:

- Women are concentrated in lower-paying occupations.
- Women enter the labor force at different and lower-paying levels than do men.
- Women as a group have less education and experience than do men; therefore, they are paid less than men.
- Women tend to work less overtime than do men.

These conditions explain only part of the earnings gap between women and men. They do not explain why female workers earn substantially less than do male workers with the same number of years of education and with the same work histories, skills, and work experience. Men with professional degrees may expect to earn almost 2 million dollars more than their female counterparts (Sklar, 2004). Study after study finds that if women were men with the same credentials, they would earn substantially more. Research on the income gap has found that women's and men's credentials explained some differences, but that experience accounted for only about one-third of the wage gap. The largest part of the wage gap is caused by sex discrimination in the labor market that blocks women's access to better-paying jobs through hiring or promotion or simply paying women less than men in any job (Dubeck and Dunn, 2002; *ISR Newsletter*, 1982; Leinwand, 1999).

Intersection of Race and Gender in the Workplace

There are important racial differences in the occupational concentration of women and men. Women of color make up 14 percent of the private sector workforce in the United States (U.S. Equal Employment Opportunity Commission, 2003:2). They are the most segregated group in the workplace. Compared with White women, they are concentrated in low-paying jobs and have few fringe benefits, poor working conditions, high turnover, and little chance of advancement. Mexican American women, for example, are concentrated in secretarial, cashier, and janitorial jobs; Central American women in jobs as household cleaners, janitors, and textile machine operators; Filipinas as nurses, nurses' aides, and cashiers; and Black women as nursing aides, cashiers, and secretaries (Andersen, 2003; Reskin, 1999). White women are a privileged group in the workplace compared with women of color. A much larger share of White women (38 percent) than Black women (30 percent) or Latinas (22 percent) hold managerial and professional specialty jobs (U.S. Department of Labor, 2005).

Workplace inequality, then, is patterned by both gender and race—and also by social class and other group characteristics. One's placement in a job hierarchy as well as the rewards one receives depend on how these characteristics "combine" (Dubeck and Dunn, 2002:48). Earnings for all workers are lowest in those areas of the labor market where women of color predominate.

Pay Equity

Women's low earnings create serious problems for women themselves, for their families, and for their children. Increasingly, families need the incomes of both spouses, and many working women are the sole providers of their families. Given these trends, equal pay is a top social concern.

The Equal Pay Act, passed in 1963, made it illegal to pay women less for doing the same work as men. However, the law is difficult to enforce because women and men are located in different occupations. For example, to be a secretary (usually a woman) requires as much education and takes as much responsibility as being a carpenter (usually a man), but the secretarial job is paid far less (Folbre, Heintz, and the Center for Popular Economics, 2000). Pay equity in jobs that are dominated by women (where women comprise 70 percent or more of the workforce) would result in an 18 percent increase in wages for women (National Organization for Women, 2005).

In the early 1980s, a number of state and local governments began addressing the pay-gap issue by institutionalizing pay-equity policies in the public sector. Pay-equity policies are a means of eliminating sex and race discrimination in the wage-setting system. Pay equity means that the criteria employers use to set wages must be gender- and race-neutral (National Committee on Pay Equity, 2002b).

Since 1980, twenty states have implemented pay-equity programs that reduced the gender wage gap. Minnesota, Oregon, and Washington were among the most successful (Folbre, Heintz, and the Center for Popular Economics, 2000). Pay-equity struggles are difficult. Yet, in recent years, women willing to fight for their rights have won multi-million-dollar pay-equity settlements from corporations such as Home Depot, Eastman Kodak, Merrill Lynch, and Texaco.

How Workplace Inequality Operates

Common explanations for gender differentials rely on women's learned behaviors. Women's socialization and aspirations are said to produce gender divisions in the workplace. But gender socialization cannot fully explain workplace inequality. The organizational structure of work itself is responsible for gender differences in the

"Before we can get married, I have to know one thing. Does your employer extend parental leave to fathers?"

workplace. Let us examine the organization of the labor force that assigns better jobs and greater rewards to men and positions of less responsibility with lower earnings to women.

The labor market is divided into two separate segments, with different characteristics, different roles, and different rewards. The primary segment is characterized by stability, high wages, promotion ladders, opportunities for advancement, good working conditions, and provisions for job security. The secondary market is characterized by low wages, fewer or no promotion ladders, poor working conditions, and little provision for job security. Women's work tends to fall in the secondary segment. For example, clerical work, the largest single occupation for women, has many of the characteristics associated with the secondary segment.

To understand women's disadvantages, we must look at the structural arrangements that women confront in the workplace. A classic study by Rosabeth Moss Kanter (1977), *Men and Women of the Corporation*, found that organizational location is more important than gender in shaping workers' behavior. Although women and men behave differently at work, Kanter demonstrated that the differences were created by organizational locations. Workers in low-mobility or blocked situations (regardless of their sex) tend to limit their aspirations, seek satisfactions in activities outside work, dream of escape, and create sociable peer groups in which interpersonal relationships take over other aspects of work. Kanter argued that "when women seem to be less motivated or committed, it is probably because their jobs carry less opportunity" (Kanter, 1977:159).

Many organizational features block women's advancement. In the white-collar workforce, the well-documented phenomenon of women going just so far—and no further—in their occupations and professions is called the **glass ceiling**. This refers to the invisible barriers that limit women's mobility despite their motivation and capacity for positions of power and prestige (Lorber, 1994:227). "Women face the twin barriers of the 'glass ceiling' and the 'sticky floor,' which combine to keep them stuck at the bottom and unable to reach the top" (Kimmel, 2004:195). The movement of women into highly skilled blue-collar jobs has been limited by the steady decline of manufacturing jobs. Those women who do enter blue-collar work often confront blatant resistance from male coworkers. Even the movement of women into male jobs does not always bring about integration. Sociologists Barbara Reskin and Patricia Roos (1990) studied eleven once-male-dominated fields that had become integrated between 1979 and 1988: book editing, pharmacy, public relations, bank management, systems analysis, insurance sales, real estate sales, insurance adjusting and examining, bartending, baking, and typesetting and composition. Reskin and Roos found that women gained entry into these fields only *after* earnings and upward mobility in each of these fields declined; that is, salaries had gone down, prestige had diminished, or the work had become more like "women's work" (Kroeger, 1994:50). Furthermore, in each of these occupations, women specialized in lower-status specialties, in different and less desirable work settings, and in lower-paid industries. Reskin and Roos call this process *ghettoization*. Some occupations changed their sex-typing completely, while some became resegregated by race as well as gender (Amott, 1993:80; Reskin and Roos, 1990).

Many fields that have opened up to women no longer have the economic or social status they once possessed. Their structures now have two tiers: (1) higher-paying, higher-ranking jobs with more authority, and (2) lower-paying, more routinized jobs with less authority. Women are concentrated in the new, more routinized sectors of professional employment, but the upper tier of relatively autonomous work continues to be male-dominated, with only token increases in female employment (Carter and Carter, 1981). For example, women's entry into three prestige professions—medicine, college teaching, and law—has been accompanied by organizational changes. In medicine, hospital-based practice has grown as more women have entered the profession. Female doctors are more likely than male doctors to be found in hospital-based practice, which provides less autonomy than the more traditional office practice. In college teaching, many women are employed in two-year colleges, where heavy teaching responsibilities leave little time or energy for writing and publishing—the keys to academic career advancement. And in law, women's advancement to prestigious positions is being eroded by the growth of the legal clinic, where much legal work is routinized.

Many of the old discriminatory patterns are difficult to change. In the professions, for example, sponsor-protege systems and informal interactions among colleagues limit women's mobility. Sponsorship is important in training personnel and ensuring leadership continuity. Women are less likely to be acceptable as proteges. Furthermore, their sex status limits or excludes their involvement in the buddy system or the old-boy network (Epstein, 1970). These informal interactions create alliances that can further chances for social mobility, but they are systematically blocked for women.

Gender in the Global Economy

Gender relations in the United States and the world reflect the larger changes of economic globalization. Private businesses make investment decisions that have a major impact on the work, community, and family lives of women and men all around the world. In their search for profit, transnational corporations have turned to developing nations and the work of women and children. The demand for less expensive labor has produced a global system of production with a strong gendered component. The international division of labor affects both men and women. As manufacturing jobs switch to low-wage economies, men are often displaced. The global assembly line uses the labor of women, many of them young, single, and from poor rural areas. Women workers of particular classes/castes and races from poor countries provide a cheap supply of labor for the manufacture of commodities distributed in the richer industrial nations.

Economic globalization is altering gender relations around the world by bringing women into the public sphere (Walby, 2000). While this presents new opportunities for women, the disruption of male dominance can also result in the reaffirmation of local gender hierarchies through right-wing militia movements, religious revivalism, and other forms of masculine fundamentalism (Connell, 1998). In addition, old forms of women's exploitation and abuse are being remade on massive scale. For example, the commodification of women in the sex industry cuts across national borders and cultures. The sex industry is closely linked to increases in transnational trade, international migration, and global systems of production and communication. (See the panel titled "Globalization: Trafficking Sex for a Globalized Market.")

Trafficking Sex for a Globalized Market

What do oil, "Big Macs," and women all have in common? Although the link may seem elusive, it is a very important one. Each of these is largely connected to the global market. They are each commodities that are bought and sold in countries across the world. Many things and many people are affected in different ways by globalization, but women especially are negatively affected. Some even find themselves in what has come to be known as the global sex industry. The global sex industry can be understood as all of the activities, legal and illegal, performed by individuals and institutions around the world that service the system by which sex is bought and sold. Those who work in the sex industry are mostly women, but children are also involved. The process by which the sex industry has taken hold is complex, involving different actions by corporations. The requirement of companies to make a profit to stay in business and the desire to increase consumption by consumers in order to gain these profits have led to increased "needs" in various places across the world. Employing diverse tactics, companies make whatever their product is seem attractive and necessary, thus increasing the need for and consumption of the product. All of this is done in the name of profit. This has pervaded all sectors of society, including the sex industry (Doezema and Kempadoo, 1998:16–17). By relocating and creating new "needs" for people, as well as by creating fractured local economies, globalization has set the stage for the development of the sex industry.

The industrialization of sex work can be best illustrated by a common practice referred to as "trafficking." Trafficking is the profit-seeking system whereby women (and children) are moved from one place to another in order to perform sexual work for money. Involved in the trafficking are groups who want these workers to be brought to a certain area to perform sex acts as a draw to increase tourist interest in the area. This heightened interest brings consumers (mostly men) to the region, thus stimulating the economy. Also involved are those who are paid to ensure that women and children are available to be bought and sold, and those who are in control of the women and children when they arrive at their new location. Trafficking, then, requires an agreement between different groups whose common goal is money. While some of those involved may enter voluntarily, the majority is coerced into their situation. This coercion can occur because of the lack of other monetary options, which is often created either by large corporations leaving a city, causing joblessness, or by large corporations entering a city, creating competition that cannot be handled by local businesses. Thus, women may migrate to find better jobs and in this migration become involved in sex work (Doezema and Kempadoo, 1998:16–17). Also, promises of a better life or a better job, which are rarely, if ever, realized, are often used to lure women. "In this sense, sex tourism is like any other multinational industry, extracting enormous profits from grotesquely underpaid local labor and . . . in the context of the global economy" (Hennessy and Ingraham, 1997:256).

Corporations and globalization, then, put women workers in a precarious position by making them work in horrible conditions for low pay, forcing migration to find better jobs. These jobs, which may include being involved in sex trafficking, whether entered voluntarily or involuntarily, are exploitative and work to undermine the autonomy and livelihood of women across the world.

Source: This essay was written expressly for *In Conflict and Order*, 11th ed. by Katie Thurman, Department of Sociology, Michigan State University (2003). Jo Doezema and Kamala Kempadoo (eds.), 1998. *Global Sex Workers: Rights, Resistance, and Redefinition.* New York: Routledge, pp. 16–17. Rosemary Hennessy and Chrys Ingraham (eds.), 1997. *Materialist Feminism: A Reader in Class, Difference, and Women's Lives.* New York: Routledge, p. 256.

The Costs and Consequences of Sexism

Who Benefits?

Clearly, gender inequality enters all aspects of social life both in the United States and globally. This inequality is profitable to certain segments of the economy, and it also gives privileges to individual men.

Transnational corporations derive extra profits from paying women less than men. Worldwide, the workplace is segregated by gender. Women's segregation in low-paying jobs produces higher profits for certain economic sectors—namely, those where most of the workers are women. Women who are sole breadwinners and those who are in the workforce on a temporary basis have always been a source of easily exploitable labor. These women provide a significant proportion of the marginal labor force capitalists need to draw on during upswings in the business cycle and to release during downswings (Edwards, Reich, and Weisskopf, 1978:333).

Gender inequality is suited to the needs of the economy in other ways as well. The U.S. economy must accumulate capital and maintain labor power. This requires that all workers be physically and emotionally maintained. Who provides the daily maintenance that enables workers to be a part of the labor force? Women. They maintain the workers through the unpaid work they do caring for home, children, and elders. This keeps the economy going and it also provides privileges for individual men at women's expense.

The Social and Individual Costs

Gender inequality benefits certain segments of society. But society at large and women and men as individuals pay a high price for inequality. Sexism diminishes the quality of life for all people. Our society is deprived of half of its resources when women are denied full and equal participation in its institutions. If women are systematically kept from jobs requiring leadership, creativity, and productivity, the economy suffers. The pool of talent consisting of half the population will continue to be underutilized.

Sexism also produces suffering for millions. We have seen that individual women pay for economic discrimination. Their children pay as well. The poverty caused by gender inequality is a pressing problem in the new century. Adult women's chances of living in poverty are still higher than men's at every age. This is called the feminization of poverty (Pearce, 1978). Economist Nancy Folbre points out that the highest risk of poverty comes from being female and having children—which helps explain the high rates of both female and child poverty in the United States. Folbre calls this trend the "pauperization of motherhood" (Folbre, 1985, cited in Albelda and Tilly, 1997:24). Of course, sexism produces suffering around the world. Some women are persecuted simply because they are women.

Women's economic problems can be compounded by divorce and widowhood, which leave them worse off than men who lose their wives. But sexism's price is not only economic. The psychological costs of sexism are also deep. Society's devaluation of women can lead to low self-esteem, and a general sense of inadequacy.

Sexism also denies *men* the potential for full human development. Gender segregation denies employment opportunities to men who wish to enter such fields as nursing, grade-school teaching, or secretarial work. Eradicating sexism would benefit such males. It would benefit all males who have been forced into stereotypic male behaviors. In learning to be men, boys express their masculinity through toughness, competitiveness, and aggression. Expressions typically associated with femininity, such as gentleness and expressiveness, are seen as undesirable for males. In rigidly following gender expectations, males pay a price. As Pleck (1981) puts it:

> The conventional expectations of what it means to be a man are difficult to live up to for all but the lucky few and lead to unnecessary self-deprivation in the rest when they do not measure up. Even for those who do, there is a price: they may be forced, for example, to inhibit the expression of many emotions. (69)

Male inexpressiveness can hinder communication between husbands and wives and between fathers and children; it has been called "a tragedy of American society" (Balswick and Peck, 1971). Certainly, it is a tragedy for the man himself, crippled by an inability to show the best part of a human being—his warm and tender feelings for other people (Balswick and Collier, 1976:59).

Fighting the System

Feminist Movements in the United States

Gender inequality in this society has led to feminist social movements. Three stages of feminism have been aimed at overcoming sex discrimination. The first stage grew out of the abolition movement of the 1830s. Working to abolish slavery, women found that they were not equal with their male abolitionist friends. They became convinced that women's freedom was as important as freedom from slavery. In July 1848, the first convention in history devoted to women's rights was held at Seneca Falls, New York. Participants in the Seneca Falls convention approved a declaration of independence, asserting that men and women are created equal and that they are endowed with certain inalienable rights.

During the Civil War, feminists turned their attention to the emancipation of Blacks. After the war and the ratification of the Thirteenth Amendment abolishing slavery, feminists were divided between those seeking broad social reforms and those seeking voting rights for women. The second stage of feminism gave priority to voting. The women's suffrage amendment, introduced into every session of Congress from 1878 on, was ratified on August 26, 1920, nearly three-quarters of a century after the demand for women's suffrage had been made at the Seneca Falls convention. From 1920 until the 1960s, feminism was dormant: "So much energy had been expended in achieving the right to vote that the woman's movement virtually collapsed from exhaustion" (Hole and Levine, 1979:554).

Feminism was reawakened in the 1960s. Social movements of that era gave rise to an important branch of contemporary feminism. The civil rights movement and other protest movements of the 1960s spread the ideology of equality. But like the early feminists, women involved in political protest movements found male dominance even in social movements seeking equality. Finding injustice in freedom movements, they broadened their protest to concerns such as health care, family life, and relationships between the sexes. Another strand of contemporary feminism emerged among professional women who discovered sex discrimination in earnings and advancement. Formal organizations such as the National Organization for Women evolved, seeking legislation to overcome sex discrimination (Freeman, 1979).

These two branches of contemporary feminism gave rise to a feminist consciousness among millions of U.S. women. During the 1960s and early 1970s, this produced many changes in the roles of women and men. However, periods of recession, high unemployment, and inflation in the late 1970s fed a backlash against feminism. Today's women's movement may be the first in U.S. history to face an *antifeminist* social movement. From the mid-1970s, a coalition of groups calling themselves profamily and prolife emerged. These groups, drawn from right-wing political organizations and religious organizations, oppose feminist gains in reproductive, family, and antidiscrimination policies. Many gains have been set back by opposition to affirmative action programs and other equal rights policies. Political, legal, and media opposition to feminism continues to undermine women's equality (Faludi, 1991).

Women's Struggles in the Twenty-First Century

The women's movement is not over. Quite the contrary, the women's movement remains one of the most influential sources of social change, even though there is not a unified organization that represents feminism (Andersen, 2005:320). Not only do mainstream feminist organizations persist, but the struggles for women's rights continue. Today, many feminist activities occur at the grassroots level, where issues of race, class, and sexuality are important. In communities across the country, women and men fight

> against the abuse of women, against corporate poisoning of their neighborhoods, against homophobia, and racism, and for people-oriented economic development, immigrants' rights, educational equity, and adequate wages. Many have been engaged in such struggles for most their lives and continue despite the decline in the wider society's support for a progressive social agenda. (Naples, 1998:1)

Whether or not they call themselves feminist, women and men activists across the country and around the world are using their community-based organizing to fight for social justice (see the panel titled "Human Agency: Empowering Poor Women and Protecting the Environment"). Instead of responding passively to the outside world, they are forging new agendas and strategies to benefit women.

Empowering Poor Women and Protecting the Environment: The Story of Wangari Maathai, Nobel Peace Laureate

In 2004 the Nobel Peace Prize was awarded to an exceptional woman, Wangari Maathai. Maathai, of Kenya, was awarded the prestigious prize in recognition of "her contribution to sustainable development, democracy and peace" (The Norwegian Nobel Committee, 2004) through her work assisting poor women to improve their ability to provide for their families and mitigate environmental degradation by planting trees. She became the first African woman and the first African person from the vast area between South Africa and Egypt to be awarded the prize. Maathai's story is one of dedication and determination, and illustrates how through human agency one person can have an immensely wide and positive impact.

Wangari Maathai was born in Nyeri, Kenya, in 1940. Her academic accomplishments would first set her apart. Educated in Kenya, the United States, and Germany, Maathai became the first woman in Kenya to earn a doctoral degree, the first woman professor at the University of Nairobi, and the first woman in the region to become chair of a Department of Veterinary Anatomy (Mjøs, 2004; The Nobel Foundation, 2004).

Maathai's impressive academic achievements would later be eclipsed only by her own accomplishments as an activist. In 1977, she resigned from her position as chair of her department and founded the Green Belt Movement. The purpose of the movement was to plant trees in an attempt to mitigate the increasing deforestation in Kenya and across the African continent (Kenya lost 90 percent of its forests in the second half of the twentieth century). Maathai began the movement simply by planting nine trees in her own backyard (Mjøs, 2004).

Trained as a biologist, Maathai was aware of the negative consequences of the deforestation, loss of biodiversity, and increasing pollution in the region; however, she was also keenly aware of the social consequences of environmental degradation. In her Nobel Peace Prize acceptance speech, Maathai explained that she began the Green Belt Movement in response "to the needs identified by rural women, namely lack of firewood, clean drinking water, balanced diets, shelter and income" (Maathai, 2004). Due to their role as primary caretakers of the family, many women's responsibilities in the region entail working with the land, livestock, and natural resources. As a result, women are often the first to notice that the environment is being compromised. Because of their labor role, women also experience unique effects of environmental degradation. For instance, due to water pollution women have to walk long distances to collect water for their families (Maathai, 2004). In explaining how these human and environmental concerns are intertwined, Maathai stated in her speech "[t]here can be no peace without equitable development; and there can be no development without sustainable management of the environment in a democratic and peaceful space" (Maathai, 2004).

To date, the Green Belt Movement has mobilized poor women to plant over 30 million trees that not only mitigate environmental damage but also provide fuel, food, shelter, and income for impoverished women and their families. This successful movement has also been expanded to other countries and is not only involved in planting trees, but has also developed education, family planning, and nutrition programs as well (BBC News, 2004; Maathai, 2004; Mjøs, 2004).

Empowering Poor Women and Protecting the Environment: The Story of Wangari Maathai, Nobel Peace Laureate continued

In addition to her academic and activist accomplishments, Maathai has also been active in politics. In the 1980s she became the Chairperson of the National Council of Women and became one of the leaders of the prodemocracy movement in her country. In 2002, when the authoritarian leader of Kenya had to relinquish power, Maathai was elected to Parliament (Mjøs, 2004), winning with an astounding 98 percent of the vote (The Nobel Foundation, 2004). Subsequently, in 2003, she was appointed Deputy Minister of Environment, Natural Resources and Wildlife in Kenya (Mjøs, 2004). Maathai went on to write a book titled The Green Belt Movement: Sharing the Approach and the Experience (2003) and to found the Wangari Maathai Foundation to facilitate the work of the movement and to promote its activities in other countries (The Wangari Maathai Foundation, 2005).

These numerous achievements, however, did not come without a cost. Maathai's activities championing sustainable development, women's rights, and democracy made her a target of the authorities: she was harassed, repeatedly sent to prison, attacked with tear gas, clubbed (Mjøs, 2004), and beaten unconscious (BBC News, 2004). Additionally, her ambition and determination have been considered by many Kenyans to be unsuitable for and unbecoming of a woman. Her ex-husband, whom she divorced in the 1980s, has been quoted as saying that his ex-wife was "too educated, too strong, too successful, too stubborn and too hard to control" (cited by the BBC News, 2004). The physical and emotional toll, however, could not dampen her resolve.

Wangari Maathai's accomplishments as an academic, activist, and politician have been remarkable. But her overall impact is even greater than her own direct actions: her accomplishments and tireless dedication can serve as inspiration for all of us to make our own positive changes in the world. Her story demonstrates that even something as seemingly inconsequential as planting nine trees in one's backyard can spark broader action and have profound social consequences.

References:

BBC News. 2004. "Profile: Wangari Maathai." Friday, October 8. Available online: http://news.bbcco.uk/1/hi/world/africa/3726084.stm Accessed June 8, 2005.

Maathai, Wangari. 2003. *The Green Belt Movement: Sharing the Approach and the Experience.* New York: Lantern.

____. 2004. "Nobel Lecture." Given December 10, in Oslo City Hall, Norway. Available online: http://nobelprize.org/peace/laureates/2004/maathai-lecture-text.html Accessed June 17, 2005.

Mjøs, Ole Danbolt. 2004. "Nobel Peace Prize 2004 Presentation Speech." Given December 10 in Oslo City Hall, Norway. Available online: http://nobelprize.org/peace/laureates/2004/presentation-speech.html Accessed June 17, 2005.

The Nobel Foundation. 2004. "Wangari Maathai—Biography." Available online: http://nobelprize.org/peace/laureates/2004/maathai-bio.html Accessed June 16, 2005.

The Norwegian Nobel Committee. 2004. "Press Release—The Nobel Peace Prize 2004." Available online: http://nobelprize.org/peace/laureates/2004/maathai-bio.html Accessed June 16, 2005.

The Wangari Maathai Foundation. 2005. Available online: http://www. wangari-maathai.org/

Source: Amy Fitzgerald, Department of Sociology, Michigan State University, 2005. Reprinted by permission.

Chapter Review

1. U.S. society, like other societies, ranks and rewards women and men unequally.

2. Gender differences are not natural. They are social inventions. Although gender divisions make women unequal to men, different groups of men exhibit varying degrees of power, and different groups of women exhibit varying levels of inequality.

3. Men as well as women are gendered beings.

4. Gender works with the inequalities of race, class, and sexuality to produce different experiences for all women and men.

5. The conflict and order perspectives provide different explanations of women's inequality. Order theorists emphasize division of labor and social integration; conflict theorists emphasize the economic structure of society in producing women's inequality.

6. Many sociologists have viewed gender inequality as the consequences of learned behavior. Sociologists tend to view gender as a characteristic of social structure.

7. Gender inequality is reinforced through language, interpersonal behavior, mass communication, religion, the law, and politics.

8. The segregation of women in a few gendered occupations contrasts with that of men, who are distributed throughout the occupational hierarchy; and women, even with the same amount of education and when doing the same work, earn less than men in all occupations.

9. Gender segregation is the basic source of gender inequality in the labor force. Work opportunities for women tend to concentrate in a secondary market that has few advancement opportunities, fewer job benefits, and lower pay.

10. The combined effects of gender and racial segregation in the labor force keep women of color at the bottom of the work hierarchy, where working conditions are harsh and earnings are low.

11. The global economy is strongly gendered. Around the world, women's labor is key to global development strategies.

12. Gender inequality deprives society of the potential contributions of half its members, creates poverty among families headed by women, and limits the capacities of all women and men.

13. Feminist movements have created significant changes at all levels of society. Despite a backlash against feminism, women across the country continue to struggle for equal rights.

Key Terms

Sex
Gendered
Feminist approach
Gender stratification
Gendered institutions

Male dominance
Compulsory heterosexuality
Sexuality
Capitalist patriarchy
Gender structure

Androgyny
Gender segregation
Pay equity
Glass ceiling

Study Questions

1. In explaining gender inequality, order theorists emphasize the gender-roles approach, whereas conflict theorists focus on structural factors. Compare and assess these two approaches.

2. What are the individual and institutional mechanisms that reinforce gender inequality in society?

3. The incomes of men and women differ significantly. Why?

4. How do female officeholders make a difference?

5. Who benefits from gender inequality?

For Further Reading

Margaret L. Andersen, *Thinking about Women*, 7th ed. (Boston: Allyn and Bacon, 2006).

Maxine Baca Zinn, Pierrette Hondagneu-Sotelo, and Michael A. Messner (eds.), *Gender through the Prism of Difference*, 3rd ed. (New York: Oxford University Press, 2005).

Irene Brown (ed.), *Latinas and African American Women at Work* (New York: Russell Sage Foundation, 1999).

Paula J. Dubeck and Dana Dunn (eds.), *Workplace, Women's Place*, 2nd ed. (Los Angeles: Roxbury Publishing Company, 2002).

Michael Kimmel and Michael A. Messner, *Men's Lives*, 6th ed. (Boston: Allyn and Bacon, 2004).

Judith Lorber, *Gender Inequality: Feminist Theories and Politcs*, 3rd ed. (Los Angeles: Roxbury Publishing Company, 2005).

Barrie Thorne, *Gender Play: Girls and Boys in School* (New Brunswick, NJ: Rutgers University Press, 1993).

Web Resources

http://www.dol.gov/wb/
The U.S. Department of Labor Women's Bureau site has important publications put out by the bureau, as well as statistics that are pertinent to women.

http://www.chicanas.com/huh.html
Making Face, Making Soul is a Chicana feminist site. The site offers news relevant to Chicana women, information on academics, including a list of Chicana professors, and other useful information.

http://www.feminist.com/fairpay/
The National Committee on Pay Equity is a coalition to eliminate discrimination in pay based on both race and sex.

http://www.cluw.org/
The Coalition of Labor Union Women looks to empower women workers in their lives, at work, and in their unions. Links and current events information are available.

http://www.catwinternational.org/about/
The Coalition against Trafficking in Women "promotes women's rights. It works internationally to combat sexual exploitation in all its forms, especially prostitution and trafficking in women and children, in particular girls."

http://www.femina.com/
Femina is a site that offers links, from A to Y, to "sites for, by, and about women."

http://www.rslevinson.com/gaylesissues/
All Things Queer is a gay and lesbian site devoted to issues surrounding the community, including coming-out stories, news, and other resources with relevant information.

http://www.hsph.harvard.edu/grhf/WoC/index.html
The Women of Color Web provides articles on different issues, such as reproductive rights and sexualities as they relate to women of color. The site also has information on teaching tools, organizations, activism, and health.

http://www.feminist.org
The Feminist Majority is a private organization dedicated to women's equality. The website provides information on a wide array of subjects, including global issues, reproductive rights, health and safety, and other subjects.

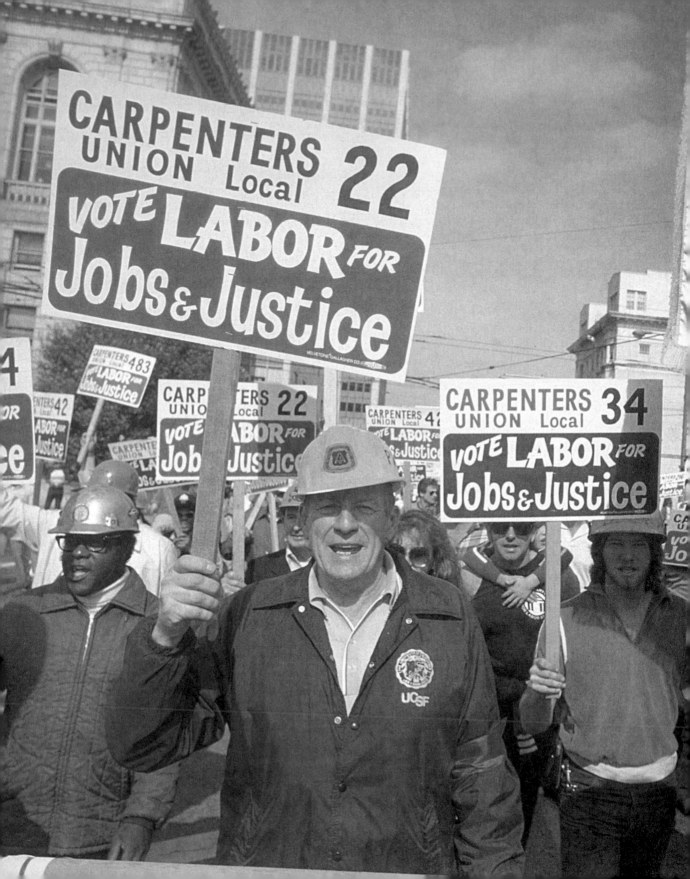

The Economy

Since 2002, Wal-Mart has been ranked in the Number One position on *Fortune's* list of the 500 biggest U.S. companies. In doing so, it underscores the economic transformation of the economy, since Wal-Mart, unlike previous Number Ones (such as General Motors or Exxon) does not make or produce anything. Thus it symbolizes the "New Economy." But just what does the ascendancy of Wal-Mart signify? For David Callahan (2002) of Demos, a New York public policy research and advocacy group, Wal-Mart shows the dark side of the "New Economy":

Low-skilled jobs: In the Wal-Mart economy, the most valued productivity gains include those that automate service transactions, allowing them to be more easily completed by low-skilled, lower-paid workers. These workers are easier to find, easier to use in part-time positions, without benefits and less likely to unionize. Wal-Mart's legions of low-paid, non-unionized workers (some 60% of whom don't have company-provided health insurance) are part of the fastest-growing labor market sector: 73.9% of new jobs created between 1989 and 1999 were in such low-wage service industries. In 2000, tech jobs comprised only 5% of all U.S. jobs. Retail and services accounted for far more.

Fewer options: Wal-Mart is famous for offering wide customer choices. But it is also famous for driving surrounding smaller competitors out of business. When they disappear, consumers' choices are decided by Wal-Mart, sometimes in disturbing ways. For example, if Wal-Mart is your only pharmacy option, and you need emergency contraception, forget it. Wal-Mart's conservative management decreed that its pharmacies would not carry the morning-after pill. In an economy of ubiquitous chains and franchises, consumer choices actually narrow, and shoppers are increasingly served by less-knowledgeable, less-well-trained employees who are less likely to know them.

Environmental woes: The real New Economy generates endless sprawl and mind-boggling waste. Again, Wal-Mart typifies the problem. Its stores can cover 100,000 square feet. With parking areas, new Wal-Marts can encompass more than 25 acres. (11A)*

*From "Wal-Mart, Not High Tech, Defines 'New Economy,'" by David Callahan, *USA Today*, April 18, 2002. Reprinted with permission.

The next five chapters of this book describe the fundamental institutions of society. As noted in Chapter 2, institutions are social arrangements that channel behavior in prescribed ways in the important areas of social life. They are interrelated sets of normative elements—norms, values, and role expectations—that the people making up the society have devised and passed on to succeeding generations in order to provide solutions to society's perpetually unfinished business. The institutions of society—family, education, religion, polity, and economy—are interrelated. But even though there are reciprocal effects among the institutions, the economy and the polity are the core institutions. The way society is organized to produce and distribute goods and services and the way power is organized are the crucial determinants of the way the other institutions are organized. We begin, then, with a chapter on the economy, followed by a chapter on the polity. The remaining three chapters focus on the supporting institutions of the family, education, and religion. Each of these institutions is strongly affected by the form of the economy and power arrangements in the contemporary United States.

This chapter describes the economy of the United States. Four areas are emphasized: the domination of huge corporations, the maldistribution of wealth, the social organization of work, and the current economic crises. We start, though, with a brief description of the two fundamental ways societies can organize their economic activities.

Capitalism and Socialism

Industrialized societies organize their economic activities according to one of two fundamental forms: capitalism or socialism. Although no society has a purely capitalist or socialist economy, the ideal types provide opposite extremes on a scale that helps us measure the U.S. economy more accurately.

Capitalism

Three conditions must be present for pure **capitalism** to exist—private ownership of the means of production, personal profit, and competition. These necessary conditions constitute the underlying principles of a pure capitalist system. The first is private ownership of the means of production. Individuals own not only private possessions but also, most important, the capital necessary to produce and distribute goods and services. In a purely capitalist society, there would be no public ownership of any potentially profitable activity.

The pursuit of maximum profit, the second essential principle, implies that individuals are free to maximize their personal gains. This means that the proponents of capitalism argue that profit seeking by individuals has positive consequences for society (i.e., job creation, economic growth).

Competition, the third ingredient, is the mechanism for determining what is produced and at what price. The market forces of supply and demand ensure that capitalists will produce the goods and services wanted by the public, that the goods will be high in quality, and that they will be sold at the lowest possible price. Moreover, competition is the mechanism that keeps individual profit seeking in check.

Potential abuses such as fraud, faulty products, and exorbitant prices are negated by the existence of competitors, who will soon take business away from those who violate good business judgment. So, too, economic inefficiency is minimized as market forces cause the inept to fail and the efficient to succeed.

These three principles—private property, personal profit, and competition—require a fourth condition if true capitalism is to work: a government policy of *laissez-faire*, allowing the marketplace to operate unhindered. Any government intervention in the marketplace will, argue capitalists, distort the economy by negatively affecting incentives and freedom of individual choice. If left unhindered by government, the profit motive, private ownership, and competition will achieve the greatest good for the greatest number in the form of individual self-fulfillment and the general material progress of society.

Critics argue that capitalism promotes inequality and a host of social problems because the object is profit, not enhancing the human condition. Consider this critique by the Reverend Jesse Jackson (1998):

> The operation of free markets is a wondrous and mighty thing. To allocate goods and services, to adjust supply with demand, the market has no equal. But the market sets the price—not the value—of things. It counts consumers, not citizens. . . . The market has no opinion on the distribution of income, wealth and opportunity in society. . . . The market does not care if kids in Appalachia or Brooklyn go to school in buildings that are dangerous to their health. The market has no opinion on whether opportunity is open to the many, or limited to the few. The market does not care that [41] million Americans go to bed every night without health insurance. . . . The market does not care if the economy is swimming in speculative capital, but large segments of the country are effectively redlined [a banking practice of not loaning money within certain boundaries, most typically where the poor and racial minorities

are located] as banks merge. The market does not care if the shows our children watch on television are filled with sex, violence, and racial stereotyping. The market measures TV shows by the price of their advertising. On the values they impart, the market has no opinion. (19)

As political observer Molly Ivins (2000) has observed: "Capitalism . . . is a dandy system for creating wealth, but it doesn't do squat for social justice. No reason to expect it to—that's not its job" (22).

The economy of the United States is not purely capitalistic. Taxes are levied on people and business operations to raise monies for the common good such as a federal interstate highway system, the air traffic control system and the subsidizing of airports, flood control projects, the defense establishment, the postal system, and disaster relief. In many ways the government interferes with the market by monitoring the safety of food and drugs, prohibiting the sale of certain products, issuing licenses, protecting the civil rights of women and minorities, taxing income, subsidizing business activities, overseeing the banking and insurance industries, and preventing monopolies.

Morever, while U.S. social programs are less generous than found in the social welfare states, there is nonetheless minimal help for victims of natural disasters, preschool training for children of the poor, low-interest student loans, Medicare, and Medicaid.

Socialism

Socialism is an economic system in which the means of production are owned by the people for their collective benefit. The five principles of socialism are democratism, egalitarianism, community, public ownership of the means of production, and planning for common purposes. True socialism must be democratic. Representatives of a socialist state must be answerable and responsive to the wishes of the public they serve. Nations that claim to be socialist but are totalitarian violate this fundamental aspect of socialism. The key to differentiating between authentic and spurious socialism is to determine who is making the decisions and whose interests are being served. Thus, it is a fallacy to equate true socialism with the politicoeconomic systems of the former Soviet Union, the People's Republic of China, or Cuba. These societies are socialistic in some respects; that is, their material benefits are more evenly distributed than those in the United States. But their economies and governments are controlled by a single political party in an inflexible and authoritarian manner. Although these countries claim to have democratic elections, in fact the citizens have no electoral choice but to rubber-stamp the candidates of the ruling party. The people are denied civil liberties and freedoms that should be the hallmark of a socialist society. In a pure socialist society, democratic relations must operate throughout the social structure: in government, at work, at school, and in the community.

The second principle of socialism is egalitarianism: equality of opportunity for the self-fulfillment of all, equality rather than hierarchy in decision making, and equality in sharing the benefits of society. For some socialists, the goal is absolute equality. For most, though, equality means a limit to inequality, with some acceptable disparities in living standards. This more realistic goal of socialism requires a fundamental commitment to achieving a rough parity by leveling out gross inequities in income, property, and opportunities. The key is a leveling of advantages so that all citizens receive the necessities (food, clothing, shelter, medical care, living wages, sick pay, and retirement benefits).

The third feature of socialism is community, which is the "idea that social relations should be characterized by cooperation and a sense of collective belonging rather than by conflict and competition" (Miller, David, 1991:406). This sense of the collective is evidenced by a relatively high taxation rate to provide for the common good—such as universal health care, paid maternity leave, subsidized child care, universal preschool programs, and a generous retirement program.

The fourth characteristic of socialism is the public ownership of the means of production. The people own the basic industries, financial institutions, utilities, transportation, and communication companies. The goal is serving the public, not making a profit.

The fifth principle of socialism is planning. The society must direct social activities to meet common goals. This means that socialists oppose the heart of capitalism, which is to let individuals and corporations acting in their own interests in the marketplace determine overall outcomes. For socialists, these uncoordinated activities invite chaos and, while possibly helping some in the society, will do damage to others. Thus, a purely socialist economy requires societal planning to provide, at the least possible individual and collective cost, the best conditions to meet the material needs of its citizens. Planning also aims to achieve societal goals such as protecting the environment, combating pollution, saving natural resources, and developing new technologies. Public policy is decided through the rational assessment of the needs of society and of how the economy might best be organized to achieve them. In this situation the economy must be regulated by the government, which acts as the agent of the people. The government sets prices and wages; important industries are run at a loss if necessary. Dislocations such as surpluses or shortages or unemployment are minimized by central planning. The goal is to run the economy for the good of the society.

Critics of democratic socialism argue that it minimizes individual freedom and choice. Government monopoly is inefficient because of a centralized bureaucracy making "one size fits all" decisions. Taxes are high to pay for the expensive social programs. And, the argument goes, the "cradle to grave" social programs for individuals and families reduce their motivation to succeed, an attitude that when held by many limits creativity, economic productivity, growth, and the striving for excellence.

The Corporation-Dominated Economy

The U.S. economy has always been based on the principles of capitalism; however, the present economy is far removed from a free enterprise system. The major discrepancy between the ideal system and the real one is that the U.S. economy is no longer based on competition among more or less equal private capitalists. It is now dominated by huge corporations that, contrary to classical economic theory, control demand rather than respond to the demands of the market. However well the economic system might once have worked, the increasing size and power of corporations disrupt it. This development calls into question the appropriate economic form for a modern postindustrial society. This section examines the consequences of concentrated economic power domestically and internationally, for they create many important social problems.

Monopolistic Capitalism

Karl Marx, more than 130 years ago, when bigness was the exception, predicted that capitalism was doomed by several inherent contradictions that would produce a class of people bent on destroying it. The most significant of these contradictions for our purposes is the inevitability of monopolies.* Marx hypothesized that free enterprise would result in some firms becoming bigger and bigger as they eliminate their opposition or absorb smaller competing firms. The ultimate result of this process is the existence of a monopoly in each of the various sectors of the economy. Monopolies, of course, are antithetical to the free enterprise system because they, not supply and demand, determine the price and the quality of the product.

For the most part, the evidence in U.S. society upholds Marx's prediction. Less than 1 percent of all corporations produce over 80 percent of the private-sector output. Most sectors of the economy are dominated by few corporations. Instead of one corporation controlling an industry, the typical situation is domination by a small number of firms. When four or fewer firms supply 50 percent or more of a particular market, a **shared monopoly** results, which performs much as a monopoly or cartel would. Most economists agree that above this level of concentration—a four-firm ratio of 50 percent—the economic costs of a shared monopoly are manifest (for example, higher prices by 25 percent). Government data show that a number of industries are highly concentrated (for example, each of the following industries has four or fewer firms controlling at least 60 percent): light bulbs, breakfast cereals, turbines/generators, aluminum, tobacco, beer, chocolate/cocoa, photography equipment, trucks, cosmetics, film distribution, soft drinks, snack foods, guided missiles, and roasted coffee.

This trend toward ever greater concentration among the largest U.S. business concerns has accelerated because of two activities—mergers and interlocking directorates.

Megamergers. There are thousands of mergers each year, as giant corporations become even larger. The ten largest mergers in U.S. history have occurred in the past fifteen years or so (for example, Time, Inc., and AOL joining with Warner Communications; Disney merging with Capital Cities/ABC; the combining of Wells Fargo and First Interstate Banks; the merger of NationsBank and Bank-America; Philip Morris taking over Miller Brewing; the AT&T buyout of Tele-Communications, Inc.; Citicorp merging with Travelers Group; Texaco buying out Getty Oil; and Exxon merging with Mobil Oil). There have also been megamergers combining U.S. and foreign firms (e.g., Daimler and Chrysler, British Petroleum and Amoco, and Deutsche Bank and Bankers Trust). The federal government encouraged these mergers by relaxing antitrust law enforcement on the grounds that efficient firms should not be hobbled.

This trend toward megamergers has at least six negative consequences: (1) it increases the centralization of capital, which reduces competition and raises prices

---

*Marx prophesied that capitalism carried the seeds of its own destruction. In addition to resulting in monopolies, capitalism (1) encourages crises—inflation, slumps, gluts, depressions—because the lack of central planning means the overproduction of some goods and the underproduction of others; (2) encourages mass production for expansion and profits, but in so doing, a social class, the proletariat (working class), is created that has the goal of equalizing the distribution of profits; (3) demands the introduction of labor-saving machinery, which forces unemployment and a more hostile proletariat; and (4) will control the state, the effect of which is that the state will pass laws favoring the wealthy, thereby incurring the further wrath of the proletariat. All of these contradictions of capitalism increase the probability of the proletariat building class consciousness, which is the condition necessary before class conflict and the ushering in of a new economic system (Marx, 1967).

for consumers; (2) it increases the power of huge corporations over workers, unions, and governments; (3) the benefits to local communities are diminished ("Superlarge companies with interests and commitments stretching from Boston to Brisbane are unlikely to focus as intensely as smaller ones do on support for the local neighborhoods—the schools, the arts, the development of research activities, the training of potential workers" [Garten, 1999:28]); (4) it reduces the number of jobs (for example, when Citicorp and Travelers combined to make Citigroup, 10,400 jobs were cut); (5) it increases corporate debt (currently, U.S. corporations spend about half their earnings on interest payments); and (6) it is nonproductive. Elaborating on this last point, mergers and takeovers do not create new plants, products, or jobs. Rather, they create profits for lawyers, accountants, brokers, bankers, and big investors.

Defenders of a free and competitive enterprise system should attack the existence of monopolies and shared monopolies as un-American. There should be strong support of governmental efforts to break up the largest and most powerful corporations.

Interlocking Directorates. Another mechanism for the ever greater concentration of the size and power of the largest corporations is **interlocking directorates**, the linkage between corporations that results when an individual serves on the board of directors of two companies (a **direct interlock**) or when two companies each have a director on the board of a third company (an **indirect interlock**). Such arrangements have great potential to benefit the interlocked companies by reducing competition through the sharing of information and the coordination of policies.

In 1914, passage of the Clayton Act made it illegal for a person to serve simultaneously on the corporate boards of two companies that were in direct competition with each other. Financial institutions and indirect interlocks, however, were exempt. Moreover, the government has had difficulty in determining what constitutes "direct competition." The result is that despite the prohibition, over 90 percent of large U.S. corporations have some interlocking directors with other corporations.

Interlocking directorates proliferate throughout U.S. industry. When directors are linked directly or indirectly, there is the potential for cohesiveness, common action, and unified power. Clearly, the principles of capitalism are compromised when this phenomenon occurs.

Transnational Corporations

The thesis of the previous section is that there is a trend for corporations to increase in size, eventually resulting in huge enterprises that join with other large companies to form effective monopolies. This process of economic concentration provides the largest companies with enormous economic and political power.

Another trend—the globalization of the largest U.S. corporations—makes their power all the greater. This fact of international economic life has very important implications for social problems, both domestically and abroad.

A number of U.S. corporations have substantial assets overseas. Why are they shifting more and more of their total assets outside the United States? The obvious answer is that the rate of profit tends to be higher abroad. Resources necessary for manufacture and production tend to be cheaper in many other nations. Most significant, U.S. corporations increase their profits by moving their production facilities from high-wage situations to low-wage nonunion countries. Moreover, foreign production costs are lower because labor safety laws and environmental protection laws are much more lax than in the United States.

The consequences of this shift in production from the United States to outside this country are significant. Most important is the reduction of, even drying up of, many semiskilled and unskilled jobs in the United States. The effects of increased unemployment are twofold: increased welfare costs and increased discontent among those in the working class. (This problem of domestic job losses through overseas capital investments was discussed in Chapter 8.)

Another result of the twin processes of concentration and internationalization of corporations is the enormous power wielded by the gigantic multinational corporation. In essence, the largest corporations control the world economy. Their decisions to build or not to build, where to relocate a plant, and to start a new product or to scrap an old one have tremendous impacts on the lives of ordinary citizens in the countries they operate from and invest in and in their disinvestment in U.S.-based operations.

Finally, multinational corporations tend to meddle in the internal affairs of other nations in order to protect their investments and maximize profits. These activities include attempts to overthrow governments considered unfriendly to corporate interests and payment of millions of dollars in bribes and political contributions to reactionary governments and conservative leaders in various countries.

Capitalism and Inequality

Inequality is endemic to capitalism. In the competition for profits there are winners and losers. But, as economist Lester Thurow puts it:

> In the theology of capitalism the distributions of wealth, income and earnings are of no consequence. There is no concept of fairness other than that those who produce in the market are fairly compensated by the market. Those who do not produce are shoved aside by the market. They do not get to consume-they do not deserve to consume. (quoted in Collins, Leondar-Wright, and Sklar, 1999:1)

We have seen how corporate wealth is concentrated through shared monopolies and interlocking directorates. Let's begin by reviewing the degree to which corporate wealth is concentrated.

Concentration of Corporate Wealth

Wealth in the business community is centralized in a relatively few corporations, and this concentration is increasing. In 2002, for example, the minimum revenue to be included among the 500 largest corporations was $2.8 billion, with the top corporation—Wal-Mart—having $244 in revenues (*Forbes*, 2003). The following examples reveal just how concentrated wealth is among the major U.S. corporations:

- Less than 1 percent of all corporations account for over 80 percent of the total output of the private sector.

- Of the 15,000 commercial U.S. banks, the largest fifty hold more than one-third of all assets.
- One percent of all food corporations control 80 percent of all the industry's assets and about 90 percent of the profits.
- Six U.S.-based transnational corporations ship 90 percent of the grain in the world market.
- Five massive conglomerates (Viacom/CBS; Disney/ABC; News Corp./Fox; NBC; and AOL Time Warner) now command 75 percent of prime-time television. Similarly, 2 conglomerates (Clear Channel and Viacom) together own radio stations with 42 percent of the nation's listeners.

Concentration of Private Wealth and Income

Capitalism generates inequality. Wealth is concentrated not only in the largest corporations but also among individuals and families. For example, in 2004, according to *Forbes* (reported in Reed, 2004), Bill Gates, head of software giant Microsoft, was the wealthiest person in 2004 at about $48 billion, followed by Warren Buffett of Berkshire Hathaway with $42 billion, and 311 other billionaires.

A few families are fabulously wealthy and colossal in corporate magnitude. The five heirs to Sam Walton, founder of Wal-Mart, for example, were worth a combined $90 billion in 2004. Dividends from their Wal-Mart stock adds a cumulative total of $1 billion annually. Michael Parenti (2002) describes the holdings of few "old-rich" families:

> A handful of giant business conglomerates, controlled by the Mellons, Morgans, DuPonts, Rockefellers, and a few others, dominate the U.S. economy. The DuPonts control ten corporations, each worth billions of dollars, including General Motors, Coca-Cola, and United Brands, along with many smaller firms. The DuPonts serve as trustees of dozens of colleges. They own about forty manorial estates and private museums in Delaware alone and have set up thirty-one tax-exempt foundations. . . .
>
> Another powerful financial empire, that of the Rockefellers, extends into just about every industry in every state of the Union and every nation of the world. The Rockefellers control five of the world's twelve largest oil companies and four of the biggest banks. (12)

Concentration of Want and Misery

The inequality generated by a capitalist economy has a dark side. Summarizing the 2000 data on poverty in the United States (found in Chapter 10), 12.5 percent of the population (35.9 million people) were below the poverty line. According to the National Council on Economic Opportunity, another 30 million were on the edge of poverty. The data indicate that the poor are concentrated among certain social categories, especially people of color and families headed by women.

Again, summarizing from earlier chapters, research strongly substantiates how the life chances of the poor are jeopardized by their lack of resources. The fewer the resources available, the greater are the possibilities for any of the following to occur:

- Premature births and babies born mentally retarded because of prenatal malnourishment

- Below-average life expectancy
- Disproportionate death from tuberculosis, influenza, pneumonia; from cancer of the stomach, lung, bronchus, and trachea; and from accidents
- Impaired health because of differences in diet, sanitary facilities, shelter, and medical care
- More frequent and longer periods of illness
- An arrest, conviction, and serving of a longer sentence for a given violation
- A lower-than-average level of educational attainment
- Spouse and child abuse, divorce, and desertion

Thus, the economic position of a family has very telling consequences on the probability of good health, educational attainment, justice, and a stable marriage.

Work in U.S. Society

Work is central to the human experience. Societies are organized to allocate work in order to produce the goods and services needed by the society and its members for sustenance, clothing, shelter, defense, and even luxury. Work provides individuals with their social identity, economic resources, and social location. Work dominates their time and is a primary source of life's meaning because it constitutes their contributions to other people.

The world of work also has a dark side, however. The structure of work is a major source of social problems. Work is alienating for many people. The organization of work sometimes exploits, does harm to workers, and often dehumanizes them. The distribution of work and how it is rewarded are major sources of inequality in society. This section focuses on the social problems generated by the social organization of work.

The Problems of Work

Work is a universal human activity. People everywhere engage in physical and mental activities that enhance the physical and social survival of themselves and others. Although people universally must work to meet their material needs, the way work is structured varies by society. Let's examine problems that emanate from the way work is structured in U.S. society.

The Control of Workers. With the advent of the Industrial Revolution, more and more families left agrarian life, moved to cities, and worked in factories. Work in these factories was sometimes difficult, often tedious, and usually boring. There was always the threat of lowered productivity and worker unrest under these adverse conditions. The factory owners and their managers used several tactics to counteract these potential problems and especially to maintain high productivity—scientific management, hierarchical control, technical control, and extortion.

Scientific management (called Taylorization, after its founder, Frederick Taylor) came to the fore in U.S. industry around 1900. The emphasis was on breaking down work into very specialized tasks, standardization of tools and procedures, and speeding up repetitive work. These efforts to increase worker efficiency and therefore to increase profits meant that workers developed a very limited range of skills. Instead of a wide knowledge of building cars or furniture, their knowledge was severely curtailed. This specialization had the effect of making workers highly susceptible to automation and to being easily replaced by cheaper workers. But the scientific-management approach also had a contradictory effect. In its attempt to increase efficiency by having workers do ever more compartmentalized tasks, it increased the repetition, boredom, and meaninglessness of work—hence, the strong tendency for workers to become alienated and restless. Consider the description by George Ritzer (2000):

> [The assembly line is clearly] a dehumanizing setting in which to work. Human beings, equipped with a wide array of skills and abilities, are asked to perform a limited number of highly simplified tasks over and over. Instead of expressing their human abilities on the job, people are forced to deny their humanity to act as robots. People cannot express themselves in their work. (32)

Closely related to scientific management is the use of bureaucracy to control workers. Work settings, whether in factories, offices, or corporations, are organized into bureaucratized hierarchies. In this hierarchy of authority (chain of command), each position in the chain gives orders to those below, taking responsibility for their actions and following orders from above. The hierarchical arrangement controls workers by holding out the possibility of advancement, with more prestigious job titles, higher wages, and greater benefits as one moves up the ladder. Those who hope to be upwardly mobile in the organization must become obedient rule followers who do not question authority.

Similarly, work organized along an assembly line permits maximum control over workers. "Workers must do certain tasks at specific points during the production process. It is immediately obvious when a worker fails to perform the required tasks" (Ritzer, 1996:25–26).

Workers are also controlled by management's use of technology to monitor and supervise them (see Chapter 6). Some businesses use lie detectors to assess worker loyalty. Psychological tests and drug tests are used to screen applicants for work. Telephone taps have been used to determine whether workers use company time for personal use. Closed-circuit television, two-way mirrors, and other devices have been used by management to determine whether workers are using their time most productively. The most common contemporary technology for worker control is the computer. The computer can count keystrokes, time phone calls, monitor frequency of errors, assess overall employee performance, and even issue warnings when the employee falls short of the ideal.

A final management tool to control workers is extortion. If workers become too militant in their demands for higher wages, safe working conditions, or benefits, management can threaten them with reprisals. In the past, owners threatened to hire cheaper labor (new immigrants, for example) or to use force to end a strike. Today, the most common and successful management tool is the threat to move the plant to a nonunion state (or even outside the United States if the union does not reduce its demands) or to replace the workers with robots or other forms of automation.

Alienation. **Alienation** refers to the separation of human beings from each other, from themselves, and from the products they create. In capitalism, according to Karl Marx, worker alienation occurs because the workers do not have any control over

Many forms of work are alienating because the work is routine, repetitive, boring, and unchallenging.

their labor; because they are manipulated by managers; because they tend to work in large, impersonal settings; and because they work at specialized tasks. Under these circumstances, workers use only a fraction of their talents and have no pride in their own creativity and in the final product. Thus, we see that worker alienation is linked with unfulfilled personal satisfaction. As Blauner (1964) describes it,

> [a]lienation exists when workers are unable to control their immediate work processes, to develop a sense of purpose and function which connects their jobs to the overall organization of production, to belong to integrated industrial communities, and when they fail to become involved in the activity of work as a mode of personal self-expression. (5)

Put another way, this time by philosopher Albert Camus: "Without work all life goes rotten. But when work is soulless, life stifles and dies" (quoted in Levitan and Johnson, 1982:63).

In the absence of satisfaction and personal fulfillment, work becomes meaningless. When this meaninglessness is coupled with management's efforts to control workers, the repetitious nature of the work, and the requirement of punching a time clock, many workers feel a profound resentment. This resentment may lead workers to join together in a union or other collective group to improve their working conditions. For many workers, though, the alienation remains at a personal level and is manifested by higher worker dissatisfaction, absenteeism, disruption in the workplace, and alcohol or other drug abuse on the job.

Alienation is not limited to manual workers. The work of white-collar workers such as salesclerks, secretaries, file clerks, bank tellers, and keypunchers is mostly routine, repetitive, boring, and unchallenging. These workers, like assembly line workers, follow orders, do limited tasks, and have little sense of accomplishment.

Studs Terkel (1975), in introducing his book *Working*, summarizes the personal impact of alienating work:

> This book, being about work, is, by its very nature, about violence—to the spirit as well as to the body. It is about ulcers as well as accidents, about shouting matches as well as fistfights, about nervous breakdowns as well as kicking the dog around. It is, above all (or beneath all), about daily humiliations. To survive the day is triumph enough for the walking wounded among the great many of us.
>
> It is about a search, too, for daily meaning as well as daily bread, for recognition as well as for cash, for astonishment rather than torpor; in short, for a sort of life rather than a Monday through Friday sort of dying. Perhaps immortality, too, is part of the quest. To be remembered was the wish, spoken and unspoken, of the heroes and heroines of this book.
>
> For the many, there is a hardly concealed discontent. The blue-collar blues is no more bitterly sung than the white-collar moan. "I'm a machine," says the spotwelder. "I'm caged," says the steelworker. "A monkey can do what I do," says the receptionist. "I'm less than a farm implement," says the migrant worker. "I'm an object," says the high-fashion model. Blue collar and white call upon the identical phrase: "I'm a robot." (xiii–xiv)

Dangerous Working Conditions. In a capitalist economy, workers represent a cost to profit-seeking corporations. The lower that management can keep labor costs, the greater will be their profits. Historically, low labor costs meant that workers received low wages, had inferior or nonexistent fringe benefits such as health care, and worked in unhealthy conditions. Mines and factories were often extremely unsafe. The labor movement early in this century gathered momentum because of the abuse experienced by workers.

After a long and sometimes violent struggle, the unions succeeded in raising wages for workers, adding fringe benefits, and making work conditions safer. But the owners were slow to change; and worker safety was, and continues to be, one of the most difficult areas. Many owners of mills, mines, and factories continue to consider the safety of their workers a low-priority item, presumably because of the high cost.

Over 10,000 workers die from on-the-job injures and another 50,000 from occupationally related diseases. Another 50,000 to 60,000 sustain permanent disability, and millions suffer from work-related illnesses (Parenti, Michael, 2002:102). Minorities, especially Latinos, have the highest work-related death rates. In 2001, the death rate per 100,000 workers was 25.8 for Latinos, 17.7 for African Americans, and 15.4 for Whites. Moreover, the Latino death rate has risen in the past 10 years. The reason for the higher Latino rate is the influx of Latino immigrants who took the dangerous and hard-to-fill jobs in construction, meat packing plants, and as farm laborers. "They took the only jobs they could get. They were often repaid with death. Poisoned by toxic fumes. Crushed by falling equipment. Burned alive" (Hopkins, 2003:1B).

Significant occupational dangers continue to plague workers, especially in certain jobs. The dangers today are invisible contaminants such as nuclear radiation, chemical compounds, coal tars, dust, and asbestos fibers in the air. These dangers from invisible contaminants are increasing because the production of synthetic chemicals has increased so dramatically. The following examples describe the specific risks of continued exposure to dangerous chemicals in certain industries:

- Workers in the dyestuffs industry (working with aromatic hydrocarbons) have about thirty times the risk of the general population of dying from bladder cancer.
- About 10 percent of coal miners suffer from black lung, caused by years of breathing coal dust in areas with inadequate ventilation.
- Migrant farm workers have a life expectancy thirty years below the national average. This low rate is a consequence of living in poverty or near-poverty and, most significant, of the exposure to herbicides and pesticides sprayed on the fields where they work.
- Workers in the semiconductor industry face special dangers from exposure to acids, gases, and solvents used in chip manufacturing. "About 75,000 workers in semiconductor plants breath or come in contact with dozens of known or suspected carcinogens, including toluene, cadmium, arsenic, benzene, and trichloroethylene" (Stranahan, 2002:45).
- Pregnant operators of video display terminals have disproportionate numbers of miscarriages or babies with birth defects, apparently from exposure to nonionizing radiation.

The record of industry has often been one of ignoring the scientific data, or of stalling through court actions, or of claims that jobs will be lost because of the cost to clean up the factories or mills, resulting in higher prices to consumers. Most important, some companies have not informed workers of the dangers.

This discussion raises some critical questions: Should profits supersede human life? Are owners guilty of murder if their decisions to minimize plant safety result in industrial deaths? Who is a greater threat, the thugs in the streets or the executives in the suites? Jeffrey Reiman (2004) answers these questions:

> Is a person who kills another in a bar brawl a greater threat to society than a business executive who refuses to cut into his profits to make his plant a safe place to work? By any measure of death and suffering the latter is by far a greater danger than the former. Because he wishes his workers no harm, because he is only indirectly responsible for death and disability while pursuing legitimate economic goals, his acts are not labelled "crimes." Once we free our imagination from the blinders of the one-on-one model of crime, can there be any doubt that the criminal justice system does *not* protect us from the gravest threats to life and limb? It seeks to protect us when danger comes from a young-lower-class male in the inner city. When a threat comes from an upper-class business executive in an office, the criminal justice system looks the other way. (81)

Sweatshops. A **sweatshop** is a substandard work environment where workers are paid less than the minimum wage, workers are not paid overtime premiums, and other labor laws are violated. Although sweatshops occur in various types of manufacturing, they occur most frequently in the garment industry. Garment sweatshops are common in New York City, San Francisco, Los Angeles, El Paso, and Seattle. The workers in these places make clothes for such brands as Levi Strauss, Esprit, Casual Corner, the Limited, and the Gap and for such merchandisers as JC Penny, Sears, and Wal-Mart. The workers, mostly Latina and Asian immigrant women, are paid much below the minimum wage, receive no benefits, and work in crowded, unsafe, and stifling conditions. See the panel titled "Human Agency: Sweatshop Workers Organize and Win."

Sweatshop Workers Organize and Win

The sweatshop is back with a vengeance. From maquiladoras in Mexico and Central America to a slave-labor factory in El Monte, California, poor young women trapped in desperate conditions are making designer clothes for upscale consumers.

Because subcontractors—not the clothing manufacturers themselves—employ these workers, the industry has managed to fend off traditional organizing efforts. But a recent victory demonstrates the value of using strategies that go beyond usual labor-organizing practice.

The Asian Immigrant Women's Association (AIWA) announced in April that it had reached a settlement with millionaire fashion designer Jessica McClintock. AIWA had been mobilizing community pressure for three years to win justice for a dozen women who lost their jobs while making clothing for McClintock, Inc. An Oakland, California, garment subcontractor for McClintock called Lucky Sewing Company declared bankruptcy in 1992, leaving its workers unpaid. Lucky owed the women more than $10,000 in back wages.

AIWA launched the Garment Workers Justice Campaign against McClintock, arguing that it had a moral responsibility to reimburse the workers even though the company was not legally liable for Lucky Sewing's financial problems. AIWA conducted a creative, multifaceted campaign in cities across the country, which included several full-page ads in the *New York Times* portraying McClintock as a heartless Marie Antoinette saying to the starving workers, "LET THEM EAT LACE."

McClintock is a purveyor of frilly prom dresses and other "romantic" clothing, an image that does not fit well with pictures of sweatshops filled with underpaid women workers.

The settlement with McClintock includes back wages for the laid-off workers, a garment-workers' education fund and scholarships, an outreach campaign to inform garment workers of their rights, and a toll-free hotline in English and Cantonese that can be used to report illegal wages and working conditions. The break in the campaign came last fall when the Department of Labor published a list of "fair labor fashion trendsetters"—corporations notable for their commitment to upholding worker protections. McClintock, Inc., was listed. AIWA contacted the Department of Labor, notifying them of the Garment Workers Justice Campaign and the glaring contradiction between McClintock's verbal commitment to worker protections and the company's use of sweatshop labor. Faced with the prospect of removal from the list, McClintock gave in.

"The clothing manufacturers are vulnerable," says Charlie Kernaghan of the National Labor Committee. "They've gotten fat and lazy, and with the right strategy we can beat them, even though we can't match their resources."

Source: John Anner, 1996. "Sweatshop Workers Organize and Win," *The Progressive* 60 (June):15. Reprinted by permission from The Progressive, 409 East Main Street, Madison, WI 53703. www.progressive.org.

U.S. corporations also sell products produced by workers in sweatshop conditions in other countries. Soccer balls are sewn together by child laborers in Pakistan. Mattel makes tens of millions of Barbies a year in China. Many of Disney's products are made in Sri Lanka and Haiti—countries notorious for their lack of labor and human rights. Nike, Reebok, and other shoe manufacturers have exploited workers in many Asian countries.

Unions and Their Decline. Historically, labor unions have been extremely important in changing management-labor relations. Joining together, workers challenged owners to increase wages, add benefits, provide worker security, and promote safety in the workplace. Through the use of strikes, work slowdowns, public relations, and political lobbying, working conditions improved and union members, for the most part, prospered. In wages and benefits, union workers earn about 34 percent more than nonunion workers. Consider the following differences between union workers and unorganized workers in comparable jobs in 2004:

- Considering all jobs, union members earn 27 percent more than union workers.
- Union women earn 33 percent more than nonunion women.
- African American union members earn 35 percent more than comparable nonunion members; and Latino unionists earn 51 percent more.
- Of union workers, 85 percent have medical benefits, compared with 74 percent of nonunion workers.
- Of unionists, 79 percent have defined-benefit retirement plans, which are federally insured with a guaranteed monthly payment, while only 44 percent of nonunion workers have such plans.
- Union workers have greater job stability, with more than 60 percent having worked for their current employers for at least ten years, compared with only 30 percent of nonunion workers (Levin, 2004).

In the past, unions were a powerful force for economic security and social justice. But that was forty years ago, when unions were strong. In the mid-1950s, 35 percent of all workers belonged to unions, 80 to 90 percent in major industries such as automaking, steel, and coal mining. But unions have lost their strength since about 1980, dropping to about 13.5 of the nonagricultural labor force in 2004. With such small and dwindling numbers, labor unions are in danger of becoming irrelevant. Most significant, they have already become enfeebled politically. This decline in power by unions is linked to the decline in progressive politics. Once, unions were a major force behind such progressive programs as Social Security, Medicare, unemployment insurance, and the minimum wage. When unions were a force politically even Republicans had to occasionally give in to their demands.

The reasons for the decline in union membership (and clout) are several. First, there was a direct assault against unions by Republican Presidents Ronald Reagan, George H. W. Bush, and George W. Bush. Each of these administrations was unsympathetic with strikes and sometimes used federal leverage to weaken them. Similarly, their appointees to the post of Secretary of Labor and the National Labor Relations Board (NLRB) were probusiness rather than prolabor. Long delays in decision making at the NLRB and their antiunion rulings have resulted in management sometimes firing prounion workers with impunity.

Second, public opinion has turned against unions because some of them are undemocratic, scandal-ridden, and too zealous in their demands. Public opinion has also turned against organized labor because of a probusiness, procapitalist bias that increased during the era of supply-side economics that dominated the Reagan and Bush administrations and much of Congress during that time. That bias, although muted a bit, continued during the Clinton administration but was resurrected during George W. Bush's administration.

Third, businesses do all they can to block unions. Typically, companies are required to have a union vote if 30 percent of workers sign a petition. When such an election does occur, companies have won more than half the time, versus 28 percent in the early 1950s. The antiunion vote by workers is the result usually of an all-out assault by the company, including information arguing that unionization may lead to downsizing or even the closing of plants, "worker appreciation" days with free barbeque or pizza, and selective firing of workers who are union activists (an illegal activity, but it happens in about one-fourth of union drives, according to a commission study established by President Clinton), and other forms of intimidation. Wal-Mart, for example, "has been formally cited more than 40 times in the past five years for using illegal tactics to deny its workers the right to join a union" (Hightower, 2003:1).

A major reason for the decline of union strength is the shift in the economy brought about by globalization (discussed in Chapter 8). Manufacturing jobs, which are in decline, have historically been prounion, while service jobs, which are increasing, have been typically nonunionized. Many businesses, faced with stiff competition from low-wage economies, have insisted on reducing wages and/or worker benefits or have said they would go bankrupt or move overseas themselves. The increased use of microchip technology threatens jobs with increased automation in the factory (robots to replace assembly-line workers) and in the office (computers to displace typists and file clerks). Similarly, the advent of computers, modems, and fax machines has increased the number of workers who work at home, as temporaries, and part-time. These workers are the least likely to join unions.

These forces have given the strong advantage to management, a trend that has several negative consequences. First, faced with the threat of plants closing or moving to nonunion localities or to low-wage nations, unions have chosen, typically, to give back many of the gains they made during the 1960s and 1970s. Thus, workers have lost real wages and benefits.

A second consequence of union decline is that the workplace may be less safe: "Some of the most injury-prone industries, like food processing and textiles, have clustered in right-to-work [nonunion] states across the South" (Lacayo, 1991:29).

A major consequence of union decline is the further dwindling of the middle class. In the words of Albert Shanker (1992), the late president of the American Federation of Teachers, "The union movement took a lot of workers who were relatively unskilled and turned them into middle class people who educated their children and supported the United States economy. Now, we've got businesses turning their employees into third-world workers" (E9). Implied in this statement is a related consequence: If businesses turn their employees into Third World workers, then these workers will not be able to purchase enough goods and services to encourage economic growth and society-wide prosperity. As Norman Birnbaum (1992) has said, "Nations with strong unions and social contracts have the highest living standards" (319).

> Another consequence is a weakened voice and political power for working people: Today, we need unions to raise money and raise hell as much as to raise wages. In politics, business is outspending labor 3 to 1, has captured the votes of Washington and sets the agenda for national debate—a debate that pits the far right against the moderate right and ignores everyone else. . . . Democracy doesn't work unless everyone has a say. Today, it's out of whack. (Gartner, 1995:11A)

A final consequence points to a possible contradiction—the precipitous decline in unions may actually lead to labor's regeneration. As the unions decline, with workers poorly compensated and ever fearful of losing their jobs, with management becoming more arrogant and demanding, the situation may get bad enough that there will be a turnaround—a surge in union membership and worker militancy. This could lead not only to a stronger collective voice in the work arena but also in the nation's politics. Those nations with strong unionized labor (for example, Canada, Germany, France, and Sweden) have a social democratic conception of society, which means universal health care, progressive income taxes, and more equitable government programs.

Of course, this scenario may not occur. Unions may continue to decline in size and influence; pay and benefits to workers may continue to erode; and workers may be fragmented rather than united.

Discrimination in the Workplace: The Perpetuation of Inequality

Women and minorities have long been the objects of discrimination in U.S. industry. Currently (and we have progressed mightily), approximately 50,000 charges of discrimination by organizations are filed annually with the U.S. Equal Opportunity Commission. The charges now and in the past have centered on hiring policies, seniority rights, restricted job placement, limited opportunities for advancement, and lower pay for equal work. A number of court suits (and those settled out of court) illustrate that discriminatory policies have been common among such major corporations as AT&T, General Motors, and Northwest Airlines and in such industries as banking and steel.

Two mechanisms operating in the U.S. economy perpetuate inequalities in the job market by social class, race, and gender—the segmented labor market and male dominance in the workplace.

Segmented Labor Market. The capitalist economy is divided into two separate sectors that have different characteristics, different roles, and different rewards for laborers within each. This organization of the economy is called the **segmented labor market**, or the *dual labor market*. The primary sector is composed of large, bureaucratic organizations with relatively stable production and sales. Jobs within this sector require developed skills, are relatively well paid, occur in good working conditions, and are stable. Within this sector there are two types of jobs. The first type, those in the upper tier, are high-status professional and managerial jobs. The pay is very good for the highly educated people in these jobs. They have a high

"How could we discriminate against minority employees... we don't even have any."

© 1991, Carol Simpson Cartoons. Reprinted by permission of Carol Simpson Productions.

"If we pay them starvation wages, why do they need a lunch break?

degree of personal autonomy, and the jobs offer variety, creativity, and initiative. Upward mobility is likely for those who are successful. The second type, the lower-tier jobs within the primary sector, are held by working-class people. The jobs are either white-collar clerical or blue-collar skilled and semiskilled. The jobs are repetitive, and mobility is limited. The jobs are relatively secure because of unionization, although they are much more vulnerable than those in the upper tier. When times are difficult, these workers tend to be laid off rather than terminated.

The secondary economic sector is composed of marginal firms in which product demand is unstable. Jobs within this sector are characterized by poor working conditions, low wages, few opportunities for advancement, and weak job security. Little education or skill is required to perform these tasks. Workers beginning in the secondary sector tend to get locked in because they lack the skills required in the primary sector and they usually have unstable work histories. A common interpretation of this problem is that secondary-sector workers are in these dead-end jobs because of their pathology—poor work history, lack of skills, and lack of motivation. Such an explanation, however, blames the victim. Poor work histories tend to be the result of unemployment caused by the production of marginal products and the lack of job security. Similarly, these workers have few, if any, incentives to learn new skills or to stay for long periods with an employer because of the structural impediments to upward mobility. And unlike workers in the primary sector, workers in the secondary sector are more likely to experience harsh and capricious work discipline from supervisors, primarily because there are no unions.

The significance of this dual labor market is threefold. First, placement in one of these segments corresponds with social class, which tends to be perpetuated from generation to generation. Second, employment in the secondary sector is often so inadequately paid that many full-time workers live in poverty, as noted in Chapter 6. And third, the existence of a dual labor market reinforces racial, ethnic,

FIGURE 13.1

Female-to-Male
Earnings Ratio
and Median Earn-
ings of Full-Time,
Year-Round Work-
ers 15 Years Old
and Over by Sex:
1960 to 2003

Note: The data points
are placed at the mid-
points of the respec-
tive years. Data on
earnings of full-time
year-round workers
are not readily avail-
able before 1960.

Source: U.S. Census
Bureau, "Income,
Poverty, and Health
Insurance Coverage in
the United States,"
*Current Population
Reports, Series,*
P60–226 (August
2004), p.6.

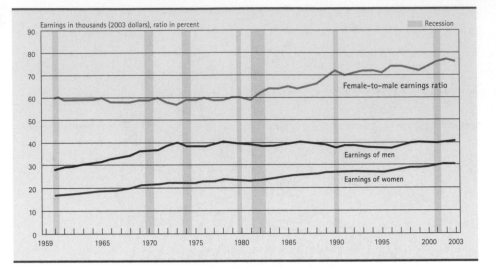

and gender divisions in the labor force. White males, while found in both segments, tend to predominate in the upper tier of the primary sector. White females tend to be clerks in the lower tier of the primary sector, and White ethnics tend to be clerks in the lower tier of the primary sector. Males and females of color are found dispro-portionately in the secondary sector. These findings explain why unemployment rates for African Americans and Latinos are consistently much higher than (usually at least double) the rate for Whites. They also explain the persistent wage differences found by race and gender.

Male Dominance at Work. Closely tied to segmented labor markets is the dominance of men in work-related roles (also known as capitalist patriarchy). This dominance is reflected in two ways—men tend to make the rules and enforce them, and men receive unequal (i.e., greater) rewards (see Figure 13.1).

Current gender inequality results from a long history of patriarchal social relations in which men have consciously kept women in subordinate roles at work and in the home. Men as workers consistently have acted in their own interests to retain power and to keep women either out of their occupations or in subordinate and poorly paid work roles. Historically, through their unions, males insisted that the higher-status and better-paying jobs be exclusively male. They lobbied legislatures to pass legisla-tion supportive of male exclusiveness in occupations and in opposition to such equal-ization measures as minimum wages for women. Also, the male unions prevented women from gaining the skills that would lead them to equal-paying jobs. The National Typographical Union in 1854, for example, insisted not only that women be refused jobs as compositors but also that they not be taught the skills necessary to be a compositor (Hartmann, 1976).

Throughout U.S. history, capitalists have used gender inequality in the work-place to their advantage. Women were hired because they would work for less money than men, which made men all the more fearful of women in the workplace. Capitalists even used the threat of hiring lower-paid women to take the place of higher-paid men to keep the wages of both sexes down and to lessen labor militancy.

In contemporary U.S. society, men and women, with some exceptions, are accorded different and unequal positions in religious, government, school, work, and family activities. Looking only at work, women and men perform different tasks in the labor force. This division of labor between the sexes preserves the differential power, privilege, and prestige of men (see Chapter 12). Men are overrepresented in administrative and supervisory roles. Women are found disproportionately in jobs in which they follow orders. Women are found, as noted earlier, more often than men in the secondary job market where jobs are menial, poorly paid, and with little or no benefits.

Unemployment

The Bureau of Labor Statistics supplies the official unemployment statistics. The official unemployment rate in the United States since 1980 has ranged from a high of 9 percent in 1982–1983 to a low of 3.9 percent in October 2000. These rates are misleading because they understate, dramatically, the actual amount of unemployment. Not included in the data are the 60 million or so people who are not in the labor force because they are in school, disabled, retired, homemakers, or not seeking work.

The data are distorted by undercounting the unemployed in two ways. First, people who have not actively sought work in the four weeks prior to being interviewed are not counted in the unemployed category. In 2004, there were about 2 million such **discouraged workers**, most of whom were once employed in the secondary sector of the segmented labor force. Women and minorities are overrepresented

There are almost five million part-time workers who want to work full-time. These people are counted in the official government statistics as fully employed.

among these discouraged workers. The rationale of the Bureau of Labor Statistics for excluding dispirited workers is that the function of the statistic is to chart fluctuations in the conditions of the active labor force, not to provide a complete portrait of the jobless. Regardless of the reasoning, the official data of the government, by undercounting joblessness, diminish the perceived severity of unemployment and therefore reduce the zeal to do anything about the problem. The extent to which the public perceives unemployment as a problem is further lessened by counting as employed anyone who had worked for as little as an hour for pay in the week before being interviewed. There are almost 5 million part-time workers who want to work full-time. Thus, people who subsist on odd jobs, temporary work, or minimal part-time work are counted as fully employed by the government. In January 2004, the official jobless rate was 5.9 percent (8.7 million officially unemployed). If those part-time workers who wanted to work full-time and the discouraged workers were added to the official numbers, the unemployed rate would have been about 10 percent, which is a huge surplus of labor (Streitfeld, 2003).

Unemployment is commonly believed to be functional (i.e., have positive consequences) for society by reducing inflationary pressures. Capitalists like high unemployment because it tends to deflate wages and therefore increases profits. When there are unemployed people willing to work, workers will not make inordinate demands for higher wages for fear that they will be replaced by cheaper labor. Thus, even unionized labor becomes relatively docile when unemployment is high. Joe and Clairece Feagin (1997) summarize the capitalist argument:

"There are plenty of jobs around. People just don't want to work."

The . . . unemployed are essential to the operation of the capitalist system because they put downward pressure on wages and provide a reserve labor force that can be drawn back into employment when profit and investment conditions require it. Not only the officially unemployed, but also other groups make up this reserve labor force: discouraged workers, part-time workers, newly arrived immigrant laborers. Workers who protest too hard in times of a glutted labor market will find themselves replaced by people from the great pool of the unemployed. (92)

Unemployment affects some groups more than others. This **reserve army of the unemployed** is disproportionately composed of people of color (Latinos, African Americans, Native Americans), immigrants, teenagers, and residents in declining cities and regions. In 2002, for example, one of every four Black males between the ages of sixteen and twenty-two were out of work and not in school (Muwakkil, 2004). Typically, the official unemployment rates for African Americans and Latinos are at least twice as high as the rate for Whites. These proportions by race tend to be relatively constant, whether the overall unemployment rate is high or low or whether the economy is in a boom or a slump. Thus, the labor market assigns people of color disproportionately not only to the low-paying jobs but also to the jobs that are most unstable, precisely the situation of the secondary sector in the segmented labor market.

An important consequence of the reserve army of the unemployed being composed primarily of racial minorities is that it inflames racial antipathies against them by people who hold unstable jobs. These job holders perceive their enemy as the people below them who will work for lower wages, rather than the capitalists who oppose full employment and adequate wages for all people.

In summary, the problems associated with work in U.S. society are structural in origin. The source is not in unmotivated or unwilling workers. To understand the work setting in our society, we must understand the nature of capitalism, for which profit rather than human consequences guides managerial decisions. And in looking at unemployment, we must recognize that the economy fails to produce enough jobs with living wages and adequate benefits for the workers to maintain a middle-class lifestyle. Finally, in examining this labor market, we must understand that the economy is undergoing a profound transformation (Chapter 8). The next few generations will be caught in the nexus between one stage and another, and many will suffer because of the dislocations. So, too, will a society that refuses to plan, but rather lets the marketplace dictate the choices of economic firms.

Capitalism in Crisis

The Negative Consequences of Private Profitability over Social Need

We have written elsewhere (Eitzen and Baca Zinn, 2006) that the major social problems in the United States are in large measure the result of the form of the economy. This is illustrated by the role of capitalists as they seek profit in the climate engendered by the economic transformation just discussed. Entrepreneurs, as they seek to maximize profit, shut down plants, reduce workforces, replace workers with machines, or threaten to move operations overseas to force workers to accept lower wages and benefits. They also continue to pollute the environment and fight government attempts to enforce worker and consumer safety. These entrepreneurs, corporate boards of directors, and corporate executives have no allegiance to consumers, workers, or the communities in which their operations are located. Their ultimate loyalty is to the bottom line. Michael Parenti (1986) describes this fundamental logic of capitalism and capitalists:

> Capitalism's purpose is not to create jobs; in fact, capitalists are constantly devising ways of eliminating jobs in order to cut labor costs. Nor is its purpose to build communities, for capitalists will build or destroy communities as investment opportunities dictate. Nor is capitalism dedicated to protecting the family or traditional life, for no system in human history has been more relentless in battering down ancient practices and destroying both rural and urban homegrown cultures. Nor is capitalism intent upon protecting the environment on behalf of generations yet to come; for corporations will treat the environment like a septic tank in order to cut production costs and maximize profits without regard for future generations or for the generation enduring it all today. Nor can we say that capitalists are committed to economic efficiency as such, since they regularly pass on their hidden diseconomies to the public in the form of overproduction, overpricing, pollution, unemployment, population dislocation, harmful products, and personal injury. And as the military budget shows, they actively court waste and duplication if it brings fatter contracts and bigger profits.
>
> Capitalism has no loyalty to anything but its own process of capital accumulation, no loyalty to anything but itself. Nor could it be otherwise if one wished to survive as a capitalist; for the first law of the market is to make a profit off other people's labor or go out of business. Private profitability rather than social need is the determining condition of capital investment. (1–2)

Can society continue to allow capitalists the freedom to make investment decisions unfettered by the concerns of society? Can corporations pollute the environment and produce waste with impunity? Should businesses be allowed to shut down a plant without sufficient warning and compensation to the affected workers and communities? Should taxes be levied on robots, with the monies spent on job retraining of workers displaced by them? As the next chapter shows, the close relationship between economic power and political power appears to preclude government curbs on the abuses created by capitalists. And the rationale provided by many people for the lack of governmental control of business will likely be that capitalism is not the problem but really the solution to society's problems—if allowed to operate without restraints.

Excesses at the Heart of Capitalism: Greed, Cronyism, and Ripoffs

In 2000 and 2001, a number of scandals, what some would call "a corporate crime wave," occurred involving a number of major U.S. corporations (e.g., Enron, WorldCom, Global Crossing, Lucent, Qwest, Tyco, Xerox, Kmart, ImClone, Adelphia), accounting firms (Arthur Andersen), and brokerage houses (Goldman Sachs, Merrill Lynch, Morgan Stanley Dean Witter). The corruption consisted of deception, cheating, and stealing on a grand scale. Before the fall, stock prices soared as corporate executives manipulated the books to make their corporation appear profitable and growing (WorldCom admitted to overstating its earnings by $3.9 billion), and stock analysts touted the stock while playing a "double game with their customers-doing investment deals with companies in their private offices while their stock analysts are out front whipping up enthusiasm for the same companies' stocks" (Greider, 2002:13).

While the prices were high, corporate insiders sold their shares and exercised their options making many millions (e.g., Gary Winnick, CEO of Global Crossing, cashed out early for $600 million), meanwhile assuring his employees who held the stocks in their retirement plans that the company was in good shape. The consequences of these acts by corporate leaders are enormous. Speaking only of the Enron situation, which led the corporate parade of scandal and sleaze, economist Paul Krugman (2002) says: "I predict that in the years ahead Enron, not September 11, will come to be seen as the greater turning point in U.S. society" (1). Consider the economic fallout from these scandals:

- From March 2000 to July 2002, the value of the U.S. stock market plunged by $3.7 trillion. While the scandals played a major role in this decline, it was triggered by other factors as well.
- The unfunded liabilities of U.S. corporate pension funds—that is, the difference between what companies expect to pay retirees and the amount of money they have on hand—soared to $111 billion in December 2001, up from $26 billion a year earlier (Dreyfuss and Leefeldt, 2002).
- The average household wealth declined an average of 16 percent in two years.
- As the value of stocks declined to nothing or next to nothing, many thousands of employees who had their savings in their company's stock lost most if not all of their retirement nest eggs (at Enron, 12,000 employees watched their 401(k) savings disappear while twenty-nine Enron insiders cashed out more than $1.1 billion of their own shares).
- Individuals also participating in pension funds such as CALPERS (employees of the state of California) watched their investments decline with the stock market swoon. For example, three pension funds invested $1.25 billion in WorldCom bonds that were worth 13 cents on the dollar in mid-2002 (Faux, 2002). In another instance, owners of pension funds and mutual funds with investments in Enron lost $25 billion to $50 billion (Greider, 2002).

These numbers mask two greater consequences of these scandals. Foremost is the loss of public trust: in the markets, in accountants who are supposed to verify the accuracy of corporate balance sheets, in corporate executives to inform the public fairly of their company's status, in the stock market touts are who supposed to be independent, and in the government to regulate and monitor the business world so that it is fair. If the public loses trust in business and the marketplace, then the economy is in a shambles. In effect, the market has lost the "glue" that holds it together. As one observer puts it: "No need to worry about Islamic terrorists sacking our economy. We are doing a fine job on our own" (Lewis, Al, 2002:1K).

The other major consequence of the scandals is that they rock the very foundations of the capitalism credo. The essence of capitalism is the *laissez-faire* ideology,

> that market place forces discipline and punishes the errant players more effectively than government does. To produce greater efficiency and innovation, government was told to back off, and it largely has. "Transparency" became the exalted buzzword. The market discipline would be exercised by investors acting on honest information supplied by the banks and brokerages holding their money, "independent" corporate directors and outside auditors, and regular disclosure reports required by the Securities and Exchange Commission and other regulatory agencies. The Enron story makes a sick joke of all these safeguards. (Greider, 2002:11)

See the panel titled "A Closer Look: The Ten Habits of Highly Defective Corporations."

The Ten Habits of Highly Defective Corporations: Titans of the Enron Economy

The pivotal lessons from the Enron debacle do not stem from any criminal wrongdoing. Most of the maneuvers leading to Enron's meltdown are not only legal, they are widely practiced. Many of the problems dramatically revealed by the Enron scandal are woven tightly into the fabric of American business. Outside the spotlight on Enron's rise and fall, government policies and accounting practices continue to reward and shelter many firms with harmful habits just like those of Enron. We've ranked the 100 worst companies for each habit and awarded "Ennys" for outstanding Enron-like performance. We've also given a Lifetime Achievement Award to the corporation with the highest combined score for Enron-like performance in all ten categories (a hint: Enron placed second).

Habit 1: Tie employee retirement funds heavily to company stock and let misled employees take the fall when the stock tanks—while executives diversify their holdings and cash out before bad news goes public. Winner: Coca-Cola.

Once upon a time the upward slope of Coca-Cola's stock price was as smooth as a cold Coke on a warm afternoon. Over the past couple of years, however, the venerable soft drink maker's stock fizzled like New Coke. Employees saw their 401(k) retirement assets evaporate, with the stock down more than 31 percent in the three years ending November 2001. Eighty-one percent of Coke's 401(k) was invested in company stock. Not all employees fared poorly. Former CEO M. Douglas Ivester left Coke under a cloud of controversy but received a severance package valued at more than $17 million; it included maintenance of his home security system and payment of his country club dues.

Habit 2: Excessively compensate executives. Winner: Citigroup.

CEO Sanford Weill took home more than $482 million between 1998 and 2000. In 2001 he made another $42 million. Weill's stock compensation plan was amazingly equipped with a "reload" feature: Each time Weill cashed in his options, he automatically received new options to replace them. Imagine if Citigroup customers had a reload ATM machine that automatically added replacement money to their

accounts after withdrawals! While throwing money at its executives, Citigroup rips off low-income Americans with predatory lending practices. The Federal Trade Commission has brought suit against Citigroup, alleging abusive lending practices; if all charges are proven, Citigroup's liabilities could reach $500 million.

Habit 3: Lay off employees to reduce costs and distract from management mistakes. Increase executive pay for implementing this cost-cutting strategy. Winner: Lucent Technologies.

Last year Lucent axed at least 42,000 jobs. While these layoffs occurred during the tech-industry tumble, Wall Street critics lay much of the responsibility for Lucent's misfortune at management's door. Lucent was the only company to end up on both the Fortune and Chief Executive 2001 "worst boards of directors" list. Though the board took action and fired CEO Richard McGinn in October 2000, it gave him a golden parachute of more than $12 million as a parting gift.

Habit 4: Stack the board with insiders and friends who will support lavish compensation and not ask difficult questions about the business. Winner: EMC Corporation.

Only two years ago this leading producer of computer storage media could have held Thanksgiving dinner in its boardroom: The chairman, Richard Egan, his wife and son all sat on EMC's board. As a member of the board Junior got to help set Dad's allowance (and help determine his own inheritance). How many kids wouldn't love that? Of course, Dad might not have needed much help, since he also sat on EMC's compensation committee, which determined his and other executives' pay. Since winning this award, EMC has added an independent director to its board.

Habit 5: Pay board members excessively for their part-time service; pay them heavily in stock so they have a disincentive to blow the whistle on bad business practices that keep the stock price up. Winner: AOL Time Warner.

AOL Time Warner is one of a growing number of companies to compensate directors solely in stock options. In 2000, according to an Investor Responsibility Research Center study, the potential value of these

The Ten Habits of Highly Defective Corporations: Titans of the Enron Economy continued

stock options (using SEC-specified formulas for computing the present value) was $843,200 per director—not bad for a part-time job. Each member of AOL Time Warner's board is annually granted 40,000 stock options. Directors make money for each dollar increase in the stock price. If AOL Time Warner's stock price rose $10 a share, the options would gain $400,000 in value.

Habit 6: Give your independent auditor generous nonaudit consultant work, creating conflicts of interest for those charged with assuring that the company follows the rules and protects shareholder interests. Winner: Raytheon.

When it comes to shooting down auditor independence, military giant Raytheon is a proven winner. According to an IRRC study, in 2000 Raytheon had the highest percentage of nonaudit fees for companies with revenue of more than $20 billion. Raytheon paid just $3 million to PricewaterhouseCoopers for audit services and an additional $48 million for consulting services. That Raytheon's independent auditor receives such large nonaudit fees creates a substantial conflict of interest and continues a pattern of board and management disregard for shareholder interests.

Habit 7: Give campaign contributions to gain access to decision-makers; diversify your political investments in a portfolio of candidates from both major parties. Winner: Financial Services Industry. Accepting for the group, Citigroup and MBNA.

After heavy lobbying and campaign contributions from the banking and credit card industry, Congress passed the Bankruptcy Reform Act in 2001 by wide margins. Credit-card giants Citigroup and MBNA were among the largest campaign contributors during the 2000–02 period. On the very day the House voted on the bankruptcy bill, MBNA contributed $200,000 to the National Republican Senatorial Committee, according to a *Time* exposé. If it becomes law, the bill will make filing for personal bankruptcy considerably more difficult; it will also put credit-card companies in a more favorable position, allowing them equal standing to claims for child support, for example.

Habit 8: Lobby lawmakers and regulators to eliminate pesky oversight, safety, environmental, and other rules, and pass favorable regulations, subsidies, tax breaks, and other items on the company wish list. Winner: Boeing.

Using its famed stealth technology in Congress, Boeing circumvented military procurement practices when the Secretary of the Air Force directly submitted a controversial contract under which the Air Force would lease 100 large tanker aircraft from Boeing. Senator John McCain challenged both the process and the terms of the deal, which he said would cause the government to pay much more for the lease than if it purchased the planes outright. He added, "It's pork, and we shouldn't be paying for it." Boeing has paid for plenty of pork and prime rib, as the nation's fifth-largest lobbyist over the three years ending in 1999.

Habit 9: Get the government to finance and insure dubious overseas investments, especially those opposed by the local citizenry. Winner: Halliburton.

While Vice President Dick Cheney was CEO of Halliburton, a leading global energy services and engineering/construction company, Halliburton received $1.5 billion in government financing and loan guarantees, a fifteenfold increase from the pre-Cheney days. The company also garnered $2.3 billion in direct government contracts, more than double the amount received in the five years preceding Cheney's half-decade tenure. Over the 1992–2000 period, in which Enron received $7.2 billion in government financing and loan guarantees, Halliburton was close behind at $6 billion. Not surprisingly, Halliburton doubled both its campaign finance and lobbying expenditures, to $1.2 million and $600,000 respectively, during Cheney's tenure.

Habit 10: Avoid taxes. Use tax deductions, credits, and clever accounting to pay little or no tax, and hopefully even get tax rebates. Winner: WorldCom.

When you send or receive e-mail from an AOL account, fly on a commercial airliner or make long-distance calls on MCI, you are consuming services provided

Clearly, the self-cleansing nature of markets failed. If the markets are to work without scandal and if the public trust is to be restored, the government must institute strict rules, monitor the corporations, and punish wrongdoers (individuals and corporations). Will the business scandals of the early twenty-first century bring about an ideological sea change, when Republicans, who have traditionally argued the *laissez-faire* philosophy, and Democrats agree on a much stronger role for government in overseeing the business world? If so, then government must not be corrupted with bribery (corporate donations to politicians, which is the topic of the next chapter).

Declining Wages, Jobs, Consumerism, and Profits

According to Karl Marx, one of the contradictions of capitalism that will bring its downfall is the "**falling rate of profit**." This refers to the propensity of employers to maximize profits by reducing labor expenses. This is accomplished by using labor-saving machines and by paying the minimum in wages and benefits. The result of this capitalist rationale, argued Marx, would actually be to reduce profits because the workers would be less and less able to purchase products. Some industrialists, such as Henry Ford, recognized this problem. "Mass production," Ford said, "requires mass consumption, which means higher wages" (cited in Harrington, 1986:13). The logic, more commonly held by capitalists, though, is to increase profits by keeping wages low.

This, as seen in Chapter 8, is evidenced by the purchase of new microelectronic technology to replace workers, the movement of production sites from relative high-wage areas to low-wage ones such as in the southern United States or to foreign countries, and the hiring of part-time or temporary workers in order to escape paying benefits.

The result is that the purchasing power of labor is declining. Two examples:

- Median family income (adjusted for inflation) has declined slightly.
- Employer-supplied health insurance and pensions have declined.

These are indicators of personal and family economic decline. The middle class is smaller. More and more workers receive substandard wages, substandard pensions, and substandard fringe benefits. The result is a reduction in lifestyle. For families on the economic margin, purchases will be limited to necessities. As more and more people in the United States are adversely affected, the sale of consumer goods and services will decline. This means that corporate profits will suffer, causing further efforts by management to reduce expenses. Thus, one possible future scenario is that of an economic downward spiral. The way out, to repeat Henry Ford's admonition, is to encourage mass consumption through higher wages. The prospect for higher-wage jobs, however, is bleak as corporations downsize and U.S. corporations and U.S. workers compete with even lower-wage economies elsewhere.

The Lack of Economic Planning

The capitalist philosophy dating back to Adam Smith argues that the government should stay out of economic affairs. According to this view, the marketplace will force businesses to make the decisions that will best benefit them and, indirectly, the citizenry. Yet, when the government does receive valuable information with which it could make decisions to avert future crises, the strong tendency in the United States is to remain aloof.

Ironically, the government is involved in central planning in the areas of space exploration, military goals, and homeland security from terrorists. As one commentator has said:

> The U.S. launched Mariner 10 on Nov. 3, 1973, and it flew to Venus and then to Mercury, which it circled for a total of a billion miles. It performed magnificently and sent back photographs. That took years of planning. But planning for a thing like that is one thing. Social planning and foreseeing energy shortages before they happen, that is different, and to some, slightly sinister. (TRB, 1975:2)

The issue of central planning revolves around whether the society is able and willing to respond to present and future social problems. Is a capitalist society capable of meeting the problems of poverty, unemployment, social injustice, population growth, energy shortages, environmental damage, and monopoly? Robert Heilbroner (1974), a distinguished economist, argues that we will not prepare for the problems of the future: "The outlook is for what we may call 'convulsive change'—change forced upon us by external events rather than by conscious choice, by catastrophe rather than by calculation" (132).

The lack of central planning points to the undemocratic nature of U.S. society. It is commonly believed that the people, through their economic choices, actually govern business decisions. While this is partially true, it ignores the manipulation of the public by business interests through advertising and other hypes. Neither the public nor its elected representatives are involved in the economic decisions of the giant corporations—and these decisions often have dire consequences domestically and internationally. As Andrew Hacker (1970) argues:

> The power to make investment decisions is concentrated in a few hands, and it is this power which will decide what kind of a nation America will be. Instead of government planning there is boardroom planning that is accountable to no outside agency; and these plans set the order of priorities on national growth, technological innovation, and ultimately, the values and behavior of human beings. Investment decisions are sweeping in their ramifications—no one is unaffected by their consequences. Yet this is an area where neither the public nor its government is able to participate. (52)

The lack of central planning is also a result of the resistance of powerful interest groups in society. Short-term goals such as employment for labor groups or profit for corporations lead special interests to block government efforts to meet future needs. Thus, the power of the economic dominants in society has the effect of superseding the interests of the nation, as shown in the next chapter.

Chapter Review

1. Economic activity involves the production and distribution of goods and services.

2. There are two fundamental ways society can organize its economic activities: capitalism and socialism.

3. Capitalism in its pure form involves (a) the private ownership of the means of production, (b) the pursuit of personal profit, (c) competition, and (d) a government policy of allowing the marketplace to function unhindered.

4. Socialism in its pure form involves (a) democracy throughout the social structure; (b) equality—equality of opportunity, equality rather than hierarchy in making decisions, and equality in sharing the benefits of society; and (c) efficiency in providing the best conditions to meet the material needs of the citizens.

5. Marx's prediction that capitalism will result in an economy dominated by monopolies has been fulfilled in the United States. But rather than a single corporation dominating a sector of the economy, the United States is characterized by the existence of shared monopolies—in which four or fewer corporations supply 50 percent or more of a particular market.

6. Economic power is concentrated in a few major corporations and banks. This concentration has been accomplished primarily through mergers and interlocking directorates.

7. The power of the largest corporations in the United States is increased by their international activities. Multinational corporations have important consequences: (a) a decline in domestic jobs, (b) a crippling of union's power, (c) a crippling of the government through lost revenues in taxes and a negative balance of payments, (d) an increase in corporate power over the world economy and world events, and (e) an exploitation of workers and natural resources in Third World countries.

8. Inequality is endemic to capitalism. Corporate wealth and private wealth are highly concentrated. Poverty, too, is concentrated disproportionately among people of color and in households headed by women.

9. Societies are organized to allocate work in order to produce the goods and services required for survival. The way work is organized generates important social problems.

10. Owners and managers of firms and factories control workers in several ways: (a) through scientific management, (b) through bureaucracy, (c) through extortion, and (d) by monitoring worker behavior.

11. Blue- and white-collar workers in bureaucracies and factories are susceptible to alienation, which is the separation of human beings from each other, from themselves, and from the products they create. Specialized work in impersonal settings leads to dissatisfaction and meaninglessness.

12. A primary goal of business firms in a capitalist society is to reduce costs and thus increase profits.

One way to reduce costs is not to provide adequately for worker safety.

13. Labor unions have declined in numbers and power. This has resulted in lower real wages and benefits, less-safe work conditions, and a declining middle class.

14. Another work-related problem is discrimination, in which women and minorities have long received unfair treatment in jobs, pay, and opportunities for advancement. Two features of the U.S. economy promote these inequities: (a) the segmented labor market and (b) capitalist patriarchy.

15. The official government data on unemployment hide the actual amount by undercounting the unemployed in two ways: (a) People not actively seeking work (discouraged workers) are not counted; and (b) people who work at part-time jobs are counted as fully employed.

16. Unemployment has positive consequences for some people. Having a certain portion unemployed tends to keep inflation in check, according to some economists. Also, unemployment benefits capitalists by keeping wages down.

17. U.S. capitalism is facing four crises: (a) the primacy of profit over human considerations; (b) the propensity of corporate managers to increase profitability by reducing the workforce and lowering wages, which means that ultimately profits will fall because workers will be forced to reduce their purchases; (c) corporate scandals that illuminate the greed and cronyism at the heart of *laissez-faire* capitalism; and (d) the lack of central planning to solve current problems and anticipate future ones.

18. Two facts about institutions of society are especially important: (a) Although they are interrelated, the economy is the most dominant and shapes each of the other institutions; and (b) the particular way that an institution is organized is at once a source of stability and a source of problems.

Key Terms

Capitalism
Laissez-faire
Socialism
Shared monopoly
Interlocking directorates

Direct interlock
Indirect interlock
Scientific management
Alienation
Sweatshop

Segmented labor market
Discouraged workers
Reserve army of the unemployed
Falling rate of profit

Study Questions

1. What are the mechanisms within the U.S. economy that work against the capitalist ideal of free enterprise?
2. Why is inequality endemic to capitalism? Is this good?
3. A major assumption of conflict theorists is that capitalism is a primary source for many social problems. Michael Parenti's critique of capitalism (in the section titled "The Negative Consequences of Private

Profitability over Social Need") is an example of this approach. Do you agree or disagree? Why?
4. Given the conditions of the "structural transformation of the economy" (Chapter 8), should the government become more involved in the economy (violating *laissez-faire*) with policies to alleviate current problems and central planning to lessen or eliminate future problems?

For Further Reading

Inequality

Chuck Collins, Betsy Leondar-Wright, and Holly Sklar, *Shifting Fortunes: The Perils of the Growing American Wealth Gap* (Boston: United for a Fair Economy, 1999).

Dollars & Sense and United for a Fair Economy, *The Wealth Inequality Reader* (Cambridge, Ma: *Dollars & Sense*).

Barbara Ehrenreich, *Nickel and Dimed: On (Not) Getting By in America* (New York: Metropolitan Books, 2001).

Robert H. Frank and Philip J. Cook, *The Winner-Take-All Society* (New York: Free Press, 1995).

Work

Carol J. Auster, *The Sociology of Work* (Thousand Oaks, CA: Pine Forge Press, 1996).

Kathleen Gerson, *No Man's Land: Men's Changing Commitments to Family and Work* (New York: Basic Books, 1993).

Jacqueline Jones, *Labor of Love, Labor of Sorrow: Black Women, Work, and the Family from Slavery to the Present* (New York: Basic Books, 1985).

Lawrence Mishel, Jared Bernstein, and Heather Boushey, *The State of Working America, 2002/2003* (Ithaca, NY: Cornell University Press).

George Ritzer, *The McDonaldization of Society: An Investigation into the Changing Character of Contemporary Social Life*, rev. ed. (Thousand Oaks, CA: Pine Forge Press, 1996).

Juliet B. Schor, *The Overworked American: The Unexpected Decline of Leisure* (New York: Basic Books, 1991).

William J. Wilson, *When Work Disappears: The World of the New Urban Poor* (New York: Knopf, 1996).

The Economy

Fred L. Block, *The Vampire State: And Other Myths and Fallacies about the U.S. Economy* (New York: New Press, 1996).

Peter F. Drucker, *Post-Capitalist Society* (New York: HarperCollins, 1993).

Thomas L. Friedman, *The World Is Flat* (New York: Farrar, Straus, and Giroux, 2005).

Robert Kuttner, *Everything for Sale: The Virtues and Limits of Markets* (New York: Knopf, 1997).

James O'Connor, *The Fiscal Crisis of the State* (New York: St. Martin's Press, 1973).

Web Resources

http://www.dol.gov/
The United States Department of Labor provides facts and statistics on labor, including unemployment.

http://www.bls.gov/
"The Bureau of Labor Statistics is the principal fact-finding agency for the Federal Government in the broad field of labor economics and statistics."

http://www.labornet.org/
Labornet offers information on the current labor movement, including news, archives, links, and protests.

http://www.northlandposter.com/cgi-bin/Web_store/web_store.cgi
This is the home of the Northland Poster Collective, which sells posters, buttons, bumper stickers, and more with slogans related to social justice, particularly labor.

http://www.umwa.org/homepage.shtml
This is the homepage of the United Mine Workers of America, a union fighting for the rights of workers since 1890.

http://unions.org/default2.asp
The Union Resource Network is a searchable index of unions on the Internet. It also contains union labor news.

http://www.sweatshops.org
Sweatshops.org provides general information on sweatshops, why they form, ideas on how to eliminate them, and links to other relevant sites. There is also the option of searching the green pages for socially and environmentally responsible products.

http://www.tao.ca/~resist/womeninglobalcapitalism.html
This site discusses the position of women in global capitalism. It includes information on sweatshops and trafficking in women, as well as links to similar sites.

http://www.cartoonweb.com/lobby.asp
Cartoons related to the economy and other issues can be found at this site.

http://www.dsausa.org/dsa.html
Democratic Socialists of America is an organization that advocates for a more humane social order with an "equitable distribution of resources, meaningful work, gender and racial equality, a healthy environment, sustainable growth, and non-oppressive relationships."

http://www.globalexchange.org/
Global Exchange is a human rights organization that looks to create environmental, political, and

social justice around the world. The site explores global campaigns, provides information on issues in different countries, and offers opportunities to get involved.

http://www.corpwatch.org/
Corpwatch is a site looking to hold corporations responsible for their actions. It contains information on issues dealing with sweatshops and politics.

http://epinet.org
The Economic Policy Institute website provides information on jobs, living wages, Social Security, and more.

Power and Politics

When the government took Microsoft to court over alleged antitrust violations, Microsoft unleashed an all-out crusade to create a political climate to discourage the Justice Department from seeking aggressive sanctions and to encourage Congress to pass helpful legislation (the following is from Chandrasekaran and Mintz, 1999). In the 1998 congressional election, Microsoft and its employees increased their political donations fivefold from the 1996 election to $1.4 million. Also in 1998, Microsoft was the tenth largest corporate giver of unregulated "soft money." The Microsoft political action committee (PAC) spent about $1 million before the 2000 election, putting it in the top tier of corporate PACs. The firm also doubled its lobbying spending to $3.7 million.

In addition to these standard efforts by corporate entities to influence politics, Microsoft also "deployed a range of far more sophisticated and subtle techniques: contributing to the pet causes of key members of Congress, airing television ads aimed at decision-makers, underwriting friendly think tanks, lobbying states involved in the antitrust case and organizing networks of 'grass-roots' supporters" (Chandrasekaran and Mintz, 1999:9).

These political activities by Microsoft are commonly employed by other corporations (and, in the Microsoft antitrust case, by those corporations who complained to the government about Microsoft's monopolistic practices), professional organizations, labor unions, and interest groups. This phenomenon of influencing policymakers can be interpreted in two opposing ways—each of which illustrates a fundamental view of the distribution of power for the whole society. The first view is that these activities are the essence of democracy, as each competing pressure group presents its best case to the decision makers. These officials, faced with these countervailing forces, tend to compromise and make decisions most beneficial to the public. The contrasting position is that these efforts to use money to influence politics are another instance of the privileged few consistently getting their way. Interest groups are not equal in power. Some have enormous power and are not challenged by effective opposition. The poor and the near-poor, for example, are not represented in the power equation. How do start-up companies fight Microsoft, not only in the marketplace, but in Washington? Clearly, from this perspective, power in Washington is centralized and represents the powerful few.

The compelling questions of this chapter are, Who are the real power wielders in U.S. society? Are they an elite, or are the people sovereign? The location and exercise of power are difficult to determine, especially in a large and complex society such as the United States. Decisions are necessarily made by a few people, but in a democracy these few are to be representatives of the masses and therefore subject to their influence. But what of nonrepresentatives who aid in shaping policy? What about the pressure on the decision makers by powerful groups? What about those pressures on the decision makers that are so diffuse that the leaders may not even know who is applying the pressure?

Models of the National Power Structure

There are two basic views of the power structure—the **elitist model of power** and the **pluralist model of power**. The elitist view of power is that there is a pyramid of power. The people at the apex control the rest of the pyramid. Pluralists, on the other hand, see power as dispersed rather than concentrated. Power is broadly distributed among a number of organizations, special interests, and the voters. This chapter examines different elitist and pluralist conceptions of power in the United States. As each is surveyed, the fundamental questions are, How does a particular model mesh with the facts of our contemporary society? Does the model portray things as they are or as they should be?

Pluralist Models

Pluralism I: Representative Democracy. Many people in the United States accept the notion promoted in high school civics books that the country is a "government of the people, by the people, for the people." **Democracy** is the form of government in which the people have the ultimate power—a government of, by, and for the people. The will of the majority prevails, there is equality before the law, and decisions are made to maximize the common good. In a complex society of almost 300 million people, the people cannot make all decisions; they must elect representatives to make most decisions. So, decision making is concentrated at the top, but it is to be controlled by the people who elect the decision makers. This model is shown in Figure 14.1. (See the panel titled "A Closer Look: Structural Barriers to Democracy.")

The most important component of a democratic model is that the representatives, because they are elected by the people, are responsive to the wishes of the people. This model, however, does not conform to reality. The United States is undemocratic in many important ways. The people, although they do vote for their representatives every few years, are really quite powerless. For example, who makes the really important

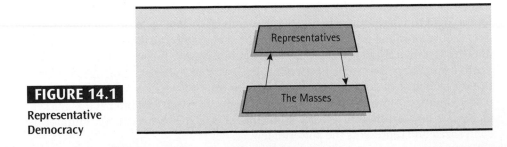

FIGURE 14.1

Representative
Democracy

decisions about war and peace, economic policies, and foreign policy? The people certainly do not. The record shows that many times the people have been deceived when the object was to conceal clandestine illegal operations, mistakes, undemocratic practices, and the like. These illicit and deceptive activities have been carried out by Democratic and Republican presidents alike.

Not only have the people in the United States been misinformed at times, but the basic democratic tenet that the public be informed has also been defied on occasion. On one hand, Congress has shown its contempt for the electorate by the use of secret meetings. The executive branch, too, has acted in secret. Recent presidents have gone months without holding a press conference, have used executive privilege to keep presidential advisors from testifying before congressional committees, and have refused to debate opponents in election campaigns. Many people who are appointed rather than elected wield tremendous power. Technical experts, for example, evaluate extremely complicated issues; they can virtually dictate to the president and Congress what is needed for defense, shoring up the economy, or winning friends abroad because they are the experts. The coterie of advisors may convince the president to act in particular ways. Members appointed to the regulatory agencies have tremendous power to shape various aspects of the economy.

Perhaps one of the most undemocratic features (at least in its consequences) of the U.S. political system is a result of how campaigns are financed. Political campaigns are becoming more and more expensive, with money needed to pay for staff, direct-mail operations, phone banks, polling, computers, consultants, and media advertising. The campaigns for Congress and president in 2004 cost more than $5 billion overall (up from $3.5 billion in 2000), including monies from the federal government, individuals, political parties, and organizations.

In 2002 Congress passed the Bipartisan Campaign Reform Act (also known as the McCain-Feingold law). This law limited the use of "soft money," in federal elections. The use of "soft money" had allowed individuals, corporations, unions, and other organizations to give unlimited amounts of money to political parties or to private organizations that are technically independent of the candidates. Since this tactic was not covered by the election laws, the amounts raised were unlimited. This loophole was used by wealthy persons to contribute to the Republican and Democratic national parties (and indirectly to the presidential candidates).

McCain-Feingold did wipe out "soft money" in federal elections (buttressed by a favorable Supreme Court ruling in 2003) but it did not limit the giving of large sums to affect election outcomes. In the 2004 election campaign activists devised ways to get large donations to build support among Democrat or Republican voters. The loophole used is called 527s, which are advocacy groups, tax exempt under Section 527 of the Internal Revenue Code, that finance political advertisements while not directly calling for the election or defeat of specific candidates (Dwyer, 2004). Democrats, for example, created such organizations as the Media Fund and America Coming Together. Working through these organizations, billionaires George Soros and Peter Lewis gave a total of $15 million, creating among other strategies the liberal Internet organization MoveOn.org. Similarly, Republicans set up comparable groups, such as the Leadership Forum, a fund-raising group headed by Washington lobbyists.

McCain-Feingold also limited maximum contributions to $2,000. While technically adhering to this limitation, corporate executives, lobbyists, and other insiders could maximize their political influence by a sophisticated system of bundling—the

Structural Barriers to Democracy

In the 2004 presidential election the actual vote by the adult U.S. population was as follows (Zinn, 2005):

- Only 60 percent of the eligible voters actually voted. Stated another way, 40 percent of those eligible chose not to vote.
- Bush won the approval of 31 percent of the eligible voters. Kerry won 28 percent of the eligible voters.

In short, George Bush became president of the United States receiving slightly more than three out of ten of the possible votes.

Those who voted were disproportionately White, relatively affluent, educated, and suburban. What about the poor and the near-poor, racial minorities, blue-collar laborers, and city dwellers who chose not to vote? Why did they not vote? What is the source of their alienation? Is the problem with these apathetic people or is it with the system? Let's look at the systemic sources that thwart democracy in the United States.

The two-party system that has emerged (it is not part of the Constitution) is a major impediment to democracy. Corporations, special interests, and wealthy individuals sponsor both parties. Since candidates from minor parties rarely win, they do not receive monetary support, which fulfills the prophecy. They also remain minor parties because the government subsidizes the two major parties in two ways: First, the Republican and Democratic Parties receive millions from the federal government to fund their nominating conventions and receive federal matching campaign funds based on their presumed viability. On the surface, this "matching funds" approach seems fair, but in practice it keeps the strong parties strong and the weak parties weak.

The bias toward the two-party system was revealed again when a "bipartisan" commission ruled that Ross Perot could not participate in the 1996 presidential debates and Ralph Nader could not be part of the 2000 and 2004 presidential debates. They could not take part, it was argued, because they had no chance of winning. Of course, not being part of the debates makes that prophecy a certainty. The commission, by the way, was composed of members selected from the Republican and Democratic Parties!

Another obstacle to third parties is that they cannot break the two-party control at every level of government. Even if the candidate of a third party were successful in winning the presidency, he or she would have difficulty in governing because both houses of Congress would be controlled by one or the other of the major parties. Moreover, since the two major parties control both houses of Congress (chairing committees, majorities on committees and in Congress), independents (in 2006 there are two, Bernie Sanders of Vermont in the House and Jim Jeffords of Vermont in the Senate) have no power.

A major problem lies with the winner-take-all system. A state with a 30 percent Latino population may not have any Latino representation in Congress because a White majority in each congressional district voted for the White candidate. Similarly, a city may have a seven-member city council elected at large by majority vote. The usual result is that not one council member represents a poor section of the city. The method used to elect the president, the electoral college, decrees that the candidate winning a plurality of votes in that state receives all of the electoral votes allocated to the state. The 2000 presidential election

pooling of a large number of contributions. This tactic is used by both political parties. The Republicans in 2004, for example, used an elite regiment of 455 "Rangers" and "Pioneers," honorary fundraisers who collected at least $200,000 or $100,000, respectively.

Another method to raise money is through contributions to a "foundation" sponsored by a candidate. Through this loophole, donors could give unlimited contributions to a candidate with their identities hidden from the public record. A fourth source of money is the contributions to the political conventions. For example, the 2004 Republican convention in New York City was underwritten by contributions of

Structural Barriers to Democracy continued

hinged on the vote in Florida, which after five weeks of disputed vote counting, declared Bush the winner by a few thousand votes; but even though the vote was virtually even in the state, Bush received all of Florida's electoral votes, giving him the presidency. The consequence is that all votes for other candidates were wasted. "Worse than antiquated, Winner Take All is downright dangerous. It distorts national policy, robs voters of representation, and pits partisan voters as well as racial, ethnic, and religious minorities against each other for a scarce commodity—political representation" (Hill, Stevens, 2002:xi).

Consider what happened in Alabama in the 1992 election. George Bush won the state handily with 47.9 percent of the vote, claiming all nine of its electoral votes. But exit polls indicated that 91 percent of African American voters in Alabama—who make up roughly two-ninths of the state's electorate—voted for Bill Clinton. Despite this overwhelming level of support, Clinton, with only 30 percent of the White vote, didn't secure a single electoral vote in Alabama. African American voters might just as well have stayed home (Hoffman, 1996:15).

Just as many voters are disenfranchised by the winner-take-all system, many are also shut out by the process in which state legislatures under partisan control deliberately shape congressional districts (called "gerrymandering") to be overwhelmingly Republican or Democrat. This rigging of the system means, in effect, that the public is denied a choice. As *USA Today* (2002d) editorialized: "Little wonder turnout at the polls has been declining for years. By trying to fix the outcomes of House races before Election Day, professional partisans are effectively disenfranchising voters" (13A).

Both parties seek the largest number of voters by appealing to those who are most likely to vote (upper-middle-class, White fiscal conservatives from the suburbs). Both parties push for middle-class tax cuts, "family values," and a tougher stance on crime. Both parties are beholden to business. As Ralph Nader put it: The difference between his major party foes was merely the "velocity with which their knees hit the floor when Big Business enters the room" (quoted in Willing, 2000:9A). All of these similarities leave out many who find each of the two major parties irrelevant to their interests. Neither party, for example, has a plan to revitalize the cities, desegregate housing, and provide affordable housing for the working poor. Neither the Republicans nor the Democrats have been willing "or professed to see the necessity to mount an attack on the economic trends that had created the inner-city ghetto and that also were keeping many Whites and non-ghetto Blacks in poverty and hopelessness" (Wicker, 1996:12). Neither party has pressed hard for further racial gains or for the enforcement of what has been accomplished. In short, many if not most of the nation's eligible voters are electorally homeless (Hightower, 1996).

The U.S. system is in sharp contrast to the multinational party systems found in the European democracies, where religious minorities, racial groups, the working class, and other special interests form viable political parties. The result is that citizens can find a political party with an agenda compatible to their interests. As a consequence, voter turnout in Canada and Europe ranges between 80 and 90 percent, compared to the 50 percent in U.S. presidential elections.

$64 million. While technically not a political contribution, the parties and candidates are beholden to the contribution corporations.

In addition to the legal ways to influence campaigns with money, there are the contributions made outside the federal law. Fred Wertheimer (1996), former president of Common Cause, who has investigated campaign abuses for twenty years, says this:

> When you add it all up—the illegality, the cheating, the evasion, as well as the arrogance and cynicism—what we have is a collapse of the system on a scale we simply haven't seen before. . . . Put simply, we've seen that the attitude of our national leaders when it comes to campaign laws is no different than that of tax evaders, deadbeat dads and welfare cheats. (29)

What do the contributors of large sums receive for their donations? Obviously, they have access to the politician, perhaps even influence. It is difficult to prove conclusively that receiving campaign contributions from a special interest buys a vote, but there is some indirect evidence that such contributors do gain advantage:

- Interest groups often give to candidates who run unopposed.
- Some interest groups give money to both sides in an election. Others contribute after the election to the candidate they opposed but who won anyway.
- Interest groups overwhelmingly support incumbents. By giving to the incumbent, the giver is almost assured of giving to the winner.
- The most money disproportionately goes to the most powerful members of the House and Senate (those in leadership roles).

See the panel titled "A Closer Look: The Best Democracy Money Can Buy."

a Closer Look

The Best Democracy Money Can Buy

About $5 billion was spent in the 2004 election campaign. The consequence of this flood of money in elections is that it sabotages democracy. This occurs in several ways. First, it makes it harder for government to solve social problems.

> How can we produce smart defense, environmental, and health policies if arms contractors, oil firms, and HMOs have a hammerlock over the committees charged with considering reforms? How can we adequately fund education and child care if special interests win tax breaks that deplete public resources? (Green, 2002:4)

Second, and related to the first, the "have-nots" of society are not represented among the decision makers. Moreover, since the successful candidate must either be wealthy or be beholden to them, they are a different class of people, from a different social world than most Americans. Thus, the money-politics connection is undemocratic because "democracy requires diversity in its legislatures in order to reflect the popular will" (Green, 2002:18)

> Since cash is the currency of elections, candidates troll for money where it is concentrated: in largely white, wealthy neighborhoods. . . . When a small wealthy group in effect decides which candidates will have enough money to run a viable campaign, it is no great surprise that the agenda of the policymakers is skewed toward its interests and not those of people of color and other underserved communities. (Gonzalez and Moore, 2003:23A)

Third, the money chase creates part-time elected officials and full-time fundraisers. For example, "senators from the ten largest states have to raise an average of over $34,000 a week, every week, for six years to stay in office" (Green, 2002:2).

Fourth, money diminishes the gap between the two major political parties because the candidates and parties seek and receive funds from the same corporate sources and wealthy individuals. Democrats in need of funds, even though they are more inclined than Republicans to support social programs and raising taxes to pay for them, must temper these tendencies or lose their monetary support from wealthy interests. As Robert Reich has observed, "it is difficult to represent the little fellow when the big fellow pays the tab" (Reich, 1989:A29).

Fifth, the money chase in politics discourages voting and civic participation (of the twenty-four Western democracies, the United States ranks twenty-third in voting turnout).

Sixth, big money in politics means that special interests get special access to the decision makers and receive special treatment from them.

> The pay-to-play mentality has so seeped into our system that there now exist two classes of citizens. There are those for whom tax breaks, bailouts, and subsidies are granted; for whom running for and winning office is plausible; and with who elected officials take time to meet. And then there are the rest of us—the non-donors for whom taxes go up, consumer prices rise, and influence evaporates. (Green, 2002:148)

Money presents a fundamental obstacle to democracy because only the interests of the wealthy tend to be served. It takes money—and lots of it—to be a successful politician. The candidate must either be rich or be willing to accept contributions from other people. In either case, the political leaders will be part of or beholden to the wealthy.

Closely related to campaign financing is the process by which political candidates are nominated. Being wealthy or having access to wealth is essential for victory because of the enormous cost. This means that the candidates tend to represent a limited constituency—the wealthy.

The two-party system also works to limit choices among candidates to a rather narrow range. Each party is financed by the special interests—especially business:

> Campaign donations from members of the corporate community and upper class are a central element in determining who enters politics with any hope of winning a nomination. . . . It is the need for a large amount of start-up money—to travel around the district or the country, to send out large mailings, to schedule radio and television time in advance—that gives members of the power elite a very direct role in the process right from the beginning and thereby provides them with personal access to politicians of both parties. (Domhoff, 1998:225)

Affluent individuals and the largest corporations influence candidate selection by giving financial aid to those sympathetic with their views and withholding support from those who differ. The parties, then, are constrained to choose candidates with views congruent with the monied interests. See the panel titled "A Closer Look: Is the United States a Plutocracy? Some Warnings," which discusses this linkage between money and power.

Pluralism II: Veto Groups. Although some groups and some individuals have more power than others, the power structure in the United States is viewed according to the veto groups' model as a plurality of interest groups (Riesman, 1950:213–217). Each interest group (for example, the military, labor, business, farmers, education, medicine, law, veterans, the aged, African Americans, and consumers) is primarily

The important question is: Do these elected officials represent the interests of the people or the narrow interests of their contributors?

concerned with protecting its own interests. The group that primarily exercises power varies with the issue at stake. There is a balance of power, since each veto group mobilizes to prevent the others from actions threatening its interests. Thus, these groups tend to neutralize each other.

a Closer Look

Is the United States a Plutocracy? Some Warnings

A plutocracy is a government by or in the interest of the rich. Many observers are concerned that the political system in the United States has become a plutocracy. Consider the following statements (all are taken from Phillips, 2002:xvi, 405).

The U.S. system of campaign finance is "an elaborate influence-peddling scheme in which both parties conspire to stay in office by selling the country to the highest bidder."

Senator John McCain

"Big money and big business, corporations and commerce are again the undisputed overlords of politics and government. The White House, the Congress and, increasingly, the judiciary, reflect their interests. We appear to have a government run by remote control from the U.S. Chamber of Commerce, the National Association of Manufacturers and the American Petroleum Institute. To hell with everyone else."

Bill Moyers

"Money not only determines who is elected, it determines who runs for office. Ultimately, it determines what government accomplishes—or fails to accomplish. Congress, except in unusual moments, will listen to the 900,000 Americans who give $200 or more to their campaigns ahead of the 259,600,000 who don't. Real reform of democracy, reform as radical as those of the Progressive era and deep enough to get government moving again, must begin by completely breaking the connection between money and politics."

Senator Bill Bradley

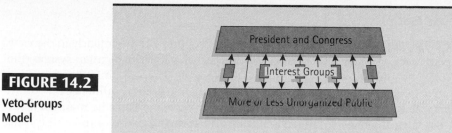

FIGURE 14.2

**Veto-Groups
Model**

The masses are sought as an ally (rather than dominated, as is the case in the various elitist models) by the interest groups in their attempts to exert power over issues in their jurisdiction. Figure 14.2 shows the relationship between the various levels in this model. This pluralist model assumes that there are a number of sectors of power. The most powerful people in each sector are usually wealthy—probably upper class. But the pluralist view is that the upper class is not a unified group—there is considerable disagreement within the upper-class category because of differing interests. Power is not concentrated but is viewed as a shifting coalition depending on the issue. The basic difference between pluralists and elitists depends on the question of whether there is a basic unity or disagreement among the powerful from different sectors (basically, those who are wealthy enough to be upper class).

Several criticisms of this pluralistic model stem from the knowledge that it, like the other pluralistic model (for representative democracy), is an idealized conception of the distribution of power—and as such, it does not conform with reality and is subject to question on several grounds. First, is the power structure so amorphous that power shifts constantly from one power source to another? Second, are the interest groups so equal in power that they neutralize each other? The special bias of this view is that it does not give attention to the power differentials among the various interest groups. It is absurd to claim that the power of big business is neutralized by the countervailing power of farmers. The business sector spends much more than does organized labor to get its way. Moreover, only 13 percent of workers now belong to unions and while union members tend to vote Democratic, a significant minority now vote Republican. Similarly, the business community has many more resources to affect the political process than do environmental groups. Then, there are the powerless, such as migrant workers, the homeless, welfare recipients, immigrants, the poor, and the near-poor, who present no countervailing power against the rich and powerful. Thus follows the conclusion that there is a hierarchy of power among these so-called "veto groups."

A final criticism is that the leaders in each sector come disproportionately from the upper economic stratum. If this assertion is correct, the possibility of a power elite that transcends narrow interest groups is present, since they may know each other, tend to intermarry, and have similar economic interests (as discussed later in this chapter).

The pluralist models are not altogether faulty. A number of possible power centers often compete for advantage. Shifting coalitions are possible. There are instances when elected officials are responsive to public opinion (e.g., the banning of soft money contributions to the political parties in 2002). However, it seems to us that most of the evidence supports an elitist view, although each of the three types described next also has its faults.

Elitist Models

The elitist views of societal power are usually structured quite similarly to the views of Karl Marx. For Marx, economics was the basis for the stratification system (that is, unequal distribution of rewards, including power). The economic elite, because of its ownership and control of the economy, exerts tremendous influence on government policies and actions and is, therefore, a ruling class. The elite manipulate the masses through religion, nationalism, control of the media, and control of the visible governmental leaders (Marx and Engels, 1947:39). Marxists agree that the state serves the interests of the capitalist class. They disagree on how this is accomplished. One position is called the **instrumentalist view** (the following is from Marger, 1987:42–44). Here, the ruling class rules by controlling political officials and institutions through money and influence. Research shows, for example, the connections (social backgrounds) between top corporate and political decision makers. The state is seen as functioning "in terms of the instrumental exercise of power by people in strategic positions, either directly through the manipulation of state policies or indirectly through the exercise of pressure on the state" (Gold, Lo, and Wright, 1975:34). In effect, then, the government is an active instrument of the ruling class, used to accomplish its goals.

The second way Marxists see the ruling class is the **structuralist view**. From this perspective, the linkage between the economic elite and the political elite is not important. Rather, the ruling class gets its way because "the structure of political and economic institutions in capitalist society makes it imperative that the state serve those interests regardless of whether big businessmen directly or indirectly take part in state affairs" (Marger, 1987:43). From this perspective, then, the system is viewed as biased in favor of the elite without their active manipulation.

Power Elite I: The Thesis of C. Wright Mills. C. Wright Mills's (1956) view of the U.S. structure of power posits that the key people in three sectors—the corporate rich, the executive branch of the government, and the military—combine to form a **power elite** that makes all-important decisions.

The elite are a small group of people who routinely interact together. They also, as Mills assumed, have similar interests and goals. The elite are the power elite because the members have key institutional positions—that is, they command great authority and resources in specific and important sectors, and each sector depends on the other sectors.

There are three levels in Mills's pyramid of power. The uppermost is the power elite—composed of the leaders of three sectors. Mills implied that of the three, the corporate rich are perhaps the most powerful (first among equals). The middle level of power is composed of local opinion leaders, the legislative branch of government, and the plurality of interest groups. These bodies, according to Mills, do the bidding of the power elite. The third level is the powerless mass of unorganized people who are controlled from above. They are exploited economically and politically. The three levels of power are depicted in Figure 14.3.

Mills (who was writing in the 1950s) believed that the power elite was a relatively new phenomenon resulting from a number of historical and social forces that have enlarged and centralized the facilities of power, making the decisions of small groups much more consequential than in any other age (Mills, 1968).

FIGURE 14.3

Mills's Pyramid of
Power

Legend:
*1 = corporate rich;
2 = executive
branch;
3 = military leaders;
4 = leaders of inter-
est groups, legisla-
tive branch, local
opinion leaders;
5 = unorganized
masses*

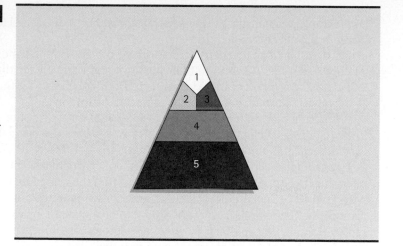

The two important and related factors giving rise to the recent emergence of the power elite are that the means of power and violence (1) are now infinitely greater than they were in the past, and (2) are also increasingly centralized. The decisions of a few people become ultimately crucial when they have the power to activate a system that has the capability of destroying hundreds of cities within minutes. Transportation, communication, the economy, and the instruments of warfare are examples of several areas that have become centralized—making a power elite possible. The federal government taxes, regulates, and passes laws so that the lives of almost all people in the United States are affected.

This same bureaucratic process is evident in the military, in which decisions are more and more centralized. The Pentagon, which oversees the largest and most expensive feature of the government, is a relatively new phenomenon. The economy in the United States was once composed of many, many small productive units that were more or less autonomous. But over time the number of semiautonomous economic units has dwindled through mergers, interlocking directorates, and chain stores, putting the financial squeeze on the small businessperson. The result is that the economy has become dominated by less than 200 giant corporations.

The tremendous advances in transportation and communication have made it much more likely that the people holding key positions in the political, economic, and military hierarchies can be in contact with each other if they wish to do so. If, as Mills assumed, they have similar interests, then they must be in contact so that their activities can be coordinated to the best mutual advantage.

The key decision makers also have instruments to influence the masses, such as television, public relations firms, and techniques of propaganda that are unsurpassed in the history of humankind. Hence, if there is a power elite and they want to manipulate the masses to accept their decisions, they have the instruments of mass persuasion at their disposal. Mills also contended that the importance of institutions has shifted. Whereas the family and religion were once the most important U.S. institutions, they (along with education) have become subordinate to the three power institutions of the economy, polity, and military—thus making the leaders of these three domains the power elite. Mills (1968) said, "Families and churches and schools adapt to modern life; governments and armies and corporations shape it; and, as they do so, they turn these lesser institutions into means for their ends" (267).

For example, religious institutions supply chaplains to the armed forces, where they increase the effectiveness of the combat units by raising morale. Schools train people for their places in the giant corporations. Fathers and sons, mothers and daughters are sometimes taken from their homes to fight and die for their country. And, Mills said, the symbols of these lesser institutions are used to legitimate the decisions of the power elite who dominate the powerful institutions.

A most important impetus for the formation of the power elite was World War II. United States participation in a worldwide war, where the possibility of defeat was very real, meant, among other things, that a reorganization of various sectors had to be accomplished. The national government, particularly the executive department, had to be granted dictatorial powers so that the war could be conducted. Decisions had to be made quickly and in secret, two qualities not compatible with a democracy. The nation's corporations had to be mobilized for war. They made huge profits. Finally, the military became very prominent in decision making. Their expertise was essential to the making of wartime strategy.

Following World War II, the United States was faced with another threat—the spread of communism. This meant, in effect, that the executive department, the corporations, and the military did not shift back to their peacetime ways. The military remained in the decision-making process, the corporations remained dependent on lucrative defense contracts, and the executive branch continued to exercise its autonomous or at least semiautonomous powers.

All these factors, according to Mills, ensured that the domains of the polity, economy, and military were enlarged and centralized. Decisions made in each of these domains became increasingly crucial to all citizens, but particularly to the leaders of the other key domains. The result had to be a linkage between the key people in each domain. It was in their interests to cooperate. Because each sector affected the others, the people at the top of each hierarchy had to interact with the leaders from the other sectors, so that the actions and decisions would benefit all. Thus, they have come to form a triangle of power, an interlocking directorate of people in the three key domains making coordinated decisions—a power elite.

An important ingredient in Mills's view is that the elite are a self-conscious cohesive unit. This unity is based on three factors: psychological similarity, social interaction, and coinciding interests.

1. *Psychological similarity.* The institutional positions men and women occupy throughout their lifetimes determine the values they will hold. For example, career military men hold certain values by virtue of being socialized into the military subculture. The famous quote "What's good for General Motors is good for the country" by Secretary of Defense (under President Eisenhower) Charles Wilson is also indicative of this probability. Thus, for Mills, the psychology of these leaders is largely shaped by the values they develop in their institutional roles. Additionally, the psychological similarity among the members of the elite is derived from their similar social origins and lifestyles.

2. *Social interaction.* Mills (1956) states that the ruling elite are involved in a set of overlapping groups and intricately connected cliques:

> The people of the higher circles may also be conceived as members of a top social stratum, as a set of groups whose members know one another, see one another socially and at business, and so, in making decisions, take one another into

account. The elite, according to this conception, feel themselves to be, and are felt by others to be, the inner circle of "the upper social classes." They form a more or less compact social and psychological entity; they have become self-conscious members of a social class. People are either accepted into this class or they are not, and there is a qualitative split, rather than merely a numerical scale, separating them from those who are not elite. They are more or less aware of themselves as a social class and they behave toward one another differently from the way they do toward members of other classes. They accept one another, understand one another, marry one another, tend to work and to think if not together at least alike. (11)

3. *Coinciding interests.* A third unifying condition hypothesized by Mills is the existence of similar interests among the elite. The interest of the elite is, among other things, maintenance of the capitalist system with themselves at the top. Additionally, the government needs adequate defense systems, to which the military agree and that the corporations gladly sell for a profit. The huge corporations have large holdings in foreign countries. They therefore expect the government to make policy decisions that will be beneficial (profitable) for these U.S. interests. These similar interests result in unity and a need for planning and coordination of their efforts. Because each sector affects the other, the people at the top of each hierarchy must interact with leaders of the other sectors so that their actions will benefit all. Top decisions, Mills argued, thus become coordinated decisions.

Much of Mills's argument seems to fit with the realities of U.S. politics. Certainly those at the top of the key sectors wield enormous power. Some elements in Mills's thesis, however, have not held completely during the intervening forty years (see Wolfe, 1999). First, Mills believed that the three sub-elites that compose the power elite are more or less equal, with the corporate rich probably having the most power. The equality of these groups is not proved. With the dismantling of the Soviet Empire, the power of the military elite diminished only to rise again after the terrorist attacks on the World Trade Center and the Pentagon in 2001. Military leaders are influential only in their advisory capacities and their ability to convince the executive branch and Congress. What looks like military power is often actually the power of the corporations and/or the executive branch carried out in military terms. In the view of many observers (especially Domhoff, as we see in the next section), business leaders compose the real power elite. Even though this is debatable, the fact is that they surpass the military in power, and because the executive branch is composed of people with close ties to the leading corporations, the logical conclusion is that business interests prevail in that sector as well.

Conflict occurs among the three sectors. There is often bitter disagreement between corporations and the government, between the military and the executive branch, and between the military and some elements in the business community. How is this conflict to be explained if, as Mills contended, the power elite is a group that acts in concert, with joint efforts planned and coordinated to accomplish the agreed-on goals? A good deal of empirical evidence shows that the heads of the three major sectors do not compose a group.

Mills relegates a number of powerful (or potentially powerful) forces to the middle ranges of power. What about the power of pressure groups that represent interests other than business or the military? Certainly, organized labor, farmers, professional organizations such as the American Medical Association, and consumers exert power over particular issues. Sometimes business interests even lose. How is this to be explained?

Finally, is Congress only in the middle level of the power structure? In Mills's view, Congress is a rubber stamp for the interests of business, the executive branch, and the military. Congress is apparently not composed of puppets for these interests, although the laws most often seem to favor these interests. But Congress does have its mavericks, and some of these people, by virtue of seniority, exert tremendous power (for either the blockage or passage of legislation). Should not the key congressional leaders be included in the power elite? The problem is that they often have interests that do not coincide with those of the presumed elite.

Power Elite II: Domhoff's "Governing Class" Theory. In the view of Mills, power is concentrated in a relatively small, cohesive elite; G. William Domhoff's model of power is more broadly based in a "**dominant class.**" Domhoff (1998) defined this dominant class as the uppermost social group (approximately 1 percent of the population), which owns a disproportionate amount of the country's wealth and contributes a disproportionate number of its members to the controlling institutions and key decision-making groups of the country:

> The owners and top-level managers in large income-producing properties are far and away the dominant power figures in the United States. Their corporations, banks, and agribusinesses come together as a corporate community that dominates the federal government in Washington. Their real estate, construction, and land development companies form growth coalitions that dominate most local governments. Granted, there is competition within both the corporate community and the local growth coalitions for profits and investment opportunities, and there are sometimes tensions between national corporations and local growth coalitions, but both are cohesive on policy issues affecting their general welfare, and in the face of demands by organized workers, liberals, environmentalists, and neighborhoods. (Domhoff, 1998:1)

This status group is composed mainly of rich businesspeople and their families, many of whom are, according to Domhoff's convincing evidence, closely knit through stock ownership, trust funds, intermarriages, private schools, social clubs, exclusive summer resorts, and corporation boards.

The dominant class in Domhoff's analysis controls the executive branch of the federal government, the major corporations, the mass media, foundations, universities, and the important councils for domestic and foreign affairs (for example, the Council on Foreign Relations, the Committee for Economic Development, the National Security Council, the National Industrial Conference Board, and the Twentieth Century Fund). Since they can control the executive branch, Domhoff argues, this dominant class controls the very important regulatory agencies, the federal judiciary, the military, the Central Intelligence Agency, and the Federal Bureau of Investigation.

The dominant class has greater influence on (but not control of) Congress and state and local governments than any other group. These parts of the formal power structure are not directly controlled by the governing class in Domhoff's analysis, but because he claims that such a class controls the executive and judicial branches, Congress is effectively blocked by two of the three divisions of government. Thus, U.S. foreign and domestic policies are initiated, planned, and carried out by members and organizations of a power elite that serve the interests of an upper class of rich businesspeople. Decisions are made that are considered appropriate for the interests of the United States—a strong economy, an adequate defense, and social stability.

While perhaps beneficial to all people in the country, policies designed to accomplish these goals especially favor the rich. Consequently, U.S. corporations overseas are protected, foreign trade agreements are made that benefit U.S. corporations, and the tax structure benefits corporations or the very wealthy (by means of allowances for oil depletion, for capital gains and capital losses, for depreciation of equipment, and for other business expenses).

Domhoff demonstrates in detail the manner in which the governing class interacts (which we examined in Chapter 10). Once he established the interlocking ties brought about by common interests and through interaction, he cites circumstances that show the impact of individuals and subgroups within the elite on the decision-making structure of the United States:

- Control of presidential nominations through the financing of political campaigns: The evidence is clear that unless candidates have large financial reserves or the backing of wealthy people, they cannot hope to develop a national following or compete in party primaries.
- Control of both major political parties: Even though the Democratic Party is usually considered the party of the common person, Domhoff shows that it, like the Republican Party, is controlled by aristocrats (Parenti, Michael, 1995; this is documented well in Greider, 1992).
- Almost total staffing of important appointive governmental positions (cabinet members, members of regulatory agencies, judges, diplomats, and presidential advisors): These appointees are either members of the upper class or people who have held positions in the major corporations, and are thereby people who accord with the wishes of the upper class.

As a result of these circumstances (and others), all important foreign and domestic decisions are seen as made by the governing class. Domhoff's view of the power structure is reconstructed graphically in Figure 14.4.

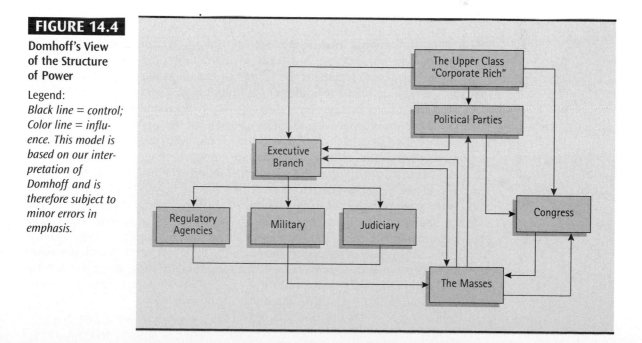

FIGURE 14.4

Domhoff's View of the Structure of Power

Legend:
Black line = control; Color line = influence. This model is based on our interpretation of Domhoff and is therefore subject to minor errors in emphasis.

In many ways, Domhoff's model of the U.S. power structure was a refinement of the one posited earlier by Mills. Domhoff's assessment of the power structure was similar to Mills's in that they both (1) view the power structure as a single pyramid, (2) see the corporate rich as the most powerful interest group, (3) relegate Congress to a relatively minor role and place the executive branch in an important role in the decision-making process, and (4) view the masses as being dominated by powerful forces rather than having much grassroots power.

The major difference between the views of Mills and Domhoff is that Domhoff has asserted the complete ascendancy of the upper class to the apex of power. The executive branch is controlled by upper-class businesspeople, industrialists, and financiers, rather than the two groups being more or less equal partners in the power elite, as Mills saw it. Moreover, the placement of the military in the pyramid of power is quite different. Mills saw the military as part of the alliance of the troika, whereas Domhoff saw the military as having much less power and being dominated by the corporate rich through the executive branch.

Domhoff's view of power is quite persuasive, but there are also several criticisms. First, much of Domhoff's proof is in the form of listing the upper-class pedigrees of presidential advisors, cabinet members, ambassadors, regulatory agency members, and so on. Even though people in these positions are disproportionately from upper-class backgrounds (as evidenced by their attendance at prestige schools, their membership in exclusive social clubs, and their placement in the various social registries), we are given no proof that these people actually promote the interests of the corporate rich. This is an assumption by Domhoff that appears reasonable, but it is an oversimplification. There are many examples of wealthy people who make decisions on bases other than economics, such as religious or moral altruism, or civil or human rights. Thus, Domhoff's assumption is one of Marxian economic determinism, and as such is subject to the criticism of oversimplification of a complex process. Even though an economic motive of some kind explains a great deal of social behavior, its operation with other prestige factors is very complex and does not explain all of human behavior.

Power Elite III: Parenti's "Bias of the System" Theory. We commonly think of the machinery of government as a beneficial force promoting the common good. The government can be organized for the benefit of the majority, but it is not always neutral. The state regulates; it stifles opposition; it makes and enforces the law; it funnels information; it makes war on enemies (foreign and domestic); and its policies determine how resources are apportioned. And in all of these areas, the government is generally biased toward policies that benefit the wealthy, especially the business community (this section is taken from Michael Parenti, 1978; 1995; 2002).

Power in the United States is concentrated among the people who control the government and the largest corporations. This assertion is based on the assumption that power is not an attribute of individuals but rather of social organizations. The elite in U.S. society is composed of people who occupy the power roles in society. The great political decisions are made by the president, the president's advisors, cabinet members, the members of regulatory agencies, the Federal Reserve Board, key members of Congress, and the Supreme Court. The individuals in these government command posts have the authority to make war, raise or lower interest rates, levy taxes, dam rivers, and institute or withhold national health insurance.

Economic activity was once the result of many decisions made by individual entrepreneurs and the heads of small businesses. Now, a handful of companies have virtual control over the marketplace. Decisions by the boards of directors and the management personnel of these huge corporations determine employment and production, consumption patterns, wages and prices, the extent of foreign trade, and the rate at which natural resources are depleted, for example.

The few thousand people who compose this power elite tend to come from backgrounds of privilege and wealth. It would be a mistake, however, to equate personal wealth with power. Great power is manifested only through decision making in the very large corporations or in government. We have seen that this elite exercises great power. Decisions are made by the powerful, and these decisions tend to benefit the wealthy disproportionately. But the power elite is not organized and conspiratorial.

The interests of the powerful (and the wealthy) are served, nevertheless, because of the way society is organized. This bias occurs in three ways—by their influence

over elected and appointed governmental officials at all levels, through systemic imperatives, and through the ideological control of the masses.

As discussed in an earlier section, the wealthy receive favorable treatment by actually occupying positions of power or by having direct influence over those who do. Moreover, the financially advantaged spend huge sums to influence Congress and the executive branch through lobbying—there are over 36,000 lobbyists in Washington, spending well over $1 billion annually to influence legislation and executive actions (Parenti, Michael, 2002:223). The laws, court decisions, and administrative decisions give advantage to those individuals, corporations, and interest groups with financial clout.

More subtly, the power elite can get its way without actually being mobilized at all. The choices of decision makers are often limited by various **systemic imperatives**; that is, the institutions of society are patterned to produce prearranged results regardless of the personalities of the decision makers. In other words, there is a bias that pressures the government to do certain things and not to do other things. Inevitably, this bias favors the status quo, allowing people with power to continue to exercise it. No change is easier than change. The current political and economic systems have worked and generally are not subject to question, let alone change. In this way, the laws, customs, and institutions of society resist change. Thus, the propertied and the wealthy benefit, while the propertyless and the poor remain disadvantaged. As Michael Parenti (1978) argues: "The law does not exist as an abstraction. It gathers shape and substance from a context of power, within a real-life social structure. Like other institutions, the legal system is class-bound. The question is not whether the law should or should not be neutral, for as a product of its society, it cannot be neutral in purpose or effect" (188).

In addition to the inertia of institutions, other systemic imperatives benefit the power elite and the wealthy. One such imperative is for the government to strive to provide an adequate defense against our enemies, which stifles any external threat to the status quo. Thus, Congress, the president, and the general public tend to support large appropriations for defense, which, in turn, provide extraordinary profit to many corporations. In addition, the government protects U.S. transnational corporations in their overseas operations, so that they enjoy a healthy and profitable business climate. Domestic government policy also is shaped by the systemic imperative for stability. The government promotes domestic tranquility by squelching dissidence.

Power is the ability to get what one wants from someone else. This can be achieved by force or by getting that someone to think and believe in accordance with your interests. "The ability to control the definition of interests is the ability to define the agenda of issues, a capacity tantamount to winning battles without having to fight them" (Parenti, Michael, 1978:41). U.S. schools, churches, and families possess this power. The schools, for instance, consciously teach youth that capitalism is the only correct economic system. This indoctrination to conservative values achieves a consensus among the citizenry concerning the status quo. In other words, each of us comes to accept the present arrangements in society because they seem to be the only options that make sense. Thus, there is a general agreement on what is right and wrong. In sum, the dominance of the wealthy is legitimized. "The interests of an economically dominant class never stand naked. They are enshrouded in the flag, fortified by the law, protected by the police, nurtured by the media, taught by the schools, and blessed by the church" (Parenti, 1978:84). Finally, the belief in democracy works to the advantage of the power elite, as Parenti (1978) notes in the following passage:

As now constituted, elections serve as a great asset in consolidating the existing social order by propagating the appearances of popular rule. History demonstrates that the people might be moved to overthrow a tyrant who shows himself provocatively indifferent to their woes, but they are far less inclined to make war upon a state, even one dominated by the propertied class, if it preserves what Madison called "the spirit and form of popular government." Elections legitimate the rule of the propertied class by investing it with the moral authority of popular consent. By the magic of the ballot, class dominance becomes "democratic" governance. (201)

The Consequences of Concentrated Power

Who benefits from how power is concentrated in the United States? At times, most everyone does; but for the most part, the decisions made tend to benefit the wealthy. Whenever the interests of the wealthy clash with those of other groups or even of the majority, the interests of the wealthy are served. Consider how the president and Congress deal with the problems of energy shortages, inflation, or deflation. Who is asked to make the sacrifices? Where is the budget cut—are military expenditures reduced or are funds for food stamps slashed? When the Congress considers tax reform, after the roar of rhetoric recedes, which groups benefit by the new legislation or by the laws that are left unchanged? When a corporation is found guilty of fraud, violation of antitrust laws, or bribery, what are the penalties? How do they compare with the penalties for crimes committed by poor individuals? When there is an oil spill or other ecological disaster caused by huge enterprise, what are the penalties? Who pays for the cleanup and the restoration of the environment? The answers to these questions are obvious—the wealthy benefit at the expense of the less well-to-do.

In short, the government is an institution made up of people—the rich and powerful or their agents—who seek to maintain their advantageous positions in society.

Two journalists, Donald Barlett and James Steele (2000), argue that there are two ways to get favorable treatment by Congress and the White House: contribute generously to the right people and spend lavishly on lobbying.

If you do both of these things success will maul you like groupies at a rock concert. If you do neither—and this is the case with about 200 million individuals of voting age and several million corporations—those people in Washington will treat you accordingly. In essence, campaign spending in America has divided all of us into two groups—first- and second-class citizens. This is what happens if you are in the latter group:

You pick up a disproportionate share of America's tax bill.

You pay higher prices for a broad range of products. . . .

You are compelled to abide by laws while others are granted immunity from them.

You must pay debts that you incur while others do not.

You are barred from writing off on your tax return some of the money spent on necessities while others deduct the cost of their entertainment.

In contrast, first-class citizens—the fortunate few who contribute to the right politicians and hire the right lobbyists—enjoy all the benefits of their special status. Among them:

If they make a bad business decision, the government bails them out.

If they want to hire workers at below-market wage rates, the government provides the means to do so.

If they want more time to pay their debts, the government gives them an extension.

If they want immunity from certain laws, the government gives it.

If they want to ignore rules their competitors must comply with, the government gives its approval.

If they want to kill legislation that is intended for the public good, it gets killed.

Call it government for the few at the expense of the many. (40–42)

The bias of the system today is nothing new. Since the nation's founding, the government's policy has primarily favored the needs of the wealthy. The founding fathers were upper-class holders of wealth. The Constitution they wrote gave the power to people like themselves—White male property owners.

This bias continued throughout the nineteenth century as bankers, railroad entrepreneurs, and manufacturers joined the landed gentry to make the power elite. The shift from local business to large-scale manufacturing during the last half of the nineteenth century saw a concomitant increase in governmental activity in the economy. Business was protected from competition by protective tariffs, public subsidies, price regulation, patents, and trademarks. Throughout that century, when there was unrest by troubled miners, farmers, and laborers, the government inevitably took the side of the strong against the weak. The militia and federal troops were used to crush the railroad strikes. Antitrust laws, which were not used to stop the monopolistic practices of business, were invoked against labor unions.

During this time, approximately 1 billion acres of land in the public domain (almost half the present size of the United States) were given to private individuals and corporations. The railroads in particular were given huge tracts of land as a subsidy. These lands were and continue to be very rich in timber and natural resources. This active intervention of the government in the nation's economy during the nineteenth century was almost solely on the behalf of business. Michael Parenti (2002) notes, "The government remained laissez-faire in regard to the needs of the common people, giving little attention to poverty, unemployment, unsafe working conditions, child labor, and the spoilation of natural resources" (59).

The early twentieth century was a time of great governmental activity in the economy, which gave the appearance of restraining big business. However, the actual result of federal regulation of business was to increase the power of the largest corporations. The Interstate Commerce Commission, for instance, helped the railroads by establishing common rates to replace ruinous competition. Federal regulations in meat packing, drugs, banking, and mining weeded out the weaker cost-cutting competitors, leaving a few to control the markets at higher prices and higher profits. Even the actions of that great trustbuster, Teddy Roosevelt, were largely ceremonial. His major legislative proposals reflected the desires of corporate interests. Like other presidents before and since, he enjoyed close relations with big businessmen and invited them into his administration (Parenti, 2002:59–60).

World War I intensified the governmental bias on behalf of business. Industry was converted to war production. Corporate interests became more actively involved in the councils of government. Governmental actions clearly favored business in labor disputes. The police and military were used against rebellious workers, because strikes were treated as efforts to weaken the war effort and therefore as treasonous.

The New Deal is typically assumed to be a time when the needs of those impoverished by the Great Depression were paramount in government policies. But, as Michael Parenti has argued, "the central dedication of the Franklin Roosevelt administration was to business recovery rather than to social reform" (Parenti, 1980:74). Business was subsidized by credits, price supports, bank guarantees, stimulation of the housing industry, and the like. Welfare programs were instituted to prevent widespread starvation, but even these humanitarian programs also advantaged the big-business community. The government provision of jobs, minimum wages, unemployment compensation, and retirement benefits obviously was aimed at people in dire economic straits. But these programs were actually promoted by the business community because of benefits to them. The government and business favored social programs at this time not because millions of people were in misery but because violent political and social unrest posed a real threat.

Two social scientists, Piven and Cloward (1993), in a historical assessment of government welfare programs, have determined that the government institutes massive aid to the poor only when the poor constitute a threat. When large numbers of people are suddenly barred from their traditional occupations, the legitimacy of the system itself may be questioned. Crime, riots, looting, and social movements bent on changing the existing social, political, and economic arrangements become more widespread. Under this threat, the government initiates or expands relief programs in order to diffuse the social unrest. During the Great Depression, Piven and Cloward contend, the government remained aloof from the needs of the unemployed until there was a surge of political disorder. Added proof for Piven and Cloward's thesis is the contraction or even abolishment of public assistance programs when stability was

The Constitutional Battle for Racial Equality

In his widely acclaimed study *In the Matter of Color* (1978), A. Leon Higginbotham dates the beginning of the inextricable link between race and the law with the colonial period. As early as the 1670s, statutes in Virginia and Maryland codified slavery into a system of permanent bondage for Africans and their descendants. These laws, moreover, became the basis for similar legislation throughout British North America.

Meanwhile, from Massachusetts to South Carolina, African peoples used the same laws to petition for freedom and rights. The case of *Quock Walker v. Jennison* (1781), for example, is widely viewed as cementing the abolition of slavery in Massachusetts in 1783. Walker sued Jennison, charging assault and battery. Jennison responded that Walker was his property and not his neighbor, and, as property, he could be punished. A jury disagreed.

The Bill of Rights, however, introduced new ambiguities and opportunities, which were exacerbated by the retreat from the ennobling principles of the Declaration of Independence and the American Revolution. As David Brion Davis sketched in *The Problem of Slavery in the Age of Revolution* (1975), the Constitution's framers evinced considerable ambivalence about the presence of slaves and the practice of slavery. Few could say they had never engaged in the "execrable commerce." Fewer yet believed Africans their equals. Consequently, scores of African-Americans found themselves in legal limbo as they traversed the nation as free or enslaved people.

Did the right to petition the government for redress of grievances include them? Could they comfortably assume that the 4th Amendment, which protected all citizens from unlawful search and seizure, safeguarded them from slave catchers and bounty hunters? Contemporaries and scholars agree: They could not be so assured. Instead, the question of citizenship and unlawful search and seizure awaited the Supreme Court's landmark ruling in *Scott v. Sandford* (1857).

The Dred Scott decision momentarily settled the question of citizenship. Writing for the majority, U.S. Supreme Court Chief Justice Roger B. Taney concluded that African-Americans could be citizens of individual states but not the United States. Although poorly reasoned and badly researched, the opinion proved politically expedient—temporarily protecting Southern and some Northern interests by limiting what it meant to be free and black in our republic. If Blacks were not citizens of the United States, they had no right to petition the court for redress, no right to claim benefit from the Bill of Rights.

Fortunately, the Bill of Rights proved a living document, open to new interpretations, new protections. Following the Civil War, the country eliminated the ambiguities of the previous century by amending the Constitution once again. The new statutes of liberty—the 13th, 14th and 15th Amendments—expanded upon the rights and privileges articulated in the Bill of Rights.

The 13th Amendment abolished slavery, putting into the Constitution language stricken from the Declaration of Independence and excluded from the Constitution altogether. The 14th Amendment determined the grounds for citizenship, ensured equal protection and due process, and, among other things, endowed Congress with the powers to enforce the laws. And the 15th Amendment granted male citizens of all races the right to vote. But to the chagrin of many, African-Americans had to remain ever vigilant lest their civil rights be eroded.

The retreat from equal protection came early and definitively. Between 1876 and 1896, a series of Supreme Court rulings severely narrowed the Bill of Rights and the post–Civil War amendments. The first substantive hint of the new social order came in The

restored. Perhaps this theory explains how African Americans have gradually attained their constitutional rights (see the panel titled "Human Agency: The Constitutional Battle for Racial Equality").

The historical trend for government to favor business over less powerful interests continues in current public policy. This bias is perhaps best seen in the aphorism enunciated by President Calvin Coolidge and repeated by subsequent presidents: "The business of America is business."

The Constitutional Battle for Racial Equality continued

Slaughter-House Cases (1873). A divided Supreme Court distinguished between the rights of a federal and a state citizen by greatly restricting the former. Three years later, in *United States v. Cruishank*, the court addressed the barbarous murder of 100 Blacks in Colfax, Louisiana, and overturned a lower court ruling and found that the defendants had not violated the 1st, 2nd and 14th Amendments. The line of judicial reasoning culminated in the 1896 Plessy decision, which legalized the doctrine of separate but equal.

Over the course of the next century, new challenges and new opportunities to refer to the Bill of Rights arose. African-Americans, in their dogged determination to fulfill the dream of equality, helped expand the meaning of the law—the Bill of Rights.

Perhaps the most heralded and surprising example dates from the '30s. In 1931, nine Black youths hopped a train and had a chance encounter with a smaller group of Whites. To the later surprise of the nine Blacks, two in the other party were females. When confronted by law officials and questioned about their presence on the train, the women alleged the most heinous of all interracial crimes had occurred: the rape of White women by Black men. The Black youths were charged and convicted.

The drama that unfolded became known nationally and internationally as the Scottsboro boys case. And, as Dan Carter noted in his classic study of Scottsboro, the case changed both the nation and the Southern social landscape.

How the case changed the Southern social landscape is another story; how it changed the nation had a direct bearing on the Bill of Rights. The 6th Amendment guaranteed all citizens a speedy trial before an "impartial jury of the state and district wherein the crime shall have been committed." It also assured all the assistance of competent counsel for their defense.

The defendants in the Scottsboro boys case charged that they were denied competent counsel and an impartial jury. During the hastily concluded initial trial, which lasted six days and resulted in the death penalty for all nine, the court-sanctioned attorneys lacked the time, the will, and the skills to defend. Moreover, African-Americans in that part of Alabama had been systematically excluded from the jury rolls. In *Powell v. Alabama* (1932), the Supreme Court upheld the right of the accused to counsel. Because the 6th Amendment granted protection to defendants in federal trials, the court turned to the equal-protection clause of the 14th Amendment, which offered protection at both the state and federal levels.

Three years later, in *Norris v. Alabama*, the U.S. Supreme Court ruled that the exclusion of Blacks from juries violated the 14th Amendment.

The men who authored the original Bill of Rights recognized what it ignored as well as what it covered. Since that time we have struggled to improve on their enduring genius. That they were imperfect is beyond dispute. Nonetheless, their undeniable concern for democratic values—despite their skirting the issue of slavery—enabled others to modify or amend their work.

Most importantly, the ideals that fueled the writings of the Bill of Rights also inspired African-Americans to struggle for two centuries to keep the Bill of Rights a living document. In the process, Blacks helped the nation examine the importance of freedom of speech, freedom of assembly, freedom of the press, due process, and justifiable bail and punishment.

Source: Earl Lewis, 1991. "African-Americans and the Bill of Rights." *In These Times* (December 18–24):12–13. Reprinted by permission.

Subsidies to Big Business

There is a general principle that applies to the government's relationship to big business—business can conduct its affairs either undisturbed by or encouraged by government, whichever is of greater benefit to the business community. The government benefits the business community with $125 billion in subsidies annually. Corporations receive a wide range of favors and tax breaks, direct government subsidies pay for advertising, research, and training costs and incentives to pursue overseas production and sales (Gillespie, Ed, 2003). The following are examples of government decisions that were beneficial to business:

- State and local governments woo corporations with various subsidies including tax breaks, low-interest loans, infrastructure improvements, and relatively cheap land. In 2001, for example, Chicago beat out the offers by Denver and Dallas, by offering $50 million in incentives to encourage Boeing to move its headquarters there from Seattle. To keep the New York Stock Exchange in New York City, the city and state of New York offered an incentive package worth more than $1 billion. To which Ralph Nader (2001) replied: "It would be hard to script a more brazen and shameless corporate giveaway from a city where nearly one in three children lives in poverty, and public investment necessities go begging" (26).

- In 1996, Congress gave broadcasters spectrum rights to broadcast one channel of super-high-resolution digital programs or several channels that could be used for digital interactive services or TV programs of high, but not super-high resolution. To which the *New York Times* (2000a) editorialized: "By giving the new spectrum away instead of auctioning it off to the highest bidders, Congress deprived the treasury, and thus taxpayers, of tens of billions of dollars" (1).

- Following the terrorist attacks of September 11, 2001, Congress appropriated $15 billion for the airline industry. The bailout went to the airline companies, *not* the workers laid off by the companies and allied industries (travel and tourism).

- The government installs price supports on certain commodities, increasing the profits of those engaged in those industries and simultaneously costing consumers. For example, sugar price supports cost consumers $3 billion a year; dairy and milk price supports increase the annual cost to consumers by $9 billion (Green, 2002:161).

- The federal government directly subsidizes the shipping industry, railroads, airlines, and exporters of iron, steel, textiles, paper, and other products.

- The government often funds research and develops new technologies at public expense and then turns them over to private corporations for their profit. This transfer occurs routinely with nuclear energy, synthetics, space communications, mineral exploration, and pharmaceuticals. Although the pharmaceutical industry, for example, argues that it must charge high prices on drugs to recoup its costly research, the Joint Economic Committee of Congress found that public research led to fifteen of the twenty-one drugs considered to have the highest therapeutic value introduced between 1965 and 1992 (reported in Goozner, 2000). Three of these drugs—Capoten, Prozac, and Zovirax—have sales of more than $1 billion each. Not incidentally, the drug makers are the most powerful lobby in Washington, with 625 registered lobbyists spending nearly $100 million a year to lobby.

- Congress subsidizes the timber industry by building roads for logging at an annual cost of $173 million (Zepezauer, 2004). Under an 1872 law, mining companies need not pay for the $2 billion worth of minerals they extract from public lands (Scher, 2000). The government subsidizes corn growers and corn processors by mandating the use of ethanol (a corn-based fuel product) in gasoline.

- Transnational corporations are permitted to set up tax havens overseas to make various intracompany transactions from a unit in one foreign country to another, thus legally sheltering them from U.S. taxes.

Perhaps the best illustration of how business benefits from government policies is the system of legal loopholes provided by the tax code. The 2001 and 2003 tax cuts slashed an estimated $175 billion in corporate taxes through 2004. Moreover, the tax code provides corporations with numerous ways to avoid taxes through generous credits and exemptions. Corporations legally escape much of the tax burden through such devices as accelerated depreciation, capital gains, the investment tax credit, and the tax havens overseas. As a result, the General Accounting Office reported that 61 percent of U.S. corporations, doing nearly $2.5 trillion in gross income, *paid no taxes* during the period from 1996 to 2000 (reported in *USA Today*, 2004:20A). The key point is that Congress has allowed the tax burden to shift from corporations to individuals—in 1940, companies and individuals each paid about half the federal income tax collected; in 2003 the companies paid 13.7 percent and individuals 86.3 percent (Byrnes and Lavelle, 2003).

Trickle-Down Solutions

Periodically, the government is faced with the problem of finding a way to stimulate the economy during an economic downturn. One solution is to spend federal monies through unemployment insurance, government jobs, and housing subsidies. In this way the funds go directly to the people most hurt by shortages, unemployment, inadequate housing, and the like. Opponents of such plans advocate that the subsidies should go directly to business, which would help the economy by encouraging companies to hire more workers, add to their inventories, and build new plants. Subsidizing business in this way, the advocates argue, benefits everyone. In effect, proponents argue, because the government provides direct benefits to businesses and investors, the economic benefits indirectly trickle down to all.

Opponents of "trickle-down" economics argue that this is an inefficient way to help the less-than-affluent.

> One way to understand "trickle-down" economics is to use a more graphic metaphor: horse-and-sparrow economics—that is, if you feed the horse well, some will pass on through and be there on the ground for the sparrow. There is no doubt that sparrows can be nourished in this manner; and the more the horses get fed, the more there will be on the ground for the sparrows to pick through. It is, however, probably not a very pleasant way for sparrows to get their sustenance, and if one's primary goal is to feed the sparrows, it is a pretty silly—and inefficient—way to do the job. . . . Why waste the money on the horses when it might go directly to the sparrows? (MacEwan, 2001:40)

There are at least two reasons government officials tend to opt for these trickle-down solutions. First, because they tend to come from the business class, government officials believe in the conservative ideology that says what is good for business is good for the United States. The second reason for the probusiness choice is that government officials are more likely to hear arguments from the powerful. Because the weak, by definition, are not organized, their voice is not heard or, if heard, not taken seriously in decision-making circles.

Although the government most often opts for trickle-down solutions, such plans are not very effective in fulfilling the promise that benefits will trickle down to the poor. The higher corporate profits generated by tax credits and other tax incentives do not necessarily mean that companies will increase wages or hire more workers.

What is more likely is that corporations will increase dividends to the stockholders, which further increases the inequality gap. Job creation is also not guaranteed because companies may use their newly acquired wealth to purchase labor-saving devices. If so, then the government programs will actually have widened the gulf between the haves and the have-nots.

The Powerless Pay the Burden

Robert Hutchins (1976), in his critique of U.S. governmental policy, characterized the basic principle guiding internal affairs in this way: "Domestic policy is conducted according to one infallible rule: the costs and burdens of whatever is done must be borne by those least able to bear them" (4). Let us review several examples that support this statement.

When threatened by war, the government institutes a military draft. A careful analysis of the draft reveals that it is really a tax on the poor. During the height of the Vietnam War, for instance, only 10 percent of men in college were drafted, although 40 percent of draft-age men were in college. Even for educated young men who ended up in the armed services, there was a greater likelihood of their serving in noncombat jobs than for the non-college-educated. Thus, the chances for getting killed while in the service were about three times greater for the less-educated than for the college-educated (Baskir and Strauss, 1978; Zeitlin, Lutterman, and Russell, 1977). Even more blatant was the practice that occurred legally during the Civil War. The law at that time allowed the affluent who were drafted to hire someone to take their place in the service.

The poor, being powerless, can be made to absorb the costs of societal changes. In the nineteenth century the poor did the back-breaking work that built the railroads and the cities. Today, they are the ones pushed out of their homes by gentrification, urban renewal, and the building of expressways, parks, and stadiums.

The government's attempts to solve economic problems generally obey the principle that the poor must bear the burden. A common solution for runaway inflation, for example, is to increase the amount of unemployment. Of course the poor, especially minorities (whose rate of unemployment is consistently twice the rate for Whites), are the ones who make the sacrifice for the economy. This solution, aside from being socially cruel, is economically ineffective because it ignores the real sources of inflation—excessive military spending, excessive profits by energy companies (foreign and domestic), and administered prices set by shared monopolies, which, contrary to classical economic theory, do not decline during economic downturns (Harrington, 1979).

More fundamentally, a certain level of unemployment is maintained continuously, not just during economic downturns. Genuine full employment for all job seekers is a myth. But why, if all political candidates extol the work ethic and it is declared national policy to have full employment? Economist Robert Lekachman (1979) has argued that it is no accident that we tolerate millions of unemployed people. The reason is that a moderate unemployment rate is beneficial to the affluent. These benefits include the following: (1) People are willing to work at humble tasks for low wages, (2) the children of the middle and upper classes avoid the draft as the unemployed join the volunteer army, (3) the unions are less demanding, (4) workers are less likely to demand costly safety equipment, (5) corporations do

The poor, being powerless, can be made to absorb the costs of societal changes. They are the ones pushed out of their homes and apartments by gentrification, urban renewal, and the building of expressways, parks, and stadiums.

not have to pay their share of taxes because local and state governments give them concessions to lure them to their area, and (6) the existing wide differentials between White males and the various powerless categories such as females, Latinos, and African Americans are retained.

Foreign Policy for Corporate Benefit

The operant principle here is that "foreign policy seems to be carried on in the light of the needs of the munitions makers, the Pentagon, the CIA, and the multinational corporations" (Hutchins, 1976:4). For example, military goods are sold overseas for the profit of the arms merchants. Sometimes arms are sold to both sides in a potential conflict, the argument being that if we did not sell them the arms, then other nations would, so we might as well make the profits.

The government has supported foreign governments that are supportive of U.S. transnational companies regardless of how tyrannical these governments might be. The Reza Shah's government in Iran, Chiang's regime in China, Chung Hee Park's dictatorship in South Korea, Somoza's dictatorship in Nicaragua, and Ferdinand Marcos's rule in the Philippines are five examples of this tendency.

The U.S. government has directly intervened in the domestic affairs of foreign governments to protect U.S. corporate interests and to prevent the rise of any government based on an alternative to the capitalist model. In Latin America, for example, the United States has intervened militarily since 1950 in Guatemala, the Dominican Republic, Chile, Uruguay, Nicaragua, Grenada, and Panama. As Michael Parenti (1988) characterizes it:

Sometimes the sword has rushed in to protect the dollar, and sometimes the dollar has rushed in to enjoy the advantages won by the sword. To make the world safe for capitalism, the United States government has embarked on a global counterrevolutionary strategy, suppressing insurgent peasant and worker movements throughout Asia, Africa, and Latin America. But the interests of the corporate elites never stand naked; rather they are wrapped in the flag and coated with patriotic appearances. (94)

In summary, this view of power argues that the power of wealthy individuals and the largest corporations is translated into public policy that disproportionately benefits the power elite. Throughout U.S. history, there has been a bias that pervades government and its policies. This bias is perhaps best seen in the aphorism once enunciated by President Calvin Coolidge and repeated by contemporary presidents: "The business of America is business."

The Order and Conflict Perspectives on the Distribution of Power

Power is unequally distributed in all social organizations. In our examination of the structure of power at the societal level, two basic views were presented—the pluralist and the elitist. The former is consistent with the world view of order theorists, while the latter is congruent with the way conflict theorists perceive reality (see Table 14.1).

One glaring weakness of many pluralists *and* elitists is that they are not objective. Their writings tend often to be polemics because so much effort is spent attempting to prove what they believe is the nature of the power structure. The evidence is presented to ensure the absolute negation of the opposite stance. This points to a fundamental research problem. Are the data reliable? Are our observations distorted by bias? Sociologists or political scientists are forced in the study of power to rely on either the perceptions of other people (who are presumed to be knowledgeable) or on

TABLE 14.1

Assumptions of the Order and Conflict Models about Politics

Order Model	*Conflict Model*
1. People in positions of power occupy bureaucratic roles necessary for the rational accomplishment of society's objectives.	1. People in positions of power are motivated largely by their own selfish interests.
2. The state works for the benefit of all. Laws reflect the customs of society and ensure order, stability, and justice—in short, the common good.	2. The state exists for the benefit of the ruling class (law, police, and courts protect the interests of the wealthy).
3. Pluralism: (1) competing interest groups; (2) majority rule; (3) power is diffused.	3. Power is concentrated (power elite).

their own observations, which are distorted by their not being present during all aspects of the decision-making process. Unfortunately, one's perceptions are also affected by one's model (conflict or order). Ideological concerns often cause either faulty perceptions or a rigidity of thought that automatically rejects conflicting evidence.

The task for sociologists is to determine the real distribution of power with our ideological distortion. Given these problems with objectivity, we must ask: (1) What is the power structure really like? (2) What facts are consonant with the pluralist model and what facts fit the elitist model?

Chapter Review

1. In answering the question of who the real power wielders are in U.S. society, there are two contrasting answers from pluralists and elitists.

2. The representative-democracy version of pluralism emphasizes that the people have the ultimate power. The people elect representatives who are responsive to the people's wishes. This version ignores the many instances in which the people have been deliberately misled by their leaders, secrecy, and the undemocratic manner in which election campaigns are funded.

3. The veto-groups version of pluralism recognizes the existence of a number of organizations and special-interest groups that vie for power. There is a balance of power, however, with no one sector getting its way. The groups tend to neutralize each other, resulting in compromise. Critics of this view of power argue that it is an idealized version that ignores reality. The interest groups are not equal in power. Power does not shift from issue to issue. Also, at the apex of each of the competing groups are members of the upper class, suggesting the possibility of a power elite.

4. Marxists assert that there is a ruling class. There are two variations on this theme. The instrumentalist view is that the ruling class (capitalists) does not govern (that is, hold office) but that it rules by controlling political officials and institutions. The structuralist view is that the state serves the interests of the capitalist class because whoever holds government office will make decisions that promote stability and a healthy business climate—both of which enhance the interests of the capitalist class.

5. In C. Wright Mills's view of power, there is a power elite composed of the top people in the executive branch of the federal government, the military, and the corporate sector. Although these people represent different interests, they tend to perceive the world in a like manner because of their similar social class backgrounds and similar role expectations, because they interact socially, because their children go to the same schools and intermarry, and because they share similar interests. There is considerable evidence for the linkages among these three sectors. There are some problems with this view, however. The equality of these three groups is not a fact. There is conflict among the three sectors. Other sectors of power are ignored.

6. In G. William Domhoff's view of power, there is a dominant class—the uppermost social class. The very rich control the nation's assets, control the corporations, are overrepresented in the key decision-making groups in society, and through contributions and activities control both major political parties. The major criticism of this view is that while the people in key positions tend to have upper-class pedigrees, there is no evidence that these people actually promote the interests of the corporate rich.

7. Michael Parenti's bias-of-the-system view is another elitist theory. The powerful in society (those who control the government and the largest corporations) tend to come from backgrounds of privilege and wealth. Their decisions tend to benefit the wealthy disproportionately, but the power elite is not organized and conspiratorial. The interests of the wealthy are served, nevertheless, by the way society is organized. This bias occurs by their influence over elected and appointed officials, systemic imperatives, and through the ideological control of the masses.

8. The pluralist model of power is congruent with the order model: (a) People in powerful positions work for the accomplishment of society's objectives; (b) the state works for the benefit of all; and (c) power is diffused through competing interest groups.

9. The elitist model of power fits with the conflict model: (a) People in powerful positions are motivated largely by selfish interests; (b) the state exists for the benefit of the ruling class; and (c) power is concentrated in a power elite.

Key Terms

Elitist model of power
Pluralist model of power
Democracy
Plutocracy

Instrumentalist view
Structuralist view
Power elite
Dominant class

Systemic imperatives
Power

Study Questions

1. How does the way political campaigns are financed have undemocratic consequences?
2. What is your reaction to the panel titled "A Closer Look: Structural Barriers to Democracy"? Is the United States a democracy? (Consider also your response to Study Question 1 here.) Elaborate.
3. Classify Mills, Domhoff, and Parenti as either instrumentalists or structuralists. Justify your placement of each.
4. Summarize the three variations of the conflict view of politics by Mills, Domhoff, and Parenti. Which variation most closely approximates politics in the contemporary United States? Why? Or, alternatively, is each variation incorrect? If so, why?
5. How have government decisions tended to increase the gap between the haves and the have-nots?

For Further Reading

Power

Robert A. Dahl, *Who Governs?* (New Haven, CT: Yale University Press, 1961).

G. William Domhoff, *Who Rules America? Power and Politics in the Year 2000*, 3rd ed. (Mountain View, CA: Mayfield, 1998).

Godfrey Hodgson, *More Equal Than Others* (Princeton, NJ: Princeton University Press, 2004).

C. Wright Mills, *The Power Elite* (New York: Oxford University Press, 1956).

Michael Parenti, *Democracy for the Few*, 7th ed. (New York: St. Martin's Press, 2002).

Michael Parenti, *Power and the Powerless*, 2nd ed. (New York: St. Martin's Press, 1978).

Max Weber, *From Max Weber: Essays in Sociology*, Hans Gerth and C. Wright Mills, trans. and eds. (New York: Oxford University Press, 1946).

Howard Zinn, *A People's History of the United States* (New York: Harper & Row, 1980).

Wealth and Power

Jeffrey H. Birnbaum, *The Money Men: The Real Story of Fund-Raising's Influence on Political Power in America* (New York: Crown, 2000).

Mark Green, *Selling Out: How Big Corporate Money Buys Elections, Rams through Legislation, and Betrays Our Democracy* (New York: HarperCollins, 2002).

Arianna Huffington, *Pigs at the Trough: How Corporate Greed and Political Corruption Are Undermining America* (New York: Crown, 2003).

Paul Kivel, *You Call This a Democracy?* (New York: Apex Press, 2004).

Peter Kobrak, *Cozy Politics: Political Parties, Campaign Finance, and Compromised Governance* (Boulder, CO: Lynne Rienner, 2002).

Greg Palast, *The Best Democracy Money Can Buy* (Sterling, VA: Pluto Press).

Kevin Phillips, *Wealth and Democracy* (New York: Broadway Books, 2002).

Darrell M. West, *Checkbook Democracy: How Money Corrupts Political Campaigns* (Boston: Northeastern University Press, 2000).

Web Resources

http://www.lib.umich.edu/govdocs/govweb.html

For government resources on the Web, go to this University of Michigan site. It has information on each branch of the U.S. government, as well as links to sites about governments in other countries.

http://www.udel.edu/htr/Psc105/Texts/whogovern.html

This site offers a discussion of the pluralist and elitist models of power and other ideas pertaining to theories of power and who governs the United States.

http://www.thirdworldtraveler.com/Book_Excerpts/PowerElite.html

This site contains excerpts from C. Wright Mills's *The Power Elite.*

http://opensecrets.org/

The Center for Responsive Politics is a group that "tracks money in politics, and its effect on elections and public policy. The Center's work is aimed at creating a more educated voter, an involved citizenry, and a more responsive government."

http://www.brook.edu/dybdocroot

The Brookings Institution "functions as an independent analyst and critic, committed to publishing its findings for the information of the public. In its conferences and activities, it serves as a bridge between scholarship and public policy, bringing new knowledge to the attention of decision makers and affording scholars a better insight into public policy issues."

http://www.ncl.org/

The National Civic League is a "non-profit, nonpartisan organization dedicated to strengthening citizen democracy by transforming democratic institutions."

http://www.commoncause.org/

Common Cause is a nonpartisan citizen's lobbying organization promoting open, honest, and accountable government.

Families   CHAPTER 15

Families are far different from what they used to be. They are more diverse; they include more diverse household arrangements; they are more easily fractured; family members spend less time together; and parents have less influence over their children, to name a few differences from earlier times. Many find these changes threatening. They yearn for a time when families were more stable, when fathers were providers and mothers stayed home to raise the children.

Family changes occurring in the last few decades have led some social analysts to conclude that the family is in serious trouble; that we have lost our **family values**, and that family decline explains many social problems. This view of the world is flawed in two fundamental respects. First, it reverses the relationship between family and society by treating families as the building blocks of society rather than as a reflection of social conditions. Second, it ignores the structural reasons for recent family changes and the profound transformations occurring throughout the world. Even in very different societies, families and households are undergoing similar shifts as a result of global economic changes. (See the panel titled "Globalization: Families in Global Perspective.")

This chapter examines the family as a social institution and relates families to the larger society. Families in the United States are diverse, with regional, social class, religious, racial, and ethnic differences; nonetheless, distinct patterns can be found in family life. The theme of the chapter is that families are not isolated units free from outside constraints, but that social forces outside the family affect life inside families.

The Mythical Family in the United States

There are a number of myths about families. These beliefs are bound up with nostalgia and cultural values concerning what is typical and true about families. The following beliefs, based on folk wisdom and common beliefs, are rarely challenged except by social scientists and family scholars.

    1. *The myth of a stable and harmonious family of the past.* The common belief is that families of the past were better than families of the present. They are thought to have been more stable, better adjusted, and happier. However, family historians have found

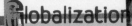
Families in Global Perspective: Family Upheavals around the World

The rapidity and depth of the most recent period of family transformation which began in the wake of the Second World War rivals any in history. In most Western nations, marriage and family relationships have become more discretionary and variegated while at the same time becoming more precarious than at any time in recorded history. Some of the particular changes that have been most dramatic:

1. In virtually all Western countries, the link between the onset of sexuality and marriage has been broken. Relatively few young people expect to wait until they wed or are about to wed to initiate sex, and only a small number now expect that their first sexual partner will be their only one. Sexual norms regarding conjugal exclusivity have always been subject to considerable violation. However, for better or for worse, the norms that once confined sex to marital relations have more or less disappeared, leaving individuals to work out their own understandings of when, why, and with whom to have sex.

2. In most Western nations, cohabitation has now become the initial stage of family formation and in some nations state-sanctioned marriage is postponed until well after childbearing begins or has declined altogether. So children in many countries now enter families where their parents have established a partnership but not a formal contract for their care and upbringing. In some places, northern Europe in particular, childbearing unions are tantamount to marriage but in others such as the United States, they are typically not. And even in northern Europe, the prospects of these unions surviving are far lower than if the couple entered matrimony.

3. When it does occur, marriage has become less enduring over the past several decades. In virtually all countries, divorce rates have risen sharply despite the fact that those marrying are a more select group whose prospects of divorce should be lower. Couples who wed are older, less likely to be pregnant at the time of marriage, more likely to hold conventional views, and more economically secure than those who do not. Despite these trends that should favour stability, conjugal unions have become less stable over time throughout Europe and North America.

Source: Frank F. Furstenberg, Jr., "Is the Modern Family a Threat to Children's Health?" *Society* 36 (July/August 1999):30–37. © 1999 by Transaction Publishers. Reprinted by permission of the publisher.

that there is no golden age of the family. Many children were raised by single parents or stepparents, just as now. Divorce rates were lower because of strong religious prohibitions and community norms against divorce, but this does not mean that love was stronger in the past. Many "empty" marriages continued without love and happiness to bind them. Historian Stephanie Coontz has reexamined our deepest assumptions about the history of the family. Her book *The Way We Never Were* (Coontz, 1992) explodes the myth that family life has recently "gone bad." In her more recent book, *Marriage, A History* (Coontz, 2005), she shows how marriage changed from an economic and political institution to a voluntary love relationship. This change, not the loss of family values, is what makes marriage more fragile today.

Family life of the past was quite different from the stereotype. Desertion by spouses, illegitimate children, and other conditions that are considered modern problems existed in the past. Part of the family nostalgia holds that there were three generations living under one roof or in close proximity. This image of the three-generational family is also false. Few examples of this "classical family of western nostalgia" (Goode, 1984:43) have been found by family historians.

2. *The myth of the family as a "haven in a heartless world"* (Lasch, 1977). This is the positive image of the family as a place of love and trust, where individuals escape the competitive forces in modern society. Of course, love and trust are the glue for

many families, but this glorification of private life tends to mask the dark side of some families, where emotional and physical aggression are commonplace, and where competition between spouses and among children sometimes destroys relationships. This myth ignores the harsh effects of economic conditions (e.g., poverty or near-poverty, unemployment, and downward mobility). It ignores the social inequalities (racism, sexism, ageism, homophobia) that prevent many people from experiencing the good things in life. And the idealized family view masks the inevitable problems that arise in intimate settings (tensions, anger, and even violence in some instances).

3. *The myth of the monolithic family form.* We get a consistent image of what the American family is supposed to look like from our politicians, from our ministers and priests, from children's literature, and from television. This is of a White, middle-class, heterosexual, father-as-breadwinner, mother-as-homemaker, and children-at-home living in a one-family house. This model, however, accounts for fewer than 10 percent of all families. Women have joined the paid labor force in great numbers. A number of family forms are common: single-parent families (resulting either from unmarried parenthood or divorce), remarried couples, unmarried couples, gay and lesbian families, step families, foster families, multigenerational families, co-resident grandparents and grandchildren, and transnational family forms. Almost half of marriages end in divorce, and half of all children will spend at least part of their childhood in a single-parent family (90 percent with their mothers). Yet children thrive in many different family forms. Research shows that what is important for them is the quality of the relationships they have with the people who care for them, rather than number, sex, or marital status of their care givers (Silverstein and Aurbach, 2001:30).

4. *The myth of a unified family experience.* We assume that all family members experience family life in the same way. This image hides the diversity *within* families. The family is a gendered institution. Women and men experience marriage differently. There are gender differences in decision making, in household division of labor, and in forms of intimacy and sexuality. Similarly, divorce affects them differently. Remarriage patterns differ by gender, as well. Girls and boys experience their childhoods differently, as there are different expectations, different rules, and different punishments according to gender.

5. *The myth of family decline as the cause of social problems.* The rhetoric about family values argues that all family arrangements *different* from the two-parent, father-working, mother-and-children-at-home are unhealthy arrangements. Fatherless families, or women working outside the home, are said to be the reasons for poverty, violence, and crime. Divorced and unwed mothers, in this view, are damaging children, destroying families, and tearing apart the fabric of society.

Families in Contemporary U.S. Society

The Family in Capitalism

Family arrangements in the United States are closely related to economic development. Industrialization moved the center of production from the domestic family unit to the workplace. Families became private domestic retreats set off from the rest of society. Men went off to earn a wage in factories and offices, while women remained in the home to nurture their children. From the rise of the industrial economy until World War II, capitalism operated within a simple framework. Employers assumed that most families included one main breadwinner—a male— and one adult working at home directing domestic work—a female; in short, jobs with wives. As a result, many men received the income intended to support a family (Albelda, 1992:7).

The private family with a breadwinner father and a homemaker mother pattern was an important historical development, but economic conditions precluded this pattern for many families. With industrialization, wave after wave of immigrants filled the industrial labor force. Through their labor, entire families became a part of society. Immigrant families did not separate themselves into privatized units. Instead, they used kinship connections to adjust in the new society. Families were crucial in assisting their newly arrived kin to adapt to the new society. Many immigrants came to the United States in family groupings, or they sent for families once they were established in cities. Kin helped in locating jobs and housing, and they provided other forms of support. Contrary to the typical portrayal of immigrants, their transplanted kinship and ethnic bonds did not disintegrate, but rather were rebuilt in the new society (Early, 1983; Vecoli, 1964).

The developing capitalist economy did not provide equal opportunities for all people. Racial-ethnic people did not have the opportunity to become part of the industrial labor force. Instead, they labored in nonindustrial sectors of the economy. This often required family arrangements that were different from those in the dominant society. The breadwinner–homemaker pattern never applied to immigrants and racial minorities because they were denied the opportunities to earn a family wage. So, many married women took jobs to make ends meet. Some women took in boarders or did piecework; some worked as maids in middle-class and upper-class homes; and some became wage workers in sweatshops, department stores, and offices. For these families, the support of the community and extended family members was crucial (Albelda, 1992:7).

Families have always varied with the social structures in which people live. From the original settlement of the American colonies through the mid-twentieth century, families of European descent often received economic and social supports to maintain families. Following World War II, the G.I. Bill, the National Defense Education Act, the expansion of the Federal Housing Authority and Veterans Administration loan subsidy programs, and government funding of new highways provided the means through which middle-class Whites were able to achieve the stable suburban family lives that became the ideal against which other families were judged (Coontz, 1992). These kinds of supports have rarely been available for people of color and, until quite recently, were actively denied them through various forms of housing and job discrimination. Family history makes it clear that society has always created many different family forms.

What we think of as "the family" is an ideal. It implies a private retreat set apart from society. This image masks the real relationship between families and the larger society. A better way to see how families are related to other social structures is by making the following distinction between families and households: A **family** is a construct of meanings and relationships; a **household** is a residential and economic unit (Osmond and Thorne, 1993:607; Rapp, 1982). To put it another way, a household is a residence group that carries out domestic functions, whereas a family is a kinship group (Holstein and Gubrium, 1999:31). A good example of the importance of distinguishing between family and household is the restructuring of family obligations and household composition after divorce (Ferree, 1991:107).

Stratification and Family Life

In previous chapters, we examined growing inequalities in the distribution of resources and rewards. These stratification hierarchies—class, race, and gender—are changing and reshuffling families and individuals. In this section, we examine the effects of social class on families in the United States. Of course, the social patterning of inequality occurs along many other dimensions including age, family characteristics, and place of residence (see Table 15.1).

Families are embedded in a class hierarchy that is "pulling apart" to shrink the middle class while more families join the ranks of the rich or the poor (Usdansky, 1992). This movement creates great differences in family living and no longer guarantees that children's placement in the class system will follow that of their parents. Still, a family's location in the class system is the single most important determinant of family life.

TABLE 15.1

People and Families in Poverty by Selected Characteristics, 2003

Characteristics	Below Poverty Percent	Characteristics	Below Poverty Percent
People		**Nativity**	
Total	12.5	Native	11.8
Family Status		Foreign born	17.2
In families	10.8	Naturalized citizen	10.0
Householder	10.0	Not a citizen	20.7
Related children under 18	17.2	**Region**	
Related children under 6	19.8	Northeast	11.3
In unrelated subfamilies	38.6	Midwest	10.7
Reference person	37.6	South	14.1
Children under 18	41.7	West	12.6
Unrelated individual	20.4	**Residence**	
Male	18.0	Inside metropolitan areas	12.1
Female	22.6	Inside central cities	17.5
Race		Outside central cities	9.1
White	8.2	Outside metropolitan areas	14.2
Black	24.4	**Type of family**	
Asian	11.8	Married-couple	5.4
Hispanic origin	22.5	Female householder	
Age		(no husband present)	28.0
Under 18 years	17.6		
18 to 64 years	10.8		
65 years and older	10.2		

Source: U.S. Bureau of the Census, 2004. *Current Population survey 2003–2004.* "Annual Social and Economic Supplement." Table 3. Online. Accessed: August 8, 2005. http://www.bis.census.gov/cps/asec/adsmain.htm.

Social and economic forces produce different family configurations. In a stratified society, family structures differ because households vary in their ability to hook into, accumulate, and transmit wealth, wages, or welfare (Rapp, 1982). Households in different parts of the class structure have different ways of acquiring the necessities of life. Inheritance, salaries, wages, welfare, or various involvements with the hidden economy, the illegal economy, or the irregular economy provide different connections with society's opportunity structures. The social networks and relationships outside the family—at work, school, church, and voluntary associations—are important in shaping class and race differences in family life.

The middle-class family form is idealized in our society. This form, composed of mother, father, and children in a self-supporting unit, has long been most characteristic of middle-class and upper-middle-class families. Middle-class families of the twenty-first century are quite different from the employed-father and homemaker-mother model that evolved with industrialization. Today, many families can sustain their class status only through the economic contributions of employed wives. Here, households are based on stable and secure resources provided by the occupations of adult women and men. Family "autonomy" is shaped by supportive forces in the larger society. When exceptional economic resources are called for, nonfamilial institutions usually are available in the form of better medical coverage, expense accounts, and credit at banks (Rapp, 1982:181).

These links with nonfamily institutions are precisely the ones that distinguish life in middle-class families from families in other economic groups. The strongest links are with the occupations of middle-class family members, especially those of the husband-father. Occupational roles greatly affect family roles and the quality of family life (Schneider and Smith, 1973). Occupations are part of the larger opportunity structure of society: Occupations that are highly valued and carry high-income rewards are unevenly distributed. The amount of the paycheck determines how well a given household can acquire needed resources.

In the working class, material resources depend on wages acquired in exchange for labor. When hourly wages are insufficient or unstable, individuals in households must pool their resources with other people in the larger family network. The pooling of resources may involve exchanging babysitting, sharing meals, or lending money. Pooling is a way of coping with the tenuous connections between households and opportunity structures of society. It requires that the boundaries of "the family" be expanded. This is one reason that the idealized nuclear family is impossible for many people to sustain. At the lower levels of the class hierarchy, people lack the material resources to form autonomous households.

The fluid boundaries of these families do not make them unstable. Instead, this family flexibility is a way of sustaining the limited resources that result from their place in the class hierarchy. Minority single-parent families, which are criticized as being disorganized, are often embedded in a network of sharing and support. Variation in family organization is often a way of adapting to society.

Middle-class families with husbands (and perhaps wives) in careers have both economic resources and built-in ties with supportive institutions such as banks, credit unions, medical facilities, and voluntary associations. These ties are intrinsic to some occupations and to middle-class neighborhoods. They are structurally determined. Such connections strengthen the autonomy of middle-class families. But the middle class is shrinking, and many middle-class families are without middle-class incomes because of changes in the larger economy. Changes in family structure have also contributed to the lowering of family income. High divorce rates, for example, create many more family units with lower incomes.

Turning to the upper class, we find that family boundaries are more open than are those of the middle class, even though class boundaries are quite closed. Among the elite, family constitutes not only a nuclear family but also the extended family. The elite have multiple households (Rapp, 1982:182). Their day-to-day life exists within the larger context of a network of relatives (Dyer, 1979:209).

The institutional linkages of the elite are national in scope. Families in various sections of the country are connected by such institutions as boarding schools, exclusive colleges, exclusive clubs, and fashionable vacation resorts. In this way, the elite remain intact, and the marriage market is restricted to a small (but national) market (Blumberg and Paul, 1975:69). Family life of the elite is privileged in every sense, as Stein, Richman, and Hannon (1977) report: "Wealthy families can afford an elaborate support structure to take care of the details of everyday life. Persons can be hired to cook and prepare meals and do laundry and to care for the children" (9). The vast economic holdings of these families allow them a high degree of control over the rewards and resources of society. They enjoy freedoms and choices not available to other families in society. These families maintain privileged access to **life chances** and lifestyles.

Kinship ties, obligations, and interests are more extended in classes at the two extremes than they are in the middle (McKinley, 1964:22). In the upper extreme and toward the lower end of the class structure, kinship networks serve decisively different functions. At both extremes they are institutions of resource management. The kin-based family form of the elite serves to preserve inherited wealth. It is intricately tied to other national institutions that control the wealth of society. The kin-based family form of the working and lower classes is a primary institution through which individuals participate in social life as they pool and exchange their limited resources to ensure survival. It is influenced by society's institutions, but it remains separate from them.

Structural Transformation and Family Life

In Chapter 8, we discussed globalization and the structural transformation of the economy. Given the magnitude of the economic transformation, we should not be surprised that families and individuals are profoundly affected by the global shifts now occurring.

As U.S. companies move production overseas, use new technology to replace workers, and engage in megamergers, jobs are lost and wages decline. Declining industries are those that historically provided high-earning positions for men. On the other hand, much of the new growth in the U.S. economy has been in sectors that are major employers of women. As the need for certain kinds of labor diminishes, more and more working-class and middle-class families are the victims of economic dislocations. Families are affected when their resources are reduced, when they face economic and social marginalization, and when family members are unemployed or underemployed. The modern economic system undermines "family values" (Thurow, 1995a:11A). (This section is adapted from Baca Zinn and Eitzen, 2005:108–114.)

Economic changes have affected not only production workers but white-collar workers and managers as well. What does downward mobility mean for families? Katherine Newman (1988) describes the experience of the downwardly mobile middle class:

They once "had it made" in American society, filling slots from affluent blue-collar jobs to professional and managerial occupations. They have job skills, education, and decades of steady work experience. Many are, or were, homeowners. Their marriages were (at least initially) intact. As a group they savored the American dream. They found a place higher up the ladder in this society and then, inexplicably, found their grip loosening and their status sliding. Some downwardly mobile middle-class families end up in poverty, but many do not. Usually they come to rest at a standard of living above the poverty level but far below the affluence they enjoyed in the past. They must, therefore, contend not only with financial hardship but with the psychological, social, and practical consequences of "falling from grace, of losing their proper place" in the world. (8)

Thus, individual self-esteem and family honor are bruised. Moreover, this ordeal impairs the chances of the children, as children and later as adults, to enjoy economic security and a comfortable lifestyle.

Downward mobility also occurs within the stable working class, whose links with resource-granting opportunity structures have always been tenuous. Many downwardly mobile families find successful coping strategies to deal with their adverse situations. Some families develop a tighter bond to meet their common problems. Others find support from families in similar situations or from their personal kin networks. But for many families, downward mobility adds tensions that make family life especially difficult. Family members experience stress, marital tension, and depression. Newman suggests that these conditions are normal, given the persistent tensions generated by downward mobility. Many families experience some degree of these pathologies and yet somehow endure. But some families disintegrate under these pressures, with serious problems of physical brutality, incapacitating alcoholism, desertion, and even suicide (Newman, Katherine, 1988:134–140).

Although families throughout society are changing as a result of macroeconomic forces, the changes are most profound among the working class. Blue-collar workers have been hardest hit by the economic transformation. Their jobs have been eliminated by the millions because of new technologies and competition from other lower-wage (much lower) economies. They have disproportionately been fired or periodically laid off. Sometimes their places of work have shut down entirely and moved to other societies. Their unions have lost strength (in numbers and clout). And their wages have declined.

The changing forms of the family are a major consequence of the economic transformation. In 1950, some 60 percent of U.S. households fit this pattern: an intact nuclear household composed of a male breadwinner, his full-time homemaker wife, and their dependent children. Sociologist Judith Stacey (1990; 1991) calls this type of family the **modern family**. But this family form was disrupted by deindustrialization and the changes in women's work roles. Stacey found that working-class families, especially the women in them, created innovative ways to cope with economic uncertainty and domestic upheavals. In effect, these women were and are the pioneers of emergent family forms. Stacey calls these new family forms **postmodern families** because they do not fit the criteria for a "modern" family. Now there are divorce-extended families that include ex-spouses and their lovers, children, and friends. Households now expand and contract as adult children leave and then return home only to leave again. The vast majority of these postmodern families has dual earners. Many now involve husbands in greater child care and domestic work than in earlier times. Kin networks have expanded to meet economic pressures. Parents now deal with their children's cohabitation, single and unwed parenthood, and divorce. The result is that fewer than 10 percent of households now conform to the "modern" family form. According to Stacey (1991):

> No longer is there a single culturally dominant family pattern, like the modern one, to which the majority of Americans conform and most of the rest aspire. Instead, Americans today have crafted a multiplicity of family and household arrangements that we inhabit uneasily and reconstitute frequently in response to changing personal and occupational circumstances. (19)

These postmodern family forms are new to working-class and middle-class families as they adjust to the structural transformation, *but they are not new to the poor.* The economic deprivation faced by the poor has always forced the poor to adapt in similar ways: single-parent families, relying on kin networks, sharing household costs, and multiple wage-earners among family members.

The Changing Composition of Households and Families

To understand current trends in family life, we must return to the distinction between households and families discussed earlier in this chapter. (The following is based on Ahlburg and De Vita [1992] and Bianchi and Casper [2000:8].) The U.S. Census Bureau defines a *household* as all persons who occupy a housing unit such as a house, apartment, or other residential unit. A household may consist of one person who lives alone or of several people who share a dwelling. A *family*, on the other hand, is two or more persons related by birth, marriage, or adoption who reside together. All families comprise households but not all households are families under the Census Bureau's definition.

Over the years, U.S. households have changed in several important ways. Households have become smaller, with the greatest differences occurring in the largest and smallest households (see Figure 15.1). Between 1970 and 2003, households with five or more people decreased from 21 percent to 9.7 percent of all households. Between 1970 and 2000, the share of households with only one or two people increased from 46 percent to 59 percent and the average number of people per household declined from 3.14 to 2.62 (Fields, 2001:4). The growth of the **nonfamily** household (i.e., persons who live alone or with unrelated individuals) is one of the most dramatic changes to occur during the past three decades, as shown in Figure 15.2. It highlights the most significant changes in the nation's households since 1970. According to Fields (2004), in the past, family households accounted for a large majority of all households. Eighty-one percent of households in 1970 were family households, but the proportion dropped to 68 percent by 2003. Figure 15. 2 divides family and nonfamily households into various categories: married couples with and without children, other family households, men and women living alone, and other nonfamily households. The most noticeable trend is the decline in the proportion of married-couple households with children. In contrast, the proportion of households that were made up of married couples without children remained relatively stable over the period—29 percent in 2003 and 30 percent in 1970. The third family component—families whose householder has no spouse present, but with other relatives, including children—increased from 11 percent of all households in 1970 to 16 percent in 2003. The top three segments of the graph represent all nonfamily household types. The figure shows that the majority of the

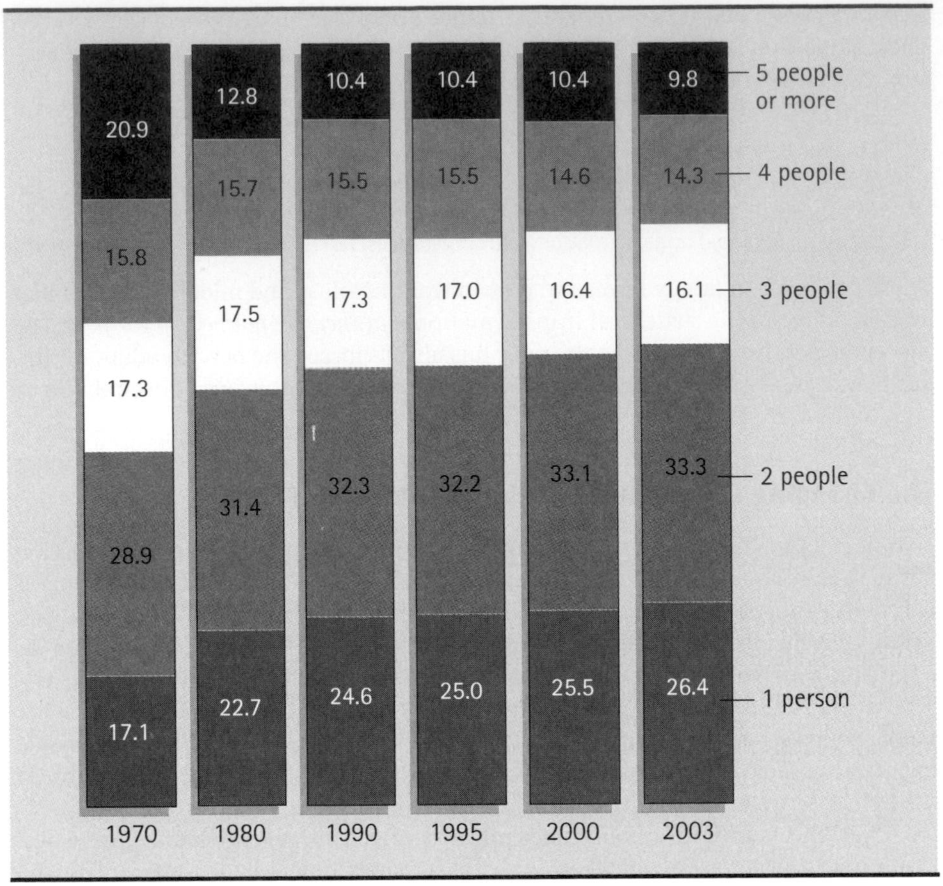

FIGURE 15.1

Households by Size: 1970 to 2003 (Percent Distribution)

Source: Jason Fields, 2004. "America's Families and Living Arrangements: 2003." *Current Population Reports,* Series P20–553 (November). Washington, DC: U.S. Bureau of the Census, p. 5.

increase in nonfamily households was due to the growth in one-person households, people living alone (Fields, 2004:2).

Nonfamily households are a diverse group. They may consist of elderly individuals who live alone, college-age youths who share an apartment, cohabiting couples, individuals who delay or forego marriage, or those who are in between marriages (Ahlburg and De Vita, 1992).

Another dramatic shift in household composition between 1970 and 2000 was the decline in the percentage of households with children. Married-couple households with their own children dropped from 40 percent of all households in 1970 to 23 percent in 2003 (U.S. Bureau of the Census, 2004). This downward trend reflects the decline in birth rates, the shift toward smaller families, and the extended period of time before young adults marry (Bianchi and Casper, 2000:8).

No one household arrangement is typical. Instead, a very diverse world of households, families, and individual life histories has emerged. Such diversity has meant great economic inequality across households. "Some of the new, nontraditional families, such as dual-earner couples, are doing very well; others, such as single-mother families, are doing poorly" (McLanahan and Casper, 1995:2).

Households headed by women account for a growing proportion of American families over the last two decades. By 2000, single-mother families accounted for 22 percent of all families with children, up from 6 percent in 1950 (Bianchi and

Casper, 2000:9). Many mothers are single by choice. New reproductive technologies and women's increased independence mean that husbands are less of a necessity. Still, families headed by a single-parent run a high risk of being poor because they lack the economic resources of dual-parent families. Furthermore, single-parent families are usually headed by women, who are at great risk of economic hardship. The earnings gap found in all occupations makes female-headed households especially vulnerable (see Chapter 9). In 2000, the poverty rate for female-headed families was 32.5 percent, roughly six times the rate for married-couple families with children (4.7 percent) (Lichter and Crowley, 2002:7). This growing class of families has profound implications for our society as a whole.

Changes in Marriage and Family Roles

Marriage is still very much the norm, with about 90 percent of the population eventually marrying. However, the marriage rate has declined in recent decades. Marriage occupies a less central place in society than it did in the past. Married people now represent a smaller proportion of adults. In 2003, about 54 percent of all adults were married, compared with 72 percent in 1970 (U.S. Bureau of the Census, 2004). The decline in marriage has many causes, including increased rates of cohabitation, later age at first marriage, and a high divorce rate. (See Figure 15.3 for changing patterns of median age at first marriage.) These trends suggest that women and men orient their lives less and less around marriage (the following is primarily from Baca Zinn and Eitzen, 2005:282–286).

How do we as a society respond to the trends that have reshaped family life over the past several decades? One of the responses to changing marital behavior is a

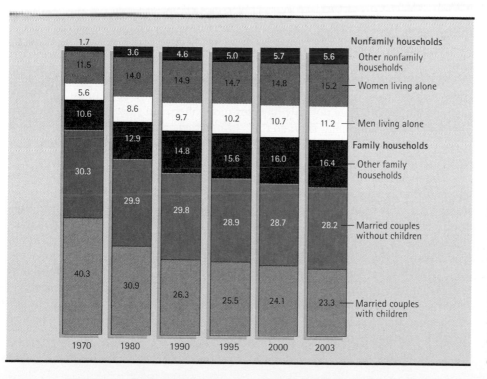

FIGURE 15.2

Households by Type: 1970 to 2003 (Percent Distribution)

Source: Jason Fields, 2004. "America's Families and Living Arrangements: 2003." *Current Population Reports,* Series P20–553 (November). Washington, DC: U.S. Bureau of the Census, p. 4.

"marriage movement" that seeks to raise public awareness of the benefits of marriage to both individuals and society. Some family scholars are even making a strong "case for marriage" by stressing the positive relationship between marriage and individual well-being. For example, sociologist Linda Waite (2000) contends that married individuals are healthier, happier, and better off financially than the never married, the divorced, and the widowed. Her arguments represent one side in a national debate between those who wish to promote traditional marriage (organizations such as the Institute for American Values) and those who argue that family forms are shaped by social and economic forces (organizations such as the Council on Contemporary Families).

The Social and Individual Benefits of Marriage

Individuals marry for a variety of reasons. These include the obvious ones, such as the desire for companionship and intimacy. But there are other benefits to being married. To begin with, the marriage relationship promotes healthy behaviors. Research shows that the unmarried are far more likely than the married to die from all causes, including heart disease, stroke, pneumonia, many kinds of cancer, automobile accidents, cirrhosis of the liver, murder, and suicide. There are many reasons why marriage promotes better health. When the married are compared with the unmarried of the same age and the divorced, the married (especially husbands) are less likely to engage in risky behaviors such as excessive drinking, dangerous driving, substance abuse, and multiple sexual partners. Waite and Gallagher (2000) posit that marriage affects health by providing individuals, again especially men, with someone who monitors their health and who encourages self-regulation. Marriage also provides individuals with a sense of meaning in their lives and a sense of obligation and responsibility to others.

The married also have better mental health than the unmarried. Summarizing the research, Waite and Gallagher say, "Married men and women report less depression, less anxiety, and lower levels of other types of psychological distress than those who are single, divorced, or widowed" (2000:67).

Marriage also enhances the sex lives of the partners. Waite and Gallagher, after surveying the research, conclude that "married people have both more and better sex than singles do. They not only have sex more often, but they enjoy it more, both physically and emotionally, than do their unmarried counterparts. . . . Marriage, it turns out, is not only good for you, it is good for your libido too" (Waite and Gallagher, 2000:70).

The married have more economic resources (income, pension and Social Security benefits, financial assets, and the value of their primary residence) than the unmarried. This economic activity stems from the increase in productivity by husbands (compared to unmarried men) and the fact that both spouses in so many marriages are now in the labor force. The greater economic advantage of married couples explain many of the benefits that Waite and others associate with the marriage bond itself. With greater affluence comes better nutrition, better access to physicians and hospitals, a greater likelihood of living in a safe neighborhood, more travel and quality leisure, and the opportunity to experience the good things in life. So it may not be true that the marriage bond itself generates better emotional and physical health for the partners, but the greater resources generated.

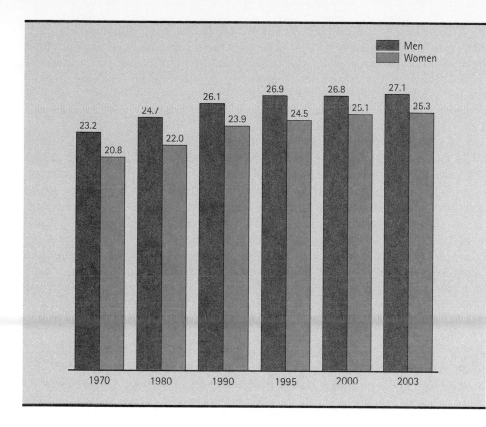

FIGURE 15.3

Median Age at First Marriage for the Population 15 Years and Over by Sex: 1970 to 2003

Source: Jason Fields, 2004. "America's Families and Living Arrangements: 2003." *Current Population Reports,* Series P20–553 (November). Washington, DC: U.S. Bureau of the Census, p. 13.

The Benefits of Marriage Reconsidered

Marriage matters. Married people have more resources, are better networked, and are healthier, leaving little doubt that marriage is beneficial. But we must evaluate this generalization cautiously. Obviously, not all marriages are advantageous to their partners. Some marriages are abusive. Some marriages are empty of love and caring. The relatively high divorce rate is ample evidence that marriages are not blissful for millions of couples. But let's go beyond these negatives. Consider, first, the generalization that marriage is beneficial economically. Recent research finds the economic benefits of marriage to be uneven; that is, they differ by social class and race. The economic transformations of the past three decades are closely associated with what has been called the "retreat from marriage" (Lichter, McLaughlin, and Ribar, 2002). A society that produces an increasing proportion of low-wage, unstable jobs is a society that is likely to have less marriage because economic insecurity discourages marriage. The "good economy" of the 1990s provided a stable economic base for most middle-class couples, but did not help poorly educated Whites or disadvantaged racial minorities provide for their families. Many women seek the economic benefits described by Waite and others. The problem many encounter is the difficulty of finding economically attractive marriage partners. Women are generally reluctant to marry men who are jobless or have unstable employment.

The obstacles to achieving economic stability through marriage are especially difficult for people of color. "The issues facing impoverished Black families [and Latino and Native American families] are different from those facing poor Whites; low-income African Americans are much more likely than low-income Whites to have an income only *half or less* of the poverty-level figure, and to be trapped in areas where at least 40 percent of the population is also poor" (Coontz, 1997:24).

The evidence documenting the economic benefits of marriage is strong; nonetheless, marriage turns out to be more economically beneficial to some groups in society than others. Gender is a crucial factor in evaluating the benefits of marriage. Each marriage is the creation of a new social unit. The two members of this unit—in which the interaction is intense and the feelings intimate—do not, strange as it may seem, always share the same interpretations and reap the same rewards from their shared life. The fundamental reason for this is that the two members in a marriage differ by gender. By dissecting the family, we see that the sex-gender system structures women's and men's family lives differently. One of the most useful ways of understanding this is Jessie Bernard's concept of "his" and "her" marriages. Bernard's classic work (1972) revealed that every marital union actually contains two marriages, which do not always coincide.

The generalization that marriage is beneficial to the spouses is too facile. We can only answer the question "Who benefits from marriage?" by examining the social location of the partners in a marriage. This means including the social class, and race/ethnicity of the spouses. And we must learn the lesson of Jessie Bernard that every marriage is actually two marriages. In effect then, marriage matters, but the degree to which it matters is affected by social class, race, and gender.

Same-Sex Marriage

Another issue dominating today's marriage debate is the definition (and legality) of marriage. At issue is whether marriage is limited to a women and a man or whether it can be between members of the same sex.

Supporters of same-sex marriage argue that homosexual couples should have the same rights as heterosexuals. Legalizing same-sex marriage would provide gays the privileges of marriage such as Social Security benefits, health care, and pension benefits. If marriage is denied to lesbians and gays, then they are being discriminated against on the basis of sexuality. (See the panel titled "Diversity: Why Family Issues Matter for Lesbians and Gays.")

Opponents argue that making same-sex unions legal denigrates marriage and abandons the basic building block of the family. This view dominates politics in the United States. President Clinton signed the "Marriage Protection Act" in 1996, which prohibits federal recognition of same-sex marriage and relieves the states of the obligation to recognize gay marriages performed in other states where it might be legal. Most states have passed legislation banning same-sex marriage. There is also a current effort by Congress and supported by President George W. Bush to pass an amendment to the Constitution prohibiting same-sex marriages.

The United States trails Canada, Europe, and Scandinavia on gay rights. Gay and lesbian couples have full marriage rights in Spain, the Netherlands, and Belgium. Canada is now on the brink of making same-sex marriages legal.

Why Family Issues Matter for Lesbians and Gays

What is a family? According to opinion polls, a majority of Americans understand family as a group of people who love one another and take care of each other in good times and bad.

What is a family? In the hands of the radical Christian Right, it has become a symbol and a weapon. A symbol of an imagined past when everything was just fine. A weapon that divides people into categories of good or bad, moral or immoral, productive citizen or irresponsible parasite. The allegedly "pro-family" rhetoric of the radical right is deeply homophobic and antifeminist, and exploits historically powerful racist stereotypes.

What is a family? For lesbians and gay men, family has become the frontier issue in our struggle for freedom, justice, and respect. Everywhere we look, family issues are surfacing — in the courts, in state legislatures, in workplaces, in the schools, in communities of faith, in the activities of our community centers and other organizations. Sometimes, picking up a copy of a gay newspaper, nothing but family issues of one sort or another seem to fill its pages.

It wasn't always so. When I was first coming out in the late sixties, as a college student influenced by the hippie counterculture and the first wave of radical feminist theory, "family" was something I could do without. It seemed that my only choices were to have a family, which meant my family of origin, or to be gay, which meant exile and escape from the constrictions of a heterosexist institution.

So why does family seem so important to us . . . ? Is the concern for family simply a defensive, reactive move on our part, a knee-jerk response to the "traditional family values" rhetoric of the Radical Christian Right? Or does the rise of family issues tell us something about how we have changed and what we want?

I think it's the latter. There are good reasons growing out of the history of our movement and communities that have pushed family issues to the front burner. One has to do with growing diversity of the public face of our movement and our community organizations. Lesbians, for instance, have often taken the lead in campaigns involving custody, adoption,

and our right to be parents. Lesbians and gays of color have spoken and written passionately of the importance of strong, extended family ties for the survival of their home communities in the face of racism, and of their unwillingness to have to choose between family ties or their sexual identity. As gays and lesbians in smaller communities come out of the closet and organize for change, family is something just around the corner, not something to escape from.

Family issues challenge homophobia in new and important ways. One of the most destructive and persistent stereotypes used to perpetuate hatred against us and keep us isolated and separated is the claim that we are a danger to children. The gay man who molests children, or the lesbian teacher who corrupts her students, have been common cultural myths. As more and more parents come out of the closet and assert their right to keep their children, as more and more of us choose to have children even after coming out, we force the issue of queers and children in proactive ways.

Parents are becoming front-line activists in institutions that reach into the lives of most Americans. Take public schools, for instance. As the children of openly gay or lesbian parents make their way through the public schools, these parents have to confront the insidious effects of homophobia in compelling ways. Will the schools, through their curriculum, be teaching these children to hate their parents? Will these children be the targets of ridicule, ostracism, and harassment? What must parents do to protect the integrity of their family relationships and to keep their children from harm? The actions they take—whether at parent-teacher conferences, at PTA meetings, or in one-on-one conversations with parents of their children's friends—is the stuff of permanent grassroots social change.

Family issues matter. Whether it be the public rituals we create to celebrate our committed relationships or our decisions to have children in our lives, the articulation of a lesbian and gay "family politics" has the power to move our freedom struggle forward.

Source: John D'Emilio, 1996. "Commentary: What Is a Family?" *Sociologists' Lesbian and Gay Caucus Newsletter* (Summer):3–4.

Divorce and Remarriage

Most people in the United States marry, but not all marriages last; some eventually are dissolved. Recent divorce rates show that the chances of a first marriage in the United States ending in divorce are about one in two. Although the U.S. divorce rate is the world's highest, divorce rates have increased dramatically in most Western countries.

Many politicians, ministers, editorial writers, and other people have shown great concern over the current high rates of marital dissolution in the United States. Although the present divorce rate is historically near its peak, it has been declining slowly for the past twenty years. Divorce and marital separation are not evenly distributed through the population, but vary according to social and economic characteristics. The following are some generalizations about divorce in the United States:

- One in five marriages ends in divorce or separation within five years.
- One in three marriages dissolves within ten years.
- Couples with children are less likely to divorce than childless couples.
- The lower the income, the greater the likelihood of divorce. In fact, poor two-parent families are twice as likely to divorce as are two-parent families not in poverty. Thus, poverty is a major factor contributing to the breakup of families (Pear, 1993:A6).
- The divorce patterns for Blacks and Hispanics differ significantly from those of Whites. From 1969 though the mid-1990s, African American divorce rates have been twice as great as those of Whites and Hispanics.
- About four out of every five people who obtain a divorce will remarry, with men more likely than women to do so.

Some of the many reasons for the increased divorce rate include the increased independence (social and financial) of women; the economic restructuring that eliminates many jobs for men and makes women's employment necessary; the greater tolerance of divorce by religious groups; and the reform of divorce laws, especially the adoption of no-fault divorce in many states (that is, no longer does one spouse have to prove that the other was at fault in order to obtain a divorce).

Despite changes in public attitudes toward divorce, many social critics persist in seeing family breakup as a main cause of social problems. Discouraging divorce is an important theme in the "marriage movement." Many states are examining their no-fault divorce laws and exploring legislation to "toughen up" divorce. Some states have instituted covenant marriages, which require marriage counseling if a relationship falters and which narrowly restrict grounds for divorce (Fletcher, 1999:2A).

Like marriage, divorce is gendered, resulting in unfair treatment of women and children. Ex-husbands have some major advantages over their ex-wives. They are almost always much better off financially. Typically, they were the major economic producers for their families, and after the separation their incomes stay disproportionately with them. A ten-year study in California, for example, found that men after divorce were much better off than were women (Peterson, 1996; Weitzman, 1985; 1996).

Divorce does not mean a permanent withdrawal from the marriage arena. The United States has the highest remarriage rate in the world. About one-third of Americans will marry, divorce, and remarry. Three-fourths of divorced men and six out of ten divorced women eventually remarry (Heatherington, 2002). The probability of remarriage is affected by four important variables: age, socioeconomic status, race, and religion. The age of women is crucial, with older women much less likely to remarry than younger women. The remarriage prospect of younger women with children is less than it is for younger women without children. Socioeconomic status is also important. Income, for example, is significant, but the relationship differs by gender. The more money a divorced man has, the more likely he is to remarry. The reverse is true for women (Coleman and Ganong, 1991:193). Race is also significant. African Americans and Latinos remarry at lower rates than Whites. Religion also affects remarriage rates. In the past, most Christian religious groups disapproved strongly of divorce, with varying severity in sanctions for those who defied the doctrines of the church on this matter. The ultimate church sanction was to consider as adulterers the divorced who remarried. Most denominations have shifted considerably on this issue and show ever greater tolerance, even bestowing the church's blessing on remarriages. The exception has been the Catholic Church, which officially does not recognize remarriage.

Remarriage may solve the economic problems of single-parent families by adding a male income. It may also relieve the many burdens of running a household alone. Partners in a remarriage should, when compared to first marrieds, be more tolerant, more willing to compromise, more aware of the need to integrate their different styles of living, and better able to anticipate problems and work them out before they snowball. Moreover, the pooling of economic resources and the greater probability of better-paying jobs (because of being older) should ease or eliminate the economic problems that plague many first marriages.

Work and Family Roles

Changes in families are closely related to changes in the workplace. The institutions of the economy and the family are linked together in many ways. The economy

"I'm staying together for the sake of my parents."

provides jobs with varying amounts of social status and economic resources for the family and in this way sets limits on its standard of living. The family supplies skilled workers to the economy. Jobs impose different constraints on families, such as the amount of time spent working and the scheduling of work, which determine the amount of time workers can spend with their families. In addition, work has psychological costs and benefits that influence family interaction. Extensive research on work and family in recent years has given us new information on how these "greedy institutions" operate.

Among the most important changes affecting U.S. families is the increase in married-couple families in which both spouses are in the labor force, or **dual-worker marriages**. Since 1960, the rise of women's participation in the labor force has been dramatic (see Chapter 12). For example, the percentage of women in two-parent families with children under six years of age who are in the workplace increased from around 19 percent in 1960 to 64 percent in 2003 (U.S. Bureau of the Census, 2004).

The demands of the family intrude more on women's work roles than on men's. If an emergency arises, requiring a choice between the two parents, the family role usually takes priority over the work role for mothers. For example, when there is child crisis in school, it is the child's working mother, rather than the working father, who will be called on to take initial responsibility. (The following is taken from Baca Zinn and Eitzen, 2005:198–200.) For fathers, the relationship is reversed. The work role takes priority over the family role. Many fathers take work home with them or use their time at home to recuperate from the stresses they face in the work role.

This gendered and uneven relationship of work and family, or the "**work-family role system**" (Pleck, 1977), reinforces traditional division of labor in both work and family. The system also ensures that wives' employment does not affect their core responsibilities for housework and child care. Employed wives generally have two jobs—work and family—while employed husbands have only one. For wives, this produces a second work shift. In her study of working families, sociologist Arlie Hochschild (Hochschild and Machung, 1989) found enormous conflicts between work and family. (See the panel titled "Research Methods: Researching Families.") Women were much more deeply torn between the demands of work and family than were their husbands. The additional hours that working women put in on the **second shift** of housework, she calculated, add up to an extra month of work each year. Even though social class is important in determining how the household labor gets done (more affluent families can afford to purchase more labor-saving services), Hochschild has found that social class, race/ethnicity, and personality give limited clues about who does and does not share the second shift. Gender is paramount. This finding is repeated in study after study. Child care, one of the most fundamental problems of employed parents, remains unsolved. In general, U.S. society is unresponsive to the needs of working parents. The traditional organization of work—an inflexible eight hour workday—makes it difficult for parents to cope with family problems or with the conflicting schedules of family members. The policies of federal and state governments lag behind the child support policies of other Western nations. (See Figure 15.4.)

Despite these different orientations to work and family, pressures are increasingly an issue for men as well as women. Rather, involvement in family life is taking place across race and class. Research on men's family lives offers a hopeful perspective in gender equality. Although true "role sharing" couples remain a minority, men

Research Methods

Researching Families: How Sociologist Arlie Hochschild Interviewed Couples about the Demands of Work and Family

With my research associates Anne Machung and Elaine Kaplan, I interviewed fifty couples very intensively, and I observed in a dozen homes. We first began interviewing artisans, students, and professionals in Berkeley, California, in the late 1970s. This was at the height of the women's movement, and many of these couples were earnestly and self-consciously struggling to modernize the ground rules of their marriages. Enjoying flexible job schedules and intense cultural support to do so, many succeeded. Since their circumstances were unusual they became our "comparison group" as we sought other couples more typical of mainstream America. In 1980 we located more typical couples by sending a questionnaire on work and family life to every thirteenth name—from top to bottom—of the personnel roster of a large, urban manufacturing company. At the end of the questionnaire, we asked members of working couples raising children under six and working full time jobs if they would be willing to talk to us in greater depth. Interviewed from 1980 through 1988, these couples, their neighbors and friends, their children's teachers, daycare workers and baby-sitters, form the heart of this book. . . .

We also talked with other men and women who were not part of two-job couples: divorced parents who were war-weary veterans of two-job marriages, and traditional couples, to see how much of the strain we were seeing was unique to two-job couples.

I also watched daily life in a dozen homes during a weekday evening, during the week-end, and during the months that followed, when I was invited on outings, to dinner, or just to talk. I found myself waiting on the front doorstep as weary parents and hungry children tumbled out of the family car. I shopped with them, visited friends, watched television, ate with them, walked through parks, and came along when they dropped their children at daycare, often staying on at the baby-sitter's house after parents waved good-bye. In their homes, I sat on the living-room floor and drew pictures and played house with the children. I watched as parents gave them baths, read bedtime stories, and said good night. Most couples tried to bring me into the family scene, inviting me to eat with them and talk. I responded if they spoke to me, from time to time asked questions, but I rarely initiated conversations. I tried to become as unobtrusive as a family dog. Often I would base myself in the living room, quietly taking notes. Sometimes I would follow a wife upstairs or down, accompany a child on her way out to "help Dad" fix the car, or watch television with the other watchers. Sometimes I would break out of my peculiar role to join in the jokes they often made about acting like the "model" two-job couple. Or perhaps the joking was a subtle part of my role, to put them at ease so they could act more naturally. For a period of two to five years, I phoned or visited these couples to keep in touch even as I moved on to study the daily lives of other working couples—black, Chicano, white, from every social class and walk of life.

I asked who did how much of a wide variety of household tasks. I asked who cooks? Vacuums? Makes the beds? Sews? Cares for plants? Sends Christmas or Hanukkah cards? I also asked: Who washes the car? Repairs household appliances? Does the taxes? Tends the yard? I asked who did most household planning, who noticed such things as when a child's fingernails need clipping, cared more how the house looked or about the change in a child's mood.

Source: "A Speed-Up in the Family," from *The Second Shift* by Arlie Hochschild and Anne Machung, copyright © 1989 by Arlie Hochschild. Used by permission of Viking-Penguin, a division of Penguin Putnam Inc.

are taking on more of the family workload, a step in the transformation of both the male role and the patriarchal family (Coltrane, 1996).

Obstacles remain to achieving a society in which men and women share equally the responsibilities for work and family. Nicholas Townsend's *The Package Deal: Marriage, Work, and Fatherhood in Men's Lives* (2002) finds that men today view their lives in terms of a "package deal" in which marriage, fatherhood, employment, and home ownership are interconnected. In this package, supporting a family is "crucial to successful fatherhood." Men who do not adequately support their families have failed to be good fathers. The ties between successful fatherhood and the good provider role encourage men to invest their energies in labor market success and make the goal of involved fatherhood difficult to achieve.

Children and Adolescents

Family changes have profoundly affected children. Over the past few decades, the living arrangements of children changed substantially. In 1980, 85 percent of children lived with two parents, but by 2000, this proportion had dropped to 69 percent (U.S. Bureau of the Census, 2000). Living arrangements of children have become more varied. For example, in the early 1990s, researchers and policymakers began to notice an increase in the number of children living in a home maintained by a grandparent. By 2003, 5 percent of children were living such homes (U.S. Bureau of the Census, 2004).

Research comparing 1990 with 1999 finds that children's well-being across the nation is improving. Many indicators of child well-being including infant mortality, child and teen death rates, and teen birth rates show improvement (Annie E. Casey Foundation, 2002). The poverty rate of children has dropped substantially in recent years. Now at 17 percent, it is still well above the lows of the late 1960s and 1970s of around 14 percent. Furthermore, the lowered child poverty rate masks disparities by race. Child poverty stands at 30 percent for African Americans and 28 percent for Latinos (Madrick, 2002).

The U.S. child poverty rate is the highest among the nineteen rich members of the Organization of Economic Cooperation and Development. Only Italy comes close at 14 percent. The next closest is Canada at 9.6 percent, then Britain at 8.4 percent. France's child poverty rate is 2.9 percent, Taiwan is 2 percent, and Sweden is at the bottom of the list at 1.3 percent. Although our society purports to value children, it turns out that our poorest children, those in the bottom 10 percent, have a lower standard of living than those in the bottom 10 percent of any other nation measured except Britain (Madrick, 2002:13).

FIGURE 15.4

Countries That Take the Best Care of Women and Children

Source: "USA Today, Snapshots." *USA Today* (May 21, 2002), p. 1A. Reprinted with permission.

Countries that take the best care of women and children, in terms of health, literacy, use of contraception, political participation, infant mortality, nutritional status, primary school enrollment, and access to safe water*:

1	Switzerland
2	Canada
3	Norway
4	Denmark
4	Sweden

*USA ranked 10th.

Source: Save the Children

Child poverty is related to the changes in family structure discussed in this chapter. A child's likelihood of experiencing poverty during the formative years is partially determined by the type of family he or she lives in. U.S. child poverty rates are often linked to the surge in families headed by single women. The share of children living in single-parent families has stabilized and inched downward over the past five years. Today, 27 percent of U.S. children live in single-parent families (U.S. Bureau of the Census, 2004). However, changes in the proportion of mother-only families are but one factor contributing to changes in child poverty rates. There are vast numbers of poor two-parent families with children. Young parents, whether living alone or as married couples, are especially vulnerable to poverty because they are likely to have less job experience than older workers. Because they have less job experience than older workers, they are often the first to lose their jobs during economic downturns (O'Hare, 1996:19–20).

Children and adolescents are strongly influenced by the amount of economic resources available to their families and the degree of esteem the family members receive from others outside the family. Most basically, social class position provides for their life chances. The greater the family's economic resources, the better the chance they have to live past infancy, to be in good health, to receive a good education, to have a satisfying job, to avoid being labeled a criminal, to avoid death in war, and to live the good life. Negatively, this means that millions of the nation's children are denied these advantages because they were born to parents who were unemployed, stuck in the lower tier of the segmented labor market, or victims of institutional racism or sexism.

Material resources produce different social resources and different ways in which families interact with society. Annette Lareau's study of middle-class and working-class families shows class differences in parenting styles, which transmit different advantages to their children. Her book *Unequal Childhoods* (2003) reveals how middle-class families engage in practices of "concerted cultivation," centering on verbal skills and organized activities. In contrast, working class families allow their children to develop more naturally. While both forms of child rearing have benefits, middle-class practices are those more highly valued by society. They transmit greater social advantages to children.

About 10 percent of the total population is between the ages of thirteen and nineteen (U.S. Bureau of the Census, 2000:16). This is a very significant category in U.S. society, for several reasons. First, teenagers are a strong economic force. For example, they account for a sizable proportion of CD sales and constitute an important movie audience. Collectively, they spend an enormous amount of money on clothes and toiletries. As they shift from fad to fad, fortunes are made and lost in the clothing and entertainment industries.

Almost all U.S. teens now work at some time during high school (Mortimer and Finch, 1996). National studies are showing that nearly three-fourths of students work for pay during their last years of high school (Crispell, 1995). Teens form the core of our low-wage retail and restaraunt work force. Teen earnings are often used for luxury items such as cars, stereos, "extra" clothing, concert tickets, and drugs. Researchers find that only a small percentage of high school seniors save all or most of their earnings for long-term purposes. This has created for many a "premature" affluence, an unrealistic level of discretionary income that is impossible to maintain at college unless they have extravagant parents (Hine, 1999; Woodward, 1990:57).

The stage of adolescence in U.S. society is a period of stress and strain for many teens. The most important reason is that it is an age of transition from one social

Middle-class family choices for children's activities are more valued by society.

status to another. There is no clear distinction between adolescence and childhood. Similarly, there is no clear line of demarcation between adolescence and adulthood. Are people considered adult when they can get a full-time job, when they are physically capable of producing children? Conversely, are they still adolescents when they continue to live at home with their parents? Unlike premodern societies, which have rites of passage serving to identify the individual as a child or an adult, adulthood in U.S. society is unclear. Surely much of the acting out by adolescents in the United States can be at least partially explained by these status ambiguities.

Recent changes in family life have altered childhood and adolescence. Along with changes in family structure, parents spend more time working and less time at home. Busy schedules create a time crunch for all family members. Kids are leading much more hectic lives, their time carefully parceled out among school, after-school care, soccer, ballet, karate, piano, horseback riding, and "play dates," with less time not only for pure play but also for family meals (down about 20 percent on weekdays), and even simple conversations within families (half of what it used to be, even on weekends) (Fishman, Charles, 1999:2). Average parents today spend eleven fewer hours per week with their children than parents did in the 1960s.

Along with the changing pace of life, technology is decreasing family interactions. Although living in the same house, parents or children may tune each other out. Watching television, often in separate parts of the house, along with using video games, personal computers, and personal stereos with headsets, have all worked to loosen the bond between parents and children. The results for some people are attenuated family relationships and adverse outcomes for infants, children, and adolescents (Hamburg, 1993). Other parents and children manage well even with these deficits in interaction time.

The Aged

During the twentieth century, the population of the United States experienced a profound change—it became older and is on the verge of becoming much older. (See Figure 15.5.) The "senior boom" discussed in Chapter 8 affects family life in many ways. First, aging has produced personal and family relationships that never existed before. Although we think of grandparenthood as a universal stage of family life, this is a post–World War II phenomenon. For the first time in history, most adults live long enough to know their grandchildren, and grandparents are a regular part of children's growing up experiences (Cherlin and Furstenberg, 1994a).

A second way in which increased longevity transforms family life involves the emergence of new family and household forms. For example, households with grandparents present are more common in the 1990s than in previous decades. According to the Census Bureau, as of 2000, there were a total of 3.9 million multigenerational households in the United States, making up 3.7 percent of the total population. There are several types of multigenerational households: (1) both grandparents and both parents present (34 percent of the total); (2) both grandparents, no parents present (17 percent of the total); (3) grandmother only, some parents present (29 percent); (4) grandmother only (14 percent); and (5) grandfather only (6 percent) (Paul, 2002).

Violence in Families

The family has two faces. It can be a haven from an uncaring, impersonal world, a place where love and security prevail. The family members love each other, care for each other, and are accepting of each other. But there is also a dark side to the family. The family is a common context for violence in society. "People are more likely to be killed, physically assaulted, sexually victimized, hit, beat up, slapped, or spanked in their own homes by other family members than anywhere else in our society" (Gelles, 1995:450). The intensity that characterizes intimate relationships can give way to conflict. Some families resolve the inevitable tensions that arise in the course of daily living, but in other families conflict gives way to violence.

Although the family is based on love among its members, the way it is organized encourages conflict. The family, like all other social organizations, is a power system; that is, power is unequally distributed between parents and children and between

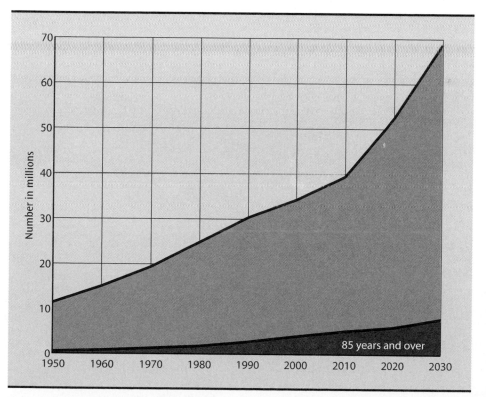

FIGURE 15.5

Population 65 Years of Age and Over: United States, 1950–2030

Source: U.S. Department of Health and Human Services, *Health: United States, 1999.* Hyattsville, MD: National Center for Health Statistics, 1999, p. 23.

spouses, with the male typically dominant. Parents have authority over their children. They feel they have the right to punish children in order to shape them in the ways they consider important. As we saw in Chapter 12, male dominance has been perpetuated by the legal system and religious teaching. Threats to male dominance are often resisted through violence.

Unlike most organizations in which activities and interests are relatively narrow, the family encompasses almost everything. Thus, there are more "events" over which a dispute can develop. Closely related to this phenomenon is a vast amount of time during each day when family members can interact. This lengthy interaction increases the probability of disagreements, irritations, violations of privacy, and the like, which increase the risk of violence.

The rule in our society that the home is private has two negative consequences. First, it insulates the family members from the protection that society could provide if a family member gets too abusive. Second, the rule of privacy often prevents victims of abuse from seeking outside help.

Violence in the family presents the ultimate paradox—the physical abuse of loved ones in the most intimate of social relationships. The bonds between wife and husband, parent and child, and adult child and parent are based on love, yet for many people these bonds represent a trap in which they are victims of unspeakable abuses.

Although it is impossible to know the extent of battering that takes place in families, the problem these forms of violence represent is not trivial. The threat of violence in intimate relationships exists for all couples and for parents and children. Violence in the family is not only a problem at the micro level of family units, it also represents an indictment of the macro level of society, its institutions, and the cultural norms that support violence.

Multi-generational households will continue to increase in the United States.

The Modern Family from the Order and Conflict Perspectives

From the *order* perspective, biology and social needs combine to produce a nuclear family that is well suited to modern society. This arrangement separates men and women into distinctive roles. Biologically, men are stronger while women bear and nurse children. Men have been the family providers, and women have "naturally" dealt with child rearing and family nurturance. Industrialization made the private family more important than ever before. Its separation from the outside world created stable families and an efficient role system, with boys and girls trained throughout their youth to take their places in society. This family prototype became the dominant sociological framework in the 1950s and 1960s. It was based on a family form that was more statistically prevalent in the 1950s than today, but by no means the only family form even then. Talcott Parsons and colleagues (1955) defined the family as a particular set of people (a married couple and their children) filling two central functions (socialization of children and emotional support) with a fixed division of labor (a stay-at-home, nurturing mother and a breadwinning father). This became known as the standard family. According to this view, the family operates most effectively when a division of labor is present in the nuclear family. Women fill the "expressive" or emotional roles of providing affection and support, while men fill the "instrumental" roles that provide economic support by working outside the family.

In the order perspective, families provide a haven from the harsh outside world of work and the marketplace. The nuclear family is the bedrock of society in an achievement-oriented world. The family fits with other social institutions and contributes to social order. The order perspective gives rise to the argument that changes in the family are destroying the country's social fabric. "Family values" is code for reinstating the two-parent family.

From the *conflict* perspective, families are closely connected to material inequalities in the larger society. Conflict theorists are especially interested in how families are affected by class, race, and gender. This perspective sees different family arrangements emerging out of different social and economic contexts.

The family is a vital part of capitalism in that it produces both workers and consumers to keep the economy going. The family is a primary mechanism for perpetuating social inequality because it is the vehicle through which property and social status are acquired. Wealth is locked up in elite families and then passed down through intergenerational inheritance. This limits the resources and opportunities of those who are lower in the socioeconomic hierarchy. As we have seen, families pass on their advantages and disadvantages to their offspring. While this transmission of social class position promotes stability in society—which the order theorists cherish—it also promotes inequality based on ascribed status.

The family serves the requirements of capitalism in another way—by glorifying the realm of the personal. This serves the economy through heightened consumerism. It also supports the interests of the dominant class by promoting false consciousness. The family is one of the primary socialization agents of youth, and as such it promotes the status quo by transmitting the culture of society. Children are taught to accept the inequalities of society as natural, and they are taught to accept the political and economic systems without question.

From the conflict perspective, the family is not the haven posited by the order theorists. Broader social systems enter into the family and reproduce the conflicts and tensions found in the rest of society. Family relations are not simply matters of love and agreement, but political arrangements as well. What is thought to be a private relationship of love is really a social relationship of power. At the micro level, conflict is generated by (1) women's resistance to men's dominance, and (2) employment and economic hardships, which work against family companionship. Thus, the modern family is not a tranquil institution, but one fraught with potential and actual conflict.

Conflict theorists argue that the nuclear family has positive consequences for capitalism, but can be negative for individuals (Zaretsky, 1976). The economic system benefits when employers can move individuals from place to place. The economy is served when employers do not have to worry about satisfying the emotional needs of workers. Finally, the system benefits when the family is isolated and therefore cannot affect society.

Conflict theorists maintain that because the family has sole responsibility for maintaining a private refuge from an impersonal society and for providing personal fulfillment, it is structured to fail. The demands are too great. The family alone cannot provide for all the emotional needs of its members, although its members try to fulfill these needs through consumerism, leisure, and family fun. Conflict theorists argue that society should be restructured so that personal fulfillment is met not only in the family but also in the community, at work, and in the other institutions of society.

Families of the Future

We have examined a number of trends that characterize contemporary families. Several key societal trends are dramatically altering the future prospects for families in the United States and around the world. (Much of the following is taken from Joseph F. Coates, 2002.)

- *Stresses on family functions will continue to reshape families.* Schools, businesses, and government institutions will be under more demand for meeting human services once provided in families.
- *Economics will continue to drive family changes.* The rise of the two-income family will make family life more complicated, but will provide women broader opportunities and will result in men's greater involvement in family life.
- *Divorce will continue.* Society will focus on creating more effective families as "pro-family" movements emerge.
- *Nontraditional family forms shaped by social and economic changes will proliferate.* Emerging patterns include cohabitation relationships; blended families resulting from divorced parents who remarry; "boomerang families" resulting from young people returning home to live with parents; single-parent families; and gay and lesbian families. Other emerging family forms include those formed through technology (surrogate parents and eventually children from cloned embryos) and transnational families in which family members live in different countries with a pattern of moving back and forth across national boundaries.
- *An aging society will redefine families.* Parents will "boomerang" back to their adult children. Elders will enter into cohabitation and other shared living arrangements including retirement communities with dorm-style living.

These trends lead to the conclusion that family variation is typical. Most significant, at the personal level most of us have been and will be participants in a variety of family forms as we move through the life cycle. This is not only the case for individuals but also for individual families, for they, too, will change forms as members enter and leave and work situations change. As the new century moves forward, many different family arrangements will emerge. They will exist alongside traditional families. This will contribute to the diversity and flexibility of the family.

Chapter Review

1. The family is idealized and mythologized. New sociological research has given us a better understanding of the U.S. family in the past and present.

2. Families are a product of social structure. They have different connections with institutions that provide resources for family support. Class and race are important determinants of family life.

3. The new economy has generated several difficulties for families. In particular, it has reduced the number of jobs providing a middle-class standard of living and has expanded the number of lower-standard-of-living jobs. Many blue-collar families have experienced underemployment or unemployment. Families have adjusted to economic difficulties by placing both spouses in the labor force.

4. As blue-collar workers in this century have experienced a rapid rise and fall in their fortunes, they moved from the modern family (an intact nuclear household of male breadwinner, his full-time homemaker wife, and their children) to the postmodern family (emergent family forms that vary considerably).

5. A major demographic trend since World War II has been the sharp rise in mothers who work outside the home. This takes a toll on the well-being of women workers, even though men in all classes and racial groups are taking on more of the family workload.

6. About one-fourth of all households with children are single-parent families; more than one-half of all Black families, one-third of Hispanic families, and one-fifth of White families are in this category. In 80 percent of these cases, these families are headed by women. Single-parent families have a number of unique problems, the most prominent one being a lack of economic resources.

7. Seventeen percent of all children in the United States live in poverty.

8. Although work and family are interdependent, husbands give priority to jobs over families, and employed wives give priority to families over jobs. Gender inequality in the larger society reinforces the gendered family. Women and men experience the family in different ways, and men benefit more than women from family arrangements.

9. Although women and men both benefit from marriage, men gain more. Marriage matters for most couples. However, the benefits are decreased, even reversed, for some poor couples, especially minority poor who face greater threats of unemployment, underemployment, and lower wages than Whites.

10. The family is not a tranquil institution, but one fraught with potential and actual conflict. Families are a major setting for violence in this society.

11. The divorce rate in U.S. society is the highest in the world. The probability of divorce is correlated with a number of variables, including socioeconomic status, age at first marriage, education, race, and religion.

12. Adolescence is a difficult time in U.S. society for many young people and their parents. A fundamental reason for this is that adolescents are in a transitional stage between childhood and adulthood, with no clear distinction to indicate when adulthood is reached. Rapidly changing social conditions are exacerbating this tension.

13. The aging of U.S. society has produced new family relationships and new household configurations, including multigenerational households.

14. Order theorists view the family as a source of stability for individuals and society. The traditional division of labor by sex contributes to social order.

15. Conflict theorists argue that the traditional family supports the economy but individuals and families pay a high price. The family is a major source of false consciousness and the primary agent by which the system of social stratification is perpetuated.

16. A number of trends indicate that families in the United States will continue to change—for example, economic changes, stress on families, the high divorce rate, and demographic changes, including the aging of society and immigration.

Key Terms

Family values
Family
Household
Modern family

Postmodern families
Nonfamily household
Marital power
Dual-worker marriages

Work-family role system
Second shift

Study Questions

1. What are the myths about U.S. families?
2. What is the relationship between the economy and family patterns?
3. Explain the following statement: Families are embedded in class and race hierarchies. What are the consequences of this fact for family life?
4. Explain how family and work are interconnected.

5. What are the benefits of marriage by class, race, and gender?
6. What social factors are related to variation in divorce rates in the United States?
7. What are the consequences for families of an aging population?
8. Contrast the differing views of families by order and conflict theorists.

For Further Reading

Maxine Baca Zinn and D. Stanley Eitzen, *Diversity in Families*, 7th ed. (Boston: Allyn and Bacon, 2005).

Suzanne M. Bianchi and Lynne M. Casper, "American Families," *Population Bulletin* 55 (4) (Washington, DC: Population Reference Bureau, December 2000).

Stephanie Coontz, *Marriage, a History* (New York: Viking 2005).

Susan J. Ferguson (ed.), *Shifting the Center: Understanding Contemporary Families* (Mountain View, CA: Mayfield, 2001).

Anita Ilta Garey, *Weaving Work and Motherhood* (Philadelphia: Temple University Press, 1999).

Karen V. Hansen, *Not So Nuclear Families: Class, Gender, and Networks of Care* (New Brunswick: Rutgers University Press, 2005).

Arlie Hochschild, with Anne Machung, *The Second Shift* (New York: Viking-Penguin, 1989).

Ronald L. Taylor (ed.), *Minority Families in the United States: A Multicultural Perspective*, 3rd ed. (Upper Saddle River, NJ: Prentice Hall, 2002).

Nicolas W. Townsend, *The Package Deal: Marriage, Work, and Fatherhood in Men's Lives* (Philadelphia: Temple University Press, 2002).

Web Resources

http://www.familiesandwork.org/index.html

The Families and Work Institute is a "non-profit center for research that provides data to inform decision-making on the changing workplace, changing family, and changing community."

http://www.contemporaryfamilies.org/

The Council on Contemporary Families, founded in 1996, is a nonprofit organization dedicated to enhancing the national conversation about what contemporary families need and how these needs can be met. Discussions on divorce, gay and lesbian families, and welfare reform are just a few of the many topics discussed.

http://laborproject.berkeley.edu/

In order to advocate for family-friendly policies in the workplace, the Labor Project for Working Families works with unions on collective bargaining, legislation, and public policy related to balancing work and family. Issues dealt with include child care, elder care, family leave, and flexible work schedules.

http://www.nationalpartnership.org/

The National Partnership for Women and Families promotes "fairness in the workplace, access to quality affordable healthcare, and policies that help women and men meet the dual demands of work and family."

http://www.trinity.edu/~mkearl/family.html

This site contains various information about families, including myths, violence, divorce, and marriage roles.

http://www.pscw.uva.nl/sociosite/TOPICS/familychild.html

Go to this site for links on family and children.

http://www.nccep.org/

The National Center for Children in Poverty promotes "strategies that prevent child poverty in the United States and that improve the lives of low-income children and families."

http://www.atask.org/

The Asian Task Force against Domestic Violence has a mission to eliminate family violence and to strengthen Asian families and communities. It addresses the need for multicultural and multilingual resources for Asian American families.

http://www.ncadv.org/

This is the home of the National Coalition against Domestic Violence, which has information on domestic violence, how to get help, and legislation dealing with domestic violence.

http://www.hrc.org/

The Human Rights Campaign works for lesbian, gay, bisexual, and transgender rights. Included in the website is information on LGBT adoption, partner benefits, and recent news related to the community.

http://www.ngltf.org/

The National Gay and Lesbian Task Force fights for the civil rights of those in the gay, lesbian, bisexual, and transgender community.

http://www.childrensdefense.org

This website for the Children's Defense Fund provides information on children's issues such as health, education, safety, and poverty.

Jonathan Kozol, in his classic *Savage Inequalities* (1991), describes how poor children are shortchanged in the United States:

> On an average morning in Chicago, about 5,700 children in 190 classrooms come to school only to find they have no teacher. Victimized by endemic funding shortages, the system can't afford sufficient substitutes to take the place of missing teachers. . . .
>
> The odds these [mostly] black kids in Chicago face are only slightly worse than those faced by low-income children all over America. Children like these will be the parents of the [future]. Many of them will be unable to earn a living and fulfill the obligations of adults; they will see their families disintegrate, their children lost to drugs and destitution. When we later condemn them for "parental failings," as we inevitably will do, we may be forced to stop and remember how we also failed them in the first years of their lives.
>
> It is commonplace that a society reveals its reverence or contempt for history by the respect or disregard that it displays for older people. The way we treat our children tells us something of the future we envision. The willingness of the nation to relegate so many of these poorly housed and poorly fed and poorly educated children to the role of outcasts in a rich society is going to come back to haunt us (Kozol, 1991).

This chapter examines one of society's basic institutions—education. The chapter is divided into four sections. The first describes the characteristics of U.S. education. The second focuses on how corporate society reproduces itself through education—in particular, how the schools socialize youth in accordance with their class position and point them toward factory, bureaucratic, or leadership roles in the economy. The third section describes the current role of education in perpetuating inequality in society. The concluding section summarizes the chapter by looking at education from the order and conflict perspectives.

The Characteristics of U.S. Education

Education as a Conserving Force

The formal system of education in U.S. society (and in all societies) is conservative, since the avowed function of the schools is to teach newcomers the attitudes, values, roles, specialties, and training necessary for the maintenance of society. In other words, the special task of the schools is to preserve the culture, not to transform it. Thus, the schools indoctrinate their pupils in the culturally prescribed ways. Children are taught to be patriotic. They learn the myths, the superiority of their nation's heritage, who are the heroes and who are the villains. Jules Henry (1963) has put it this way:

> Since education is always against some things and for others, it bears the burden of the cultural obsessions. While the Old Testament extols without cease the glory of the One God, it speaks with equal emphasis against the gods of the Philistines; while the children of the Dakota Indians learned loyalty to their own tribe, they learned to hate the Crow; and while our children are taught to love American democracy, they are taught contempt for the totalitarian regimes. (285–286)

There is always an explicit or implicit assumption in U.S. schools that the American way is the only really right way. When this assumption is violated on the primary and secondary school level by the rare teacher who asks students to consider the viability of world government, or who proposes a class on the life and teachings of Karl Marx or about world religions, then strong enough pressures usually occur from within the school (administrators, school board) or from without (parents, the American Legion, Daughters of the American Revolution) to quell the disturbance. As a consequence, creativity and a questioning attitude are curtailed in school, as Michael Parenti (2002) points out forcefully:

> From grade school to graduate school, students are instructed to believe in America's global virtue and moral superiority and to hold a rather uncritical view of U.S. politico-economic institutions. Surveys show that most youngsters believe that our political leaders are benevolent and know best. Teachers tend to concentrate on the formal aspects of representative government and accord scant attention to the influences that wealthy, powerful groups exercise over political life. . . . School texts seldom give more than passing attention to the history of labor struggle and the corporate exploitation of working people at home and abroad. Almost nothing is said of the struggles of First Nation People (also known as Native Americans or "Indians"), indentured servants, small farmers, and Latino, Asian, and European immigrants. The history of resistance to slavery, racism, and U.S. expansionist wars is largely untaught in our schools. (29–30; see also Loewen, 1995).

Mass Education

People in the United States have a basic faith in education. This faith is based on the assumption that a democratic society requires an educated citizenry so that individuals can participate in the decisions of public policy. It is for this reason that they not only provide education for all citizens, but also compel children to go at least to the eighth grade or until age sixteen (although this varies somewhat from state to state).

Who can quarrel with the belief that all children should be compelled to attend school, since it is for their own good? After all, the greater the educational attainment, the greater is the likelihood of larger economic rewards and upward social mobility. However, to compel a child to attend school for six hours a day, five days a week, forty weeks a year, for at least ten years, is quite a demand. The result is that many students are in school for the wrong reason. The motivation is compulsion, not interest in acquiring skills or curiosity about their world. This involuntary feature of U.S. schools is unfortunate because so many school problems are related to the lack of student interest.

As a result of the goal of and commitment to mass education, an increasing proportion of persons have received a formal education. In 1940, for example, 38 percent of the people in the United States age twenty-five to twenty-nine had completed high school. This proportion increased to 74 percent in 1970 and 88 percent in 2001. For Whites, 93 percent had completed high school, compared to 87 percent for African Americans, and 63 percent for Latinos (National Center for Education Statistics, 2002:80).

Local Control of Education

Although the state and federal governments finance and control education in part, the bulk of the money and control for education comes from local communities. There is a general fear of centralization of education—into a statewide educational system or, even worse, federal control. Local school boards (and the communities themselves) jealously guard their autonomy. Because, as it is commonly argued, local people know best the special needs of their children, local boards control allocation of monies, curricular content, and the rules for running the schools, as well as the hiring and firing of personnel.

There are several problems with this emphasis on local control. First, tax money from the local area traditionally finances the schools. Whether the tax base is strong or weak has a pronounced effect on the quality of education received (a point we return to later in this chapter). Second, local taxes are almost the only outlet for a taxpayers' revolt. Dissatisfaction with high taxes (federal, state, and local) on income, property, and purchases is often expressed at the local level in defeated school bonds and school tax levies. A current population trend increases the likelihood of the defeat of school issues—the increasing proportion of people age sixty-five and older. Third, because the democratic ideal requires that schools be locally controlled, the ruling body (school board) should represent all segments of that community. Typically, however, the composition of school boards has overrepresented the business and professional sectors and overwhelmingly underrepresented blue-collar workers, the poor, and various minority groups. The result is a governing body that is typically conservative in outlook and unresponsive to the wishes of people unlike themselves.

Fourth, local control of education may mean that the religious views of the majority (or at least, the majority of the school board) may intrude in public education. An explicit goal of the Christian Coalition, a conservative religious organization founded by Pat Robertson (see Chapter 17), is to win control of local school boards. Their agenda opposes globalism, restricts sex education to abstinence from sexual intercourse, promotes the teaching of biblical creationism in science classes, encourages school prayer, and censors books that denigrate Christian values (favorite targets are, for example, J. D. Salinger's *The Catcher in the Rye* and John Steinbeck's *The Grapes of Wrath*).

The following are some examples by states and cities to install religious values in schools:

- In 1999 the state school board of Kansas removed from the science curriculum all references to dinosaurs, geological time lines, and other tenets of evolution. In the next election, voters gave moderates the edge on the school board, which promptly dropped all efforts to revise the science curriculum. In 2004, however, conservatives retook the board.
- In Cobb County, Georgia, the school board inserted into a new biology textbook this statement: "This textbook contains material on evolution. Evolution is a theory, not a fact, regarding the origin of living things. This material should be approached with an open mind, studied carefully, and critically considered."
- In 2002, the Texas Board of Education objected to a sixth-grade social studies book that read, "Glaciers formed the Great Lakes millions of years ago," because this was counter to the creation time line of religious fundamentalists. The book was changed to read, "Glaciers formed the Great Lakes in the distant past" (Russell, 2003).

A final problem with local control is the lack of curriculum standardization across the nation's 15,367 school districts and fifty states: "Unlike virtually every other industrialized country, the United States has no national curriculum and no agency that services the development of classroom materials. *Each of the nation's 15,367 school districts is a kingdom unto itself*—with the power to decide what its students will be taught" (Kantrowitz and Wingert, 1992:59; italics added.)

Arguing for a common curriculum, Albert Shanker (1991), the late president of the American Federation of Teachers, stated:

> A common curriculum means that there is agreement about what students ought to know and be able to do and, often, about the age and grade at which they should be able to accomplish these goals. . . . In most countries with a common curriculum, linkage of curriculum, assessment and teacher education is tight. . . . In the U.S., we have no such agreement about curriculum—and there is little connection between what students are supposed to learn, the knowledge on which they are assessed, and what we expect our teachers to know. (E7)

The lack of a common curriculum has at least two negative consequences. First, there is a wide variation in the preparation of students. Second, because families move on the average of once every five years (and the rate is probably higher for families with school-age children), there are large numbers of children moving from district to district who find the requirements of their new schools different, sometimes very different, from their previous schools.

There are certain trends that indicate that the educational system in the United States is moving toward greater fragmentation rather than less. More and more parents are opting to send their children to private schools (about 12 percent) or to school them at home (2 percent). Taxpayer-funded charter schools are growing rapidly. These schools are based on a hybrid "free market" system in which educators, students, and parents choose a curriculum and educational philosophy free from the dictates of school boards and educational bureaucracies but financed publicly. In 2004, there were some 3,000 charter schools with more than 600,000 students.

Vouchers are another plan that splinters the educational system. This plan gives parents a stipulated amount of money per child that can be used to finance that child's education in any school, public or private. This plan sets up an educational "free market" in which schools have to compete for students. This competition will, theoretically, improve schools because they must provide what parents want for their children, whether that be better discipline, emphasis on learning the fundamentals, religious instruction, focus on the arts, vocational training, or college preparation. While some parents will use vouchers to send their children to other public schools outside their district, there is the constitutional question as to whether it is appropriate to use public funds to pay tuition in religious-based schools (most commonly, Catholic parochial schools). The Supreme Court ruled (5 to 4) in 2002 that spending public money to pay tuition costs at religious schools was constitutional and did not violate the separation of church and state.

Each of these educational reforms that are underway has strengths and weaknesses. Most important, they represent a trend that is rapidly dividing and subdividing the educational system. For many, this is viewed as a strength, representing the core American values of individualism and competition. Others see this trend as fragmenting further an already disaggregated educational system. Moreover, they see this trend as increasing the gap between the "winners" and "losers" in U.S. society. The voucher plan, for example, gives a set amount (typically about $2,000 a year) per student. This meager amount does not pay the full amount in private schools, thus allowing children of affluent parents to pay the difference but limiting the choice for less-than-affluent parents. The *Los Angeles Times* (2002) mentioned two additional problems: "A widespread voucher program would siphon off the involved parents and striving students who keep up the pressure for programs. No private schools need accept or keep a student with a troubled discipline history, increasing the concentration of violent or disruptive students in public school classes" (1).

Countering these trends, in 2001 Congress passed the "No Child Left Behind Act," which has the potential to reduce the fragmentation of education. The goal of this legislation is to close the gaps that plague education in the United States. For example, according to National Assessment of Educational Progress data, only 29 percent of the nation's eighth-graders are proficient in mathematics and just 32 percent read at their level (reported in Symonds, 2004). Compared with other industrialized nations, which have prescribed national curricula or highly specified national standards, U.S. students rank near the bottom in achievement. To improve performance, the "No Child Left Behind" legislation requires states to develop academic standards in reading, math, and science. States, districts, and schools would then be responsible to ensure that all children achieve these state standards by 2013–2014. Adequate yearly progress is measured by a single statewide assessment system given annually to all students from third to eighth grade. On the basis of these tests, schools are given a grade of "passing" or "failing." Another provision in this legislation is that all teachers are to meet a federal definition of "highly qualified."

While this legislation has been heralded as the most ambitious federal overhaul of public schools since the 1960s, the first years have resulted in a number of problems:

- Instead of one system, we have fifty. Each state is permitted to set its own proficiency benchmarks, with some high and others setting a low standard. Since the federal government rewards those who meet the standards, the ones with high standards are punished, while the ones with low standards are unfairly rewarded.
- Some conservative critics are concerned that this legislation intrudes on the traditional twin pillars of U.S. education—local control and states' rights.
- The emphasis on testing results in teaching a narrow range of skills for those tests.
- There is no attempt to address the funding inequities among rich and poor districts within a state that perpetuate the achievement gaps, the chronic underfunding of poorer schools, or child poverty itself (Metcalf, 2002).
- "If making the grade is statistically tough for many schools with lots of minority students, it's almost impossible in schools with large numbers of students who arrive speaking little English" (Schrag, 2004:39).
- The legislation is underfunded. The federal government was short $8 billion in 2004 of what was authorized in the bill. The cash-strapped states, which pay 90 percent of the bill for public education, have, typically, also cut their appropriations for education.

For how this legislation has worked in one city—Baltimore—see the panel titled "Diversity: How to Leave No Child Behind."

The Competitive Nature of U.S. Education

Not surprisingly, schools in a highly competitive society are competitive. Competition extends to virtually all school activities. The compositions of athletic teams, cheerleading squads, pom-pom squads, debate teams, choruses, drill teams, bands, and dramatic play casts are almost always determined by competition among classmates. Grading in courses, too, is often based on the comparison of individuals (grading on a curve) rather than on measurement against a standard. To relieve boredom in the classroom, teachers often invent competitive games such as spelling baseball or hangman. In all these cases, the individual learns at least two lessons: (1) your classmates are enemies, for if they succeed, they do so at your expense, and (2) fear of failure is the great motivator, not intellectual curiosity or love of knowledge.

The Sifting and Sorting Function of Schools

Schools play a considerable part in choosing the youth who come to occupy the higher-status positions in society. Conversely, school performance also sorts out those who will occupy the lower rungs in the occupational prestige ladder. Education is, therefore, a selection process. The sorting is done with respect to two different criteria: a child's ability and his or her social class background. Although the goal of education is to select on ability alone, ascribed social status (the status of one's family, race, and religion) has a pronounced effect on the degree of success in the educational system. The school is analogous to a conveyor belt, with people of all social classes getting on at the same time but leaving the belt in accordance with social class—the lower the class, the shorter the ride (see the panel titled "Diversity: Cooling Out the Failures").

How to Leave No Child Behind

In late 2001, Congress passed an education bill that had been promoted by President George W. Bush. The key part of this bill was that schools will test every student in grades three to eight every year in reading and mathematics. In addition a sample of pupils from each state will be required to take a national test to measure progress. This reverses, somewhat, the trend toward ever greater local control. Now students and schools will be measured against students and schools in a state, and to a degree against students and schools across the nation. The problem is that the use of standardized tests across districts and states does not take into account the imbalance in resources in disparate schools and school districts. That is the argument by DeWayne Wickham that follows.

"No child left behind," the education-reform mantra President Bush popularized, has run aground in Baltimore. In that city, nearly 30% of public elementary and middle school students today begin a new school year in the same grades they attended during the previous year.

About 20,000 of 70,000 Baltimore youngsters in grades one through eight were held back after they failed to pass specific classes and performed poorly on a national standardized test, and either didn't attend or failed summer school. Many of these under-achieving students fit a disturbing profile: They are African-Americans in a "high-poverty" school district whose teachers disproportionately lack degrees in the subjects they teach.

Baltimore is not alone. In many states, students in schools with large numbers of minorities are more likely to be in classes taught by teachers who did not major or minor in that subject field, according to a recent report by The Education Trust, a Washington-based non-profit organization that works to boost student academic achievement.

The amount of out-of-field teaching "remains unacceptably high, with classes in high-poverty and high-minority schools much more likely to be assigned to a teacher lacking minimal academic qualifications in the subject being taught," the report concluded.

In Baltimore's case, slightly less than a quarter of its 6,000 teachers were classified as provisional in the last school year. That means they didn't meet the minimum requirements for teacher certification. Nationally, 29% of the teachers in schools with high concentrations of minority students lack a degree or minor in the subject they teach.

"The research shows that teachers with weak academic backgrounds have a hard time teaching students in high minority districts," said Craig Jerald, who wrote the report, "All Talk, No Action: Putting an End to Out-of-Field Teaching."

This problem is compounded by the findings of another report—this one on the gap in school funding—released last month by The Education Trust. In 30 of 47 states reviewed, the school districts with the greatest populations of poor students got "substantially less" state and local money per student than did those with the lowest proportions of poor students.

When The Education Trust applied the same measurement to the minority population of these districts, it found that those with the highest concentrations of minority students received far fewer state and local education dollars per student than districts that had the lowest proportions of minority students.

This suggests that the education reforms Bush champions have little chance of succeeding without a more equitable distribution of state and local money—the bulk of school funding—to public schools, and a bigger push to increase the number of certified teachers in schools with high concentrations of poor and minority students. If this doesn't happen soon, a lot more students will be left behind.

Increasingly, students are being required to take standardized tests, not just to move from one grade to another, but also to graduate. Already students must pass an exit exam in 18 states to get a high school diploma. That number is expected to grow to 24 by 2008 and encompass 80% of the nation's minority students.

Before the nation's education system becomes too dependent on standardized tests, it must ensure that the funding of public schools is more balanced—and that teachers at all schools are qualified to teach the subjects on which the students will be tested.

Source: DeWayne Wickham, 2002. "Standardize Teachers before Standardizing Tests." *USA Today* (September 3), p. 15A. Copyright 2002, USA Today. Reprinted with permission.

Cooling Out the Failures

Although our schools can be a golden avenue of opportunity for those who succeed in them, they are also the arena in which many confront failure that condemns them to the more subservient positions in our society. How are those who "fail" handled so they do not become bitter revolutionaries intent on over-throwing the system that so brutally used them?

"Cooling out" is the process of adjusting victims to their loss. When someone has lost something that is valuable to him, it leads to intense frustration. This frustration and its accompanying anger are dangerous to society because they can be directed against the social system if the social system is identified as being responsible for the loss. But our educational system is insidiously effective, and many who fail within it (per-haps most) never even need to be cooled out. They learn early in grade school that they are stupid and that higher education is meant for others. They suffer miserably in school as they continue to be confronted year after year with more evidence of their failure, and they can hardly wait until they turn sixteen so they can leave for greener pastures. Such persons are relieved to end their educational miseries and need no cooling out.

For those who do need to be cooled out, however, a variety of techniques is used. The primary one makes use of the ideology of individualism. To socialize students into major cultural values means to teach them more values than conformity and competition. . . . Two other major values students consistently confront in our educational system are the ideologies of indi-vidualism and equal opportunity. They are taught that people make their own way to the top in a land of equal opportunity. Those who make it do so because of their own abilities, while those who do not make it do so because of a lack of ability or drive on their own part. They consequently learn to blame themselves for failure, rather than the system. It was not the educa-tional system that was at fault, for it was freely offered. But it was the fault of the individual who failed to make proper use of that which society offered him. Individualism provides amazing stabiliza-tion for the maintenance of our social system, for it results in the system going unquestioned as the blame is put squarely on the individual who was himself conned by the system.

If this technique of cooling out fails to work, as it does only in a minority of cases, other techniques are put into effect. Counselors and teachers may point out to the person that he is really "better suited" for other tasks in life. He may be told that he will "be happier" doing something else. He might be "gradually disen-gaged" from the educational system, perhaps be directed to alternate sources of education, such as vocational training.

The individual may also be encouraged to blame his lack of success on tough luck, fate, and bad breaks. In one way or another, as he is cooled out, he is directed away from questioning the educational sys-tem itself, much less its relationship to maintaining the present class system and his subservient position within it. . . .

Finally, the malcontent-failure has the example before him of those from similar social class circum-stances as his own who did "make it." This becomes incontrovertible evidence that the fault does lie with himself and not the system, for if they could make it, so could he. This evidence of those who "made it" is a powerful cooling out device, as it directly removes any accusatory finger that might point to the educational social systems.

Having our educational system set up in such a way that some lower class youngsters do manage to be successful and are able to enter upper middle class positions serves as a pressure valve for our social sys-tem. In the final analysis, it may well be this pressure valve which has prevented revolutions in our country—as the most able, the most persistent, and the most conforming are able to rise above their social class cir-cumstances. And in such instances, the educational system is pointed to with pride as representing the gateway to golden opportunity, freely open to all.

Source: James M. Henslin, Linda K. Henslin, and Steven D. Keiser, 1976. "Schooling for Social Stability: Education in the Corporate Society." In *Social Problems in American Society*, 2nd ed., James M. Henslin and Larry T. Reynolds (eds.). Boston: Allyn and Bacon, pp. 311–312. © 1976 by Pearson Education. Reprinted by per-mission of the publisher.

Schools are preoccupied with order and control. To what degree is this emphasis appropriate? Does it stifle creativity and learning?

The Preoccupation with Order and Control

Most administrators and teachers share a fundamental assumption that school is a collective experience requiring subordination of individual needs to those of the school. U.S. schools are characterized, then, by constraints on individual freedom. The school day is regimented by the dictates of the clock. Activities begin and cease on a timetable, not in accordance with the degree of interest shown or whether students have mastered the subject. Another indicator of order is the preoccupation with discipline (i.e., absence of unwarranted noise and movement, and concern with the following of orders).

In their quest for order, schools also demand conformity in clothing and hair styles. Dress codes are infamous for their constraints on the freedom to dress as one pleases. School athletic teams also restrict freedom, and these restrictions are condoned by the school authorities. Conformity is also demanded in what to read, where to set the margins on the computer or typewriter, and how to give the answers the teacher wants.

The many rules and regulations found in schools meet a number of expressed and implicit goals. The school authorities' belief in order is one reason for this dedication to rules: Teachers are rated not on their ability to get pupils to learn but rather on the degree to which their classroom is quiet and orderly. The community also wants order. An excerpt from a famous (or infamous) book titled *The Student as Nigger* dramatizes the demands for order in U.S. schools:

> [Students] haven't gone through twelve years of public school for nothing.
> They've learned one thing and perhaps only one thing during those twelve years.
> They've forgotten their algebra. They've grown to fear and resent literature. They
> write like they've been lobotomized. But Jesus, can they follow orders! . . . Students
> don't ask that orders make sense. They give up expecting things to make sense

long before they leave elementary school. Things are true because the teacher says they're true. At a very early age we all learn to accept "two truths," as did certain medieval churchmen. Outside of class, things are true to your tongue, your fingers, your stomach, your heart. Inside class things are true by reason of authority. And that's just fine because you don't care anyway. Miss Wiedemeyer tells you a noun is a person, place or thing. So let it be. You don't give a rat's ass; she doesn't give a rat's ass. The important thing is to please her. Back in kindergarten, you found out that teachers only love children who stand in nice straight lines. And that's where it's been at ever since. (Farber, 1970:92)

The paradoxes listed below indicate the many profound dilemmas in U.S. education. They set the foundation for the remaining sections of this chapter, which deal with the crises facing education and with some alternative modes.

- Formal education encourages creativity but curbs the truly creative individual from being too disruptive to society.
- Formal education encourages the open mind but teaches dogma.
- Formal education has the goal of turning out mature students but does not give them the freedom essential to foster maturity.
- Formal education pays lip service to meeting individual needs of the students but in actuality encourages conformity at every turn.
- Formal education has the goal of allowing all students to reach their potential, yet it fosters kinds of competition that continually cause some people to be labeled as failures.
- Formal education is designed to allow people of the greatest talent to reach the top, but it systematically benefits certain categories of people regardless of their talent: the middle- and upper-class students who are White.

Education and Inequality

Education is presumed by many people to be the great equalizer in U.S. society—the process by which the disadvantaged get their chance to be upwardly mobile. The data in Figure 16.1 show, for example, that the higher the educational attainment, the

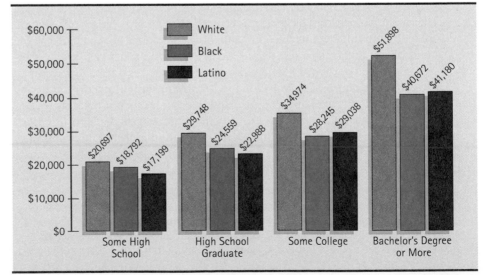

FIGURE 16.1

Median Annual Income for Full-Time Workers by Educational Attainment for People 25 Years Old and Over by Race and Hispanic Origin: 2000

Source: U.S. Bureau of the Census, 2000. "Educational Attainment in the United States: March 2000." *Current Population Reports*, Series P20–536. Washington, DC: U.S. Government Printing Office.

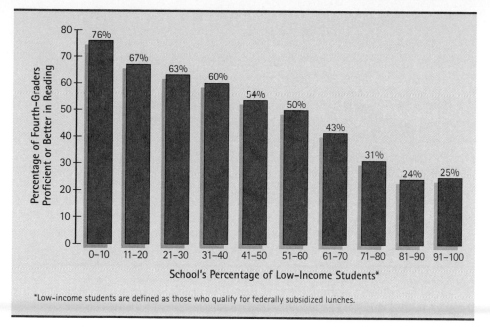

FIGURE 16.2

Poverty and Achievement in Denver Schools, 1999

Source: "Taking the Test," by Charles Illescas and Janet Bingham in *The Denver Post* (February 27, 2000):1A. Reprinted by permission of *The Denver Post.*

Y-axis: Percentage of Fourth-Graders Proficient or Better in Reading

X-axis: School's Percentage of Low-Income Students*

Values: 0–10: 76%; 11–20: 67%; 21–30: 63%; 31–40: 60%; 41–50: 54%; 51–60: 50%; 61–70: 43%; 71–80: 31%; 81–90: 24%; 91–100: 25%

*Low-income students are defined as those who qualify for federally subsidized lunches.

higher the income. But these data do not in any way demonstrate equality of opportunity through education. They show clearly that African Americans and Latinos with the same educational attainment as Whites receive lower economic rewards. These differences by race reflect discrimination in society, not just in schools. This section focuses on how the schools help perpetuate class and race inequities.

The evidence that educational performance is linked to socioeconomic background is clear and irrefutable (we include race/ethnicity along with economic status since they are highly correlated).

- There is a strong relationship between test scores in reading, writing, and mathematics and poverty (see Figure 16.2).
- Children in the poorest families are six times as likely as children in wealthier families to drop out of high school (Children's Defense Fund, 2004:88).
- College students whose families are in the top income quartile earn eight times as many bachelor's degrees by age twenty-four as students from the bottom quartile (Scott, 2001).
- Achievement gaps in reading, writing, and mathematics persist between minority and White students (see Figure 16.3).
- African American, Latino, and Native American students lag behind their White peers in graduation rates and most other measures of student performance.
- Black, Latino, and Native American students are suspended or expelled in numbers disproportionate to those of Whites. In 1998–1999, only one state (South Carolina) suspended 9 percent or more of its White students, but 35 states suspended that percentage of Blacks, according to the Civil Rights Project at Harvard University. The syndrome has even acquired a catchphrase: "learning while Black" (Morse, 2002:50).

These social class and racial gaps in academic achievement are found in almost every school and district in the United States. On the surface these patterns reinforce

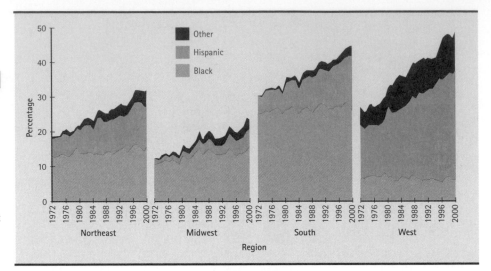

FIGURE 16.3

Enrollment: Percentage of Public School Students Enrolled in Grades K–12 Who Were Minorities, by Region: October 1972–2000.

Source: U.S. Department of Commerce, Bureau of the Census, 1972–2000. *Current Population Surveys*

the social Darwinist assumptions that the affluent are successful because they are intelligent, and, conversely, the poor and minorities are at society's bottom because they do not have the requisite abilities to be successful. Similarly, dysfunctional families, unmotivated students, and the culture of poverty are commonly believed to explain why the poor and minorities are disadvantaged in our supposedly meritocratic educational system. In effect, though, the educational system is stacked in favor of middle- and upper-class children and against children from the lowest classes.* At least three interrelated factors explain why the education system tends to reinforce the socioeconomic status differentials in the United States: finances, curriculum, and segregation.

Finances

Schools in the United States reflect the economic divide that exists in society: "In America, the type of education provided, the way it is funded, and the content of the curriculum are local matters directed by local authorities. The result is easy to see. Across America one sees the extremes: from schools that resemble shining mansions on a hill to ramshackle, dilapidated structures" (Kamau, 2001:81).

Approximately 86 percent of U.S. children attend public schools. These schools receive funds from three governmental sources—about 10 percent from the federal government, and depending on the allocation within each state, about 40 percent from the state, and 50 percent from property taxes in each district within the state. The result of this distribution is that schools are funded unequally in the United States, with public schools being more successful in educating children in middle-class communities but often failing children in poor neighborhoods.

---

*We have phrased the question to focus on the system, not on the victims, contrary to the typical response, which is to center on the cultural deprivation of the poor. That approach attacks the home and culture of poor people. It assumes that these people perform inadequately because they are handicapped by their culture. Observers cannot, however, make the value judgment that a culture is deprived. They can note only that their milieu does not prepare children to perform in schools geared for the middle class. In other words, children of the poor and/or minority groups are not nonverbal—they are very verbal, but not necessarily in the language of the schools—that is, the middle class.

SEPARATE BUT EQUAL

Equal opportunity in education (at least as measured by equal finances) has not been accomplished nationwide because wealthier states are able to pay much more per pupil than are poor states. The top-spending states, for example, invest more than double the amount per pupil than those states spending the least. Because the federal government provides only about 10 percent of the money for public schools, equalization from state to state is impossible as long as education is funded primarily by state and local governments because both entities vary in wealth and commitment to public education.

The disparities in per-pupil expenditures within a given state are also great, largely because of the tradition of funding public schools primarily through local property taxes. This procedure is discriminatory because rich school districts can spend more than poor ones on each student—and at a lower taxing rate. Thus, suburban students are more advantaged than are students from the inner city; districts with business enterprises are favored over agricultural districts; and districts with natural resources are better able to provide for their children than are districts with few resources. Some examples:

- In Illinois, each child of all-Black East St. Louis receives an education worth $8,000 yearly, while a child in Lake Forest, a predominantly White Chicago suburb, receives on worth $18,000 (Kozol, 2004).
- In New York City, per pupil spending of $10,500 is half the $21,000 per student in the Long Island suburb of Manhasset (Kozol, 2004).
- Including all the costs of operating a public school, a third-grade class of twenty-five children in the schools of Great Neck, New York, receives at least $200,000 more per year than does a class of the same size in Mott Haven, New York, where 99.8 percent of the children are African American or Latino (Kozol, 2002).
- In the Los Angeles area, the students of McKittrick School in the Central Valley receive $17,000 each, more than twice as much as students in Laguna Beach schools (*Los Angeles Times*, 2003).

This gap is even greater when one considers the monies raised in each district from bake sales and other fund-raisers, soda machine contracts, and foundation contributions. In Colorado, for example Pitkin County (the location of various affluent mountain communities) schools in 1999 raised an extra $2,194 per student compared to just $163 in Saguache County (an arid, rural area with a high concentration of poverty) (*Denver Post*, 2001).

There have been a number of court challenges to unequal funding within states with systems in several states judged unconstitutional. Various schemes have been proposed to meet the objections of the courts, but inequities remain even in the more progressive states. Progressive plans to address financial inequities are fought by the affluent districts and their constituents because, they argue, their taxes should be spent on their children, not others.

Some have argued that the money spent per pupil in a district is not related to educational performance. Bob Chase (1997), president of the National Education Association, argues the opposite, while acknowledging that money alone will not suffice:

> Money matters because books matter, because small classes matter, and the one-on-one interactions between teacher and student matter. Generations of wealthy families who have sent their children to expensive private schools have long understood the importance of money in education. . . . The crucial point is this: You need money to create excellent schools. (20)

Research shows that poor students and the schools serving them:

- Have one computer for every sixteen students, compared to one computer for every seven students in the affluent schools (Mendels, 2000);
- Have teachers that are underpaid relative to their peers in affluent schools;
- Are more likely than their more affluent peers to be taught by teachers who did not major in the subject area in which they teach;
- Are more likely to attend schools in need of repairs, renovations, and modernization;
- Are more likely to attend schools that lack some necessary classroom materials; and
- Have higher pupil/teacher ratios.

Family Economic Resources. The average combined SAT (Scholastic Aptitude Test) scores for youth from families whose income was $70,000 or more is about 200 points higher than youth from families whose income is $10,000 less. By race, Whites score 100 points higher than African Americans on average (U.S. Department of Education, 2001). How are we to explain these differences on the SATs by income and race? Among the reasons are the benefits that come from economic privilege. Poor parents (disproportionately people of color), most without health insurance, are unable to afford prenatal care, which increases the risk of babies being born at low birth weight, a condition that may lead to learning disabilities. As these poor children age, they are less likely than more affluent children to receive adequate nutrition, decent medical care, and a safe and secure environment. These deficiencies increase the probability of their being less alert, less curious, and less able to interact effectively with their environment than are healthy children.

Poor children are more likely than the children of the affluent to attend schools with poor resources, which, as we have seen, means that they are less likely to receive an enriched educational experience. Similarly, most poor young people live in communities that have few opportunities to apply academic skills and build new ones because they are either not available or not accessible (libraries, planetariums, summer camps, zoos, nature preserves, museums). The lack of community resources is especially destructive during the summer months, the time when children doing least well in school (a group that is disproportionately poor) slide backward the farthest.

Children from poor families cannot afford private early development programs, which prepare children for school. They can be in Head Start, but these government programs have the funding for only about 60 percent of those eligible.

The level of affluence also affects how long children will stay in school, because schools, even public schools, are costly. There are school fees (many school districts charge fees for participation in music, athletics, and drama), supplies, meals, transportation, and other costs of education. These financial demands pressure youngsters from poorer families to drop out of school prematurely to go to work. The children from the middle and upper classes, not constrained by financial difficulties, tend to stay in school longer, which means better jobs and pay in the long run.

The affluent also give their children edu-

Scene from Fairfield Country Day, a private boys' school for grades K–9. The affluent often send their children to private elite schools, which serve, among other functions, to place their students in the most elite universities and later to placement in top professional and corporate posts.

cational advantages such as home computers, travel experiences abroad and throughout the United States, visits to zoos, libraries, and various cultural activities, and summer camps to hone their skills and enrich their experiences in such activities as sports, music, writing, and computers. Another advantage available to the affluent is the hiring of tutors to help children having difficulty in school or to transform good students into outstanding ones.

Affluent parents may also use their privilege to get other advantages for their children. For example, in addition to spending money for their children to enroll in SAT preparation classes, they may get a psychologist's or medical doctor's recommendation for a youth to be identified as having a learning disability so that he or she would be given extra time to complete tests such as the SAT. The College Board reports that while only a tiny fraction—1.9 percent—of students nationwide are given special accommodations for taking the SAT, the percentage jumps fivefold for students from New England prep schools (exclusive private schools that send their students to elite colleges and universities). In contrast, at ten Los Angeles inner-city high schools, no students bought the time accommodation. This, despite the fact that learning disabilities are frequently found in economically disadvantaged populations (Weiss, 2000).

The well-to-do often send their children to private schools (about 12 percent of U.S. children attend these schools). Parents offer several rationales for sending their children to private schools. Some do so for religious reasons. Some choose them because private schools, unlike public schools, are selective in whom they accept. Thus, parents can ensure that their children will interact with children similar to theirs in race (some private schools were expressly created so that White children could avoid attending integrated public schools) and social class. Similarly, private schools are much more likely than are public schools to get rid of troublesome students (those with behavioral problems and low achievers), thereby providing an educational environment more conducive to achievement. A final reason for attending private schools is that the most elite of them provide a demanding education and entry to the most elite universities, which, in turn, lead to placement in top positions in the professional and corporate occupational worlds.

Higher Education and Stratification. Obtaining a college degree is the most important avenue to later success (the annual rate of return on the cost of a college degree is about 11 percent for life) (Farrell, 1996). One's family finances are directly related to whether one attends college and, if so, what type.

The cost of college is high and getting higher (as noted in Chapter 10). These high costs, coupled with declining scholarship monies, preclude college attendance not only for the able poor but also increasingly for the children of the working and lower middle classes. The ability to pay for college reinforces the class system in two ways: The lack of money shuts out the possibility of college for some students, and for those who do attend college, money stratifies. The poorest, even those who are talented, are most likely to attend community colleges, which are the least expensive; they emphasize technical careers and are therefore limiting in terms of later success (about 45 percent of the nation's college students attended community colleges). Students with greater resources are likely to attend public universities. Finally, those with the greatest financial backing are most likely to attend elite and prestigious private schools, where the annual cost can exceed $40,000. It is important to note that, although ability is an important variable, it is money—not ability—that places college students in this stratified system. Children of the affluent are also advantaged in admittance to elite universities because of admission criteria that favor the children of alumni and the children of big contributors to the university's fund-raising campaigns.

Minorities and Higher Education. Because racial minorities are much more likely than Whites to be poor or near-poor, they are underrepresented in college education. The following facts make this point.

First, even though more minorities are attending college than ever, they continue to be underrepresented in higher education. Moreover, racial minorities are more likely than Whites to attend community colleges and schools that are less funded, and they are more likely to leave college with greater debts than White students.

Racial minorities also receive a disproportionately low number of college degrees. This is reflected in the relatively low number of minority students who attend and graduate from graduate school. For example, in 2003, African Americans earned only 6.5 percent of all doctorates awarded. Since Blacks are almost 13 percent of the population, Black doctoral awards were earned at only one half the level that racial parity would call for (*Journal of Blacks in Higher Education*, 2004). This, of course, results in a low proportion of minorities in the various professions. Of special significance is their low representation among full-time faculty in higher education now and projected for the future.

Curriculum. U.S. schools are essentially middle or upper class. The written and spoken language in the schools is expected to be middle class. This is always a problem to some extent because some children, especially some children from economically disadvantaged backgrounds, do not speak English (at least middle-class English) and, for many, English may be a second language (see Figure 16.3 on page 472 for the trend of increasing minority children in schools). This language gap is increasing with the recent wave of immigrants from Latin America and Asia. As a result, the number of students with limited English skills has doubled to 5 million in the last decade (Zhao, 2000). This presents problems for the schools not only in urban areas such as Los Angeles but also in many rural areas. English is clearly a second language for many Latino youngsters, making their success in U.S. schools especially problematic. Standardized tests often ask the student to determine how objects are similar. For students whose first language is Spanish, this presents a problem. "Spanish, which separates words into masculine and feminine categories, tends to emphasize the differences between objects. This interferes with tasks that require the subject to describe how objects are similar" (Philippus, 1989:59). The schools, in general, have failed to recognize the special needs of these and other bilingual students, which results in their overall poor student performance.

In these and other matters, the curriculum of the schools does not accommodate the special needs of the poor. To the contrary, the schools assume that the language and behaviors of the poor are not only alien but also wrong—things to be changed. This assumption denigrates the ways of the poor and leads to loss of ego strength (a trait already in short supply for the poor in a middle-class world).

The curriculum also is not very germane to the poor child's world. What is the relevance of conjugating a verb when you are hungry? What is the relevance of being able to trace the path of how a bill becomes law when your family and neighbors are powerless? Irrelevancy for the poor is also seen in the traditional children's primers, which picture middle-class surroundings and well-behaved blond children. There is little effort at any educational level to incorporate the experience of slum children in relation to realistic life situations of any kind. Schools also have a way of ignoring real-life problems and controversial issues. Schools are irrelevant if they disregard topics such as race relations, poverty, and the distribution of community power.

The typical teaching methods, placement tests, and curricula are inappropriate for children from poor families. This factor, along with the others mentioned earlier, results in failure for a large proportion of these youngsters. They perceive themselves (as do others in the system) as incompetents. As Silberman (1970) puts it:

> Students are not likely to develop self-respect if they are unable to master the reading, verbal, and computational skills that the schools are trying to teach. Children must have a sense of competence if they are to regard themselves as people of worth; the failure that minority-group children, in particular, experience from the beginning can only reinforce the sense of worthlessness that the dominant culture conveys in an almost infinite variety of ways, and so feed the self-hatred that prejudice and discrimination produce. Chronic failure makes self-discipline equally hard to come by; it is these children's failure to learn that produces the behavior problems of the slum school . . . and not the behavior problems that produce the failure to learn. (67)

Silberman's discussion of the problems of minority-group children can be broadened to include all poor children (who are, after all, also a minority group). The poor of all races experience prejudice and discrimination. They quickly learn that they are considered misfits by the middle class (teachers, administrators, citizens).

Segregation. U.S. schools tend to be segregated by social class and race, both by neighborhood and, within schools, by ability grouping. Schools are based in neighborhoods that tend to be relatively homogeneous by socioeconomic status. Racial and economic segregation is especially prevalent at the elementary school level, carrying over to a lesser degree in the secondary schools. Colleges and universities, as we have seen, are peopled by a middle- and upper-class clientele. Thus, at every level, children tend to attend a school with others like themselves in socioeconomic status and race. A study by Harvard University found that public schools are highly segregated and becoming more so: "Although minority enrollment now approaches 40 percent nationwide, the average White student attends a public school that is 80 percent White. At the same time, one-sixth of Black students—the figure is one-quarter in the Northeast and Midwest—attend schools that are nearly 100 percent non-White" (reported in the *New York Times*, 2003:1). In short, the progress toward desegregation peaked in the late 1980s and has retreated over the past 15 years.

Tracking and Teachers' Expectations

In 1954, the Supreme Court declared segregated schools unconstitutional. As we have seen, many schools remain at least partially segregated by social class and race because schools draw students from residential areas that are more or less homogeneous by class and race. Segregation is reinforced further by the tracking system within the schools. **Tracking** (also known as ability grouping) sorts students into different groups or classes according to their perceived intellectual ability. The decision is based on grades and teachers' judgments but primarily through standardized tests. The result is that children from poor families and from ethnic minorities are overrepresented in the slow track, while children from advantaged backgrounds are disproportionately in the middle and upper tracks. The rationale for tracking is that it provides a better fit between the needs and capabilities of the student and the demands and opportunities of the curriculum. Slower students do not retard the progress of brighter ones, and teachers can adapt their teaching more efficiently to the level of the class if the students are relatively homogeneous in ability. The special problems of the different ability groups, from gifted to challenged, can be dealt with more easily when groups of students share the same or similar problems. The arguments are persuasive.

Although these benefits may be real, tracking is open to serious criticisms. First, students in lower tracks are discouraged from producing up to their potential. They tend to be given repetitive and unchallenging tasks. Students labeled as *low ability* tend to be taught a "dumbed-down" curriculum. They are given low-level work that increases the gap between them and students in the higher tracks. Rather than seeing the remedial track as a way to get students up to speed, many "teachers see themselves as weeders, getting rid of the kids who can't make it, rather than nurturers trying to make all grow to their potential" (Rachlin, 1989:52).

Second, students in the upper track develop feelings of superiority, whereas those in the lower track tend to define themselves as inferior. As early as the second grade, students know where they stand on the smart-or-dumb continuum, and this knowledge profoundly affects their self-esteem. These psychological wounds can have devastating effects.

Third, the low-track students are tracked to fail. The negative labels, low teacher expectations, poor education resources (the highest track is much more likely to have access to computers and to have the most talented teachers), and because teachers typically do not want to teach these classes (there is a subtle labeling among teachers regarding who gets to teach what level) all lead to a high probability of failure among students assigned to the lowest track. Given all of these negatives, it is not surprising that students who are discipline problems or who eventually drop out come disproportionately from the low track.

Fourth, the tracking system is closely linked to the stratification system—that is, students from low-income families are disproportionately placed in the lowest track, resulting in a reinforcement of the social class structure. Data from a nationwide study of 14,000 eighth-grade students in English classes reveal that this is true (see Table 16.1). Thus, U.S. schools deny equality of educational opportunity, which is contrary to the ideal of the school system as open and democratic.

Finally, and most telling, recent research calls into serious question whether tracking has educational value. Research at Johns Hopkins University found, for example, that "given the same curriculum in elementary and middle-grade schools, there is no difference in achievement between advanced students in a tracked school and students in the top third of a class made up of students with varying abilities" (cited in Rachlin, 1989:52). The Carnegie Corporation, in a report assessing the state of middle-grade schools, advocated "abolishing tracking on the grounds that it discriminates against minorities, psychologically wounds those labeled slow, and doesn't work" (cited in Rachlin, 1989:51).

To summarize, Claude Fischer and his colleagues (1996) find that social class has powerful effects on student placement in the tracking system and that the track location

TABLE 16.1

Ability Grouping by Race and Class (from a National Study of 14,000 Eighth-Grade Students in English Classes)

| Category | Percent in | | | |
	High Ability	Middle Ability	Low Ability	Mixed
Race/ethnicity				
Asian	40%	37%	16%	7%
White	32	40	14	15
Hispanic	18	42	29	12
Black	15	38	34	13
Native American	9	44	35	13
Scocioeconomic status				
Top one-fourth	39	39	14	8
Bottom one-fourth	13	36	37	14

Source: U.S. Department of Education, National Center for Educational Statistics, 1990. *National Education Longitudinal Study of 1988.* Washington, DC: U.S. Government Printing Office.

has powerful effects on students' success, regardless of preexisting cognitive differences. Thus, inequality in learning is increased by tracking. They also note: "There is . . . a broader sense in which American schools are tracked. The great decentralization and local control of schools in the United States—much more than is common in other Western nations—means that entire schools and even school districts are tracked" (Fischer et al., 1996:167). The tracking system appears not to accomplish its educational goals, but it is powerful in its negative effects. There are four principal reasons this system stunts the success of students who are negatively labeled.

Stigma. Assignment to a lower track carries a strong **stigma** (a label of social disgrace). Such students are labeled as intellectual inferiors. Their self-esteem wanes as they see how other people perceive them and behave toward them. Thus, individuals assigned to a track other than college prep perceive themselves as second class, unworthy, stupid, and in the way. Clearly, assignment to a low track is destructive to a student's self-concept.

The Self-Fulfilling Prophecy. A **self-fulfilling prophecy** (see Chapter 7) is an event that occurs because it is predicted and people alter their behavior to conform to the prediction. This effect is closely related to stigma. If placed in the college-prep track, students are likely to receive better instruction, have access to better facilities, and be pushed more nearly to their capacity than are those assigned to other tracks. The reason is clear: The teachers and administration expect great things from the one group and lesser things from the other. Moreover, these expectations are fulfilled. Those in the higher track do better, and those in the lower track do not. These behaviors justify the greater expenditures of time, faculties, and experimental curricula for those in the higher track—thus perpetuating what sociologist Robert Merton has called a "reign of error" (Merton, 1957:421–436).

An example comes from a controversial study by Rosenthal and Jacobson (1968). Although this study has been criticized for a number of methodological shortcomings, the findings are consistent with theories of interpersonal influence and with the labeling view of deviant behavior. In the spring of 1964, all students in an elementary school in San Francisco were given an IQ test. The following fall the teachers were given the names of children identified by the test as potential academic spurters, and five of these were assigned to each classroom. The spurters were chosen by means of a table of random numbers. The only difference between the experimental group (those labeled as spurters) and the control group (the rest of the class) was in the imaginations of the teachers. At the end of the year all the children were again tested, and the children from whom the teachers expected greater intellectual gains showed such gains (in IQ and grades). Moreover, they were rated by their teachers as being more curious, interesting, and happy, and more likely to succeed than the children in the control group.

The implications of this example are clear and profound. Teachers' expectations have a profound effect on students' performance. When students are overrated, they tend to overproduce; when they are underrated, they underachieve. The tracking system is a labeling process that affects the expectations of teachers (and fellow students and parents). The limits of these expectations are crucial in the educational process. Yet the self-fulfilling prophecy can work in a positive direction if teachers have an unshakable conviction that their students can learn. Concomitant with this belief, teachers should hold themselves, not the students, accountable if the latter should fail (Silberman, 1970:98). Used in this manner, the self-fulfilling prophecy can work to the benefit of all students.

Future Payoff. School is perceived as relevant for students going to college. Grades are a means of qualifying for college. For the non-college-bound student, however, school and grades are much less important for entry into a job. At most, they need a high school diploma, and grades really do not matter as long as one does not flunk out. Thus, non-college-bound students often develop negative attitudes toward school, grades, and teachers. These attitudes for students in the lower tracks are summed up by sociologist Arthur Stinchcombe:

> Rebellious behavior is largely a reaction to the school itself and to its promises, not a failure of the family or community. High school students can be motivated to conform by paying them in the realistic coin of future advantage. Except perhaps for pathological cases, any student can be motivated to conform if the school can realistically promise something valuable to him as a reward for working hard. But for a large part of the population, especially the adolescent who will enter the male working class or the female candidates for early marriage, the school has nothing to offer. . . . In order to secure conformity from students, a high school must articulate academic work with careers of students. (quoted in Schafer, Olexa, and Polk, 1972:49)

As we have seen, being on the lower track has negative consequences. These students are more rebellious both in school and out and do not participate as much in school activities. Finally, what is being taught is often not relevant to their world. Thus, we are led to conclude that many of these students tend to feel that they are not only second-class citizens but perhaps even pariahs (outcasts). What other interpretation is plausible in a system that disadvantages them, shuns them, and makes demands of them that are irrelevant?

The Student Subculture. The reasons given previously suggest that a natural reaction of students in the lower track would be to band together in a subculture that is antagonistic toward school. This subculture would quite naturally develop its own system of rewards, since those of the school are inaccessible.

These factors (stigma, negative self-fulfilling prophecy, low future payoff, and a contrary student subculture) show how the tracking system is at least partly responsible for the tendency of students in the lower tracks to be low achievers, unmotivated, uninvolved in school activities, and more prone to break school rules and drop out of school. To segregate students either by ability or by future plans is detrimental to the students labeled as inferior. It is an elitist system that for the most part takes the children of the elite and educates them to take the elite positions in society. Conversely, children of the non-elite are trained to repeat the experiences of their parents. In a presumably democratic system that prides itself on providing avenues of upward social mobility, such a system borders on immorality (Oakes, 1985).

The conclusion is inescapable: Inequality in the educational system causes many people to fail in U.S. schools. This phenomenon is the fault of the schools, not of the children who fail. To focus on these victims is to divert attention from the inadequacies of the schools. The blame needs to be shifted:

> We are dealing, it would seem, not so much with culturally deprived children as with culturally depriving schools. And the task to be accomplished is not to revise, and amend, and repair deficient children but to alter and transform the atmosphere and operations of the schools to which we commit these children. Only by changing the nature of the educational experience can we change its product. (Ryan, 1976:60)

Education from the Order and Conflict Perspectives

From the order perspective, schools are crucially important for the maintenance of social integration. They are a vital link between the individual and society, deliberately indoctrinating youth with the values of society and teaching the skills necessary to fit into society. Most important, the schools sift and sort children so that they will find and accept their appropriate niche in the societal division of labor.

The conflict perspective emphasizes that the educational system reinforces the existing inequalities in society by giving the advantaged the much greater probability of success (in grades, in achievement tests, in IQ tests, in getting an advanced education; all of which translate into economic and social success outside school). Conflict adherents also object to the **hidden curriculum** in schools—that is, learning to follow orders, to be quiet, to please people in authority regardless of the situation. In short, students learn to fit in, to conform. This may be functional for society and for students who will act out their lives in large bureaucracies, but it is not conducive to personal integrity and to acting out against situations that ought to be changed.

1. The U.S. system of education is characterized by (a) conservatism—the preservation of culture, roles, values, and training necessary for the maintenance of society; (b) belief in mass education; (c) local control; (d) competition; (e) reinforcement of the stratification system; and (f) preoccupation with order and control.

2. The belief that U.S. society is meritocratic, with the most intelligent and talented at the top, is a myth. Education, instead of being the great equalizer, reinforces social inequality.

3. Schools perform four functions that maintain the prevailing social, political, and economic order: (a) socializing the young; (b) shaping personality traits to conform with the demands of the culture; (c) preparing youngsters for adult roles; and (d) providing employers with a disciplined and skilled labor force.

4. The curricula, testing, bureaucratic control, and emphasis on competition in schools reflect the social class structure of society by processing youth to fit into economic slots similar to those of their parents.

5. The schools are structured to aid in the perpetuation of social and economic differences in three ways: (a) by being financed principally through property taxes; (b) by providing curricula that are irrelevant to the poor; and (c) by tracking according to presumed level of ability.

6. The tracking system is closely correlated with social class; students from low-income families are disproportionately placed in the lowest track. Tracking thwarts the equality of educational opportunity for the poor by generating four effects: (a) stigma, which lowers self-esteem; (b) self-fulfilling prophecy; (c) a perception of school as having no future payoff; and (d) a negative student subculture.

Key Terms

Tracking

Stigma

Self-fulfilling prophecy

Hidden curriculum

Study Questions

1. Formal education reinforces the status quo. Should it? Must it? Should there be some point in the educational process when schools promote a critical assessment of society? If so, when?

2. What is meant by the political economy of education?

3. What's right about the "No Child Left Behind" legislation? How could it be improved?

4. How does the formal system of education reinforce the social stratification system in society?

5. Contrast the order and conflict perspectives on formal education.

For Further Reading

James W. Loewen, *Lies My Teacher Told Me: Everything Your American History Textbook Got Wrong* (New York: Simon & Schuster, 1996).

National Center for Education Statistics, *The Condition of Education 2002*, NCES 2002-025, (Washington, DC: U.S. Department of Education).

Mitchell L. Stevens, *Kingdom of Children: Culture and Controversy in the Homeschooling Movement* (Princeton, NJ: Princeton University Press, 2001).

Schools and Inequality

Claude S. Fischer, Michael Hout, Martin Sanchez Jankowski, Samuel R. Lucas, Ann Swidler, and

Kim Voss, *Inequality by Design: Cracking the Bell Curve Myth* (Princeton, NJ: Princeton University Press, 1996).

Jonathan Kozol, *Savage Inequalities: Children in America's Schools* (New York: Crown, 1991).

Myra Sadker and David Sadker, *Failing at Fairness: How America's Schools Cheat Girls* (New York: Scribner, 1994).

Anne Wheelock, *Crossing the Tracks: How "Untracking" Can Save America's Schools* (New York: New Press, 1992).

Web Resources

http://www.census.gov/statab/www/
Go to this site to download the Statistical Abstract, which contains U.S. education statistics.

http://nces.ed.gov/
The National Center for Education Statistics collects and analyzes educational data.

http://www.crede.ucsc.edu/
The Center for Research on Education, Diversity and Excellence is a "federally funded research and development program focused on improving the education of students whose ability to reach their potential is challenged by language or cultural barriers, race, geographic location, or poverty."

http://nafeo.org/
This is the home of the National Association for Equal Opportunity in Higher Education. There are over 100 Black colleges and universities associated with NAFEO.

http://www.aauw.org/home.html
American Association of University Women "promotes education and equity for all women and girls."

http://dragon.ep.usm.edu/~caerda/
Chinese American Educational Research and Development Association (CAERDA) is a non-profit, international organization. It was founded in 1992 to "promote excellence in education for all students, particularly among Chinese and Chinese Americans."

http://www.sacnas.org/
The mission of SACNAS, Society for the Advancement of Chicanos and Native Americans in Science, is to "encourage Chicano/Latino and Native American students to pursue graduate education and obtain the advanced degrees necessary for research careers and science teaching professionals at all levels."

http://www.alternative-learning.org/
The Alternative Learning Organization promotes the education of children in a more "child-directed" way; that is, it looks to promote learning based on each child's "unique being."

http://www.uscharterschools.org
U.S. Charter Schools organization serves and supports the U.S. charter schools and educates others about them.

http://www.glsen.org/templates/about/index.html?section=25

The Gay, Lesbian and Straight Education Network (GLSEN) is an organization that looks to end anti-gay bias in schools. The network "strives to assure that each member of every school community is valued and respected regardless of sexual orientation or gender identity/expression."

http://www.edliberation.org/

A group of activists, educators, and researchers make up the Education for Liberation Network. This network of people is concerned about the lack of opportunity in education for African American young people. The site offers resources and information for people who share these concerns.

http://www.mpi-fg-koeln.mpg.de/index_en.html

The Max Planck Institute for the Study of Societies conducts research on the "self-organization and governance of society." The theme of research focuses on "the conditions under which modern societies may be able to solve problems through collective action."

http://learninfreedom.org/

This site talks about home schooling and some of the negative implications of socialization in schools.

The following excerpt is from a sermon by Robert H. Meneilly (1993), when he was senior pastor of the Village Presbyterian Church, Prairie Village, Kansas:

> Religion can be the greatest thing on earth or the worst. It can be the greatest healing therapy in society, or the greatest hazard to a society's health. It can be a democratic republic's greatest good or its worst threat.
>
> Look at the hot spots of the earth and you see religious extremists lighting the fuses—whether in Northern Ireland, Israel, Bosnia, or California. Religious extremists are breeding all kinds of "culture wars." Religion can breed all kinds of harassment, bigotry, prejudice, intolerance and deception.
>
> Religion is peculiar. When it is not in earnest, it doesn't hurt anyone, but it doesn't do any good either. When it is in earnest, it is a most powerful force for good or evil. . . . We Christians must face up to the fact that our Christianity has propagated, in the name of Jesus, devilish acts, bloody wars, awful persecutions, hate crimes and political chaos. . . . (E15)

In this regard, consider the statement by Osama bin Laden before September 11, 2001:

> By God's leave, we call on every Muslim who believes in God and hopes for reward to obey God's command to kill the Americans and plunder their possessions wherever he finds them and whenever he can. Likewise we call on the Muslim ulema and leaders and youth and soldiers to launch attacks against the armies of the American devils and against those who are allied with them from among the helpers of Satan. (quoted in Lewis, Bernard, 2001:5B).

Following the attacks on September 11, 2001, someone scribbled these words on a wall in Washington, DC: "Dear God, save us from the people who believe in you." To which columnist Maureen Dowd (2002) responded: "The atrocities and brutalities and repressions committed in the name of God fill us with a greater need for God or some spiritual solace" (7B).

Sociologists study religion for two fundamental reasons. First, religion is a ubiquitous phenomenon that has a tremendous impact on human behavior. Surveys find consistently that six out of ten Americans say that religion is "very important" to them in daily life and that religion can solve "all or most of today's problems" (summarized in Harper, 2004). In the words of sociologist Meredith McGuire (1992): "Religion is one of the most powerful, deeply felt, and influential forces in human society. It has shaped people's relationships with each other, influencing family, community, economic, and political life. . . . Religious values influence their actions, and religious meanings help them interpret their experiences" (3).

Second, sociologists study religion because of its influence on society and society's impact on religion. Religion is part of a larger social system, affected by and affecting the other institutions of the society—that is, patterns of the family, the economy, education, and the polity. Because religious trends may be responses to fundamental changes in society, and some religious ideas may constrain social behaviors in a narrowly prescribed manner, the understanding of any society is incomplete unless one comprehends the religion of that society.

But what is religion? The variety of activities and belief systems that have fallen under this rubric is almost infinite. There are some elements essential to religion, however, that allow us to distinguish it from other phenomena (taken from Nottingham, 1954:1–11). A starting point is that religion is a social construction—that is, it is created by people and is a part of culture. It is an integrated set of ideas by which a group attempts to explain the meaning of life and death. Religion is also a normative system, defining immorality and sin as well as morality and righteousness. Let us amplify some of these statements further.

- Religion deals with the ultimate of human concerns—the meaning of life and death. It provides answers as to the individual's place in society and in the universe.
- There is an emphasis on human conduct. There are prescriptions for what one ought to do as well as the consequences for one's misconduct.
- There is a distinction between the sacred and the secular. Some objects and entities are believed to have supernatural powers and are therefore treated with respect, reverence, and awe. What is sacred and what is not are a matter of belief. The range of items believed to be sacred is limitless. They may be objects (idols, altars, or amulets), animals or animal totems, parts of the natural world (sun, moon, mountains, volcanos, or rivers), transcendental beings (gods, angels, devils), or people (living or dead, such as prophets, messiahs, or saints).
- Because the sacred is held in awe, there are beliefs (theologies, cosmologies) to express and reinforce proper attitudes among believers about the sacred. The set of beliefs attempts to explain the meaning of life. McGuire (1992) says: "Religion shapes what the adherent knows about the world. This cosmic knowledge organizes the individual's perceptions of the world and serves as a basis for action" (16).
- **Ritual** consists of symbolic actions (for example, processions, sacraments, candles, chanting, singing) that reinforce the collective remembering of the group's shared meanings. Ritual, then, evokes shared understandings among the believers (awe, reverence, ecstasy, fear), which lead to group unity.
- An essential ingredient of religion is the existence of a community of believers. There must be a social group that shares a set of beliefs and practices, moral values, and a sense of community (a unique identity). Again, turning to McGuire (1992), "Coming together with fellow believers reminds members of what they collectively believe and value. It can also impart a sense of empowerment to accomplish their religious and everyday goals" (20).

One important consequence of a group of people having the same religious heritage and beliefs is unity. All believers, whether of high or low status, young or old, are united through the sharing of religious beliefs. Thus, religion, through the holding of common values to be cherished, sins to be avoided, rules to be followed, and symbols to be revered, integrates. Group unity is also accomplished through the universal feeling that God or the gods look on this particular group with special favor (the ethnocentric notion that "God is on our side"). An example of this is found in a verse of the national anthem of Great Britain:

> O lord our God, arise
> Scatter our enemies
> And make them fall.
> Confound their politics,
> Frustrate their knavish tricks,
> On thee our hopes, we fix,
> God save us all.

Another consequence of religion is that it constrains the behavior of the community of believers, thus providing a social control function. This is accomplished in two ways. First, there are explicit rules to obey that, if violated, are punished. Second, in the process of socialization, children internalize the religious beliefs and rules. In other words, they each develop a conscience, which keeps them in line through guilt and fear.

A final consequence of religion is the legitimation of social structures that have profane origins (Berger, 1967a:343–344). There is a strong tendency for religious beliefs to become intertwined with secular beliefs, thereby providing religious blessings to the values and institutions of society: "As recently as twenty years ago, clergy in the Dutch Reformed Church of South Africa still used the Bible (Genesis 9:18–27; Joshua 9:21–27) to defend apartheid, arguing that Blacks were considered the children of Ham and therefore destined to be the 'hewers of wood and the drawers of water'" (Parenti, Michael, 1994:121).

Similarly, in U.S. society, the church has endorsed a number of secular activities. The Puritan Church of the early settlers condoned witch hunts. The defeat of the Native Americans was justified by most Christian groups on the grounds that the Indians were heathens and in need of Christianity. Finally, most religious denominations sought biblical rationalizations for slavery (van den Berghe, 1967:82).

The same religious bases that promote group integration also divide. Religious groups tend to emphasize separateness and superiority, thereby defining others as inferior (infidels, heathens, heretics, or nonbelievers). There are some ten thousand extant religious sects—each with its own cosmology, each with its own answer for the meaning of life and death. Most assert that the other 9,999 not only have it completely wrong but are instruments of evil, besides (Krakauer, 2003:338). This occurs because each religious group tends to feel it has the way (and often the only way) to achieve salvation or reach nirvana or whatever the goal.

Religious differences accentuate the differences among societies, denominations, and even within local churches. Because religious groups have feelings of superiority, there may be conflict brought about by discrimination, competition for converts, or feelings of hatred. Also, because religious ideas tend to be strongly held, groups may split rather than compromise. Liberals and fundamentalists, even within

The Global Reach of the World's Major Religions

Some 70 percent of the world's inhabitants identify with one of five major world religions. The largest is Christianity, with some 2 billion followers (one-third of the world's population). This religion originated with a cult of the followers of Jesus of Nazareth. Its source of truth is the Bible.

Islam is the world's second largest religion (1.2 billion—about 20 percent of the world's population). It is also growing the fastest as eight of the ten countries in the world with the most rapid growth have Islamic majorities. Islam is the word of God (Allah) as revealed to Muhammad, God's messenger (born A.D. 570), who wrote the Koran (Qur'an). Its roots go back to Abraham (as do the roots of Christianity and Judaism). While Islam is found everywhere (there are 7 million in the United States), it is concentrated in the Arab countries of the Middle East, northern Africa, and Indonesia.

Judaism began with God's covenant with Abraham some 4,000 years ago, granting Abraham and his descendents exclusive rights to what is now Palestine and the designation as "God's chosen people." Following numerous battles and enslavement in Old Testament times, the Jews scattered during the first century, experiencing prejudice and persecution wherever they settled. There are only 15 million Jews worldwide, with 6 million residing in the United States.

Hinduism is the oldest of the world's major religions, dating back about 4,500 years. It is the third largest with over 800 million followers (14 percent of the world's population). Hinduism differs from Christianity, Islam, and Judaism in that it is polytheistic (several gods and goddesses with no one supreme being), and it has no single sacred text, but many. Also, unlike Christianity and Islam, Hindus do not proselytize or use force to add to their numbers. Hinduism grows primarily through high birth rates in India, its primary location. Hinduism is also found in Pakistan, southern Africa, and Indonesia (there are 1.4 million in the United States).

Buddhism has 350 million followers (6 percent of the world's population), primarily in Asia, with majorities in Thailand, Cambodia, Japan, and Myanmar (Burma). Siddhartha Gautama, born in 563 B.C., became the "Buddha." His message was that by living a rigidly prescribed life of meditation and proper conduct, one could achieve enlightenment, the highest level of human consciousness. Buddhism does not recognize a god or gods, since each human being has the potential of godliness.

These brief descriptions of the world's major religions mask the diversity of religious expression found within each (e.g., Christianity split into the Eastern Orthodox Church and the Roman Catholic Church in the eleventh century and then split again with the Protestant Reformation in the sixteenth century). Each religion is a powerful source of unity among its followers as well as division within the religion (fundamentalists and liberals, radicals and moderates, as well as denominations). For our purposes here, however, we focus on the global dimensions of these religions.

• Through missionary activity, the followers of a religion travel to various countries trying to convert nonbelievers to their religious beliefs (called proselytizing). For example, in 1900, about 9 percent of Africa's population was Christian. By 2000, that number had risen to 46 percent, with much of the increase the result of missionary activity (Jenkins, 2002:55). Or take the global reach of The Church of Latter-Day Saints (Mormons). This religion began in the United States and had (in 2000) some 5.1 million members in the United States. Because of a strong

the same religion, denomination, or local church, will, doubtless, disagree on numerous issues. A common result, of course, is division.

A major divisive characteristic of religion is its tendency, through established churches, to accept the acts of the state. Within the church, there have always been people who spoke out against the church's cohabitation with the secular. This ability of the church to rationalize the activities of the state, no matter how onerous, has split many churches and denominations. The slavery issue, for example, split Baptists into American Baptists and Southern Baptists.

The Global Reach of the World's Major Religions continued

missionary zeal (young Mormon men give two years to missionary activity), there are now some 2.5 million Mormons in South America, 711,000 in Asia, 228,000 in Europe, as well as hundreds of thousands each in Mexico, Central America, the South Pacific, United Kingdom, Canada, Africa, and the Caribbean (Sheler, 2000:61).

- Historically, some religions have used military actions to convert nonbelievers (e.g., the Crusades were attempts by European Christians to drive Muslims out of the Holy Land; part of the zeal behind the colonial expansion of the sixteenth and seventeenth centuries was a missionary zeal to convert the indigenous peoples of these non-Christian lands to Christianity).
- Religious ideology is the source of tensions, political instability, terrorism, and wars. In contemporary times, there are many examples, such as Muslims versus Hindus in India and Pakistan; Muslims versus Jews in the Middle East; Catholics versus Protestants in Northern Ireland; Catholics and Christian Serbs fighting Bosnian and Kosovar Muslims in the Balkans; Muslim guerrillas versus Catholics in the Philippines; clashes between Christians and Muslims in Indonesia and Nigeria; Hindus fighting Buddhists in Sri Lanka; and Muslim extremists using terrorist attacks against Christian targets worldwide.
- While there are nations in which one religion prevails (e.g., Saudi Arabia is 99 percent Muslim), immigration brings religious diversity to other nations. Both Europe and the United States, for example, are experiencing an influx of non-Christian immigrants. These immigrants practice the religions of their country of origin, build churches, mosques, or temples, and often send their children to religious-based schools.

- Policy decisions by governments are sometimes affected by religious ideology. For example, the voting in the United Nations often divides Muslim and Christian nations. U.S. policy toward Israel is consistently pro-Jewish, regardless of whether Republicans or Democrats are in power. Abortion politics in the United States, which divide liberals and conservatives and have a strong religious component for some (e.g., the Christian Right), have implications for policy. For instance, in 2002, President George W. Bush canceled the financial contribution of the United States to the United Nations Population Fund, a fund providing poor women worldwide with access to prenatal care, family planning, and other reproductive health services. Similarly, some religious traditions are a primary force of backlash against modernization (e.g., the Taliban in Afghanistan, the Muslim clerics in Iran).

The globalization of religion is ironically creating crises within nations. Sociologist David Newman (2000) says:

> Exposure to competing worldviews challenges traditional beliefs. In some cases, religions have reacted with a forceful revitalization of ancient, fundamentalist traditions. Witness the growing trend toward governments defining themselves in narrowly religious terms. The ascension of fundamentalist Islamic governments in Iran and Afghanistan, the growing influence of orthodox Jews in Israeli politics, and the continuing conflict between Christians and Muslims in Bosnia and Kosovo attest to the fact that many people today believe religion cannot be separated from a nation's social and political destiny. (295)

Conflict itself can occur between religious groups (with the sanction of each religion). Recent events in Iraq, Lebanon, Palestine, Ireland, Nigeria, the Philippines, Indonesia, and Bosnia provide bloody evidence of this occurrence (see the panel titled "Globalization: The Global Reach of the World's Major Religions"). Religious conflict has also occurred within the United States at various times. Confrontations between Catholics and Protestants, Christians and Muslims, between warring sects of Muslims, as well as between Protestants and Jews, have been fairly commonplace. Clearly, religious values are reason enough for individuals and groups to clash.

Classical Sociology's Differing Interpretations of Religion

The great classical sociologists—Emile Durkheim (1858–1917), Karl Marx (1818–1883), and Max Weber (1864–1920)—wrote perceptively about religion. From different perspectives and asking different questions, each theorist adds to our sociological understanding of the differing consequences of religion on society and its members.

Religion from the Order Perspective of Emile Durkheim

Durkheim, the French sociologist, wrote *The Elementary Forms of Religious Life* in 1912 (1965). This classic work explored the question of why religion is universal in human societies. He reasoned that religion must help maintain society. Durkheim studied the religion of the Australian aborigines to understand the possible role of religion in societal survival.

Durkheim found that each aborigine clan had its own totem, an object it considered sacred. The totem—a kangaroo, lizard, tree, river, or rock formation—was sacred because the clan believed that it symbolized the unique qualities of the clan. Two of Durkheim's interpretations are important in this regard. First, people bestow the notion of the sacred onto something, rather than that object being intrinsically sacred. Second, what the group worships is really society itself. Thus, people create religion.* Because the members of a society share religious beliefs, they are a moral community and as such the solidarity of the society is enhanced.

The society is held together by religious rituals and festivals in which the group's values and beliefs are reaffirmed. Each new generation is socialized to accept these beliefs, ensuring consensus on what is right and wrong. Religion, then, whether it be among the preindustrial Australian aborigines, the Muslims of the Middle East, the Buddhists of Asia, or the Christians of North America, serves the same functions of promoting order and unity. In short, as people meet to affirm common beliefs and values, they are bound together in a moral community.

Religion from the Conflict Perspective of Karl Marx

Whereas Durkheim interpreted the unity achieved through religion as positive, Marx viewed it as negative. Religion inhibits societal change by making existing social arrangements seem right and inevitable. The dominant form of economics in society, the type of government, the law, and other social creations are given religious sanction. Thus, the system remains stable, which the order theorists see as good, when it perhaps should be transformed to meet the needs of all of the people.

---

*This raises an important question: Do we create God or is there a supernatural force somewhere that human beings grope to find? Durkheim is correct in stating that religion is a social product. This universal response, however, does not prove or disprove the existence of God (or gods). Sociologists as individuals may have strong religious beliefs, but as sociologists they focus on the complex relationship between religion and society.

Religion promotes the status quo in other ways. The powerless are taught to accept religious beliefs that are against their own interests. The Hindus, for example, believe that it is each person's duty to accept his or her caste. Failure to do so will result in being reincarnated to a lower caste or even as an animal.

> A good example of [the legitimation of inequality through religion] occurs in Hinduism in which the concepts of karma, dharma, and samsara combine to explain and justify the continuous inequality generation after generation. Karma indicates the belief that a person's present situation is the result of his or her actions in a previous life, and dharma refers to the duties and norms attached to each caste. Finally, samsara refers to the continual birth and rebirth of life. In other words, central beliefs in Hinduism absolve society or others from responsibility for social inequality. It is the result of individual actions. (Hurst, 2001:309–310)

Christianity proclaims that the poor should accept their lot in this life, for they will be rewarded. As the Bible says, "The meek shall inherit the earth." This says, in effect, do not assert yourself, accept oppression, and good things will happen ultimately. From this perspective, oppression and poverty are reinterpreted by religion to be a special form of righteousness. Thus, religion is the ultimate tool to promote false consciousness.

Max Weber's View of Religion and Social Change

Max Weber disagreed fundamentally with Marx's notions that (1) religion impedes social change by being an **opiate of the masses** and by encouraging the oppressed to accept their lot, and that (2) economic considerations supersede ideology. Weber's 1904 classic *The Protestant Ethic and the Spirit of Capitalism* (1958) refuted Marx on both grounds. Weber demonstrated that the religious beliefs of John Calvin (1509–1564) were instrumental to the rise of capitalism in Europe. The Calvinist doctrine of predestination was the key. Because God, by definition, knows everything, God knows who will go to heaven (the elect) and who will be condemned to hell *even before they are born.* This view was disconcerting to believers because it meant that one's future was locked in (predestined). Calvinists dealt with their anxiety by emphasizing economic success as the indicator to themselves and others of being one of God's elect. The rationale for this emphasis was that surely God would reward the chosen in this life as well as in the afterlife. This belief led Calvinists to work very hard, to live frugally, to accumulate savings, and to invest those savings in more land, equipment, and labor. Thus, the particular religious beliefs of the Calvinists were conducive to the development of capitalism in Europe and later among the colonies in America. Religious ideology, in this case, led to economic change.

Religious ideology has led to social changes in other settings as well. Martin Luther King, Jr., and the Southern Christian Leadership Council used religion to inspire followers to break down racial segregation in the United States. Liberation theology practiced by many priests and nuns and their followers in Central and South America fueled protest against many Latin American dictatorships. Similarly, Catholicism was a force for change in communist Eastern Europe (Hurst, 2001:311).

Some Distinctive Features of U.S. Religion

Civil Religion

One feature of U.S. religion, traditionally, has been the separation of church and state (established by the First Amendment to the Constitution). This is both a consequence and the cause of the religious diversity found in the United States. There is a relationship between religion and the state in the United States, but it differs from the usual conception of one dominant church that is inseparable from the state. In many respects, "God and country" are conceived by most people as one. This notion that the United States and its institutions are sanctified by God has been labeled the civil religion of the United States (Bellah, 1967).

Civil religion in the United States is seemingly antithetical to the constitutional demand for separation of church and state. The paradox is that the government sanctions God as "religious imagery, language, and concepts [that] pervade public discourse, appear on the currency, and are present in the pledge to the flag" (Wilcox, 2000:16). Every presidential inaugural address except Washington's second has mentioned God; and present-day presidents have regularly scheduled prayer breakfasts, while at the same time declaring it illegal to have prayer and/or religious instruction in the public schools. The basis for the paradox is that the civil religion is not a specific creed. It is a set of beliefs, symbols, and rituals that are broad enough for all citizens to accept. The God of the civil religion is all things to all people. One thing is certain—politicians, if they want to be successful, must show some semblance of piety by occasionally invoking the blessings of this nondenominational, nonsectarian God.

Several central themes of the civil religion are important for understanding U.S. society. First, there is the belief that God has a special destiny for the United States, that it has been chosen by God to fulfill His will (Wilcox, 2000:16). This implies that God is actively involved in history and, most important, that the country has a holy

Globalization

Outsourcing Prayer

Outsourcing is the practice of shifting work done domestically to an entity in another society. An unusual version of outsourcing is where Catholic clergy, in short supply in the United States, Canada, and Europe, ask priests in India to say Mass for special intentions.

In Kerala, [the Indian state with the largest concentration of Catholics] often receive intentions from overseas. The Masses are conducted in Malayalam, the native language. The intention—often a prayer for the repose of the soul of a deceased relative, or for a sick family member, thanksgiving for a favor received, or a prayer offering for a newborn—is announced at Mass.

The requests are mostly routed to Kerala's churches through the Vatican, the bishops or through religious bodies. Rarely, prayer requests come directly to individual priests.

In Kerala's churches, memorial and thanksgiving prayers conducted for local residents are said for a donation of 40 rupees (90 cents), whereas a prayer request from the United States typically comes with $5. . . .

Bishop Adayanthrath said sending Mass intentions overseas was a way for rich churches short on priests to share and support smaller churches in poorer parts of the world. (Rai, 2004:13)

mission to carry out God's will on earth. John F. Kennedy phrased this message well in the conclusion to his inaugural address: "With a good conscience our only sure reward, with history the final judge of our deeds, let us go forth to lead the land we love, asking His blessing and His help, but knowing that here on earth God's work must truly be our own" (quoted in Bellah, 1967:1–2). This belief has been the source of self-righteousness in foreign relations. It has allowed people to subdue the pagan Indians, win the frontier, follow a policy of manifest destiny, and defeat fascism and communism. President Reagan, for example, exhorted people in the United States to understand that communism was evil and that God wanted us to be strong. Thus, he invoked Scripture to justify a strong defense:

> I found myself wanting to remind you of what Jesus said in Luke 14:31: "Oh, what king, when he sets out to make [war]—or meet another king in battle will not first sit down and take counsel whether he is strong enough with 10,000 men to encounter the one coming against him with 20,000. Or else, while the other is still far away, sends a delegation and asks the terms of peace." I don't think the Lord that blessed this country, as no other country has ever been blessed, intends for us to have to some-day negotiate because of our weakness. (quoted in Pierard and Linder, 1988:280)

Similarly, President George H. W. Bush argued that God was on our side in the Persian Gulf War: "During the 1992 presidential campaign, Bush cited Jesus Christ as the moral force behind his military interventionism, claiming that during the Persian Gulf war 'America, as Christ ordained' was 'a light unto the world'" (Parenti, Michael, 1992:43).

President George W. Bush in an address to the nation on the first anniversary of the terrorist acts said this:

> We cannot know all that lies ahead. Yet we do know that God has placed us together in this moment, to grieve together, to stand together, to serve each other and our country. And the duty we have been given—defending America and our freedom— is also a privilege we share.
>
> We are prepared for this journey. And our prayer tonight is that God will see us through, and keep us worthy.

As a final example of the presidential invoking of God, recent presidents, including George W. Bush, end their speeches with the prayer "God bless America."

A second aspect of the civil religion is maintenance of the status quo. The God of civil religion is more closely allied to law and order than to changing the system. Thus, civil religion tends strongly toward uncritical endorsement of U.S. values and the system of stratification. Order and unity are the traditional ways of God, not change and dissent. Thus, public policy tends to receive religious sanction.

At the same time, however, the civil religion enjoins people in the United States to stand up for certain principles—freedom, individualism, equal opportunity. Consequently, there are occasions when current governmental policy or the policy of some group is criticized because it does not measure up to certain ideals. The civil religion of the United States, then, accomplishes both the **priestly role of religion** (acceptance of what is) and the **prophetic role of religion** (challenging the existing system), with emphasis, however, on the former.

The Variety of Religious Beliefs in the United States

Some societies are unified by religion. All people in those societies believe the same religious ideas, worship the same deities, obey the same moral commandments, and identify strongly with each other. Superficially, through its civil religion, the United States appears to be homogeneous along religious lines. In 2004, some 96 percent of Americans professed to believe in God or a universal spirit. About 85 percent of Americans identify themselves as Christians. And, 6 out of 10 Americans say that religion is "very important" to them in daily life (Harper, 2004). While Christians are the clear majority in the United States, there are also about 7 million Jews, 7 million Muslims, and millions of other non-Christians, including Buddhists and Hindus as well as atheists (see the panel titled "Diversity: Islam in the United States").

There are about seven million Muslims in the United States, outnumbering Jews, or Episcopalians, or Presbyterians.

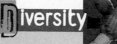

Islam in the United States

Islam has about 1.2 billion followers worldwide, second only to Christianity (the following is taken from Culver, 2001; and Grossman, 2001; Power, 1998a; Sheler, 2001). Muslims believe in one god, Allah, as their creator and the sustainer of the universe. They accept the Hebrew Bible, and venerate Jesus as a prophet. The founder of Islam was Muhammad, an Arab born in Mecca about A.D. 570 who is believed to be Allah's messenger. Islamic scripture, the Koran, is a recording of divine revelation as revealed by the prophet Muhammad. Observant Muslims perform five key duties (the Five Pillars of Islam): accepting no god but Allah and Muhammed as his prophet, prayer five times a day, fasting during the ninth month in the Islamic lunar year, giving to charity, and making a pilgrimage to Mecca at least once in a lifetime.

Islam is the nation's fastest-growing faith, with about 7 million adherents in the United States, nearly double the number of a decade ago. Muslims outnumber Jews, Episcopalians, and Presbyterians in the United States. About 1 million Muslims live in California, 800,000 in New York, and 420,000 in Illinois (300,000 in Chicago). Their growth in the United States is evidenced by the fifteenfold growth in the number of Islamic houses of worship (mosques) since 1960—from 104 to 1,209 in 2001. More than half of American Muslims reside in ten states—California, New York, Illinois, New Jersey, Indiana, Michigan, Virginia, Texas, Ohio, and Maryland.

American Muslims are not a monolithic group. Some 64 percent were born in 80 different countries; 35 percent were born in the United States. The ethnic makeup in mosques is 33 percent South Asian, including people from such countries as India, Pakistan, Bangladesh, and Sri Lanka, 30 percent African American, and 25 percent from the Arab world. Of the U.S.-born converts to Islam, 42 percent are African Americans. Although most Muslims are conservative on social issues (opposing abortion, premarital sex, homosexuality, divorce, alcohol use, and dancing), there are differences in beliefs and levels of activism. For example, although Muslim women are encouraged to dress modestly, their clothing varies from head scarfs and floor-length dresses to fashions not unlike that of other U.S. women. Only 10 percent of U.S. Muslims practice Islam's five pillars. Like any other religious group, Muslims have different sects within; there are Sunnis and Shiites (they differ on who are the descendents of Muhammad); there are about 20,000 who belong to Louis Farrakhan's Nation of Islam.

Their religion differs from Christianity, they are typically people of color, and they are stereotyped as religious and political zealots. Therefore, Muslims in the United States are often objects of discrimination, hostility, and hate crimes. During the Gulf War of the early 1990s and following the September 11, 2001, terrorist attacks, hate crimes (arsons, bombings, physical assaults) against Arab Americans surged. In both historical instances, FBI agents surveilled business and community leaders of Arab descent. Immediately after the terrorist attacks on the Trade Center and Pentagon, Arabs were singled out at airports and other sensitive places for surveillance and questioning. Four years after 9/11, Muslim, South Asian, and Arab-American employees continue to report discrimination on the job (Armour, 2005). In short, Muslims are marginalized. As Ghazi Khankan, president of the National Council on Islamic Affairs, has put it: "To demonize, to dehumanize my people, my way of life, my religion is unfair, un-American and undemocratic" (quoted in Sontag, 1993:19).

The proportions by religious affiliation are:

- Protestant, 52 percent
- Catholic, 23 percent
- Jewish, 4 percent
- Muslim, 4 percent
- No affiliation, 14 percent (this category includes atheists, but it consists mostly of people who believe in Christian basics) (Van Biema, 2004).

The range of attitudes and beliefs among U.S. Christians is fantastically wide. Among Roman Catholics, for example, there are radical priests, nuns, and parishioners who disobey the instructions of bishops, cardinals, and even the pope. At the same time, however, there are Catholics who rigidly adhere to all the rules set down by the church authorities. Some even insist on Masses where Latin is spoken. The range within Protestantism is even greater. Many Protestants believe that the Bible is to be taken literally, word for word; for others, the Bible is purely allegorical. Some religious groups have so much faith in the healing power of religion that their members refuse to see physicians under any circumstances. Within Protestantism are Amish, Hutterites, Quakers, high-church Episcopalians, Pentecostal Holiness groups, Congregationalists, and even snake handlers.

Religious Organization

Very broadly, U.S. religious organizations can be divided according to their secular commitments into two categories—churches and sects (Troeltsch, 1931). Religious groups have a choice—to reject and withdraw from the secular society, or to accommodate to it. The basis for a decision to reject the social environment is maintenance of spiritual and ethical purity. Such a choice, by definition, entails withdrawal from the world, thereby consciously avoiding any chance to change it. The opposite choice—accommodation—requires compromise and the loss of distinctive ideals, but it also means that the groups can influence the larger society. The accommodation or resistance to the secular world is the fundamental difference between a church and a sect.

A **church**, as an ideal type (that is, in its purest form), has the following attributes:

- The tendency to compromise with the larger society and its values and institutions.
- Membership that tends to occur by being born to parents who belong.
- Membership, moreover, takes place through infant baptism, which implies that all members are saved.
- A hierarchy of authority, with those at the top being trained for their vocation.
- Acceptance of a diversity of beliefs, because the membership is large; for many, the scriptures are interpreted metaphorically rather than literally.
- Tolerance of the popular vices.

"We're thinking maybe it's time you started getting some religious instruction. There's Catholic, Protestant, and Jewish—any of those sound good to you?"

A **sect** in its perfect form is exactly opposite a church in every way:

- There is a fundamental withdrawal from and rejection of the world. A sect is a moral community separate from and in many ways hostile toward the secular world.
- Membership is only through a conversion experience. Membership is therefore voluntary and limited to adults. Hence, adult baptism is the only accepted form of baptism.
- Organization is informal and unstructured. Ministers are untrained. They became ministers by being called from the group.
- The belief system is rigid. The Bible is the source, and it is interpreted literally. The goal of the membership is spiritual purity as found in the early Christian Church.
- There are rigid ethical requirements restraining the members from the popular vices of drinking, smoking, card playing, dancing, and cursing.

The church–sect dichotomy does not exhaust all the possibilities. Some religious groups fit somewhere in between—as institutionalized sects. These groups (for example, Mormons, Disciples of Christ, and Southern Baptists) incorporate features of both a church (trained leadership, some accommodation to the larger society) with the sectlike attributes of adult baptism and an unwillingness to compromise on some theological questions.

For our purposes, however, the church–sect dichotomy, while oversimplifying the situation, is useful in two ways: to depict a form of social change, and to show why certain categories of people are attracted to one type and not the other.

The church–sect dichotomy illustrates an important sociological phenomenon—the process of organization deflects away from the original goal of the group. A group may form to pursue a goal such as religious purity, but in so doing it creates a new organization, which means that some of the group's energies will be spent in organizational maintenance. Consequently, a sect may form with the explicit intention of eliminating a hierarchy and a codification of beliefs. Patterns of behavior emerge, however, as certain practices are found to be more effective. In particular, the selection of ministers tends to become routinized, and a system of religious instruction for children is developed so that they will learn the catechism in the proper sequence.

Sects, then, tend to become churches. This is illustrated by the type of leader found in each. Often a sect is formed by a charismatic person and his or her followers. This person is followed because he or she is believed to possess extraordinary qualities of leadership, saintliness, gifts of prophecy, or ability to heal.

What happens to such an organization when this leadership is gone? The organization is faced with a crisis of succession. Groups typically find ways to pass on the charisma (the extraordinary attributes) of the original leader. This process is called the **routinization of charisma** (whereby an organization attempts to transmit the charisma of the former leader to a new one). This is done by (1) selection of the successor by the original charismatic leader, (2) designation of a successor by the group closest to the original leader ("disciples"), (3) hereditary transmission, or (4) transmission of charisma by ritual ("laying on of hands") (Weber, 1947:358–366). In this last instance there is the recognition of a **charisma of office**—that is, whoever holds the position possesses charisma. When this occurs, the organizational machinery is advanced enough to move the group away from its sectlike qualities toward a church. The important sociological point here is that organizations seldom remain the same. The simple tends to become complex. But the process does not stop at complexity; as the original goal of the sect (religious purity with the necessity of separation from the world) is superseded when the organization gets larger and more bureaucratic, some persons will become dissatisfied enough to break away and form a new sect. Thus, the process tends to be cyclical.

Increased bureaucratization (and subsequent splintering) is characteristic of modern urban society. This leads us to a final consideration relative to the church–sect dichotomy—the motivation to join sects. At the risk of oversimplification, two important features of sects help explain why some categories of people are especially prone to join sects rather than churches. The first is that a sect (more so than a church) may provide a total world of meaning and social identity and a close circle of people to whom members can turn when troubled. The sect provides precisely those things missing in the lives of many who live in large metropolitan areas and work in huge bureaucracies, and whose world is rapidly changing. They find meaning in a meaningless world. They find friends in a sea of strangers. They find stability in a setting that is rapidly undergoing change. Thus, the alienated are especially attracted to sects. So, too, are new migrants to the city. In the city, they are confronted with a variety of new and difficult problems—industrialized work, work insecurity, loss of kinship ties, and disruption of other primary-group ties. The sects, unlike the established city churches, appeal to such people through their form of worship, emphasis on individual attention, and lack of formal organization (Yinger, 1961:21–25).

A second variable affecting attraction to a sect or church is social class. Generally, low-status people tend to be attracted to sects rather than to churches because religious status is substituted for social status (or as the Bible puts it, "and the last shall be first"). It makes sense for people of low social or economic status to reject this world and the religious bodies that accommodate to it. Such people would be especially attracted to a religious group that rejects this world and assures its followers that in the next world true believers—those who are religiously pure—will have the highest status. The sect represents to its followers a reaction against or escape from the dominant religious and economic systems in society. It is a protest against the failure of established churches to meet the needs of marginal groups (Pope, 1942:140). The sect, moreover, rejects the social class as irrelevant and, in fact, as a system of rewards that is in exact reverse order from God's will.*

Churches, on the other hand, attract the middle and upper classes. Since these people are successful, they obviously would not turn to a religious organization that rejects their world. As Max Weber (1963) has said: "Other things being equal, classes with high social and economic privilege will scarcely be prone to evolve the ideas of salvation. Rather, they assign to religion the primary function of legitimizing their own life pattern and situation in this world" (107).

Both the sect and the church, consequently, have well-developed theodicies (Berger, 1967b). A **theodicy** is a religious legitimation for a situation that otherwise might cause guilt or anger (such as defeat in a war or the existence of poverty among affluence). Sects tend to have a theodicy of suffering—that is, a religious explanation for their lack of power and privilege. Churches must explain the inequalities of soci-

---

*It is incorrect to say, however, that all lower-class people who are alienated will join religious sects in order to attack the establishment. Their estrangement may lead them to join other kinds of social movements (for example, labor or political) or toward social isolation.

The Heaven's Gate Cult

The Heaven's Gate cult began in 1975 when Marshall Applewhite (known in the cult as "Do") and his colleague Bonnie Lee Trusdale ("Ti") persuaded followers to leave their families and belongings behind and join them in their quest to leave the "Human Kingdom" and join the "Kingdom of Heaven." Twenty-two years later, in 1997, Do, Ti, and thirty-seven of their followers engaged in a mass suicide in San Diego. Suicides by cult members are not like suicides in the traditional sense of despair and hopelessness. Rather, it is following the orders of a charismatic leader who had convinced them that through suicide they would pass to a higher state of being (Hinman, 1997).

Applewhite's message was that the end of the world is near and that by leaving their fleshly container (their bodies), they would join with others in an enraptured state. His message was "part Christian, part Asian mystic, part Gnostic, part X-Files" (Lacayo, 1997:45). Or, as Stephen Jay Gould characterized it: "[The Heaven's Gate mixed] traditional millenarianism [an apocalyptic prediction of the end times] with American pop culture myths of science fiction in general, and UFOlogy in particular" (Gould, 1997:53). When the comet Hale-Bopp appeared, Applewhite taught that its tail was a shield for a UFO that would transport his followers to the "Kingdom of Heaven." He chose March 22 as the time for the mass suicide, a time when Hale-Bopp was approaching its closest point to earth. This time also coincided with a full moon, a lunar eclipse in parts of the United States, and the next day was Palm Sunday, the beginning of the Christian Holy Week. The following is from the Heaven's Gate website:

As was promised–the keys to Heaven's Gate are here again to Ti and Do (the UFO two) as they were in Jesus and His Father 2000 years ago. [The arrival of Hale-Bopp] is joyously very significant to us at "Heaven's Gate." The joy is that our Older Member in the Evolutionary Level above Human (the "Kingdom of Heaven") has made it clear to us that Hale-Bopp's approach is the "marker" we've been waiting for—the time for the arrival of the spacecraft from the Level Above Human to take us home to "Their World"—in the literal Heavens. Our 22 years of classroom here on planet Earth is finally coming to conclusion—"graduation" from the Human Evolutionary Level. We are happily prepared to leave "this world" and go with Ti's crew. (Heaven's Gate, 1997)

ety, too, but their emphasis is on legitimation of possessing power and privilege. This tendency to develop theodicies has the important social function of preserving the status quo. Churches convince their adherents that all is well, that one should accept one's fate as God-given. This makes people's situations less intolerable and the possibility of revolution remote—the suffering know they will be rewarded, while the guilt of the well-off is assuaged. Consequently, there is no reason to change the system.

Cults. A **cult** is a new religion with practices and teachings at odds with the dominant culture and religion. In other words, a cult rejects society and established religions. Typically, the members of a cult give extreme devotion to a charismatic leader who requires much of them (their material goods, their work, a demanding lifestyle, and a total, intense commitment). A cult differs from a sect in one fundamental way. A sect is a religious group that leaves an established church to recapture what it considers the essence of its religious tradition. A cult, on the other hand, represents religious innovation, a new religious expression.

We tend to think of cults and their followers as bizarre (for example, the mass suicides by the followers of Jim Jones's People's Temple and Heaven's Gate). (See the panel titled "A Closer Look: The Heaven's Gate Cult.") They are, by definition, different from the rest of us; they reject society and claim to have religious experiences that are alien to most of us. Many of these groups ultimately fail. The message fades; the predictions misfire; the charismatic leader dies and his or her replacement disappoints. But while we tend to think of these groups as weird and transitory, we should remember that many of the major religious groups of today, including Christianity, Mormonism, Islam, and Judaism, began as cults.

Class, Race, Gender, Sexuality, and Religion

The Relationship between Social Class and Religion

The dominant religion in the United States, Christianity, stresses the equality of all people in the sight of God. All people, regardless of socioeconomic status, are welcomed in Christianity. We might expect, therefore, that the distribution of members by socioeconomic status within any denomination would be randomly distributed. We might also assume that the organization of any local congregation would ignore status distinctions. Although these two assumptions seem to have surface validity, the empirical situation refutes them.

We have seen that sects and churches tend to have a social-class bias—the lower the socioeconomic status, the greater the probability of belonging to a sect. There also seems to be a ranking of denominations in terms of the socioeconomic status of their members. Although there is always a range of social classes within any one denomination, there is a modal status that characterizes each. The reasons for this are varied: the proportion of members living in rural or urban areas, which immigrant groups brought the religion to the colonies or United States and during what historical period, and the appeal of the religious experience (ritual, evangelism, close personal ties, salvation, legitimation of the social system, or attacks on the establishment). This last point is especially important because "life conditions affect men's religious propensities, and life conditions are significantly correlated with the facts of stratification in all societies" (O'Dea, 1966:60).

There is a relationship between economic status, educational attainment, and denominational affiliation. Judaism has the highest proportion of high-education and high-income members, followed in order by Episcopalian, Presbyterian, Methodist, Lutheran, Catholic, and Baptist. This is an oversimplification, however, since each denomination includes people of high, middle, and low economic and educational status.

Local churches, even more so than denominations, tend to be homogeneous in socioeconomic status. This is partly the result of residential patterns—that is, neighborhoods are relatively homogeneous by socioeconomic status, and the local churches are attended mostly by people living nearby. Another reason, and perhaps just as important, is the tendency for people to want to belong to organizations composed of people like themselves. They do not want to feel out of place, so they are attracted to churches where the members have the same lifestyle (for example, speech patterns, clothing tastes, and educational backgrounds). The result, then, is that people belonging to a particular denomination often seek out the local congregation where they feel most comfortable.

There is some range, however, in every local church. Probably no one congregation is composed totally of people from exactly the same status niche. Although the status differentials may be minimal within a local congregation, they are evidently important to the parishioners. The rule is that the higher the socioeconomic status of the member, the greater his or her influence in the running of the local church. There is greater likelihood that such people will be elected or appointed to office (elder, deacon, trustee, Sunday school superintendent) and that their opinions will carry greater weight than those of people of lower social status. This may be partly a function of the disproportionately large financial contributions by the more well-to-do, but the important point here is that the secular world intrudes in the organization of each local congregation. The common indicators of religious involvement—church membership, attendance at church services, and participation in the church's activities—demonstrate a relationship to socioeconomic status. On each of these measures, people of high status are more involved than those of low status. Unfortunately, these are not very good measures of religiosity, although they are often assumed to be. The problem is that upper-class people are much more likely to join and actively participate in all sorts of organizations. The joining of churches and attending services are the manifestations of a more general phenomenon—the tendency for middle- and upper-class people to be joiners, while lower-class individuals tend to isolate themselves from all types of organizations. The spuriousness of the relationship between socioeconomic status and religiosity is more clearly seen when we analyze the importance of religion to people of varying socioeconomic circumstances, as well as differences in religious beliefs and the degree to which church activities are secular by social class.

William J. Goode (1966), after comparing white-collar church members with working-class church members, found that while the former were more likely to belong to and participate in formal activities of the church, the latter were actually more religious:

> They participate less in formal church activities, but their religious activity does not appear to be nearly so secularized. It is more specifically religious in character. This is indicated by the fact that on a number of other religious dimensions, dimensions not dependent on extraneous nonreligious variables, individuals of manual-status levels appear to display a considerably higher level of religious response. This is true particularly of psychological variables, such as religious "salience," the greater feeling that the church and religion are great forces in the lives of respondents. It is also true for "religiosity" as measured by a higher level of religious concern, and for religious "involvement," the extent to which the individual is psychologically dependent on some sort of specifically religious association in his life. (111)

There is evidence for the "secularization of religion" by social class. Polling data reveals that the more education and income one has, the less likely one is to find religion important and to hold traditional religious beliefs. Table 17.1 provides data to support this.

In summary, there is a rather complex relationship between socioeconomic status and religion. Although the relatively poor and uneducated are more likely to be indifferent to religion than are the better educated and financially well-off, those who are religious tend to make religion a more integral part of their lives than do better-off people. They go to church more for religious than secular reasons. They believe much more strongly than do the well-to-do in the fundamental beliefs as expressed in the Bible. Thus, we have the paradox that on many objective measures of religious involvement—church attendance and participation in formal church activities—middle- and upper-status people exceed those of less status, whereas if

TABLE 17.1

The Importance of Religion Question: How Important Would You Say Religion Is in Your Own Life?

Variable	Very Important	Fairly Important	Not Very Important
Income			
$75,000+	46%	36%	17%
$50,000–74,999	51	33	15
$30,000–49,999	62	26	11
$20,000–29,000	56	29	13
Under $20,000	76	18	6
Education			
Beyond BA	50%	30%	18%
Bachelor's degree	55	31	12
Some college	58	27	14
High school or less	69	25	6

Source: The Gallup Poll Monthly, 1997. No. 378 (March):26.

importance of religion in the lives of the individual is considered, the poor who go to church outstrip their more economically favored brethren.

Religion and Race: The Case of African Americans

As with other social phenomena, race and religion separate people. As noted earlier, historically most White churches in the United States chose to ignore or to actively support racial segregation. The issue of the legitimacy of slavery divided some White congregations and denominations. For example, the Southern Baptist Convention was a denomination conceived out of support for slavery. In 1995, 150 years after taking that proslavery stand, the Southern Baptist Convention passed a resolution confessing to a sin of historic proportion: "We lament and repudiate historic acts of evil such as slavery from which we continue to reap a bitter harvest" (quoted in Sheler, 1995:10). Similarly, Pope John Paul II apologized for the church's complicity in the African slave trade. Also, of historic importance to Blacks everywhere, the Dutch Reformed Church in 1991 formally apologized to Black South Africans for having provided religious justification for apartheid. While these sweeping apologies are important symbolically, we should note that they were slow in coming. It took the Southern Baptists, for example, 150 years—and a full thirty years after the height of the civil rights struggle—to finally admit to their support of racism.

Local churches are among the most segregated organizations. They tend to be exclusively of one race or predominantly White or African American. Some observers have suggested, for example, that the most segregated hour left in the United States is eleven o'clock on Sunday morning.

This segregation by race is the consequence of a number of factors: a reflection of residential segregation patterns, past and present discrimination, and denominational loyalty (Jaynes and Williams, 1989:92). Most significant for African Americans is that their local churches are one of the few organizations over which they have control. Moreover, these historic Black churches have been not only the focus of their religion but also a key component of the Black community's social life, sources for helping those in need, and centers for Black political activities. Segregated churches gave African Americans, who were denied equal opportunity in the larger society, opportunities for the talented to express and hone their abilities. Significantly, the leaders of the civil rights movement in the 1960s were almost exclusively African American clergy.

Religion and Gender

The three dominant religions in the United States—Christianity, Judaism, and Islam—have been and remain patriarchal. Each worships a male God, recognizes only males as prophets, and has historically given men the highest religious leadership roles. Significantly, their belief systems have been used to legitimize female subordination to males (see the panel titled "Diversity: Religion and Patriarchy").

These religions began in historical times and places where women were clearly subservient to men in all aspects of society. However, this patriarchal tradition continues. Women are formally denied the role of pastor, minister, priest, or rabbi in the Missouri Synod Lutheran Church, the Greek Orthodox Church, the Church of Latter-Day Saints (Mormon), the Catholic Church, the Southern Baptist Church, the Mennonite Brethren Church, and Orthodox Judaism. Pope John Paul II, for example, stated in 1995 that the Roman Catholic Church's ban on women priests is "founded on the written Word of God and that it is to be held always, everywhere and by all" (quoted in Religion News Service, 1995). In other denominations there have been bitter disputes over this matter, with some dissidents breaking away to form separate organizations when women were allowed to become ministers. The majority of Protestant denominations now has women in the ministry, as do Reformed and Conservative Judaism. These breakthroughs are relatively recent in origin. The United Methodist Church and the Presbyterians began ordaining women in 1956, Evangelical Lutherans in 1960, and Episcopalians in 1979. Clearly, though, female clergy are not only underrepresented but have not kept up with the gains by women in other professions—women now account for 25 percent of lawyers and 21 percent of physicians, but only 15 percent of the mainline Protestant clergy. Moreover, female clergy with the same training as male clergy were much less likely to be senior pastors, thereby receiving less annual salary and fewer benefits than their male peers.

Religion and Sexuality

The Judeo-Christian tradition considers homosexual behavior a heinous sin. The Old Testament approves of sexual intercourse only within marriage and for the purpose of procreation. The New Testament continued this tradition. The apostle Paul, for example, wrote in Corinthians that homosexuals would never inherit the kingdom of God.

Contemporary Christian churches and denominations have varied in their response to homosexuality. For fundamentalists the twin pillars of their fight in the culture wars are to outlaw abortions and same-sex marriages. Regarding the latter,

Religion and Patriarchy

The great religions and their leaders have consistently taught that women were secondary to men. Consider the following examples of this thought, which supported men as God's chosen leaders:

- One hundred women are not worth a single testicle. —Confucius (551–479 B.C.)
- In childhood a woman must be subject to her father; in youth to her husband; when her husband is dead, to her sons. A woman must never be free of subjugation. —The Hindu Code of Manu (circa A.D. 100)
- If . . . the tokens of virginity are not found in the young woman, then they shall bring out the young woman to the door of her father's house, and the men of the city shall stone her to death with stones because she has wrought folly . . . so you shall purge the evil from the midst of you. —Deuteronomy 22:20–21 (Old Testament)
- Blessed art thou, O Lord our God and King of the Universe, that thou didst not create me a woman. —Daily prayer (ancient and contemporary) of the Orthodox Jewish male
- Let a woman learn in silence with all submissiveness. I permit no woman to teach or to have authority over men; she is to keep silent. —I Timothy 2:11–15 (New Testament)

- Men are superior to women. —The Koran (circa A.D. 650)
- Women should remain at home, sit still, keep house, and bear and bring up children. —Martin Luther (1438–1546)
- Woman in her greatest perfection was made to serve and obey man, not rule and command him. —John Knox (1505–1572)

Given these pronouncements, we should not be surprised that women traditionally have not held positions of spiritual leadership within organized religion. But these statements were made long ago at historical times when women were clearly subservient to men in all aspects of society.

Serious questions remain: Will congregations accept female clergy in the same way they do men? Will female clergy be called to lead the largest and most prestigious congregations? Will the hierarchy in the various denominations promote women to the highest offices? And will some religious groups continue to deny women the clergy role?

Source: The quotations were taken from a list compiled by Meg Bowman, 1983. "Why We Burn: Sexism Exorcised." *The Humanist* 43 (November/December):28–29.

there is no issue—homosexuality is a sin. The Reverend Jerry Falwell, fundamentalist preacher and founder of the Moral Majority, for example, called the outbreak of AIDS among homosexuals a "form of judgment of God upon a society" (quoted in Crooks and Baur, 1987:312). The fundamentalists also try to affect public and corporate policy regarding their values. The Southern Baptist Convention in 1996, for instance, voted to boycott the Walt Disney Corporation because Disney provides the same health care benefits for the live-in mates of gay employees as it does for the spouses of straight workers (while still denouncing homosexuality, the Southern Baptists did rescind its boycott of Disney in 2005). Even some mainline churches have taken a stand against homosexuals, especially their ordination into the clergy and same-sex marriages. The United Methodist Church added these words to its Book of Discipline in 1996: "Ceremonies that celebrate homosexual unions shall not be conducted by our ministers and shall not be conducted in our churches" (Kerr, 1999:37A). On the other hand, the United Church of Christ in 2005 declared that it would sanction same-sex marriages.

As an example of an inclusive church, consider this statement in its weekly church service bulletin:

Fundamentalists believe that homosexuality is a sin. At the extreme, some believe that heterosexuals who accept homosexuality as a viable lifestyle also should be condemned as sinners.

> Bethel College Mennonite Church [North Newton, Kansas] welcomes into fellowship and membership all persons who confess faith in Jesus Christ, without regard to their race, ethnic background, gender, age, sexual orientation, education, ability, and other factors which give rise to discrimination and marginalization.

In the more liberal denominations and churches, the issue has often been divisive, with some resisting doctrinal change while others seek the acceptance of homosexuals, the recognition of loving unions outside of marriage, and even the ordination of gay and lesbian clergy. For example, in defiance of the Methodist ban on same-sex marriages, ninety United Methodist ministers married two women before more than 1,000 clergy, lay leaders, gay men, lesbians, and other supporters in the Sacramento Convention Center in early 1999.

One Christian denomination, the Universal Fellowship of Metropolitan Community Churches, was founded in 1968 as a fellowship of Christian Churches with a special outreach to the world's gay, lesbian, bisexual, and transgender communities. It has grown from twelve worshipers to a denomination claiming 42,000 members in the United States and 352 churches in nineteen countries. More than twenty of their churches in the United States have been bombed or set on fire by arsonists.

Religious Trends

Religion in U.S. society is a paradox. On the one hand, religion seems to be losing its vitality. The data show that in the past forty years or so there has been a downward trend, a leveling off, and most recently a slight increase in regular church atten-

THE DECLINE OF MORALITY IN AMERICA

dance (see Table 17.2). There are several trends within these data. First, attendance by Protestants during this period has remained about the same, while the percentage of Catholics attending church at least once a week has fallen dramatically. The data also show that the percentage of young adults attending church regularly has fallen, and that the largest denominations—Episcopal, Methodist, and Presbyterian—are declining in both attendance and membership.

On the other hand, however, there are indications that people in the United States are just as religious as ever, and in some areas there is even dramatic growth. Bill Moyers (1996) argues that there is a current surge in the search for an understanding of core principles of belief. "We shouldn't be surprised by all this stirring. It's a confusing time, marked by social and moral ambivalence and, for many, economic insecurity. People yearn for spiritual certainty and collective self-confidence" (4). This theme is amplified by sociologist Rodney Stark: "Besides providing a sense of orientation and insecurity in an insecure world, one of the functions of religion is to satisfy the need to know where we come from and where we're going" (quoted in Morin, 1998:37).

Americans have consistently and overwhelmingly believed in God, with survey findings that about 96 percent of adults in the United States believe in God or a universal spirit. The World Values Survey of sixty nations, conducted by the University of Michigan (reported in Morin, 1998) found that Americans are far more likely than their counterparts in Europe and Scandinavia to attend church regularly and to respond that religion is important in their lives.

Contrary to the experience of the mainline churches, some religious groups are growing rapidly in members and interest. The fastest growing in percentage gain is the Church of Jesus Christ of Latter-Day Saints (Mormons). More significant because of their growing numbers nationwide and their political leverage are the evangelical denominations and sects. In this section we highlight three major trends of U.S. religion: (1) the decline of the mainline churches, (2) the rise of the evangelicals, and (3) the new political activism of the evangelicals and the decline of religious pluralism. Because social conditions have led to these shifts, the focus is on the societal conditions that have given impetus to these trends.

TABLE 17.2

Percentage Attending Church during Average Week (1954–2004)

Year	Percentage	Year	Percentage	Year	Percentage	Year	Percentage
1954	46	1967	43	1980	40	1993	41
1955	49	1968	43	1981	41	1994	38
1956	46	1969	42	1982	41	1995	44
1957	47	1970	42	1983	40	1996	39
1958	49	1971	40	1984	40	1997	35
1959	47	1972	40	1985	42	1998	40
1960	47	1973	40	1986	40	1999	41
1961	47	1974	40	1987	40	2000	42
1962	46	1975	40	1988	42	2001	42
1963	46	1976	41	1989	43	2002	46
1964	45	1977	41	1990	43	2003	46
1965	44	1978	41	1991	43	2004	42
1966	44	1979	40	1992	43		

Source: The Gallup Poll Monthly, various issues, and www.pollingreport.com/religion.html.

The Decline of the Mainline Denominations

Together, the mainline denominations of the United Church of Christ (which includes most Congregationalists), Presbyterians, Episcopalians, American Baptists, United Methodists, Evangelical Lutherans, and the Disciples of Christ (Christian) have lost millions of members since the 1960s (more than 1 million during the 1990s) and continue to do so. At the same time, the Mormons, African American Protestant groups, and the conservative evangelical groups have increased membership substantially.

The reasons for the decline in the mainline denominations are not altogether clear, but the following appear plausible. These denominations have lost their vitality as they have become more and more churchlike (i.e., they have moved away from the qualities characterizing sects) and do not require enough commitment, theologically or evangelistically, from congregants (Van Biema, 2004). The beliefs within these churches have become so pluralistic that to many people the faith seems watered down. Many churchgoers want authority, but they too often receive only more ambiguity. The mainline churches also have lost members because of a preoccupation with political and social issues at the expense of an emphasis on an old-fashioned faith and biblical teachings for personal growth (Reeves, 1996).

Because other parts of society emphasize rationality, efficiency, and bureaucracy, many people seek a religion that will emphasize feelings and fellowship. However, the mainline churches, for the most part, are just as impersonal and ossified as the other bureaucracies in society.

The Catholic Church has been especially vulnerable to losses in attendance. In this case, the rigidity of the Catholic hierarchy is partly responsible. The Church has taken strong stances against contraception, abortion, gender equality, homosexuality, and divorce. Many Catholics feel that church authorities are out of step with contemporary life. The current revelations of the pedophilia scandals (priests sexually abusing children) engulfing a number of Catholic parishes and the subsequent coverups by church officials have turned many away from Catholicism. The prohibition on marriage by priests is, in large part, the cause of a drastic reduction in the number of priests (an average of one for every 1,400 Catholics with an average age of nearly 60) (Kristof, 2005). The Catholic and some other traditional churches have also lost credence with some people for their refusal to accept women in leadership roles. This patriarchal emphasis by some churches, however, is a positive attraction for some individuals, as we discuss later.

An interesting recent development has been the defection of many Latino Catholics for Evangelical Protestant denominations. In 2001 slightly less than 1 million Latinos were Pentecostal and another 1.1 million were Baptists (Kornblum, 2002). There are several reasons for this shift away from traditional membership patterns. First, the emotional power of the evangelicals appeals to many Whites and Latinos alike. Second, evangelical churches often provide a sense of community and social services sometimes lacking in Catholic Churches. Third, Latino Catholics often find linguistic and cultural barriers in the church. Only 2 percent of Catholic priests (fewer than 2,000), for example, are Latino. Meanwhile, the Southern Baptists, to name just one evangelical denomination, have 2,300 Latino pastors and 500 more in seminary training. Finally, critics charge that Latino Americans suffer various forms of discrimination within the U.S. Catholic Church. These charges include the failure of the church hierarchy to encourage religious vocations among Latino Americans, a hesitancy to elevate Latino priests to higher posts, and a reluctance to accept rituals meaningful to Latinos, such as devotions to the Virgin of Guadalupe.

The Rise of Christian Fundamentalism

Beginning in the late 1960s, there has been a rise in Christian fundamentalism. Although there are variations among fundamentalists, they share four central features. First, there is a personal relationship with Jesus brought about by being born again and a repentance of sins. This personal experience is reflected in a believer's daily life. Second, there is an emphasis on evangelism, a responsibility to convert others to their faith. Not only is this an effort to change individuals, it also includes an intense wish to bring the wider culture back to its religious roots, to restore the Christian character of American society. A third feature of fundamentalism is the belief that every word of the Bible is literally true. Scripture, thus, provides an exact description of history and absolute moral truths. Moreover, it provides prophecy of future world events. Fourth, fundamentalists are true believers separate from those who do not take the Bible literally. As holders of certain truth, they reject religious pluralism.

There are two categories of fundamentalists—evangelicals and pentecostals. Evangelicals emphasize a personal relationship with Jesus, public declaration of their faith, and spreading the faith to nonbelievers. Pentecostals share these beliefs with fundamentalists and also emphasize the active presence of the Holy Spirit in their lives and church services. Their church services are very emotional (crying, laughing, shouting, applauding, moving about) with special emotional experiences involving faith healing and "speaking in tongues."

Both of these strands of religious fundamentalism are growing rapidly in the United States. This growth caught many religious observers and sociologists by surprise, because they assumed that modernizing societies undergo processes that tend to make religion increasingly irrelevant to the affairs of society (Lechner, 1989). What, then, are the reasons for this unforeseen rise?

The most obvious reason that fundamentalists are increasing in number is their great emphasis on converting other people to their faith. They stress this activity because Christ commanded, "Go ye into all the world and preach the gospel to every creature."

Second, fundamentalist congregations emphasize community. The people are friendly, accepting, and caring in a world that for many people is unfriendly, unaccepting, and uncaring. Thus, fundamentalists tend to provide for many people the ingredients they find missing in the mainline churches and in the other impersonal bureaucracies of which they are a part.

Third, fundamentalists offer the truth. They believe intensely that they are right and other people are wrong. In a society characterized by rapid change and a plurality of ideas and choices, many people seek authority, a foundation to provide consistency and constancy in their lives. Fundamentalists provide a rigid set of beliefs based on the infallibility of the Bible as the word of God.

A fourth appeal of fundamentalists is their insistence that society has made wrong choices and that we must go back to laws and customs based on biblical truths. For example, in keeping with their reading of the Bible, the Southern Baptists declared at their 1998 convention that a woman should "submit herself graciously" to her husband's leadership and a husband should "provide for, protect and lead his family" (Niebuhr, 1998). Thus, fundamentalism offers not only a critique of modern society but also an action program based on its set of absolute beliefs.

Fifth, evangelicals appeal directly to youth and young adults. The approach to people is warm rather than aloof (parishioners and clergy are more apt to hug). The buildings, lighting, staging, and music are contemporary. Compare evangelical music, for example, with that found in mainline churches. Instead of hymns and organ music, there is music of praise, music with a beat with guitars and drums.

Sixth, some of these churches have become huge (the Lakewood megachurch in Houston has 30,000 people attending services on an average Sunday). There are about 2,000 of these **megachurches** (with at least 2,000 in attendance each week). Their growth is fueled by entertaining church services (fast-paced, scripted productions, with high-energy music, dramatic skits, and sermons with real-life applications), a number of services during the week (for example, child care, aerobics, weight rooms, saunas, movies, gardening, and crafts), and specialized ministries for targeted groups (elderly, newly divorced, parents of teenagers, Vietnamese immigrants, compulsive eaters) (Symonds, 2005).

Finally, fundamentalists have increased their popularity through an emphasis on modern marketing techniques (for example, direct-mail advertising, radio, and television). This type of ministry, which is particularly effective in reaching the disabled and the elderly, began with the advent of radio in the 1920s and expanded greatly with the growth of television in the 1950s and 1960s, cable television in the late 1970s, and satellite transmission in the 1980s.

The Spread of the Evangelical Message via Savvy Marketing

Many religious leaders have become entrepreneurs using contemporary marketing techniques and various forms of the media to reach millions and to make millions. Let's look at four examples.

- Pastor Joel Osteen of Houston's Lakewood's megachurch is the largest church in the United States with 30,000 members. They contribute $55 million each year.

The Sunday service at the Lakewood megachurch in Houston fills 18,000 seats in the former Houston Rockets basketball arena.

Each week 7 million people watch his sermon on national cable and network channels. His book *Your Best Life Now* sold 2.5 million in it's first year (Symonds, 2005). In 2005, the congregation moved into the newly renovated 18,000-seat complex at Houston's Compaq Center. The $75 million remodel features 2 waterfalls, 3 large television screens, and a state-of-the-art lighting system (Rieken, 2005).

- Willow Creek Community Church in suburban Chicago has a $48 million budget and $143 million in assets and 427 employees. Its bookstore brings in $3.2 million; its restaurants another $2.5 million; and its auto repair has revenue of $1 million. An arm of the church, the Willow Creek Association, provides consulting services for other churches, running workshops and conferences on Willow Creek's methods for creating effective services. It attracts more than 21,000 people to its weekly services (Symonds, 2005).

- Rick Warren, pastor of a California megachurch, launched a book, *The Purpose-Driven Life,* in 2002. In 3 years his book has been taught in 20,000 churches in 162 countries, translated into 25 languages, and sold 23 million copies. The marketing tool identified evangelical pastors who would take their church members on a 40-day period of spiritual reflection that the book recommends (Symonds, 2005).

- James Dobson has a $147 million Focus on the Family ministry with 1,400 employees based in Colorado Springs, Colorado. Dobson has a syndicated column in 500 newspapers and his broadcasts are carried in the United States on 80 television outlets and 3,500 radio stations and reach 7 million to 8 million listeners a week. Focus on the family receives so much mail it has its own ZIP code. It receives 8,000 to 10,000 calls, e-mails, and letters a day. It has a website *Plugged In* that registers 1 million visitors a month (Gorski, 2005).

Contemporary Christianity and Politics

Religious organizations are sometimes organized for political action. The National Council of Churches, for example, tends to take liberal political positions on social issues, while the Christian Coalition supports far-right causes and candidates. Political concerns tend to unite fundamentalist churches, while the membership of many mainline churches is split on political issues.

The Religious Right

Fundamentalists and evangelicals believe that they live in a society that is suffering from a moral breakdown. The family is no longer stable, with both spouses working outside the home and a high divorce rate. Crime is rampant. The public schools give away condoms but will not allow Bible study. The media promote sexual promiscuity, violence, and drug use. Abortion is legal. Gays and lesbians openly espouse what the Religious Right considers a sinful lifestyle. Thus, they fight for practices consistent with their biblical view of the Christian family and the Christian society. The political beliefs that emanate from this view are described by sociologist Sara Diamond:

> [The political beliefs of the Christian Right have a] consistent yet contradictory pattern. That is that the right, typically, [these are generalizations] supports state institutions or government institutions or government action when the role that's being played is what I call an "enforcer" role. So the right, for example, has historically supported U.S. military intervention all over the world, until fairly recently; supports, under the rubric of "law and order," very tough law enforcement, draconian measures, even, draconian police power, even violations of people's civil liberties. Also, the right typically supports what they call a "traditional morality," a religiously-derived code of behavior and therefore supports a very strong role for the state in regulating, if not outlawing abortion, access to contraception, sex education; and wants the government to maintain sodomy laws.
>   At the same time the right is anti-government, rhetorically, at least, when it comes to the state's role as distributor of wealth and power. The right does not want the government to be active in terms of anti-poverty programs, spreading the wealth more equitably throughout society via the tax structure, or through funding various welfare programs. (quoted in Barsamian, 1996:36–37)

The Religious Right has become especially politically energized recently by what they feel is a move away from the Christian roots of the United States. The courts, composed of judges with lifetime appointments, have been responsible, in their view, for this shift. Since the 1960s court decisions have ruled against prayer in schools, against religious displays in public spaces, and have made abortion legal. In 2005, with two Supreme Court vacancies conservative religious leaders aggressively pressured President George W. Bush to appoint replacements compatible with their views.

The Religious Right is a social movement with a network of leaders and organizations. There is Pat Robertson's Christian Coalition, James Dobson's Focus on the Family Action (the political arm of Focus on the Family), Beverly LaHaye's Concerned Women of America (which promotes traditional roles for women), Donald Wildmon's American Family Association (which opposes pornography), Robert Simond's Citizens for Excellence in Education, Phyllis Schlafly's The Eagle Forum,

and Gary Bauer's Family Research Council. But the Christian Right is as much a political force as a religious movement. Its organizations use their bloc voting and substantial financial resources to support politicians (almost always Republicans) who share their religion-based agenda and to influence the positions of the Republican Party (nationally and in each of the states). In the 2004 presidential election, 40 percent of Bush's votes came from religious conservatives. They also organize cadres of church-based workers as volunteers to disseminate political information to people most likely to be compatible with their religious and political views. Also, the Christian Coalition actively works to defeat candidates who they feel hold what they believe to be antibiblical positions.

The Role of Mainline Churches: Comfort or Challenge?

The political activism among fundamentalists is different from that found in mainline churches. The difference is that while fundamentalist congregations are relatively homogeneous in religious and political ideologies, mainline congregations are much more pluralistic. This pluralism places the clergy in a precarious position, a dilemma brought about by the two contradictory roles (analogous to the order and conflict approaches to the social order) of the church—to comfort the afflicted and to afflict the comforted (or to comfort and to challenge). The comforting role is one of aiding individuals in surmounting trials and tribulations of sickness, the death of loved ones, financial woes, and social interaction with family, neighbors, colleagues, or enemies. The church helps by such means as pastoral counseling and collecting and distributing food and clothing to the needy. Another way the church comforts the afflicted is through providing a rationale for suffering (theodicy), the consequence of which is sanctification of the status quo.

Three related criticisms of the comforting function are immediately apparent. First, some would say that the church (and the clergy) have allowed this function to supersede the other role of challenger. Second, if the church would do more challenging and less comforting, evils such as poverty would be reduced. By helping people to accept an imperfect society, the church preserves the status quo—that is, the injustice and inequality that caused the problems in the first place. In this way, religion is an "opiate of the masses" because it persuades them to accept an unjust situation rather than working to change it from below. Third, the comfortable will not feel guilty, thereby preventing them from working to change the system from above.

The other function of the church—to challenge—is the injunction to be an agent of social protest and social reform. The church, through its pronouncements and leadership, seeks to lead in the fight to right the inequities of the society. A fundamental problem is in winning the support of the members. Change is almost by definition controversial, because some people benefit under the existing social arrangements. When the church takes a stand for or against patriarchy, abortion, same-sex marriage, war, or the abuses of business or labor, some members will become alienated. They may withdraw their financial support or even leave the church. The church, of course, has a commitment to its members. Because it cannot afford to lose its membership, the church may compromise its principles. Such an action, however, may make other members angry at the church because of its hypocrisy. Consequently, the church is in the unenviable position of trying to maintain a precarious balance between compromise and purity.

Of course, the clergy vary in their interpretation of the role of the church. They are truly people in conflict. There are conflicting expectations of the clergy from all sides (resulting in **role conflict**). The church hierarchy expects the clergy to behave in a particular way (consider the rules issued by the Catholic hierarchy, such as celibacy and absolute obedience to authority). Most parishioners favor the comforting role. They want counsel in times of personal crisis. If poor, they want to be assured that they will be rewarded later, and if rich, they want their holding of wealth and power legitimized.

Although they are a minority in most congregations, some parishioners wish the clergy to take stands on controversial issues and work for social change. This wish puts their clergy in a bind because to take a public stand on controversial issues is divisive.

A final source of the clergy's role conflict arises from their own definition of the role. These various expectations, and the resulting role conflict of the clergy, amount to one reason they may drop out. Another is that if they take a stand (or do not), they may automatically alienate a segment of the parish and perhaps the church hierarchy. They may, consequently, be forced to resign.

Clergy who do not resign may solve their dilemma by being noncontroversial. This non-boat-rocking stance is all too familiar and results in another problem—irrelevancy. By not talking about social problems, one in fact legitimates the status quo. Hence, the inequities of the society continue, because the moral force of the churches is mainly quiet.

Not all clergy are content with the emphasis on comfort. As noted in the previous section, increasing numbers of clergy have become politically active on the moral issues of abortion, homosexuality, and pornography. Typically, though, this view of morality ignores the social problems of inequalities and injustices. Other clergy are not content to let the church continue to perpetuate injustice by not speaking and acting out. They are committed to a socially relevant church, one that seeks social solutions to social problems.

A recent trend appears to be a resurgence in religious activism on social issues, not only by religious fundamentalist groups opposed to such things as sex education in the schools, gay rights, and abortion, but also by the leadership in the mainline churches. The leaders in almost every mainline religious organization have gone on record as opposing the government's budget cuts to the disadvantaged, U.S. military aid to dictatorships, and the arms race. For example, the bishops of the Roman Catholic Church in the United States have formally challenged the fundamental assumptions and strategies of the U.S. defense system. Justifying this new wave of social concern by the church, the late Joseph Bernardin, archbishop of Chicago, said:

> Some people say we shouldn't talk politics and that we should address ourselves to truly religious issues. Well, it's not as simple as all that. It's our responsibility to address the moral dimension of the social issues we face. These issues, of course, do have a political dimension as well as a moral dimension. I don't deny that, but that doesn't mean we're not permitted to talk about them. But our perspective must always be from the moral or ethical dimension. I reject out of hand that we have taken a leftward swing. What we are trying to do is focus on the teaching of the Gospel as we understand it, and to apply that teaching to the various social issues of the day. Our central theme is our respect for God's gift of life, our insistence that the human person has inherent value and dignity. (quoted in *Time*, 1982:77; see also National Conference of Catholic Bishops, 1986)

But political stands from the general leadership of a denomination are viewed quite differently than political activism by local ministers or priests. When local ministers or priests speak out, participate in marches, work for integrated housing, and demonstrate against the Iraq War, many of their parishioners become upset. As a result, the socially active clergy often become objects of discrimination by their parishioners. Another consequence is that the laity trust their clergy less and less. As behavior in one area is questioned (for example, social activism), church members are likely to withdraw confidence in others as well. Finally, churches have divided on this issue. Some want social action instead of just pious talk. Others want to preserve the status quo. The hypocrisy found in many churches forces splits, the formation of underground churches, or total rejection of Christianity as the source of social action. Other members may leave because they feel that the church has wandered too far from the beliefs on which the faith was founded. This dilemma accelerates the current dropout problem among mainline churches—by parishioners and clergy alike. The problem seems to be that for the most part those who drop out are the social activists who leave the church with a residue of comforters. If this is the case, the future of the church is bleak unless there is a reversal, and prophets of social action ascend—an unlikely possibility, given the propensity of most parishioners for the message of comfort over the message of challenge. Meanwhile, the political message and action from the religious right unite and energize its clergy and followers.

Religion from the Order and Conflict Perspectives

As usual, order and conflict theorists view this social phenomenon—religion—very differently. Also, as usual, the unity and diversity found within this institution suggest that both models of society are partially correct.

Proponents of the order model emphasize the solidarity functions of religion. Religion helps individuals through times of stress, and it benefits society by binding people together through a common set of beliefs, reaffirmed through regularly scheduled ceremonial rituals.

Conflict theorists acknowledge that religion may unify in small societies, but in diverse societies religious differences divide. Religious conflict occurs commonly at all levels, however, from intersocietal religious warfare to schisms in local congregations. From the conflict perspective, religious unity within a society, if it does occur, has negative consequences. Such unity is used to legitimate the interests of the powerful (for example, slavery, racial segregation, conquest of pagans, and war; see Spong, 2005). Similarly, the interests of the powerful are served if the poor believe that they will be rewarded in the next life. Such a theodicy prevents revolutions by the oppressed and serves, as Marx suggested, as "an opiate of the masses."

Chapter Review

1. Religion is socially created and has a tremendous impact on society. It is an integrated set of beliefs by which a group attempts to explain the meaning of life and death. Religion defines immorality and sin as well as morality and righteousness.

2. The consequences of religion are unity among the believers, conformity in behavior, and the legitimation of social structures. Religion also divides. It separates believers from nonbelievers, denominations, religions, and even the members of local religious groups.

3. Emile Durkheim, an order theorist, explored the question of why religion is universal. He reasoned that what any group worships is really society itself. The society is held together by religious rituals and festivals in which the group's values and beliefs are reaffirmed.

4. Karl Marx, a conflict theorist, saw religion as inhibiting social change by making existing social arrangements seem right and inevitable. Religion further promotes the status quo by teaching the faithful to accept their condition—thus, religion is the ultimate tool to promote false consciousness.

5. Max Weber, contrary to Marx, saw religious ideology as the catalyst for economic change. He demonstrated this with his analysis of the relationship between Calvinist ideology (predestination) and the rise of capitalism.

6. Civil religion is the belief that "God and country" are one. God is believed to have a special destiny for the United States. Order and unity are thus given religious sanction.

7. Although most people in the United States identify with Christianity, there is a wide variety of religious belief in U.S. society.

8. U.S. religious organizations can be divided according to their secular commitment into two categories. A church tends to compromise with the larger society, tolerates popular vices, and accepts a diversity of beliefs. A sect, in sharp contrast, rejects the world. It is a moral community with rigid ethical requirements and a narrow belief system.

9. A theodicy is a religious legitimation for a situation that otherwise might cause guilt or anger. Sects tend to have a theodicy of suffering, explaining their lack of power and privilege. Churches have theodicies that legitimate the possession of power and privilege.

10. A cult is a religious group that rejects the society and religions of the mainstream. It provides a new religious expression that some are willing to follow completely. A cult differs from a sect in one fundamental way. A sect results from a breakoff from an existing religious organization. The members do not seek a new religion but rather seek to recapture the true faith. Cults, on the other hand, represent a new religion. Most cults fail, but a few have become major religions.

11. There is a relationship between social class and religion: (a) The lower the social class, the greater the probability of belonging to a sect; (b) there is a relationship between social class and denominational affiliation (for example, the lower the social class, the more likely to be Baptist, and the higher the social class, the more likely to be Episcopalian); (c) the higher the social class of the member, the greater his or her involvement and influence in the local church.

12. Religious groups hold beliefs or behave in ways that support the racial, gender, and sexuality norms of society.

13. One trend is the decline in the mainline denominations. These churches are often bureaucratic and impersonal. Their beliefs are pluralistic. The Catholic Church is losing members because its stands against contraception and divorce are out of tune with contemporary life.

14. Another trend is the rise of Christian fundamentalism. The two categories of fundamentalists are evangelicals and pentecostals. They are alike except that pentecostal congregations are more emotional—personally experiencing the Holy Spirit. Fundamentalists are growing (while the mainline churches are declining) because they (a) emphasize evangelism; (b) tend to be friendly, accepting, and caring communities; (c) have the truth based on the infallibility of the Bible; (d) offer a critique of modern society and a prescription for its change back to a God-centered society; and (e) use modern marketing techniques and radio and television.

15. The contemporary mainline Christian churches are faced with a basic dilemma brought about by their two contradictory roles—to comfort the afflicted and to afflict the comforted. The comforting function is criticized because it focuses on helping the individual but ignores the problems of society. The challenging function—the injunction to be an agent of social protest and social reform—is criticized because it is divisive, alienating some members who disagree with the position taken. The evidence is clear that the majority of clergy is opting for the comforting function over the challenging function.

16. The order model emphasizes the solidarity functions of religion, which order theorists interpret as good.

17. From the conflict perspective, religious beliefs have negative consequences because they sanctify the status quo; that is, religion legitimates the interests of the powerful while also justifying the existence of inequality. Thus, revolutionary activity by the oppressed is suppressed by religion because it serves, as Marx suggested, as "an opiate of the masses."

Key Terms

Religion
Ritual
Opiate of the masses
Civil religion
Priestly role of religion

Prophetic role of religion
Church
Sect
Routinization of charisma
Charisma of office

Theodicy
Cult
Megachurches
Role conflict

Study Questions

1. What are the social consequences for a community of believers?
2. Explain the contradiction that religion is both a source of stability and a source of conflict.
3. Contrast the views of religion by Durkheim, Marx, and Weber.
4. Is religion generally supportive of existing class and gender hierarchies? Give evidence to support your position.
5. Explain the contrast in growth patterns by the mainline denominations and the more fundamentalist denominations.

For Further Reading

Religion, General

Karen Armstrong, *The Battle for God* (New York: Ballantine, 2000).

Frederick Clarkson, *Eternal Hostility: The Struggle between Theocracy and Democracy* (Monroe, ME: Common Courage Press, 1997).

Harvey Cox, *Fire from Heaven: The Rise of Pentecostal Spirituality and the Reshaping of Religion in the Twenty-First Century* (Reading, MA: Addison-Wesley, 1995).

Stephen Jay Gould, *Rocks of Ages: Science and Religion in the Fullness of Life* (New York: Ballantine, 1999).

Michael Harrington, *The Politics at God's Funeral: The Spiritual Crisis of Western Civilization* (New York: Penguin, 1983).

The Hedgehog Review, special issue on "Religion and Violence," Volume 6 (Spring 2004).

Charles Kimball, *When Religion Becomes Evil* (New York: HarperCollins, 2002).

D. L. Kimbrough, *Taking Up Serpents: Snake Handlers of Eastern Kentucky* (Chapel Hill: University of North Carolina Press, 1995).

C. Eric Lincoln and Lawrence H. Mamiya, *The Black Church in the African-American Experience* (Durham, NC: Duke University Press, 1990).

Richard V. Pierard and Robert D. Linder, *Civil Religion and the Presidency* (Grand Rapids, MI: Zoldervan, 1988).

Stephen Sharot, *A Comparative Sociology of World Religions: Virtuosos, Priests, and Popular Religion* (New York: New York University Press, 2001).

John Shelby Spong, *The Sins of Scripture: Exposing the Bible's Texts of Hate to Reveal the God of Love* (New York: HarperSanFrancisco, 2005).

Rodney Stark, *The Rise of Christianity: A Sociologist Reconsiders History* (Princeton, NJ: Princeton University Press, 1996).

Max Weber, *The Protestant Ethic and the Spirit of Capitalism* (New York: Scribner, 1958; orig., 1904).

David Sloan Wilson, *Darwin's Cathedral: Evolution, Religion, and the Nature of Society* (Chicago: University of Chicago Press, 2002).

Religious Trends in the United States

Amy E. Ansell, *Unraveling the Right: The New Conservatism in American Thought and Politics* (Boulder, CO: Westview, 1998).

Carol P. Christ and Judith Plaskow (eds.), *Womanspirit: A Feminist Reader in Religion* (San Francisco: Harper, 1992).

Sara Diamond, *Not by Politics Alone: The Enduring Influence of the Christian Right* (New York: Guilford Press, 1998).

Thomas C. Reeves, *The Empty Church: The Suicide of Liberal Christianity* (New York: Free Press, 1996).

Jim Wallis, *God's Politics: Why the Right Gets It Wrong and the Left Doesn't Get It* (New York: HarperCollins, 2005).

Clyde Wilcox, *Onward Christian Soldiers? The Religious Right in American Politics*, 2nd ed. (Boulder, CO: Westview, 2000).

Walter Wink (ed.), *Homosexuality and Christian Faith: Questions of Conscience for Churches* (Minneapolis MN: Fortress Press, 1999).

Alan Wolfe, *The Transformation of American Religion* (Chicago: University of Chicago Press, 2004).

Web Resources

http://durkheim.itgo.com/main.html

This page is the home of the Emile Durkheim Archive. It offers excerpts from Durkheim's work and some explanation on his theories, including those that he held on religion.

http://www.angelfire.com/or/sociologyshop/msor.html

This page offers a look at Karl Marx's theories on religion and how they pertain to the study of religion in sociology.

http://www.ne.jp/asahi/moriyuki/abukuma/

The Weberian Sociology of Religion page contains texts about religion written by Max Weber and links to other pertinent sites.

http://www.infidels.org/index.shtml

The Secular Web is "an online community of nonbelievers dedicated to the pursuit of knowledge, understanding, and tolerance."

http://www.religioustolerance.org/welcome.htm#new

For information on current and historical events in the news related to religion, as well as descriptions of different religions and links to other religion sites, visit ReligiousTolerance.org.

http://www.earlham.edu/~libr/acrlwss/wsstheo.html

Part of WSSLINKS, created by the Women's Studies Section of the Association of College and Research Libraries, this site has links to websites that are generally related to women and religion, as well as those that pertain to specific religions, including Christianity, Judaism, and Buddhism.

http://www.calltorenewal.com/about_us.html

Call to Renewal is a faith-based group attempting to overcome racism and poverty.

http://www.barna.org

This is the website for the Barna Research Group. This group specializes in research on religious issues.

http://www.parishioners.org/

This site provides information on various religious issues.

http://www.princeton.edu/~nadelman/csar/csar.html

This is the site for the Center for the Study of American religion. It has links to many other sites for the study of American religion.

http://www.igc.apc.org/culturewatch

Culture Watch provides information about the religious right in the United States.

LIFE, LIBERTY
AND

Human Agency: Individuals and Groups in Society Changing Social Structures

The Sociological Paradox: Social Structure and Agency

Sociology is the study of all things social. This book, focusing on the societal level, emphasizes the social context and the social forces that so strongly affect human behavior. As sociologist Peter Berger (1963) says (as quoted in Chapter 1): "Society not only controls our movements, but shapes our identity, our thoughts and our emotions. The structures of society become the structures of our own consciousness. Society does not stop at the surface of our skins. Society penetrates us as much as it envelops us" (121).

This view of **determinism** is too strong, however. While society *constrains* what we do, it does not *determine* what we do (Giddens, 1991:863). While society and its structures are powerful, the members of society are not totally controlled. We are not passive actors. We can take control of the conditions of our own lives. Human beings cope with, adapt to, and change social structures to meet their needs. Individuals, acting alone or with others, can shape, resist, challenge, and sometimes change the social institutions that impinge on them. These actions constitute human agency. This chapter focuses on the macro dimensions of agency—that is, those collective actions that change and overcome societal constraints.

The paradox of sociology—the power of society over its members versus the power of social actors to change society—has several important meanings and implications (see Chapters 1 and 2). Foremost, society is not a rigid, static entity composed of robots. People in interaction are the architects of society in an ongoing project; that is, society is created, sustained, and changed by people.

Second, the social forms that people create often take on a sacred quality—the sanctity of tradition—that constrains behavior in socially prescribed ways. The sociological insight is, to restate the previous point, that what many consider sacred and therefore unchangeable is a social construction and can, therefore, be reconstructed.

A third implication is that since social structures are created and sustained by people, they are imperfect. There are positive and negative consequences of the way people have organized. Many are content with the status quo because they benefit from it. Others accept it even though they are disadvantaged by it. But there are also those who seek change to improve it or, perhaps, to change it completely. They are the agents of change.

In sum, the essence of agency is that individuals through collective action are capable of changing the structure of society and even the course of history. But, while agency is important, we should not minimize the power of the structures that subordinate people, making change difficult or, at times, impossible.

This chapter is divided into two major parts. The first is conceptual, considering social movements, the collective and organized efforts of human actors to change society. This section describes the types of social movements and the conditions under which they succeed or fail. The second part is illustrative, providing two case studies of agency—the civil rights movement and the movement to bring gender equity to sport.

Social Movements

Individuals seeking to change social life in some way are limited in what they can accomplish by themselves. We need to join with others who share our goals, if we are to have any hope of success. Sociologists Kenneth Kammeyer, George Ritzer, and Norman Yetman (1997) show the importance of social movements if we are to be effective agents of change:

> As individuals, we are limited in our ability to make the societal changes we would like. There are massive social forces that make change difficult; these forces include the government, large and powerful organizations, and the prevailing values, norms, and attitudes. As individuals going to a voting booth, we have minimal power. As individuals protesting to officials, we have minimal power. As individuals standing against the tide of public opinion, we have little hope of exerting influence. As individuals confronting a corporate structure, we are doomed to frustration and failure. But if we combine with others who share our convictions, organize ourselves, and map out a course of action, we may be able to bring about numerous and significant changes in the social order. Through participation in a social movement, we can break through the social constraints that overwhelm us as individuals. (632–633)

Individual actors seeking change typically join with others for greater power to become part of a social movement. A **social movement** is a collective attempt to promote or resist change. These movements arise when people are sufficiently discontented that they will work for a better system. Hence, social movements are inherently political because they seek to affect public policy. A social movement is a goal-directed effort by a substantial number of people. It is an enduring organization with leaders, a division of labor, an ideology, a blueprint for collective action, and a set of roles and norms for the members (see Blumer, 1951; Smelser, 1962). Although money and organizational skills are important, ideology is the key to a movement's success. The ideology provides the goal and the rationale for action, binds diverse members together in a common cause, and submerges individuals to the movement. An **ideology** is a set of ideas that explains reality, provides guidelines for behavior, and expresses the interests of a group. An ideology may be elaborate, such as Christianity, Marxism, or capitalism. Such an ideology provides a consistent framework from which to act and believe on a number of issues. Or the ideology may be narrowly aimed at one side or the other on issues such as animal rights, abortion, protection of the environment, capital punishment, gun control, gay rights, U.S. involvement in preemptive war, nuclear energy, universal health insurance, pay equity, living wage, and welfare. For each of these issues, groups on either side have an ideology that explains their position, provides the goal, brings members together, and offers a compelling argument used to recruit new members.

Types of Social Movements

Three types of social movements are political in nature: resistance movements, which are organized to prevent changes; reform movements, which seek to alter a specific part of society; and revolutionary movements, which seek radical changes.

A resistance movement is organized to either resist change or to seek to reverse changes that have already occurred and restore "traditional values."

One type of social movement—**resistance movements**—is explicitly organized either to resist change or it is reactionary in that it seeks to reverse changes that have already occurred and restore "traditional values."

Because periods of rapid change foster resistance movements, there are numerous contemporary examples of this phenomenon. There are current efforts to stop the trend toward the use of nuclear power for energy. People have organized to stop the damming of rivers or the logging of forests because they want to protect the environment. The move to make the Equal Rights Amendment part of the Constitution was met with considerable organized resistance, even from women. Antiabortion groups have formed to reverse legislation and judicial acts that make abortion legal or easy to obtain. Evangelicals in a number of communities have organized to pressure school boards to reverse school policies that they consider opposite to Christian principles. As examples, they oppose the teaching of evolution and seek to have the schools also teach creationism or intelligent design. They want prayer in the schools. They want Christian symbols in public spaces. They oppose the teaching of sex education (unless it teaches abstinence). They oppose same-sex marriage.

Reform movements seek to alter a specific part of society. These movements commonly focus on a single issue, such as women's rights, gay rights, or global warming. Typically, there is an aggrieved group such as women, African Americans, Native Americans, gays, people with disabilities, farmers, or workers that focuses its strategy on changing the laws and customs to improve its situation (see the panel titled "Human Agency: The Political Muscle of Americans with Disabilities"). At various times in U.S. history, oppressed groups have organized successful drives to change the system to provide more equity. The civil rights movement of the 1950s and 1960s provides an example. Another example is the student movement in the late 1990s to eliminate foreign sweatshops that produce goods that bring profits to U.S. colleges and universities (see the panel titled "Globalization: Students against Sweatshops").

The third type of social movement—the **revolutionary movement**—seeks radical changes. Such movements go beyond reform by seeking to replace the exist-

The Political Muscle of Americans with Disabilities

In 1989, Congress passed historic legislation to protect the civil rights of people with disabilities. This bill, the Americans with Disabilities Act, extends to people with disabilities the same protections against discrimination that were given African Americans and women in the 1960s and 1970s.

Some 20 percent of people in the United States have some form of impairment (more than 55 million). About 5 percent of people with a disability were born with it, 85 percent will experience a disabling condition in the course of their lives, usually from accidents, disease, environmental hazards, or criminal victimization (Russell, 2000). This category of disability includes a wide range of people, such as people with mental retardation, paraplegics, the blind, those with cerebral palsy, and those with AIDS, and those with Alzheimer's disease.

Before the Americans with Disabilities Act became law with President George H. W. Bush's signature in 1990, people with disabilities faced discrimination in jobs, social situations, and transportation. The new law prohibited stores, hotels, restaurants, and theaters from denying access to people with disabilities. Employers could no longer reject qualified workers just because they are disabled. Moreover, employers had to modify the workplace to make it accessible to their workers with disabilities. Public buildings under construction or undergoing remodeling now must be made accessible to wheelchair users under the new legislation. So, too, must public transportation vehicles be equipped with lifts to accommodate wheelchair users. Finally, telephone companies must now have operators who can take messages typed by deaf people on a Telecommunications Device for the Deaf and then relay it orally to a hearing person on another phone.

People with disabilities are one of the last minority groups to win their civil rights. They were behind racial minorities and women because they did not mobilize a vast movement with highly visible protests. They also lacked a charismatic leader, as had Blacks with Martin Luther King, Jr., and women with Betty Friedan. Nevertheless, they achieved some early victories with a 1973 law that protected people with

disabilities from discrimination by institutions receiving federal funding (similar to Title IX legislation prohibiting discrimination against women in education) and 1975 legislation that ensured access to schools to all children with disabilities.

The sweeping 1989 victory for people with disabilities was won despite the contrary efforts of many in the business community who argued that the provisions were too costly to businesses. Success was achieved over this considerable opposition through a number of means. Foremost, people with disabilities have developed a common identity (class consciousness) through a shared outrage at the discrimination they experience. Now, instead of feelings of isolation, feelings of a common bond and empowerment have emerged among the disabled. Many became active in what became known as the disabilities movement. Some of these people joined advocacy groups; others joined together to use tactics of civil disobedience, such as disrupting public transportation or blocking access to city hall, in order to make their plight more visible. In one celebrated case, the students at Gallaudet University, a college for the deaf, protested the selection of a hearing president in 1988. They refused to go to classes and occupied the administration building, eventually forcing the newly appointed president to resign and the governing board to appoint the university's first deaf president.

The 1989 Americans with Disabilities Act victory was also fueled by increased numbers of people with disabilities, including people with AIDS and the aged, who had become disabled with Alzheimer's, blindness, deafness, arthritis, and the like. With the realization that about one-fifth of Americans have disabilities, politicians have found it difficult to vote against them. As a cohesive group, people with disabilities have considerable potential political clout. Their growing sense of a shared condition and common identity has made their voting as a bloc on certain issues more likely than ever. The result has been, finally, legislation guaranteeing their civil rights.

Sources: The content of this essay has been taken from a number of sources, especially De Parle, 1989; Eitzen and Baca Zinn 2006; Johnson, 1991; Russell, 1998; 2000; and Shapiro, Joseph, 1989:ch. 11.

ing social institutions with new ones that conform to a radically different vision of society. For example, throughout Eastern Europe, new nations have been created out of the Soviet Union and its satellites. These nations, newly independent, are adopting new forms of government and new economies that are drastically different from what they had in the last fifty years. These changes will dramatically change all areas of social life.

525

CHAPTER 18
Human Agency:
Individuals and
Groups in Society
Changing Social
Structures

The Life Course of Social Movements

Social movements move through predictable stages. For a movement to begin, it must attract members. Usually there is some societal condition—institutional racism, institutional sexism, economic depression, war, an immigration wave, the passage of a controversial law or court decision, technological change—that threatens or harms some segment of society. This causes social unrest, but it is unfocused.

The second stage of a movement is when grievances become focused. A leader or leaders emerge who use ideology and charisma (extraordinary personal attributes) to define the central problem(s) they face, and to challenge and inspire followers to join in a common quest to change society for the better. Sometimes there are individuals whose acts of personal courage, such as provoking the powerful, or getting jailed, injured, or killed serve to coalesce the previously unfocused. This is especially important in an age of instant communication, in which public attention is centered on the charismatic leader's message and personal valor, the heroism of martyrs, the repressive acts by authorities, the terrorism of those opposing the movement, and the continuing inequities in society on which the movement is centered. This is a critical stage when those in similar situations realize that others share their feelings of discontent, anger, or injustice and that together they can make a difference. They begin to acquire a collective identity and a sense of common purpose. It is a time of excitement over the possibilities for collectively bringing about needed social change.

The third phase involves moving toward organization. Resources (money, equipment, and members) are mobilized. A formal organizational structure is developed

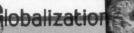

Students against Sweatshops

The collegiate apparel industry generates $2.5 billion annually, with each university receiving a share of the sales using its logo on sweatshirsts, caps, and other items. Each university sells its right to use the logo to the Collegiate Licensing Corporation, a trademark company that acts as an agent for Nike, Champion, and Reebok and the more than 200 universities involved. Major universities earn several million dollars annually from these sales.

Students on a number of campuses have taken this opportunity to indicate to the world that they do not want their universities engaged in enterprises that manufacture clothing made in foreign sweatshops. A baseball cap with a university logo selling retail for $19.95, for example, earns the university $1.50, while the worker in the Dominican Republic who made it earns eight cents (Capellaro, 1999).

To right the injustices accompanying sweatshops and the complicity of U.S. corporations and universities in these injustices, students on a number of campuses have battled to ensure that collegiate apparel is made under humane conditions. The students used various tactics: Students at the University of Michigan occupied a dean's office for a three-day "sweat-in," students at the University of Arizona blocked an administration building for an afternoon; students at the University of Wisconsin, Madison, defied the use of pepper spray and night sticks by campus police to sit-in at the chancellor's office; students at Purdue held an eleven-day hunger strike; at Yale, forty students engaged in a "knit-in," doing needlework in the center of campus; at Holy Cross and the University of California at Santa Barbara, students held mock fashion shows, lecturing on sweatshops while parading down the catwalk; at Harvard, 350 students held a rally, as did 250 at Princeton, to demand that their schools not use sweatshops to create merchandise; and students at the University of North Carolina held a nude-optional party titled "I'd Rather Go Naked Than Wear Sweatshop Clothes." Students at other colleges and universities circulated petitions, picketed college bookstores, and launched websites calling for "sweat-free" clothing. These protests were coordinated through United Students against Sweatshops (USAS), which was founded in 1997 and now has chapters at more than 200 schools.

As a result of these protests, individual universities have changed their policies. Duke University, for example, notified Nike and other licensees of Duke products that they must disclose to the school the locations of their factories or Duke would not renew their contracts (similar demands were made by the University of Wisconsin, Madison, the University of Michigan, and Georgetown University). The presidents of various universities ended up agreeing to the demands of student activists and, in turn, demanding the monitoring of factories independent of industry influence (through the Worker Rights Consortium) that make college-name apparel, full disclosure, living wages, and women's rights guarantees.

By 2004 the social movement initiated by students against sweatshops in the garment industry seven years earlier, had enlarged its goals to include worker struggles in other industries and to struggle against racism, sexism, homophobia, classism, and other forms of oppression. The thrust is to bring justice to workers who are being exploited in the global economy.

Clearly, students acting collectively on their campuses have been and continue to be change agents from the bottom up, changing the policies of their universities and those of corporations to create more humane working conditions for those who labored to make profits for those universities.

Sources: Appelbaum and Bonacich, 2000; Featherstone, 2000; Harris, 2000; Pereira, 2004; and Street, 2000.

with rules, policies, and procedures to be followed. Power is centralized and levels of organization are delineated. Strategies are formed to confront the authorities, attract new members, and keep older members energized. Alliances may be formed with other groups with similar goals (allowing them to share computerized mailing lists of likely contributors or new members, and the like). In short, this is a bureaucratization (or formalization) stage when a once unfocused number of people now have become an organization. Where once leadership was charismatic, it is now composed of administrators and managers (this is called the routinization of charisma).

The final stage occurs if the movement is successful. If so, the movement becomes integrated into society. The goals of the movement have been accomplished. This is the stage of **institutionalization**. While this is the goal of the social movement, this stage has its dangers. A common danger is **goal displacement**. This occurs when the goal of maintaining the formal structure of the movement's organization supersedes the original goals of the social movement. Another threat involves power struggles within the movement, which divert effort from the common goal. Finally, and related to the last point, success can lead to the leadership elite using its power to keep power and the extraordinary status and rewards that come with that power. In effect, then, "organizational success and its consequences can corrupt the original goals of the movement" (Hess, Markson, and Stein, 1993:596).

527

CHAPTER 18
Human Agency:
Individuals and
Groups in Society
Changing Social
Structures

Agency: Social Change from the Bottom Up

Often the people lead and the leaders of government and business follow. Harlan Cleveland (1992) states:

> The tidal waves of social change of our lifetimes—environmental sensitivity, civil rights for all races, the enhanced status of women, recognition of the rights of consumers and small investors—were not generated by the established leaders in government, business, labor, religion, or higher education. They boiled up from people (and new leaders) who had not previously been heard from. (16)

This section provides two case studies in which the efforts of seemingly powerless individuals and groups changed powerful social structures. The first case involves the centuries-long struggle by African Americans to obtain the civil rights due all citizens. The second case study is of the specific situation in which recent actions by individuals and groups have brought significant changes moving toward gender equity within athletics.

The Civil Rights Movement

Many believe that the civil rights movement began when Rosa Parks was arrested for not giving up her seat to a White man on a bus in Montgomery, Alabama, in 1955, and a successful bus boycott followed. The civil rights movement is not the result of one event but the "inevitable outcome of centuries of mistreatment of black people by white people and their governments" (Powledge, 1991:xi). Or, as Vincent Harding (1981) puts it, the movement is long and continuous,

> flowing like a river, sometimes powerful, tumultuous, and roiling with life; at other times meandering and turgid. . . . The river of black struggle is people, but it is also the hope, the movement, the transformative power that humans create and that create them, us, and makes them, us, new persons. So we black people are the river; the river is us. The river is in us, created by us, flowing out of us, surrounding us, re-creating us and this entire nation. (xix)

Africans were brought to this country as slaves and as slaves they were exploited, demeaned, and kept powerless (this section is taken in part from Berry, 1994; Harding,

1981; Powledge, 1991; and Zinn, 1980). The laws and the customs permitted the oppression of the slaves:

> Beginning in Virginia at the end of the 1630s, laws establishing lifelong African slavery were instituted. They were followed by laws prohibiting black-white inter-marriage, laws against the ownership of property by Africans, laws denying blacks all basic political rights. . . . In addition, there were laws against the education of Africans, laws against the assembling of Africans, laws against the ownership of weapons by Africans, laws perpetuating the slavery of their parents to African children, laws forbidding Africans to raise their hands against whites even in self-defense. . . . [The laws] outlawed many rituals connected with African religious practices, including dancing and the use of drums. In many places they also banned African languages. Thus they attempted to shut black people out from both cultures, to make them wholly dependent neuters. (Harding, 1981:27)

Despite the oppressive control of Blacks and the severe punishments for their violations of the laws and customs, many African men and women struggled against the domination of White power. Some engaged in individual acts of rebellion. Some ran away, heading north. At times, Black fugitives formed small guerrilla bands, creating bases from which to harass neighboring plantations and places to which others might flee. These fugitives (known as outlyers) were very significant to the oppressed. Their existence meant that the apparently total institution of slavery was not all-encompassing. Most important, "the outlyers represented a hidden, submerged black power that the masters could not break. They were a radical presence, challenging blacks and whites alike" (Harding, 1981:40). For those who remained in bondage, some chose to resist, using such tactics as refusing to learn how to use a tool without breaking it, work slowdowns, persistent noncooperation, arson, and even poisoning.

Around 1800, Blacks constituted about 20 percent of the U.S. population. Of the 1 million, 900,000 were held in legal slavery. In that year, Gabriel Prosser and forty other slaves were executed for daring to revolt against their masters. This insurrection and the punishment ushered in a period of some thirty-five years of intensified slave rebellions. Efforts to escape also escalated, as the chances for success increased with the Underground Railroad, a network of Blacks and Whites who smuggled thousands of slaves to the North. Among the slaves who stayed behind, agency took many forms such as keeping African traditions, fighting to keep family ties, maintaining community solidarity, and creating their own rituals that recognized marriage and parenthood. Summarizing the pre–Civil War situation for Blacks, historian Vincent Harding (1981) states:

> [The slave community] was not a community caught in the flatness of despair. It was not a community without hope. It lived with brutality, but did not become brutish. Often it was treated inhumanely, but it clung to its humanity. There was too much in the river [Harding's metaphor of the cumulative effects of the Black struggle] which suggested other possibilities, announced new comings, and hurled restless movements against the dam of white oppression. Always, under the surface of slavery, the river of black struggle flowed with, and was created by, a black community that moved actively in search of freedom, integrity, and home—a community that could not be dehumanized. (74)

After the Civil War, the Emancipation Proclamation, and the passage of the Thirteenth, Fourteenth, and Fifteenth Amendments to the Constitution, Blacks were freed from slavery and given certain rights. But while they were technically free, they remained oppressed. One form of oppression—slavery—was lifted, only to be replaced by other modes of oppression—economic slavery through low-wage jobs and share-cropping arrangements with landowners, and being treated as inferiors by Whites. In the 1880s, the average wage of Black farmworkers in the South was about fifty cents a day. They were usually paid in "orders," not money, which could only be used at a store controlled by the landowner. The sharecropper had to borrow from the store to get the seed to plant the crop. "When everything was added up at the end of the year he was in debt, so his crop was constantly owed to someone, and he was tied to the land, with the records kept by the planter and storekeeper so that the Negroes are swindled and kept forever in debt" (Zinn, 1980:204).

Despite these roadblocks, there was more freedom than before, and many Blacks found ways to reinforce their liberty such as hunting with guns, driving carriages, meeting with other Blacks in public places, forming political unions, changing their names, asserting their rights to Whites, and omitting the long-standing and deeply understood signs of inferior status:

> One of the most significant movements toward the definition of freedom came as black families all over the South made a momentous decision to withdraw their women from the full-time agricultural labor force. In many cases children moved out of the role of full-time field hands as well. Everywhere in slavery's former domain, black families were openly declaring the autonomy they had fought so hard to develop and maintain under the old regime; they were establishing their right to decide who should work and how. Now mothers and wives were often free to give more attention to their own families and work; children could attend the schools now being created at great cost by blacks and their white allies. (Harding, 1981:282)

White violence toward Blacks escalated in response to the behavioral changes of the former slaves. The Ku Klux Klan and local vigilante groups used raids, lynchings, beatings, and burnings to intimidate Blacks. The courts were much more likely to send Blacks to prison than Whites. And in the penitentiary system of the South there were beatings, chain gangs, and forced labor as contractors purchased their labor cheaply.

The Black Codes were laws passed by Southern states and local governments to keep Blacks "in their place." These codes were intended to keep Blacks from achieving equality, to control Blacks, and to keep Blacks bound to jobs and land controlled by Whites. Although the laws varied from state to state and city to city, the patterns were essentially the same. There were restrictions against land ownership or rental by Blacks. There were vagrancy laws insisting that Blacks have lawful employment. In South Carolina, for example, a vagrant could be sentenced to a year of hard labor and be hired out to an individual. The laws created harsh penalties against Black workers who broke contracts with landowners or other employers. Other laws placed severe restrictions on the kinds of work that Blacks could do. In effect these laws meant that Blacks were subjected to many special punishments that did not apply to Whites. "The patterns were clear: in almost every situation having to do with black-white relationships, freedom of movement, freedom of choice in jobs, a personal sense of independence, and control over their own families, the Black Codes were the slave codes revived" (Harding, 1981:314).

Moving to the early twentieth century, a rigid system of segregation emerged in the South, where interaction between the races as equals was denied. These "Jim

529
CHAPTER 18
Human Agency:
Individuals and
Groups in Society
Changing Social
Structures

Crow" laws (supported by an 1896 U.S. Supreme Court decision *Plessy* v. *Ferguson*, which justified the principle of "separate but equal") meant that all public facilities in the South such as restaurants, restrooms, schools, and public transportation could be segregated. Nevertheless, African Americans often banded together to fight injustice, share resources, and maintain control over their lives. The National Association for the Advancement of Colored People (NAACP) was founded in 1909, and the National Urban League began a year later. Both fought for civil rights in public opinion and in the courts, but with little success until after World War II.

The military was segregated during World War II, although defense industries were prohibited from discrimination based on racial differences (by executive order of President Roosevelt). Toward the conclusion of the war, the Black press and a few Whites in the media pushed for integration, arguing that since Blacks had fought in the war for the principles of equality, freedom, and democracy, they should have the same rights.

Shortly after World War II, the NAACP challenged the concept of separate but equal schooling in the courts. This effort was rewarded in 1954 when the Supreme Court ruled in *Brown* v. *Board of Education of Topeka, Kansas*, that "separate educational facilities are inherently unequal." This ruling was resisted in the South by the Ku Klux Klan, White Citizens Councils, mayors, school boards, and governors.

In addition to this momentous court decision, two events in the next year galvanized Blacks into a mass movement that ultimately changed race relations in the United States. The first incident was the lynching of Emmitt Till in Mississippi. Till, a fourteen-year-old African American from Chicago, was visiting relatives. To show off to his cousins, he violated the unwritten code of conduct for Blacks in the rural South by making a "smart" remark to a White woman. The woman's husband and brother-in-law kidnapped Till from his uncle's house. Later, young Till's mutilated body was found in a river. In court, Till's uncle identified the two men who took his nephew from his house (the first time in Southern history that a Black man accused Whites of a felony crime in court). Despite this heroic act, the all-White jury found Till's murderers not guilty (who later admitted, with pride, that they had killed him).

The second case involved the jailing of a Black woman, Rosa Parks, in Montgomery, Alabama, for not giving her seat on a bus to a White man as was the custom fortified by the law. As a result of this courageous act, the Black community in Montgomery mobilized to bring down the segregated public busing system. A leader emerged, a young local minister, Martin Luther King, Jr., who inspired African Americans to use nonviolent resistance to overthrow their oppressors and their unfair laws and practices. The Blacks boycotted the transportation system for 381 days, walking to work or using a carpooling network. The city eventually abolished segregation in public transportation—a clear case of agency, as the powerless successfully changed an unfair system.

Under King's leadership, Blacks and White sympathizers mobilized to desegregate other public facilities. There were sit-ins in restaurants, waiting rooms, and churches, and wade-ins at public beaches. Economic boycotts were organized. Court cases were initiated. Brave students became the first African Americans to integrate schools. And there were protest marches to publicize grievances. These efforts were violently resisted by Whites. King and others were jailed. Demonstrators were abused verbally and physically. There were lynchings, the most infamous being the murder by Klansmen of three civil rights workers in Mississippi. Birmingham police commissioner "Bull" Conner ordered the police to disperse protesters with fire hoses, clubs, and police dogs, an event watched by millions on television. There were also drive-by shootings and other forms of intimidation to keep Blacks from registering to vote. King's reform movement was bent on tearing down the segregationist norms and values and substituting new ones. To a limited, but nonetheless significant extent, the movement succeeded. Schools were desegregated with the help of federal troops. The 1964 Civil Rights Bill banned discrimination in public facilities, education, employment, and in any agency receiving government funds. The 1965 Voting Rights Act prohibited the use of literacy and similar tests to screen voting applicants and allowed federal examiners to monitor elections.

But the civil rights movement has not achieved equality. As noted in various parts of this text, considerable residential segregation occurs in the North and the South, many schools remain racially segregated, African Americans have less spent on their education than Whites, Black unemployment is twice that of Whites, wages are considerably less for Blacks, the poverty rate for Blacks is triple that of Whites, racial discrimination continues in receiving loans, and the economic position of Black women is far worse than that of White women.

In short, while civil rights battles have been won, the war for equality is still being fought in legislatures, in the courts, in school districts, and in neighborhoods. As before, individuals and groups are taking agency seriously, working to change institutional racism in all its forms.

Gender Equity in Sports

In the last century or so, women have made several significant advances. The courts have ruled that women are not the property of their husbands. Women now own property. Women vote. Women serve on juries. Women are now elected to public office. In each case, women fought against a patriarchal social order where it just seemed "natural" for men to have the power to win these rights (Kuttner, 1996). The battles for gender equity are ongoing, especially regarding equal employment and promotion opportunities and the acceptance of women in leadership roles (religion, government, education, corporations). One of the most recent, interesting, and successful battles for gender equity has occurred in sports, the case study described here.

Historically, sport has been a male preserve (this section is dependent on a number of sources: Coakley, 2005:ch. 8; Eitzen, 2003; Eitzen and Sage, 2003:ch. 14; and Malec, 1997). When women did participate, they were ignored by fans and the media, trivialized (given team nicknames such as the "Wildkittens" or the "Teddy Bears") (Eitzen and Baca Zinn, 1989a), or demeaned for being "masculine" or lesbians. Thus, sport was (and is) an institution that contributed to and perpetuated male dominance in society (Hall, 1985).

With a few exceptions, U.S. sport in the early 1970s was for men and boys. At that time, *Sports Illustrated* writers Bil Gilbert and Nancy Williamson (1973) said: "There may be worse (more socially serious) forms of prejudice in the United States, but there is no sharper example of discrimination today than that which operates against girls and women who take part in competitive sports, wish to take part, or might wish to if society did not scorn such endeavors" (90).

531

CHAPTER 18
Human Agency:
Individuals and
Groups in Society
Changing Social
Structures

These women are celebrating their gold medal-winning performance in the 2004 Olympics. Women's sports programs in the United States have made tremendous progress since 1972. These changes were not initiated by the powerful, but came about because of a wider social movement for women's rights and the acts of individual parents, athletes, and groups who challenged patriarchal tradition, laws, and policies in athletics.

Compare this statement with the situation now. United States women were celebrated in the 1996, 2000, and 2004 Olympic Games for their successes. Female professionals in tennis and golf are on television and highly rewarded for victories. New professional leagues for women are springing up in basketball, soccer, and other sports. At the collegiate level, schools with successful teams, especially in basketball, are given strong fan and media support (in some cases more than for the men's teams). In 1972, women athletes received a total of $100,000 in athletic scholarships. Now, more than 150,000 women play college sports and share almost $400 million a year in scholarships. At the high school level, just 1 girl in 27 (less than 300,000) participated in interscholastic competition in 1971. Now almost 3 million girls participate. Youth sports now have girls' teams, and some have boys and girls playing on the same teams, in sharp contrast to a generation ago when many youth sports programs had formal policies excluding girls from any participation.

These important changes were *not* initiated by the powerful—by the federal government, state governments, the National Collegiate Athletic Association, the various state high school associations, local school boards, Little League Baseball, or other youth sports organizations. The changes came about because of a wider social movement for women's rights and the acts of individual parents, athletes, and groups who challenged patriarchal tradition, laws, and the policies of various athletic and school organizations. As a result of their acts of agency, sport has been changed so that "the next generation of sportswomen will likely find equality in athletics so ordinary and natural that they could forget where it came from" (Kuttner, 1996:5).

The 1960s and early 1970s were a time of societal upheaval. Rebellion was ubiquitous. The powerless (for example, racial minorities, people with disabilities, gays and lesbians) challenged discriminatory laws and practices. Students confronted school administrations about their archaic and paternalistic practices. Young people contested the government's war in Southeast Asia. Rather than be drafted to serve in a war they did not believe in, some young men fled to Canada and others chose jail. Youth defied traditions and the materialistic ways of their parents and the older generation. In this time of insurgence, insubordination, defiance, and reforms, the women's movement took root. Actually, women had fought for equality for a hundred years or more, but in the 1960s the movement gained many followers and significant momentum. There were intellectual strands such as Betty Friedan's *The Feminine Mystique* (1963), which argued for an all-out effort to remove the obstructions that had restricted women's access to equal opportunities in society. Feminist intellectuals argued also that girls and women are enhanced as human beings when they are given the opportunities to become competent intellectually and physically. The women's movement also redefined occupational and family roles for women, providing them with increased time and resources for other pursuits.

Organizations emerged, such as the National Organization for Women (NOW), with branches throughout the United States. This organization was instrumental in promoting progress in women's sports in two major ways. First, it asked local organizations to gather information about the differences for boys and girls and men and women in local schools and community programs (number of teams, participants, budgets, equipment, and facilities). This provided a national database for proposed legislation and court cases, as well as information for each participating community so that strong arguments for equity could be made before school boards or the courts. Indirectly, this survey was important because local women learned about the inequities of their communities firsthand and thus were likely candidates for more activist responses later.

The second contribution of NOW was its lobbying effort for national legislation to correct gender inequities. Armed with national data, women as individuals and as members of women's groups applied pressure on political representatives. After two years of intense lobbying, Congress passed Title IX of the Educational Amendments of 1972, which declared, "No person in the United States shall, on the basis of sex, be excluded from participation in, be denied the benefits of, or be subjected to discrimination under any educational program or activity receiving federal financial assistance."

Title IX was resisted vigorously by the male establishment in athletic organizations and schools as being too radical, impractical, and burdensome. As a result, enforcement in the early years was sporadic at best. There was a setback in 1984 when the Supreme Court in *Grove City* v. *Bell* ruled that Title IX did not apply to school athletic programs because they did not receive federal monies directly (even though the schools did). Congress made Title IX stronger in 1988 with the passage of the Civil Rights Restoration Act (over President Reagan's veto), which mandated equal opportunity to all programs in any organization receiving federal money. Most significant, the U.S. Supreme Court ruled that schools could be sued for financial damages if the schools had intentionally violated Title IX.

Court cases have been used throughout the struggle for gender equity in sports. Regarding youth sports, in 1973 Little League Baseball's ban against participation by girls was challenged and overturned in several lawsuits by individual parents. As a result, the various youth sports have permitted female participation.

At the high school level, lawsuits have been brought by girls and their parents against school districts or state high school regulatory bodies. Typically, these cases involve one of three situations: (1) a girl wishing to participate on a boys' team because

533

CHAPTER 18
Human Agency:
Individuals and
Groups in Society
Changing Social
Structures

her school did not provide a girls' team (the courts generally ruled in favor of the girl in these cases); (2) a girl wanting to be on a boys' team even though her school provided a girls' team (the courts generally ruled against her in this type of case because equal opportunity had not been denied her); and (3) girls wanting a team because neither a boys' team nor a girls' team exists in a particular sport. As an example of this last situation, Nebraska settled four class-action lawsuits in 1996, agreeing that high schools must provide girls' softball, with facilities and equipment equal to boys' baseball (Pera, 1996).

Gender inequity in intercollegiate athletics has been challenged officially in two ways (Eitzen and Sage, 2003). Between 1972, when Title IX became law, and 1992, for example, over 1,000 complaints were filed on behalf of women with the Department of Education's Office of Civil Rights. In addition, dozens of lawsuits have been filed against colleges and universities because of gender inequity. For example, in 1992 Colorado State University dropped several sports, including the women's softball team, because of budgetary constraints. Nine members of the softball team filed suit against CSU, claiming the university violated Title IX. The Colorado Supreme Court ruled that CSU had to reinstate women's softball. In another case, the California chapter of NOW filed a sex-discrimination lawsuit against the California State University system in 1993, claiming that only 30 percent of its participants in sports are women and that women's sports receive less than 25 percent of the athletics budget. Within a year, the California State University system agreed to increase significantly its athletics opportunities and finances for women. In 1994, a U.S. district court, reacting to a suit brought by female athletes at Brown University, ordered that the school reinstate women's gymnastics and volleyball teams and provide "equal treatment" to women's athletics.

Aside from the courts, there are other challenges by women to the male-dominated system of athletics. Some female athletes compete with men in the traditional male sports of football and wrestling. There are a few female coaches of men's teams. There are also female athletic directors (even a few at NCAA Division I-A schools), female sportswriters, and a few women umpires and referees. In each instance, these women invaded a male domain, and, as a result, they have often encountered hostility, disrespect, and various uncooperative actions from men. But by crossing traditional gender boundaries, these pioneers are extremely important players in this struggle for gender equity.

The past thirty years have seen dramatic changes in sports opportunities for women and girls. Participation is way up. Public interest in women's sports is growing rapidly. The number of sports for girls and women offered by schools has risen dramatically. Budgets, resources, and facilities are enormously better. Gender equality in sport, however, is still a goal, not a reality. For example, while 53 percent of college students are women, women receive only 42 percent of the athletic scholarship money that is distributed in Division I-A schools. Men's football is the culprit, since it has been allowed to be exempt from the accounting. It is not uncommon for a school with a big-time football program to spend twice as much on its men's football team as it spends on all women's sports. A second area of concern is the decrease, since Title IX, in the proportion of women's teams with women in leadership positions (the number of men exceed the number of women as head coaches and top administrator of women's athletics) at both the high school and college levels. Third, media attention is not equal. The argument by television networks and newspapers is that they give the public what they want, and the public wants male sports. This, of course, is a self-fulfilling prophecy. Fourth, opportunities in sports careers (professional sports,

sports journalism, athletic trainers, referees) for women still lag behind the opportunities and rewards for men. Fifth, female athletes, especially those involved in sports requiring strength and aggression, continue to battle stereotypes, because they do not conform to the dominant cultural definitions of femininity.

So, despite dramatic and positive changes, sport is still a battleground for those wishing to achieve gender equity. Continued acts of agency, collectively and individually, are required if the positive trend is to stay on track.

535

CHAPTER 18
Human Agency:
Individuals and
Groups in Society
Changing Social
Structures

Conclusion

This book is an introduction to sociology. The primary purpose was to make you more perceptive and more analytical regarding things social. Our hope is that you will build on this knowledge in a lifelong quest to understand society and your place in it.

The theme of this last chapter is the importance of human beings in constructing and reconstructing society. This has two important implications for each of us. First, we do not have to be passive actors who accept society's institutional imperatives as inevitable. To the contrary, we can be actively engaged in social life, working for the improvement or even radical change of faulty social structures. Second, the personal is political. While there are broad political struggles within society that involve us, politics also occurs at the micro level. Issues of social justice may be present in our work situations, at church and other organizations to which we belong, in our neighborhoods, in our families, and in our personal relationships. We can promote social justice in these situations or thwart it. In each instance, our actions have political implications.

At the macro level, the most important struggles involve overturning existing structures of exploitation and domination. These include collective efforts to bring about universal programs for greater equality such as universal health care, pensions, equal opportunity education, and expanding and upgrading the societal infrastructure (highways, bridges, water supply, airports, mass transit). New family forms require programs such as paid parental leave and a national system of dependent care. The changing economy requires management-labor cooperation to increase productivity while providing fair wages and protecting job security, job safety, job training, and collective bargaining rights. Issues of social justice involve progressive taxation (the more money made, the higher proportion paid in taxes), pay equity, and programs to guard against race, gender, and sexuality biases in employment, housing, and lending practices.

In sum, society's structural arrangements are not inevitable. Individuals converging across lines of race, ethnicity, gender, and sexual orientation can work at the grassroots level organizing opposition, educating the public, demonstrating to promote a cause, electing allied candidates, using the courts, or employing other tactics to transform society. Human beings are agents of change if they choose to be. The choice is ours.

Frances Fox Piven (1996), the eminent social scientist, in writing about the need for social change to solve our current social problems, says: "No one has ever successfully predicted the movements when ordinary people find their footing, discover new capacities for solidarity and power and new visions of the possible. Still, the development of American democracy depended on the perennial emergence of popular revolt in the past, and it does once again" (67).

1. The sociological paradox is that while society has power over its members, social actors have the power to change society. This means that (a) society is not a rigid entity, composed of robots; (b) what people consider sacred, and therefore unchangeable, is a social construction that can be reconstructed; and (c) since social structures are created by people, they are imperfect, always in need of reform or transformation.

2. A social movement is a collective attempt to promote or resist change.

3. There are three types of social movements: (a) resistance movements, which are organized to resist change or to reverse changes that have occurred; (b) reform movements, which seek to alter a specific part of society; and (c) revolutionary movements, which go beyond reform by seeking the transformation of the entire society.

4. Social movements move through predictable stages. Initially, a number of people share feelings of discontent or anger over some societal condition. The second stage is when the grievances of these people become more focused. A leader emerges who defines the goals, identifies the enemies, and challenges and inspires followers to work together for positive change. The followers are further galvanized as their target is provoked and the powerful attack them. Stage three involves organization, with formal rules, policies, procedures, and tactics. Alliances are formed with similar groups for mutual advantage. When the goals of the movement are accepted by society, the movement has arrived at the final stage, institutionalization.

5. The point of social movements and individual acts of agency is that institutional changes tend not to come from the leaders of government and business, but rather boil up from the people.

6. The civil rights movement did not begin in the 1960s, but rather from the time Blacks arrived here as slaves. Moreover, the civil rights movement is not the result of a single event. It carries the cumulative effects of centuries of mistreatment of Blacks by Whites and White governments.

7. Despite the oppressive control of Blacks, many of them exhibited agency by individual acts of rebellion, work slowdowns, and running away to join with others in bands that harassed Whites. Others fought the slave codes by promoting community solidarity, fighting to keep family ties, and creating their own rituals that recognized marriage and parenthood. After the Civil War, Blacks remained oppressed by low wages and sharecropping arrangements. Black Codes, laws that were biased against Blacks, were passed to keep Blacks from achieving equality. Similarly, in the early twentieth century, Jim Crow laws enforced rigid segregation. Again, in the face of these indignities, Blacks engaged in various forms of agency.

8. The civil rights movement came together in the 1950s, with the passage of the Supreme Court decision desegregating the schools, the outrage of the lynching of Emmitt Till, and the Montgomery bus boycott. Sit-ins were organized. Economic boycotts against White businesses were initiated. Grievances were taken to court. The movement was partially successful, as segregationist laws and practices were soon abolished. Racial equality has not yet been achieved, however, as measured by wages, employment opportunities, unemployment rates, poverty rates, desegregated neighborhoods, and differences in money spent on education.

9. Before 1970, U.S. sport was almost exclusively for men and boys. However, as a consequence of court cases; individual acts of courage by women pioneers in sport as athletes, coaches, administrators, and referees; and the efforts of women's organizations, dramatic moves toward gender equity in sports have been accomplished. Archaic rules by athletic organizations prohibiting girls from competition were overturned. Legislation, most prominently Title IX, was passed which gave impetus to greater participation by girls and women in school sports. Rulings by the courts have given women greater equity in this previously male preserve. Full gender equity, however, has not yet been reached.

10. Society's structural arrangements are not inevitable. Individuals acting alone or with others in grassroots organizations can be agents of change.

Key Terms

Determinism
Social movement
Ideology

Resistance movements
Reform movements
Revolutionary movement

Institutionalization
Goal displacement

Study Questions

1. What is the fundamental sociological paradox?
2. Provide contemporary examples (in the United States and worldwide) of the three types of social movements.
3. Using the case study of the civil rights movement (beginning with Rosa Parks), show how that movement has gone through the various stages of social movements.
4. What are the implications of this chapter's thesis— that human beings construct and reconstruct society?

For Further Reading

Human Agency: General

Herbert Blumer, "Collective Behavior," in Alfred M. Lee (ed.), *Principles of Sociology*, 2nd ed. (New York: Barnes and Noble, 1955), pp. 165–198.

Robert A. Goldberg, *Grassroots Resistance: Social Movements in Twentieth-Century America* (Belmont, CA: Wadsworth, 1991).

Neil Smelser, *Theory of Collective Behavior* (New York: Free Press, 1962).

Howard Zinn, *A People's History of the United States* (New York: Harper & Row, 1980).

Human Agency: Case Studies

Teresa Amott, *Caught in the Crisis: Women and the U.S. Economy Today* (New York: Monthly Review Press, 1993).

Taylor Branch, *Parting the Waters: America in the King Years 1954–63* (New York: Simon & Schuster Touchstone, 1988).

Robert D. Bullard. 1994. *Unequal Protection: Environmental Justice and Communities of Color*. San Francisco: Sierra Club Books.

Dudley Clendinen and Adam Nagourney, *Out for Good: The Struggle to Build a Gay Rights Movement in America* (New York: Simon & Schuster, 1999).

D. Stanley Eitzen, *Fair and Foul: Beyond the Myths and Paradoxes of Sport*, 3rd ed. (Lanham, MD: Rowman & Littlefield, 2006).

John Hope Franklin and Loren Schweninger, *Runaway Slaves: Rebels on the Plantation* (New York: Oxford University Press, 1999).

John C. Hammerback, Richard J. Jensen, and Jose Angel Gutierrez, *A War of Words: Chicano Protest in the 1960s and 1970s* (Westport, CT: Greenwood Press, 1985).

Vincent Harding, *There Is a River: The Black Struggle for Freedom in America* (New York: Harcourt Brace Jovanovich, 1981).

Fred Powledge, *Free at Last? The Civil Rights Movement and the People Who Made It* (Boston: Little, Brown, 1991).

Marta Russell, *Beyond Ramps: Disability at the End of the Social Contract* (Monroe, ME: Common Courage Press, 1998).

Joseph P. Shapiro, *No Pity: People with Disabilities Forging a New Civil Rights Movement* (New York: Times Books/Random House, 1993).

http://www.wsu.edu:8001/~amerstu/smc/smcframe.html

The Social Movements and Culture website offers a listing of some of the major historical and current social movements.

http://www.selfadvocacy.com/

This is a website for the disability rights organization Advocating Change Together. It is "run by and for people with developmental and other disabilities" and is "committed to freedom, equality, and justice for all people with disabilities."

http://www.glaad.org/org/index.php

The Gay and Lesbian Alliance against Defamation website offers news related to gays and lesbians and proactive ideas for creating visibility and awareness surrounding the gay and lesbian community.

http://www.colorlines.com/

Produced by the Applied Research Center, Color Lines is the "nation's leading magazine on race, culture, and organizing."

http://civilrights.org/

Civilrights.org's mission is to "empower the civil rights community to lead the fight for equality and social justice in the emerging digital society through the establishment of an online social justice network."

http://www.thp.org/index.html

The Hunger Project is committed to ending world hunger. The organization has projects in many parts of the world.

http://www.cuadp.org/index.html

Citizens United for Alternatives to the Death Penalty is a grassroots activist group with the goal of ending the death penalty in the United States.

http://members.aol.com/rasphila/linkspage.html

This site is a comprehensive list of peace-related websites. It includes links to activist groups advocating for peace, as well as alternative media sources.

Glossary

Accommodation. Acceptance of one's position in a situation without struggle.

Achieved status. A position in a social organization attained through personal effort.

Age cohort. Individuals from the same generation and thus affected by similar societal events such as an economic depression or war.

Ageism. Discrimination against the elderly.

Aggregate. A collection of individuals who happen to be at the same place at the same time.

Alienation. An individual's feeling of separation from the surrounding society.

Altruistic suicide. The sacrificing of one's life for the good of the group.

Androgyny. Having the characteristics of both males and females.

Anomic suicide. Durkheim's term *anomie* indicates a social condition characterized by the absence of norms or conflicting norms. At the individual level, the person is not sure what the norms are, which leads to a relatively high probability of suicide.

Anticipatory socialization. Learning and acting out the beliefs, norms, and values of a group before joining it.

Argot. The specialized or secret language peculiar to a group.

Ascribed status. Social position based on such factors as age, race, and family over which the individual has no control.

Assimilation. The process by which individuals or groups voluntarily or involuntarily adopt the culture of another group, losing their original identity.

Baby boom. A term referring to a fifteen-year period in U.S. history following World War II in which an extraordinary number of babies were born.

Bias theories. An explanation that blames the prejudiced attitudes of majority members for the secondary status of the minority.

Blaming the victim. The belief that some individuals are poor, criminals, or school dropouts because they have a flaw within them.

Bourgeoisie. Marx's term for the class of people that owns the means of production in a capitalist society.

Bureaucracy. A system of administration that is characterized by specialized roles, explicit rules, and a hierarchy of authority.

Bureaucratization. The trend toward greater use of the bureaucratic mode of organization and administration within society.

Capital flight. The investment choices that involve moving corporate monies from one investment to another (for example, investments in other countries, plant relocation, and mergers).

Capitalism. The economic system based on private ownership of property, guided by the pursuit of maximum profits.

Capitalist patriarchy. A condition of capitalism in which male supremacy keeps women in subordinate roles at work and in the home.

Case study. The research strategy that involves detailed and thorough analysis of a single event, community, or organization.

Caste system. The closed system of social stratification. Membership is fixed at birth and is permanent.

Caveat emptor. The Latin phrase that means "let the buyer beware."

Charisma. The extraordinary attributes of an individual that enable the possessor to lead and inspire without the legal authority to do so.

Charisma of office. Instead of charisma based on personal attributes, in some organizations, the holder of a particular position is believed to possess charisma.

Church. The highly organized, bureaucratic form of religious organization that accommodates itself to the larger society.

Civil religion. The set of religious beliefs, rituals, and symbols outside the church that legitimates the status quo.

Class. Ranking in a stratification system based on economic resources.

Class consciousness. Karl Marx's term that refers to the recognition by people in a similar economic situation of a common interest.

Class segregation. Barriers that restrict social interaction to the members of a particular social class.

Cloning. The artificial production of genetically identical offspring.

Cohabitation. The practice of two people living together as a couple without being married.

Colonial theory. A structural explanation of minority subordination that rests on use of power by the dominant group to oppress a racial minority group.

Commune. A small, voluntary community characterized by cooperation and a common ideology.

Compulsory heterosexuality. The system of sexuality that imposes negative sanctions on those who are homosexual or bisexual.

Conflict model. A view of society that posits conflict as a normal feature of social life, influencing the distribution of power and the direction and magnitude of social change.

539

Consensus. Widely held agreement on the norms and values of society.

Conspicuous consumption. The purchase and obvious display of material goods to impress other people with one's wealth and assumed status.

Constraint. The state of being controlled by some force.

Contingent workers. Those involved in an employment arrangement in which employees work for an employer as temporaries or as independent contractors.

Control group. A group of subjects in an experiment who are not exposed to the independent variable but are similar in all other respects to the group exposed to the independent variable.

Co-optation. The process by which representatives of a potentially destabilizing subgroup are incorporated into the leadership or management level of an organization to avert problems.

Corporate crime. The illegal and/or socially harmful behaviors that result from the deliberate decisions of corporate executives in accordance with corporate goals.

Correlation. The degree of relationship between two variables.

Counterculture. A subculture that fundamentally opposes the dominant culture.

Crime. An act that is prohibited by the law.

Cult. A religion with practices and teachings at odds with the dominant culture and religion.

Cultural deficiency theories. Explanations that argue that some flaw in a social group's way of life is responsible for its secondary status.

Cultural deprivation. An ethnocentric term implying that the culture of another group is not only deficient but also inferior.

Cultural diffusion. The spread of one culture's characteristics to another.

Cultural relativity. The belief that customs of another society must be viewed and evaluated by their standards, not by an outsider's.

Cultural tyranny. The belief that the socialization process forces narrow behavioral and attitudinal traits on people.

Culture. The knowledge that the members of a social organization share.

Culture of poverty. The view that the poor are qualitatively different in values and lifestyles from the rest of society and that these cultural differences explain continued poverty.

Deferred gratification. The willingness to sacrifice in the present for expected future rewards.

Deficiency theories. Explanations that view the secondary status of minorities as the result of their own behaviors and cultural traits.

Deflation. The part of the economic cycle when the amount of money in circulation is down, resulting in low prices and unemployment.

Deindustrialization. The widespread, systematic diversion of capital (finance, plant, and equipment) from investment in the nation's basic industries into service and knowledge sectors of the economy or overseas.

Democracy. The form of government in which the citizens participate in government, characterized by competition for office, public officials being responsive to public opinion, and the citizenry having access to reliable information on which to make their electoral choices.

Demographics. The scientific study of the size, composition, and changes in human populations.

Dependency ratio. The relationship between old-age Social Security recipients and those workers paying Social Security taxes.

Dependent variable. A variable that is influenced by the effect of another variable (the independent variable).

Deprogramming. The process in which people believed to have been brainwashed by cults are abducted and retrained against their will.

Derogation. Discrimination in the form of words that put a minority down.

Determinism. The belief that human behavior is controlled by some force, whether genetic, economic, or political. Taken to the extreme, deterministic theories leave no room for human beings to adapt to and change social structures to meet their needs.

Deviance. Behavior that violates the expectations of society.

Dialectic. The clash between conflicting ideas and forces.

Differential association. The theory that a person becomes deviant because of an excess of definitions favorable to the violation of societal expectations over definitions supporting the norms and values.

Direct interlock. A type of interlocking directorate in which an individual serves on the board of directors of two companies.

Direct social control. Direct intervention by the agents of society to control the behavior of individuals and groups.

Discouraged workers. People who have not actively sought work for four weeks. They are not counted as unemployed by the Bureau of Labor Statistics.

Discrimination. To act toward a person or group with partiality, typically because they belong to a minority.

Disengagement. The process of removing oneself from society.

Division of labor. The specialization of economic roles resulting in an interdependent and efficient system.

Dominant class. Domhoff's model of power that posits that the very wealthy in society contribute a disproportionate number of people to the controlling institutions and key decision-making groups.

Dual-worker marriages. Marriages in which a husband and wife are both employed outside the home.

Dysfunctions. Consequences that are disruptive for the stability and cohesion of the social organization.

Economic inequality. The gap between the rich and the poor.

Economy. The institution that ensures the maintenance of society by producing and distributing the necessary goods and services.

Egalitarianism. Fundamental belief in equality.

Ego. According to Freud, the conscious, rational part of the self.

Egoistic suicide. Durkheim's finding that people lacking ties to social groups are more susceptible to suicide than are those with strong group attachments.

Elitist model of power. The assumption that power is concentrated in a few, rather than dispersed (the pluralist view).

Environmental racism. The disproportionate exposure of some racial group to toxic substances.

Epistemology. The philosophical position that all reality is socially constructed.

Ethnic group. A social group with a common culture distinct from the culture of the majority because of race, religion, or national origin.

Ethnicity. Shared cultural heritage.

Ethnocentrism. The universal tendency to deprecate the ways of people from other societies as wrong, old-fashioned, or immoral and to think of the ways of one's own group as superior (as the only right way).

Ethnomethodology. The subdiscipline in sociology that studies the everyday living practices of people to discover the underlying bases for social behavior.

Eugenics. The attempt to improve the human race through the control of hereditary factors.

Experimental group. A group of subjects in an experiment who are exposed to the independent variable, in contrast to the control group, which is not.

Falling rate of profit. One of the contradictions of capitalism argued by Karl Marx. This refers to the propensity of employers to maximize profits by reducing labor expenses (using technology and paying the lowest possible wages). The result of this capitalist rationale, argued Marx, would actually be to reduce profits because the workers would be less and less able to purchase products.

False consciousness. In Marxian theory, the idea that the oppressed may hold beliefs damaging to their interests.

Family. A particular societal arrangement whereby people related by ancestry, marriage, or adoption live together, form an economic unit, and raise children.

Family values. The conservative term supporting the heterosexual two-parent family. The implication is that all other family arrangements are the source of social problems.

Feminist approach. An approach based on support for women's equality.

Feminization of poverty. A reference to the relatively large number of female-headed households living in poverty.

Feral children. Children reputedly raised by animals; they have the characteristics of their peers (animals) rather than of human beings.

Folkways. Relatively unimportant rules that if violated are not severely punished.

Function. Any consequence of a social arrangement that contributes to the overall stability of the system.

Functional integration. Unity among divergent elements of society resulting from specialized divisions of labor.

Functionalism. The theoretical perspective that emphasizes the order, harmony, and stability of social systems.

Gender. The cultural and social definitions of feminine and masculine. Differs from sex, which is the biological fact of femaleness or maleness.

Gendered. Behavior patterned as feminine or masculine.

Gendered institutions. Entire institutions that are patterned by gender.

Gender roles. The understanding of gender differences that emphasize the characteristics that individuals learn in the socialization process.

Gender segregation. The location of women and men in different job categories throughout the workforce.

Gender stratification. The differential ranking and rewarding of women's and men's roles.

Gender structure. Features of social organization that produce gender inequality.

Generalized other. Mead's concept that refers to the internalization of the expectations of the society.

Genetic engineering. The scientific effort to manipulate DNA molecules in plants and animals.

Glass ceiling. Invisible barriers that limit women's mobility in organizations.

Global culture. The diffusion of a single culture throughout the world.

Globalization. The economic, political, and social connections and interdependence among the societies in the world.

Glossolalia. The emotional religious experience involving the incoherent "speaking in tongues."

Goal displacement. When the original goals of an organization are displaced by the goals of maintaining the organization.

Group. A collection of two or more people who, because of sustained interaction, have evolved a common culture.

Hedonism. The pursuit of pleasure and self-indulgence.

Hidden curriculum. That part of the school experience that has nothing to do with formal subjects but refers to the behaviors that schools expect of children (obedience to authority, remaining quiet and orderly, and so on).

Hierarchy. The arrangement of people or objects in order of importance.

Home-based work. Women working for pay in their homes.

Horizontal mobility. Changes in occupations or other situations without moving from one social class to another.

Household. A residential unit of unrelated individuals who pool resources and perform common tasks of production and consumption.

Human agency. When individuals, acting alone or with others, shape, resist, challenge, and sometimes change the social institutions that impinge on them.

Id. Freud's term for the collection of urges and drives people have for pleasure and aggression.

Ideal type. An abstraction constructed to show how some phenomenon would be characterized in its pure form.

Ideological social control. The efforts by social organizations to control members by controlling their minds. Societies accomplish this, typically, through the socialization process.

Ideology. A set of ideas that explain reality, provide guidelines for behavior, and express the interests of a group.

Immigration. The movement of people from one nation to another for permanent residence.

Independent variable. A variable that affects another variable (the dependent variable).

Indirect interlock. A type of interlocking directorate in which two companies each have a director on the board of a third company.

Individual racism. Overt acts by individuals of one race to harm a member or members of another race.

Inflation. The situation when too much money purchases too few goods, resulting in rising prices.

Institutions. Social arrangements that channel behavior in prescribed ways in the important areas of societal life.

Institutional derogation. Occurs when the normal arrangements of society act to reinforce the negative stereotypes of minority groups.

Institutional discrimination. When the social arrangements and accepted ways of doing things in society disadvantage some social category.

Institutionalization. Occurs when a movement's beliefs are accepted by the larger society and its goals are achieved.

Institutional process. The concept designating the forces that resist change, which emanate from the assumed human need for certainty and stability.

Institutional racism. Occurs when the social arrangements and accepted ways of doing things in society disadvantage a racial group.

Institutional sexism. Occurs when the social arrangements and accepted ways of doing things in society disadvantage females.

Institutional violence. Occurs when the normal workings of the society do harm to a social category.

Instrumentalist view. A view of power held by some Marxists that the ruling class controls political institutions through money and influence. Other Marxists accept the structuralist view of power.

Instrumental process. The search for technological solutions to human problems as an impetus for change.

Interest group. A group of like-minded persons who organize to influence public policy.

Intergenerational mobility. The difference in social class position between (typically) a son and his father.

Interlocking directorates. The linkages between corporations that results when an individual serves on the board of directors of two companies (a direct interlock) or when two companies each have a director on the board of a third company (an indirect interlock).

Internalization. In the process of socialization, society's demands become part of the individual, acting to control his or her behavior.

Intragenerational mobility. The movement by an individual from one social class to another.

"Iron cage" of rationality. The dehumanizing aspects of bureaucracy. Max Weber saw bureaucracies as cages with people trapped in them, denied of their basic humanity.

Labeling theory. The explanation of deviant behavior that stresses the importance of the society in defining what is illegal and in assigning deviant status to particular individuals, which in turn dominates their identities and behaviors.

Laissez-faire. The government policy of allowing the marketplace to operate unhindered.

Latent consequence. An unintended consequence of a social arrangement or social action.

Life chances. Weber's term for the chances throughout one's life cycle to live and experience the good things in life.

Looking-glass self. Cooley's concept of the importance of how other people influence the way we see ourselves.

Machismo (macho). An exaggerated masculinity, evidenced by male dominance, posturing, physical daring, and an exploitative attitude toward women.

Macro level. The large-scale structures and processes of society, including the institutions and the system of stratification.

Majority group. The social category in society holding superordinate power and which successfully imposes its will on less-powerful groups (minority groups).

Male chauvinism. Exaggerated beliefs about the superiority of the male and the resulting discrimination.

Male dominance. The beliefs, values, and cultural meanings that give higher value and prestige to masculinity than to femininity and that institutionalize male control of socially valued resources.

Manifest consequence. An intended consequence of a social arrangement or social action.

Marginality. The condition resulting from taking part in two distinct ways of life without belonging fully to either.

Marital power. The ability to control the spouse and to influence or control family decisions and activities.

Master status. A status that has exceptional importance for social identity, overshadowing other statuses.

Material technology. Refers to the technical knowledge needed to use and make things.

Matriarchal family. A family structure in which the mother is dominant.

Matrix of domination. The intersections of the hierarchies of class, race, and gender in which each of us exists.

McDonaldization. George Ritzer's term for the process by which the principles of fast-food restaurants are coming to dominate more and more sectors of American society as well as the rest of the world.

Megachurches. A trend among evangelicals is toward very large churches. Their growth is fueled by entertaining church services, the provision of services, and specialized ministries for targeted groups.

Meritocracy. A system of stratification in which rank is based purely on achievement.

Micro level. The social organization and processes of small-scale social groups.

Military-industrial complex. The term that refers to the direct and indirect relationships between the military establishment (the Pentagon) and the corporations.

Minority group. A social category composed of people who differ from the majority, are relatively powerless, and are the objects of discrimination.

Modal personality type. A distinct type of personality considered to be characteristic of the members of a particular society.

Model. The mental image a scientist has of the structure of society. This influences what scientists look for, what they see, and how phenomena are explained.

Modern family. The nuclear family that emerged in response to the requirements of an urban, industrial society. It consisted of an intact nuclear household unit with a male breadwinner, his full-time homemaker wife, and their dependent children.

Monogamy. The form of marriage in which an individual may not be married to more than one person at a time.

Monopolistic capitalism. The form of capitalism prevalent in the contemporary United States, where a few large corporations control the key industries, destroying competition and the market mechanisms that would ordinarily keep prices low and help consumers.

Monopoly. Occurs when a single firm dominates an industry.

Mores. Important norms, the violation of which results in severe punishment.

Mortality rate. The frequency of actual deaths in a population.

Myth of peaceful progress. The incorrect belief that throughout U.S. history, disadvantaged groups have gained their share of power, prosperity, and respectability without violence.

Myth of separate worlds. The belief that work and family roles operate independently of each other.

New immigration. Unlike previous waves of immigration in which the immigrants were primarily White and European, the latest wave of immigration is composed primarily of people of color (from Latin America and Asia).

New poor. The poor who are displaced by new technologies or whose jobs have moved away to the suburbs, to other regions of the country, or out of the country.

Nominalist position. A philosophical position that a group is nothing more than the sum of its parts.

Nomos. Literally, meaningful order. The opposite of anomie.

Nonfamily household. People who live alone or with unrelated individuals.

Norms. Cultural rules that specify appropriate and inappropriate behavior (in other words, the shared expectations for behavior).

Nuclear family. A kinship unit composed of a husband, a wife, and children.

Nuptiality. The proportion of married people.

Offshoring. When a company moves its operations to another country.

Ontology. The philosophical position that accepts the reality of things because their nature cannot be denied.

Opiate of the masses. Marx's term for religion's effect on society. In this view, religion inhibits societal change by making existing social arrangements seem right and inevitable. The dominant form of economics in society, the type of government, the law, and other social creations are given religious sanction.

Order model. The conception of society as a social system characterized by cohesion, consensus, cooperation, reciprocity, stability, and persistence.

Outsourcing. The practice of corporations of contracting work outside the company and its relatively well-paid (usually unionized) workers to companies inside and outside the United States where costs are cheaper.

Paradigm. The basic assumptions a scientist has of the structure of society (see *Model*).

Participant observation. A method in which researchers engage in the activities of the people they are observing.

Participatory socialization. The mode of socialization in which parents encourage their children to explore, experiment, and question.

Patriarchal family. A family structure in which the father is dominant.

Patriarchy. A form of social organization in which males dominate females.

Pay equity. Policies designed to bring the pay levels of women in closer alignment with those of men. Also called comparable worth.

Peer group. Friends usually of the same age and socioeconomic status.

Peter Principle. The view that most people in an organization will be promoted until they eventually reach their level of incompetence.

Pluralism. A situation in which different groups live in mutual respect but retain their racial, religious, or ethnic identities.

Pluralist model of power. The diffuse distribution of power among various groups and interests.

Plutocracy. Government by or in the interest of the rich.

Political crime. Either crime against the state (the order model's view) or crime by the state (the conflict model's view).

Polity. The societal institution especially concerned with maintaining order.

Population implosion. The trend for people to live in ever denser localities (the movement of people from rural areas to the urban regions).

Positivism. The scientific model for understanding reality.

Postmodern families. Judith Stacey's term for the multiplicity of family and household arrangements that has emerged as a result of a number of social factors, such as women in the labor force, divorce, remarriage, and cohabitation arrangements.

Poverty. A standard of living below the minimum needed for the maintenance of adequate diet, health, and shelter.

Power. The ability to get what one wants from someone else.

Power elite. Mills's term for the coalition of the top echelon of the military, the executive branch of the federal government, and business.

Prestige. The respect of an individual or social category as a result of his or her social status.

Priestly role of religion. One role of the church and the clergy is to comfort individuals, helping them through difficult times. The church also celebrates the various important stages in life (birth, marriage, death). This role is conservative since it does not challenge the system.

Primary deviance. The original illegal act preceding the successful application of the deviant label.

Primary groups. Small groups characterized by intimate, face-to-face interaction.

Privilege. The distribution of goods and services, situations, and experiences that are highly valued and beneficial.

Progressive tax. A tax rate that escalates with the amount of income.

Proletariat. Marx's term for the industrial workers in a capitalistic society.

Prophetic role of religion. One function of the church is to challenge the existing system, leading the fight to right the inequities of society.

Protestant ethic. The religious beliefs, traced back to Martin Luther and John Calvin, that emphasize hard work and continual striving in order to prove by material success that one is saved.

Psychosurgery. A form of brain surgery used to change the behavior of the patient.

Pygmalion effect. Students placed in a track are treated by teachers in a way that ensures that the prophecy is fulfilled.

Race. A group socially defined on the basis of a presumed common genetic heritage resulting in distinguishing physical characteristics.

Racial-ethnic groups. Groups labeled as races by the wider society and bound together by their common social and economic conditions, resulting in distinctive cultural and ethnic characteristics.

Racial formation. The sociohistorical processes by which races are continually being shaped and transformed.

Racism. The domination of and discrimination against one racial group by the majority.

Radical nonintervention. Schur's term for the strategy of leaving juvenile delinquents alone as much as possible rather than processing (and labeling) them through the criminal justice system.

Random sample. The selection of a subset from a population so that every person has an equal chance of being selected.

Realist position. The philosophical position that a group is more than the sum of its parts (referring to the emergence of culture and mechanisms of social control that affect the behavior of members regardless of their personalities).

Recidivism. Reinvolvement in crime.

Reference groups. Groups to which one would like to belong and toward which one therefore orients his or her behavior.

Reform movements. Social movements that seek to alter a specific part of society.

Regressive tax. A tax rate that remains the same for all people rich or poor. The result is that poor people pay a larger proportion of their earned income than do affluent people.

Reliability. The degree to which a study yields similar results when repeated.

Religion. The social institution that encompasses beliefs and practices regarding the sacred.

Repressive socialization. The mode of socialization in which parents demand rigid conformity in their children, enforced by physical punishment.

Reserve army of the unemployed. Unemployed people who want to work. Their presence tends to depress the wages of workers and keeps those workers from making demands on employers for fear of being replaced.

Resistance movements. The organized attempt to reinforce the traditional system by preventing change.

Revolutionary movement. The collective attempt to bring about a radical transformation of society.

Rites of passage. The ritual whereby the society recognizes the adult status of a young member.

Ritual. Symbolic actions that reinforce the collective remembering of the group's shared meanings.

Role. The behavioral expectations and requirements attached to a position in a social organization.

Role conflict. Occurs when an individual cannot fulfill the expectations of one status without violating those of another.

Role performance (role behavior). The actual behavior of people occupying particular positions in a social organization.

Routinization of charisma. The process by which an organization attempts to transmit the special attributes of the former leader to a new one. This is done by various means, for example, laying on of hands and the old leader choosing a successor.

Sacred. That which inspires awe because of its believed supernatural qualities.

Sample. A representative part of a population.

Sanctions. Social rewards or punishments for approved or disapproved behavior.

Scientific management. Efforts by business managers to increase worker efficiency by breaking work down into very specialized tasks, standardizing tools and procedures, and speeding up repetitive work.

Secondary deviance. Deviant behavior that is a consequence of the successful application of the deviant label.

Secondary groups. Large, impersonal, and formally organized groups.

Second shift. Women's responsibilities for housework, child care, and home management that they must do in addition to their labor in the workforce.

Sect. A religious organization, in contrast to a church, that tends to be dogmatic, fundamentalistic, and in opposition to the world.

Secular. Of or pertaining to the world; the opposite of sacred.

Segmented labor market. The capitalist economy is divided into two distinct sectors, one in which production and working conditions are relatively stable and secure; the other is composed of marginal firms in which working conditions, wages, and job security are low.

Segregation. The separation of one group from another.

Self. George Herbert Mead's term for an individual's personality.

Self-esteem. The opinion of oneself.

Self-fulfilling prophecy. An event that occurs because it was predicted. The prophecy is confirmed because people alter their behavior to conform to the prediction.

Severely poor. Those at least 50 percent *below* the official poverty line.

Sex. Biological identity as male or female.

Sex-gender system. A system of stratification that ranks and rewards gender roles unequally.

Sexism. The individual actions and institutional arrangements that discriminate against women.

Sex roles. The learned patterns of behavior expected of males and females by society.

Sexuality. A way of organizing the social world based on sexual identity.

Sexual stratification. A hierarchical arrangement based on gender.

Shared monopoly. When four or fewer companies control 50 percent or more of an industry.

Sibling. A brother or sister.

Significant others. Mead's term referring to people who are most important in determining a child's behavior.

Social class. A number of people who occupy the same relative economic rank in the stratification system.

Social construction of reality. The process by which individuals learn how to define reality from other people in interaction and by learning the culture.

Social control. The regulation of human behavior in any social group.

Social Darwinism. The belief that the principle of the survival of the fittest applies to human societies, especially the system of stratification.

Social determinism. The assumption that human behavior is explained exclusively by social factors.

Social differentiation. The process of categorizing people by some personal attribute.

Social facts. Durkheim's term referring to the forces outside individuals that constrain them in their behaviors.

Social group. Two or more people who identify with each other and who share a distinctive set of relationships.

Social inequality. The ranking of people by wealth, family background, race, ethnicity, or sex.

Social interaction. When individuals act toward or respond to each other.

Socialism. The economic system in which the means of production are owned by the people for their collective benefit.

Socialization. The process of learning cultural values, norms, and expectations.

Socialization agents. The individuals, groups, and institutions responsible for transmitting the culture of society to newcomers.

Social location. One's position in society based on family background, race, socioeconomic status, religion, and other relevant social characteristics.

Social mobility. Movement by an individual from one social class or status group to another.

Social movement. A collective attempt to promote or resist change.

Social organization. The order of a social group as evidenced by the positions, roles, norms, and other constraints that control behavior and ensure predictability.

Social problems. There are two types of social problems: (1) societally induced conditions that cause psychic and material suffering for any segment of the population; and (2) acts and conditions that violate the norms and values of society.

Social relationship. Occurs when two or more people engage in enduring social interaction.

Social roles. The expectations of what individuals should do in various statuses.

Social stratification. Occurs when people are ranked in a hierarchy that differentiates them as superior or inferior.

Social structure. The patterned and recurrent relationships among people and parts in a social organization.

Social system. A differentiated group whose parts are interrelated in an orderly arrangement, bounded in geographical space or membership.

Social technology. The knowledge necessary to establish, maintain, and operate the technical aspects of social organization.

Society. The largest social organization to which individuals owe their allegiance. The entity is located geographically, has a common culture, and is relatively self-sufficient.

Socioeconomic status. The measure of social status that takes into account several prestige factors, such as income, education, and occupation.

Sociological imagination. The view that individual troubles are inextricably linked to social forces.

Sociological theory. A set of ideas that explain a range of human behavior and a variety of social and societal events.

Sociology. The scholarly discipline concerned with the systematic study of social organizations.

Stagflation. The contemporary economic phenomenon that combines the problems of inflation and deflation—high prices, high unemployment, a wage-price spiral, and a profits squeeze.

Status. A socially defined position in a social organization.

Status anguish. A fundamental concern with the contradictions in the individual's status set.

Status group. People of similar status. They view each other as social equals.

Status inconsistency. The situation in which a person ranks high on one status dimension and low on another.

Status withdrawal. The loss of status that occurs with downward mobility.

Stereotype. An exaggerated generalization about some social category.

Stigma. A label of social disgrace.

Structural approach to sexual inequality. The understanding of gender differences resulting from factors external to individuals.

Structural discrimination theories. Explanations that focus on the institutionalized patterns of discrimination as the sources of the secondary status of minorities.

Structuralist view. A Marxian interpretation of power arguing that the ruling class gets its way because the political and economic institutions are biased in its favor. Other Marxists hold the instrumentalist view of power.

Structural transformation of the economy. The shift to a new era evidenced by the move from a manufacturing to a service/information economy with microchip technology, the global economy, and the rapid movement of capital.

Structured social inequality. The patterns of superiority and inferiority, the distribution of rewards, and the belief systems that reinforce the inequities of society.

Subculture. A relatively cohesive cultural system that varies in form and substance from the dominant culture.

Subsidy. Financial aid in the form of tax breaks or gifts granted by the government to an individual or commercial enterprise.

Suburb. A community adjacent to a city.

Sunrise industries. Industries characterized by increased output and employment.

Sunset industries. Industries declining in both output and employment.

Superego. Freud's term for the internalization of society's morals within the self.

Survey research. The research technique that selects a sample of people from a larger population in order to learn how they think, feel, or act.

Sweatshop. A substandard work environment in which workers are paid less than the minimum wage, workers are not paid overtime premiums, and other labor laws are violated.

Symbol. A thing that represents something else, such as a word, gesture, or physical object (cross, flag).

Synthesis. The blending of the parts into a new form.

Systemic imperatives. The economic and social constraints on the decision makers in an organization that promote the status quo.

Tax expenditures. Legal tax loopholes that permit certain individuals and corporations to pay lower taxes or no taxes at all.

Technology. The application of science to meet the needs of society.

Theodicy. The religious legitimation for a situation that might otherwise cause guilt or anger (such as defeat in a war or the existence of poverty among affluence).

Tracking. A practice of schools of grouping children according to their scores on IQ and other tests.

Transnational corporation. A corporation that operates in more than one country.

Transcience. Toffler's term for the rapid turnover in things, places, and people characteristic of a technological society.

Underemployment. Being employed at a job below one's level of training and expertise.

Undocumented immigrants. Immigrants who have entered the United States illegally.

Urbanism. The ways in which city life characteristically affects how people feel, think, and interact with one another.

Urbanization. The movement of people from rural to urban areas.

Urban region (megalopolis, conurbation, strip city). The extensive urban area that results when two or more large cities grow together until they are contiguous.

Validity. The degree to which a scientific study measures what it attempts to measure.

Value neutrality. The attempt by scientists to be absolutely free of bias in their research.

Values. The shared criteria used in evaluating objects, ideas, acts, feelings, or events as to their relative desirability, merit, or correctness.

Variable. An attitude, behavior, or condition that can vary in magnitude from case to case (the opposite of a constant).

Vertical mobility. Movement upward or downward in social class.

Voluntary associations. Organizations that people join because they approve of their goals.

Wealthfare. Receipt by the affluent of financial aid and/or services from the government.

Welfare. Receipt of financial aid and/or services from the government.

White flight. Whites leaving the central cities for the suburbs to avoid interaction with Blacks, especially the busing of children.

Work–family role system. The traditional uneven division of labor in which men's work role takes priority over the family role, and women, even those who work outside the home, are to give priority to the family role.

Academe. 1999. *Bulletin of the American Association of University Professors.* 85 (January/February). Washington, DC: American Association of University Professors.

———. 2001. *Bulletin of the American Association of University Professors.* 87 (March/April).

Acker, Joan. 1973. "Women and Stratification: A Case of Intellectual Sexism." *American Journal of Sociology* 78 (January): 936–945.

———. 1992. "Gendered Institutions: From Sex Roles to Gendered Institutions." *Contemporary Sociology* 21 (September):565–568.

Ahlburg, Dennis A., and Carol J. De Vita. 1992. "New Realities of the American Family." *Population Bulletin* 47 (August):entire issue.

Albelda, Randy. 1992. "Whose Values, Which Families?" *Dollars & Sense* 182 (December):6–9.

———. 1996. "Farewell to Welfare." *Dollars & Sense* 208 (November/December):16–19.

Albelda, Randy, and Chris Tilly. 1996. "It's a Family Affair." In *For Crying Out Loud: Women's Poverty in the United States,* D. Dujon and A. Withorn (eds.). Boston: South End Press.

———. 1997. *Glass Ceilings and Bottomless Pits: Women's Work, Women's Poverty.* Boston: South End Press.

Allen, Walter R., and Angie Y. Chung. 2000. "Your Blues Ain't Like My Blues: Race, Ethnicity and Social Inequality in America." *Contemporary Sociology* 29 (November):796–805.

American Association of University Professors. 2004. "Faculty Salary and Faculty Distribution Fact Sheet 2003–2004" Available online: http://www.aaup.org/Issues/WomeninHE/sal&distribution.htm.

American Association of University Women [AAUW]. 1992. "How Schools Shortchange Girls." Executive Summary. *AAUW Report.* Washington, DC: American Association of University Women Educational Foundation.

American Association of University Women. 1999. *Gender Gaps: Where Schools Still Fail Our Children.* New York: Marlowe and Company.

American Civil Liberties Union, Rhode Island Affiliate. 2005. "The Persistence of Racial Profiling in Rhode Island: An Update" (August). Available online: http://www.aclu.org/Files/OpenFile.cfm?id=18892.

American Community Survey. 2003. Available online: http://factfinder.census.gov.

American Council on Education. 2000. "ACE Study Shows Gains in Number of Women College Presidents, Smaller Gains for Minority CEOs." Available online: www.acenet.edu/news/press_release.

American Lung Association State of the Air. 2001. "American Lung Association Fact Sheet: African Americans and Lung Disease" (January). Available online: www.lungusa.org/diseases/.

American Psychological Association. 1993. *Violence and Youth.* Washington, DC: American Psychological Association.

American Society for Aesthetic Plastic Surgery. 2005. Available online: http://www.surgery.org/press/statistics-2004.php.

American Sociological Association. 2003. *The Importance of Collecting Data and Doing Scientific Research on Race.* Washington, DC: American Sociological Association.

Americans for Democratic Action. 2004. *Income and Inequality: Millions Left Behind,* 3rd. ed. Washington, DC: Americans for Democratic Action.

Amott, Teresa. 1993. *Caught in the Crisis: Women and the U.S. Economy Today.* New York: Monthly Review Press.

Andersen, Margaret L. 1997. *Thinking about Women: Sociological and Feminist Perspectives,* 4th ed. Boston: Allyn and Bacon.

———. 2003. *Thinking about Women,* 6th ed. Boston: Allyn and Bacon

———. 2005. *Thinking about Women,* 7th ed. Boston: Allyn and Bacon.

———. Forthcoming. "Diversity without Oppression: Race, Ethnicity and Power." In *Critical Ethnicity: Countering the Waves of Identity Politics,* Mary Kenyatta and Robert Tai (eds.). Lanham, MD: Rowman & Littlefield.

———. Forthcoming. "Whitewashing Race: A Critical Review Essay on 'Whiteness.'" In *Deconstructing Whiteness, Deconstructing White Supremacy,* Woody Doane and Eduardo Bonilla-Silva (eds.). New York: Routledge.

Andersen, Margaret L., and Patricia Hill Collins (eds.). 1992. *Race, Class, and Gender: An Anthology.* Belmont, CA: Wadsworth.

———. 1995. *Race, Class, and Gender: An Anthology,* 2nd ed. Belmont, CA: Wadsworth.

———. 1998. *Race, Class, and Gender: An Anthology,* 3rd ed. Belmont, CA: Wadsworth.

Andersen, Margaret L., and Howard F. Taylor. 2000. *Sociology: Understanding a Diverse Society.* Belmont, CA: Wadsworth.

Anderson, Jack. 1983. "Plans to Test Adolescents Smack of 1984." *Rocky Mountain News* (October 13):106.

Anderson, Sarah, and John Cavanagh. 1997. "The Top 10 List: A Four-Star Feast, But Who Gets the Check?" *Nation* (December 8):8–9.

Angier, Natalie. 2000. "Scientists: DNA Shows Humans Are All One Race." *Denver Post* (August 22):2A, 5A.

Anner, John. 1996. "Sweatshop Workers Organize and Win." *The Progressive* 60 (June):15.

Annie E. Casey Foundation. 2002. *Kids Count Pocket Guide.* Baltimore, MD: Annie E. Casey Foundation.

Aponte, Robert. 1991. "Urban Hispanic Poverty: Disaggregations and Explanations." *Social Problems* 38 (4):516–528.

Appelbaum, Richard P., and Edna Bonacich. 2000. "Choosing Sides in the Campaign against Sweatshops." *Chronicle of Higher Education* (April 7):B4–B6.

Appelbaum, Richard P., and William J. Chambliss. 1995. *Sociology.* New York: HarperCollins.

Applebome, Peter. 1989. "Scandals Aside, TV Preachers Thrive." *New York Times* (October 8):12A.

Armas, Genaro C. 2002. "In Course of a Lifetime, Doctor Worth $3.2M More Than High School Grad." Associated Press (July 18).

Armas, Genaro. 2003. "White Male with Degree Still Earns the Most." *The Denver Post* (May 21):21A.

Armour, Stephanie. 2002. "Security Checks Worry Workers." *USA Today* (June 19):B1.

———. 2005. "Post-9/11 Charges of Bias Continue." *USA Today* (July 6):3B.

Armstong, Karen. 2000. *The Battle for God*. New York: Ballantine Books.

Asch, Solomon E. 1958. "Effects of Group Pressure upon the Modification and Distortion of Judgments." In *Readings in Social Psychology*, 3rd ed., Eleanor E. Maccoby, Theodore M. Newcomb, and Eugene L. Hartley (eds.). New York: Holt, Rinehart and Winston.

Associated Press. 1976. "Jungle Boy Remains More Like Monkey." (May 15).

———. 1994. "Study: Poor, Minorities Pay More for Insurance." (December 23).

———. 2002. "FBI and Gov. Reagan Targeted 'Subversives.'" (June 14).

———. 2003. "Keeping Native Tongues." (October 9).

Auge, Karen. 1998. "Mass Appeal." *Denver Post* (April 26):1A, 16A, 17A.

Baca Zinn, Maxine. 1990. "Family, Feminism and Race in America." *Gender and Society* 14 (March):62–86.

Baca Zinn, Maxine, and Bonnie Thornton Dill. 1994. "Difference and Domination." In *Women of Color in U.S. Society*, Maxine Baca Zinn and Bonnie Thornton Dill (eds.). Philadelphia: Temple University Press, pp. 3–12.

———. 1996. "Theorizing Difference from Multicultural Feminism." *Feminist Studies* 22 (Summer):1–11.

Baca Zinn, Maxine, and D. Stanley Eitzen. 2002. *Diversity in Families*, 6th ed. Boston: Allyn and Bacon.

———. 2005. *Diversity in Families*, 7th ed. Boston: Allyn and Bacon.

Baca Zinn, Maxine, Pierrette Hondagneu-Sotelo, and Michael A. Messner. 2006. "Sex and Gender through the Prism of Difference." In *Through the Prism of Difference: A Sex and Gender Reader*, 2nd ed., Maxine Baca Zinn, Pierrette Hondagneu-Sotelo, and Michael A. Messner (eds.). Boston: Allyn and Bacon, pp. 1–8.

Baca Zinn, Maxine, Pierrette Hondagneu-Sotelo, and Michael A. Messner. 2006. *Gender through the Prism of Difference*, 3rd ed. New York: Oxford University Press.

Baca Zinn, Maxine, and Angela Y. H. Pok. 2002. "Tradition and Transition in Mexican-Origin Families." In *Minority Families in the United States: A Multicultural Perspective*, Ronald L. Taylor (ed.). Upper Saddle River, NJ: Prentice Hall.

Baig, Edward C., Marcia Stepanek, and Neil Gross. 1999. "Privacy." *Business Week* (April 5):84–90.

Bailey, Garrick. 2000. *An Introduction to Cultural Anthropology*, 5th ed. Belmont, CA: Wadsworth.

Balswick, Jack, with James Lincoln Collier. 1976. "Why Husbands Can't Say 'I Love You.'" In *The Forty-Nine Percent Majority*, Deborah S. David and Robert Brannon (eds.). Reading, MA: Addison-Wesley.

Balswick, Jack, and Charles Peck. 1971. "The Inexpressive Male: A Tragedy of American Society." *Family Coordinator* 20: 363–368.

Baltzell, E. Digby. 1958. *Philadelphia Gentlemen: The Making of a National Upper Class*. New York: Free Press.

Bandura, Albert. 1977. *Social Learning Theory*. New York: General Learning Press.

Bamshad, Michael J., and Steve E. Olson. 2003. "Does Race Exist?" *Scientific American* (December):78–85.

Banfield, Edward C. 1974. *The Unheavenly City Revisited*. Boston: Little, Brown.

Bannon, Lisa. 2000. "Gender-Specific Toy Marketing Irks Some." *Wall Street Journal* (February 17):7D.

Barber, Benjamin R. 1992. "Jihad vs. McWorld." *Atlantic Monthly* 269 (March):53–63.

———. 1995. *Jihad vs. McWorld*. New York: Ballantine Books.

———. 2001. "The Uncertainty of Digital Politics." *Harvard International Review* 23 (Spring):42–47.

———. 2002. "Beyond Jihad vs. McWorld." *The Nation* (January 21):11–18.

Barlett, Donald L., and James B. Steele. 2000. "Soaked by Congress." *Time* (May 15):64–75.

Barlow, Dudley. 1999. "AAUW Gender Equity Research: Scholarship or Partisanship?" *Education Digest* 64 (March):15–60.

Barna Research. 2001a. "The Faith of Hispanics Is Shifting." *Barna Update* (January 3). Available online: www.barna.org.

———. 2001b. "More Americans Are Seeking Net-Based Faith Experiences." *Barna Update* (May 21). Available online: www.barna.org.

Barnouw, Victor. 1979. *Culture and Personality*, 3rd ed. Homewood, IL: Dorsey.

Barrera, Mario. 1979. *Race and Class in the Southwest: A Theory of Racial Inequality*. Notre Dame, IN: University of Notre Dame Press.

Barringer, Felicity. 1992. "As American as Apple Pie, Dim Sum or Burritos." *New York Times* (May 31):section 4, p. 2.

Barsamian, David. 1996. "Politics of the Christian Right: An Interview with Sara Diamond." *Z Magazine* 9 (June): 36–41.

———. 1997. "Howard Zinn." *The Progressive* 61 (July): 37–40.

Bartik, Timothy. 2002. "Poverty, Jobs, and Subsidized Employment." *Challenge* 45 (May/June):100–111.

Bartik, Timothy. 2002. "Poverty, Jobs, and Subsidized Employment." *Challenge* 45 (May/June):100–111.

Baskir, Laurence M., and William A. Strauss. 1978. *The Draft, the War, and the Vietnam Generation*. New York: Knopf.

Basow, Susan. 1996. "Gender Stereotypes and Roles." In *The Meaning of Difference*, Karen E. Rosenblum and Toni-Michelle Travis (eds.). New York: McGraw-Hill, pp. 81–96.

Bauer, Karlin S. 2000. "Promoting Gender Equality in Schools." *Contemporary Education* 71 (2):22–25.

Bauman, Zygmunt. 1990. *Thinking Sociologically*. Cambridge, MA: Basil Blackwell.

Bean, Frank D., Jennifer Lee, Jeanne Batalova, and Mark Leach. 2004. *Immigration and Fading Color Lines in America*. New York: Russell Sage Foundation and Population Reference Bureau.

Beck, Allen J., and Christopher Mumola, 1999. "Prisoners in 1998." *Bureau of Justice Statistics Bulletin*, NCJ175687 (August).

Beck, Joan. 1995. "Preschool Can Help Close the Poverty Gap." *Denver Post* (January 19):7B.

Becker, Howard S. 1963. *The Outsiders: Studies in the Sociology of Deviance*. New York: Free Press.

———. 1967. "Whose Side Are We On?" *Social Problems* 14 (Winter):239–247.

Beckman, L. J., and B. B. Houser. 1979. "The More You Have, the More You Do: The Relationship between Wife's Employment, Sex-Role Attitudes and Household Behavior." *Psychology of Women Quarterly* 4 (Winter): 160–174.

Begley, Sharon. 1997. "The Science Wars." *Newsweek* (April 21):54–56.

Bellah, Robert N. 1967. "Civil Religion in America." *Daedalus* 96 (Winter):1–21.

Belluck, Pam. 1997. "Hispanic Lawsuit Cracks Housing Bias." *Denver Post* (August 8):2A.

Bengtson, Vern L., Carolyn Rosenthal, and Linda Burton. 1990. "Families and Aging: Diversity and Heterogeneity." In *Handbook of Aging and Social Sciences*, 3rd ed., Robert H. Binstock and Linda K. George (eds.). San Diego: Academic Press.

Bennefield, Robert L. 1998. "Health Insurance Coverage: 1997." *Current Population Reports*, Series P60–202 (September).

Benokraitis, Nijole, and Joe R. Feagin. 1974. "Institutional Racism: A Review and Critical Assessment of the Literature." Paper presented at the American Sociological Association, Montreal, Canada (August).

———. 1995. *Modern Sexism*, 2nd ed. Upper Saddle River, NJ: Prentice Hall.

Berenson, Alex. 1996. "Quickie Lenders Popular." *Denver Post* (July 4):1C.

Berger, Peter L. 1963. *Invitation to Sociology: A Humanistic Perspective*. Garden City, NY: Doubleday Anchor Books.

———. 1967a. "Religious Institutions." In *Sociology*, Neil J. Smelser (ed.). New York: Wiley.

———. 1967b. *The Sacred Canopy*. Garden City, NY: Doubleday.

———. 1975. "Religion and World Construction." In *Life as Theatre*, Dennis Brissett and Charles Edgley (eds.). Chicago: Aldine.

Berger, Peter L., and Hansfried Kellner. 1975. "Marriage and the Construction of Reality." In *Life as Theatre*, Dennis Brissett and Charles Edgley (eds.). Chicago: Aldine.

Berger, Peter L., and Thomas Luckmann. 1967. *The Social Construction of Reality*. Garden City, NY: Doubleday.

Berkowitz, Bill. 2002. "The Marriage Movement." *Z Magazine* 15, no. 7/8 (August):12–16.

Bernard, Jessie. 1972. *The Future of Marriage*. New York: Bantam.

Berry, Mary Frances. 1994. *Black Resistance, White Law*, rev. ed. New York: Penguin Books.

Bernstein, Aaron. 2004. "Women's Pay: Why the Gap Remains a Chasm." *Business Week* (June 14):58–59.

Bianchi, Suzanne M. 1995. "Changing Economic Roles of Women and Men." In *State of the Union: America in the 1990s*, Vol. 1, Reynolds Farley (ed.). New York: Sage, pp. 107–154.

Bianchi, Suzanne M., and Lynn M. Casper. 2000. "American Families." *Population Bulletin* 55 (December):entire issue.

Bianchi, Suzanne M., and Daphne Spain. 1996. "Women, Work, and Family in America." *Population Bulletin* (December):entire issue.

Biema, David. 1995. "Bury My Heart in Committee." *Time* (September 18):48–51.

Bierstedt, Robert. 1974. *The Social Order*, 4th ed. New York: McGraw-Hill.

Birnbaum, Norman. 1992. "One Cheer for Clinton." *Nation* (September 28):318–320.

Blau, Peter M., and Otis Dudley Duncan. 1967. *The American Occupational Structure*. New York: Wiley.

Blau, Peter M., and Otis Dudley Duncan. 1967. *The American Occupational Structure*. New York: Wiley.

Blau, Peter M., and W. Richard Scott. 1962. *Formal Organizations: A Comparative Approach*. San Francisco: Chandler.

Blauner, Robert. 1964. *Alienation and Freedom*. Chicago: University of Chicago Press.

———. 1972. *Racial Oppression in America*. New York: Harper & Row.

———. 2001. *Still the Big News: Racial Oppression in America*. Philadelphia: Temple University Press.

Blum, William. 1999. "A Brief History of U.S. Interventions: 1945 to the Present." *Z Magazine* 12 (June):25–30.

Blumberg, Paul M., and P. W. Paul. 1975. "Continuities and Discontinuities in Upper-Class Marriage." *Journal of Marriage and Family* 37 (February).

Blumer, Herbert. 1951. "Collective Behavior." In *Principles of Sociology*, 2nd ed., Alfred McClung Lee (ed.). New York: Barnes & Noble, pp. 167–222.

Blumstein, Philip, and Pepper Schwartz. 1983. *American Couples: Money, Work, Sex*. New York: Morrow.

Bonacich, Edna. 1992a. "Class and Race." *Encyclopedia of Sociology*, vol. 1. New York: Macmillan, pp. 204–208.

———. 1992b. "Inequality in America: The Failure of the American System for People of Color." In *Race, Class, and Gender, an Anthology*, Margaret L. Andersen and Patricia Hill Collins (eds.). Belmont, CA: Wadsworth, pp. 96–109.

Bonilla-Silva, Eduardo. 1996. "Rethinking Racism: Toward a Structural Interpretation." *American Sociological Review* 62 (June):465–480.

———. 2003. *Racism without Racists*. Lanham, MD: Rowman and Littlefield.

Bowman, Lee. 2001. "Violence Prevalent in Video Games Rated OK for Kids." *Rocky Mountain News* (August 20):11B.

Bowman, Meg. 1998. "Why We Burn: Sexism Exorcised." *The Humanist* 43 (November/December):28–29.

Boyd, Robert. 1996. "Biologists Reject Notion of Race." *Denver Post* (October 20):37A.

Boyle, D. Ellen, Nancy L. Marshall, and Wendy W. Robeson. 2003. "Gender at Play: Fourth-Grade Girls and Boys on the Playground." *The American Behavioral Scientist* 46 (10):1326–1345.

Bradshaw, York W., Joseph F. Healey, and Rebecca Smith. 2001. *Sociology for a New Century*. Thousand Oaks, CA: Pine Forge Press.

Branigin, William. 1997. "Sweatshops Are Back." *Washington Post National Weekly Edition* (February 24):6–7.

Brecher, Jeremy, Tim Costello, and Brendan Smith. 2000. *Globalization from Below: The Power of Solidarity*. Cambridge, MA: South End Press.

Breines, Wini, and Linda Gordon. 1983. "The New Scholarship on Family Violence." *Signs* 8 (Spring):490–531.

Brenner, Lynn. 1999. "How Did You Do This Year?" *Parade* (February 14):4–6.

Breslow, Marc. 1996. "The Real Un(der)employment Rate." *Dollars & Sense* 207 (September/October):51.

Briggs, David. 1995. "Women's Gains Fall Short in Pulpit." *Denver Post* (May 5):2A.

Briggs, Tracey Wong. 2002. "Do the Math: High Cost Locks Kids Out of College." *USA Today* (June 27):11D.

Briscoe, D. 1999. "Faltering Pledge Leaves 275M Kids Uneducated." Associated Press (March 27).

Brogan, Pamela. 1994. "Gender Pay Gap Runs Deep in Congress, Study Finds." *Denver Post* (February 26):17A.

Bronfenbrenner, Urie, Peter McClelland, Elaine Wethington, Phyllis Moen, and Stephen J. Ceci. 1996. *The State of Americans*. New York: Free Press.

Bronowski, J. 1978. *The Common Sense of Science*. Cambridge, MA: Harvard University Press.

Brooks, James. 1993. "Slavery on Rise in Brazil, as Debt Chains Workers." *New York Times* (May 23):3A.

Brouillette, John R., and Ronny E. Turner. 1992. "Creating the Sociological Imagination on the First Day of Class: The Social Construction of Deviance." *Teaching Sociology* 20 (October):276–279.

Brown, Dee. 1971. *Bury My Heart at Wounded Knee*. New York: Holt, Rinehart and Winston.

Buchanan, Patrick. 1994. "Is U.S. Culturally Superior?" *Denver Post* (May 19):B7.

Bureau of Labor Statistics. 2002. "The Employment Situation: May 2002." Available online: ftp://ftp.bls.gov/pub/news. release/history/empsit.06072002.new.

Bureau of Justice Statistics. 2002. "Recent Trends in the U. S.: Recidivism." Available online: www.ojp.usdoj.gov/bjs.

———. 2005. "Nation's Prison and Jail Population Grew by 932 Inmates per Week, Number of Female Inmates Reached More Than 100,000." (April 24). Available online: http://www.ojp .usdoj.gov/bjs/pub/press/pjimo04lpr.htm.

Buriel, Raymond, and Terri De Ment. 1997. "Immigration and Sociocultural Change in Mexican, Chinese, and Vietnamese American Families." In *Immigration and the Family*, Alan Booth, Ann C. Crouter, and Nancy Landale (eds.). Mahwah, NJ: Erlbaum, pp. 165–200.

Burns, John F. 1996. "Stonings Mark Return to Primal Afghan Law." *New York Times* (November 3):8Y.

Burt, Keith B, and Jacqueline Scott. 2002. "Parent and Adolescent Gender Role Attitudes in 1990s Great Britian." *Sex Roles* 46 (7/8):239–245.

Business Week. 2001. "The 21st Century Corporation." (August 28):278.

———. 2002. "The Global 1000: The World's Most Valuable Companies." (July 15):58–84.

Byrnes, Nanette, and Louis Lavelle. 2003. "The Corporate Tax Game." *Business Week* (March 31):79–87.

Callahan, David. 2002. "Wal-Mart, Not Hi-Tech, Defines New Economy." *USA Today*. Available online: www.demos-usa. org/Pubs/Callahan/walmart/walmart.pdf.

Campbell, Frances A., and Craig T. Ramey. 1994. "Effects of Early Intervention on Intellectual and Academic Achievement: A Follow-Up Study of Children from Low-Income Families." *Child Development* 65 (April):684–698.

Campenni, C. Estelle. 1999. "Gender Stereotyping of Children's Toys: A Comparison of Parents and Nonparents." *Sex Roles* 40, no. 1/2:121–138.

Cannon, Angie. 1999. "DWB: Driving While Black." *U.S. News & World Report* (March 15):72.

Capellaro, Jennie. 1999. "Students for Sweat-Free Sweatshirts." *Progressive* 63 (April):16.

Caplan, Nathan, and Stephen D. Nelson. 1973. "On Being Useful: The Nature and Consequences of Psychological Research on Social Problems." *American Psychologist* 28 (March):199–211.

Carey, Anne R., and Genevieve Lynn. 1998. "Earnings by Degree." *USA Today* (September 11):1A.

Carey, Anne R., and Quin Tian. 1998. "More Women of the Cloth." *USA Today* (December 23):1A.

Carmichael, Stokely, and Charles V. Hamilton. 1967. *Black Power: The Politics of Liberation in America*. New York: Random House.

Carnegie Foundation Report. 1981. Cited in "Hispanics Make Their Move." *U.S. News & World Report* (August 24):64.

Carre, Francoise, and Chris Tilly. 1998. "Part-Time and Temporary Work." *Dollars & Sense* 215 (January/February): 22–25.

Carroll, John B. (ed.). 1956. *Language, Thought, and Reality: Selected Writings of Benjamin Lee Whorf*. Cambridge, MA: MIT Press.

Carter, Michael J., and Susan Boslego Carter. 1981. "Women Get a Ticket to Ride after the Gravy Train Has Left the Station." *Feminist Studies* 7:477–504.

Carville, James. 1996. *We're Right, They're Wrong: A Handbook for Spirited Progressives*. New York: Random House.

Cassidy, John. 1997. "The Melting Pot Myth." *The New Yorker* (July 14):40–43.

Catanzarite, Liza, and Vilma Ortiz. 1996. "Family Matters, Work Matters? Poverty among Women of Color and White Women." In *For Crying out Loud: Women's Poverty in the U.S.*, Diane Dujon and Ann Withorn (eds.). Boston: South End Press, pp. 122–139.

Center on Budget and Policy Priorities. 2001. "Pathbreaking CBO Study Shows Dramatic Increase in Both 1980s and 1990s in Income Gaps between the Very Wealthy and Other Americans" (May 31). Available online: www.centeronbudget.org/ 5-31-01tax-pr.htm.

Center on Social Welfare and Law. 1996. "Welfare Myths: Fact or Fiction?" Washington, DC: Center on Social Welfare and Law.

Center for American Women and Politics. 2005. "Women in Elective Office 2005." Available online: http://www. cawp.rutgers .edu/Facts/Officeholders/cawpfs.html.

Center for Disease Control, Office of Minority Health. 2005. "About Minority Health. Available online: http:// www .cdc .gov/ omh/AMH/AMH.htm.

Chafel, Judith A. 1997. "Societal Images of Poverty." *Youth and Society* 28 (June):432–463.

Chafetz, Janet Saltzman. 1997. "Feminist Theory and Sociology: Underutilized Contributions for Mainstream Theory." *Annual Review of Sociology* 23:97–120.

Chambliss, William J. 1969. *Crime and the Legal Process*. New York: McGraw-Hill.

———. 1973. "The Saints and the Roughnecks." *Society* 11 (November–December):24–31.

———. 1974. *Functional and Conflict Theories of Crime*. Module 17. New York: MSS Modular Publications.

———. 1976. "Functional and Conflict Theories of Crime: The Heritage of Emile Durkheim and Karl Marx." In *Whose Law, What Order? A Conflict Approach to Criminology*, William J. Chambliss and Milton Mankoff (eds.). New York: Wiley.

Chandler, Clay. 1998. "A Market Tide That Isn't Lifting Everybody." *Washington Post National Weekly Edition* (April 13):18.

Chandrasekaran, Rajiv, and John Mintz. 1999. "Microsoft Hits All the Right Buttons." *Washington Post National Weekly Edition* (May 17):9.

Chase, Bob. 1997. "All Children Are Equal But Some Children Are More Equal Than Others." *Washington Post National Weekly Edition* (April 28):20.

Chawkins, Steve. 1982. "Holy Tortilla: Burden or Blessing?" *Rocky Mountain News* (June 6):10.

Cherlin, Andrew, and Frank F. Furstenberg, Jr. 1983. "The American Family in the Year 2000." *Futurist* 17 (June).

———. 1994a. "The Modernization of Grandparenthood." In *Family in Transition*, 8th ed., Arlene S. Skolnick and Jerome H. Skolnick (eds.). New York: HarperCollins, pp. 104–111.

———. 1994b. "Stepfamilies in the United States: A Reconsideration." *Annual Review of Sociology* 20: 359–381.

Chideya, Farai. 1999. "A Nation of Minorities: America in 2050." *Civil Rights Digest* 4 (Fall):35–41.

Children's Defense Fund. 1998. *The State of America's Children: Yearbook 1998*. Washington, DC: Children's Defense Fund.

———. 2001. *The State of America's Children: Yearbook 2001*. Washington, DC: Children's Defense Fund.

———. 2002. Available online: www.childrensdefense.org/.

———. 2004. "While Corporations and the Wealthy Benefit from Huge Tax Cuts, Poor Families Still Struggle." Press release (April 14).

Children Now. 2004. "Fall Colors, 2003–04 Prime Time Diversity Report." Available online: http://www.childrennow.org/assets/ pdf/fco3/fall-colors-03-y5.pdf.

Christian Science Monitor. 1994. "Will Computers in Schools Make the Poor Poorer?" (February 25):1.

Chronicle of Higher Education. 1998. "Note Book." (January 9): A55.

Clark, Roger, Rachel Lennon, and Leanna Morris. 1993. "Of Caldecotts and Kings: Gendered Images in Recent Children's Books by Black and Non-Black Illustrators." *Gender and Society* 7 (2):227–245.

Cleveland, Harlan. 1992. "The Age of People Power." *Futurist* 26 (January/February):14–18.

Clifford, Lee. 2001. "Fortune 500." *Fortune* (April 16):101–103.

Coakley, Jay J. 2001. *Sport in Society: Issues and Controversies,* 7th ed. Boston: Irwin McGraw-Hill.

———. 2001. "Truth and Context References," personal communication (September 25).

———. 2005. *Sport in Society: Issues and Controversies,* 8th ed. New York: McGraw-Hill.

Coates, Joseph F. 2002. "What's Ahead for Families: Five Major Forces of Change." In *Annual Editions: The Family 2002/2003,* Kathleen Gilbert (ed.). Sluice Dock, CT: Dushkin/McGraw-Hill.

Cocco, Marie. 2005. "It's Not Just Pensions That We're Losing." *Newsday* (May 17);A32.

Cohen, Albert K. 1955. *Delinquent Boys: The Culture of the Gang.* Glencoe, IL: Free Press.

———. 1966. *Deviance and Control.* Englewood Cliffs, NJ: Prentice Hall.

Cohen, Elizabeth. 1997. "Virtual Sisterhood: Feminism Goes Online." *New York Times* (February 2):1–5. Available online: http://nytimes.com/yr/mo/day/cyber/index.html.

Cohen, Robin, and Paul Kennedy. 2000. *Global Sociology.* New York: New York University Press.

Cole, David. 1994. "Five Myths about Immigration." *Nation* (October 17).410–412.

———. 1999. "When the Reason Is Race." *Nation* (March 15):22–24.

———. 2001. "Ashcroft Justice," *The Nation* (December 17): 3–5.

Cole, Stephen. 1975. *The Sociological Orientation: An Introduction to Sociology.* Chicago: Rand McNally.

Coleman, Marilyn, and Lawrence H. Ganong. 1991. "Remarriage and Stepfamily Research in the 1980s: Increased Interest in an Old Family Form." In *Contemporary Families: Looking Forward, Looking Back,* Alan Booth (ed.). Minneapolis, MN: National Council on Family Relations, pp. 192–207.

Collins, Chris. 1998. "Hispanic Kids Less Likely to Be Enrolled in Medicaid." *USA Today* (April 27):3A.

Collins, Chuck, Betsy Leondar-Wright, and Holly Sklar. 1999. *Shifting Fortunes: The Perils of the Growing American Wealth Gap.* Boston: United for a Fair Economy.

Collins, Patricia Hill. 1990. *Black Feminist Thought.* Cambridge, MA: Unwin Hyman.

———. 1997. "Comment on Heckman's 'Truth and Method: Feminist Standpoint Revisited': Where's the Power?" *Signs: Journal of Women in Culture and Society* 22(2):375–381.

Collins, Randall. 1975. *Conflict Sociology.* New York: Academic Press.

———. 1988. "Women and Men in the Class Structure." *Journal of Family Issues* 9 (March):27–50.

———. 1992. *Sociological Insight: An Introduction to Non-Obvious Sociology,* 2nd ed. New York: Oxford University Press.

Coltrane, Scott. 1996. *Family Man: Fatherhood, Housework, and Gender Equity.* New York: Oxford University Press.

Comer, Lee. 1978. "Women and Class, the Question of Women and Class." *Women's Studies International Quarterly* 1:165–173.

Conant, Jennet. 1986. "The New Pocketbook Issue." *Newsweek* (December 1):72.

Confessore, Nicholas. 2002. "Swinging Seniors." *American Prospect* (June 17):10–11.

Conley, Dalton. 2001. "The Black–White Wealth Gap," *The Nation* (March 26):20–22.

Connell, Robert W. 1992. "A Very Straight Gay: Masculinity, Homosexual Experience, and the Dynamics of Gender." *American Sociological Review* 57:735–751.

———. 1998. "Masculinities and Globalization," *Men and Masculinities* 1 (July):3–23.

Consumer Reports. 2002. "Your Body, Your I.D.?" Vol. 67 (August):12–13.

Contemporary Sociology. 1995. "Symposium: The Bell Curve." Vol. 24 (March):149–161.

Cook, Christopher D. 2000. *The Nation* "Temps Demand a New Deal." (March 27):13–20.

Cook, James. 1981. "The American Indian through Five Centuries." *Forbes* (November 9).

Cooley, Charles Horton. 1922. *Human Nature and the Social Order.* New York: Scribner.

Coontz, Stephanie. 1992. *The Way We Never Were.* New York: Basic Books.

———. 1997. *The Way We Really Are: Coming to Terms with America's Changing Families.* New York: Basic Books.

———. 2005. *Marriage: A History.* New York: Viking.

Coser, Lewis. 1966. *The Functions of Social Conflict.* New York: Free Press.

Corbett, Sara. 2001. "The Breast Offense." *New York Times* (June 6). Available online: http://www.nytimes.com/2001005/06/magazine/06NURSING.html.

Cox, Harvey. 1999. "The Market as God." *Atlantic Monthly* 283 (March):18–23.

Crabb, Peter, and Dawn Bielawski. 1994. "The Social Representation of Material Culture and Gender in Children's Books." *Sex Roles* 30 (1/2):69–79.

Crispell, Diane. 1992. "The Brave New World of Men." *American Demographics* 14 (January):38–43.

———. 1995. "Why Working Teens Get into Trouble." *American Demographics* 17 (February):19–20.

Crooks, Robert, and Karla Baur. 1999. *Our Sexuality,* 3rd ed. Menlo Park, CA: Benjamin Cummings.

Crossette, Barbara. 1996. "Caste May Be India's Moral Achilles Heel." *New York Times* (October 20):3E.

Crowley, Sheila. 2002. "The National Low Income Housing Coalition." *Poverty and Race* 11 (January/February): 24–26.

Culver, Virginia. 2001. "U.S. Muslim Population Embraces Activism." *Denver Post* (April 27):5B.

Cunningham, Shea. 1994. "Farm Workers in the '90s." *Food First Action Alert* 16 (Fall):1–4.

Currie, Elliott, and Jerome H. Skolnick. 1988. *America's Problems: Social Issues and Public Policy,* 2nd ed. Boston: Little, Brown.

Curtis, Emory. 2000. "The Poor Pay More." *Exodus* (March 30). Available online: http://www.exodusnews.com/editorials/editoriall-065.htm.

Cutler, James E. 1905. *Lynch-Law: An Investigation into the History of Lynching in the United States.* New York: Longmans, Green.

Cuzzort, R. P. 1969. *Humanity and Modern Sociological Thought.* New York: Holt, Rinehart and Winston.

———. 1989. *Using Social Thought: The Nuclear Issue and Other Concerns.* Mountain View, CA: Mayfield.

Dahl, Robert. 1961. *Who Governs?* New Haven, CT: Yale University Press.

Dahrendorf, Ralf. 1959. *Class and Class Conflict in Industrial Society.* Stanford, CA: Stanford University Press.

———. 1968. "Out of Utopia: Toward a Reorientation of Sociological Analysis." *American Journal of Sociology* 64 (September).

Dalaker, Joseph. 2001. "Poverty in the United States: 2000." *Current Population Reports,* Series 060–214. Washington, DC: U.S. Bureau of the Census.

David, Deborah S., and Robert Brannon. 1980. "The Male Sex Role." In *Family in Transition: Rethinking Marriage, Sexuality, Child Rearing and Family Organization,* 3rd ed., Arlene S. Skolnick and Jerome H. Skolnick (eds.). Boston: Little, Brown.

Davies, James A. 1966. "Structural Balance, Mechanical Solidarity, and Interpersonal Relations." In *Sociological Theories in Progress I,* Joseph Berger, Morris Zelditch, Jr., and Bo Anderson (eds.). Boston: Houghton Mifflin.

Davies, Karin. 1996. "Fat-Man Contest Trumpets Wealth." *Denver Post* (November 29):60A.

Davis, Kingsley. 1940. "Extreme Social Isolation of a Child." *American Journal of Sociology* 45 (January):554–564.

———. 1948. *Human Society.* New York: Macmillan.

Davis, Kingsley, and Wilbert E. Moore. 1945. "Some Principles of Stratification." *American Sociological Review* 10 (April):242–249.

Davis, Nanette J. 1975. *Sociological Constructions of Deviance Perspectives and Issues in the Field.* Dubuque, IA: Wm. C. Brown.

Death Penalty Information Center. 2005. "Facts about the Death Penalty." Available online: www.deathpenaltyinfo. org.

Defreitas, Gregory. 1994. "Fear of Foreigners: Immigrants as Scapegoats for Domestic Woes." *Dollars & Sense* 191 (January/February):8–9, 33.

Deibel, Mary. 2000. "CEOs Pay Hikes Far Outpace Workers." *Rocky Mountain News* (September 3):G1.

De Lone, Richard H. 1979. *Small Futures: Children, Inequality, and the Limits of Liberal Reform.* New York: Carnegie Council on Children.

del Pinal, Jorge, and Audrey Singer. 1997. "Generations of Diversity: Latinos in the United States." *Population Bulletin* 52 (October):entire issue.

D'Emilio, John. 1996. "Commentary: What Is a Family?" *Sociologists' Lesbian and Gay Caucus Newsletter* (Summer): 3–4.

DeNavas-Walt, Carmen, Bernadette D. Proctor, and Robert J. Mills. 2004. "Income, Poverty, and Health Coverage in the United States: 2003." U.S. Bureau of the Census, *Current Population Reports,* P60–226.

Dentler, Robert A., and Kai T. Erikson. 1959. "The Functions of Deviance in Groups." *Social Problems* 7 (Fall): 98–107.

Denver Post. 2001. "The Haves and the Have-Nots."(June 17):6D.

De Parle, Jason. 1989. "Realizing the Rights of the Disabled." *New York Times* (December 17): Section 4, pp. 1, 5.

Department of Labor. 2005. Bureau of Labor Statistics. "Employment Status of the Civilian Non Institutional Population by age, sex, and race." Available online: http://www.bls.gov/cps/cpsaat3.pdf. Retrieved on June 15, 2005.

di Leonardo, Micaela. 1992. "Boyz on the Hood." *Nation* (August 17–24):178–186.

Dill, Bonnie Thornton, Maxine Baca Zinn, and Sandra Patton. 1993. "Feminism, Race, and the Politics of Family Values." *Report from the Institute for Philosophy and Public Policy* (University of Maryland) 13 (Fall).

Dill, Bonnie Thornton, Lynn W. Cannon, and Reeve Vanneman. 1987. "Race, Gender, and Occupational Segregation." In *Pay Equity: An Issue of Race, Ethnicity, and Sex.* Washington, DC: National Committee on Pay Equity.

Doezema, Jo, and Kamala Kempadoo (eds.). 1998. *Global Sex Workers: Rights, Resistance, and Redefinition.* New York: Routledge.

Domhoff, G. William. 1970. *The Higher Circles: The Governing Class in America.* New York: Random House.

———. 1998. *Who Rules America? Power and Politics in the Year 2000,* 3rd ed. Mountain View, CA: Mayfield.

Donahue, Phil. 2002. Segment of "Take This Media . . . Please." *Nation* (January 7/14):13–14.

Dowd, Maureen. 2002. "What Hath Abraham Wrought?" *Denver Post* (April 8):7B.

Doyle, Jack, and Paul T. Schindler. 1974. "The Incoherent Society." Paper presented at the American Sociological Association, Montreal, Canada (August 25–29).

Dreyfuss, Joel, and Ed Leefeldt. 2002. "Mutual Funds Feel Bear's Big Squeeze." *Rocky Mountain News* (August 24):1C, 5C.

Drucker, Peter F. 1989. "The Rise and Fall of the Blue-Collar Worker." In *The Reshaping of America: Social Consequences of a Changing Economy,* D. Stanley Eitzen and Maxine Baca Zinn (eds.). Englewood Cliffs, NJ: Prentice Hall, pp. 81–84.

———. 1993. *Post-Capitalist Society.* New York: HarperCollins.

———. 1999. "Beyond the Information Revolution." *Atlantic Monthly* 284 (October):44–57.

———. 2001. "The Next Society." *Economist* (November 3): 1–20.

Dubeck, Paula J., and Dana Dunn (eds.). 2002. *Workplace/Women's Place: An Anthology.* Los Angeles: Roxbury.

Duncan, Greg J. 1984. *Years of Poverty, Years of Plenty: The Changing Economic Fortunes of American Workers and Families.* Ann Arbor, MI: Institute of Social Research.

Duncan, Greg J., W. Jean Yeung, Jeanne Brooks-Gunn, and Judith R. Smith. 1998. "How Much Does Childhood Poverty Affect the Life Chances of Children?" *American Sociological Review* 63 (June):406–423.

Dunn, Dana. 1996. "Gender and Earnings." In *Women and Work: A Handbook,* Paula J. Dubeck and Kathryn Borman (eds.). New York: Garland, pp. 61–63.

Durkheim, Emile. 1951. *Suicide,* reprinted ed. Glencoe, IL: Free Press.

———. 1958. *The Rules of Sociological Method,* 8th ed., Sarah A. Solovay and John H. Mueller (trans.). Glencoe, IL: Free Press.

———. 1960. *The Division of Labor in Society,* George Simpson (trans.). New York: Free Press.

———. 1965. *The Elementary Forms of Religious Life,* Joseph Ward Swain (trans.). New York: Macmillan.

Dwyer, Paula. 2004. "The New Fat Cats." *Business Week* (April 12):32–35.

Dyer, Everett D. 1979. *The American Family: Variety and Change.* New York: McGraw-Hill.

Early, Frances H. 1983. "The French-Canadian Family Economy and Standard of Living in Lowell, Massachusetts, 1870." In *The American Family in Social Historical Perspective,* 3rd ed., Michael Gordon (ed.). New York: St. Martin's Press, pp. 482–503.

Ebony. 1995. "Amazing Grace: 50 Years of the Black Church." Vol. 50 (April):87–96.

Echaveste, Maria, and Karen Nussbaum. 1994. "96 Cents an Hour: The Sweatshop Is Reborn." *New York Times* (March 6):13F.

Eckel, Sarah. 1999. "Single Mothers, Many Faces." *American Demographics* 21 (May):63–66.

Economist. 1993. "The Other America." (July 10):17–18.

Edgley, Charles, and Ronny E. Turner. 1975. "Masks and Social Relations." *Humboldt Journal of Social Relations* 3 (Fall–Winter).

Edin, Kathryn J. 1995. "The Myths of Dependence and Self-Sufficiency: Women, Welfare, and Low-Wage Work." *Focus* 17 (Fall–Winter):1–9.

Edmondson, Brad. 1996. "Work Slowdown." *American Demographics* 18 (March):4–7.

———. 1998. "Wealth and Poverty." *American Demographics* 20 (May). Available online: http://marketingtools.com/ publications/ad/98_9805.

Education Trust. 2002. "The Funding Gap: Students Who Need the Most Get the Least." (August 8). Available online: www.edtrust.org/main/.

Edwards, Renee, and Mark A. Hamilton. 2004. "You Need to Understand My Gender Role: An Empirical Test of Tannen's Model of Gender and Communication." *Sex Roles* 50 (7/8):491–504.

Edwards, Richard C., Michael Reich, and Thomas E. Weisskopf. 1978. "Sexism." In *The Capitalist System: A Radical Analysis of American Society*, 2nd ed. Englewood Cliffs, NJ: Prentice Hall.

Ehrenreich, Barbara. 1989. *Fear of Falling: The Inner Life of the Middle Class*. New York: Pantheon.

———. 1991. "Welfare: A White Secret." *Time* (December 16):84.

———. 2000. "Warning: This Is a Rights-Free Workplace." *New York Times* (March 5). Available online: nytimes.com/library/magazine/home/20000305mag workrights.html.

———. 2004. "Gouging the Poor." *The Progressive* 68:48.

Eisenstein, Zillah. 1979. "Developing a Theory of Capitalist Patriarchy and Socialist Feminism." In *Capitalist Patriarchy and the Case for Socialist Feminism*, Zillah Eisenstein (ed.). New York: Monthly Review Press, pp. 5–40.

Eitzen, D. Stanley. 1996. "Is Dismantling the Welfare State the Solution to America's Social Problems?" *Vital Speeches of the Day* (June 15):532–536.

———. 2000a. "The Fragmentation of Social Life: Some Critical Societal Concerns for the New Millennium." *Vital Speeches of the Day* 66 (July 1):563–566.

———. 2000b. "Social Control and Sport." In *Handbook of Sport Studies*, Eric Dunning and Jay J. Coakley (eds.). London: Sage.

———. 2003. *Fair and Foul: Beyond the Myths and Paradoxes of Sport*, 2nd ed. Lanham, MD: Rowman & Littlefield.

———. 2006. *Fair and Foul: Beyond the Myths and Paradoxes of Sport*, 3rd ed. Lanham, MD: Rowman & Littlefield.

Eitzen, D. Stanley, and Maxine Baca Zinn. 1989a. "The De-Athleticization of Women: The Naming and Gender Marking of Collegiate Sport Teams." *Sociology of Sport Journal* 6 (December):362–370.

———. 1989b. "The Forces Reshaping America." In *The Reshaping of America: Social Consequences of a Changing Economy*, D. Stanley Eitzen and Maxine Baca Zinn (eds.). Englewood Cliffs, NJ: Prentice Hall, pp. 1–13.

———. 1998. "The Shrinking Welfare State: The New Welfare Legislation and Families." Paper presented at the annual meeting of the American Sociological Association, San Francisco (August 21–25).

———. 2003. *Social Problems*, 9th ed. Boston: Allyn and Bacon.

———. 2006. *Globalization: The Transformation of Social Worlds*. Belmont, CA: Wadsworth.

———. 2006. *Social Problems*, 10th ed. Boston: Allyn and Bacon.

Eitzen, D. Stanley, and George H. Sage. 2003. *The Sociology of North American Sport*, 7th ed. Madison, WI: Brown & Benchmark.

Eitzen, D. Stanley, and Kelly Eitzen Smith (eds.). 2003. *Experiencing Poverty: Voices from the Bottom*. Belmont, CA: Wadsworth.

Ekman, Paul, Wallace V. Friesen, and John Bear. 1984. "The International Language of Gestures." *Psychology Today* 18 (May):64–69.

El Nasser, Haya. 2005. "Recent Arrivals Better Educated." *USA Today* (February 22):1A.

Engardio, Pete, and Catherine Belton. 2002. "Global Capitalism." *Business Week* (September 6):72–76.

Epstein, Cynthia Fuchs. 1970. *Woman's Place*. Berkeley: University of California Press.

Epstein, Joseph. 1997. "How Revolting: Why What Disgusts Us Defines Us." *The New Yorker* (July 14).78–82.

Erikson, Kai T. 1966. *Wayward Puritans: A Study in the Sociology of Deviance*. New York: Wiley.

Eshleman, J. Ross. 1988. *The Family*, 5th ed. Boston: Allyn and Bacon.

Espiritu, Yen Le. 1996. "Asian American Panethnicity." In *The Meaning of Difference*, Karen E. Rosenblum and Toni-Michelle Travis (eds.). New York: McGraw-Hill, pp. 51–61.

Etzioni, Amitai. 1999. *The Limits of Privacy*. New York: Basic Books.

———. 2000. "Balancing Privacy, Public Good." *USA Today* (April 27):17A.

Fahim, Dareem. 2003. "The Moving Target." *Amnesty Now* 29 (Winter):6–9.

Fall Colors. 2000. "How Diverse Is the 1999–2000 TV Season's Prime Time Lineup? (January). Oakland, CA.

Farrell, John Aloysius, and Anne C. Mulkern. 2005. "Dobson Seen as Driven, Divisive." *Denver Post* (April 27):1A, 14A.

Faludi, Susan. 1991. *Backlash: The Undeclared War against Women*. New York: Crown.

Farber, Jerry. 1970. *The Student as Nigger*. New York: Pocket Books.

Farberman, Harvey, and Erich Goode. 1973. *Social Reality*. Englewood Cliffs, NJ: Prentice Hall.

Farrell, Christopher. 1996. "The New Math of Higher Education." *Business Week* (March 18):39.

Fausto-Sterling, Anne. 1992. *Myths of Gender: Biological Theories about Women and Men*. New York: Basic Books.

Faux, Jeff. 2002. "Faux Urges Curbs on Corporate Lawlessness." Press release by Economic Policy Institute (August 24). Available online: http://epinet.org/webfeatures/ release/corp070802.html.

Feagin, Joe R. 2000. *Racist America*. New York: Routledge.

Feagin, Joe R., and Clairece Booher Feagin. 1993. *Racial and Ethnic Relations*. Englewood Cliffs, NJ: Prentice Hall.

———. 1997. *Social Problems: A Critical Power–Conflict Perspective*, 5th ed. Upper Saddle River, NJ: Prentice Hall.

Feagin, Joe R., and Melvin P. Sikes. 1994. *Living with Racism: The Black Middle-Class Experience*. Boston: Beacon Press.

Featherstone, Liza. 2000. "The New Student Movement." *The Nation* (May 15):11–18.

Feminist News Feminist Majority Fund. 1999. (January 13); 1–3.

Ferree, Myra Marx. 1991. "Feminism and Family Research." In *Contemporary Families: Looking Forward, Looking Back*, Alan Booth (ed.). Minneapolis, MN: National Council on Family Relations, pp. 103–121.

Festinger, Leon, Henry W. Riecken, Jr., and Stanley Schachter. 1956. *When Prophecy Fails*. Minneapolis: University of Minnesota Press.

Fields, Jason, and Lynne M. Casper. 2001. "American Families and Living Arrangements." *Current Population Reports*, P20–537. Washington, DC: U.S. Census Bureau.

Fields, Jason. 2004. "America's Families and Living Arrangements: 2003." *Current Population Reports*, Series P20–553 (November). Washington, DC.: U.S. Bureau of the Census.

Fischer, Claude S., Michael Hout, Martin Sanchez Jankowski, Samuel R. Lucas, Ann Swidler, and Kim Voss. 1996. *Inequality by Design: Cracking the Bell Curve Myth*. Princeton, NJ: Princeton University Press.

Fishman, Charles. 1999. "Smorgasbord Generation." *American Demographics* 21 (May):1–5.

Fishman, Pamela M. 1978. "Interaction: The Work Women Do." *Social Problems* 25 (April):397–406.

FitzGerald, Frances. 1979. *America Revised: History Schoolbooks in the Twentieth Century.* Boston: Atlantic/Little, Brown.

Fletcher, Michael A. 1998. "All Fighting for a Piece of the Dream." *Washington Post National Weekly Edition* (May 18):8–9.

———. 1999. "Marriage Loses Luster in America." *Denver Post* (July 2):2A.

Folbre, Nancy, and the Center for Popular Economics. 1995. *The New Field Guide to the U.S. Economy.* New York: New Press.

Folbre, Nancy, James Heintz, and the Center for Popular Economics. 2000. *The Ultimate Field Guide to the U.S. Economy.* New York: New Press.

Food First. 1998. "Should America Be Measured by Its 3.5 Million Millionaires . . . or by Its 30 Million Hungry?" *Nation* (October 5):24–25.

Foner, Eric. 1996. "Plessy Is Not Passe." *Nation* (June 3):6.

Forbes. 1997. "Steel vs. Silicon." (July 7):129–131.

———. 1998. "The 100 Largest U.S. Multinationals." (July 27):162–164.

———. 2001. "The Forbes 400." (October 8):127–298.

———. 2002. "Billionaires: United States." (March 18):128–132.

———. 2003. "America's Top 500 Companies." (April 14):144–198.

———. 2004. "The Forbes 400." (October 11):103–278.

Forrest, Christopher B., and Ellen-Marie Whelan. 2000. "Primary Care Safety-Net Delivery Sites in the United States: A Comparison of Community Health Centers, Hospital Outpatient Departments, and Physicians' Offices." *JAMA*, Vol. 284, No. 16 (October 25):2077– 2083.

Fost, Dan. 1991. "American Indians in the Nineties." *American Demographics* 13 (December):26–34.

Frankenberg, Ruth (ed.). 1997. *Displacing Whiteness: Essays in Social and Cultural Criticism.* Durham, NC: Duke University Press.

Franklin, Deborah. 1989. "What a Child Is Given." *New York Times Magazine* (September 3):36–41, 49.

Franklin, Jeffrey. 2001. "Logic of 'Holy War' on Terror Morally Evil." *Rocky Mountain News* (September 28):46A.

Freedman, Alex M. 1993. "Peddling Dreams: A Marketing Giant Uses Its Sales Prowess to Profit from Poverty." *Wall Street Journal* (September 22):A1, A12.

Freedom from Gender Society. n.d. "What Is a Gender-Free Person?" Brookline, MA.

Freeman, Jo. 1979. "The Women's Liberation Movement: Its Origins, Organizations, Activities, and Ideas." In *Women: A Feminist Perspective,* 2nd ed., Jo Freeman (ed.). Palo Alto, CA: Mayfield, pp. 557–574.

Freud, Sigmund. 1946. *Civilization and Its Discontents,* Joan Riviére (trans.). London: Hogarth Press.

Friedan, Betty. 1963. *The Feminine Mystique.* New York: W. W. Norton.

Friedman, Thomas L. 2005. *The World Is Flat.* New York: Farrar, Straus, and Geroux.

Fuller-Thompson, Erma, Meredith Minkler, and Diane Driver. 1997. "A Profile of Grandparents Raising Grandchildren in the United States." *Gerontologist* 37 (3):406–411.

Fussell, Paul. 1983. *Class.* New York: Ballantine.

Galbraith, James K. 1998. "With Economic Inequality for All." *Nation* (September 7):24–26.

Gallinsky, Ellen, and James T. Bond. 1996. "Work and Family: The Experiences of Mothers and Fathers in the U.S. Workforce." In *The American Woman, 1996–1997,* Cynthia Costello and Barbara Kivimae Krimgold (eds.). New York: W. W. Norton, pp. 79–103.

Galst, Liz. 1994. "The Right Fight." *Mother Jones* 19 (March/April):58–59.

Gans, Herbert J. 1962. *The Urban Villagers.* New York: Free Press.

———. 1971. "The Uses of Power: The Poor Pay All." *Social Policy* 2 (July–August):20–24.

———. 1979. *Deciding What's News.* New York: Pantheon.

———. 1990. "Second Generation Decline." *Ethnic Racial Studies* 15:173–192.

Garfinkel, Harold. 1967. *Studies in Ethnomethodology.* Englewood Cliffs, NJ: Prentice Hall.

Garfinkel, Simson. 2000a. *Database Nation.* New York: O'Reilly.

———. 2000b. "Privacy and the New Technology," *The Nation* (February 28):11–15.

Garrahy, Deborah A. 2001. "Three Third-Grade Teachers' Gender-Related Beliefs and Behavior." *The Elementary School Journal* 102 (1):81–94.

Garten, Jeffrey E. 1999. "Megamergers Are a Clear and Present Danger." *Business Week* (January 25):28.

Gartner, Michael. 1995. "Unions Can Still Speak for the Little Guy." *USA Today* (June 20):11A.

Gelles, Richard J. 1977. "No Place to Go: The Social Dynamics of Marital Violence." In *Battered Women: A Psychosociological Study of Domestic Violence,* Maria Roy (ed.). New York: Van Nostrand.

———. 1995. *Contemporary Families: A Sociological View.* Thousand Oaks, CA: Sage.

Gentry, Curt. 1991. *J. Edgar Hoover: The Man and His Secrets.* New York: W. W. Norton.

Gergen, David. 2001. "Bush as a Global Steward." *U.S. News & World Report* (February 5):64.

Gerrard, Nathan L. 1968. "The Serpent Handling Religions of West Virginia." *Transaction* 5 (May).

Gerson, Michael J. 1998. "A Righteous Indignation." *U.S. News & World Report* (May 4):20–24, 29.

Gerth, Hans, and C. Wright Mills. 1953. *Character and Social Structure: The Psychology of Social Institutions.* New York: Harcourt, Brace, & World.

Gibbs, Jack P. 1966. "Conceptions of Deviant Behavior: The Old and the New." *Pacific Sociological Review* 9 (Spring):9–14.

Giddens, Anthony. 1991. *Introduction to Sociology.* New York: W. W. Norton.

Giele, Janet Z. 1988. "Gender and the Sex Roles." In *Handbook of Sociology,* Neil J. Smelser (ed.). Newbury Park, CA: Sage, pp. 291–323.

Gilbert, Bil, and Nancy Williamson. 1973. "Sport Is Unfair to Women." *Sports Illustrated* (May 28).

Gillespie, Dair. 1972. "Who Has the Power? The Marital Struggle." In *Family, Marriage, and the Struggle of the Sexes,* Hans Peter Dreitzel (ed.). New York: Macmillan, pp. 105–157.

Gillespie, Ed. 2003. "The Embedded Lobbyist." *Public Citizen* (June 16). Available online: http://www.citizen.org/ congress/welfare/index.ifm.

Gilman, Richard. 1971. "Where Did It All Go Wrong?" *Life* (August 13).

Glassman, James K. 1997. "Corporate Welfare in the Sky." *U.S. News & World Report* (July 28):49.

Gold, Allan R. 1989. "The Struggle to Make Do without Health Insurance." *New York Times* (July 30):1, 11.

Gold, David A., Clarence Y. H. Lo, and Erik Olin Wright. 1975. "Recent Developments in Marxist Theories of the Capitalist State." *Monthly Review* 27 (October): 29–45.

Goldsen, Rose K. 1977. *The Show and Tell Machine: How Television Works and Works You Over.* New York: Delta.

Goode, Erica. 1999a. "For Good Health It Helps to Be Rich and Important." *New York Times* (June 1):1F.

———. 1999b. "Lack of Status Weighs Heavily on Health." *Denver Post* (June 1):1A, 13A.

Gonzalez, Antonio, and Stephanie Moore. 2003. "Wealthy Campaign Donors Stifle Minority Voices." *USA Today* (December 11):23A.

Goode, William J. 1963. *World Revolution and Family Patterns.* New York: Free Press.

———. 1966. "Social Class and Church Participation." *American Journal of Sociology* 72 (July).

———. 1984. "Idealization of the Recent Past: The United States." In *Family in Transition: Rethinking Marriage, Sexuality, Child Rearing, and Family Organization,* 4th ed., Arlene S. Skolnick and Jerome H. Skolnick (eds). Boston: Little, Brown, pp. 43–53.

Goodgame, Dan. 1993. "Welfare for the Well-Off." *Time* (February 22):36–38.

Goozner, Merrill. 2000. "The Price Isn't Right." *American Prospect* (September 11):25–29.

Gorski, Eric. 2005. "Focus' Family Tree Sows Seeds Personal, Political." *Denver Post* (July 10):1A, 14A.

Gottfredson, Michael R., and Travis Hirschi. 1990. *A General Theory of Crime.* Stanford, CA: Stanford University Press.

Gould, Stephen Jay. 1994. "Curveball." *The New Yorker* (November 28):139–149.

———. 1997. *Questioning the Millennium: A Rationalist's Guide to a Precisely Arbitrary Countdown.* New York: Harmony Books.

———. 1998. "The Sharp-Eyed Lynx, Outfoxed by Nature." *Natural History* (May):16–21, 70–72.

Gouldner, Alvin W. 1962. "Anti-Minotaur: The Myth of Value-Free Sociology." *Social Problems* 9 (Winter).

Gove, Walter R., Carolyn Briggs Style, and Michael Hughes. 1990. "The Effect of Marriage on the Well-Being of Adults." *Journal of Family Issues* 11 (March):4–35.

Graham, Hugh Davis, and Ted Robert Gurr. 1969. *The History of Violence in America.* New York: Bantam Books.

Green, Mark. 2002. *Selling Out.* New York: HarperCollins.

Greenhouse, Steven. 2001. "Unions Hit Lowest Point in 6 Decades." *New York Times* (January 21). Available online: www.nytimes.com/2001/01/21/national/ 22LABO.html.

Greider, William. 1992. *Who Will Tell the People: The Betrayal of American Democracy.* New York: Simon & Schuster.

———. 2000. "Crime in the Suites." *The Nation* (February 4): 11–14.

———. 2002. "Crime in the Suites." *The Nation* (February 4): 11–13.

Greim, Lisa. 1998. "Working Women Protest Pay Gap." *Rocky Mountain News* (April 4):1B.

Grossman, Cathy Lynn. 1998. "Anti-Gay Prejudice No Longer Permissible, Psychoanalysts Say." *USA Today* (December 21):10D.

———. 2001. "Community Now 'Coming into Its Own.'" *USA Today* (April 26):7D.

Grunwald, Michael. 1999. "The HUD Chief Finds His Own Pulpit." *Washington Post National Weekly Edition* (June 7):29.

Guastello, Denise D., and Stephen J. Guastello. 2003. "Androgyny, Gender Role Behavior, and Emotional Intelligence among College Students and Their Parents." *Sex Roles* 49 (1/2):663–673.

Gushee, Steve. 1997. "Female Ministers Gradually Finding Acceptance." *Denver Post* (September 27):21A, 27A.

Hacker, Andrew. 1970. *The End of the American Era.* New York: Atheneum.

Hafner, Katie. 1994. "Getting Girls Online." *Working Woman* (April):60–61.

———. 1998. "Girl Games: Plenty and Pink." *New York Times* (September 10):8G.

Hall, M. Ann. 1985. "Knowledge and Gender: Epistemological Questions in the Social Analysis of Sport." *Sociology of Sport Journal* 2:25–42.

Hamburg, David A. 1993. "The American Family Transformed." *Society* 31 (January/February):60–69.

Hancock, LynNell. 1995. "The Haves and the Have-Nots: The Computer Gap." *Newsweek* (February 27):50–53.

Hannan, Annette, and Tamar Murachver. 1999. "Gender and Conversational Style as Predictors of Conversational Behavior." *Journal of Language and Social Psychology* 18 (2):153–174.

Hansen, James. 1997. "On Average Union Workers Earn 33 Percent More." *Rocky Mountain News* (October 18):4B.

———. 1998. "Organized Labor Just as Relevant in Robust Times." *Rocky Mountain News* (December 13):5B.

Harding, Vincent. 1981. *There Is a River: The Black Struggle for Freedom in America.* New York: Harcourt Brace Jovanovich.

Harjo, Susan Shown. 1996. "Now and Then: Native Peoples in the United States." *Dissent* 43 (Summer):58–60.

Harper, Jennifer. 2004. "Religion 'Very Important' to Most Americans." *Washington Times* (June 25). Available online: http://www.washingtontimes.com/national/ 20040625-120817-7896r.htm.

Harper's Magazine. 1998. "Balanced, Objective Gay-Bashing." (December):26.

Harrington, Michael. 1963. *The Other America: Poverty in the United States.* Baltimore: Penguin.

———. 1979. "Social Retreat and Economic Stagnation." *Dissent* 26 (Spring):131–134.

———. 1984. *The New American Poverty.* New York: Holt, Rinehart and Winston.

———. 1985. *Taking Sides: The Education of a Militant Mind.* New York: Holt, Rinehart and Winston.

———. 1986. *The Next Left.* New York: Henry Holt.

Harris, Kathleen Mullan. 1996. "The Reforms Will Hurt, Not Help, Poor Women and Children." *Chronicle of Higher Education* (October 4):B7.

Harris, Marvin. 1974. *Cows, Pigs, Wars, and Witches: The Riddles of Culture.* New York: Random House.

———. 1978. "India's Sacred Cows." *Human Nature* 1 (February).

Harris, Roderick J., and Claudette Bennett. 1995. "Racial and Ethnic Diversity." In *State of the Union: America in the 1990s,* Vol. 2, "Social Trends," Reynolds Farley (ed.). New York: Sage, pp. 141–210.

Harris, Stein. 2000. "Students against Sweatshops." *Multinational Monitor* 22 (January/February):27–28.

Hartjen, Clayton A. 1974. *Crime and Criminalization.* New York: Praeger.

Hartmann, Heidi I. 1976. "Capitalism, Patriarchy, and Job Segregation by Sex." *Signs* 1 (Spring):137–169.

Heatherington, E. Mavis (2002). "Marriage and Divorce American Style." *American Prospect* (April 8):62–63.

Heaven's Gate. 1997. Available online: www.sunspot.net/news/ special/heavensgatesite/2index.shtml.

Heilbroner, Robert L. 1974. *An Inquiry into the Human Prospect.* New York: W. W. Norton.

Henley, Robert J. 1994. "The Role of Women in Catholic Parish Life." *American* 171 (September):6–7.

Henneberger, Melinda, and Michael Marriott. 1993. "For Some, Youthful Courting Has Become a Game of Abuse." *New York Times* (July 11):1A, 14A.

Hennesey, Rosemary, and Chrys Ingrahm (eds.). 1997. *Materialist Feminism: A Reader in Class, Difference, and Women's Lives.* New York: Routledge.

Henry, Jules. 1963. *Culture against Man.* New York: Random House.

Henry, Tamara. 1998a. "Girls Face Technology Gap." *USA Today* (October 14):A1.

———. 1998b. "Girls Lagging as Gender Gap Widens in Tech Education." *USA Today* (October 14):A1, D4.

———. 2000. "Report: Education Not Equal Yet." *USA Today* (March 1):1A.

Henslin, James M., Linda K. Henslin, and Steven D. Keiser. 1976. "Schooling for Social Stability: Education in the Corporate Society." In *Social Problems in American Society,* 2nd ed., James M. Henslin and Larry T. Reynolds (eds.). Boston: Allyn and Bacon, pp. 311–312.

———. 1996. "America the Meritocracy." *Z Magazine* 9 (July/August):34–39.

Henwood, Doug. 2001. "Wealth Report." *The Nation* (April 9):8.

Hermann, Andrew. 1994. "Muslims Plan Census to Chart Growth Here." *Chicago Sun-Times* (February 12):4.

Herrnstein, Richard. 1971. "I.Q." *Atlantic* 228 (September): 43–64.

———. 1973. *I.Q. in the Meritocracy.* Boston: Little, Brown.

Herrnstein, Richard, and Charles Murray. 1994. *The Bell Curve: Intelligence and Class Structure in American Life.* New York: Free Press.

Herz, Diane E., and Barbara H. Wootton. 1996. "Women in the Workforce: An Overview." In *The American Woman, 1996–1997,* Cynthia Costello and Barbara Kivimae Krimgold (eds.). New York: W. W. Norton, pp. 44–78.

Hess, Beth B., Elizabeth W. Markson, and Peter J. Stein. 1993. *Sociology,* 4th ed. New York: Macmillan.

Higginbotham, Elizabeth. 1994. "Black Professional Women: Job Ceilings and Employment Sectors." In *Women of Color in U.S. Society,* Maxine Baca Zinn and Bonnie Thornton Dill (eds.). Philadelphia: Temple University Press, pp. 113–131.

Higginbotham, Elizabeth, and Margaret L. Anderson. 2005. "Introduction." In *Race and Ethnicity in Society,* Elizabeth Higginbotham and Margaret L. Anderson (eds.). Belmont, CA: Wadsworth.

Hightower, Jim. 1987. "Where Greed, Unofficially Blessed by Reagan, Has Led." *New York Times* (June 21):25.

———. 1996. "Homeless Electorate." *Dollars & Sense* 206 (July/August):7.

———. 2002. "Looting the Treasury under Cover of the Flag." *The Hightower Lowdown* 4 (February):1–4.

———. 2003. "Wal-Mart Rides Again." *The Hightower Lowdown* 5 (November):1–2.

Hill, Shirley A., and Joey Sprague. 1999. "Parenting in Black and White Families: The Interaction of Gender with Race and Class." *Gender & Society* 13 (4):480–502.

Hill, Steven. 2002. *Fixing Elections: The Failure of America's Winner Take All Politics.* New York: Routledge.

Himes, Christine L. 2001. "Elderly Americans." *Population Bulletin* 56 (December):entire issue.

Hinden, Stan. 2001. "Some Snags in the Safety Net." *Washington Post National Weekly Edition* (May 28):18.

Hine, Thomas. 1999. "The Rise and Decline of the American Teenager." *American Heritage* (September): 69–82.

Hinman, Al. 1997. "Mass Suicides Raise the Question: Why?" Available online: cnn.com/health/9703/27/nfm/ suicide. psychology/index.html.

Hirschi, Travis. 1969. *Causes of Delinquency.* Berkeley: University of California Press.

Hoch, Paul. 1972. *Rip Off the Big Game.* New York: Doubleday.

Hochschild, Arlie, with Anne Machung. 1989. *The Second Shift.* New York: Viking Penguin.

Hodge, Robert W., Paul M. Seigel, and Peter H. Rossi. 1964. "Occupational Prestige in the United States, 1925–63." *American Journal of Sociology* 70 (November):286–302.

Hodge, Robert W., Donald J. Treiman, and Peter H. Rossi. 1966. "A Comparative Study of Occupational Prestige." In *Class, Status, and Power,* 2nd ed., Reinhard Bendix and S. M. Lipset (eds.). New York: Free Press, pp. 309–321.

Hofferth, Sandra. 2002. "Did Welfare Reform Work? Implications for 2002 and Beyond." *Contexts: Understanding People in Their Social Worlds* 1(2):45–51.

Hoffman, Matthew. 1996. "Electoral College Dropouts." *The Nation* (June 17):15–16.

Hole, Judith, and Ellen Levine. 1979. "The First Feminists." In *Women: A Feminist Perspective,* 2nd ed., Jo Freeman (ed.). Palo Alto, CA: Mayfield.

Hollingshead, August B., and Frederick C. Redlich. 1958. *Social Class and Mental Illness.* New York: Wiley.

Holmes, Stanley. 2002. "Boeing's High-Speed Flight." *Business Week* (August 12):74–75.

Holmes, Steven A. 1999. "Both a Victim of Racial Profiling— And a Practitioner." *New York Times* (April 25):2A.

Holstein, James A., and Jay Gubrium. 1999. "What Is Family? Further Thoughts on a Social Constructionist Approach." *Marriage and Family Review* 28 (3/4): 3–20.

Holstein, William J. 1996. "Santa's Sweatshop." *U.S. News & World Report* (December 16):50–60.

Homans, George. 1964. "Bringing Men Back In." *American Sociological Review* 29 (December):809–818.

Horne, Gerald. 1992–1993. "Race Backwards: Genes, Violence, Race, and Genocide." *Covert Action* (Winter): 29–35.

Hopkins, Jim. 2003. "Fatality Increases for Hispanic Workers." *USA Today* (March 13):1B–2B.

Horton, John. 1966. "Order and Conflict Theories of Social Problems as Competing Ideologies." *American Journal of Sociology* 71 (May):701–713.

Hosenball, Mark. 1999. "It Is Not the Act of a Few Bad Apples." *Newsweek* (May 17):34–35.

Howard, Ina. 2002. "Power Sources: On Party, Gender, Race, and Class: TV News Looks to the Most Powerful Groups." FAIR: Fairness and Accuracy in Reporting. Available online: http://www.fair.org/index.php?page=1109.

Huaco, George A. 1966. "The Functionalist Theory of Stratification: Two Decades of Controversy." *Inquiry* 9 (Autumn):215–240.

Hudson, Christopher G. 2005. "Socioeconomic Status and Mental Illness: Tests of the Social Causation and Selection Hypotheses." *American Journal of Orthopsychiatry* 75 (1). Available online: http:www.apa.org/journals/ releasest/ort7513.pdf.

Hudson, Michael. 1996a. "Cashing In on Poverty." *The Nation* (May 20):11–14.

———. 1996b. *Merchants of Misery.* Monroe, ME: Common Courage Press.

Hulbert, Ann. 1993. "Home Repairs." *New Republic* 209 (August):26–32.

Hunter, Floyd. 1953. *Community Power Structure.* Chapel Hill: University of North Carolina Press.

Hurst, Charles E. 2001. *Social Inequality: Forms, Causes, and Consequences*, 4th ed. Boston: Allyn and Bacon.

Hutchins, Robert M. 1976. "Is Democracy Possible?" *Center Magazine* 9 (January–February):2–6.

Idle, Tracey, Eileen Wood, and Serge Desmarias. 1993. "Gender Role Socialization in Toy Play Situations: Mothers and Fathers with Their Sons and Daughters." *Sex Roles* 28 (11/12):679–691.

Ignatius, David. 1999. "Minding Your Own Business." *Washington Post National Weekly Edition* (March 1):27.

Internet Filter Review. 2005. Available online: http://internet-filter-review.toptenreviews.com/internet-pornography-statistics.html.

Inter-Parliamentary Union [IPU]. 2001. National Parliaments Database. (July 1). Available online: www.ipu.org/wmn-eclassif.htm.

Ireland, Doug. 2002. "'New' FBI, Same Old Problems." *In These Times* (July 8):12–13.

ISR Newsletter. 1982. "Why Do Women Earn Less?" Institute for Social Research, University of Michigan (Spring/ Summer).

Ivins, Molly. 2000. "Capitalism Gets a Really Bad Name." *Progressive Populist* (May 15):22–23.

———. 2002. "The Watchdoggie in the Window." *The Progressive* 66 (July):46.

Jackson, Jesse. 1998. "Market Rules and New Democracy." *Progressive Populist* 4 (June):19.

———. 2002. "Fettered Fathers." *Progressive Populist* (July 15):14.

Jackson, Maggie. 1999. "Minority Women Report Obstacles." *Denver Rocky Mountain News* (July 14):6B.

Jackson, Pamela Braboy. 1997. "Role Occupancy and Minority Mental Health." *Journal of Health and Social Behavior* 38 (September):237–255.

Jacobs, Jerry. 1999. "Gender and the Stratification of Colleges." *Journal of Higher Education* 70 (2):161–187.

Janzen, David. 1974. "Love 'Em and Leave 'Em Alone." *Mennonite* (June 11):390.

Jaynes, Gerald David, and Robin M. Williams, Jr. 1989. *A Common Destiny: Blacks and American Society*. Washington, DC: National Academy Press.

Jeffries, Vincent, and H. Edward Ransford. 1980. *Social Stratification: A Multiple Hierarchy Approach*. Boston: Allyn and Bacon.

Jencks, Christopher, Marshall Smith, Henry Ackland, Mary Jo Bane, David Cohen, Herbert Gintis, et al. 1979. *Who Gets Ahead? The Determinants of Economic Success in America*. New York: Basic Books.

Jenkins, Philip. 2002. "The Next Christianity." *Atlantic Monthly* 290 (October):53–68.

Jensen, Arthur R. 1969. "How Much Can We Boost IQ and Scholastic Achievement?" *Harvard Educational Review* 39 (Winter):1–123.

———. 1980. *Bias in Mental Testing*. New York: Free Press.

Johnson, Kevin. 1999. "ACLU: Racial Profiling Threatens Justice System." *USA Today* (June 2):3A.

Johnson, Mary. 1991. "Disabled Americans Push for Access." *The Progressive* 55 (August):21–23.

Johnston, David Cay. 1999. "Gap between Rich and Poor Found Substantially Wider." *New York Times* (September 5):16.

Jones, Barry. 1990. *Sleepers, Wake! Technology and the Future of Work*, new ed. Melbourne, Australia: Oxford University Press.

Jones, Del. 1997. "Firms Fighting, Winning to Keep Unions at Bay." *USA Today* (September 19):1B, 2B.

Jones, J. H. 1981. *Bad Blood*. New York: Free Press.

Jones, Rachel L. 1996. "Hispanic Children Biggest Minority." *Denver Post* (July 2):A1, A11.

Journal of Blacks in Higher Education. 2004. "Good News! A Record Number of Doctoral Degrees Awarded to African Americans." Available online: http://www.jbhe.com/nenws/46_blacks_doctoraldegrees.html.

Joyce Foundation. "Welfare to Work: What Have We Learned?" Available online: www.joycefdn.org/welrept/.

Kagan, Jerome. 1977. "The Child in the Family." *Daedalus* 106 (Spring):33–56.

Kamau, Puis. 2001. "Educational Funding Unfair." *Denver Post* (April 8):81.

Kammeyer, Kenneth C. W., George Ritzer, and Norman R. Yetman. 1997. *Sociology*, 7th ed. Boston: Allyn and Bacon.

Kanter, Rosabeth Moss. 1977. *Men and Women of the Corporation*. New York: Basic Books.

Kantrowitz, Barbara, and Pat Wingert. 1992. "One Nation, One Curriculum?" *Newsweek* (April 6):59–60.

Karlgaard, Rich. 1999. "Digital Rules: Technology and the New Economy." *Forbes* (March 22):43.

Keating, Frank. 2002. "Dishwasher or Stockbroker: A Life Is a Life." *Fort Collins Coloradoan* (January 25):A10.

Keleher, Terry. 1999. "ERASE—Towards a New Model of School Reform." *ColorLines* (Spring):22.

Keller, Helen. 1954. *The Story of My Life*. Garden City, NY: Doubleday.

Kelley, Jack. 2001. "Devotion, Desire Drive Youths to 'Martyrdom.'" *USA Today* (June 26):1A.

Kennedy, David. 1996. "Can We Still Afford to Be a Nation of Immigrants?" *Atlantic Monthly* (November):51–80.

Kennedy, Paul. 2001. "Introduction: Globalization and the Crisis of Identities." In *Globalization and National Identities: Crisis or Opportunity*, Paul Kennedy and Catherine J. Danks (eds.). London: Pallgrave.

Kent, Mary M., Kelvin M. Pollard, John Haaga, and Mark Mather. 2001. "First Glimpses from the 2000 U.S. Census." *Population Bulletin* 56 (June):entire issue.

Kerbo, Harold R. 1983. *Social Stratification and Inequality: Class Conflict in the United States*. New York: McGraw-Hill.

Kerr, Jennifer. 1999. "A Kiss, a Promise and an Act of Defiance." *Rocky Mountain News* (January 17):37A.

Kesey, Ken. 1962. *One Flew Over the Cuckoo's Nest*. New York: Signet Books.

Kibria, Nazli. 1997. "The Concept of 'Bicultural Families' and Its Implications for Research on Immigrant and Ethnic Families." In *Immigration and the Family*, Alan Booth, Ann C. Crouter, and Nancy Landale (eds.). Mahwah, NJ: Erlbaum, pp. 205–210.

Kilborn, Peter T. 1996. "Build a Better Welfare System, and the World . . ." *Denver Post* (September 19):17A.

Kim, Marlene. 1998. "Are the Working Poor Lazy?" *Challenge* 41 (May/June):85–99.

Kimmel, Michael. 1992. "Reading Men, Masculinity, and Publishing." *Contemporary Sociology* 21 (March): 162–171.

Kimmel, Michael, and Michael A. Messner. 1995. *Men's Lives*, 3rd ed. Boston: Allyn and Bacon.

———. 1998. *Men's Lives*, 4th ed. Boston: Allyn and Bacon.

———. 2004. *The Gendered Society*, 2nd ed. New York: Oxford University Press.

Kiser, Jim. 2005. "A Tattletale May Be Riding In Your Car." *Arizona Daily Star* (June 5):1H.

Kitson, Gay. 1996. "Chair's Notes." *Family Forum: Newsletter of the American Sociological Association Family Section* (Summer):1–2.

Kivel, Paul. 2004. *You Call This a Democracy? Who Benefits, Who Pays and Who Really Decides?* New York: Apex Press.

Klein, Edward. 2002. "'We're Not Destroying Rights, We're Protecting Rights.'" *Parade Magazine* (May 19):4–6.

Klinger, Scott, and Holly Sklar. 2002. "Titans of the Enron Economy: The Ten Habits of Highly Defective Corporations." *The Nation* (August 5/12):16–17.

Kloos, Peter. 2000. "The Dialectics of Globalization and Localization." In *The Ends of Globalization*, Don Kalb, Marco van der Land, Richard Staring, Bart van Steenbergen, and Nico Wilterdink (eds.). Lanham, MD: Rowman & Littlefield, pp. 281–298.

Kluckhohn, Clyde, and D. Leighton. 1946. *The Navaho.* Cambridge, MA: Harvard University Press.

Knottnerus, J. David. 1987. "Status Attainment Research and Its Image of Society." *American Sociological Review* 52 (February):113–121.

Knowles, Louis L., and Kenneth Prewitt (eds.). 1965. *Institutional Racism in America.* Upper Saddle River, NJ: Prentice Hall.

Kochanek, Kenneth D., Betty L. Smith, and Robert N. Anderson. 2001. "Deaths: Preliminary Data for 1999." National Center for Health Statistics, *National Vital Statistics Reports* 49, no. 3 (June). Hyattsville, MD.

Kopkind, Andrew. 1993. "The Gay Moment." *The Nation* (May 3):577, 590–602.

Kornblum, Janet. 2002. "More Hispanic Catholics Losing Their Religion." *USA Today* (December 12):12D.

Kotkin, Joel. 1997. "Rebuilding Blocks." *Washington Post National Weekly Edition* (April 28):21–22.

Kozol, Jonathan. 1991. *Savage Inequalities: Children in America's Schools.* New York: Crown.

———. 2002. "Malign Neglect." *The Nation* (June 10):20–23.

———. 2004. "An Interview with Jonathan Kozol." *The Nation* (May 3):23–24.

Kramer, R. C. 1982. "Corporate Crime." In *White Collar and Economic Crime*, P. Wickman and T. Dailey (eds.). New York: Lexington, pp. 75–94.

Krakauer, Jon. 2003. *Under the Banner of Heaven.* New York: Doubleday.

Kristof, Nicholas D. 2005. "Let Fathers Be Fathers." *New York Times* (April 10):wk13.

Kroeger, Brook. 1994. "The Road Less Rewarded." *Working Woman* (July):50–55.

Krugman, Paul. 2002. "The Great Divide." *New York Times* (January 29). Available online: http://nytimes.com/2002/01/29/opinion/29KRUG.html.

Kulik, Liat. 2002. "Like-Sex versus Opposite-Sex Effects in Transmissions of Gender Role Ideology from Parents of Adolescents in Israel." *Journal of Youth and Adolescence* 31 (6):451–457.

Kulman, Linda. 2004. "Our Consuming Interest." *U.S. News & World Report* (June28/July 5):58–60.

Kuttner, Robert. 1996. "Fair Play for Female Athletes." *Washington Post National Weekly Edition* (August 26– September 1):5.

———. 2002. "Can Liberals Save Capitalism (Again)?" *New American Prospect* (August 12):22–26.

Labi, Nadya. 1998. "Burning Out at Nine?" *Time* (November 23):86.

Lacayo, Richard. 1991. "Death on the Shop Floor." *Time* (September 16):28–29.

———. 1997. "The Lure of the Cult." *Time* (April 7): 45–46.

———. 2000. "The Rain of Dollars." *Time* (August 14):36–37.

Ladner, Joyce A. 1971. *Tomorrow's Tomorrow.* New York: Doubleday.

Lareau, Annette. 2003. *Unequal Childhoods: Class, Race, and Family Lives.* Berkeley: University of California Press.

———. 2003. *Unequal Childhoods.* Berkeley: University of California Press.

Lasch, Christopher. 1977. *Haven in a Heartless World.* New York: Basic Books.

Lauer, Nancy Cook. 2002. "Studies Show Women's Role in Media Shrinking." Available online: www.equality2020.org/media.htm.

Lechner, Frank J. 1989. "Fundamentalism Revisited." *Society* 26 (January/February):51–59.

Lee, Jennifer, and Frank D. Bean. 2004. "America's Changing Color Lines: Immigration, Race/Ethnicity, and Multiracial Identification." *Annual Review of Sociology* 30:221–242.

Lee, Ronald, and John Haaga. 2002. "Government Spending in an Older America." *Reports on America* 3 (May): entire issue.

Lee, Sharon M. 1998. "Asian Americans: Diverse and Growing." *Population Bulletin* 53 (June):entire issue.

Leinwand, Donna. 1999. "Debate Rages on Remedies for Women's Pay Gap." *Denver Post* (October 11):15A.

Leondar-Wright, Betsy, Meizhu Lui, Gloribell Mota, Decrick Mohammed, and Mara Voukydis. 2005. *State of the Dream 2005: Disowned in the Ownership Society.* Boston: United for a Fair Economy.

Lekachman, Robert. 1979. "The Specter of Full Employment." In *Crisis in American Institutions*, 4th ed., Jerome H. Skolnick and Elliott Currie (eds.). Boston: Little, Brown, pp. 50–58.

Leland, John. 2000. "Shades of Gay." *Newsweek* (March 20): 46–49.

LeMasters, E. E. 1974. *Parents in Modern America: A Sociological Analysis*, rev. ed. Homewood, IL: Dorsey.

Lemert, Edwin M. 1951. *Social Pathology: A Systematic Approach to the Theory of Sociopathic Behavior.* New York: McGraw-Hill.

———. 1967. *Human Deviance, Social Problems and Social Control.* Upper Saddle River, NJ: Prentice Hall.

Lenski, Gerhard. 1966. *Power and Privilege: A Theory of Social Stratification.* New York: McGraw-Hill.

———. 1970. *Human Societies: A Macrolevel Introduction to Sociology.* New York: McGraw-Hill.

Leonard, Mary. 1997. "Abortion: 25 Years after *Roe v. Wade*, Middleground in Battlefield." *Boston Globe* (December 14):1F, 3F.

Leondar-Wright, Betsy. 2001. "As Economy Tumbles, The Poor Will Suffer Most." *San Jose Mercury News* (October 19). Available online: http://inequality.org/ econtumble2.html.

Leondar-Wright, Betsey, Meizhu Lui, Gloribell Mota, Decrick Mohammad, and Mara Voukydis. 2005. *State of the Dream 2005: Disowned in The Ownership Society.* Boston: United for a Fair Economy.

Leonhardt, David. 2000. "Lingering Job Worries Amid a Sea of Plenty." *New York Times.* Available online: www. nytimes. com/library/tech/yt/mo/bizrtech/articles/ 29worry.html.

Lever, Janet. 1976. "Sex Differences in the Games Children Play." *Social Problems* 23 (April):478–487.

Levin, Andy. 2004. "Speech." C-Span (September 6).

Levine, Susan. 1997. "To Grandmother's House We Go." *Washington Post Weekly National Edition* (March 3):35.

Levitan, Sar A., and Clifford M. Johnson. 1982. *Second Thoughts on Work.* Kalamazoo, MI: W. E. Upjohn Institute for Employment Research.

Levy, Steven. 2004. "A Future with Nowhere to Hide?" *Newsweek* (June 7):76.

Lewin, Tamar. 1998. "How Boys Lost Out to Girl Power." *New York Times* (December 13):3D.

———. 2000. "Majority of Married Couples with Children Now Both Work." *Rocky Mountain News* (October 24):24.

Lewis, Al. 2002. "Trust Takes a Holiday." *Denver Post* (June 30):1K.

Lewis, Anthony. 2001. "Wake Up, America." *New York Times* (November 30). Available online: www.nytimes.com/2001/11/30/opinion/30LEWI.html.

Lewis, Bernard. 2001. "Understanding bin Laden." *Rocky Mountain News* (September 22):4B–5B.

Lewis, Earl. 1991. "African-Americans and the Bill of Rights." *In These Times* (December18–24):12–13.

Liazos, Alexander. 1972. "The Poverty of the Sociology of Deviance: Nuts, Sluts, and Perverts." *Social Problems* 20 (Summer):103–120.

———. 1985. *Sociology: A Liberating Perspective.* Boston: Allyn and Bacon.

Lichtenberg, Judith. 1992. "Racism in the Head, Racism in the World." *Report from the Institute for Philosophy and Public Policy* (University of Maryland) 12 (Spring/ Summer):3–5.

Lichter, Daniel T., and Martha L. Crowley. 2002. "Poverty in America: Beyond Welfare Reform." *Population Bulletin* 57 (June):entire issue.

Lichter, Daniel T., and Nancy S. Landale. 1995. "Parental Work, Family Structure, and Poverty among Latino Children." *Journal of Marriage and the Family* 57 (May): 346–353.

Lichter, Daniel T., Diane K. McLaughlin, and David C. Ribar. 2002. "Economic Restructuring and the Retreat from Marriage." *Social Science Research* 31:230–256.

Liebow, Elliot. 1967. *Tally's Corner.* Boston: Little, Brown.

Lincoln, C. Eric. 1996. *Coming through the Fire: Surviving Race and Place in America.* Durham, NC: Duke University Press.

Lipman-Blumen, Jean. 1984. *Gender Roles and Power.* Englewood Cliffs, NJ: Prentice Hall.

Locke, John L. 1998. *The De-Voicing of Society: Why We Don't Talk to Each Other Anymore.* New York: Simon & Schuster.

Lockheed, Marlaine. 1985. "Sex Equity in the Classroom Organization and Climate." In *Handbook for Achieving Sex Equity through Education,* Susan S. Klein (ed.). Baltimore: Johns Hopkins University Press, pp. 189–217.

Loewen, James W. 1995. *Lies My Teacher Told Me: Everything Your American History Textbook Got Wrong.* New York: Simon & Schuster.

Lofholm, Nancy. 1999. "A Matter of Faith, Justice: Is Withholding Care a Crime?" *Denver Post* (March 15): 1A, 4A, 5A.

Lorber, Judith. 1994. *Paradoxes of Gender.* New Haven, CT: Yale University Press.

———. 2005. *Gender Inequality: Feminist Theories and Politics.* Los Angeles: Roxbury.

Lord, Walter. 1955. *A Night to Remember.* New York: Henry Holt.

Los Angeles Times. 2002. "A Blow to U.S. Education." (June 28). Available online: www.latimes.com/news/opinion/ editorials.

———. 2003. "A Formula for Inequity." (December 13). Available online: http://www.latimes.com/news/opinion/ editorials/la-ed-schoolfund13d.

Lott, Juanita Tamayo, and Judy C. Felt. 1991. "Studying the Pan Asian Community." *Population Today* 19 (April 1): 6–8.

Love, Alice Ann. 1998. "Gender Wage Gap Shrinks Slightly." *USA Today* (June 10):1A.

Lowy, Joan. 1998. "On a Mission." *Rocky Mountain News* (March 29):3A, 63A.

Lucal, Betsy. 1994. "Class Stratification in Introductory Textbooks: Relational or Distributional Models?" *Teaching Sociology* 22 (April):139–150.

———. 1996. "Oppression and Privilege: Toward a Relational Conceptualization of Race." *Teaching Sociology* 24 (July):245–255.

Luker, Kristin. 1991. "Dubious Conceptions: The Controversy over Teen Pregnancy." *American Prospect* 5 (Spring):73–83.

Lydersen, Kari. 2002. "Banking on Poverty: Predatory Lenders Take Advantage of the Poor." *In These Times* (October 14):19.

MacEwan, Arthur. 1994. "Markets Unbound: The Heavy Price of Globalization." *Dollars & Sense* 195 (September/ October):8–9, 35–37.

———. 2001. "Ask Dr. Dollar." *Dollars & Sense,* no. 233 (January/February):40.

Madrick, Jeff. 2002. "A Rise in Child Poverty Rates Is at Risk in U.S." *New York Times* (June 13). Available online: www. nytimes.com/2002/06/13/business/13SCEN.html.

Mahler, Jonathan. 2004. "The Soul of the New Exurb." *New York Times Magazine* (March 27):30–46, 50, 54–57.

Malec, Michael A. 1997. "Gender Equity in Athletics." In *Perspectives on Current Social Problems,* Gregg Lee Carter (ed.). Boston: Allyn and Bacon, pp. 209–218.

Males, Mike. 1993. "Infantile Arguments." *In These Times* (August 9):18–20.

———. 1994. "The Real Generational Gap." *In These Times* (February 7):18–19.

———. 1996. *The Scapegoat Generation: America's War on Adolescents.* Monroe, ME: Common Courage Press.

Malveaux, Julianne. 2002. [no title], *The Nation* (January 7/14):34–35.

Mandel, Michael J. 2004. "Where Wealth Lives." *Business Week* (April 19):34–37.

Marcus, David L. 1999. "Mothers with Another's Eggs." *U.S. News & World Report* (April 12):42–44.

Marger, Martin N. 1987. *Elites and Masses: An Introduction to Political Sociology,* 2nd ed. Belmont, CA: Wadsworth.

Marklein, Mary Beth. 2002. "Poor Continue to Lose Ground in College Finances." *USA Today* (May 2):9D.

Marsden, Peter. 1998. *The Taliban: War, Religion and the New Order in Afghanistan.* London: Zed Books.

Martin, Philip, and Elizabeth Midgley. 1999. "Immigration to the United States." *Population Bulletin* 54 (June):entire issue.

Martin, Philip, and Jonas Widgren. 1996. "International Migration: A Global Challenge." *Population Bulletin* 51 (April):entire issue.

———. 2002. "International Migration: Facing the Challenge." *Population Bulletin* 57 (March):entire issue.

Martin, Teresa Castro, and Larry L. Bumpass. 1989. "Recent Trends in Marital Disruption." *Demography* 26:37–51.

Marx, Karl. 1967. *Capital: A Critique of Political Economy.* Vol. 1. New York: International.

Marx, Karl, and Friedrich Engels. 1947. *The German Ideology.* New York: International.

———. 1959. *Marx and Engels: Basic Writing on Politics and Philosophy,* Lewis S. Feuer (ed.). Garden City, NY: Anchor Books.

Maschinot, Beth. 1995. "Behind the Curve." *In These Times* (February 6):31–34.

Massey, Douglas S. 1993. "Latino Poverty Research: An Agenda for the 1990s." *Items* (Social Science Research Council) 47 (March):7–11.

———. 1996. "Concentrating Poverty Breeds Violence." *Population Today* 24 (June/July):5.

Massey, Douglas S., and Nancy Denton. 1993. *American Apartheid: Segregation and the Making of the Underclass.* Cambridge, MA: Harvard University Press.

Matza, David. 1964a. *Delinquency and Drift.* New York: Wiley.

———. 1964b. "Position and Behavior Patterns of Youth." In *Handbook of Modern Sociology,* Robert E. L. Faris (ed.). Chicago: Rand McNally.

McAdoo, John. 1988. "Changing Perspectives on the Role of the Black Father." In *Fatherhood Today: Men's Changing Role in the Family*, P. Bronstein and C. P. Cowan (eds.). New York: Wiley, pp. 79–92.

McCaghy, Charles H. 1976. *Deviant Behavior: Crime, Conflict, and Interest Groups*. New York: Macmillan.

McCarthy, Sarah J. 1979. "Why Johnny Can't Disobey." *Humanist* (September–October).

McClam, Erin. 2000. "Less Teens Smoked in '99, CDC Says." Associated Press (August 25).

McCleary, Paul. 2002. "Information, Please." *In These Times* (June 24):22–23.

McGee, Reece. 1975. *Points of Departure: Basic Concepts in Sociology*, 2nd ed. Hinsdale, IL: Dryden Press.

McGeorge, Erina L., Angela R. Graves, Bo Feng, Seth J. Gillihan, and Brant R. Burleson. 2004. "The Myth of Gender Cultures: Similarities Outweigh Differences in Men's and Women's Provision of and Responses to Supportive Communication." *Sex Roles* 50 (3/4):143–175.

McGrath, Peter. 1999. "Knowing You All Too Well." *Newsweek* (March 29):48–50.

McGuire, Meredith B. 1992. *Religion: The Social Context*, 3rd ed. Belmont, CA: Wadsworth.

McIntosh, Peggy. 1992. "White Privilege and Male Privilege." In *Race, Class, and Gender, an Anthology*, Margaret L. Andersen and Patricia Hill Collins (eds.). Belmont, CA: Wadsworth, pp. 70–81.

McIsaac, Jenny. 2002. "Human Rights for All." *Dollars & Sense*, no. 240 (March/April):6–7.

McKelvey, Tara. 2001. "Father and Son Target Kids in a Confederacy of Hate." *USA Today* (July 16):3D.

McKinley, Donald Gilbert. 1964. *Social Class and Family Life*. Glencoe, IL: Free Press.

McKissack, Frederick L., Jr. 1998. "Cyberghetto: Blacks Are Falling through the Net." *Progressive* 62 (June):20–22.

McLanahan, Sara, and Lynne Casper. 1995. "Growing Diversity and Inequality in the American Family." In *State of the Union, America in the 1990s*. Vol. 2, "Social Trends," Reynolds Farley (ed.). New York: Russell Sage, pp. 1–45.

McWhirter, Norris, and Ross McWhirter. 1972. *Guinness Book of World Records*, 11th ed. New York: Sterling.

Mead, George Herbert. 1934. *Mind, Self, and Society*. Chicago: University of Chicago Press.

Meckler, Laura. 1999. "Poor Going from Welfare to Low-Paying Jobs." *Rocky Mountain News* (June 18):23.

Media Report to Women. 2002. "Industry Statistics." Available online: www.mediareporttowomen.com/statistics. htm.

Mendels, Pamela. 2000. "Crumbling Schools Have Trouble Getting Online." *New York Times* (February 23). Available online: www.nytimes.com/library/tech/yr/mo/cyber/education/23education.html.

Meneilly, Robert H. 1993. "Government Is Not God's Work." *New York Times* (August 29):15E.

Merton, Robert K. 1957. *Social Theory and Social Structure*, 2nd ed. Glencoe, IL: Free Press.

Messner, Michael A. 1996. "Studying Up on Sex." *Sociology of Sport Journal* 13:221–237.

Metcalf, Stephen. 2002. "Reading between the Lines." *The Nation* (January 28):18–22.

Michels, Robert. 1966. *Political Parties*, Eden Paul and Cedar Paul (trans.). New York: Free Press.

Miles, Robert. 1989. *Racism*. New York: Tavistock.

Miller, D. W. 1999. "Scholars of Immigration Focus on Children." *Chronicle of Higher Education* (February 5):A19–A20.

Miller, David. 1991. "A Vision of Market Socialism." *Dissent* 38 (Summer):406–414.

Miller, Jason. 2005. "Liberating the 'Liberal Media.'" *Znet* (May 4). Available online: http://www.zmag.org/ content/showarticle.cfm?ItemID=7780.

Miller, Jerome G. 1996. *Search and Destroy: African-American Males in the Criminal Justice System*. New York: Cambridge University Press.

Miller, Juanita E. 2000. "The Working Poor." *Ohio State University Extension Fact Sheet*. Available online: www.ag.ohio-state.edu/.

Miller, Mark Crispin. 2002. "What's Wrong with This Picture." *The Nation* (January 7/14):18–22.

Miller, Walter B. 1958. "Lower Class Culture as a Generating Milieu of Gang Delinquency." *Journal of Social Issues* 14(3):5–19.

Miller, William Ian. 1997. *The Anatomy of Disgust*. Cambridge, MA: Harvard University Press.

Mills, C. Wright. 1956. *The Power Elite*. New York: Oxford University Press.

———. 1959. *The Sociological Imagination*. Fair Lawn, NJ: Oxford University Press.

———. 1968. "The Power Elite." In *Reader in Political Sociology*, Frank Lindenfeld (ed.). New York: Funk & Wagnalls, pp. 263–276.

Mishel, Lawrence, Jared Bernstein, and John Schmitt. 1998. "A Boom for Whom? The State of Working America 1998–99." *Progressive Populist* 4 (October):1, 11–12.

———. 2000. *The State of Working America 2000–2001*. Ithaca, NY: Cornell University Press.

Mishel, Lawrence, Jared Bernstein, and Sylvia Allegretto. 2004. *The State of Working America 2004/2005*. Washington, DC: The Economic Policy Institute.

Moberg, David. 1995. "Reviving the Public Sector." *In These Times* (October 16):22–24.

Mogelesky, Marcia. 1996. "The Rocky Road to Adulthood." *American Demographics* 18 (May):26–35.

Mohan, Geoffrey, and Ann M. Simmons. 2004. "Diversity Spoken in 39 Languages. *Los Angeles Times* (June 16). Available online: http://www.latimes.com/news/locak/ la-me-multilingual16jun16,1,157.

Mokhiber, Russell, and Robert Weissman. 2002. "The Age of Inequality." Available online: www.inequality.org/mokhiber2.html.

———. nd. "The Age of Inequality." Available online: http://www.inequality.org/ageofinequality.html.

Monthly Forum for Women in Higher Education. 1995. "Women College Presidents." *Monthly Forum for Women in Higher Education* 1 (December):9.

Moore, Joan, and Raquel Pinderhughes (eds.). 1994. *In the Barrios: Latinos and the Underclass Debate*. New York: Sage.

Moore, Joan, Robert Garcia, Carlos Garcia, Luis Cerda, and Frank Valencia. 1978. *Homeboys: Gangs, Drugs, and Prison in the Barrios of Los Angeles*. Philadelphia: Temple University Press.

Moore, Wilbert E. 1969. "Social Structure and Behavior." In *The Handbook of Social Psychology*, 2nd ed., Vol. IV, Gardner Lindzey and Elliot Aronson (eds.). Reading, MA: Addison-Wesley.

Morin, Richard. 1998. "Keeping the Faith." *Washington Post National Weekly Edition* (January 12):37.

Morse, Jodie. 2002. "Learning While Black." *Time* (May 22):50–52.

Mortimer, Jeylan T., and Michael D. Finch. 1996. "Work, Family, and Adolescent Development." In *Adolescents, Work, and Family*, Jeylan T. Mortimer and Michael D. Finch (eds.). Newbury Park, CA: Sage, pp. 1–24.

Moskos, Charles C., Jr. 1975. "The American Combat Soldier in Vietnam." *Journal of Social Issues* 31 (Fall):25–37.

Mother Jones. 1996. "Corporate Welfare Poster Boys." *Mother Jones* 60 (June):15.

Mott, Paul E. 1965. *The Organization of Society.* Englewood Cliffs, NJ: Prentice Hall.

Mott, Tracy. 2005. "American Dream: Is It Fading?" *Denver Post* (July 10):E1, E4.

Moyers, Bill. 1996. "America's Religious Mosaic." *USA Weekend* (October 11):4–5.

Mukhopadhyay, Carol, and Rosemary C. Henz. 2003. "How Real Is Race? Using Anthropology to Make Sense of Human Diversity." *Phi Delta Kappan* (May): 669–678.

Muller, Joanne. 2002. "Autos: A New Industry." *Business Week* (July 15):98–106.

Multinational Monitor. 1997a. "The Great Digital Giveaway." Vol. 18 (May):5.

———. 1997b. "Nike: Swooshes and Sweatshops." Vol. 18 (December):13–14.

Mulvaney, Jim. 1993. "Skinhead Founder Sorry Now." *Denver Post* (August 1):21A–22A.

Murphy, Cait. 2000. "Are the Rich Cleaning Up?" *Fortune* (September 4):252–262.

Murray, Jim. 1976. "Vocabulary Takes on a Ruddy-Faced Look." *Rocky Mountain News* (December 9):150.

Muwakkil, Salim. 1994. "Dangerous Curve." *In These Times* (November 28):22–24.

———. 1998a. "Movin' on Apart." *In These Times* (March 22):11–12.

———. 1998b. "Real Minority, Media Majority: TV News Needs to Root Out Stereotypes about Blacks and Crime." *In These Times* (June 28):18–19.

———. 2002. "Forgotten Freedoms." *In These Times* (January 7):17–18.

———. 2004. "The Best and Worst of Times." *In These Times* (August 30):14.

Myers, Jerome K., and Lee L. Bean. 1968. *A Decade Later: A Follow-Up of Social Class and Mental Illness.* New York: Wiley.

Myrdal, Gunnar. 1944. *An American Dilemma.* New York: Pantheon.

Nader, Ralph. 2001. "Corporate Welfare Spoils." *Nation* (May 7):7, 26.

Naples, Nancy A. 1998. "Women's Community Activism and Feminist Action Research." In *Community Activism and Feminist Politics,* Nancy A. Naples (ed.). New York: Routledge, pp. 1–27.

NARAL. 2005. *State and Federal Legislation.* Available online: http://naral.org/legislation/index.cfm.

The Nation 2002. "Big Media, Bad News." (January 7/14):3.

The Nation 2002. "The Big Ten." (January 7/14):27–30.

National Center for Education Statistics. 1997. *Digest of Education Statistics.* Washington, DC: U.S. Department of Education.

———. 2002. "The Condition of Education 2002." NCES 2002025. Washington, DC: U.S. Department of Education.

———. 2004. Available online: http://nces.ed.gov/programs/coe/2004/section4/indicator25.asp.

National Committee on Pay Equity. 1998. "Questions and Answers on Pay Equity," pp. 1–4.

———. 2002a. "Little Progress on Closing the Wage Gap in 2000." Available online: www.feminist.com/fairpay.

———. 2002b. "Questions and Answers on Pay Equity." Available online: www.feminist.com/fairpay.

National Conference of Catholic Bishops. 1986. *Economic Justice for All: Pastoral Letter on Catholic Social Teaching and the U.S. Economy.* Washington, DC: United States Catholic Conference, Inc.

National Council of Bioethics. 2005. "Genetics and Human Behaviour: the Ethical Context." Available online: http://www.nuffieldbioethics.org.

National Council of La Raza. 1999. "The Mainstreaming of Hate: A Report on Latinos and Harassment, Hate Violence, and Law Enforcement Abuse in the '90s." (July). Washington, DC.

National Institute on Drug Abuse. 2005. "Monitoring the Future Survey." University of Michigan's Institute for Social Research. Available online: http://www.drugabuse.gov/DrugPages/MTF.html.

National Opinion Research Center. 1994. *General Social Surveys, 1972–1994: Cumulative Codebook.* Chicago: National Opinion Research Center.

National Opinion Research Center. 1996. *Social Surveys, 1972–1996: Cumulative Codebook.* Chicago: National Opinion Research Center.

National Organization for Women. 2002. *Watch Out, Listen Up! 2002 Feminist Primetime Report.* Washington, DC: National Organization for Women.

National Organization for Women. 2005. Facts about Pay Equity. Available online: http://www.now.org/issues/economic/factsheet.html.

———. 2004. *Reproductive Rights Historical Highlights.* Available online: http://www.now.org/issues/abortion/roe30timeline.html?printable.

Navarro, Vincente. 1991. "Class and Race: Life and Death Situations." *Monthly Review* 43 (September):1–13.

Nelson, Mariah Burton. 1999. "Learning What 'Team' Really Means." *Newsweek* (July 19):55.

Nettler, Gwynn. 1974. *Explaining Crime.* New York: McGraw-Hill.

Neubauer, Diane. 2000. "Assaying the Frontiers of Globalization: Exploration in the New Economy." *American Studies* 41 (Summer/Fall):13–32.

Neugarten, Bernice L. 1980. "Grow Old along with Me! The Best Is Yet to Be." In *Growing Old in America,* Beth Hess (ed.). New Brunswick, NJ: Transaction Books, pp. 180–197.

Newcomb, Peter. 1999. "The First Billion Takes a Lifetime . . . Except in the Internet Age." *Forbes* (April 19): 246–247.

Newman, David M. 2000. *Sociology: Exploring the Architecture of Everyday Life,* 3rd ed. Thousand Oaks, CA: Pine Forge Press.

Newman, Katherine S. 1988. *Falling from Grace: The Experience of Downward Mobility in the American Middle Class.* New York: Free Press.

Newsweek. 1998. "The Face of the Nation." (November 2):63.

New York Times. 2000a. "A Fix for the Broadcast Giveaway." (October 11). Available online: http://nytimes.com/2000/10/11/opinion/11WED2.html.

———. 2000b. "The Religious Wars." (March 2). Available online: http://nytimes.com/yr/mo/day/editorial/02THU1.html.

———. 2003. "Fighting School Resegregation." (January 27). Available online: http://www.nytimes.com/2003/01/27/opinion/27MON1.html.

———. 2005. "Revising the Patriot Act." (April 20):wk 11.

Nguyn, Alexander. 2000. "The Souls of White Folk." *American Prospect* 11 (July 31):46–49.

Nichol, Gene. 1999a. "Equality Has Been Taken off the Table." *Rocky Mountain News* (January 22):59A.

———. 1999b. "Unhealthy Times for Have-Nots." *Rocky Mountain News* (May 14):55A.

Niebuhr, R. Gustav. 1995. "Where Shopping Mall Culture Gets a Big Dose of Religion." *New York Times* (April 16): 1A, 12A.

———. 1998. "Doctrine Defines Wives' Roles." *Rocky Mountain News* (June 10):3A.

Nielson, Joyce McCarl. 1990. *Sex and Gender in Society*. Prospect Heights, IL: Waveland Press.

Nilges, Lynda M., and Albert F. Spencer. 2002. "The Pictorial Representation in Notable Children's Picture Books; 1995–1999." *Sex Roles* 45 (1/2):89–101.

Nilsen, Alleen Pace. 2000. "Sexism in English: A 1990s Update." In *The Gender Reader*, 2nd ed., Evelyn Ashton-Jones, Gary A. Olson, and Merry G. Perry (eds.). Boston, MA: Allyn and Bacon, pp. 301–313.

North, C. C., and Paul K. Hatt. 1947. "Jobs and Occupations: A Popular Evaluation." *Public Opinion News* 9 (September):3–13.

Norton, Arthur J., and Louisa F. Miller. 1992. "Marriage, Divorce, and Remarriage in the 1990s." *Current Population Reports*, P23–180. Washington, DC: U.S. Government Printing Office.

Nottingham, Elizabeth K. 1954. *Religion and Society*. New York: Random House.

Novak, Viveca. 1991. "Why Workers Can't Win." *Common Cause Magazine* 17 (July/August):28–32.

Nussbaum, Bruce. 2002. "Can You Trust Anybody Anymore?" *Business Week* (January 28):31–32.

Oakes, Jeannie. 1985. *Keeping Track: How Schools Structure Inequality*. New Haven, CT: Yale University Press.

Obeidallah, Dawn A., Susan M. McHale, and Rainer K. Silbereisen. 1996. "Gender Role Socialization and Adolescents' Reports of Depression: Why Some Girls and Not Others?" *Journal of Youth and Adolescence* 25(6): 775–785.

O'Dea, Thomas. 1966. *The Sociology of Religion*. Upper Saddle River, NJ: Prentice Hall.

Office of Minority Health. 2005. Center for Disease Control. "About Minority Health." Available online. http://www.cdc.gov/omh/AMH/AMH.htm.

O'Hare, William P. 1985. "Poverty in America: Trends and New Patterns." *Population Bulletin* 40 (June):entire issue.

———. 1992. "America's Minorities: The Demographics of Diversity." *Population Bulletin* 47 (December):entire issue.

———. 1993. "Diversity Trend: More Minorities Looking Less Alike." *Population Today* 21 (April):1–2.

———. 1996. "A New Look at Poverty in America." *Population Bulletin* 51 (September):entire issue.

———. 1998. "Managing Multiple-Race Data." *American Demographics* 20 (April):1–4.

———. 2001. "The Rise—and Fall?—of Single Parent Families." *Population Today* 29 (July):1, 4.

O'Hare, William P., and Brenda Curry-White. 1992. "Is There a Rural Underclass?" *Population Today* 20 (March): 6–8.

O'Harrow, Robert, Jr. 2005. *No Place to Hide*. New York: Free Press.

O'Harrow, Robert, Jr., and Liz Leyden. 1999. "The True Colors of a Check Fraud Database." *Washington Post National Weekly Edition* (March 1):30.

O'Kelly, Charlotte. 1980. *Women and Men in Society*. New York: Van Nostrand.

Oldenburg, Ray. 1997. *The Great Good Place*. New York: Marlowe.

Oliver, Melvin L., and Thomas M. Shapiro. 1995. *Black Wealth/White Wealth: A New Perspective on Racial Equality*. New York: Routledge.

Olsen, Marvin E. 1976. *The Process of Social Organization*, 2nd ed. New York: Holt, Rinehart and Winston.

Omi, Michael, and Howard Winant. 1986. *Racial Formation in the United States*. London: Routledge.

———. 1994. *Racial Formation in the United States*, 2nd ed. New York: Routledge.

O'Neill, Tom. 2003. "Untouchable." *National Geographic* 203 (June):4–31.

Orfield, Gary. 1999. "The Resegregation of Our Nation's Schools." *Civil Rights Journal* 4 (Fall):8–12.

Ortner, Sherry B. 1974. "Is Female to Male as Nature Is to Culture?" In *Woman, Culture, and Society*, Michelle Zimbalist Rosaldo and Louise Lamphere (eds.). Stanford, CA: Stanford University Press, pp. 66–88.

Orwell, George. 1946. *Animal Farm*. New York: Harcourt Brace.

Oskamp, Stuart, Karen Kaufman, and Liannaa Atchison Wolterbeek. 1996. "Gender Role Portrayal in Preschool Books." *Journal of Social Behavior and Personality* 11 (5):27–39.

Osmond, Marie Withers, and Barrie Thorne. 1993. "Feminist Theories: The Social Construction of Gender in Families and Society." In *Sourcebook of Family Theories and Methods: A Contextual Approach*, P. G. Boss, W. J. Doherty, R. LaRousse, W. R. Schumm, and S. K. Steinmetz (eds.). New York: Plenum Press, pp. 591–623.

Outtz, Janice Hamilton. 1995. "Higher Education and the New Demographic Reality." *Educational Record* 76 (Spring/Summer):65–69.

Palast, Greg. 2002. *The Best Democracy Money Can Buy*. London: Pluto Press.

Papper, Bob. 2004. "Recovering Lost Ground: Minorities Gain Ground and Women Make Management Strides in Radio and TV Newsrooms in 2004." *Communicator* (July/August):24–28.

Parenti, Christian. 2001. "Big Brother's Corporate Cousin." *The Nation* (August 6):26–30.

———. 2002. "DC's Virtual Panopticon." *The Nation* (June 3):24–26.

Parenti, Michael. 1978. *Power and the Powerless*, 2nd ed. New York: St. Martin's Press.

———. 1980. *Democracy for the Few*, 3rd ed. New York: St. Martin's Press.

———. 1983. *Democracy for the Few*, 4th ed. New York: St. Martin's Press.

———. 1986. *Inventing Reality: The Politics of the Mass Media*. New York: St. Martin's Press.

———. 1988. *Democracy for the Few*, 5th ed. New York: St. Martin's Press.

———. 1992. *Make-Believe Media: The Politics of Entertainment*. New York: St. Martin's Press.

———. 1993. *Inventing Reality: The Politics of the News Media*, 2nd ed. New York: St. Martin's Press.

———. 1994. *Land of Idols: Political Mythology in America*. New York: St. Martin's Press.

———. 1995. *Democracy for the Few*, 6th ed. New York: St. Martin's Press.

———. 2002. *Democracy for the Few*, 7th ed. New York: Bedford/St. Martin's Press.

Parker, Laura. 2001. "U.S. Hispanics' Youth Assures More Growth." *USA Today* (May 10):3A.

Parlee, Mary Brown. 1979. "Conversational Politics." *Psychology Today* 12 (May):48–56.

Parsons, Talcott, and Robert R. Bales. 1955. *Family, Socialization and Interaction Process*. Glencoe, IL: Free Press.

Pascale, Celine-Marie. 1995. "Normalizing Poverty." *Z Magazine* 8 (June):38–42.

Passel, Jeffrey S. 2005. "Estimates of the Size and Characteristics of the Undocumented Population." Pew Hispanic Center (June 14).

Paul, Pamela. 2002. *The Starter Marriage and the Future of Matrimony*. New York: Villard.

Paulson, Michael. 2000. "More Women Embracing the Study of Jewish Faith." *Boston Globe* (March 13):1B, 5B.

562

Pear, Robert. 1993. "Poverty Is Cited as Divorce Factor." *New York Times* (January 15):A6.

———. 2004. "Selling to the Poor, Stores Bill U.S. for Top Prices." *New York Times* (June 6):1.

Pearce, Diana. 1978. "The Feminization of Poverty: Women, Work, and Welfare." *Urban and Social Change Review* II:28–36.

Pera, Gina. 1996. "School Sports: Girls Take the Field." *USA Weekend* (September 6):26.

Perry, Bruce D. 2002. "Childhood Experience and the Expression of Genetic Potential: What Childhood Neglect Tells Us about Nature and Nurture." The Child Trauma Academy. Available online: http://www.feralchildren.com/en/pager.php?df=perry2002.

Peterson, Linda, and Elaine Enarson. 1974. "Blaming the Victim in the Sociology of Women: On the Misuse of the Concept of Socialization." Paper presented at the Pacific Sociological Association, San Jose, California (March).

Peterson, Richard R. 1996. "A Re-Evaluation of the Consequences of Divorce." *American Sociological Review* 61 (June):528–536.

Peyser, Marc. 1999. "Home of the Gray." *Newsweek* (March 1):50–53.

Philippus, M. J. 1989. "Hispanics Fail Tests because Tests Fail Them." *Rocky Mountain News* (June 15):59.

Phillips, Kevin. 2002. *Wealth and Democracy: A Political History of the American Rich*. New York: Broadway Books.

Phillips, Lisa E. 1999. "Love, American Style." *American Demographics* 21 (February):1–3.

Pierard, Richard V., and Robert D. Linder. 1988. *Civil Religion and the Presidency*. Grand Rapids, MI: Zondervan.

Pike, Jennifer J., and Nancy A. Jennings. 2005. "The Effects of Commercials on Children's Perceptions of Gender Appropriate Toy Use." *Sex Roles* 52(1/2):83–91.

Piven, Frances Fox. 1996. "Welfare and the Transformation of Electoral Politics." *Dissent* 43 (Fall):61–67.

Piven, Frances Fox, and Richard A. Cloward. 1971. "The Relief of Welfare." *Transaction* 8 (May).

———. 1993. *Regulating the Poor: The Functions of Public Welfare*, updated ed. New York: Vintage Books.

Plagens, Peter. 1991. "Violence in Our Culture." *Newsweek* (April 1):46–52.

Pleck, Joseph. 1977. "The Work–Family Role System." *Social Problems* 24 (April):417–427.

———. 1981. "Prisoners of Manliness." *Psychology Today* 15 (September).

Pogatchnik, Shawn. 2002. "Northern Ireland Tots Learn Hate." Associated Press (June 25).

Pollard, Kelvin M., and William P. O'Hare. 1999. "America's Racial and Ethnic Minorities." *Population Bulletin* 54, no. 3 (September). Washington, DC: Population Reference Bureau.

Pollitt, Katha. 2001. "Childcare Scare." *The Nation* (May 14):10.

Pope, Harrison G., Katharine A. Phillips, and Roberto Olivardia. 2000. *The Adonis Complex: The Secret Crisis of Male Body Obsession*. New York: Simon & Schuster.

Pope, Liston. 1942. *Millhands and Preachers*. New Haven, CT: Yale University Press.

Popper, Bob. 2004. "Recovering Lost Ground: Minorities Gain Ground and Women Make Management Strides in Radio and TV Newsrooms in 2004." *Communicator* (July/August):24–28.

Population Today. 1998. "Census Race and Ethnic Categories Retooled." Vol. 26 (January):4.

———. 2001. "Median Net Worth of U.S. Households by Race and Ethnicity." Vol. 29 (April):4.

Port, Otis. 1999. "They're Listening to Your Calls." *Business Week* (May 31):110–111.

Porter, Eduardo. 2005. "Boon from Illegal Labor." *Denver Post* (April 5):1A.

Portes, Alejandro, and Min Zhou. 1993. "The New Second Generation: Segmental Assimilation and the Variants." *Annals of the American Academy of Political and Social Science* 530:74–96.

Poulantzas, Nicos. 1974. *Classes in Contemporary Capitalism*. London: New Left Books.

Power, Carla. 1998a. "The New Islam." *Newsweek* (March 16):34–37.

———. 1998b. "When Women Are the Enemy." *Newsweek* (August 3):37–38.

Powers, Edwin, and Helen Witmer. 1951. *An Experiment in the Prevention of Delinquency*. New York: Columbia University Press.

Powledge, Fred. 1991. *Free at Last? The Civil Rights Movement and the People Who Made It*. Boston: Little, Brown.

Prewitt, Kenneth. 2003. *Politics and Science in Census Taking*. New York: Russell Sage Foundation.

Price, Sharon J., and Patrick C. McKenry. 1988. *Divorce*. Beverly Hills, CA: Sage.

Progressive. 1980. "An Editorial." Vol. 44 (August):27–28.

Purdum, Todd S. 2000. "Shift in the Mix Alters the Face of California." *New York Times* (July 4). Available online: http://nytimes.com/library/national/070400calatin.html.

Quinn, Jane Bryant. 2000. "Fighting the Cookie Monster." (February 28):63.

Quinney, Richard. 1970. *The Social Reality of Crime*. Boston: Little, Brown.

———. 1973. *Critique of Legal Order: Crime Control in Capitalist Society*. Boston: Little, Brown.

———. 1974. *Criminal Justice in America: A Critical Understanding*. Boston: Little, Brown.

Quittner, Joshua. 1997. "Invasion of Privacy." *Time* (August 25):18–35.

Rachlin, Jill. 1989. "The Label That Sticks." *U.S. News & World Report* (July 3):51–52.

Radio-Television News Directors Association and Foundation [RTNDA]. 2002. "More Women News Directors Than Ever, Study Shows." Available online: www.rtnda.org/news/2002/071502.html.

Rai, Saritha. 2004. "Short on Priests, U. S. Catholics Outsource Prayers to Indian Clergy." *New York Times* (June 13):13.

Rain, Diana. 1999. *Internet*, 2nd ed. New York: DDC.

Rapp, Rayna. 1982. "Family and Class in Contemporary America." In *Rethinking the Family: Some Feminist Questions*, Barrie Thorne and Marilyn Yalom (eds.). New York: Longman.

Rasmus, Jack. 2005. "CAFTA and the Legacy of Free Trade." *Z Magazine* (July/August):86–89.

Record, Jane C., and Wilson Record. 1965. "Ideological Forces and the Negro Protest." *Annals* 357 (January): 89–96.

Reed, Adolph, Jr. 1990. "The Underclass as Myth and Symbol: The Poverty of Discourse about Poverty." *Radical America* 24 (January/March):21–40.

———. 1994. "Looking Backward." *Nation* (November 28): 654–662.

Reed, Madlen. 2004. "USA Sets Record for Billionaires." *USA Today* (September 24):8B.

Reeves, Thomas C. 1996. *The Empty Church: The Suicide of Liberal Christianity*. New York: Free Press.

Reich, Robert. 1989. "Yes: Blame Election Funds." *New York Times* (October 12):A29.

———. 2000. "The Great Divide." *American Prospect* (May 8):56.

———. 2002. *I'll Be Short: Essentials for a Decent Working Society.* Boston: Beacon Press.

Reiman, Jeffrey H. 2004. *The Rich Get Richer and the Poor Get Prison: Ideology, Class, and Criminal Justice,* 7th ed. Boston: Allyn and Bacon.

Religion News Service. 1995. "Vatican Declares 'Infallible' Its Ban on Women Priests."

Renzetti, Claire M., and Daniel J. Curran. 1992. *Women, Men, and Society,* 2nd ed. Boston: Allyn and Bacon.

———. 1995. *Women, Men, and Society,* 3rd ed. Boston: Allyn and Bacon.

———. 1998. *Living Sociology.* Boston: Allyn and Bacon.

———. 2003. *Women, Men, and Society,* 5th ed. Boston: Allyn and Bacon.

Reskin, Barbara F. 1999. "Occupational Segregation by Race and Ethnicity among Women Workers." In *Latinas and African American Women at Work: Race, Gender, and Economic Inequality,* Irene Browne (ed.). New York: Russell Sage Foundation.

Reskin, Barbara F., and Irene Padavic. 1994. *Women and Men at Work.* Thousand Oaks, CA: Pine Forge Press.

Reskin, Barbara F., and Patricia A. Roos. 1990. *Job Queues, Gender Queues.* Philadelphia: Temple University Press.

Reuss, Alejandro. 2001. "Cause of Death: Inequality." *Dollars & Sense,* 235 (May/June):10–12.

Reuteman, Rob. 2004. "Sobering Statistics to Ponder over Labor Day." *Rocky Mountain News* (September 4):2C.

Richburg, Keith B. 2004. "A Smorgasbord of Cultures." *The Washington Post National Weekly Edition* (November 1–7):17.

Riche, Martha Farnsworth. 1991. "We're All Minorities Now." *American Demographics* 13 (October):26–31.

———. 2000. "America's Diversity and Growth: Signposts for the 21st Century." *Population Bulletin* 55 (June):entire issue.

Richmond, Julius B. 1994. "Give Children an Earlier Head Start." *USA Today* (April 12):13A.

Richmond-Abbott, Marie. 1992. *Masculine and Feminine: Sex Roles over the Life Cycle,* 2nd ed. New York: McGraw-Hill.

Ridgeway, Cecilia L., and Lynn Smith-Lovin. 1999. "The General System and Interaction." *Annual Review of Sociology* 25:191–216.

Ridley, Matt. 2003. "What Makes You Who You Are." *Time* (June 2):55–63.

Rieken, Kristie. 2005. "Megachurch's Choice of Home a Slam-Dunk: Basketball Arena." *Rocky Mountain News* (July 16):29A.

Riesman, David. 1950. *The Lonely Crowd.* New Haven, CT: Yale University Press.

Rifkin, Jeremy. 1995. *The End of Work: The Decline of the Global Labor Force and the Dawn of the Post-Market Era.* New York: Putnam.

———. 1996. "Civil Society in the Information Age." *Nation* (February 26):11–16.

Risman, Barbara J. 1998. *Gender Vertigo.* New Haven, CT: Yale University Press.

Ritz, Mary Kaye. 2002. "Church Attendance Rose Following 9/11." *Honolulu Advertiser* (September 7). Available online: http://the.honoluluadvertiser.com/article/2002/sep/07/In/In04a.html.

Ritzer, George. 1995. *Expressing America: A Critique of the Global Credit Card Society.* Thousand Oaks, CA: Pine Forge Press.

———. 1996. *The McDonaldization of Society: An Investigation into the Changing Character of Contemporary Social Life,* rev. ed. Thousand Oaks, CA: Pine Forge Press.

———. 2000. *The McDonaldization of Society: New Century Edition.* Thousand Oaks, CA: Pine Forge Press.

Rizvi, Haider. 1995. "Slaves to Fashion." *Multinational Monitor* 16 (October):6–7.

Roberts, Sam. 2005. "More Africans Enter U.S. Than in Days of Slavery." *New York Times* (February 21):A1.

Robey, Renate. 1997. "Grandparents Learn to Cope with Raising a Second Generation." *Denver Post* (July 4):4B.

Robins, Natalie. 1987. "The Defiling of Writers." *Nation* (October 10):367–372.

———. 1992. "The Secret War against American Writers." *Esquire* 117 (March):106–109, 158–160.

Roediger, David R. 1991. *The Wages of Whiteness: Race and the Making of the American Working Class.* New York: Verso.

Rogers, Susan Carol. 1978. "Women's Place: A Critical Review of Anthropological Theory." *Comparative Studies in Society and History* 20(1):123–162.

Romaine, Suzanne. 1999. *Communicating Gender.* Mahwah, NJ: Erlbaum.

Rosaldo, Michelle Zimbalist. 1974. "Woman, Culture and Society: A Theoretical Overview." In *Woman, Culture, and Society,* Michelle Zimbalist Rosaldo and Louise Lamphere (eds.). Stanford, CA: Stanford University Press, pp. 17–42.

———. 1980. "The Use and Abuse of Anthropology." *Signs* 5 (Spring):389–417.

Rosen, Jeffrey. 2000. *The Unwanted Gaze: The Destruction of Privacy in America.* New York: Random House.

Rosen, Ruth. 2000. "When Women Spied on Women." *The Nation* (September 4):18–25.

Rosenblum, Karen E., and Toni-Michelle C. Travis. 1996. "Introduction." In *The Meaning of Difference,* Karen E. Rosenblum and Toni-Michelle C. Travis (eds.). New York: McGraw-Hill, pp. 1–34.

Rosenthal, Robert, and Lenore Jacobson. 1968. *Pygmalion in the Classroom: Teacher Expectations and Pupils' Intellectual Development.* New York: Holt, Rinehart and Winston.

Ross, Catherine E., John Mirowsky, and Karen Goldsteen. 1991. "The Impact of the Family on Health: The Decade in Review." In *Contemporary Families: Looking Forward, Looking Back,* Alan Booth (ed.). Minneapolis, MN: National Council on Family Relations, pp. 341–360.

Rossie, Dave. 1994. "Pendulum Swings in Florida." *Fort Collins Coloradoan* (May 19):B6.

Rotello, Gabriel. 1996. "To Have and to Hold: The Case for Gay Marriage." *Nation* (June 24):11–18.

Rothfeder, Jeffrey. 1992. *Privacy for Sale: How Computerization Has Made Everyone's Life an Open Secret.* New York: Simon & Schuster.

Rubenstein, Richard E. 1970. *Rebels in Eden: Mass Political Violence in the United States.* Boston: Little, Brown.

Rubin, Lillian B. 1973. *Worlds of Pain.* New York: Basic Books.

———. 1983. *Intimate Strangers.* New York: Harper & Row.

Rubington, Earl, and Martin S. Weinberg. 1973. *Deviance: The Interactionist Perspective,* 2nd ed. New York: Macmillan.

Russell, Jan Jarboe. 2003. "Religious Right Monkeying with Our Kids' Textbooks Again." *San Antonio Express-News* (September 14):1H.

Russell, Marta. 1998. *Beyond Ramps: Disability at the End of the Social Contract.* Monroe, ME: Common Courage Press.

———. 2000. "The Political Economy of Disablement." *Dollars & Sense,* no. 231 (September/October):13–15, 48–49.

Ryan, Joanna. 1972. "IQ—The Illusion of Objectivity." In *Race and Intelligence,* Ken Richardson and David Spears (eds.). Baltimore: Penguin.

Ryan, William. 1972. "Postscript: A Call to Action." *Social Policy* 3 (May–June).

———. 1976. *Blaming the Victim*, rev. ed. New York: Vintage Books.

Sacks, Karen. 1974. "Engels Revisited: Women, the Organization of Production, and Private Property." In *Woman, Culture, and Society*, Michelle Zimbalist Rosaldo and Louise Lamphere (eds.). Stanford, CA: Stanford University Press, pp. 207–222.

Sacks, Oliver. 1993. "To See and Not See." *The New Yorker* (May 5):59–73.

Sadker, David. 1998. "Gender Equity: Still Knocking at the Classroom Door." *Educational Leadership* 56 (April): 22–26.

———. 2002. "An Educator's Primer on the Gender War." *Phi Delta Kappan* (November):235–244.

Sadker, Myra, and David Sadker. 1994. *Failing at Fairness: How America's Schools Cheat Girls*. New York: Scribner.

Saenz, Rogelio. 2004. *Latinos and the Changing Face of America*. New York: Russell Sage Foundation and the Population Reference Bureau.

Sampat, Payal. 2001. "Last Words." *World Watch* 14 (May/June):34–40.

Sanders, Bernard. 1993. "Clinton Must Go to the People." *Nation* (June 21):865–867.

———. 1998. "The International Monetary Fund Is Hurting You." *Z Magazine* 11 (July/August):94–96.

———. 2000. "The 'Booming' Economy." *Sanders Scoop* (Spring):3.

———. 2004. "We Are the Majority." *The Progressive* 68 (February):26–28.

Sanderson, Stephen K. 1988. *Macrosociology; An Introduction to Human Societies*. New York: Harper & Row.

Sapiro, Virginia. 1999. *Women in American Society*, 4th ed. Mountain View, CA: Mayfield.

Savage, David G. 2001. "U.S. Lays Out Aid for Kin of Terror Attack." *Los Angeles Times* (December 21):A1, A38–A39.

Scarpitti, Frank R., and Margaret Andersen. 1992. *Social Problems*, 2nd ed. New York: HarperCollins.

Schafer, Walter E., Carol Olexa, and Kenneth Polk. 1972. "Programmed for Social Class." In *Schools and Delinquency*, Kenneth Polk and Walter E. Schafer (eds.). Upper Saddle River, NJ: Prentice Hall.

Scher, Abby. 2000. "Corporate Welfare: Port for All." *Dollars & Sense*, no. 229 (May/June):11.

Scheff, Thomas J. 1966. *Mentally Ill*. Chicago: Aldine.

Schneider, David M., and Raymond T. Smith. 1973. *Class Differences and Sex Roles in American Family and Kinship Structure*. Englewood Cliffs, NJ: Prentice Hall.

Schorr, Lisbeth B., with Daniel Schorr. 1988. *Within Our Reach: Breaking the Cycle of Disadvantage*. New York: Doubleday Anchor Press.

Schrag, Peter. 2004. "Bush's Education Fraud." *American Prospect* (February):38–41.

Schur, Edwin. 1971. *Labeling Deviant Behavior: Its Sociological Implications*. New York: Harper & Row.

———. 1973. *Radical Non-Intervention: Rethinking the Delinquency Problem*. Upper Saddle River, NJ: Prentice Hall.

———. 1980. *The Politics of Deviance*. Englewood Cliffs, NJ: Prentice Hall.

Schwartz, Herman. 1983. "Reagan's Bullish on Bugging." *Nation* (June 4):697–699.

Schwarz, John E., and Thomas J. Volgy. 1993. "Above the Poverty Line—But Poor." *The Nation* (February 15): 191–192.

Scott, Janny. 2005. "Life at the Top in America Isn't Just Better. It's Longer." *New York Times* (May 16). Available online: http://www.nytimes.com/2005/05/16/national/class/HEALTH-FINA.

Scott, Janny, and David Leonhardt. 2005. "Class in America: Shadowy Lines That Still Divide America." *New York Times* (May 15):15–18.

Scott, Katherine Hutt. 2001. "Factors Conspire to Keep Poor Students out of College." *USA Today* (March 5):8D.

Sennett, Richard, and Jonathan Cobb. 1973. *The Hidden Injuries of Class*. New York: Random House Vintage.

Sesser, Stan. 1992. "A Nation of Contradictions." *The New Yorker* (January 13):37–68.

Shanker, Albert. 1991. "Improving Our Schools." *New York Times* (May 17):7E.

———. 1992. "How Far Have We Come?" *New York Times* (August 16):9E.

Shapiro, Joseph P. 1989. "Liberation Day for the Disabled." *U.S. News & World Report* (September 18):20–24.

Shapiro, Judith. 1981. "Anthropology and the Study of Gender." In *A Feminist Perspective in the Academy*, Elizabeth Langland and Walter Gove (eds.). Chicago: University of Chicago Press, pp. 110–129.

Shapiro, Thomas M. 2004. *Houses Dividend: The Hidden Cost of Being African American*. New York: Oxford University Press.

Sharn, Lori. 1997. "Clergy Still a Tough Career for Women." *USA Today* (July 7):1A–2A.

Sheler, Jeffrey L. 1995. "The Era of Collective Repentance." *U.S. News & World Report* (July 3):10–11.

———. 2000. "The Mormon Moment." *U.S. News & World Report* (November 13):58–65.

———. 2001. "Muslim in America." *U.S. News & World Report* (October 29):50–52.

Sherif, Muzafer. 1958. "Group Influences upon the Formation of Norms and Attitudes." In *Readings in Social Psychology*, 3rd ed., Eleanor E. Maccoby, Theodore M. Newcomb, and Eugene L. Hartley (eds.). New York: Holt, Rinehart and Winston, pp. 219–232.

Sherif, Muzafer, and Carolyn W. Sherif. 1966. *Groups in Harmony and Tension*. New York: Harper, Brace & Giroux.

Shils, Edward A., and Morris Janowitz. 1948. "Cohesion and Disintegration in the Wehrmacht in World War II." *Public Opinion Quarterly* 12 (Summer):280–315.

Shreve, Anita. 1984. "The Working Mother as Role Model." *New York Times Magazine* (September 9):43.

Shute, Nancy. 2004. "Makeover Nation." *U.S. News & World Report* (May 31):53–59.

Sidel, Ruth. 1994. *Battling Bias*. New York: Penguin Books.

———. 1996. *Keeping Women and Children Last: America's War on the Poor*. Baltimore: Penguin.

Silberman, Charles E. 1970. *Crisis in the Classroom*. New York: Random House.

Silverstein, Louise B., and Carl F. Auerbach. 2001. "The Myth of the 'Normal' Family." *USA Today, the Magazine of the American Scene* 129 (January):30–31.

Simon, David R., and D. Stanley Eitzen. 1993. *Elite Deviance*, 4th ed. Boston: Allyn and Bacon.

Simon, Rita J., Angela J. Scanlan, and Pamela Madell. 1993. "Rabbis and Ministers: Women of the Book and Cloth." *Sociology of Religion* 54(1):115–122.

Sinderbrand, Rebecca. 2005. "A Shameful Little Secret." *Newsweek* (March 28):33.

Skinner, B. F. 1972. *Beyond Freedom and Dignity*. New York: Knopf.

Sklar, Holly. 1992. "Reaffirmative Action." *Z Magazine* 5 (May/June):9–15.

———. 1993. "The Upperclass and Mothers and the Hood." *Z Magazine* 6 (March):22–36.

——. 2001. "CEO Ponzi Scheme." Available online: www.inequality.org/ceopayedit2.html.

——. 2003. "CEO Pay Still Outrageous." *Progressive Populist* (June 15):1, 18.

——. 2004. "Don't Get Duped Out of Your Social Security." Knight Ridder/Tribune News Service (March 8).

——. 2004. "Break That Glass Ceiling." *Progressive Populist* (June 15):16.

Sklaroff, Sara. 1999. "E-Mail." *U.S. News & World Report* (March 22):54–55.

Skolnick, Jerome. 1969. *The Politics of Protest*. New York: Ballantine Books.

Skolnick, Jerome, and Elliott Currie. 1970. "Approaches to Social Problems." In *Crisis in American Institutions*, Jerome H. Skolnick and Elliott Currie (eds.). Boston: Little, Brown.

Slater, Philip. 1970. *The Pursuit of Loneliness: American Culture at the Breaking Point*. Boston: Beacon Press.

Slevin, Peter. 2001. "Super Bowl Surveillance." *Denver Post* (February 1):10A.

Smeeding, Timothy M., and Peter Gottschalk. 1998. "Gross-National Income Inequality." *Focus* (University of Wisconsin, Madison, Institute for Research on Poverty), vol. 19 (Summer/Fall):15–19.

Smeeding, Timothy M., and Lee Rainwater. 2002. "Comparing Living Standards across Nations: Real Incomes at the Top, the Bottom, and the Middle." Unpublished paper.

Smelser, Neil. 1962. *Theory of Collective Behavior*. New York: Free Press.

Smith, Elliot Blair. 2001. "Migrants Flex Muscles Back Home in Mexico." *USA Today* (June 28):9A.

Smith, Maureen. 2001. "An Exploration of African American Preschool-Aged Children's Behavioral Regulation in Emotionally Arousing Situations." *Child Study Journal* 31(1):13–45.

Snider, Mike. 2001. "Technology Offers a Feeling of Security." *USA Today* (November 15):1D–2D.

Snipp, Matthew. 1996. "The First Americans: American Indians." In *Origins and Destinies: Immigration, Race, and Ethnicity in America*, Silvia Pedraza and Ruben G. Rumbaut (eds.). Belmont, CA: Wadsworth, pp. 390–403.

Snyder, Eldon. 1972. "Athletic Dressing Room Slogans and Folklore." *International Review of Sport Sociology* 7:89–102.

Solow, Robert M. 2000. "Welfare: The Cheapest Country." *New York Review of Books* (March 23):20–24.

Sontag, Deborah. 1993. "Muslims in the United States Fear an Upsurge in Hostility." *New York Times* (March 7):1, 19.

Southern Poverty Law Center [SPLC]. 1998. "Wrath of Angels." *Southern Poverty Law Center Report* 91 (Summer): 32–39.

——. 1999. "Crime Study: Violent Prime Hit Native Americans Hardest." *Southern Poverty Law Center Report* 94 (Spring):1.

——. 2001a. "Hate Group Numbers Rise." *Southern Poverty Law Center Report* 31 (May):3.

——. 2001b. "Reevaluating the Net." *Intelligence Report* 102 (Summer):54–56.

——. 2002. "Hate Group Growth Continues." *Southern Poverty Law Center Report* 32 (April):3.

——. 2005. "Hate Group Numbers Up Slightly in 2004." Vol. 35 (March):3.

Spain, Daphne. 1999. "America's Diversity: On the Edge of Two Centuries." *Reports on America* 1 (May):entire issue.

Spencer, Porche, and Ek. Toleman. 2003. "We've Come a Long Way—Maybe: New Challenges for Gender Equity in Education." *Teachers College Record* 105 (9): 1774–1807.

Spong, John Shelby. 2005. *The Sins of Scripture: Exposing the Bible's Texts of Hate to Reveal the God of Love*. New York: HarperSanFrancisco.

Srinivasan, Kalpana. 1998. "IBM Claims World's Speediest Computer." Associated Press (October 28).

Stacey, Judith. 1990. *Brave New Families: Stories of Domestic Upheaval in Late Twentieth-Century America*. New York: Basic Books.

——. 1991. "Backward toward the Postmodern Family: Reflections on Gender, Kinship, and Class in the Silicon Valley." In *America at Century's End*, Alan Wolfe (ed.). Berkeley: University of California Press, pp. 17–34.

Stack, Carol B. 1990. "Different Voices, Different Visions: Gender, Culture, and Moral Reasoning." In *Uncertain Terms: Negotiating Gender in American Culture*, Faye Ginsburg and Anna Lowenhaupt Tsing (eds.). Boston: Beacon Press, pp. 19–27.

Stashenko, Joel. 2001. "Cost of Trade Center Loss May Reach $105 Billion." *Denver Post* (October 5):21A.

Stein, Peter J., Judith Richman, and Natalie Hannon. 1977. *The Family: Functions, Conflicts, and Symbols*. Reading, MA: Addison-Wesley.

Steinberg, David. n.d. "Racism in America: Definition and Analysis." Detroit, MI: People against Racism.

Stivers, Richard. 1975. "Introduction to the Social and Cultural Control of Deviant Behavior." In *The Collective Definition of Violence*, F. James Davis and Richard Stivers (eds.). New York: Free Press.

Stolberg, Sheryl Gay. 2002. "Minorities Got Inferior Care, Even if Insured, Study Finds." *New York Times* (March 21).

Stranahan, Susan Q. 2002. "The Clean Room's Dirty Secret." *Mother Jones* (March/April):44–49.

Strauss, William, and Neil Howe. 1991. *Generations: The History of America's Future, 1584 to 2069*. New York: Morrow.

Street, Paul. 2000. "The Anti-Sweatshop Movement." *Z Magazine* 13 (May):16–20.

——. 2001a. "Race, Prison, and Poverty." *Z Magazine* 14 (May):25–31.

——. 2001b. "Free to Be Poor." *Z Magazine* 14 (June): 25–29.

——. 2002. "Marriage as the Solution to Poverty?" *Z Magazine* 15 (April):33–39.

Streitfeld, David. 2003. "Jobless Count Skips Millions." *Los Angeles Times* (December 29): Available online: http://www.latimes.com/business/la-fi-jobs29dec29,1,626151.story?c.

Suarez-Orozco, Marcelo M., and Mariela M. Paez. 2002. "Introduction: The Research Agenda." In *Latinos: Remaking America*, Marcelo M. Suarez-Orozco and Mariela M. Paez (eds.). Berkeley: University of California Press.

Sutherland, Edwin H., and Donald R. Cressey. 1966. *Principles of Criminology*, 7th ed. Philadelphia: Lippincott.

Sykes, Gresham M. 1974. "Criminology: The Rise of Critical Criminology." *Journal of Criminal Law and Criminology* 65 (June).

Symonds, William C. 2003. "College Admissions: The Real Barrier Is Class." *Business Week* (April 14):66–67.

——. 2004. "No Child: Can It Make the Grade?" *Business Week* (March 8):78–80.

——. 2005. "Earthly Empires: How Evangelical Churches Are Borrowing from the Business Playbook." *Business Week* (May 23):78–88.

Szasz, Thomas. 1974. *Ceremonial Chemistry*. Garden City, NY: Doubleday.

Szymanski, Albert. 1978. *The Capitalist State and the Politics of Class*. Cambridge, MA: Winthrop.

Takaki, Ronald. 1993. *A Different Mirror: A History of Multicultural America*. Boston: Little, Brown.

Tannen, Deborah. 1990. *You Just Don't Understand: Women and Men in Conversation.* New York: Ballantine Books.

———. 1991. "Teachers' Classroom Strategies Should Recognize That Men and Women Use Language Differently." *Chronicle of Higher Education* 37(40):B3.

Taub, Amy. 1998. "Oligopoly! Highly Concentrated Markets across the U.S. Economy." *Multinational Monitor* 20 (November):9–12.

Ten Kate, Nancy. 1998. "Two Careers, One Marriage." *American Demographics* 20 (April):1.

Terkel, Studs. 1975. *Working: People Talk about What They Do All Day and How They Feel about What They Do.* New York: Avon Books.

Thorne, Barrie. 1993. *Gender Play: Girls and Boys in School.* New Brunswick, NJ: Rutgers University Press.

Thornton, Russell. 1996. "North American Indians and the Demography of Contact." In *Origins and Destinies: Immigration, Race, and Ethnicity in America,* Silvia Pedraza and Ruben G. Rumbaut (eds.). Belmont, CA: Wadsworth, pp. 43–59.

Thurow, Lester. 1995a. "Companies Merge: Families Break Up." *New York Times* (September 3):11A.

———. 1995b. "Why Their World Might Crumble." *New York Times Magazine* (November 19):78–79.

Tienda, Marta, and Susan Simonelli. 2001. "Hispanic Students Are Missing from Diversity Debates." *Chronicle of Higher Education* (June 1):A16.

Time. 1982. "Bishops and the Bomb." (November 29):77.

———. 2002. "Tongues That Go out of Style." (June 5):22.

Timmer, Doug A., and D. Stanley Eitzen. 1992. "The Root Causes of Urban Homelessness in the United States." *Humanity and Society* 16 (May):159–175.

———. (eds.). 1989. *Crime in the Streets and Crime in the Suites.* Boston: Allyn and Bacon.

Timmer, Doug A., D. Stanley Eitzen, and Kathryn D. Talley. 1994. *Paths to Homelessness: Extreme Poverty and the Urban Housing Crisis.* Boulder, CO: Westview Press.

Townsend, Nicholas W. 2002. *The Package Deal: Marriage, Work and Fatherhood in Men's Lives.* Philadelphia: Temple University Press.

TRB. 1975. "The Case for More Planning." *Rocky Mountain News* (March 30):2.

Tribe, Lawrence H. 1996. "Toward a Less Perfect Union." *New York Times* (May 26):E11.

Troeltsch, Ernst. 1931. *The Social Teaching of the Christian Churches,* Olive Wyon (trans.). New York: Macmillan.

Townsend, Nicholas W. 2002. *The Package Deal: Marriage, Work, and Fatherhood in Men's Lives.* Philadelphia: Temple University Press.

Tumin, Melvin M. 1953. "Some Principles of Stratification." *American Sociological Review* 18 (August):387–393.

———. 1973. *Patterns of Society.* Boston: Little, Brown.

Tye, Larry. 1997. "Playing under Pressure." *Boston Globe* (September 28):1A, 30A.

Uchitelle, Louis. 2001. "U.S. Jobless Rate Rose to 4.5% in April." *New York Times* (May 5). Available online: www.nytimes.com/2001/05/05/business95ECON.html.

United for a Fair Economy. 2004. "Wealth Inequality by the Numbers." *Dollars & Sense,* no. 251 (January/February): 20–21.

United Nations. 1997. *Men and Women in Politics: Democracy Still in the Making—A World Comparative Study.* Geneva, Switzerland: United Nations, Inter-Parliamentary Union.

USA Today. 1991. "Let Stockholders Vote on Executive Pay." (May 23):10A.

———. 1993. "Whose 'Objectivity' Are We Getting?" (September 1):11A.

———. 1996. "Smoke and Mirrors Can't Cure Fast-Failing Medicare." (June 6):12A.

———. 1997. "Messages Reinforce Sexual Stereotypes." (December):3A.

———. 1999a. "Evidence Mounts That Police Target Minorities Excessively." (June 3):14A.

———. 1999b. "A Small but Useful Start on Providing Long-Term Care." (January 5):16A.

———. 1999c. "Web Sites, Silence Invited Racist's Weekend Rampage." (July 7):12A.

———. 2000. "FBI Eavesdrops on E-mail, Crashes Privacy Barriers." (July 24):16A.

———. 2002a. "Alzheimer's Rate May Triple in USA by 2050." (July 23):8D.

———. 2002b. "Gender Equity: Suit Unfairly Attacks Effort to Boost Women's Sports." (January 21):10A.

———. 2002c. "Rigged Voting Districts Rob Public of Choice." (August 28):13A.

———. 2002d. "30 Years after Watergate, Money Trail Is Still Crooked." (June 21):12A.

———. 2004. "More Corporations Shirk Their Shares of Tax Burden." (April 12):20A.

U.S. Bureau of the Census. 1998. "1997 Population Profile of the United States." *Current Population Reports,* Special Studies P23–194 (September).

U.S. Bureau of the Census. 2003. "The Hispanic Population of the United States: March 2002." *Current Population Reports* (June) P20–545. Washington, DC: U.S. Government Printing Office.

U.S. Bureau of the Census. 2004. *We the People: Asians in the United States.* Census 2000 Special Reports (Dec. 2004) CENSR-17. Washington, DC: U.S. Government Printing Office.

———. 1998. *Statistical Abstract of the United States, 1998,* Washington, DC: Government Printing Office.

———. 2000. "Marital Status of People 15 Years and Over." Available online: www.census.gov/population/ socdemo/hh-fam/p20-537/2000.

———. 2001a. "Health Insurance: 2000." *Current Population Survey Reports,* P60–215 (March).

———. 2001b. "Income 2000: Median Income of Families by Selected Characteristics, Race, and Hispanic Origin of Householder: 2000, 1999, and 1998." (September). Available online: www.census.gov/hhes/income00/inctab4.html.

———. 2001c. "Population Profile of the United States 1999." *Current Population Reports,* P23–205. Washington, DC: Government Printing Office.

———. 2001d. "Poverty in the United States: 2000." *Current Population Reports,* P60–214.

———. 2001e. "Profile of General Demographic Characteristics: 2000." *American Fact Finder.* Washington, DC: U.S. Bureau of the Census.

———. 2001f. "Selected Characteristics of Families by Total Money Income in 2000." *Current Population Survey Reports* (November).

———. 2001g. *Statistical Abstract of the U.S., 2001.* Washington, DC: U.S. Government Printing Office.

———. 2001h. "Overview of Race and Hispanic Origin: Census 2000 Brief." *Current Population Reports* (March). Washington, DC: U.S. Government Printing Office.

———. 2002. "Historical Income Tables—Households by Race and Hispanic Origin: 1967–2000." *Current Population Survey Reports* (March). Washington, DC: U.S. Bureau of the Census.

———. 2003. *Statistical Abstract of the United States: 2004–2005.* Available online: http://www.census.gov/prod/2004pubs/04statab/labor.pdf.

———. 2004. "Hispanic and Asian Americans Increasing Faster Than Overall Population." (June). Available online: http://www.census.govPress-Release/www/release/archives/rarc/001839.htm.

———. 2004. "America's Families and Living Arrangements: 2003." *Current Population Reports*, P20–553. Available online: http:www.census.gov/prod/2004pubs/ p20553.pdf.

———. 2004. "Annual Social and Economic Supplement." *Current Population Survey*. Available online: http://www. census.gov/population/socdemo/hh-fam/cps2003/tabFG8all.pdf.

———. 2004. "Income Stable, Poverty Up, Numbers of Americans with or without Health Insurance, Census Bureau Reports." Available online: http://www. census.gov/Press-Release/www/release/archives/income_wealth/002484.html.

———. 2004. "Income, Poverty, and Health Insurance Coverage in the United States: 2003. *"Current Population Reports,"* P60–226.

———. 2005. "College Degree Nearly Doubles Annual Earnings, Census Bureau Reports." U.S. Census Press Release. Available online: http://www.census.gov/ Press-Release/www/release/archives/education/ 004214.html.

Usdansky, Margaret L. 1991. "Minorities a Majority in 51 Cities." *USA Today* (September 17):1A, 9A.

———. 1992. "Middle Class Pulling Apart to Rich, Poor." *USA Today* (February 20):1A.

U.S. Department of Education. 2001. *Digest of Education Statistics 2000*. NCES 2001–034. Washington, DC: U.S. Government Printing Office.

U.S. Department of Health and Human Services. 2004. "Health Gap." Available online: http://www.healthgap. omhrc.gov/cancer.htm. Retrieved on July 12, 2004.

U.S. Department of Health and Human Services. 2004. "Health Gap." Available online: http://www.healthgap. omhrc.gov/cancer.htm. Retrieved on July 12, 2004.

U.S. Department of Justice. 1998a. "Serious Violent Crime Victimization Rates by Race, 1973–1998." Available online: www.ojp.usdoj.gov/bjs/glance/race.txt.

U.S. Department of Justice. 2004. Bias Motivated by Location, 2003." Hate Crime Statistics, 2003. Available online: http://www.fbi.gov/ucr/03hc.pdf. Retrieved on June 1, 2005.

———. 1998b. *Sourcebook of Crime Justice Statistics—1997*. Washington, DC: Government Printing Office

———. 1999. "Correctional Population in the United States, 1996." *Bureau of Justice Statistics Bulletin*, NCJ 171684 (March).

———. 2004. "Bias Motivated by Location, 2003." Hate Crime Statistics, 2003. Available online: http://www. fbi.gov/vcr/03hc.pdf.

———. 2005. "Victim Characteristics." Bureau of Justice Statistics. Available online: http://www.ojp.usdoj. gov/bjs/cvict-v.htm.

U.S. Department of Labor. 1965. *The Negro Family: The Case for National Action*. Washington, DC: Office of Policy Planning and Research.

U.S. Department of Labor. 2005. Bureau of Labor Statistics. "Employment Status of the Civilian Non Institutional Population by Age, Sex, and Race." Available online: http://www.bls.gov/cps/cpsaat3.pdf Retrieved on May 15, 2005.

U.S. Department of Labor. 2005. *Women in the Labor Force: A Databook*. Washington, DC: U.S. Government Printing Office.

———. 1997. "20 Leading Occupations of Employed Women." Washington, DC: Women's Bureau, Division of Labor Statistics.

———. 1998a. "Employment and Earnings." *Current Population Survey* (January). Washington, DC: Division of Labor Statistics.

———. 1998b. "Non-Traditional Occupations for Women in 1998." Washington, DC: Women's Bureau, Division of Labor Statistics.

———. 1999. *Bureau of Labor Statistics, Employment and Earnings* (January). Washington, DC: Division of Labor Statistics.

———. 2003. "College Enrollment and Work Activity of High School Graduates." Available online: http://www.nccs. ed.gov/programs/digest/d03/tablels/pdf/table382.pdf.

———. 2004. *Women in the Labor Force: A Databook*. Washington, DC: Division of Labor Statistics.

U.S. Department of Labor, Women's Bureau. 2000. *20 Facts on Women Workers*. Washington, DC: Division of Labor Statistics.

———. 2001a. *Employment and Earnings 2001*. Washington, DC: Division of Labor Statistics.

———. 2001b. *Twenty Leading Occupations of Employed Women*. 2001 Annual Averages. Available online: www.dol.gov/wb/wb_pubs/20lead2001.htm.

———. 2002a. *Employment and Unemployment* (May). Washington, DC: Division of Labor Statistics.

———. 2002b. "National Unemployment Rate." (August). Available online: http://databls.gov/cgio-bin/dsru.

———. 2004. "Employment Status of the Civilian Noninstitutional Population by Age, Sex, and Race. Available online: http://www.bls.gov/cps/cpsaat3.pdf.

———. "Employed Persons by Occupation, Race, Hispanic or Latino Ethnicity, and Sex." Available online: http:// www. bls.gov/cps/cpsaat10.pdf.

———. 2004. "20 Leading Occupations of Employed Women." Available online: http://www.dol.gov/wb/factsheets/20lead2004.htm.

U.S. Bureau of Labor Statistics. 2005. "Employment Status of the Civilian Population by Race, Sex, and Age." Available online: http:www.bls.gov/news.release/pdf/empsit.pdf.

———. 2005. *Women in the Labor Force: A Databook*.

———. 2005. "Employment Status of the Hispanic or Latino Population by Sex and Age." Available online: http: www.bls.gov/news.relelase/pdf/empsit.pdf.

U.S. Equal Employment Opportunity Commission. 2003. *Women of Color: Their Employment in the Private Sector*. Available online: http://www.eeoc.gov/stats/reports/womenofcolor/womenofcolor.pdf.

U.S. News & World Report. 1999. "Campus Drinking: Who, Why, and How Much." (June 20):21.

———. 2002. "Our Cheating Hearts." (June 6):4.

Valdmanis, Thor. 2000. "Big Merger Wave Appears to Be Winding down to a Trickle." *USA Today* (January 2):2B.

Valian, Virginia. 1998. "Running in Place." *Sciences* 38 (January/February):18–23.

Van Biema, David. 2004. "Rising above the Stained-Glass Ceiling." *Time* (June 28):59–61.

———. 2004. "Roll over, Martin Luther." *Time* (August 16):53.

van den Berghe, Pierre L. 1967. *Race and Racism: A Comparative Perspective*. New York: Wiley.

Vanneman, Reeve, and Lynn Weber Cannon. 1987. *The American Perception of Class*. Philadelphia: Temple University Press.

Varney, Wendy. 2002. "Of Men and Machines: Images of Masculinity in Boys' Toys." *Feminist Studies* 28(1):153–174.

Vascenda, Vanessa. 2000. "The Toy Store with a Twist." *Discount Merchandiser* 40(4):15–16.

Vecoli, Rudolph J. 1964. "Contadini in Chicago: A Critique of the Uprooted." *Journal of American History* 51:405–417.

Verdin, Tom. 2000. "Minorities in the Majority." Associated Press (August 31).

Vonnegut, Kurt. 1999. "Technology and Me." *Harper's Magazine* 293 (September):26.

Waite, Linda J. 1995. "Does Marriage Matter?" *Demography* 32 (November):483–507.

———. 1999. "The Importance of Marriage Is Being Over-looked." *USA Today: The Magazine of the American Scene* (January):46–48.

———. 2000. "Trends in Men's and Women's Well-Being in Marriage." In *The Ties That Bind: Perspectives on Marriage and Cohabitation*, Linda Waite (ed.). Hawthorne, NY: Aldine de Gruyter.

Wage Gap, The. 2003. Available online: http://www.infoplease.com/ipa10/7/6/1/7ao76317.phtml.

Waite, Linda, and Maggie Gallagher. 2000. *The Case for Marriage: Why Married People Are Happier, Healthier, and Better Off Financially.* New York: Doubleday.

Walby, Sylvia. 2000. "Gender, Globalization, and Democracy." *Gender and Development* 8 (March):20–28.

Waldron, Ingrid, and Thomas Exter. 1991. "The Legacy of the 1980's." *American Demographics* (March): 32–38.

Wali, Alaka. 1992. "Multiculturalism: An Anthropological Perspective." *Report from the Institute for Philosophy and Public Policy* (University of Maryland) 12 (Spring/Summer): 6–8.

Wall Street Journal. 1992. "TV Violence Measured." (August 17):6B.

Walton, John. 1990. *Sociology and Critical Inquiry: The Work, Tradition, and Purpose,* 2nd ed. Belmont, CA: Wadsworth.

Warren, Carol A. B., and John M. Johnson. 1973. "A Critique of Labeling Theory from the Phenomenological Perspective." In *Theoretical Perspectives on Deviance,* Jack D. Douglas and Robert Scott (eds.). New York: Basic Books.

Warriner, Charles K. 1956. "Groups Are Real: A Reaffirmation." *American Sociological Review* 21 (October): 549–554.

Waters, Mary C. 1996. "Optional Ethnicities: For Whites Only?" In *Origins and Destinies: Immigration, Race, and Ethnicity in America,* Silvia Pedraza and Ruben G. Rumbaut (eds.). Belmont, CA: Wadsworth.

Weber, Lynn. 2001. *Understanding Race, Class, Gender, and Sexuality: A Conceptual Framework.* New York: McGraw-Hill.

Weber, Max. 1947. *The Theory of Social and Economic Organization,* A. M. Henderson and Talcott Parsons (trans.). New York: Free Press.

———. 1958. *The Protestant Ethic and the Spirit of Capitalism,* Talcott Parsons (trans.). New York: Scribner.

———. 1963. *The Sociology of Religion,* Ephraim Fischoff (trans.). Boston: Beacon Press.

Weinstein, Deena, and Michael Weinstein. 1974. *Living Sociology: A Critical Introduction.* New York: McKay.

Weisbrot, Mark. 2002. "Spying and Lying: The FBI's Dirty Secrets." *Progressive Populist* (July 1):14.

Weiss, Kenneth R. 2000. "More Rich Kids Get to Take Extra Time on SAT." *Denver Post* (January 9):2A.

Weitzman, Lenore J. 1985. *The Divorce Revolution: The Unexpected Social and Economic Consequences for Women and Children in America.* New York: Free Press.

———. 1996. "Comment: Consequences of Divorce Are Still Unequal." *American Sociological Review* 61 (June): 537–538.

Weitzman, Lenore J., Deborah Eifler, Elizabeth Hokada, and Catherine Ross. 1972. "Sex-Role Socialization in Picture Books for Preschool Children." *American Journal of Sociology* 77 (May):1125–1150.

Wellman, David T. 1977. *Portraits of White Racism.* Cambridge, England: Cambridge University Press.

Wells, Barbara, and Maxine Baca Zinn. 2000. "Spatial Inequality and Marriage Matters." Unpublished paper.

Wellstone, Paul. 1998. "The People's Trust Fund." *Nation* (July 27/August 3):4–5.

Werner, Erica. 2001. "Some See 'Minority' as an Outdated Term in No Majority California." *Denver Post* (May 8):5A.

Wertheimer, Fred. 1996. "The Dirtiest Election Ever." *Washington Post National Weekly Edition* (November 11):29–30.

West, Candace, and Don Zimmerman. 1987. "Doing Gender." *Gender and Society* 1:125–151.

West, Cornel. 1992. *Race Matters.* Boston: Beacon Press.

Westhues, Kenneth. 1982. *First Sociology.* New York: McGraw-Hill.

Wheat, Andrew. 2002. "System Failure: Deregulation, Political Corruption, Corporate Fraud and the Enron Debacle." *Multinational Monitor* 23 (January/February):34–44.

Wheelis, Allen. 1958. *The Quest for Identity.* New York: W. W. Norton.

Whorf, B. L. 1956. "Science and Linguistics." In *Readings in Social Psychology,* Eleanor E. Maccoby, Theodore M. Newcomb, and Eugene L. Hartley (eds.). New York: Holt, Rinehart and Winston.

Whyte, William Foote. 1956. *Street Corner Society: The Social Structure of an Italian Slum,* rev. ed. Chicago: University of Chicago Press.

———. 1988. *City: Rediscovering the Center.* New York: Doubleday.

Wicker, Tom. 1996. "Deserting the Democrats." *The Nation* (June 17):11–15.

Wickham, DeWayne. 1999. "Racial Inequality on Radio." *Fort Collins Coloradoan* (January 20):1A.

Wilcox, Clyde. 2000. *Onward Christian Soldiers: The Religious Right in American Politics,* 2nd ed. Boulder, CO: Westview Press.

Wilgoren, Jodi. 1999. "Police Profiling Debate: Acting on Experience or on Bias." *New York Times* (April 9):1, 5.

Williams, David R. 1990. "Socioeconomic Differentials in Health: A Review and Redirection." *Social Psychology Quarterly* 53 (June):81–99.

———. 1996. "The Health of the African American Population." In *Origins and Destinies: Immigration, Race, and Ethnicity in America,* Silvia Pedraza and Ruben G. Rumbaut (eds.). Belmont, CA: Wadsworth, pp. 404–416.

Williams, J. Allen, JoEtta A. Vernon, Martha C. Williams, and Karen Malecha. 1987. "Sex Role Socialization in Picture Books: An Update." *Social Science Quarterly* 68 (March):148–156.

Williams, Juan. 1994. "The New Segregation." *Modern Maturity* 37 (April/May):24–33.

Williams, Robin M., Jr. 1970. *American Society: A Sociological Interpretation,* 3rd ed. New York: Knopf.

Williamson, Thad. 2001. "The Real Y2K Crisis: Global Economic Inequality." *Dollars & Sense,* no. 227 (January/ February):42.

Willing, Richard. 2000. "Nader Finds 5% Goal Elusive." *USA Today* (November 8):9A.

Wilson, Everett K. 1966. *Sociology: Rules, Roles and Relationships.* Homewood, IL: Dorsey Press.

Wilson, William J. 1987. *The Truly Disadvantaged: The Inner City, the Underclass, and Public Policy.* Chicago: University of Chicago Press.

———. 1996. *When Work Disappears: The World of the New Urban Poor.* New York: Knopf.

Wilson, William J., and Andrew J. Cherlin. 2001. "The Real Test of Welfare Reform Still Lies Ahead." *New York Times* (July 13). Available online: www.nytimes.com/2001/07/13/opinion/13WILS.html.

Winant, Howard. 1994. *Racial Conditions, Politics, Theory, Comparisons.* Minneapolis: University of Minnesota Press.

———. 1997. "Behind Blue Eyes: Whiteness and Contemporary U.S. Racial Politics." In *Off White: Readings on Race, Power, and Society,* Michelle Fine, Lois Weis, Linda C. Powell, and L. Mun Wong (eds.). New York: Routledge, pp. 40–53.

———. 2001. *The World Is a Ghetto.* New York: Basic Books.

Winfield, Nicole. 2000. "U.S. Scores an 'F' on Efforts to Cut Poverty among U.S. Women." Associated Press (June 8).

Witt, Susan. 1997. "Parental Influence on Children's Socialization to Gender Roles." *Adolescence* 32 (126):253–259.

Wolfe, Alan. 1999. "The Power Elite Now." *American Prospect* 44 (May/June):90–96.

Wolff, Edward N. 2001. "The Rich Get Richer . . . and Why the Poor Don't." *American Prospect* (February 12):15–17.

———. 2002. *Top Heavy: The Increasing Inequality of Wealth in American and What Can Be Done about It,* updated and expanded edition. New York: New Press.

Woodward, Kenneth L. 1990. "Young beyond Their Years." *Newsweek Special Issue on the Family* (November):54–60.

World Watch. 2001. "Unspoken Words." Vol. 14 (May/ June):33.

Wright, Erik Olin, David Hachen, Cynthia Costello, and Joey Sprague. 1982. "The American Class Structure." *American Sociological Review* 47 (December):709–726.

Wrong, Dennis. 1969. "The Oversocialized Conception of Man in Modern Sociology." In *Sociological Theory,* 3rd ed., Lewis A. Coser and Bernard Rosenberg (eds.). New York: Macmillan.

Yancey, Kitty Bean. 1999. "Gone with the Guests." *USA Today* (December 7):D1.

Yates, Michael D. 2005. "A Statistical Portrait of the U. S. Working Class." *Monthly Review* 56 (April):12–31.

Yetman, Norman R. 1991. "Introduction." In *Majority and Minority: The Dynamics of Race and Ethnicity in American Life,* 5th ed., Norman R. Yetman (ed.). Boston: Allyn and Bacon, pp. 1–29.

Yinger, J. Milton. 1961. *Sociology Looks at Religion.* New York: Macmillan.

———. 1962. "Contraculture and Subculture." *American Sociological Review* 25 (October):625–635.

Yorburg, Betty. 1983. *Families and Societies: Survival or Extinction?* New York: Columbia University Press.

Zaldivar, R. A. 1997. "Men Still Rare in Women's Work." *Denver Post* (February 2):19A.

Zaretsky, Eli. 1976. *Capitalism, the Family, and Personal Life.* New York: Harper Colophon.

Zeitlin, Maurice, Kenneth G. Lutterman, and James W. Russell. 1977. "Death in Vietnam: Class, Poverty, and the Risks of War." In *American Society, Inc.,* 2nd ed., Maurice Zeitlin (ed.). Chicago: Rand McNally, pp. 143–155.

Zelizer, Gerald L. 1999. "Year 2000 Looms . . . Or Is It 5760? 1421?" *USA Today* (March 11):15A.

———. 2004. "Time to Break the Stained Glass Ceiling." *USA Today* (September 16):1A.

Zepezauer, Mark, and Arthur Naiman. 1996. *Take the Rich Off Welfare.* Tucson, AZ: Odonian Press.

———. 2004. *Take the Rich Off Welfare,* New, Expanded Edition. Cambridge, MA: South End Press.

Zhao, Yilu. 2000. "Wave of Pupils Lacking English Strains Schools." *New York Times* (August 5). Available online: www.nytimes.com/2002/08/05/education/05ESL.html.

Zhou, Min. 1997. "Growing Up American: The Challenge Confronting Immigrant Children and Children of Immigrants." *Annual Review of Sociology* 23:63–95.

Zimbardo, Philip G. 1972. "Pathology of Imprisonment." *Society* 9 (April).

Zinn, Howard. 1980. *A People's History of the United States.* New York: Harper & Row.

———. 2005. "Harness That Anger." *The Progressive* 69 (January):20–21.

Zuckerman, M. J. 2000. "Chances Are, Somebody's Watching You." *USA Today* (November 30):1A–2A.

Name Index